The History
of Special Education

The History of Special Education

From Isolation to Integration

Margret A. Winzer

Gallaudet University Press
Washington, D.C.

Gallaudet University Press
Washington, DC 20002

Library of Congress Cataloging-in-Publication Data

Winzer, M. A. (Margret A.), 1940–
    The history of special education : from isolation to integration /
Margret A. Winzer.
        p.   cm.
    Includes bibliographical references (p.) and index.
    ISBN 1-56368-018-1 : $55.95
    1. Special education—History.   2. Special education—United
States—History.   3. Handicapped—Education—History.
    4. Handicapped—Education—United   States—
History.   5. Mainstreaming
    in education—History. I. Title.
    LC3965.W56   1993
    371.9—dc20   93-12433
                                                            CIP

The paper used in this publication meets the minimum requirements of
American National Standard for Information Sciences—Permanence of
Paper for Printed Library Materials, ANSI Z39.48-1984.∞

Photographs courtesy of Gallaudet University Archives
Cover design by Dorothy Wachtenheim

Contents

List of Tables

List of Boxes

For my family

Preface

The way that children are trained and schooled is a crucial demonstration of the way that they are perceived and treated in a given society. Many complex threads—social, political, economic, and even religious—must interweave to create a propitious climate that respects the rights of all individuals in a certain society. Hence, the changing nature of the social climate and its manifestations in the treatment of, attitudes toward, and schooling provided for exceptional individuals is the essential story of the development of special education.

This text is wedded to the notion that economic and social conditions both define and drive educational arrangements and possibilities. A history of the development of special education, then, must attempt to answer certain questions. These concern the various ways in which societies responded to handicaps and deviance. Discovering who was taught, and when and how, is related far more to the social, political, legislative, economic, and religious forces at work in a society than it is to the unique social and educational needs of disabled persons. At the same time, this history mirrors our progress toward appreciating the basic humanity of all people.

The legacy of philosophers, philanthropists, evangelicals, and reformers (and not a few reprobates) who founded institutions, developed innovative instructional methodologies, and generally directed attention toward groups traditionally considered as objects of charity and unworthy recipients of education must also be considered. The most important questions revolve around the disabled children for whom the enterprise was undertaken, their parents, and the teachers who worked in the classrooms.

It is important to know if exceptional pupils enjoyed and appreciated their schooling and how their education differed from that provided to other youngsters. Additionally, we should know who taught in the special schools, how the parents reacted to sending a small child off to an institution for ten months of the year or to losing an older child who may well have been an important source of economic contributions to the family, what the prospects were for disabled adults in society and whether schooling provided them with the skills to successfully negotiate the adult world. Did their schooling prepare them for adult life and allow them to reach their full potential, or did it serve as a structure to train young handicapped people for societal and occupational positions deemed consonant with their handicap and social class? If disabled people married and had children—as we know they did given the railing against hereditary disabilities that runs like a red thread through special education—how did they meet their spouses? When did they marry—and how did they achieve the economic stability necessary for marriage?

Many of these questions are difficult to answer. Unlike the reformers who initiated and guided the venture, exceptional people failed to put their thoughts and feelings on paper. We must rely on the occasional comments of observers and the retrospective writings of educational chroniclers to gloss over the mute evidence. Those educators and reformers who contributed their time and talents to the enterprise offer the most comprehensive body of evidence. Little is available from disabled persons themselves or from contemporaries not directly involved in education. Until the middle of the nineteenth century, the plight of disabled children and adults drew meager public attention.

This is an introductory history and, like many introductory and comprehensive histories, it is vulnerable in many areas. In the enormous body of data pertaining to the history of disability and of special education not every area can be addressed or every theme pursued. Inescapable limitations are imposed, sometimes by the sheer weight of the evidence and just as often by the paucity of data. Special education development in Canada, for example, remains a relatively unexplored area, as does the contribution of women to the enterprise in North America.

This book is written by a special educator for special educators. Historical writing inevitably mirrors the concerns of the present; any historian is apt to use his or her own perspective. Hence, in this attempt to resurrect and interpret the past for the present, my overriding objective is to detail some of the major issues in our field in the belief that an intimate knowledge of special education in its historical context can enhance and enrich our efforts today.

Many of the issues and problems that beset contemporary special education have their roots in the past; other issues were confronted by our forebears. Today's special educators grapple with many questions, among them the educational placement and instruction of exceptional students, unbiased and non-discriminatory identification procedures, labeling and generic approaches for children with mild disabilities, teacher training, the Regular Education Initiative and inclusive schooling, identification and intervention in early childhood, program eligibility, support for families with disabled members, transition programs for adolescents, the relative impact of nature and nurture on development, institutionalization, sterilization, and life management strategies for mentally handicapped persons. Many of these cogent and controversial issues are not new to the field; pioneer special educators also dealt with them. The way these dilemmas were handled lends at least some light to current solutions. With so much of today's special education determined and shaped by historical imperatives and precedents, close scrutiny can only serve to aid special educators in forming a balanced understanding and evaluation of our profession.

A number of people contributed significantly to the background research for this book. Special appreciation is extended to my graduate assistants, Patti Tudor and John Russel for their invaluable assistance, their patience, and their good humor. Helen Ford's assistance is also appreciated. Ivey Pittle Wallace of Gallaudet University Press lent assistance, guidance, and encouragement for which I am most grateful.

Part 1

Lessons of a Dark Past

Introduction

A history of special education and a history of exceptionality are not the same. One deals with educational and institutional arrangements first formally established in the eighteenth century, the other, with people who have been present in society since its beginnings. Nevertheless, the two histories are inextricably meshed, and the essential theme of both is the varying treatment afforded the disabled population.

A society's treatment of those who are weak and dependent is one critical indicator of its social progress. Social attitudes concerning the education and care of exceptional individuals reflect general cultural attitudes concerning the obligations of a society to its individual citizens. Every society recognizes certain extreme forms of human difference as abnormality. Along the range of human behavior from normal to abnormal there is some point at which a social judgment is made and an individual comes to be regarded as exceptional, disabled, different, or deviant. To what extent a society can accept such differences and how to deal with them are perennial problems. History reveals many solutions to these problems.

In any society attitudes and values are fashioned by the prevailing culture, religion, government, and economic conditions. As societies change, so do their values. Classical Greece heaped honors on the philosopher and the teacher; Rome lauded the statesman, the orator, and the soldier. With the Middle Ages, and later the Renaissance, the craftsman and the artist assumed prominence and were highly valued. By the same token, the treatment of disabled people varied, as prevailing political, social, economic, and religious pressures changed.

3

Throughout the long, dark centuries before about 1700 individual deviation, whether social, political, religious, intellectual, or physical, was rarely tolerated. Those who differed from, or differed with, what a society deemed appropriate and normal were subject to abuse, condemnation, or destruction. With rare exceptions, disabled persons were regarded with aversion and subjected to astounding cruelty; in most cultures they were scorned as inferior beings and were deprived of rights and privileges. Their afflictions were misunderstood, frequently looked upon as having supernatural causes and therefore being unamenable to human treatment. Legal mandates denied them basic civil rights; theological canons excluded them from church membership; and philosophy pronounced them incapable of mental or moral improvement (Hodgson, [1952] 1973; H. P. Peet, 1851; W. W. Turner, 1858).

The great waves of change that swept across Europe after the fall of Rome caught disabled persons in their net. The carnage of the perpetual wars and the incursions of invading tribes that ravaged Europe for centuries, leaving death, destruction, and famine in their wake, must have been even more devastating for those who could not fight and protect themselves. Plagues and epidemics decimated populations and recast large numbers of survivors into the role of handicapped people. When witch hunters roamed Europe seeking the deviant and the heretical, disabled people were singularly suspect but scarcely able to mount a cohesive defense.

During this dark and troubled period there are isolated references to aid, education, and cures for handicapped individuals. Much of the early evidence is surrounded by an aura of magic, however, and it was only at the close of the fifteenth century that the recitation of miracle and legend receded and more stable compilation of authenticated records arose. In the sixteenth and seventeenth centuries a scattered handful of disabled persons were educated, chiefly in pursuit of philosophical knowledge. But still the vast majority were rarely looked upon with humane concern.

Much of the early history of exceptionality is speculative. Historians bothered to record little about the deviant and the different, and disabled people left no records of their own pertaining to their daily lives. The contradictory nature of the evidence we have leaves us with only a dim outline. Very few mentions are made of exceptional persons in the extant literature of early societies; it was not until about the 1600s that authentic data began to lend details to the picture. Pioneer special educators wrote tantalizing but incomplete accounts of their students, their approaches, and their successes.

In the middle of the eighteenth century Britain and Europe turned, for the first time, to the systematic instruction of disabled people. France was the crucial place; there, the broad intellectual movement known as the Enlightenment stimulated rational modes of thought and enhanced novel perceptions of handicapped individuals. Under *l'esprit philosophique,* as preached by Jean Jacques Rousseau, Voltaire, Denis Diderot, and many others, people from all strata of society were stirred as never before on social questions. Philanthrophy became a sort of fashion, and the movement for the elevation of individual independence, self-respect, and dignity became common enterprises.

Enlightenment ideas were germane to the development of special education; early special education had a sociopolitical base, conditioned especially by the philosophical views of Étienne Bonnot de Condillac, Diderot, and Rousseau. The phenomenal growth of special education in the latter half of the eighteenth century was part of the wider movement that involved the abolition of social classes, the establishment of a just society, and the accession to full human rights of all members of that society. Educational pioneers adopted the essential tenets of *l'esprit philosophique,* illuminating it with specific techniques and methods for training and education (Winzer, 1986a).

By the close of the eighteenth century special education was accepted as a branch of education, although often charity, not education, served as the underlying motive. Schooling did not become a social norm for exceptional youngsters any more than it did for other children of the period, but the advances resulted in wide-ranging pedagogical experimentation, broadly based educational enterprises, the establishment of charitable foundations and state-administered schools, and the emergence of professional teachers.

Chapter 1

Disability and Society before the Eighteenth Century: Dread and Despair

Chronology of Important Events in Europe

400 B.C.	The height of classical Greece; infanticide widely practiced
460–377 B.C.	Hippocrates; medical treatment of a range of exceptional conditions
384–322 B.C.	Aristotle; philosophy inspires derogatory views of exceptional persons
34 B.C.	Imperial Rome under the control of Augustus; deaf Quintus Pedius is taught painting
A.D. 130–200	Galen; further medical treatment, much of it founded on Hippocratic dictums
4th century	The rise of monasticism; first hospices are established for blind persons
476	Fall of Rome; barbarian tribes roam Europe
533	The Code of Justinian; legal mandates that describe and classify disabled persons in great detail
1348–1350	The Black Death; one-third of the population of Europe dies
1487	The Inquisition moves into a new stage as Tomás de Torquemada assumes leadership
1500	The height of the Renaissance; marginal improvements for handicapped persons appear
1578	Pedro Ponce de León undertakes the first authenticated education of handicapped persons, in Spain
17th century	European pioneers are involved in a variety of attempts to educate disabled persons

1620   Jean Pablo Bonet writes what is essentially the first book on special education

1662   The Royal Society of London receives charter, inspires philosophical inquiry into the nature of language and the teaching of deaf and blind individuals

1720   Daniel Defoe writes *The History of the Life and Surprising Adventures of Mr. Duncan Campbell,* the first popular exposé of the problems of deaf people

The treatment the members of any society extend to the exceptional persons in their midst cannot be understood or evaluated in a vacuum. We must know, first, something about the physical and social conditions confronting all people in a society. Our exploration, then, of the fate of disabled persons in the premodern societies of the Middle East and Europe begins with an overview of daily life in these cultures.

The vast distances of time and differences between our conditions and those of the far past so cloud our perceptions of the lives of our ancestors that it is difficult to visualize daily life in earlier societies. However, it is not so difficult to imagine that poverty, dirt, disease, and vermin were constant accompaniments to the daily round. Life for most people before the rise of modern medicine and public health was difficult and short. As late as the year 1800 the population of Europe reached only 150 million; half of the population were aged below twenty-one years, and the average life expectancy was only about thirty-five years (Mahendra, 1985).

Plague, disease, and malnutrition decimated the ranks of the great as well as the common. Women faced the continual peril of childbirth; until well into the nineteenth century, most females were perpetually in a state of pregnancy. Women spent their adult life, in addition to their other duties, in bearing, rearing and, all too often, burying their children. The male population was periodically decimated by war, at home or abroad. Besides the miseries of almost constant war, early societies suffered the incursions of great hordes of raiders, political and social chaos, and the dreadful affliction of inescapable, mysterious, and deadly diseases. People suffered not only from the evil effects of diseases now vanquished such as smallpox and typhus but also from the results of unsophisticated medical treatment and ubiquitious dental decay.

Social conditions also were very unlike our own. Illiteracy flourished among all classes. Although schools have been an integral part of society for centuries, probably emerging with the first literate city states of Mesopotamia, the ethical imperative to provide universal education for all children is a relatively recent phenomenon. Today the education of children is linked with the age of the child, but young people in earlier times lived lives we would consider adult. It was not until the seventeenth century that children were thought worthy of a teacher's attention and not until the middle decades of the nineteenth century that the acquisition of literacy skills constituted a principal developmental task for children between the ages of six and twelve.

Imperatives for universal schooling were closely tied to concerns for children as a separate and important part of society. Until a society recognized the

child as an active, feeling person who had a value independent of any other purpose and saw childhood as a discrete stage of development, not merely minia-
ture adulthood, special facilities for the care and training of children would not
be made available. Indeed, until fairly recently in recorded history, children were
not even considered legally to be persons: they had no rights and were usually
considered the property of their parents.

In premodern western societies infant mortality was high. Even in the mid-
eighteenth century less than half the children born were expected to reach
adulthood. Those who did survive infancy had little to look forward to. There
were no special nurseries, no playgrounds, certainly no special toys. Children's
books appeared as early as the fifteenth century, but until the beginning of the
nineteenth, they were instructive or moralistic, not intended for the pleasure of
the child. For most children, growing up was a haphazard experience, and
among poorer classes even very young children were expected to contribute
economically to the family.

In such a social setting, where general hardship was the norm and dependent persons, children included, were not viewed as problems for social solution, the status of exceptional children and adults was radically different from
what it is today. In the thousands of years of human existence before 1800, life
for most exceptional people appears to have been a series of unmitigated hardships. The great majority of disabled persons had no occupation, no source of
income, limited social interaction, and little religious comfort. Conspicuously
abnormal persons were surrounded by superstition, myth, and fatalism—especially fatalism. Their lives were severely limited by widely held beliefs and
superstitions that justified the pervasive prejudice and callous treatment. Individuals seen as different were destroyed, exorcised, ignored, exiled, exploited—
or set apart because some were even considered divine (Hewett, 1974).

THE INVISIBLE MINORITY: THE PREVALENCE OF DISABILITY

It is difficult even to estimate the true numbers of handicapped people in
any early society. Confined by the uncertainty of historic data and the paucity of
records, we can only guess at prevalence, although the most easily supported
assumption is that handicapping conditions were noticeably more prominent
than they are today. Plague, pestilence, and poverty—all precursors of major
and minor disabling conditions—were the constant companions of humans in
their trek through history.

Moreover, scattered evidence in early writings supports the notion that
handicapping conditions were widespread and that disabled people have been
present from the earliest times. Beginning with Homer, Greek and Roman writers portrayed a very wide range of human behavior, including instances so unusual as to be considered abnormal and requiring some special explanation.
The ancients regarded history as a genre of storytelling and not as a careful
record of fact; nevertheless, such historical writings as Herodotus' portrayal of
a deaf prince (Herodotus, 1954, book 2) or Suetonius' references to handicapped
people in Imperial Rome (Suetonius, [A.D. 120] 1957) offer glimpses into the past.

Later, after storytelling and history diverged, the authors of fictional stories continued to incorporate exceptional persons into their tales. The roles they assigned to handicapped characters likewise offer important insights into the prevailing social attitudes about exceptionality down through the years (see Box 1-1).

Legal mandates are more telling: legislators did not enact laws to control the orderly but to sanction divisive elements and others who were the focus of concern. Fragments remaining from the writings of the great jurists of the ancient world imply that careful consideration was directed toward the disabled population (Gaw, 1906, 1907; Hodgson, [1952] 1973).

The widespread occurrence of debilitating physical and mental conditions in premodern times probably resulted from a combination of factors. The absence of modern prenatal care and enlightened medical assistance, combined with poor maternal nutrition, meant that many infants did not survive or were born with physical or mental anomalies. Epidemics, plagues, and fevers periodically decimated the population, leaving survivors with a range of handicapping conditions. For example, scarlet fever got its modern name in 1685, but it is one of the oldest known diseases. It was common in the pre-Christian era and may have been responsible for many of the deaf, blind, insane, and retarded cases mentioned in ancient writings (MVD, 1925). The problems of unchecked virulent fevers and other illnesses were compounded by unsanitary conditions and the primitive state of medical knowledge. Limited mobility and consequent inbreeding ensured the passage of inherited conditions from one generation to the next; at the same time, the movement of troops in the constant wars that beset the ancient and medieval world spread many epidemics.

Fascinating conjunctions of epidemics or plagues and the resurgence of laws designed to control or eliminate the disabled population occur from time to time, but the evidence for a cause-and-effect connection remains too slim to support more than bare surmise. We could speculate, for example, that the plague that ravaged Athens in the fourth century B.C. led Plato to suggest that only the mental and physical elite be allowed to marry and procreate and Aristotle to advocate infanticide laws. Or that the great plague named for the Emperor Justinian prompted that monarch's jurists to direct minute attention to the status of disabled people in society.

No doubt throughout premodern history the disabled population formed a small though resilient minority—a minority always exposed to the prejudices of the majority, not only because they could not partake of normal life, but also because they represented evil or were seen as public threats. Being different drew cruel and callous reactions from society, yet the penalities society inflicted—legal sanctions, church expulsion, starvation, exile, or even death—were too unevenly administered to exterminate all persons with handicaps.

The concept of exceptionality throughout history has not been static. The paucity of information we have on prevalence is compounded by the pervasive lack of clarity in the differentiations among disabling conditions and by difficulties in determining just who constituted the disabled population. Individuals who challenged the political, social, or value systems of some earlier societies were apt to be judged mad, insane, heretical, or blasphemous and so were destined to be subjected to harsh sanctions. How many political and religious

Box 1-1

Literary Sources

Disability per se has rarely been the central subject of literature because it is not a universal concern. But literature offers some insight into the status of exceptional people in the past. It is not possible to know if in any instance literature reflected or molded prevailing attitudes toward the disabled; it does, however, give us some insight into the opinions concerning special people that were held by a society. When exceptional or disabled people do appear in literature and other artistic works, they are usually rendered as stereotypes, appearing to be either more or less than human (see Biklen, 1986; Brulle and Mihail, 1991; D. Kent, 1986; Kriegel, 1986).

Literary and artistic works show disability by means of a number of common images—disabled persons are portrayed as criminals or monsters or as people who are suicidal, maladjusted, or sexually deviant (Brulle and Mihail, 1991; Klobas, 1985; Longmore, 1985). Disabled people are often seen as suffering punishment for doing evil; they are portrayed as embittered by their fate, or as resentful of non-disabled people, whom they seek to destroy (Longmore, 1985). Such images reinforce negative stereotypes and foster common prejudices.

Traditionally, certain disabled groups appealed more to writers' imaginations, sometimes as part of a general societal concern. Insanity, madness, possession, seen as manifestations of divine punishment, form a common literary theme (Byrd, 1974). It may be no coincidence that the literature of the sixteenth and early seventeenth centuries—the time of the Spanish Inquisition, the witch hunts, and the establishment of the great lunatic hospitals—is so rich with portrayals of distraught and insane characters. Hamlet, Lear, Timon, and Ophelia, for example, all wear the mask of madness (Rosen, 1968). But Shakespeare's characters are simply among some of the best known of a whole gallery of characters to be found in such diverse contemporary sources as the plays of John Fletcher, John Webster, John Ford, Ben Jonson, and works by other Elizabethan and Jacobean writers (Rosen, 1968).

Shakespeare's Richard III serves as the prototype of the deformed villain whose outward manifestations illustrate his inward malignity (Fiedler, 1982). This villain emerges again and again, especially in Victorian literature. He is seen in the peg-legged sea captains Ahab and Long John Silver created by Herman Melville and Robert Louis Stevenson, in Victor Hugo's hunchback, and in the sinister Quilp who pursues Little Nell throughout Charles Dickens's *Old Curiosity Shop* (Fiedler, 1982).

In literature deaf persons often had their place in comedies; the blind, often in tragedies. In the early eighteenth century Daniel Defoe presented *The History of the Life and Surprising Adventures of Mr. Duncan Campbell* ([1720] 1903), a sensitive portrait of a deaf fortune teller in London and the first popular examination of the problems of the deaf person (Defoe 1903). Other writers treated deaf people with less kindness; some, like Oliver Goldsmith, made them fools, buffoons, and the butt of jokes. Blind individuals fared somewhat better in literature. From the time of Homer, blind persons have generally been portrayed in sympathetic terms; the arts abound with blind poets, storytellers and musicians, and literature presents blind heroes for our contemplation.

Truly retarded individuals rarely appear in pre-Victorian literature—the fools of Shakespeare and his contemporaries were comics who were anything but foolish. Dickens paints gentle portraits of retarded and slower functioning characters; there is Little Dorritt's friend Maggy, forever a ten-year-old because of a childhood fever; Barnaby Rudge, a young man unable to cope with the complexities of emerging industrial society; and David Copperfield's droll friend Mr. Dick. John Steinbeck adopted the theme with Lennie Small in *Of Mice and Men.*

Charles Dickens was deeply concerned with heroes oppressed by the unfortunate circumstances of their environment. The master of pathos, Dickens awakens strong sentimental responses with characters such as Tiny Tim. Most poignant are Dickens's characterizations of vagrant and delinquent children. No sadder character exists than Jo, the vagrant crossing sweeper in *Bleak House.*

Dickens's Artful Dodger and his gang of small thieves were of the ilk that drew the attention of reformers in the latter half of the nineteenth century. But the foundling child, the epitome of poverty, emerged as a common figure in literature a century earlier. Henry Fielding's *The History of Tom Jones: A Foundling* (1749), for example, proved enormously popular. In *The Expedition of Humphry Clinker* (1771) Tobias Smollett developed the theme of reconciliation between an old man and his illegitimate son (Ramsland, 1989).

From the first, the movies have made dramatic statements about society's negative reactions to people who were different. Charles Chaplin's wonderful *City Lights* (1930) tells the story of a tramp and a blind woman; *Johnny Belinda* (1948) is about a deaf girl; and *The Miracle Worker* (1962) portrays the relationship of Helen Keller and her brilliant teacher, Anne Sullivan (see Michal-Smith, 1987).

---

nonconformists were confused in the public mind with the genuinely disabled population is unknown.

Our ability to assess the scope of the problem in earlier societies is further obscured by the lack of a consistent, sound means of discriminating between people who had physical disabilities (i.e., were crippled, dwarfed, epileptic, or deaf) and those who were intellectually handicapped or mentally ill. All were considered to form one, all-encompassing category. The lack of clear definitions means that the history of disability tends to focus on particular disabilities, those that were more clearly distinguished from the others. Until the close of the eighteenth century those who fell under the broad, elastic categories labeled as insane or blind or deaf and dumb commanded most notice.

Madness particularly attracted attention, although "idiocy" (mental retardation) as a discrete and separate condition was rarely mentioned (Mahendra,

1985).[1] The etiology and character of deafness eluded early physicians and philosophers; the condition was usually attributed to supernatural causes. Blindness was more clearly conceptualized, and blind persons throughout the centuries generally attracted more humane treatment than did those suffering other conditions. History records how some blind persons, estranged from their families and rejected by society, became bards, wandering from court to court, singing "strains divine." The tradition is reflected in many legends; for example, Ossian, the son of the Caledonian king Fingal, was just such a heroic figure of the third century. After losing his sight in a battle, he is said to have wandered about the countryside playing a harp and singing songs of battle and freedom (Farrell, 1956b).

Given the social and occupational requisites for survival in early societies, some groups that we so assiduously label and classify today were not even recognized as the logical or deserving recipients of social or legal concern. Before the advent of widespread literacy, when pushing the plow was more important than pushing the pen, mildly intellectually disabled people—those labeled today as learning disabled and those at the upper end of the spectrum of mental retardation, for example—would simply have merged into the general populace. In early times it seems probable that only the grossest examples of mental defect would have been considered remarkable (Penrose, [1949] 1966). However, those far down the continuum, affected perhaps with multiple handicaps or medically fragile conditions, could not have been expected to survive.

THE MANAGEMENT OF DISABLING CONDITIONS IN ANTIQUITY

Prehistoric and Egyptian Practices

Preagricultural societies could provide little aid and minimal solace to disabled persons; high survival rates are unlikely. Severely impaired individuals would have been incapable of enduring the hardships of nature, unlikely to have been able to detect and ward off enemies, and unable to hunt or forage for food. Moreover, as noncontributing members of the group, they would have constituted an economic hazard.

Archeological findings indicate that aberrant behavior was treated by shamans, priests, or magicians. The shaman or witch doctor, with his skill in invoking help from the spirit world, probably served as the physical and mental healer, and shamanic law was as real to early civilizations as that of today's medicine is to us. Paleontologists, working with remnants of the Stone Age and later, hypothesize that bits of bone, teeth of animals, and vertebrae of snakes found in amulet bags were thought to contain magic force that shamans used to ease their patients (Schmidt, 1936). Cave dwellers treated sufferers by chipping holes in their skulls in order to allow the possessing demons to escape (Apter and Conoley, 1984; Harms, 1976). Hebrew writings indicate that in that society bizarre behavior was interpreted as evidence of the invasion of the body by evil spirits. Terrible exorcism rites were performed by priests, who sometimes succeeded in ridding the people of possession only by killing them (Apter and Conoley, 1984).

---

[1]On the perceptions of and treatment for mental illness in antiquity, see Gill (1985).

After about 10,000 B.C. humanity began a gradual, remarkable transformation: the revolution was the introduction of farming, which began in the Middle East and from there spread over most of Europe. Hunting and food gathering began to give way to agriculture in the areas that constitute present-day Syria, Iran, Iraq, and Turkey. Eventually, in the warm and fertile lands between the great rivers Tigris and Euphrates in present-day Iran the Sumerians built the world's first hill towns of mud and brick and created the essential foundation of civilization—the literate city state.

Up to this point in history humans had only been figures on the landscape. Following game, a single family needed many miles of land over which to roam in search of food; but for sowing crops and raising livestock a few dozens of acres were enough, and food could be stored. Now, as humans began to dominate and change their environment, shaping it to their own purposes, they moved on from nomadic hunting to agriculture, symbolic reasoning, verbal communication, and life in ever larger groups. Towns and cities began to emerge.

With the advent of agriculture and urbanization, opportunities for disabled persons, at least for mere survival, seem to have increased. The ancient Egyptians were the first to document an interest in disabilities and disabled individuals. The Egyptian Ebers papyrus (1550 B.C.), which is probably based on even earlier writing (Feldman, 1970) woven around Imhotep, the Egyptian physician (3000 B.C.), contains a collection of ancient recipes, sober advice, and magic for physicians covering many human ailments, from abortion and tumors. The papyrus contains oblique references to mental retardation and specific discussions of epilepsy, as well as the first known reference to deafness (Moores, 1987).

Given the amount of water-borne blindness and other visually impairing conditions prevalent in Egypt even today, it is not surprising that physicians of ancient Egypt directed much attention to blindness. Early manuscripts described trachoma and gave prescriptions for its cure. To the accompaniment of incantations, a solution of copper, myrrh, and cyprus seeds as well as other ingredients was applied to the patient's eyes with a goose quill (Farrell, 1956b).

The Egyptians were concerned not only with the study of causes and cures of disabilities but with the personal and social well-being of afflicted individuals. At Karmah the priests trained blind persons in music, art, and massage; they participated in religious ceremonies, and in some periods blind persons represented the largest portion of poets and musicians (Moores, 1987). Mentally retarded and other disabled children may have been protected by the followers of Osiris, the most revered of all Egyptian gods (Harms, 1976; Scheerenberger, 1982). Deaf persons garnered less regard: "There is no use wasting words upon the dumb," succinctly commented one early Egyptian (De Land, 1931, p. 7).

Infanticide, the Family, and the State

Ancient medicine seems to have made very little of the life of the newborn, and many early societies practiced infanticide. The Greeks and Romans shared the notion that a vital state arises from the innate strength of its citizens, and they enacted laws designed to weed out early those who could not contribute. "As to the exposure and rearing of children," said Aristotle in his *Politics,* "let there be a law that no deformed child shall live." In a similar vein Hippocrates found it natural to raise the question "Which children should be raised?" Later

Soranus (early second century A.D.) defined the art of child rearing as that of recognizing "the newborns that are worth bringing up" (Etienne, 1976, p. 131).

To the Greeks, children were the property not of their parents, but of the commonwealth. In Sparta, under the laws of Lycurgus, newborn babies were routinely brought before the elders to be examined for their fitness for citizenship. Those seen as being physically capable of developing into warriors were formally adopted by the state, although they were left in the charge of their mothers until age seven. Infants found to be idiotic, blind, or otherwise disabled were exposed to the elements in a gorge in the Taygetus Mountains, thrown into the River Eurotes, or abandoned in the wilderness. Following Solon's laws, Athenians killed their weak children outright or placed them in clay vessels and left them to die by the wayside (French, 1932; Pritchard, 1963). Similar customs, repellent to us for their astounding cruelty, were found in other Mediterranean and European cultures. In Carthage, for example, blind children were burned on a slow fire as a sacrifice to the sun (Bowen, 1847).

Cicero intimated that Rome readily adopted the Greek attitude toward handicapped infants (Barr, [1904b] 1913), although the Romans looked to the family, rather than the state, as the basic unit of socialization (Despert, 1970). The ancient Roman legal code, the Law of the Twelve Tables, dating from the fifth century B.C., was essentially a codification into statutory law of existing customs, reflecting the preponderantly agricultural character of the Roman community (see Steinberg, 1982). Following mandates detailed in the Tables, the family was regarded as sacred; all descendants were subject to the authority of the male head of the human family, the *paterfamilias*. He, as the sole family member considered as a Roman citizen with full legal rights, possessed the power of life and death over family members. As child rearing was the responsibility of the family rather than the state, the father, with his absolute power in the family, had the right to reject a child at birth (de Mause, 1974), to kill, mutilate, exile, or sell his children, or to divorce a wife on any grounds. Any child under three who might someday become a burden on society was thrown into the Tiber by the father. Infants were also left to die in the sewers that ran through the streets of ancient Rome.

Despite the existence of such practices, there are indications of a reluctance to resort to infanticide in ancient times. Early sources contain references to sickly or deformed children and illegitimate sons—the ones who could have been exposed and were not (Bell and Harper, 1977). Greece and Rome began to place restrictions on infanticide; some cities began to limit the right of the parents to kill their newborns; some required that the approval of five neighbors be obtained before infants could be killed; and others halted the infanticide of firstborn males. Thebes outlawed infanticide altogether (de Mause, 1981).

By the time of the Empire (from about 30 B.C.) the rural character of Rome had altered, and strict adherence to the Twelve Tables relaxed. The inflexible authority of the *paterfamilias* was gradually reduced; he no longer held absolute authority over his wife and could not exile his children. Now, unwanted infants were sometimes placed at the base of the Columna Lactaria, and the state provided wet nurses to feed and save the children found there (Scheerenberger, 1982, 1983). In the second century A.D. the *paterfamilias* was deprived of the right to expose his children; by the third century child exposure was the equivalent of murder, although it was not until the fourth century that male parents finally lost all power of death over members of the family. Edward Gibbon (1952) surmises that great numbers of infants who might have been exposed by their parents were rescued and then baptized, educated, and maintained by the early Christians. By the fourth century the Emperor Constantine offered financial assistance to families who might otherwise have abandoned or killed their newborn children (Gibbon, 1952).

Disabled children who survived these Draconian measures—and there appear to have been many, possibly the result of parental solicitude, undetected congenital conditions, or postnatal handicaps—were tolerated if they were of economic or social value. In Rome many blind boys were trained to become beggars or were sold as rowers; blind girls became prostitutes (French, 1932). Mentally retarded people were sold as slaves, taken for beggars, or sometimes deliberately maimed to add to their value as objects of charity. Some disabled people served Rome as amusements or diversions; a wealthy family occasionally kept a mentally retarded person as a fool for the amusement of the household and its guests (Kanner, 1964). Seneca, sometime tutor of Nero, speaks of a blind imbecile (*fatua*) who belonged to his wife (Barr, 1904b). By the second century Roman tastes led to greater popularity for handicapped people as a source of household amusement. A special market was established where a buyer might purchase legless, armless, or three-eyed men, giants, dwarfs, or hermaphrodites (Durant, 1944).

Aversion and distaste characterized the general attitudes of Romans toward disabled persons. Suetonius, premier gossip of the doings of Imperial Rome, confided that the Emperor Augustus "loathed people who were dwarfish or in any way deformed, regarding them as freaks of nature and bringers of bad luck" (Suetonius, [A.D. 120?] 1957, p. 100). It must then be assumed that Augustus avoided the stage performances of the well-born Lycius, a dwarf less than two feet tall with a tremendous voice. Yet, in deference to the will of Julius Caesar, Augustus assumed responsibility for the education of deaf Quintus Pedius; the lad was taught painting, the first recorded evidence of the education of a deaf person (H. P. Peet, 1851).

Medical Treatment

Throughout history, the medical aspects of disabilities have been paramount; other concerns relating to disability have been secondary, where they have been considered at all. What Harlan Lane (1991) and Steven Gelb (1989) refer to as the "medicalization" of special education can be traced back to the Greeks and beyond. Medical investigation typically preceded attempts at education; certainly, no formal training facilities for disabled people were available until the mid-eighteenth century, though attempts to treat medically were widespread long before that. Typically, the causes of a condition have garnered far more attention than its impact.

In the eyes of the Greeks and Romans three categories of disability warranted attention—insanity, deafness, and blindness. Of these, madness (joined as it was with retardation and epilepsy) assumed the gravest proportions in the opinion of physicians, philosophers, and the general population.

Hippocrates (460–377 B.C.?), who founded one of the great medical schools on the island of Cos, illuminated the path that later physicians would follow. In the treatment of disabilities Hippocrates adopted accounts of medical techniques from ancient Egypt. He attempted to treat a variety of handicapping conditions—visual impairment, deafness, epilepsy, and mental retardation—and, in doing so, largely discounted older conceptions of etiology.

For many centuries humans believed that there was a pantheon of gods who lived on mountains or in trees or wherever, and that the afflictions of disabled persons were a visitation of divine or demonic origin (Hodgson, [1952] 1973; H. P. Peet, 1851; Zinsser, 1935). It was widely supposed that disabilities were in the charge of invisible superhuman entities who behaved unpredictably. Early humans deeply believed that the power to cause physical and mental derangement was carried by the gods, who inflicted disability as a punishment upon those who incurred their anger. If the gods were not to blame, then a malignant being who disliked humanity was seen as responsible for evil and unhappiness.

With the rise of Christianity came the belief in the devil, or Satan, as the prime suspect in handicapping conditions. Although early Christianity saw itself as having vanquished a pantheon of gods, piety now conceived the notion of punishment or vengeance from a Divine Master in retaliation for the sins of the affected individual or the parents. Rampant superstition, for example, placed deaf individuals "under the special curse of God" (Stone, 1869, p. 97). Madness signified divine punishment, and blindness was "one of those instruments by which a mysterious Providence has chosen to afflict man" (Dunscombe, 1836, p. 96). Many disabled persons were viewed as polluted, creatures of evil omen, dangerous to the community and to themselves. They were shunned by all who did not wish to be defiled or corrupted, or who had any regard for the safety of their own body and soul. Yet physicians, beginning with Hippocrates, inveighed against the notion that evil spirits and demons caused mental derangement and other disabling conditions (Rosen, 1968).

Hippocrates stressed physiological diagnosis but still retained a nodding acquaintance with the supernatural. He practiced a "rational supernaturalism" (Edelstein, 1937); he assumed that the mystical origins of mental and physical anomalies were less important than causes explainable through observation and diagnosis. Hippocratic medicine was based on knowledge obtained by butchering animals and examining battle wounds, not by examining the human body. Wounds rising from external causes were studied in terms of cause and effect; symptoms without a wound were variously attributed to a common physiological cause, to the spirits, or to the gods.

Fundamental to Hippocratic medicine were the four humors (fluids)—blood, lymph, yellow bile, and black bile—of which the ancients deemed blood to be the most important. Each humor was endowed with a basic quality, such as heat, cold, dryness, and moistness, from which arose certain traits and conditions. A sanginous person, for example, was thought to be subject to inflammatory diseases but could sustain much blood letting; a choleric person was thought to be one who acted hastily and rashly. Disease developed when internal or external factors produced an excess of one of the humors or when an imbalance of these basic qualities acted on organs to produce deleterious effects.

To Hippocrates, mental abnormality was a disease, or a symptom of one, caused in the same way as diseases of the body (Rosen, 1968). Madness was produced by excess of a humor. When present in abundance and under certain conditions, black bile was thought to be a particularly potent cause of various forms of mental illness, especially the condition called melancholia (Rosen, 1968).

Misunderstandings about the nature and causes of sensory handicaps prevailed, partly because of reluctance to dissect the human body and to indulge in self-study and partly because of the difficulties in studying the ear, the eye, and the brain resulting from their inaccessibility and extreme delicacy. Blindness, both in its manifestations and its consequences, was more clearly conceptualized than deafness. When dealing with hearing loss, the ancients considered only the middle and the outer ear; Hippocrates attempted no more than the treatment of otitis media (middle ear infection) (Hodgson, [1952] 1973).

In the time of Augustus and Tiberius Caesar (the first half of the first century A.D.), the medical knowledge of the world was collected and probably amplified by Aulus Cornelius Celsus (25 B.C.–A.D. 50) in *De Medicina* (Hodgson, 1973). Celsus described how he followed the prescriptions of his great predecessors, especially Hippocrates (Rosen, 1968), although he diverged from Hippocratic dictums in treatment regimes. For insanity, Hippocrates prescribed rest, useful work, and understanding companionships. In contrast, Celsus prescribed a wide variety of animal, vegetable, and mineral substances. Probably the most widely used was hellebore, which, given the numerous references in the nonmedical literature, may have been used in antiquity much as aspirin is today (Rosen, 1968). The violently purgative effect of hellebore was employed in the standard treatment of insanity (Rosen, 1968). Celsus recommended black hellebore for depression and, if the patient was "hilarious," white hellebore (Bromberg, 1975). If herbs and medication failed, then Celsus approved correction by blows, stripes, and chains (Beck, 1811).

The primitive state of anatomical knowledge led Celsus to prescribe for ear problems cures and agents that could only have aggravated the damage to an ear drum already subject to chronic otitis media. For example, for ears with pus he recommended that the sufferer "pour in box-thorn juice by itself . . . or leek juice with honey . . . or the juice of sweet pomegranate warmed in its rind, to which a little myrrh is added . . . to wash out the ear with diluted wine, through an ear syringe, and then pour in dry wine mixed with rose-oil, to which a little oxide has been added" (Hodgson, [1952] 1973, p. 64). For those dull of hearing because of age, Celsus suggested "hot oil poured in, or verdigris mixed with honey wine," and for other hearing problems "oil in which worms have been boiled" (Hodgson, [1952] 1973, p. 64).

Of all the physicians who thronged toward Rome, Galen (A.D. 130–200) was one of the most influential. He extended the humoral theory of Hippocrates into a body of medical writing that influenced medical progress until the Renaissance (Bromberg, 1975). Galen maintained the Hippocratic stance that rejected supernatural explanations of mental disorder and viewed the condition in essentially physiological terms (Rosen, 1968). He held conventional attitudes toward deafness, assuming a common cerebral origin for speech and hearing (Hodgson, 1973). In treating deaf persons, Galen and later physicians often

performed an operation "to cure their dumbness by an operation on the liga-
ment of the tongue" (De Land, 1931), a procedure that persisted well into the
twentieth century.

Philosophical Speculation

In the ancient world philosophy and medicine were closely intertwined:
medical prescriptions and philosophical assumptions about handicapping conditions mirrored each other, to be echoed in legal mandates. In searching out
the effects of sensory deprivation, Aristotle (384–322 B.C.) concluded, in essence, that if one of the faculties is lost, some knowledge must also inevitably be
lost. Of the three senses of smell, hearing, and sight, he noted that sight was the
most valuable as far as the necessities of life were concerned but that hearing
was more important in the development of the intellect. Aristotle viewed blindness as the more serious handicap but less debilitating intellectually than deafness; he assumed that those blind from birth were more intelligent than those
born deaf. With his contention that, of all the senses, hearing contributed most
to intelligence and knowledge, Aristotle was led to characterize deaf individuals
as "senseless and incapable of reason," and "no better than the animals of the
forest and unteachable" (McGann, 1888, p. 9).

Deafness baffled Hippocrates—he understood the mechanism of speech but
assumed a common cerebral origin for speech and hearing (H. P. Peet, 1851),
and he finally surmised that there was something supernatural about deafness
(Hodgson, [1952] 1973). Aristotle viewed speech as an instinct, not as a skill acquired by imitation, and also saw speech and hearing as arising from a common
site. "Men that are born deaf," he stated in *Historia Animalium,* iv, 9, "are in all
cases dumb; they can make vocal noises but they cannot speak" (Aristotle, 1910).

With his pronouncements on the status and intelligence of deaf people, Aristotle determined their fate for nearly two thousand years. In the domains of
science and philosophy Aristotle's statements were accepted without reservation by the medieval scholars; what the Scriptures were to theology, his work
became to science and philosophy (H. C. Barnard, 1922). Hence, Aristotle's notion that speech was divine and his teaching that nothing can exist in the human
mind that has not been received through the senses (Smith and Ross, 1910) profoundly affected the way deaf people were perceived in society as recently as the
eighteenth century. Coupled with this was Hippocrates' establishment of an intimate relation between the nerves of speech and hearing, which further exacerbated the plight of deaf individuals. They were treated as not only deaf but as
dumb, owing to some defect of the brain, some incapacity of the vocal organs,
or to possession by some diabolical spirit (see Ferrari, 1906). On the other hand,
Aristotle attributed to blind people equal intellects with the sighted; that, combined with the overt nature of visual impairment, explains why they were accorded marginally more humane treatment.

Legal Mandates

A march through the centuries shows that disabled people were always the
object of social concern, but whether community attention was a boon or a li-

ability depended on many different factors. No two societies viewed their disabled populations in precisely the same way.

Hebraic law contains some of the first known provisions for the disabled, founded on the biblical question "Or who maketh the dumb or deaf, or the seeing or the blind? Have not I, the Lord?" (Exodus 4:10 ff.). Under strictures outlined in the Talmud and Midrash, blind and deaf persons, widows, orphans, and the needy were all treated with special consideration; this rabbinical law was in turn based on certain key passages in Hebrew scripture (Deuteronomy 24:17–18 and 26:18; Leviticus 19:9–10, 14, and 23:22, for example). The Old Testament enjoined: "Thou shalt not curse the deaf nor put a stumbling block before the blind" (Leviticus 19:14) and cursed those "that maketh the blind to wander out of the path." Benign protection under Hebraic law was later reiterated by Maimonides or Moses ben Maimon in the twelfth century and by Shulhan Aruch in the sixteenth (Hodgson, [1952] 1973).

The Greeks sought medical answers to disabilities, but Greek law took little account of the disabled; it was left to the legal minds of Rome to wrestle with the social problems of disabled children and adults. The Roman jurists were not concerned with the nature and cause of disabilities; their sole concern was to ascertain the fact of unsoundness of mind or body and its consequences for the performance of acts judged before the law. This focus led them to create a legal framework characterized by institutions such as guardianships that provided a pattern for later legal developments affecting exceptional persons (see Gaw, 1906, 1907; Hodgson, [1952] 1973).

When confronting mental illness, Roman law took madness into account chiefly to protect property and the members of the community. Under Roman law mental defectives (*mente capti*) were designated as deficient in intellect and provided with guardians. Roman law recognized that those who were born deaf but were capable of speech were persons at law and proficient to discharge legal obligations; those deaf from birth without speech, however, were considered incapable and were classed with madmen and infants, unable to perform any legal act on their own behalf (Gaw, 1906). The law was based on the belief that deaf persons who could not speak had not been deprived of their rights; rather, they had been relieved of the responsibilities of citizenship they could not meet (Gaw, 1906).

In 533 the Roman emperor Justinian (d. 565) commanded that a revised collection of the statute laws be compiled. Scholars brought together many scraps of ancient laws and edicts and finally compiled a fifty-volume rendering of judicial interpretations, the *Corpus Juris Civilis,* which contained the *Digest* as well as a four-volume handbook of civil law, the *Institutes.* Justinian did not make many changes in the law regarding handicapped individuals (Gaw, 1907) but simply codified the ancient edicts that encompassed mental defectives (*mente capti, fatui*), the deaf, the dumb, and those subject to incurable malady (*cura debilium*).

The Code of Justinian classified disabled persons in infinite detail, allowing or denying rights and responsibilities to the different grades of handicap. Under Justinian's law, for example, lunatics and idiots were considered incapable of contracting marriage. The consent of an insane father was not necessary for the marriage of his children, and a person with an insane descendant was permitted to name substitute persons as heirs. There were five classes of deafness, ranging from those who were deaf but could speak to those totally without hearing and without speech (Gaw, 1906).

Although only two manuscripts of the original *Corpus* survived, we do know that Justinian's laws were merged with the codes of the Germanic invaders to form the basis of the law in most European countries. Thanks in part to the uniformity supplied by Justinian, the status of disabled individuals did not alter materially in those countries where the civil law prevailed from the time of Justinian in the sixth century to the mid-eighteenth.

DISABILITY AND THE RISE OF CHRISTIANITY

The Early Christian Era

Beginning in the third century great hordes of ravaging barbarians invaded the Roman Empire. In 410 Alaric and his Visigoths sacked Rome and humiliated the imperial city when its proud senators refused to pay the landless barbarians protection money. With the fall of Rome, those parts of western Europe that had developed urban centers retreated to an agrarian form of society, and systems of feudalism arose. Education, culture, and learning now were relegated to a far less elevated status.

From the death throes of Rome arose a new religion that rapidly overwhelmed paganism and its many cults. In three short centuries Christianity grew from the creed of a tiny handful of believers to become the official religion of most of the Western world. Constantine, the first of the Holy Roman Emperors, legitimized Christianity, declaring it to be the official religion of the Roman Empire in 312. For many centuries to come, civil and religious affairs in Europe were to be inextricably mingled.

The fall of Rome ushered in long centuries of disaster in Europe—social turbulence, plague, warfare, hunger, and famine threatened the lives of the entire population. Life for most people was short; less than half the population survived to maturity (Mahendra, 1985). Cruelty at the hands of humans and hardship at the vicissitudes of nature were commonplace. In a period when disaster periodically threatened the survival of the fit, disabled persons must have fared badly. Little if any aid was proffered on their behalf, and even then, solace was granted only a few.

Monasticism proved to be singularly suited to the needs of the chaotic age that followed the collapse of Roman Empire. By the fourth century strict cloistering was prevalent, as monastic life attracted increasing numbers of men and women who strove for moral perfection through asceticism. By the sixth and seventh centuries monks and nuns had become the principal agents of civilization; in fact, throughout the Middle Ages little work that was rooted in learning and enlightenment was produced outside the cloisters.

The cloistering of handicapped persons seemed a natural outgrowth of the monastic impulse, and, in the context of these dark times, it proved advantageous, as it protected them from the dangers confronting them in the general society. A hospice for the blind was established in the fourth century in Caesarea in Cappadocia (in present-day Turkey). As the centuries passed, hospices—many offering facilities for other special groups—gradually spread across Europe.

For example, in the fifth century Saint Lymnaeus built special cottages adjoining his hermitage at Syr in Syria where he taught blind persons to sing pious songs and they, in turn, accepted alms from those who were moved by their singing. Saint Herre (d. 565) was born in a tiny village in Brittany. Tradition presents him as a sightless, barefooted man who, led by a white dog, wandered throughout the countryside teaching children. Apparently, Herre later formed a small monastery in Brittany that became a shrine for blind musicians (Farrell, 1956b). Saint Bertrand, bishop of Le Mans in France, founded an institution for the blind in the seventh century (see Farrell, 1956b; French, 1932).

Cloistering was not restricted to blind persons. Saint Basil, bishop of Caesarea in A.D. 370, gathered all types of disabled people into the monastic institutions that he controlled. Each handicapped group had separate quarters, but all engaged in common work and worship. Legend holds that during the same century Nicholas, the bishop of Myra, a town in present-day southern Turkey, provided dowries for poor girls and cared for idiots and imbeciles (Barr, [1904b] 1913). For his contributions, Saint Nicholas became the patron saint of the retarded and of pawn brokers, although we remember him as Santa Claus. And the Belgian village of Gheel is famous for its unique system of caring for the mentally ill. Here was located an infirmary and a church centered on the shrine of Saint Dympna. Retarded children were given work in the fields and in the household under the guidance of country folk and the spirit of the saint (Bromberg, 1975; Scheerenberger, 1982).

Even more rare in the early Christian era than isolated attempts to provide care for disabled persons are any indications of attempted cures. Although most references to cures are permeated by an aura of magic, some may well point to what were valid educational attempts posing as miracles. In 504, for example, Saint Severinus "healed Eululius, Bishop of Nevers, who has for some time been deaf and dumb" (De Land, 1931, p. 13). Saint John of Beverley in England was said to have "cured a dumme man with blessing him" (Porter, 1847), the reason that Saint John later became patron saint of the deaf (see Bede, 1849). The life and miracles of Saint Louis, attributed to Guillaume Pathos, confessor of Queen Margaret of Provence, and composed in 1302 or 1303, contains the story of an eight-year-old boy who had never heard or spoken but who regained his hearing at the tomb of Saint Louis (P. B. Fay, 1923). Saint Elizabeth of Hungary was reported to have cured a boy's deafness and dumbness, and Saint Claire is credited with the cure of one Sister Christine (De Land, 1931; H. P. Peet, 1851).

Accounts of treatment in this period point to the influence of the church. Nevertheless, the early Christian church, a potent and stern overseer of people's lives, proved to be equivocal in its attitudes toward those with disabling conditions. The early Christians aspired to create a spiritual revolution rather than a series of coherent social changes. As they preached the spiritual equality of all and diligently promised the kingdom of heaven to the meek in spirit, the hierarchy marked for heavenly attainment systematically omitted certain groups.

Saint Augustine of Numidia, bishop of Hippo in the late fourth century and early fifth century, for example, exalted marriage and formulated the basic

Christian attitude that marriage provides a lawful channel for the relief of lust, results in the procreation of children, and establishes a Christian atmosphere for their rearing. However, Augustine renounced any claims of disabled people for participation in the covenant of the Lord. He may have interpreted Paul's charge to "comfort the feeble-minded" as applicable to those unfortunates weak in intellect, not weak in faith (Barr, [1904b] 1913, p. 25), but he interpreted the Pauline dictum "Faith comes by hearing" to mean that "those who are born deaf are incapable of ever exercising the Christian faith, for they cannot hear the Word, and they cannot read the Word" (OSD, 1895, p. 12). Augustine's declarations effectively denied church membership to deaf persons; they were restricted from the celebration of mass, disallowed the sacrament of communion, and generally excluded because they were unable to express their sins. Until the twelfth century an express dispensation of the pope was necessary to authorize the marriage of a deaf person (H. P. Peet, 1851).

Augustine further paved a troubled route for other disabled groups when his opinions on miraculous healing were accepted by the Council of Toledo in the fifth century. The church fathers avowed that "demonic seizures can be cured only by miracles, whereas diseases . . . can also be overcome by human medical effort" (Veith, 1965). With this ruling, epilepsy and other nervous disorders ceased to be primarily viewed as bodily diseases in the Hippocratic convention, but instead fell totally within the purview of the church.

The Medieval Mind and Disability

By the mid-eleventh century a more settled world began to emerge from the troubled feudal society of Europe. Populations were growing, nomadic invaders had finally been repelled, commerce was expanding, and the cities were reviving after their long neglect. The church led in establishing the new tone of society; the Gregorian Revolution of the late eleventh century built on a revived papacy and focused on basic church reforms that eventually led to new centralized institutions. Secular society was quick to follow the lead of the church.

One might assume that when ecclesiastical thought more closely concerned itself with the social and political conditions of society, more help for disabled persons would develop. But those concerned with the creation of a whole society operating on moral principles ignored the exceptional or questioned their capacity for spiritual achievement and social responsibility. Church law discriminated against disabled individuals, and the conventions of secular society subjected them to unjust laws and treatment. The early legal code of nearly every European country imposed strict civil disabilities on handicapped people—they were deprived of the rights of inheritance, forbidden to testify in a court of justice, and not allowed to make a deed, contract, note, or will (see Gaw, 1906).

With both crown and church disinclined to defend them and indeed often arrayed against them, disabled persons drew small regard and little compassion from the people around them. In the thirteenth century when Henry III of England found his small daughter, Catherine, to be deaf, Matthew Paris, a contemporary historian, described the child as "dumb, and fit for nothing, though possessing great beauty" (De Land, 1931, p. 14). Often disabled persons became the butts of crude humor, as we see in the 1425 tale of four blind men. Encased in full armor and armed with clubs, the men were placed in a square with a large hog, a prize going to the one who could kill the animal (French, 1932). People were likely to interpret the behavior of mentally retarded persons as evil and their mutterings as conversations with the Devil. In sixteenth-century Hamburg, in Germany, for example, mentally retarded individuals were confined in a tower in the city wall, appropriately named the Idiot's Cage (Burdett, 1891).

Most disabled persons in medieval Europe seem to have led an insecure and precarious existence; only a scattered few were granted aid. There is no evidence of public support, but under the aegis of the church hospices to care for exceptional persons did develop, though painfully slowly. In the thirteenth century three hundred French knights captured by the Moslems had their eyes put out. After Louis IX ransomed them, he established the Hospice des Quinz-Vingts to care for the blinded soldiers. Inmates were provided an allowance from the privy purse provided they made soup for the poor. Illiterates and paupers were taken in but provided little training. This establishment later played a role in setting the direction of the education of the blind as well as establishing the pattern for future institutions for blind children and adults (see Farrell, 1956b; French, 1932; discussion of Haüy in Chapter 2, below).

Throughout medieval times varied attitudes to mentally retarded persons are evident. Some observers interpreted the mutterings of mentally retarded persons as dialogues with the devils, but others held them to be mysteriously connected with the unknown and their talk as evidence of divine inspiration (Barr, [1904b] 1913; Burdett, 1891). In some societies a house into which an imbecile was born was considered blessed of God (Barr, 1904b). And yet exploitation and ridicule was common. Following the tradition of the Romans, some lords granted mentally retarded people the freedom of their castles to serve as household fools. Pope Leo X was said to have retained a number of mentally retarded dwarfs to serve as entertainment (Hibbert, 1975).

As the Middle Ages drew to a close, the feudal order slowly gave way to political absolutism and the national state, and new urban social groups arose. Plagues and the disruptions of social change and urbanization created a pervasive pessisimism; discontent within the monolithic church mounted. There developed a widespread sense that all of Christendom was sick, and the world seemed to be falling apart. A new order, the outlines of which could be seen but dimly, was struggling to emerge.

The medieval Christian commonwealth, fashioned and guided by the church of Rome, was wracked by dissension, hatred, and violence. Abuses within the church led many to a desire to return it to its original state, to lend it new life, a process begun as early as 1095 when Pope Urban II called the First Crusade. A little later, in 1150, the church embraced the doctrine of original sin (Durant, 1950, p. 820), which meant that from then on Christians viewed themselves and all humans as inherently evil, saved only by the grace of the good God.

Medieval life was further disrupted in the fourteenth century by the appearance of the Black Death, also called the pestilence or the Great Mortality. Beginning in Central Asia, the plague spread outward to reach the heart of Europe around 1348. This was not the first or only plague to attack Europe, but it was one of the most virulent. It is estimated that between 1347 and 1351 in the whole of Europe, about 25 million persons, as much as one-third of the population, were lost (see Slack, 1985; Zinsser, 1935).

In the face of devastating plague, humans stood helpless and terrified, trapped by a peril against which they had no defense. Responses to the crisis were often extreme. In the early days of the Black Death, mental derangement was obvious in the behavior of those belonging to the sects of flagellants and of those in some parts of central Europe who were caught up in the dancing manias. All who were deranged, whether as a consequence of the disease itself or of the terror it inspired, were prime candidates for the witch hunters who were just beginning to fan out on their grisly search across the Continent. Many believed that the sins of Adam, cast upon his children, was what brought death and dissension to life. With so much evil in the world, apocalyptic thinkers predicted that God would destroy the world and substitute a new one for the old. The final struggle of Armageddon would be between the hosts of Christ and the hosts of the AntiChrist.

Belief in the power of the Devil grew, and his might appeared capable of overthrowing the church and with it, all existing order (Rosen 1968). As awareness of the Devil and his powers was carried to new and terrifying heights, the search for the Antichrist assumed dreadful proportions. By the late thirteenth century conceptions of Armegeddon, of pervasive evil, and of social chaos slowly fused into the intertwined threads of the Inquisition and the prevailing stereotypes about heretics.

As dissension within the church and disruption everywhere assumed alarming proportions, society and the church increasingly proclaimed heresy to be rampant. People believed that the extermination of the agents of the Antichrist was a prerequisite for the salvation of all humanity, and a popular movement arose as church, state, and indeed all of European society demanded the suppression of heresy. Medieval churchmen invented a grotesque ideology, which came to be massively embodied in the Inquisition, of an evil unity between heresy, sorcery, and witchcraft. It was the belief of the church that heretics were the authors, the patrons, and the objects of witchcraft. Hence, the witch hunts grew out of the hunt for heretics, just as the witch trials evolved out of the trials for heresy (Rosen, 1968).[2]

By 1484 Pope Innocent VIII declared open war on witches. Then in 1487 two Dominicans, the chief inquisitors for Germany, a center of intense witch hunting, produced the notorious *Malleus Maleficarum* [The hammer of witches], which provided intimate details of the habits and characteristics of witches. It served as well as a manual of procedures and theory for witchcraft trials. By the time Martin Luther posted his ninety-five theses to a church door in Wittenburg (1517), Europe already possessed excellent descriptions of witches, and all Europe seemed to swarm with them (Rosen, 1968). Many believed that a preternatural dominion of the earth was exercised by old women and widows, and by any person who was unusual, different, deviant, or, no doubt, disabled.

Until the eighteenth-century Enlightenment, European civilization was haunted by the idea of witches. Witch hunting was prosecuted with vigor; for

---

[2]The witch hunts in their various manifestations have received intense attention from scholars. Herein, my concern is with but one facet, the implications for disabled people. On the witch hunts in general see Anglo (1977); Estes (1984); MacFarlane (1970); E. Midelfort (1968); H. C. Midelfort (1982); Monter (1972, 1977); Thomas (1971); Trevor-Roper (1969).

almost three centuries Europe and its overseas colonies were the sites of organized witch hunts. The hunts and the trials led to the deaths of hundreds of
thousands of people by burning, hanging, drowning, or other methods. The full
count of victims of the witchcraft mania cannot be calculated; the likeliest guess
is that the total number of trials exceeded 100,000 and the number of executions
was below this number (Monter, 1977). Witchcraft became the most important
capital crime for women in early modern Europe; perhaps 80 percent of the accused were women.[3]

How many disabled persons were accused or perished is unknown; that they
were implicated seems beyond question. Much earlier, Saint Augustine had included madness and epilepsy within the domain of the religious authorities.
Now the *Malleus* prescribed measures to differentiate witches from normal persons: "If the patient can be relieved by no drugs, but rather, seems to be aggravated by them, then the disease is caused by the devil" (quoted by Alexander
and Selesnick, 1966, p. 68). One treatise on exorcism asserted that symptoms of
possession were obvious in those feigning to be mad, or those who became deaf,
dumb, insane, or blind (Bromberg, 1975). Another expert enumerated the signs
that indicated possession and included diseases that doctors could not diagnose
and treat (Bromberg, 1975). With many handicapping conditions such as deafness, retardation, insanity, and epilepsy already linked by tradition to the supernatural and unamenable to medieval medical treatment, the consequences
for disabled individuals of assertions like these from the authorities must have
been devastating. Take a case reported by Ambroise Paré, a medieval surgeon
who treated a young nobleman who suffered "convulsions that involved different parts of his body such as the left arm, or the right, or on occasion only a
single finger, one loin or both, or his spine, and then his whole body would become so suddenly convulsed and disturbed that four servants would have difficulty in keeping him in bed" (quoted in Bromberg, 1975, p. 48). It was
discovered that the Devil, forced to reveal himself by means of religious exorcism, caused this malady. Many of the people put to death for witchcraft were
likely not possessed by satanic spirits at all, but instead may have been the victims of neurological or emotional disorders (D. H. Tuke, 1882).

Mentally ill persons were turned over to the clergy and the secular powers,
who combined to punish the "agents of the devil" by burning them at the stake
or otherwise disposing of them. Mentally retarded people may have also fallen
into the witch hunters' net. Scheerenberger (1982) states that during the Inquisition some mentally retarded individuals were executed, either because they
were perceived as being the offspring of witches or because their own behavior
seemed bizarre or threatening.

John Calvin preached that mentally retarded persons are possessed by Satan; Martin Luther was of the opinion that a mentally retarded child is merely a
mass of flesh (*massa carnis*) with no soul (Kanner, 1964). Luther further subscribed to the belief that the Devil is the father of idiots; he denounced the mentally handicapped as "filled with Satan" (Barr, [1904b] 1913, p. 26) and even
suggested that one child be taken to the nearest river and drowned (Kanner,
1964).

---

[3]On the gender bias of the witch hunters, see Quaife (1987).

It is also possible that handicapped people or the parents of handicapped children would attribute a disorder to witchcraft as a last resort, when prayers or medicines had failed and exorcism seemed the last hope of a cure. Sawyer (1989) points out that witchcraft lies at the intersection of the biological, existential, and social worlds of the infirm. Of all the afflictions attributed to witchcraft, none was more common among adults than disturbances of the mind; the next largest category among children and adults was lameness with a chronic wasting away of the body or limbs that boded permanent disability and probable death (Sawyer, 1989). When the onset of a disorder was sudden and unexpected, or when naturalistic medicine offered little or no relief, then witchcraft might well have seemed an unavoidable alternative.

The response to witch hunting included dismay and disagreement from many quarters throughout the course of its unhappy history, and it must not be assumed that the ideas embodied in the *Malleus* received universal assent (Teall, 1962). However, it was not until the late seventeenth century that the light of reason began to drive the long prevalent beliefs in witchcraft underground.

DISABILITY IN A MORE HUMANISTIC WORLD

The witchcraft mania, indeed, many forms of superstition, actually began to subside in the liberal atmosphere of the Renaissance, which brought about new knowledge in medicine and psychiatry, and, in all fields of learning, as well as unprecedented activity in exploration and colonization. Philosophers in the sixteenth and seventeenth centuries scrutinized the old shibboleths and fostered an increased skepticism. Adventurous thinkers, those of a liberal turn of mind and novel ideas, spoke against witch hunts and their trappings.

For example, Gironimo Cardano, an Italian physician of the sixteenth century (see Box 1-2), not only railed against witch hunting but proposed some of the earliest known measures for special education. Witchcraft as a crime gradually faded from the European scene. In England, for example, the penal laws against witchcraft were repealed in 1736. As witch hunts became less frequent and the very existence of witches came into question more often and more openly, the safety of disabled people increased, and their lives became somewhat less precarious.

The experience of handicapped people in medieval times was not a tale of unmitigated hardship, deprivation, isolation, and gruesome witch hunts. Even as some fanatics pursued the swarms of witches they imagined were polluting daily and ecclesiastical life, others, following more humanistic impulses, pursued ideas more in tune with emerging Renaissance thought.

Primarily an Italian experience, the Renaissance began in the fourteenth century and reached its heighth in the fifteenth and sixteenth centuries. With the movement arose a new interest in humanistic principles, individuality, learning, and the secular arts. Humanism in art led to a more intense focus on the human body and so to the development of more sophisticated surgery and medical practices. The age-old fear of dissecting the human body subsided, and the fields of anatomy and physiology enjoyed a period of vigorous development. The ear, for example, one of the smallest and most complex organs of the body,

Box 1-2

Gironimo Cardano (1501–1576)

New philosophies wrought by the many social and intellectual changes of the Renaissance began to burn away the mists of superstition and fear and to lead away from the medieval reliance on supernatural explanations for any phenomenon. One of the liveliest speculative thinkers of the Renaissance was Gironimo Cardano (in English, Jerome Cardan), the illegitimate son of a lawyer who rose to become the rector of Padua University, the leading medical facility in Europe. A genius, a physician by profession, a mathematician by natural taste and talent, Cardano is sometimes described as the first psychiatrist. He railed against the obscenities of the witch hunts; as early as 1550 he described those called vulgarly *stigae* as miserable, beggarly old women, and attributed their unusual or aberrant behavior to poverty, hunger, and hardship.

When one of his sons was found to have defective hearing, Cardano was drawn into philosophical speculation about the potentialities of disabled individuals and methods for their education. He disregarded Aristotelian imperatives and, adopting principles that would characterize the empirical psychology of John Locke a century later, was probably the first to see the true relationship among the senses. He believed that the instruction of the sensorily handicapped was possible (Monroe, 1926) and surmised that it would be successful through the use of alternative stimuli.

It would be possible, assumed Cardano, to teach the blind by means of feeling, and so he devised a sort of Braille code. He also held that "the instruction of the deaf is difficult, but it is possible" and further reasoned that "writing is associated with speech, and speech with thought," so therefore "written characters and ideas may be connected without the intervention of sound" (quoted by Monroe, 1926, p. 257). Although Cardano elaborated a sort of raised print code for the use of deaf people, he did not essay a practical application of his theories. Nevertheless, his statements mark a turning point in attitudes toward sensorily deprived persons (see Hodgson, [1952] 1973).

was examined and its basic mechanisms traced. Two Italian anatomists made important discoveries about the structure of the ear: Gabriello Fallopio (1523–1562) described the bony labyrinth of the ear, and Bartolommeo Eustachio (1524?–1574) identified the tensor tympani muscle and the Eustachian tube (Hodgson, [1952] 1973). Others added to the understanding of the ear: Costanzo Varoli identified the stapedius muscle in 1570, and Aquapendente described the function of middle ear muscles in 1598.

At the same time, the invention of printing resulted in a wider dissemination of knowledge and a surge in the spread of literacy. More books were produced during the half-century after Johann Gutenberg's press began operating in the

1450s than were likely to have issued from all the scriptoria of Europe and the Roman Empire since the first years A.D. Literacy grew rapidly (Bromberg, 1975). Moreover, the availability of reading materials motivated efforts to understand the mechanics of the visual system and to seek ways of improving sight for reading. Legend claims that eye glasses were invented by Saint Jerome (340?–420), perhaps because Jerome was the most notable student of Didymus (308–395), the blind scholar of Alexandria. Whoever the inventor may have been, spectacles began to appear in Italy in the fourteenth century and were in common use by the sixteenth.

The State of Medicine

Medieval society was not a medical desert; it was replete with empirics or quacks, divines, parsons, and magicians, as well as responsible physicians. From the thirteenth century on, these practitioners created a mixture of the rational and the unreasoned in a body of medical literature that described an enormously wide range of disabling conditions and their cures. A science of medicine emerged slowly, although Renaissance anatomy, physiology and medicine continued to draw from the notions of Hippocrates, Celsus, and Galen, often grafting onto these occasional bizarre notions taken from religion and demonology to construct its understanding of the etiology and treatment of disease. Anatomy and physiology were not exact sciences, and the treatments proposed for epilepsy, madness, and sensory impairments often amounted to nothing more than incantations, spells, and witches' brews, in short, little more than quackery.

Bromberg (1975) offers insight into Renaissance medicine with a glance at the table of contents of one medical treatise, Karl F. Paullini's *Flagellum salutis* [From sickness arises health] (1698). Paullini dealt with "the usefullness of voluntary beatings in many diseases of the head; Beatings in meloncholia; in frenzy; in paralysis; in epilepsy; in facial expression of feebleminded; in hardness of hearing; in toothache; in dumbness; hysterical crying; in nymphomania" (original punctuation, quoted by Bromberg, 1975, p. 53).

Epilepsy particularly was subject to a wide range of treatments. The condition drew considerable attention from Hippocrates, Celsus, and Galen, and during the Middle Ages its importance is testified to by its inclusion in nearly every medical treatise concerning children (see Zilboorg and Henry, 1941). Considered a particularly virulent manifestation of madness, epilepsy was long thought to abate under the influence of blood, the most important bodily humor. The Romans lined their epileptics up at the Forum to drink the supposedly curative blood of slain gladiators. Cures of the Middle Ages were little more appealing. One involved the consumption of "the brain of a mountain goat drawn through a golden ring." In another, the afflicted person could ingest "the gall still warm from a dog who should have been killed the moment the epileptic fell in the fit" (D. H. Tuke, 1882, p. 8) . The Scots suggested that the sacrifice of a live cock would benefit epileptics, probably with the passage of the evil spirit from the afflicted person to the cock. To carry out the cure it was suggested: "On the spot where the patient falls, the black cock is buried alive, along with a lock of the patient' s hair and some parings of his nails" (D. H. Tuke, 1882, pp. 20–21).

For those manifesting "idiocy and folly" the cure consisted of putting "into ale cassia, and lupins, bishopwort, alexander, githfife, fieldmore, and holy water, then let him drink" (D. H. Tuke, 1882, p. 4). For "mad and furious men" one treatment echoed Celsus—the black hellebore of the Christmas rose "purgeth all melancholy humors" (D. H. Tuke, 1882, p. 31).

Attempts during the Middle Ages and Renaissance to alleviate hearing problems were varied. One treatment forced deaf persons to shout so loudly that blood flowed from their mouths, in order to awaken their latent hearing (Hiedsiek, 1898). In other treatments, the occipital bone was struck hard enough to fracture it, in the hope that the blow might shake something loose (Hodgson, [1952] 1973). Sufferers from earaches were advised to drop the juice of a baked onion in the affected ear or to plug the ear with lint saturated with laudanum (Kile, 1916). Or they could take "Earth Wormes and fry them with Goose-grese, and drop a little thereof warme into the Deafe or, pained eares" ("Cures," 1926, p. 393). Cases of infection were treated with a white-hot iron applied to the mastoid, or the burning of a cottony material in contact with the skin from the back of the neck around to the chin in order to draw off the pus and "feculent humours" (Hodgson, [1952] 1973; "On attempted," 1851, p. 244).

More benign cures, if not more effective ones, began to appear in British periodicals in the seventeenth century. Jean Paul Seigel (1969) relates the story of a reader of the *British Apollo* who observed that normally he had to speak as loud as he was able in order to communicate with his deaf friend. But when riding in a coach with him on stone, the friend could hear distinctly every word he said. *Apollo* explained: "we shall impute the Cause of this Gentlemen's Deafness to a vitiation or laxity of the Drum of the Ear. Now, by the Impulse of the continu'd and more Vehement Sound, This Thin Membrane or Drum is Enforc'd to its due Extension, and is thereby in some measure Enabled to Perform its Proper Office" (quoted in Seigel, 1969, p. 102).

Institutionalization

Antiquity had no institutions for the care of disabled or indigent persons, and the early Christian era saw only scattered hospices and asylums established across Europe beginning in the fourth century. Public institutionalization for health problems developed between the sixth and the thirteenth centuries when leprosy became a major health concern. Leprosariums multiplied—there were perhaps as many as 19,000 throughout the Christian world (Foucault, 1965).

As the leprosy epidemic in Europe began to subside at the beginning of the seventeenth century, many of these institutions were converted, especially to the needs of those who were considered insane. Early medieval society made no effort to conceal the insane and mental defectives from public view. They were a visible part of everyday society, and, by and large, community attitudes toward these individuals were a compound of fear and contempt, mingled to a lesser extent with an element of compassion (Rosen, 1968). Insane persons occupied a special place in society; they were seen as outcasts characterized by disorder and incoherence, particularly the most dangerous among them, namely, the frenzied, the angry, the threatening, and the maniacal (Doermer, [1969] 1981).

Though many outcasts wandered freely through the squalor and cruelty of the late Middle Ages, society eventually reached the point where it could no longer tolerate the potential dangers posed by the insane. Converted leprosariums became the focal points of a complex of institutions, variously termed madhouses, bedlams, or lunatic hospitals. Rarely were these places named *asylums*—this gentler term was generally reserved for places of protection, retreat, and shelter, which little resembled the realities of seventeenth-century madhouses. It was not until the late eighteenth century that the word *asylum* was used to describe a hospital for lunatics.

Institutions do not exist in a vacuum, nor do they arise without precedent. The practice of confining mad people and other exceptional persons that became widespread in the mid-seventeenth century constituted a response to both their higher visibility in society and the perceived need for society to protect itself against the harm that the deviant, the defective, or the dependent person might incur. Witch hunters had not managed to exterminate all of society's troubling elements; now alternative methods were sought, and the confined congregate institution seemed a logical solution. Unlike the monasteries and hospices that arose to save handicapped persons from a vile world, the institutions that developed from the early seventeenth century served to protect society from the physically, intellectually, and socially deviant and dependent persons in its midst.

The early lunatic hospitals housed many more people than just those who were mentally ill; about 10 percent of the inmates, on the average, were labeled as insane. The lunatic hospitals also incarcerated heretics, social dissidents, and others who threatened the established order without actually committing any crimes. Beggars and vagabonds; those without property, jobs, or trades; political gadflies and heretics; prostitutes; libertines, syphilitics, and alcoholics; idiots and eccentrics; rejected wives, deflowered daughters, and spendthrift sons—could all be incarcerated and thus rendered harmless and virtually invisible (Doermer, [1969] 1981).

In London the Hospital of St. Mary of Bethlehem, first established in 1247, arose again in 1676 from the ashes of the Great Fire (Byrd, 1974) to become a major lunatic hospital. The name quickly degenerated into the nickname "Bedlam," which eventually became a generic designation for any lunatic hospital and has come to mean any noisy chaos.

Similar centers were established in Paris in 1630 under the tutelage of Saint Vincent de Paul (1581–1660). Cardinal Richelieu had begun to turn the ancient chateau of St. Lazare into a military hospital but ceded the property to Vincent de Paul, who gathered there the homeless, the outcast, and the feeble in mind and body. Bicêtre, as the institution soon came to be called, rapidly assumed the character of a congregate institution (large, multicelled) with entrance criteria based solely on need. Vincent de Paul also obtained the property known as Salpêtrière, which the government later managed as a house for beggars. By the eighteenth century Salpêtrière had become the women's lunatic hospital, Bicêtre the men's (see Ireland, 1877).

Callous treatment was the hallmark of all early lunatic hospitals. In England prescriptions for "the curing of Mad people" were based on "their reverence or standing in awe of such as they think their Tormentors." It was believed that

"Furious Mad-men are sooner, and more certainly cured by punishments, and hard usage, in a straight room, than by Physick or Medicines." Hence, overseers were advised to "Let the diet be slender and not delicate, their clothing coarse, their beds hard, and their handling severe and rigid" (quoted by Doermer, [1969] 1981 p. 26).

Whether to raise funds, to illustrate the potential rationality of the disabled, or simply to titillate a curious public, those whose responsibility it was to care for exceptional people exhibited them to the public in a variety of contexts, a practice that persisted until the close of the nineteenth century. Indeed, the exhibiting of deviance and disability in their various forms for money can be traced to the first lunatic hospitals, where inmates were shown as caged monsters to a paying populace (Doermer, [1969] 1981). City folk, searching entertainment, flocked to see the lunatics and their antics. For a few pennies' admission, Londoners could visit Bedlam on a Sunday and promenade past cells arrayed like a circus sideshow (Byrd, 1974). So popular were the lunatic exhibitions that contemporary accounts from London, Paris, and various German cities tell how they vied for audiences with animal acts (Doermer, [1969] 1981).

Educational Advances

The gathering humanistic and philosophical spirit of the Renaissance flowered into genuine educational attempts that, though nascent and primitive, demonstrated that disabled persons could learn and achieve. Some of the major principles that were to guide special education were established during the late Renaissance period. It was deaf persons who were first granted consideration in educational contexts, followed by blind, and, much more tardily, mentally retarded people. Closely linked to this progression was the philosophical precept that underlay special education at its founding. Teachers, writers, and philosophers based their interventions on the belief that discovering the manner in which deaf persons learned, especially the way in which they acquired language, would provide a key to the history of thought and of humankind in general.

The Beginnings in Spain

However, it was Spain, not Renaissance Italy, that spawned the first authenticated special educational efforts, and it was fiscal considerations, not philosophy, that provided the immediate motive for this first attempt. From the Benedictine monastery of San Salvador, near Burgos in northern Spain, comes the earliest evidence of formal and systematic instruction of any disabled individuals. A strong trait of hereditary deafness haunted Spain's ruling families. Under laws of inheritance that harked back to the Justinian legal codes, deaf boys could not claim their inheritance if they could not speak. Thus, the laws of inheritance that affected great estates became the educational spur for the establishment of the means to educate the deaf sons of Spanish aristocrats.

Pedro Ponce de León (1520–1584), a Benedictine monk, employing methods of his own devising, assumed the instruction of the scions of some of Spain's wealthiest families. Detailed descriptions of Ponce's methods are not available, but his own testimony and that of his pupils and impartial observers indicates that the lads learned to speak with facility. Apparently, Ponce "instructed the boys in writing, then pointed out the objects signified by the written characters, and finally exercised them in the repetition of the vocal organs of the utterances which corresponded to the characters" (OSD, 1884, p. 10). In a legal document of 1578 Ponce detailed the advances of the boys under his tutelage:

> I have had for my pupils, who were deaf and dumb from birth, sons of great lords and notable people, whom I have taught to speak, read, write and reckon; to pray, and assist at mass, to know the doctrines of Christianity, and to know how to confess themselves by speech; some of them also learn Latin, and some both Latin and Greek, and to understand the Italian language; and one was ordained, and held office and emolument in the Church, and performed the services of the Canonic Hours; and he also, and some others, arrived at a knowledge of natural philosophy and astrology; and another succeeded to an estate and marquisate, and entered the army, and in addition to his other attainments, as has been related, was skilled in the use of all kinds of arms, and was especially an excellent rider. And besides all this, some were great historians of Spanish, and foreign history; and, above all, they were versed in the doctrine, Politics and Discipline from which Aristotle excluded them. (Quoted in Mathison, 1906, p. 416)

To observers steeped in ancient prejudices, Ponce's achievements seemed miraculous, but his own reports hold a great deal of colorful exaggeration. Moreover, as Susan Plann (1991) argues, Ponce's work was less of an "astounding cognitive leap" than an astute application of the sign language he and his brother Benedictine monks used daily. Ponce's great achievements may not have been teaching speech and language to the deaf boys but more his recognition that disability did not hinder learning and his use of alternative stimuli, in this case, sign language. Most importantly, perhaps, Ponce de Leon was the first successful special educator, and 1578 the year in which special education truly began.

The Constable of Castile had a deaf younger brother, so it is not surprising that the constable's secretary, a former soldier named Jean Pablo Bonet (1579–1629), continued the work, assisted by Ramirez de Carrion. Whereas Ponce used conventional signs but not fingerspelling or speechreading, Bonet added a manual component, employing a methodology that incorporated a hand alphabet, signs, writing, speech, and a stress on lipreading, which, he claimed, could not be taught but only acquired through concentrated attention (Lane, 1976). To stimulate and teach speech, Bonet suggested the use of a flexible leather tongue to imitate the positions of the living tongue (Seguin, 1876).

In 1620 Bonet published the first practical treatise on the art of teaching the deaf, his *Simplification of the Letters of the Alphabet, and a Method of Teaching Deaf Mutes to Speak* (see H. P. Peet, 1850). Bonet's work did not appear in English until 1890; only coincidence and good luck sent a version to London by a circuitous route in 1644.

The British Pioneers

Sir Kenelm Digby, son of one of the Gunpowder Plot conspirators, visited Spain with the Prince of Wales, later Charles I, in 1623 and met one of Bonet's pupils, Luis de Valesco. In exile in Paris in 1644, Digby wrote *Treatise on the Nature of Bodies,* in which he recounted the unprecedented accomplishments in Spain with the deaf (see Digby, 1665, 1827). Through his close correspondence with John Wallis on philosophical subjects, Digby presented the Spanish accomplishments to a small British audience avidly searching for new lines of philosophical inquiry. Over the following half-century Bonet's work guided and inspired a quintet of British works on the nature of language, the elements of speech, and practical methodologies for teaching deaf persons.

In seventeenth-century England philosophical inquiry rather than pragmatic considerations underlay early designs for intervention with disabled individuals. Philosophers, avidly probing the origin and development of language, recruited deaf people as objects of study. Blind people were also studied. The philosophers wished to discover whether a person who had never seen could, if sight were suddenly restored, recognize through vision what had previously been learned by touch.

The Royal Society of London, an organization of thinkers and scientists, gained a royal charter in 1662 with an informal mandate to find "histories of phenomena," the universal and natural "history of things."

Paralleling the quest for a universal history was a desire for a universal language, frequently marked by a demand for a dictionary of words to provide accuracy and precision to the language. Calls for a universal language, first heard in the mid-seventeenth century, echoed again and again across the next three hundred years, always to the ultimate advantage of deaf persons. For example, the search was continued in the next century by such redoubtable characters as John Cleland, who wrote the immortal (or immoral) *Fanny Hill* to finance his elusive search. And as we shall see, in the nineteenth century Alexander Melville Bell's quest for a universal alphabet altered the education of deaf children for nearly a hundred years.

With their strong emphasis on language, it is little wonder that members of the Royal Society issued so many studies of deafness; examples are those undertaken by William Holder, George Dalgarno, John Bulwer, and John Wallis. Their purpose was to learn from deaf persons the secret of what people were like before language, what their ideas were before being filtered and shaped by conversation. These philosopher-scientists elucidated their work with deaf children and adults in philosophical papers written for the society: Wallis's *De loquela* (1653) and "A Letter to Robert Boyle Esq." ([1670] n.d.); William Holder's *Elements of Speech* ([1699] 1967); George Dalgarno's *Didascalocophus* ([1680] 1971); and George Sibscota's *Deaf and Dumb Man's Discourse* ([1670] 1967). These were chiefly philosophical treatises concerning the nature of language that contained elaborate analyses of the different elements of speech. The teaching of deaf people was used to illustrate the new theories that were beginning to take hold. Some, depending on the bent of the author, stressed the acquisition of artificial speech (Mathison, 1906). The reports of these pioneers thus hold interest today chiefly as early instances of educational efforts; they did not represent advances in the comprehension of the psychology of deafness. Most of the members of the Royal Society interested in deafness were dilettantes who had little or no insight into the epistemological and psychological complexities of deafness (Seigel, 1969). In concert with notions prevalent since the days of Hippocrates, they viewed deaf people as curiosities and were more often concerned with speculations of the physiological causes and cures for deafness than with the psychological, social, and educational applications of their findings.

John Wallis (1616–1703), a professor of geometry at Oxford and one of the founding members of the Royal Society, was the most influential British authority on deafness in the seventeenth and eighteenth centuries (Hoolihan, 1985). As an internationally respected mathematician, a prolific author, a correspondent with some of the best minds in Europe, and one of the greatest of Newton's English precursors (Hoolihan, 1985), Wallis's reputation in his own and later ages was such that he exerted a profound influence on the nascent field of special education.

Wallis's *Grammatica linguae anglicanae. Cui praefigur, De loquela sive sonorumm formastione, tractacus grammaticophysicus* was a grammar of the English language for non-English speakers printed at Oxford in 1653 and written in Latin. Prefaced to the *Grammatica* was a treatise of particular importance to the education of deaf persons. Wallis's "De loquela" [On speech] described the organs of speech and the nature of voice; it also presented a detailed analysis of the phonetic elements of English pronunciation, which was useful, according to the author, to foreigners and deaf people.

When Wallis assumed the instruction of twenty-five-year-old Daniel Whalley in 1661, "De loquela" served as the basis for his teaching. Wallis attempted to make Whalley understand the structural elements of language, that is, "to teach him to understand the significance of words and their relations" (OSD, 1884, p. 11). Wallis relied on instruction in written language, and then he used some method of signs for speech, most likely a hand alphabet designed by his friend and contemporary George Dalgarno (1626–1687), which Wallis appropriated without credit (*AADD*, 1850). To stimulate speech, Wallis showed Whalley how the organs of speech moved for specific sounds so that the student "may, by art, pronounce those sounds, which others do by custome" (Wallis, [1670] n.d., p. 1089). So proficient did Whalley become that John Wallis presented him before the Royal Society to demonstrate his speech ability, which he did, "though not elegantly, yet so as to be understood" (OSD, 1884, p. 11).

William Holder (1616–1698), musician, clergyman, fellow of Royal Society, and brother-in-law of Christopher Wren, also taught deaf students through the use of a finger alphabet and stylized signs. George Dalgarno (1626–1687), brought to deaf education original conceptions that anticipated some of the methods that are used even today (see Dalgarno, 1971). Sensing that language development required early intervention, Dalgarno suggested that mothers and nurses could make "successful addresses" to the dumb child if "the mother or nurse had but as nimble a hand as they usually have a tongue" (quoted by A. G. Bell, 1884b, p. 32).

Unlike Holder, Wallis, and Dalgarno who instructed individual deaf persons, John Bulwer was a theorist who pointed out safe routes for other teachers to follow. Bulwer preceded Wallis by producing in 1648 the first English work in deafness, *Philocophus* [The deaf man's friend], which he dedicated to Sir Edward Gosticke, a deaf and dumb gentleman who knew signs and fingerspelling but who wanted to learn to speak. In 1654 John Bulwer published a companion vol-

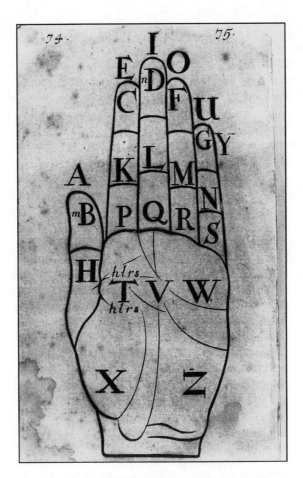

Figure 1-1   Diagram of Dalgarno's glove.
Photograph courtesy of the Gallaudet University Archives.

ume, *Chirologia, or, the Naturall Language of the Hand* ([1654] 1975). Bulwer's stress was not in the acquisition of artificial speech but in finding means to overcome, or at least accommodate to, the handicap of deafness. Rejecting the Hippocratic dictum that there existed a common site in the brain for hearing and speech, Bulwer argued that "the truth is they speak not, because they cannot hear" (quoted by Farrell, 1956a, p. 6). And, as Bonet had done earlier, Bulwer emphasized the value of lipreading: "a Man Born Deaf and dumbe," he stated, "may be taught to Heare the sound of words with the Eie" (Bulwer, 1648, preface).

Even more startling was Bulwer's petition for "an academy for the mute," possibly the first time that anyone had suggested special schooling for a disabled group. But the ramparts of entrenched superstition were as yet unassailable, as Bulwer "soon perceived by falling into discourse with some rationall men." The design, he wrote, appeared "so paradoxicall, prodigious and Hyperbolicall, that it did rather amuse them than satisfie their understandings" (quoted by J. C. Gordon, ed., 1892b, p. xx), it being the prevailing opinion that "original deafness and dumbness is not curable but by miracle" (quoted by Mathison, 1906, p. 414).

As the British philosophers and teachers labored to discover causes and cures for deafness, their efforts touched the lives of very few deaf people. However, in 1720, the year following the publication of *Robinson Crusoe,* Daniel Defoe made the hero of one of his tales a deaf man. *The Life and Adventures of Mr. Duncan Campbell* was based on a real person, a deaf seer who had captivated London society. In this first popular exposé of the problems of deaf people, Defoe pointed out that "a great many more believe it impossible for persons born deaf and dumb to write and read" (Defoe, [1720] 1903, p. 43), a myth he punctured by interweaving the pedagogy of John Wallis with his tale of Duncan Campbell.

Henry Baker (1698–1774), naturalist and a fellow of the Royal Society, read Defoe's book (and married his daughter, Sophia) and thus learned about the methods of Dr. Wallis there enumerated. Baker's interest in deafness and its implications originally developed when he visited a relative who had a deaf daughter. Jane Forester was Baker's first pupil. After succeeding with her, he became a visiting teacher; he had no school, but lived with his pupils (Oxley, 1930). Baker was very secretive, so much so that he extracted securities for as much as £100 from pupils not to disclose his methods. He took only those pupils with whom success was assured and, as the work soon became his sole livelihood, Baker is remembered more as the first professional teacher of deaf persons than for any methodological or psychological insights.

Oral Methodologies

Almost since its inception the education of deaf people has been marred by divisive controversy concerning the most appropriate modes of communication. One school, that of the manualists, views deafness as a human difference, deserving its own unique language that would circumvent the major deficits of hearing impairment. The opposing faction, the oralists, sees deafness as a handicap that can, and should, be overcome if deaf people will assume normal positions in society. Although the controversy regarding communication methods reached its most divisive pitch in late-nineteenth-century North America, the seeds of the debate were unwittingly sown by the pioneers of the seventeenth century.

As the British teachers all employed methodologies reliant on finger alphabets, possibly combined with stylized sign languages, a contrasting pedagogy arose in Europe. John Conrad Amman and Franciscus Mercurius endeavored to maintain the primacy of spoken language; they "made the essence to consist of the artificial restoration and use of the voice" (Mathison, 1906, p. 420).

John Conrad Amman (1669–1724), a Swiss doctor of medicine who emigrated to the Netherlands, was fascinated by the problem of language development, especially what he saw as its mystical and divine origin: "the Voice," he cried, "is an Emanation from that very Spirit, which God breathed into Man's nostrils, when He created him a living soul" (Amman, [1694] 1972, p. 6). Echoing Aristotelian imperatives, Amman held that speech was a mysterious gift of God and the only means for the expression of language, which led him to develop an extravagant estimate of the importance of oral language and of its absolute necessity in the cultivation of the intellect (Rae, 1848c). Amman asserted that speech that "is performed by signs and Gestures" is "base and deficient" (Amman, [1694] 1972, preface), and he bemoaned the "miserable . . . condition of those deaf individuals compelled to employ such modes" (Amman, [1694] 1972, p. 4).

Beginning with Baker and Amman, it became characteristic of those who were developing methods to impart speech to deaf persons to guard their pedagogy closely; it was equally characteristic of manual promoters to share their methods with all comers. Amman cloaked his methods in secrecy and, although he published two influential books, *Surdus loquens* [The talking deaf man] (1694) and *Dissertatio de loquela* (1700), they revealed much of his philosophy but merely a taste of his pedagogy (Amman, [1694] 1972, [1700] 1873). As Édouard Seguin (1876a) pointed out, Amman's books fail to delineate how he "developed the minds and hearts of his pupils" or even how he applied speech to other teaching. All we know is that Amman encouraged perfect articulation through the use of touch and a mirror, teaching the vowels first, and insisted that his pupils be "neither too young nor too stupid" (Amman, 1873). Nevertheless, Amman's philosophy, with its extravagant estimate of the importance of speech, introduced a line of reasoning that was fundamental to the formulation of oral methods of deaf instruction and that, from the first, exerted a leading influence in Germany (E. A. Fay, 1874).

Franciscus Mercurius, the Baron van Helmont (1614?–1699), a Belgian chemist and oculist, produced less impact on the developing field of the education of deaf persons; in fact, the peculiar bent he adopted is more curious than valuable. Van Helmont believed in a metaphysical origin of language and theorized that Hebrew was the natural language of humanity. He demonstrated how the shape and character of each letter of the alphabet in Hebrew conformed to the position of the organs of speech when making the sound (Bender, 1970; E. A. Fay, 1875). In pursuit of his firm conviction that the Hebrew tongue was superior to all other languages, van Helmont instructed deaf students in Hebrew (*AADD*, 1875, p. 172). Their progress in language is unknown. Van Helmont was also interested in the insane and recommended submersion in water as the cure, but again, the patients' progress toward rationality is unknown.

The establishment of the Royal Society and the speculations of its members, the early attempts to unravel the mysteries of the human body and the senses, and the first attempts to instruct persons handicapped by deafness, all signaled a new, emergent attitude toward exceptionality. In the age of enlightenment to come, new hope for all forms of exceptionality would flourish.

Chapter 2

Education and Enlightenment: New Views and New Methods

Chronology of Landmark Events in the Education of the Disabled Population

1690	John Locke publishes his *An Essay Concerning Human Understanding*
1745	Jacob Rodrigue Péreire begins his work with deaf students
1749	Denis Diderot publishes his study on blind people
1751	Diderot publishes his study on deaf people
1760	Abbé Charles Michel de l'Épée founds a school for deaf children in Paris
1762	Jean Jacques Rousseau's *Social Contract* is published
1784	Valentin Haüy establishes a school for blind children in Paris
1789	Abbé Roche Ambroise Cucurron Sicard takes over the Paris school for deaf children; the French Revolution erupts
1790	Schools for deaf and blind people combined under Sicard
1791	First British school for blind people opens
1792	William Tuke's Retreat near York opens; first British charity school for deaf children opens
1793	Philippe Pinel intervenes in cases of insanity at Bicêtre
1800	Jean Marc Gaspard Itard begins to work with the feral boy Victor
1810	Jean Étienne Dominique Esquirol succeeds Pinel at Salpêtrière
1825	Public hospitals for insane people open in Britain
1826	G. M. A. Ferrus opens a school for mentally retarded people (idiots) at Bicêtre
1841	The first public school for mentally retarded people (idiots) opens at Hospice des incurables de la rue St. Martin in Paris
1842	Édouard Seguin assumes leadership of the Bicêtre school

1846   First British public institution for mentally retarded people is founded

1848   Seguin emigrates to the United States

It was not until the middle of the eighteenth century that Britain and Europe turned to the education and training of their disabled populations. Onto the empty stage of special education stepped the pioneers—brilliant, innovative, often controversial and erratic philosphers, physicians, and pedagogues—who fashioned a new era in human history and paved the route that other educators could follow. Within the context of the broad intellectual movement known as the Enlightenment, they nurtured and reared the seeds sown in the previous century.

France was the crucial place; the period beginning about 1740, the critical time. The French *philosophes* (loosely defined as those who were intellectually involved in the Enlightenment) assumed the natural goodness of humans, and they erected on that base a conception of an ideal society that would protect everyone's natural rights. The intellectual power, honesty, lucidity, courage, and disinterested love of the truth of the most gifted thinkers of this era remains to this day without parallel (Berlin, 1956). Aligned with general humanistic principles, *l'esprit philosophique* of the Enlightenment generated new concepts, theories, and speculations about sensorily deprived persons that inevitably led to concerns for individuals impaired by mental retardation and mental illness. The unprecedented efforts of the French educational pioneers—Jacob Rodrigue Péreire, Abbé Charles Michel de l'Épée, Valentin Haüy, and others—adumbrated the major elements of Enlightenment philosophy. Educators were joined by the *idealogues*—young physicians who incorporated new and novel psychological notions into their practices.

So fertile were the seeds sown by Enlightenment thought that, by the close of the eighteenth century, special education was accepted as a branch of education, albeit a minor enterprise. The instruction of disabled persons was no longer confined to isolated cases or regarded merely as a subject of philosophic curiosity; now it was demonstrated that they could learn as well as their fellow beings. Effective procedures were devised for teaching many disabled groups—the recorded history of the language of signs for deaf persons and raised print for blind and deaf-blind people can be traced to this era. The education of mentally retarded groups developed, and rapid advances were apparent in the care of the emotionally disturbed. Impelled by the same motives that led to the emergence of special education, psychology and psychiatry emerged as separate disciplines and branches of medical science.

THE BASIC TENETS OF ENLIGHTENMENT THOUGHT

Primarily French in inspiration and leadership, the Enlightenment brought about a revolution in the way people perceived their world and their role in it. The *philosophes* built their theories upon a combination of rationalism and empiricism that differed fundamentally from views that had prevailed earlier. The three main branches of philosophy—metaphysics, the study of existence; epistemology, the study of knowledge; and ethics, the code of values that guides one's actions—came under scrutiny. The *philosophes* discarded the speculative metaphysics of the preceding century; they turned humanity from its preoccupation with God to an acute social consciousness and awareness of its fellows. They taught people to question, or to suspend judgment, rather than routinely to accept traditions. The central concept was that human beings were entitled to pass through life with a minimum of prejudgment; that there was innate goodness and ability in everyone that could be developed, and the species, as a whole, could be perfected; that civilizing social influences, education in particular, could help those innate abilities and qualities grow to fruition (Winzer, 1986a). It was accepted as a basic premise that the world has been established by the Creator according to a definite plan, within which there were ordered ways to behave. These ordered ways were the laws of nature, which redounded to the glory of the Creator and the greater good of humanity.

During the early part of the eighteenth century the *philosophes'* criticism focused mainly on religion, literature, and art; only slowly did their moral intention develop into a political one (Doermer, [1969] 1981). As the century progressed, writers, savants, and philosophers moved from intellectual speculation to social outrage—they became increasingly troubled by the inequities of traditional social structures and demanded extensive reconstruction. They were convinced that the world, and especially France, needed making over, from the tiniest and most insignificant details to the great moral and legal principles (Brinton, 1965). Such disparate matters as education, weights and measures, the calendar, and justice and equity came under their scrutiny. They increasingly questioned the legal, moral, and religious foundations of French society, becoming more and more critical of the established order of church and state.

The prevailing mode of the French *philosophes* was attack: they attacked the philosophical traditions, the church, the state, warfare, intolerance, social hierarchies, the educational system, and the economic organization, intending, said Denis Diderot, "to change the general way of thinking" (quoted by I. Knight, 1968, p. vii). Their ultimate objective was not only the elimination of everything they regarded as evil in contemporary life but extensive reconstruction of French society and institutions (Church, 1964). At the same time, the *philosophes* attempted to understand the world, and especially humans themselves, in their moral, psychological, and social lives; to awaken a sense of individuals' social responsibilities as well as a sense of the community's responsibility toward its members.

The prolonged campaign against church and state was more than just destructive criticism: the *philosophes* of the French Enlightenment were animated by the idea of progress through science and psychology, which, they believed, would allow a corresponding liberation from superstition. Inspired by the scientific revolution of the seventeenth century, the *philosophes* saw Isaac Newton and Newtonian science as models worthy of their emulation. If Newton could explain the mechanisms of heaven and earth in three mathematical laws, then scientific reasoning would seem to offer endless possibilities for the reform of the social sciences. The state, the economy, education, and the very structures of society itself could now be analyzed and scrutinized, and outmoded ideas and prejudices must yield to the test of criticism.

Novel and provocative ideas about equality and human rights, first generated by middle- and upper-class intellectuals, rapidly filtered down to influence all levels of society. Under the pervasive *l'esprit philosophique,* charity was active and philanthrophy a sort of fashion. A movement toward the elevation of individual independence, self-respect, and dignity became common enterprises.

The question of the action of philosophical ideas and literary works upon social and political events has divided historians sharply, and the impact of Enlightenment thought on the American and French revolutions has been widely debated (e.g., Brinton, 1965; Church, 1964). Some view eighteenth-century French philosophy as a movement that chiefly attacked church and state; some view the *philosophes* as enemies of the existing political system who became irresponsible fomentors of revolution as they progressed toward impiety and even atheism. Others see the Enlightenment as an inevitable stage in the social and political development of France, and regard the movement as a progressive liberation from religious superstition and ecclestiastical tyranny (Copleston, 1985). Even if one interpretation of Enlightenment influence could be agreed upon, it would be difficult to assess its impact on revolutionary leaders.

It is easier to assess its impact on the genesis and development of special education. The French savants, endeavoring to dissipate the clouds of authority and the fogs of error, were quick to see how new ideas and discoveries might affect important psychological questions and forward the cause of humanity. They first directed their attention to those in society denied equality by social status; then they attempted to solve the vexing problems of those denied equality by nature. The philosophical influence precipitated a complex of intellectual activities that in turn shaped efforts in special education and proved decisive in initiating the systematic training of disabled persons.

Enlightenment ideas, in short, were germane to special education. Educational pioneers adopted the essential tenets of *l'esprit philosophique* and applied them in the form of specific techniques and methods for training and education. This is not to suggest that the *philosophes* directly pointed their theories toward special education any more than it is to imply that the teachers were *philosophes.* Étienne Bonnot de Condillac, Jean Jacques Rousseau, Diderot, and their colleagues were theorists, ultimately concerned with knowledge itself. The educators were people of practical abilities who adopted the reforming zeal and basic optimism of the *philosophes* while translating speculation to the arena of action (Winzer, 1986a).

The educational advances were accomplished within a new set of social boundaries constructed by Enlightenment thought. Special education answered some of the questions about what it takes to be counted in the ranks of humanity, how important it is to grow up in those ranks, what is owed to nature and what to nurture, and how perfectible humans are. In addition, very specific threads of Enlightenment thought—those concerning Lockean sensationalism, language, and the application of alternate sensory stimuli—were woven in to this new fabric to create major pedagogical and social advances for exceptional individuals.

Empiricism and John Locke

Much of the new-found optimism regarding the education and training of handicapped persons arose from the epistemological and psychological speculations of John Locke (1632–1704). Locke was one of the outstanding figures of his period; he represented the spirit of free inquiry, of rationalism, and of the dislike of all authoritarianism that was characteristic of the age (Copleston, 1985). As a physician, humanist, and philosopher, Locke's name can be found at almost all of the century's crossroads of ideas. Isaiah Berlin (1956) observed that in his tentative and modest fashion, Locke appeared to be the genius who had done for the understanding of the human mind what Newton had done for the understanding of nature.

Locke's ideas galvanized the whole European Enlightenment. In France his philosophy was enthusiastically embraced and assimilated, to become the official epistemology of the emerging school of philosophers (Wilson, 1972). They believed that, by the scrupulous use of Locke's empirical philosophy, the functioning of everything in humanity and nature could be explained. They could thus put an end to the dark mysteries of theology, dogma, and superstition (Berlin, 1956).

Locke's expression of his political theory remains one of the most important documents in the history of liberal thought (Copleston, 1985). Locke exerted considerable influence on practices of child rearing. As a physician, Locke spoke against such traditional methods as the use of tight swaddling clothes and the overfeeding of infants with sweetmeats, cakes, and other rich foods. Instead, he advocated the importance of breast feeding. In keeping with his philosophy regarding the rights of individuals, Locke recognized the child as emotionally responsive; he stressed the importance of an empathetic understanding of children (Illick, 1974) and was concerned that children be raised with thought and care. Locke's stance on raising children was clearly enunciated in *Thoughts Concerning Education* ([1693] 1964), a somewhat revised and expanded version of advice Locke wrote to Edward Clarke on how best he might bring up his eldest son. The letters were written from 1684 to 1691; in 1689 Clarke and others began to urge Locke to publish them. In this and other works, Locke linked virtue with rationality, sociality, and humanity; his comments on children, rationality, obligation, and moral law occur in the context of a doctrine about the rights of children and the duties of parents toward them.

However, Locke's enduring fame rests on his victories over the great seventeenth-century champions of infallible rational knowledge. He focused his inquiry on human understanding, its scope and its limits (Berlin, 1956). In *An Essay Concerning Human Understanding* ([1690] 1956] Locke advanced the classical empirical thesis of eighteenth-century epistemology: All our ideas come from experience.

In propounding the notion that all ideas arise from sensation (sensationalism), Locke rejected the concept of innate ideas. He began with the principle that the infant is a *tabula rasa,* a blank slate on which is written all the experiences of the senses. He then expanded on this to say that only simple ideas come directly from experience; complex ideas are built from simple notions by operations of the mind, although they are rooted in experience (Locke, [1690]

1956). The qualities of objects are either primary or secondary. Primary qualities such as solidity, extension, figure, mobility, and number are inseparable
from objects; secondary qualities such as colors and odors are in the observer
and therefore take mental work to perceive and are subjective. In other words,
all of our ideas arise from two sources—sensations and reflection. And, although humans have natural tendencies, there are no innate ideas, or primary
notions.

Locke thus struck the greatest if not the first blow for empiricism (Berlin,
1956). Before Locke, ideas were generally believed to be innate, that is,
"stamped upon the mind of man, which the soul receives in its very first being;
and brings into the world with it" (Locke, [1690] 1894, p. 37). If disabilities are
also innate and imprinted before birth by God, the Devil, or nature, then they
would not be amenable to amelioration except by miracle. Such a conception of
disability, even when it was modified by scientific and psychological advances,
focused on the inevitability of a disabling condition. The fatalistic mindset born
of prevailing philosophical premises determined society's attitudes toward disabled individuals up to the time of the Enlightenment. But Locke's sensationalism implied that capacities are not innate, not printed on the mind before birth,
but rather, are gained through experience and the senses. Sensationalist theories came to be widely held, and they led to a general optimism about the prospects for the habilitation and rehabilitation of exceptional people (Winzer, 1986a).

Arising from the provocative notion of the *tabula rasa* and the idea that all
knowledge arises from sense perceptions was the central question around
which most epistemological and psychological problems of the eighteenth century revolved. The theoretical issues concerned whether the experience derived
from one sense was a sufficient basis on which to construct another field of perception, even when that perception had different content and structure (Seigel,
1969). In other words, is it possible for a blind person to learn to discriminate
objects by touch as finely as a sighted person does by vision? Can a blind person, recovering sight, distinguish forms by sight alone without reference to
touch, or a deaf individual learn to communicate as effectively with a sign language that bypasses hearing?

The question had originally been posed by William Molyneux (1656–1698),
a scholarly writer, philosopher, astronomer, and member of the Irish parliament,
who claimed that a blind person on regaining sight would not recognize by sight
objects that he had learned to know through touch. Molyneux held a personal
interest in the problem because of his wife's increasing visual problems. Locke
supported Molyneux, as did Bishop George Berkeley in his "Essay toward a New
Theory of Vision" ([1709] 1901). Locke, Berkeley, and Molyneux all agreed that a
person, on suddenly being able to see, would not be able to distinguish objects
by sight because that person had never had visual experiences of objects. The
new visual sensations would have no prior sensations to support them or to
lend support to them (Park, 1969). The problem eventually reached France with
Voltaire's popularization of the philosophies of Locke, Newton, and Berkeley
(Voltaire, 1738; Yolton, 1985).

The philosophical speculation was lent credence by the case of a thirteen-
year-old lad who, in 1728, was successfully operated on for cataracts by William
Cheselden, the celebrated surgeon and anatomist. Even with his repaired vision,

the boy found it difficult to form any visual judgment regarding the shape of familiar objects. He could not distinguish between his dog and his cat and was observed one day passing his hand over the cat and saying, "So, puss, I shall know you another time." He still had more confidence in the judgment of his hands than of his eyes (French, 1932).

Locke also had much to say about language and its place in human development (see Givner, 1962). Virtually all the major philosophers since Plato and Aristotle have considered the problems of the origin and role of human language. Debates centered on the role of language in the progressive differentiation of humans from other creatures and the way in which reason, if an original endowment of humans, manifested itself in language. It was their speculation on language development that led the British dilettantes of the Royal Society to recruit deaf people for their pedagogical experiments, and indeed, it was the deaf person's typical paucity of language that explains why special education seemed always to turn attention towards their needs first.

A rigorous analysis of the structures and functions of language formed an important element of Enlightenment thought. The origin of speech and language was seen as the key to the history of thought (Knowlson, 1965), and the use of language was viewed as critically important because it is the means by which people would be taught to think rationally, clearly and, above all, scientifically (Seigel, 1969). The focal interest was on language as a system of communication that somehow is able to explain reflective thought, not on language as a functional system of syntactic, morphological, and semantic elements.

For many centuries it was believed that if children were raised in an environment in which no language was spoken, they would naturally speak the most ancient of tongues. Herodotus (1954, book 2, par. 3) in the fifth century B.C. reported that various monarchs tried the experiment. Later, in the thirteenth century, the Holy Roman Emperor Frederick II of Hohenstaufen tried the same experiment to settle a controversy as to whether children would speak Hebrew, Latin, Arabic, or the language of their parents. Unfortunately, the children died. James IV, king of the Scots in the fifteenth century, repeated the experiment with more successful results. He claimed that his children "spak verey guid Ebrew" (Fromkin et al., 1974, p. 82).

Locke pointed to the arbitrary nature of language. He asserted that words derive their meaning from a culture that accepts certain relationships and certain designations: "words in their primary or immediate signification stand for nothing but the ideas in the mind of him that uses them" (Locke, [1690] 1894, p. 9). Basing their own work on Locke, the French *philosophes* used accounts of feral children and the communication of the deaf as basic data for their debate. This widespread concern for language among thinkers of the period led to a systematic study of communication, language, and symbol, and ultimately to imaginative experiments with deaf persons and their sign language.

Enlightenment Thought and Special Education

The *philosophes* of the French Enlightenment were theorists; they never passed the boundaries of abstract psychological speculation nor proposed any really practical plan for the instruction and training of disabled individuals.

Nevertheless, they created the climate and profoundly influenced the development and thrust of special education in eighteenth-century France. Rousseau, Condillac, and especially Diderot articulated ideas that provided the theoretical bases of the work of the pioneer special educators.

If the French Enlightenment had a chief architect, it was Jean Jacques Rousseau (1712–1778), a most gifted and perhaps the most complex of all the *philosophes,* the one who epitomized the underlying spirit of the French Enlightenment. Rousseau was the thinker who emotionalized the thinking of the period and gave the clearest expression to the values of the middle class. Rousseau's longing for the state of nature, his egotism and emotionalism, his celebration of the sanctity of childhood, together with his fascination with childhood as a condition of innocence, have led some scholars to classify him as a Romantic rather than an Enlightenment figure. Yet although Rousseau's solutions sometimes challenged the beliefs and values of his contemporaries, he focused on the same basic problems as the other *philosophes.* He showed that coercion and suppression were not so much the fault of the absolutist state as they were the product of humans and society—of the learned enlightened sector in particular (Doermer, [1969] 1981; see Rousseau, [1762b] 1968). So wide was Rousseau's appeal that he expanded the reading public, and with it the political public, in France far beyond the confines of high society.

Like Rousseau, Voltaire (1694–1778) increased the prestige and understanding of the new empiricism; he was successful in presenting the ideas in lucid and witty writings and making them intelligible to French society (see Yolton, 1985).

The Abbé Étienne Bonnot de Condillac (1715–1780), a devoted follower of Locke, offered the most popular version of sensationalism, the notion that all learning arises primarily from the senses (Yolton, 1985). Condillac was more radical than Locke in his conception of the mind as a *tabula rasa.* Locke was willing to endow the newborn child with capacities for sensation and reflection, but Condillac believed sensation to be enough; he was convinced that all mental processes could be analyzed into constituents consisting of basic irreducible units of sensation. In *Traité des sensations* ([1754] 1930) Condillac rejected Locke's notion of the dual origin of ideas—ideas of sensation and ideas of reflection. Instead, he saw the whole edifice of psychic life as being erected solely on sensation. The abbé's approach to the problem of the origin of ideas was stimulated by the data provided by the experiences of blind people who had undergone successful cataract removal and by Diderot's (1751) study of deaf and dumb persons (Copleston, 1985).

To demonstrate his theory, Condillac used the example of a statue that he would first endow with smell, which he regarded as the least valuable sense in contributing knowledge. He then traced the way smell would give rise to such perceptions as comparison, judgment, preference, motivation, and memory to illustrate how one sense could generate all the faculties. Finished with smell, he then used touch in the same manner. In this way Condillac attempted to construct the mental world of normal human beings bit by bit and to show that everything arises from the senses and their interplay (Berlin, 1956; Condillac, [1754] 1930).

Condillac viewed humans as intelligent beings, capable of reflection, because of the gift of language; therefore, he saw the progress of the human intellect basically as a study of the growth and development of language (Copleston, 1985; Seigel, 1969). Contemporary arguments concerning language centered on whether gesture is the natural antecedent of speech or whether gesture and speech are completely unrelated in evolution (Knowlson, 1965; Rudowski, 1974). As a strong gestural theorist, Condillac suggested that sounds were initially added to a natural gesture language, and he believed that the recall of ideas could be aided by the use of signs (Kyle, 1980–81). Condillac placed great stress on the part played by language and saw ideas as becoming fixed by association with a sign or a word. Although he believed that learning is primarily through the senses, Condillac theorized that it is shaped by language, as is the acquisition of theoretical knowledge (see Formigari, 1974).

Of all the *philosophes* who influenced the course of special education, none was more powerful and influential than the brilliant and paradoxical Denis Diderot (1713–1784) who, with Jean Le Rond' d'Alembert, sought to bring all the knowledge of the world together, arrange it alphabetically, and make it easily accessible in the *Encyclopédie*. Assézat, a contemporary and his editor, pointed out Diderot's profound influence:

> It was Diderot who, perhaps, had the privilege to give Haüy, Épée and Sicard the first idea for their philanthropic work. He had anticipated in his thinking the observations they made subsequently about deaf-mutes and blind-born people, and these observations are so widespread today that they prove in effect that he guessed very accurately.[1]

Diderot's work focused attention on the misery and exploitation of those deprived of their senses, and he stimulated renewed speculation about the education and training of deaf, blind, and deaf-blind individuals. He discussed the problems of visual impairment in his *Lettre sur les aveugles à l'usage de ceux qui voient* [Letter on blind persons for the use of those who see] (1749), in which he proposed a method for educating those who were blind and deaf-blind; he observed that a child could be taught through touch sensations by patient and insistent connection of tangible signs with the object touched (French, 1932; Seigel, 1969). Diderot's *Lettre sur sourds et muets* . . . [Letter on deaf and dumb persons . . .] (1751) also involved sense deprivation and has been characterized as the first essentially scientific study of deaf individuals (Seigel, 1969).

Diderot's letters set Paris ablaze with enthusiasm and inquiry. Many were fascinated by the novelty of the ideas and responded to the encyclopedist's examination of handicapped persons and their educational possibilities. Diderot's erudition commanded the respect of the savants of the time, but his psychological speculations also contained hints of atheism, and he courted official censure. Incarceration for three months in Vincennes followed the publication of his 1749 *Lettre*. The public outrage that followed Diderot's imprisonment, however, made him the champion of blind persons. His psychological and educational

---

[1]The original text reads: "C'est Diderot qui, peut-être, a eu l'honneur de fournir a Haüy, à de l'Épée, à Sicard, la première idée de leurs philantrophiques travaux. Il avait prevenu par la pensée les observations qu'ils ont faites depuis sur les Sourds-Muets et les Aveugles-nes: et ces observations sont assez multipliées aujourd'hui pour prouver qu'il a devine juste" (quoted by Seigel, 1969).

speculations were widely disseminated and enlisted general interest in their cause (see French, 1932).

THE PIONEERS OF EUROPE

The pioneers who undertook the education and training of disabled individuals were practical men who adopted the reforming zeal and basic optimism of the *philosophes* and translated their speculation into action. Educational ventures were initiated in an altered milieu created by Enlightenment thought; drawing on the heightened social consciousness permeating French society, the pioneer educators railed against the condition of the disabled, which they found to be wretched, unjust, and illogical. They were disinclined to preach the patient resignation of former eras; rather, they voiced a new ideal for this long-ignored population. Onto the emerging concepts about the social rights of all individuals, the French pioneers grafted their vision of enlightened education that would be rooted in sensationalism and a fuller understanding of language and alternate sensory stimuli (Winzer, 1986a).

Jacob Rodrigue Péreire

The empirical psychology of John Locke, filtered through the ideas of the French sensationalists, found early expression in the work of Jacob Rodrigue Péreire (1715–1780), an exiled Spanish Jew whose name was originally Giacomo Rodríguez Pereira. He was the first professional teacher of deaf students in France (Vaisse, 1879, 1883). Péreire's efforts to alleviate the consequences of deafness owed more to Rousseau than to any other contemporary thinker, perhaps because they were neighbors and acquaintances, or perhaps because the subtle blend of Romanticism and empiricism manifested in Rousseau's pedagogy appealed to Péreire. Péreire adopted Rousseau's sensationalist prescriptions for individual instruction and especially for structured and systematic sense training.

Rousseau often visited Péreire's school (Seguin, [1866], 1907), and according to Édouard Seguin (1876), the philosopher's theory of pedagogy, rooted in empirical principles and given concrete expression in *Émile, ou Traité de l'Éducation* (1762a), was indebted both to the experience of Péreire and his own experiments (Seguin, 1876). In turn, the pedagogical theory described in *Émile* eventually became one of Péreire's guides.

Despite his belief that all ideas arise from the senses, Condillac did not advocate specific training of the senses. In contrast, Rousseau believed that if children were left alone to play, their motor development would occur naturally although their senses would have to be trained. He suggested that each sense required individual and deliberate training, not just to increase sensitivity but also to develop the ability to discriminate between objects; only then could sense be used to exert judgment. In concert with Rousseau, Péreire believed that all ideas originated from the senses; he believed that the senses strengthened each other and could be substituted for one another. He therefore shifted the educational emphasis from training the faculties to training the senses (Magdol,

1976). In *Émile* Rousseau stressed tactile curiosity and tactile responses, which led Péreire to view touch as the basis of all learning and to rigorously train that sense (Magdol, 1976). He attempted to demonstrate that all senses are modifications of the sense of touch (Barr, [1904b] 1913).

Exact reconstruction of Péreire's methods is not possible. Like other oral proponents, such as Henry Baker and John Conrad Amman, Péreire cloaked his work in secrecy, "expressly forbidding his pupils to tell how he instructed them" (Seguin, 1876, p. 23). It seems that in his work with deaf children and youth Péreire employed alternate sensory stimuli—Jean Pablo Bonet's one-handed Spanish alphabet—to which he added forty signs of his own devising (Barr, [1904b] 1913). In 1767 Péreire incorporated speaking trumpets into his instruction to demonstrate how residual hearing could be effectively stimulated to improve speech production.

Before Péreire, stimulation of the auditory mechanism of deaf persons had been attempted by Archigenes in the first century, Alexander of Tralles in the sixth, Guido Guidi in the sixteenth (Goldstein, 1920), and probably by Bonet. However, Péreire's innovative approach to auditory training (Gillespie, 1884; Goldstein, 1920) anticipated methods still employed by teachers of very young deaf children today (e.g., see D. Pollack, 1970).

Péreire's pupils attained high levels of learning; one, Saboureux de Fontenay, achieved an extraordinarily high level of culture for a deaf-born person. Péreire's successes were certified on three separate occasions by the French Académie des Sciences, and he earned the acclaim of the *philosophes* Georges Louis Leclerc de Buffon, Diderot, and Rousseau (Seigel, 1969; Vaisse, 1879). "Nothing could show more conclusively how much the senses are alike at bottom, and to what point they may supply one another," observed Buffon after watching a demonstration by Péreire's deaf pupils (quoted by Barr, [1904b] 1913, p. 27). Diderot was inspired to write his *Lettre sur les sourds et muets* (1751) after observing Péreire's demonstrations before the academy of sciences (Meyer, 1965). In his essay on the origin of language Rousseau spoke highly of Péreire's "ingenuity in securing the natural development of language in the deaf" and lauded the teacher as the first person in France to put into practice the "admirable method" (quoted by Hodgson, [1952] 1973, p. 123). Officialdom admired Péreire and rewarded him with a pension from the king of France and election to the French Royal Society.

Abbé Charles Michel de l'Épée

Péreire was an inconsistent and erratic genius (Barr, [1904b] 1913) who devised methods that directly anticipated Jean Marc Gaspard Itard, Seguin, and Maria Montessori and provided basic principles that were axiomatic to later intervention in the cases of deaf and mentally retarded students (see Lewis, 1960; Seguin, 1846). But although he avidly promoted sensationalism and employed alternate sensory stimuli, Péreire's ideology was built over a psychological abyss that he was not ready to explore; he failed to incorporate the novel theories of language spawned by Enlightenment philosophy. He extravagantly overestimated the importance of oral language, viewing it as an absolute necessity in the cultivation of the intellect. He regarded the acquisition of speech as *the* goal of the instruction of his deaf students.

Nevertheless, the provocative new concepts regarding language allowed a departure from an emphasis on speech for people who were born deaf and the adoption of methods that relied entirely on alternate stimuli. It was Péreire's bitter enemy, the French priest Charles Michel de l'Épée (1712–1789), who astutely applied the theories regarding the psychology of deafness and the evolution of language to the education of deaf persons. The story of how Épée became involved in special education appears in Box 2-1.

When visiting parishioners in Troyes Épée met two deaf children whose plight led him eventually to found a school for poor deaf children. In 1760, when he was almost fifty years old, Épée opened a class for six poor deaf children in his home on rue de Moulins in Paris (Rae, 1848c), unfortunately very close to Péreire's well-established school on rue de la Platriere. Except for his experience in Troyes, the abbé know little about teaching deaf children or, indeed, teaching anyone else. But, having planted the seed, he nurtured it with the writings of earlier teachers and an ideology drawn from the sensationalist theories circulating in France. As a start, Épée conscientiously studied the works of Amman and Bonet; he learned Spanish to read the latter.

Épée's pioneering work not only echoed the philosophical theories of language propounded by John Locke, Diderot, Condillac, and Rousseau (Seigel, 1969), it also reflected Jansenist educational ideas regarding the special nature of childhood and a desire to devise methods suited to the psychology of the child (Ariès, 1962; I. Knight, 1968). As his fundamental assumption, the abbé took Locke's notion that language is artificial and arbitrary; that there exists "no more natural connection between metaphysical ideas and the articulate sounds which strike the ear, than between the same ideas and the written characters which strike the eye" (Épée, [1784] 1860, p. 62). Grafted onto this was the conception advanced by the French *philosophes* that images, the basis of thought, are often not representable in speech, but are perhaps more directly related to gesture (Kyle, 1980–81). The abbé speculated that "it would be possible to instruct the Deaf and Dumb with written characters, always accompanied by sensible signs" (Épée, [1784] 1860, p. 26).

Before adopting a method of alternate stimuli, Épée observed his students closely. He became convinced that the signs they made naturally with their hands when trying to communicate with each other were the basis of a mother tongue for them. "The natural language of the deaf and dumb," concluded the abbé, "is the language of signs" (Épée, [1784] 1860, p. 127). Convinced that his students needed a system of communication not of sound but of signs, and unalarmed that the language he proposed would differentiate them from the greater society, Épée proceeded to systemize the signs of his students into a new language. To *le language des signes naturalles,* the core group of signs he observed his students using spontaneously, Épée added many of his own, sometimes basing them on those employed by his pupils, sometimes inventing entirely original ones. His pupils' signs largely designated objects, qualities, and events, but the abbé's *signes méthodiques* corresponded to grammatical functions in French. He developed signs to indicate tense, person, grammatical category, and so on, and also signs to relay abstract relationships and metaphysical and religious concepts (Épée, [1784] 1860). Under the abbé's tutelage, the whole system evolved into a manual-visual equivalent of spoken language, a

Box 2-1

Abbé Charles Michel de l'Épée (1712–1789)

Abbé Charles Michel de l'Épée was nearly fifty years old when he adopted the cause of the disabled. As a French cleric advocating the ideas of the Jansenists, a sect opposed to the Jesuits, Épée found his religious career stopped at the deaconhood because of his disputes with the church hierarchy ("How the deaf mutes," 1928). The Jansenists, with the Oratorians, introduced a new spiritual and philosophical attitude into education. His Jansenist leanings were apparent in Épée's advocacy of a new approach in education; he wished to introduce mathematics, physics, history, and geography into the curriculum and to instruct in French, rather than Latin. The Jansenists' pedagogical unorthodoxy, combined with their potentially heretical questioning of church tenets such as predestination, placed them in direct conflict with the Jesuits, long the leaders of France's ecclesiastical and educational worlds. The chronic struggles within the Catholic church resulted in political as well as theological dissension (see O'Brien, 1985).

Because he could not conscientiously sign the articles of faith required of a prelate of the church, Épée spent decades in ecclesiastical exile. When his career faltered, he entered a brief period of legal practice and study and seems to have immersed himself in the philosophical concepts circulating in France. Épée's rise to prominence coincided with the condemnation, suppression, and subsequent fall and expulsion of the Jesuits from France that began about 1762.

The abbé was well into middle age when he entered the work for which he would be so widely recognized. In 1760 he finally confessed his faith to his uncle, the bishop of Troyes, who then helped Épée to become ordained and receive a parish (Pritchard, 1963). As the newly appointed deacon in the cathedral at Troyes, the abbé met two deaf daughters of a parishioner; the girls had previously been taught by a priest. Inspired by religion, sympathy, and humanity, Épée undertook instruction of the girls, teaching them to read but not to speak. While working with the deaf girls, Épée developed "an interest for a truly deplorable class of beings . . . reduced . . . to the condition of brutes" (Épée, [1784] 1860, pp. 2, 3).

Épée opened a school in Paris in the 1760s with six pupils; by 1785 the clientele had risen to seventy-two (Lane, 1976). Unlike his oral cohorts, the abbé proselytized widely; his *L'instruction des sourds et muets par la voie des signes méthodiques* [The instruction of the deaf and dumb by the sign method] (1776) and *La véritable manière d'instruire les sourds et muets* [The true method of educating the deaf and dumb] (1784) explicitly detailed his methods.

In his personal attitudes and attributes Charles Michel de l'Épée epitomized all that was good in early special education. His frankness and generosity and his devotion to the poor complemented his visionary conceptions of education and his astute application of psychological principles. In France his influence was pervasive, his stature almost heroic, and his system regarded as the sole French method by compatriots and foreigners alike. Royalty smiled on him, learned bodies vied with each other in patronizing him, his pupils adored him, and teachers came to be trained by him. From Épée's school, which eventually became known as the Institution Nationale des Sourds Muets, Paris, arose the education of deaf-blind children and mentally retarded people; from his influence came the education of blind persons, as well.

Épée played a crucial role in the transformation of special education from philosophical inquiry to educational enterprise. To scattered educational attempts he brought regularity: if it is necessary to name the father or true founder of special education, then it must be Charles Michel de l'Épée.

---

fully articulated language of signs. Fingerspelling was also incorporated, probably the same system as employed by Péreire, which de Fontenay, one of Péreire's pupils, presented to Épée at a public demonstration (Lane, 1976).

Épée saw his deaf students as *tabulae rasae,* akin to the statue of Condillac, who required bringing to life. Hence, he adopted a rigorous intellectual approach to education; once he had awakened their reason by stimulating their senses, he focused his efforts on teaching deaf individuals "to think with order, and to combine their ideas" (Épée, [1784] 1860, p. 3). Épée insisted that the central concern of education was to make deaf individuals think logically, and in this sense his aim, patently different from Péreire's, closely reflected the intellectual spirit of the French moralists. Because he recognized language as more than a verbal system only of sounds and orthography, the abbé assumed an adamant stance toward the teaching of speech. Épée insisted on a distinction between imitating sounds and expressing legitimate language, and he viewed articulation training as merely auxiliary to the main object of awakening and stimulating deaf minds. He asserted that the "deaf mute can speak like us, when they are instructed." Viewing the process as neither long nor painful, the abbé assigned the task to "simple females" to whom he taught the art "in the course of a fortnight at most" (Épée, [1784] 1860, p. 6).

In striking contrast to the oral pioneers, Épée did not shroud his work in secrecy but, rather, welcomed the curious, the critical, and the cynical. From 1771 to 1774 he presented annual, highly celebrated exhibitions of the attainments of his pupils held in the chapel he added to the spacious house built by his father, the king's architect (Lane, 1976). Épée used these displays to convince educators, academicians, and the public that deaf individuals could not only acquire language but were as "capable of education as well as those who hear and speak" (Épée, [1784] 1860, p. 38). For example, at an important demonstration in August 1773, attended by the pope's nuncio and other church dignitaries, the pupils were asked two hundred questions in three languages, a number of them concerning the mysteries of the church (Épée, [1784] 1860, pp. 129–31).

Épée's sign system and pedagogy, as well as his underlying philosophical principles, drew high praise from educators, legislators, churchmen, and *philosophes.* Earlier, Condillac had denied deaf people the faculty of memory and hence the power of reasoning because he believed that language was needed for memory (Kyle, 1980–81). Now the philosopher extravagantly lauded the abbé as the one who "transformed a language of action into a simple methodical skill in order to teach his pupils ideas of all sorts." "The ideas thus gained," noted Condillac, were probably "more exact, more precise, than those commonly acquired with the help of hearing" (Épée, [1784] 1860, p. 50).

Épée's work formed the kernel of future intervention in cases of deafness and profoundly influenced other forms of special education. The Abbé Roche Ambroise Cucurron Sicard (1742–1822) came from Bordeaux to learn Épée's methods and in 1789 took over Épée's school, which was in 1791 established as a national institution by the National Assembly. Sicard wholly adopted his mentor's philosophy and pedagogy: he made the signs more systematic and sophisticated, and he added hugely to the French eminence in the field of special education.

However, in France the disruptions of the Revolution, the Reign of Terror, Napoleon's ascendancy, and Sicard's own political leanings brought grave consequences. Because he remained a devoted royalist and correspondent of the exiled Bourbons, Sicard found himself carried before the Committee of the National Assembly twice in 1792. In August of that year he was seized and thrown into prison because he refused to take one of the oaths required of the priesthood by the National Assembly (Rae, 1847a). Sicard escaped and made his way to the Hall of the Committee. The enraged mob, recognizing the escapee, would have killed him except for a watchmaker named Monnet, who leapt to Sicard's defense. Speaking for himself, Sicard pleaded to the assembly: "I am the Abbé Sicard. I teach the deaf and dumb, and, since the number of these unfortunates is always greater among the poor than among the rich, I am of more use to you than them" (Rae, 1847, p. 19). The story of Sicard's narrow escape from the mob is told by Thomas Carlyle in *The French Revolution.*

Sicard and his school, despite his political bent, survived the Terror. Sicard remained a devout royalist and must have cheered the Bourbon return with Napoleon's exile to Elba. In fact, the reinstated Louis XVIII awarded Sicard the Legion of Honor. When Napoleon regained France, it is little wonder that Sicard and two of his pupils, Jean Massieu and Laurent Clerc, fled to London, a critical event to the future course of special education in North America (see Chapter 3).

Samuel Heinicke

As Épée was creating a system of instruction in Paris, there simultaneously arose an opposing methodology in Germany. Samuel Heinicke (1727–1790) developed an alternate ideology, an oral method for instructing deaf children that constituted a more logical and systematic application of the principles expounded by the earlier European oral advocates and teachers, Amman and Baron van Helmont.

Heinicke had a varied career. Refusing to marry the woman chosen for him by his father, he left the family farm in 1750 and went to Dresden, where he became a private soldier in the bodyguard of the elector of Saxony (Patterson, 1926). He was taken prisoner by the Prussians during the Seven Years' War but escaped in an elaborate disguise—dressed as a hunchback violinist—and fled to Jena, where he enlisted in the Dresden Royal Life Guards. He also entered the

Box 2-2

The Development of Manual Systems

When Épée developed a formalized sign language for his deaf students, he drew on an existing body of gestures, signs, and finger alphabets. He did not build the house from the foundations up; rather, he systemized and standardized the design and layout.

The manual components of the systems were not original. Dactylology or fingerspelling is a borrowed art, formulated neither by deaf persons nor by their teachers. Although the origins of dactylology are unknown, there is evidence of the use of manual alphabets dating from preclassical times that probably owe their origin to the development of manual signs for numbers. That manual alphabets served a useful if limited purpose is suggested by the fact that through the centuries they continued to be invented and improved (Hodgson, [1952] 1973).

Evidence of the existence of finger alphabets can be traced from Assyrian antiquity to the seventeenth century, and there are numerous references in the literature to single- and double-handed alphabets (Elizabeth Peet, 1922). The earliest finger alphabet is contained in a later reproduction of the Venerable Bede's *Historia Ecclesiastica Gentis Anglorum* [History of the Anglo-Saxon church] of 731, which refers to three different forms of manual alphabets used by the ancient Greeks, Egyptians, and Romans (*AADD,* 1848; Porter, 1847). Early Vatican manuscripts show the hands making numbers to one million; European paintings, from the late fifteenth to the seventeenth century, also depict manual rhetoric. There is evidence that two-handed or mixed alphabets of various forms were in use among school boys in Spain, France, and England centuries ago, and monks under rigid vows of silence and other scholars who had special reasons to prize silent, secret methods of communication doubtless used many forms of manual communication (Lane, 1976; Plann, 1991).

In 1593 Melchor Yebra, a Franciscan monk, published *A Refuge for the Infirm,* which contained prayers for sick people, each accompanied by a sketch of hand configurations that the author attributed to Saint Bonaventure. This may have been the source of the one-handed alphabet published by Bonet in 1620 (Lane, 1976) and which, transmitted through French educational sources, is used today by deaf persons in North America. The two-handed alphabet appeared in the anonymous *Digita lingua* [Finger language] of 1698. With few changes, it is employed by deaf people in Great Britain and many Commonwealth countries.

Sign language is ancient. Plato mentioned that we could signify meaning by the hands and head and other parts of the body. The Roman writer Quintilian observed that sign language originated in heroic times and met with the approval of the Greeks. "Amidst the great diversity of tongues pervading all nations and people," noted Quintilian, "the language of the hands appears to be common to all men" (quoted by Pettengill, 1873, p. 10).

Sign systems were widely used by the Egyptians, the Greeks and Romans, Moslems, Tahitians, Arabs, and Mexicans (Mallory, 1882;

Tyler, 1879). In Rome the pantomimes, which maintained their reputation from the time of Augustus until the sixth century, expressed through stylized sign and mime fables about the gods and ancient heroes. Elizabethan theater used stylized gestures to communicate emotions such as doubt and repulsion, and many remained in conventional use on the stage until the talkies of the early twentieth century.

Sign-language systems also served more nefarious purposes, and a variety of hand signals and gestures have been used by people who needed to communicate covertly—spies and members of secret societies. A medieval secret society called the Thugs, for example, specialized in ritual murder and had formal signs for "all clear" (touching the ear lobe) and the very useful "kill"—placing a hand on the chest with the second and third fingers crossed (Daraul, 1961).

Although early sign language used by deaf people would have tended to be local and idiosyncratic, it is obvious that sign formed the major mode of communication and lent credence to the argument that deaf persons are competent. Late in the twelfth century a canon of Pope Innocent III, for example, allowed deaf couples to marry if they could "express their consent in unequivocal signs" (Gaw, 1907, p. 170). Later, during the reign of Elizabeth I of England, Ursula Russet was married to deaf Thomas Filsby, who used "understandable signs throughout the ceremony" ("Marriages," 1858, p. 250).

Questions about language development fascinated Enlightenment philosophers. During that period there appeared suggestions that sign language preceded spoken language and that linked the evolved sign language of deaf people to a more primitive gestural origin. Giovanni Bonifacio, who wrote on oration and sign, for example, suggested that the language of gesture, if universally adopted, could break down the barriers raised at Babel (Knowlson, 1965). John Bulwer believed that the language of signs differs from all spoken languages and, as gesture was a natural language, is the obvious language to be adopted by humankind as a common language (Knowlson, 1965). Diderot held that gesture preceded language and is in fact more sublime than verbal utterances. In his 1751 *Lettre sur sourds et muets,* he suggested that the natural order of the development of language would be best examined by studying the sign language used by deaf persons (Kyle, 1980–81). Julien Offroy de La Mettrie wrote on language in *L'historie naturelle de l'âme* [The natural history of the soul] ([1745] 1912) and *L'homme machine* [The human machine] ([1748] 1912). He suggested trying to educate orangutans in the same way as deaf persons are taught (Lane and Pillard, 1978). Language was also discussed by Rousseau, Claude Adrien Helvétius, Charles Bonnet, and Marie Jean Antoine Nicholas de Caritat, the Marquis de Condorcet (Seigel, 1969).

The interest reached such a point of speculation that the Paris Société de Linguistique finally banned all communication on language evolution in 1866 (Kyle, 1980–81). However, the argument lingered on. Isaac Taylor, the British archeologist and philologist, analyzed sign language in 1874 with a great deal of insight and presented it as a basic communication system of primary importance in language development (Kyle, 1980–81).

university to train as a teacher and in his spare time studied Latin, French, and mathematics. He tutored a deaf and dumb boy (Pritchard, 1963), and, by 1754 was directing his attention toward the education of deaf persons.

In 1768 Heinicke organized a school at Eppendorff (Patterson, 1926) but he left in 1775 when the local pastor preached against his work, declaring "that it was presumptuous to interfere with the decree of God that has created certain persons" (Patterson, 1926, p. 184). In 1778, under the aegis of the elector of Saxony, the school moved to Leipzig (Karth, 1927).

Heinicke brought together various threads and wove them into a complete method of oral instruction for deaf students. He affirmed that speech was to hold the first place and become the sole instrument for the mental development of deaf students. In pursuit of this objective, he devised a method totally at variance with that espoused by Épée, making "artificial language . . . the fundamental point; the hinge upon which everything turns" (quoted by Garnett, 1968, p. 42). Heinicke could see no possible compromise between speech and signing; he held that people could think only with the aid of words and could conceive words only when able to articulate them (H. P. Peet, [1846] 1847). "[H]uman thought" he argued, "is impossible either by gesture or in writing, but most assuredly by the spoken word only" (quoted by Mathison, 1906, p. 492). Heinicke contended that the deaf child lacking spoken language could never become "more than a writing machine, or have anything beyond a succession of images passing through his mind" (quoted by I. L. Peet, 1890, pp. 138–39). Eschewing signs and defying the French stress on writing, he aimed chiefly "to enable his pupils to communicate orally . . . to understand others, and be understood by them" (Greenberger, 1876, p. 103).

Little is known of Heinicke's actual methodology. Clothed in the secrecy that was now so characteristic of the oral savants, he published nothing about his pedagogy, although he did write a number of children's books (Karth, 1927). David Greenberger (1876) explained that Heinicke's chief endeavor was to enable his pupils to communicate orally, and to accomplish this he provided much practice in the art of lipreading. Then he taught his students to articulate as distinctly as possible all the sounds of speech, especially the vowels, which in his estimation were the most essential.

His belief that speech formed the alpha and omega in the instruction of deaf students led Heinicke to denigrate teachers who adhered to other methods, as well as earlier oral advocates. He boasted that he was "the first and only one who had invented and put into practice the true method of instructing the deaf and dumb" (Épée, [1784] 1860, p. 86); contended that those exposed to his methods learned "to read and think clearly and with understanding" (quoted in Garnett, 1968, p. 26); claimed that "he achieved in a few months more than others had done in many years" (Mathison, 1906, p. 421); and boldly taxed with ignorance or imposture all who had written on the subject, or who had undertaken to instruct deaf and dumb persons in any way, before himself (Bender, 1970).

So great was the animosity between Heinicke and Épée, the oralist and the manualist, that they embarked upon a vigorous written debate concerning the value of and the methods and motives underlying their work. The appointment of one of Épée's protégés, Frederick Stork, as principal of a school for deaf persons in Vienna effectively elevated the argument to the public sphere with its

submission to the Academy at Zurich, a group of European scholars who served
as arbiters of philosophical and scientific disputes, for judgment. After Stork visited Heinicke's school incognito, he reported that what he saw did not correspond to Heinicke's claims; in fact, he said, those claims were exaggerated, if not
fraudulent. The academy could obtain little specific information on Heinicke's
methodology and were "not much more disposed than others seem to be, to sacrifice a large sum to obtain the knowledge of it." On the basis of the "paucity of
information" with which Heinicke had "indulged the world on the subject"
(Épée, [1784] 1860, p. 123) and the testimony of independent observers, the vote
tipped overwhelmingly in favor of the methods of Épée (Épée, [1784] 1860, p.
110). Said the Zurich academy to Épée: "[N]o articulated language whatsoever in
use among mankind is fuller or of greater compass than that language which
you have established for the deaf and dumb" (quoted in "How best," 1891, p. 15).

The Beginnings of the Oral-Manual Controversy

The controversy concerning the most appropriate communication modes to
use with deaf students did not in fact start with Heinicke and Épée. It can be
traced back to the British and European pioneers. However, Épée and Heinicke
established the boundaries of an enduring argument that has riven the education of deaf students up to the present day.

Essentially, Épée and those of a manual persuasion saw deafness as a human difference deserving of its own language. In contrast, oral advocates saw
deafness as a human difference that could be overcome with the astute application of oral principles—speech and lipreading would serve to normalize deaf
persons so that they could meld into the greater society.

The controversy did not remain within the domain of school instruction. It
spilled over to affect, and be affected by, other aspects of education and socialization. In the eighteenth century the oral-manual controversy was clearly
marked by the social class of the pupils and the status of the teacher. In the late
nineteenth century, when the argument reached its most divisive pitch, it continued to be bounded by social class but also affected which was the dominant
sex among teachers, the status of deaf teachers, teacher training and organizations, the adult status of deaf persons, and their right to marry and procreate.

It is hardly surprising that Épée, first trained in philosophical speculation by
his tutor (Épée, [1784] 1860) and later immersed in the philosophical and psychological speculations permeating France, should have embraced the novel
psychological concepts regarding language and translated these into specific
pedagogical and linguistic principles. Heinicke, however, was guided by thinkers
of the German Enlightenment, specifically Georg Wilhelm Friedrich Hegel and
Immanuel Kant. In fact, Karth notes that Heinicke was especially attracted by the
philosophy of Kant and seemed to be "entirely under the influence of the philosopher" (1927, p. 279).

Not only did Épée come to the enterprise with a broad knowledge of the new
psychological principles but he possessed the financial resources to fund his
venture. The abbé welcomed the cynical, the critical, and the curious to examine the products of his method. Heinicke, on the other hand, existed on grants
that depended on his success; it is understandable that he clothed his methods

in secrecy, steadfastly refusing to divulge his methods except for money (Épée, [1784] 1860, p. 123). He argued that "the invention and arrangement of it cost me incredible labor and pains and I am not inclined to let others have the benefit of it for nothing" (Épée, [1784] 1860, p. 123).

The abbé contended that he labored for the poor while Heinicke preferred paying pupils, one of the most obvious reasons for the effect of class on manual and oral instruction in the nineteenth century. Wealthy parents wished their children to acquire the social graces and the language competencies that would allow them access to polite society, so oralism became largely the province of the middle and upper classes, while indigent children went to public institutions where they were instructed through manual methods.

Valentin Haüy

With the education of deaf students firmly established in France and moving across the Continent, increasing concern was manifested for those afflicted by blindness. Some little education of blind persons had been attempted, but still many blind individuals eked out meager existences by begging or sometimes as musicians. Philosophical speculation during the Enlightenment period on the problems and potentialities of blind persons was not lacking: Molyneux, Berkeley, Locke, Diderot, and others explored various aspects of blindness. But if anything concrete was to be accomplished, there needed to emerge a catalyst, a teacher of the caliber and commitment of Épée, to translate philosophy into action.

In some ways the first teacher of blind persons was remarkably similar to Épée in background and motivation. Like Épée and many of the *philosophes,* Valentin Haüy (1745–1822) championed the common people but sprang from the upper echelons of Parisian society and led an aristocratic life. Épée's father was a renowned architect, Haüy's brother a celebrated mineralogist. Both teachers were members of the clergy, although Haüy's two marriages make his vows somewhat suspect. Too, Haüy moved in the same social circles as the leading *philosophes* and was steeped in the philosophy of Diderot (French, 1932).

In fact, Diderot's philosophy provided the foundation for Haüy's venture. Diderot's interest was wholly theoretical, arising from the problem formulated by Molyneux and Locke—if a blind man learns through touch, would he, on regaining sight, be able to distinguish forms by sight alone without reference to touch? Diderot discussed the problem in his *Lettre sur les aveugles;* he suggested that the senses of the blind are not especially sharpened by sight but that the loss of one sense compels increased attention to the other senses. Diderot believed that the education of blind persons must be built on what the person already has; that is, on the individual's contacts with the world through the remaining senses (French, 1932). Rousseau also deserves some of the credit. He contemplated the application of metaphysical speculation to the education of the blind and suggested teaching through raised print and embossed books.

Haüy, according to his own accounts, was also deeply impressed by Épée, who inspired his thought to take a more general turn (French, 1932). Haüy also had the experience of others to draw upon, occasional instances of the instruction of blind individuals and the use of specialized materials.

A series of propitious events moved Haüy from speculation into action. On a Paris street one day in 1771 Haüy was attracted by loud hooting and laughter coming from a cafe where ten blind men were performing on rough stringed instruments. They wore huge pasteboard spectacles, grotesque robes, and dunces' caps with asses' ears. The spectacle repelled Haüy, who thought it "dishonourable to humanity" (French, 1932).

Haüy's interest was piqued further when he met Maria Theresia von Paradis, a blind pianist from Vienna, in Paris in 1784. Von Paradis not only inspired Haüy's direct involvement in special education but assisted him in developing methods and selecting materials (French, 1932). An approach for teaching reading developed as Haüy watched von Paradis practicing. He took the large pincushion in which she stuck pins to represent the notes of music and converted it into a book with embossed letters.

Now, armed with a method, an inspiration, and a philosophical base grounded on psychology and social studies, Haüy was finally ready to build. He searched for a star pupil, one who might show his accomplishments at exhibitions to raise funds, much as Épée's pupils had done (French, 1932). Haüy found his star in François Lesueur, a beggar boy, with whom he experimented with the print method he had developed with von Paradis's pins. After exhibiting seventeen-year-old Lesueur before the Académie Royale des Sciences, Haüy was able to open a small school in 1784 under the auspices of the Philanthropic Society of Paris, which collected and funded twelve indigent blind children. This venture is recognized as the first school in the world for blind persons.

Haüy continued to seek public patronage through exhibitions; royalty smiled on his efforts after a demonstration piqued the interest of Queen Marie Antoinette. In December 1786 Haüy and his twenty-four pupils were granted an audience with the king at Versailles. Among other honors conferred, the king appointed Haüy as royal interpreter and professor of ancient inscriptions (Perkins Inst., 1881).

Haüy described his methods in *Essai sur l'éducation des aveugles* (1786). His raised print was in the Illyrian letter format, printed on the school press, along with embossed maps and musical notes. However, Haüy's raised print was not a separate system especially formulated for blind students as sign language was for deaf individuals. Raised print was designed to be read by sighted persons as well. It was not until 1832 that Louis Braille formulated a reading and writing method exclusively for blind persons (see Chapter 6).

Although sensationalist principles guided Haüy's thinking in providing alternate sensory stimuli in the form of raised print, he diverged sharply in pedagogical emphasis; he did not match education to the specified needs of his blind students but instead attempted to overcome the limits of the disability by fitting his pupils to the sighted world. Grafting temporal concerns to philosophical speculation and pedagogical experimentation, Häuy stressed vocational training; his pupils learned weaving, basket and mat making, chair caning, and the rope trade (Guillie, 1817). By making intellectual development subservient to remunerative employment, Haüy did not, wrote one critic, "live up to the light of his own age" (French, 1932, p. 90).

In 1790 the National Assembly ordered Sicard's school for deaf persons and Haüy's for blind persons to be united under Sicard. Students were moved to the

convent of the Celestines, and the joint school was partly financed by seques-
tered ecclesiastical revenues. But Haüy and Sicard bitterly quarreled over ownership and organization until the existence of both schools seemed in jeopardy.
Then in 1791 Haüy's financial base evaporated when the Société Philanthropique
was broken up and its members were imprisoned, exiled, or guillotined. The National Assembly decreed that responsibility for the school would be assumed by
the state. But although the school was placed under state support, Haüy had to
pay for upkeep himself, as the treasury of the new republic was empty. To keep
at least moral patronage, pupils and the teacher printed handbills and pamphlets for the new regime (Perkins Inst., 1881).

Shared adversity failed to ease the tension between Sicard and Haüy and,
ultimately, the school for the blind moved to separate quarters in 1794. But Haüy
was a poor administrator, and six years later Napoleon moved all the blind children to the Quinze-Vingts, the asylum supposedly founded by Louis IX for men
blinded in the Crusades. Haüy, never a favorite of Napoleon because of his royalist leanings, was allowed a meager pension, then was totally dismissed in 1801.
So complete was his fall from official grace that when a history of blindness was
later published (Guillie, 1817), the origin of the school was attributed to Louis
XVI, not Haüy.

Following his dismissal by Napoleon, Haüy opened a private school that
functioned for three years. But in 1803, when Napoleon returned from Elba in a
frenzy of public adulation, Haüy opted for exile. He accepted an invitation from
the tsar of Russia to establish an asylum for the blind in St. Petersburg. Stopping
in Berlin en route, he was reported to have influenced the development of a
school there (Brockett, 1857).

The Emergence of a Science of Medicine

Péreire, Épée, and Haüy demonstrated that sensorily deprived persons were
intelligent beings who could, with the astute application of sensationalist principles and the use of alternate sensory stimuli, achieve in areas not previously
thought attainable with their handicaps. Success with deaf and blind persons
meant that opportunities could be extended to other disabled groups, first to
those labeled insane and then to mentally retarded persons (Winzer, 1988).
However, early efforts with mentally ill and mentally retarded populations were
not subsumed under education but were considered part of the newly emerging
disciplines of psychology and psychiatry. Physicians rather than churchmen
were at the helm of these enterprises.

The late eighteenth century saw medicine supplant theology as the touch-
stone in human matters. Medical advances were shaped by the predominance of
the taxonomic point of view, the conviction that general laws could be derived
from the collection and analysis of particular facts and that genera and species
had a natural and independent existence apart from the subjective perceptions
of a human observer. Carolus Linnaeus revolutionized biological science by suggesting a classification of animals and plants based on similarities of structure
or function; Baron Georges Cuvier, the father of paleontology, brought order to
comparative zoology (Bromberg, 1975).

Physicians believed that just as plants and minerals could be classified, so
could diseases. The classification of a bewildering array of human illnesses was

founded upon two fundamental goals—first, to provide clear and precise definitions of disease, and then to exhibit the relationships and inner nature of diseases by grouping together those with similar characteristics (L. F. King, 1958). Once this was done, it was believed that it would be possible to identify the conditions that determined health and disease, and so alter them.

The *ideologues,* an alliance of physicians and *philosophes,* were concerned with empirical principles of learning, the faculties of the mind, and methods of analysis. With the ultimate goal of perfecting the human species, they adopted sensationalist principles and the new philosophical spirit. With Condillac's method of gathering facts and an analytic approach to phenomena as the starting point (Doermer, 1969), the *ideologues* conceptualized medicine as not only the science of curing disease but also the study of the mind in order to promote mental health (Mahendra, 1985).

Alienation was the term under which the early *ideologues* subsumed the first paradigm of psychiatry in France. They conceived insanity not only as case history but also as mainly erupting from within humans, as disturbances of their self-command, self-control, self-preservation, and identity, which is why *alienation*—partly synonymous with *mania*—was chosen as the generic term for the various forms of madness (see Doermer, 1969).

Although leadership of the *ideologues* is generally attributed to Pierre Jean Georges Cabanis (1757–1808), physician to the Comte de Mirabeau, the physicians of greatest interest to the development of special education are Philippe Pinel, Jean Marc Gaspard Itard, and Édouard Seguin.

The Treatment of Mental Illness

Beginning in the early sixteenth century insane persons were locked away in lunatic hospitals and other facilities chiefly for the protection of society. Medical theory asserted that lunatics should be "confined in some convenient place, in order to prevent the commission of crimes, to which they are all more or less liable" (Beck, 1811, p. 32). Institutionalization was not used only for the mentally ill; the hospitals that had sprung up during the Middle Ages housed mixed groups that included the truly insane, mentally retarded individuals, aged derelicts, albinos, and epileptics. Dissenters, heretics, and others causing disruption of the social or religious order, without actually being criminal, also formed part of the institutionalized insane population (see Doermer, [1969] 1981).

When Philippe Pinel began his work at the end of the eighteenth century, two major lunatic hospitals were found in Paris at this time. Males from Paris and its surrounds were concentrated in Bicêtre (which also served as a prison until 1836 and was the scene of the first experimental use of the guillotine), while females were in the Salpêtrière. In Paris, with its 100,000 population, these two hospitals became catch basins for the city's hopeless and dependent.

Most eighteenth-century physicians held that insane persons could be dealt with only by animal force (Doermer, [1969] 1981); ascendancy of keepers and physicians over insane patients was viewed as vital. Institutional life was characterized by harsh treatment, violent remedies, and punishments that included whipping and starving. Inmates were brutalized, treated like animals, and, legally speaking, they had the status of animals (Doermer, [1969] 1981).

Mad persons were generally considered to be insensible to pain and temperature changes; at Salpêtrière and Bicêtre, inmates were chained naked in rat-infested cubicles below ground and fed on bread and soup (Lane and Pillard, 1978). A 1787 report of the Salpêtrière described how patients were "massed in fours or more in narrow cells; a dirty sack of straw, with vermin crawling through; rats running in troops by night, eating the clothes, the bread, and in time, the flesh of the patients" (in Bromberg, 1975, p. 93). So bad were conditions at the institutions that it is not surprising that in 1780, when an epidemic spread through Paris, its origin was attributed to infection at Bicêtre among its inmates. A commission of inquiry concluded that Bicêtre was subject to a "putrid fever" that was linked to the bad quality of the air but denied that this was the source of the disease (Doermer, [1969] 1981, p. 115).

Early conceptions of mental illness blamed a constellation of outside agencies for the condition. From at least the time of classical Greece until the seventeenth century, it was assumed that the gods inflicted madness as a punishment upon those who incurred their anger by some act of omission or commission.

Voltaire, Rousseau, and other French writers, intent on mocking demonology, witchcraft, and their trappings. denied supernatural explanations for madness. They insisted that a belief in such causes was not only a species of madness itself but was a fallacy perpetuated by a bombastic clergy. Such superstition, they argued, was dismissible in the light of rationality and science. One replacement for demonology, readily accepted by Rousseau, Voltaire, and others, was the notion of self-induced causes, most especially the idea of masturbatory insanity (Hare, 1962). Yet the notion of masturbatory insanity, popular until at least the close of the nineteenth century, became a fallacy in itself and one particularly resistant to dismissal.

Warnings about the medical dangers of masturbation were first widely circulated with the publication of *Onania, or the Heinous Sin of Self-Pollution* (c. 1726) by an unknown author, probably not a medical person, perhaps a clergyman or a quack (Hare, 1962). So popular was *Onania* that it was published in nineteen editions and sold 38,000 copies before 1750 (Neuman, 1985). Although this anonymous writer attributed "the troubles and agonies of a wounded conscience," the vapors, and "lying, foreswearing, perhaps murder" to the practice of masturbation and felt that masturbators "sometimes fall into a slight madness," he did not include serious mental disorders in his catalogue of woes (Hare, 1962). However, in an early assertion of what was to become a particularly pervasive view, he held that masturbation is a common cause of epilepsy. Shortly after, Samuel Auguste David Tissot, thought to be an unimpeachable medical authority, published a work essentially agreeing that sexual excesses cause a host of serious bodily and mental disorders. Tissot (1766) argued that his condemnation of masturbation was based on scientific, not moral, grounds (Neuman, 1985). The most serious effect of habitual masturbation, he believed, was the insanity caused by the reduction of the flow of blood to the brain. The medical professionals, quacks, and clergy were not alone in railing against the "flagrant crime" (Tissot, 1766); Voltaire and Rousseau offered strictures on the subject. In fact, Tissot praised Rousseau for his *Émile* (1762), which included a warning about masturbation (Neuman, 1975).

By the end of the eighteenth century the masturbatory hypothesis was widely accepted throughout Europe and America (Hare, 1962; McDonald, 1967), and the practice was seen as both a moral and a medical problem. The physicians who supported the masturbatory hypothesis believed that prevention of the practice was clearly important because the condition would only worsen in adults. Preventive measures included a spare diet, the avoidance of salt meat, moderate exercise, and proper medicines (*Onania,* 1737). Tissot (1766) added cold baths and the avoidance of boredom and excessive sleep. Many eighteenth-century physicians thought that adults would cease the habit if apprised of its dangers; those in the next century employed other means besides moral exhortation—various ointments, pharmacological agents, manual restraints, or sometimes radical surgery.

Philippe Pinel

Medical reform was one expression of the Enlightenment quest for social reform, clearly personified in Philippe Pinel (1745–1826), a distinguished French physician and one of the earliest psychiatrists. Pinel allied the concepts of the sensationalists with the practices of medicine, bringing a new emphasis on mental as well as bodily health. Many of Pinel's medical interventions were founded on the ideas of Rousseau who, directing attention away from the outer to the inner person, presented theories that were to become an integral part of psychiatric theory and practice. Pinel himself credited Locke, Voltaire, and the encyclopedists with his ideas (Goshen, 1967).

Before Pinel, clinical medicine had not developed sufficiently to nurture a union between the new humanitarian philosophies and medical science for the treatment of mental illness. With the rise of inductive science, however, philosophers and *ideologues* began to view emotional illness as a secular rather than a supernatural sickness (Carlson and Dain, 1960). Pinel firmly believed that the Creator had so designed the human body that it would flourish when it lived in harmony with its political and social environment; likewise, the Creator had so framed the political order that human health was fostered by good social institutions (Rosen, 1968). Pinel contemplated the possibility that the most significant cause of mental disorders is the failure of society to make adequate provision for conditions essential to mental health in its members. By its failure to create such conditions, society is ultimately responsible for stresses that produce mental conflicts and breakdowns.

Pinel conceived the idea of applying to the insane the same benefits of liberty and equality that Jean Paul Marat and Georges Jacques Danton were proclaiming in the National Assembly. To provide some comfort and liberty for those traditionally discarded as societal outcasts, Pinel mounted a two-pronged attack. First, he dispensed with contemporary etiological conceptions of mental illness; second, he addressed aspects previously overlooked in the treatment of insanity, most specifically, institutional change and a novel style of psychological mediation. His work focused on

> the purely philosophical viewpoint of the derangement of understanding, the
> knowledge about the physical and moral causes likely to produce it, the dis-

tinction between the various kinds of mental derangement, the exact history of the precursory symptoms, the course and end of the attack if it is an intermittent one, the rules of interior policy in the hospitals, the careful definition of those circumstances which may make certain remedies necessary and of those which make them superfluous. (Goshen, 1967, p. 258)

Pinel's identification with the alienists and his sensationalist bent led him to reject the traditional hypotheses of the etiology of insanity. Pinel first created the latitude for his scientific approach by rejecting all contemporary systems; he discredited the notion that the condition was caused by the devil, witchcraft, or the moon, and he disregarded the three traditional "exhausting factors"—libertinism, intoxicating liquor, and masturbation (Hare, 1962). Nor would he accept insanity as simply a product of a person's inner nature; dispositions, propensities, passions, or morality are not the root of mental illness, he said, for it is a physical disorder unrelated to inner nature.

Ignoring superficial forces, Pinel viewed the dramatic exigencies of life as the prime factors in emotional disturbance. Pinel surmised that patients would not respond to violence or coercion but, rather, deserve sympathy, respect, and assistance in conquering this life-produced situation. Successful therapy, he believed, requires active participation from the patient; treatment and cure rests on an historical depiction of symptoms and their relationship to the patient's background. With such facts in hand, the physician would be naturally led to the individual history of the origin of the illness and the development of its symptoms (Doermer, [1969] 1981).

Pinel's solution was the *traitement moral,* an integrated total treatment approach (A. Brigham, 1847) that implicitly included all nonmedical techniques and specifically stressed altering the patient's psychology. The emphasis of the *traitement moral* was on constructive activity, kindness, minimum restraint, structure, routine, and consistency in treatment (Kauffman, 1976).

When Pinel was appointed physician of Bicêtre in 1793, the commissioners granted his request to implement his mode of treatment. He began with frequent visits and conversations with patients (Pinel, [1806] 1962), for, if patients were to play an active role in the therapy, they could not be intimidated into passivity, goaded into violence, or treated as faceless members of a diagnostic category. At the same time, Pinel drastically altered the management of patients at Bicêtre. Convinced "that these madmen are so unbearable only because they are deprived of fresh air and freedom" (quoted by Doermer, [1969] 1981, p. 134), he advocated a less authoritarian approach. His scientific motive of reform was born of the belief that methodologically controlled and comparable observation was possible only if cases could move freely without chains (Doermer, [1969] 1981). During periods when patients were unshackled, Pinel would closely observe their behavior and, on the basis of increased knowledge, initiate further treatment.

To the derision and amusement of the warders, Pinel first entered the cell of an English captain who had been shackled for forty years and had earned a reputation as dangerous for killing an attendant with a blow of his manacles. He treated the captain and his second patient, a drunkard, with kindness, and was rewarded by dramatic improvements in their behavior. After that, forty patients were unchained and set at liberty, their movements restrained only by the "strait waistcoat" (Galt, [1842] 1846, p. 41). When allowed to move freely, treated with kindness and respect and the expectation that they would behave appropriately, the formerly deranged patients demonstrated dramatic improvements in their behavior (Kauffman, 1981). Not only were they quieter, but there was an end to the killing of attendants (Galt, [1842] 1846).

There is no question that Pinel's treatment represented enormous advances in the humane treatment of insane persons. Even so, it was a rocky road to administered morality; Pinel demanded that the patients develop an inner moral restraint but held ready external coercion and punishment should the patient refuse to obey (Doermer, [1969] 1981). Violence toward patients as a daily norm was terminated but recalcitrant patients were still subject to "straight waistcoats, superior force and seclusion for a limited time" (Pinel, [1806] 1962). As supplementary treatments, Pinel used douches—water dripping on the head—and warm baths.

Pinel's publications, such as *Nosographic philosophique ou la méthode de l'analyse appliquée à la médicine* [The philosophical method of analysis applied to medicine] (1798), became authoritative references in the area. Following Pinel, a dramatically increased interest in the care and training of insane persons was manifested in the rising number of calls for asylums and retreats (Beck, 1811). His influence was such that an official bulletin issued in 1819 for the first time contained protective provisions not against but for the insane. The infamous subterranean cells were prohibited; rooms for the inmates had to have flooring and windows; the insane were not to be confined with other inmates of hospitals or prisons; food had to be served several times a day; chains were to be supplanted by straitjackets, bullwhips were forbidden, and even therapy was indirectly alluded to—a daily visit by a physician was ordered (Doermer, [1969] 1981).

Equally important was Pinel's differentiation of five distinct forms of mental aberration, a scheme that not only advanced insanity from a homogeneous category to one constituted of a variety of illnesses and conditions but also separated retardation as a distinct and identifiable entity. The first form of insanity Pinel described was melancholia, a partial derangement of the mind in which monomania dominates the faculties of sound reason. The second form, manic sans deline, Pinel described as a pure disorder of the will and an undisturbed mind; that is, a bodily tension with no emotional causes, manifesting itself merely as a spontaneous blind drive. Pinel's third disease form was the most frequent form of alienation, manic frenzy, a periodic phenomenon that affected one or more mental functions. Dementia, the fourth form, robbed the patient of all judgment. Idiocism, innate or acquired, was described as a more or less complete atrophy of reasoning and free will (Ackerknecht, 1959; Doermer, [1969] 1981).

Later life treated Pinel little better than it did Haüy. Suspected of having opposed the delivery to the authorities of a number of priests and émigrés who had sought refuge at Bicêtre, Pinel was denied his teaching post. He was also believed to harbor royalist sentiments, so he lived out his life in comparative destitution (Bromberg, 1975).

In 1796 Jean Étienne Dominique Esquirol (1782–1840), a royalist and moderate conservative of the Restoration, came to Paris to study and, with Itard, studied and worked under Pinel. In 1810 Esquirol succeeded Pinel as head doctor at Salpêtière; later he became the physician in chief of the Maison royale des aliéné's de Charenton.

Esquirol adopted the paradigm outlined by Pinel both theoretically and practically, although he assumed a more narrow stance. Esquirol viewed moral treatment as "the application of the faculty of intelligence and of emotions in the treatment of mental alienation," an equivalent of what is now called milieu therapy (Carlson and Dain, 1960). To Esquirol, mentally ill patients required calm and order together with mechanical labor. He used a variety of treatments, including medications such as hellebore, music, isolation, and altering the environment to make it bright and airy; he abandoned treatments that included total immersion, flogging, and leeching (Galt, [1842] 1846).

Jean Marc Gaspard Itard

The social, political, and therapeutic climate of France that had nurtured efforts with other handicapped groups now propelled mental subnormality into prominence and led to important discoveries regarding its essential features. Certainly, in the past mental retardation had not been neglected. As Mahendra (1985) stresses, such conditions as cretinism were recognized and studied with remarkable prescience by some of the great names in medicine long before mental subnormality became a subject of special interest. But the long-held conception of mental retardation as a type of insanity meant that medical treatment of mentally ill persons preceded educational intervention for the intellectually disabled population.

In 1800, when Sicard created the position of resident physician at the Institution Nationale des Sourds Muets, Jean Marc Gaspard Itard (1775–1850) joined the medical staff in order to study the consequences of deafness, research hereditary aspects, and medically examine the organs of speech and hearing. But Itard's interest tacked sharply toward a new course when reports reached Paris of a young boy seen running with the wolves in the Forest of Aveyron. Apparently the lad, who was later named Victor, was first noticed when peasants in the region of Lacaune in south-central France spied him fleeing through the woods. In 1798 he was again seen by woodsmen in the woods of Caure seeking acorns and nuts and, despite his violent resistance, captured by a group of sportsmen (Barr, [1904b] 1913). He was put on public display but did not accept readily the company of polite society, and he subsequently escaped again to the forest. For the next fifteen months Victor was glimpsed on a number of occasions digging up potatoes and turnips or seeking acorns to eat. On July 25, 1799, three hunters spotted him in the same woods, captured him, brought him back to Lacaune, and entrusted him to the care of an elderly widow. After eight days Victor again succeeded in escaping, although this time he did not return to his original forest but instead climbed the mountains and traveled across the broad plateau of the department of Aveyron. For some unknown reason he approached the workshop of a dyer, Vidal, who recaptured him. The government commission for

St.-Sernin, Constans-St. Exteve took charge of the boy and on the following day sent Victor to an orphanage at St.-Affrique. Still not reconciled to society, Victor escaped from St.-Affrique on several occasions, only to be recaptured (see Barr, [1904b] 1913; Lane, 1976).

By this time Victor was already well known throughout France and had, in fact, been somewhat of a *cause célèbre*. Crowds of visitors came to see the lad, and his story appeared in newspapers throughout France, bringing him to the attention of teachers, philosophers, and others. Abbé Pierre Joseph Bonnaterre, professor of natural history at the central school in Aveyron, was one of the first to come into contact with the boy. According to various descriptions of Victor at that time, he appeared to be congenitally deaf and mute, twelve years of age, and nice looking. Bonnaterre observed that the child was unaccustomed to prepared food, lay flat on the ground, and immersed his chin in the water to drink, tore all sorts of garments, and was trying constantly to escape. He walked often on all fours, fought with his teeth, gave few marks of intelligence, had no articulate speech, and even appeared devoid of natural speech, but he was complaisant, even pleased, at receiving caresses (Barr, [1904b] 1913).

Sicard, Itard, and other scholars were anxious to get Victor to Paris in order to observe his behavior before it lost some of its wildness (Lane, 1976). But Bonnaterre was reluctant to have Victor moved. Having written a section on zoology for Diderot's *Encyclopédie,* Bonnaterre reasoned that he knew how to study a feral child and in so doing could "furnish to philosophy and natural history important ideas on the original condition of man" (Barr, [1904b], 1913, p. 31). However, insisting on his privileges, Sicard sought the intervention of Napoleon's brother, Lucien Bonaparte, who ordered the boy brought to Paris. It took five months before Victor finally left Aveyron, and during the three-week trip to Paris he caught smallpox, although few visible signs remained once he recovered.

When he finally reached the capital on Bastille Day, 1800, Victor was placed in the school for the deaf because of his muteness. But the Abbé Sicard "soon tired of the uncouth boy who was throwing away his clothes, and trying to escape even by the windows; and left him to wander neglected in the halls of the school for deaf-mutes" (Seguin, [1866] 1907, pp. 19–20). Consequently, one Madame Guerin was allocated 150 francs a year by the ministry to attend Victor in a nearby house belonging to the school.

Itard seized the opportunity to work with the boy but, when they first met, teacher and unwilling pupil, Itard was not confronted with the noble savage of Rousseau's romantic philosophy, but instead with an *enfant sauvage* who was dirty and insensitive to basic sensations. He bit people and spent most of his time sleeping or rocking back and forth. Itard's (1932) description was no more promising than that of Bonnaterre: "a disgustingly dirty child afflicted with spasmodic movements and often convulsions who swayed back and forth ceaselessly like certain animals in the menagerie who bit and scalded those who opposed him, who showed no sign of affection for those who had attended him, and who was in short, indifferent to everything and attentive to nothing" (Itard, 1932, p. 4).

Still, the sudden advent of a feral child was a golden opportunity for putting the theories of Rousseau, Diderot, and other philosophers into practice. Through educational intervention, Itard hoped to solve "the metaphysical problem of determining what might be the degree of intelligence and the nature of the ideas in a lad, who, deprived from birth of all education, should have lived entirely separated from the individuals of his kind" (Seguin, [1866] 1907, p. 21). With his deep belief in Condillac's view that human nature is the product of human interaction, Itard based his teaching on Condillac's *Traité des sensations* [Treatise on the senses] (Talbot, 1964) and sought to prove the theory by socializing Victor. The boy was to become a living exposition of Condillac's epistemology and linguistics (Formigari, 1974).

Victor appeared at the dawn of psychology and psychiatry; no one knew how to study a feral child, much less how to treat and teach one. Itard asserted that Victor was retarded because he had been left in the woods; he believed him to be mentally arrested because of social and educational neglect, and held that he had acquired idiocy through isolation, having a sort of mental atrophy from disuse (Kanner, 1964). Philippe Pinel took the opposing view; he maintained that the lad had been thrown into the woods because he was retarded. Pinel believed that retardation largely results from hereditary influences and that such neurological damage is irreversible (Blanton, 1976).

Itard disregarded the arguments of his old mentor. So optimistic was Itard that it was he who named the boy "Victor," perhaps to represent the victory of education over idiocy (Seguin, [1864] 1976). Itard hoped that environmental changes would completely restore Victor to normal society and was convinced that the boy could be taught practical skills, including speech. In collaboration with Madame Guerin, who assumed the material and housekeeping responsibilities for Victor, Itard engaged his student in a wide range of carefully conceived educational activities, generalized from the sensorial experiments of Péreire. Our knowledge of Itard's methods comes from reports he transmitted to the French Ministry of the Interior (Talbot, 1964) and from his brief text, *L'enfant sauvage,* usually translated as *The Wild Boy of Aveyron* (Itard, 1932).

Itard organized his reports around five principal aims governing his educational strategy (Ball, 1971)—socialization, sensory stimulation, concept development, speech, and transfer of learning. Barr ([1904b] 1913) described the sequence of activities and objectives and the five specific ideals that Itard set up for Victor in order to develop the functions of the senses, the intellectual functions, and the emotional faculties. According to Barr ([1904b] 1913), Itard first endeavored "to endear Victor to social life, by making it more congenial than the one he was then leading and, above all, more like that he had but recently quitted." He also attempted "to awaken Victor's nervous sensibility by the most energetic stimulants, and at other times by quickening the affection of the soul." To "extend the sphere of his ideas," Itard first centered his teaching on Victor's immediate physical wants and then moved toward creating new wants. To lead Victor in the use of speech, Itard used "imitation, under the spur of necessity" (p. 31).

In the time that Itard worked with Victor, from 1800 to 1804, the boy progressed in the areas of touch, taste, and smell fairly quickly, but vision and hearing were trained much more slowly and with far less success (Magdol, 1976). After four years of work Victor "did not, however, progress beyond a low degree of civilization, and at last came to a stand" (Edward Peet, 1852, p. 116). Indeed, Victor was never truly restored to society, and Itard mourned his work as a failure. As well, Victor developed what seemed to be grand mal seizures (Stevens, 1954).

Notes from Itard's memoirs and his authoritative reports on progress (1801, 1804, 1807) reveal the dedication that impelled him to devote himself to an almost impossible task. But the study was abruptly ended one day when Itard, in a flare of temper, threatened to throw the boy out the window because he seemed particularly obstinate (Stevens, 1954). Overwhelmed by disappointment, Itard stormed: "Unfortunate! Since my pains are lost and my efforts fruitless, take yourself back to your forest and primitive tastes; or, if your new wants make you dependent on society, suffer the penalty of being useless, and go to Bicêtre, there to die in wretchedness" (Barr, [1904b] 1913, pp. 31–32).

Itard finally joined Pinel's camp and became convinced of the incurability of imbecility (Barr, 1904b). Although, after Victor, Itard worked with a large range of cases from "idiotic to morally depraved" (Seguin, [1866] 1907, p. 28), he came to believe that the condition of innate idiocy could be minimized but not eradicated, and he finally lent sanction to the doctrine of letting the idiot alone. Nevertheless, Itard's work stimulated later intervention in cases of retarded children and provided the basis of the teaching approaches of Édouard Seguin and Maria Montessori. Moreover, contemporary methods for retarded and disturbed children are grounded in many of the principles expounded by Itard (Lane, 1976). Nor did he abandon his original commitment to deafness; in this area Itard wrote twenty articles and books, experimented with aural teaching for deaf children, invented and perfected several ear trumpets, investigated congenital deafness, divided the congenitally deaf into specific classes, and wrote on pneumothoracic problems and stammering (Edward Peet, 1852, pp. 111–17).

And what of poor Victor, the child who exchanged the freedom of the woods for the conventions of society only to meet rejection and distaste when he failed to prove a philosophical principle? Victor died in the little house he shared with Madame Guerin in 1828 when he was in his forties.

Édouard Seguin

The French Académie des Sciences admitted in 1806 that Itard had not fully succeeded with Victor, but it acknowledged that Itard could not have added more "intelligence, sagicity, patience, courage" in his lessons and blamed "the imperfection of the organs of the subject upon which he worked" (Seguin, [1866] 1907, p. 26). It was left to Édouard Seguin (1812–1880), who had studied medicine and surgery under Itard and Esquirol, to move forward to the next logical step in the care and education of mentally retarded individuals.

As Itard had suffered the scrutiny of Pinel, so Seguin worked under the benign though skeptical gaze of Esquirol, who believed that idiocy is incurable. To Esquirol, idiocy was "not a disease, but a condition in which the intellectual faculties are never manifested, or have never been developed sufficiently to enable the idiot to acquire such amount of knowledge as persons of his own age and placed in similar circumstances with himself are capable of receiving" (Esquirol, [1838] 1845, p. 446).

However, Seguin, following the French sensationalists, held that mental retardation, except for cases of brain damage, was caused by sensory isolation or deprivation: atrophy of the brain, like atrophy of the muscles, resulted from disuse. In Seguin's view, the dormant brain could be aroused through powerful stimuli, especially motor and tactile ones. Stimulation of the brain, Seguin argued, would produce electrical excitement in the nervous system, which in turn would result in vascular dilation and increased blood flow and finally in adequate nutrition, growth, and development (Blanton, 1976).

Itard's approach to rehabilitation—education of the senses—gained breadth and momentum in the hands of Seguin. With his assertion that mentally retarded children could learn if taught through specific sensory motor exercises, Seguin expanded the techniques into a complex systematic sequence of training—the physiological method—that encompassed three main components: motor and sensory physical training; intellectual training, including academic and speech techniques; and moral training or socialization (see Ball, 1971; Holman, 1914; Kanner, 1964; Talbot, 1964).

Like Itard, Seguin acknowledged his debt to Péreire. His 1846 volume contained a seven-page account of Péreire's work and comments on Épée; a biography published in 1847 compared at length the methods and results of Épée and Péreire (Talbot, 1964). "I am not unaware," said Seguin, "that the problem of educating deaf-mutes was attacked and even solved in the last century from the wider stand point, that of Periere, which is strikingly analogous to that which I have used to solve the problem of healing mental defect" (quoted by Lewis, 1960). Seguin took Péreire's work one conceptual step further in order to treat mental retardation (see Chapter 6) and drew an analogy between Péreire's basic principles and those that enabled him to, or so he thought, solve the problem of treating mental defect. He observed that mental retardation shared with deafness and congenital blindness the early age of onset and the permanence of the condition (Seguin, 1846).

With implicit faith in Itard's discoveries, G. M. A. Ferrus, a physician who had earlier been invited by Pinel to join staff at Bicêtre, opened a school for mentally retarded children at Bicêtre in 1826. In 1830 Seguin and Esquirol opened a private school for mentally retarded children (Blanton, 1976). Seguin began another private school in Paris in 1837, although he left within a year to work with private pupils. Then in 1842 an aging Itard and Esquirol made arrangements for Seguin to test some of his ideas at Bicêtre. Seguin was convinced that his own physiological method (sense training) and Esquirol's *traitement moral* were applicable to all retarded children, regardless of the level of retardation. In the same year a commission of the Paris Academy declared that Seguin had definitely solved the problem of idiot education (Kanner, 1964).

Seguin's regular reports and textbooks became the standard references in the field, the physiological method was widely adopted in the nineteenth century, and the work established the education of mentally retarded individuals worldwide. Seguin emigrated to the United States in 1848 and there continued to work in the field of mental retardation (see Chapter 3).

ADVANCES IN GREAT BRITAIN

As the eighteenth century drew to a close, Britain initiated education for her handicapped population but, confined by social and political pressures,

diverged sharply from the route illuminated by the French *philosophes* and practitioners. Political differences and fears fueled by the French Revolution spilled
over to affect all aspects of British life, including the education of disabled individuals. France was Britain's ancient and enduring enemy on the battlefield—
and would become so again under Napoleon. The violence of the Revolution and
the ensuing Reign of Terror shook all of Europe, and nowhere was this more apparent than in Britain. Still smarting from the loss of the American colonies,
fearful after the internal civil disruptions of the 1780s, and beginning to face internal dissension with the onset of the Industrial Revolution, the British may not
yet have feared for their empire, but they fretted for their stability, bound up as
it was in the British class and political system. Even if the common people ap-
plauded the strength of their peasant brethren, the ruling classes quaked at the
specter of internal dissension and revolution sparked by news of the French experience. To protect themselves against the corrupting miasma drifting across
the Channel, the British closeted themselves in mounting conservatism, one
manifestation of which was animosity to all things French.

Although the British isolated themselves, their disregard of French philosophers and teachers did not ultimately translate into ignorance of the new social
philosophies circulating in Europe. By the close of the eighteenth century the
social climate in Britain promoted education for exceptional persons. Nevertheless, religious zealotry, political conservatism, and a stereotyped social philosophy inhibited the creative and speculative thinking that might have occurred in
Great Britain (Seigel, 1969). Rather than following the rigorous intellectual approach used by the French in special education, the British embarked on a
basically utilitarian method of education. They brushed aside the novel psychological and philosophical principles concerning the disabled population and
sought to make exceptional individuals fit neatly into regular society.

In Great Britain the care and training of exceptional children was a logical
extension of the schemes for managing those who are impecunious and dependent that emerged in the early decades of the eighteenth century. The 1730s saw
an upsurge of infanticide, particularly in the turbulent city of London, a trend
that hastened public acceptance of the need for a foundling hospital, which the
English had heretofore resisted (Ramsland, 1989). Orphanages and workhouses
sprung up, and greater demands were aired for the extension of schools for the
poor and of Sunday schools.

The task of educating disabled individuals in Britain was most often undertaken by fierce evangelical reformers who were rising to prominence among English social thinkers. The moral and religious priorities of Evangelicals were far
removed from those of the Enlightenment, although there were significant links
between them. In particular, the Enlightenment emphasis upon the human capacity for improvement helped to ensure that the Evangelical movement, despite its return to seventeenth-century Puritan morality, moved away from
emphasizing original sin (L. A. Williams, 1989). The Evangelicals believed that
children had the capacity for sin but that on the whole theirs, unlike adults', was
excusable. Following this thread, they segregated handicapped children partly to
protect impressionable youngsters from adult contamination.

Zealously concerned with the saving of souls, the British protected the disabled under the sponsorship of private charities and private teachers. Special

education was not heralded as philosophical inquiry, or even as an exercise in humanitarianism, but rather as a process by which exceptional people could be educated and evangelicalized so that they could earn entry into the next world. Evangelicals believed in the educability of exceptional children but placed more emphasis on religious improvement than on intellectual development.

Following a sequence now well established in special education, deaf persons were the first to be educated. But, as Jean Paul Seigel (1969) stresses, almost through Victorian times, the education of deaf persons in Britain was marked by ignorance of the psychology of deafness and by an unwillingness or inability on the part of the British theorists to apply fresh concepts of psychology and philosophy. The rising British educators ignored the contributions of John Wallis, Bulwer, and the others who laid the foundation for the enterprise in that country as well as the psychological principles that had evolved in France. In Britain the emphasis was very simple: sign language was thought dehumanizing, and therefore speech must be developed as quickly and effectively as possible (Kyle, 1980–81). Consequently, the education of deaf students in Britain focused on the primacy of speech. Teachers wished, said the philosopher Dugald Stewart, "to astonish the vulgar by the sudden conversion of a dumb child into a speaking *automan*" (original italics, quoted by McGann, 1863, p. 11).

Even as Dugald Stewart and other commonsensical Scots philosophers promoted the accomplishments of Épée and Sicard, an opposing faction devoted as much time to denouncing the French system (Seigel, 1969). Épée's sign system was characterized as "altogether useless" and "an absurd and inexcusable waste of time" (quoted by Seigel, 1969, p. 115). These critics disregarded the complexities of language and the broadened communication horizons inherent in the method, as well as the ruling of the Zurich Academy; they allowed no credence to teaching "a complicated artificial language, which was perfectly unintelligible to the whole rest of the world" (*Edinburgh Encyclopedia,* 1813, pp. 13, 14).

In 1760, the year of Épée's initial trial in Paris, the first organized establishment for deaf students in Britain was founded in Edinburgh by Thomas Braidwood (1715–1806), an advocate of oral principles. Originally a teacher of mathematics, Braidwood undertook to instruct the deaf son of a wealthy merchant from Leith in 1760. So successful was his venture and so sure was Braidwood of his powers, that he advertised to "undertake to teach anyone of a tolerable genius in the space of about three years to speak and to read distinctly" (*Scots Magazine,* 1767, p. 12). His house in Edinburgh, which became a school especially for deaf students, is mentioned in Walter Scott's *Heart of Midlothian.* It came to be called Dumbiedikes because Braidwood lived there with his deaf pupils ("Thomas Braidwood," 1888). Samuel Johnson and his biographer, James Boswell visited Braidwood; after examining the pupils, Dr. Johnson was led to intone that "it was pleasing to see one of the most desperate of human calamities capable of so much help" (S. Johnson, [1775] 1924, p. 148).

As secretive as his oral colleagues, Braidwood guarded his methods jealously. Seekers of information and enlightenment were informed by his teachers that they were under a bond to Braidwood to teach charity scholars for a specific time and not to communicate to anyone a knowledge of the method of instruction, an edict that was to have a decisive effect in the course of North American deaf education. In 1806 Braidwood's nephew published *Instruction of the Deaf and Dumb.* This and various other reports (e.g., Samuel Porter, 1848a, 1848b) indicate that Braidwood used lipreading and writing. He taught speech by placing a small silver rod on the tongue in various positions in the mouth. He first taught single sounds, then syllables, and finally words.

More important than his methodology is the peak of self-aggrandizement Thomas Braidwood attained. He created a remarkable situation: a monopoly on British education of deaf persons that was to last for fifty-nine years. In 1773 Braidwood moved to London with his nephew, Joseph Watson, to open a second school for deaf persons in Hackney, which prospered as a private institution. From these beginnings the family gained virtual control of the organization and pedagogy of their own private schools and the charity establishments that were being formed at about that time. So tightly did the Braidwoods hold onto the education of deaf people that, without their express permission, no one else could attempt the venture.

Once private enterprises, in the form of Braidwood's schools, were under way, evangelical reformers moved to form charity schools for indigent children. After meeting the mother of a deaf child who had paid £1,500 to the Braidwoods, John Townshend, the minister of the Congregational church at Bermondsey and a member of the Clapham sect, envisaged "the *necessity* and *practicability* of having a charitable institution for the deaf and dumb children of the poor" (original italics, Samuel Porter, 1848c, p. 231). The Clapham sect, so called because they gathered at a house on Clapham Common to discuss social problems, was a vigorous reforming minority closely aligned to the Quakers. It counted among its members such prominent figures as Henry Thornton, Henry Cox Mason, and William Wilberforce, the power behind the British ban on slavery. With their assistance, and the advice and encouragement of the American Francis Green, Townshend established the Bermondsey Institution for indigent deaf children in 1792 (see Hawker, 1805, [1805] 1905; Townshend, 1831). Six pupils were installed in a rented house with Joseph Watson as their teacher. At the outset, the organizers had to contend with the ingrained belief that nothing could be done for deaf people. But the list of potential students rapidly grew, and what had been intended as a local institution soon became established as an important national charity with applications far exceeding capacity. Moreover, the organizational plan of the Bermondsey Institution was adopted by most other British charity schools that opened in the period (Samuel Porter, 1848b). By 1834 the British Poor Law had a clause that empowered boards of guardians to pay for deaf or blind children in asylums (Hodgson, [1952] 1973) and exempted deaf and blind persons from the rigorous "workhouse test" by which one gave up everything to enter the workhouse (Young and Ashton, 1956).

In 1802 another Braidwood opened the General Institution for Instruction of the Deaf and Dumb at Birmingham. In 1810 the Bermondsey Institution moved to Old Kent Road and became the Old Kent Road Institution, later the Asylum for the Deaf and Dumb Poor (Bender, 1970). The Refuge for the Destitute Deaf and Dumb opened in Holburn in 1840; it later became the Royal Association in Aid of the Deaf and Dumb (Heassman, 1962).

British interest in the training and education of blind individuals was inspired by Edward Rushton, a blind poet who lost his sight on a slave ship while helping in an epidemic of ophthalmia. Rushton opened a school for the indigent blind persons in Liverpool in 1791 where pupils, aged fourteen to forty-five, were taught to work in trades, to sing in churches, and to play the organ. The year 1793 witnessed the opening of the Edinburgh Blind Asylum and the Bristol Asylum and Industrial School for the Blind (see Chapin, 1846). At the London School for Blind, which opened in 1799, and most others of the genre, no intellectual education was provided, merely trade teaching with a little musical instruction. Indigent blind people, it was assumed, did not need knowledge beyond their calling (Dunscombe, 1836), that is, beyond their assumed social class.

Psychiatry and psychology in England is said to have begun with the opening of William Tuke's Retreat near York in 1796. Tuke (1732–1822), an English merchant, was dismayed at the conditions in lunatic hospitals and, with the assistance of the Society of Friends (Quakers), opened a decidedly more humane establishment (Scheerenberger, 1982). The Tuke family brought new light to the care of insane persons, essentially adopting the tenets of Pinel's *traitement moral.* With sometimes gentle, often firm discipline and a system of rewards and punishments, the Tukes pioneered a nonmedical approach to insanity. The emphasis was on participation in a set of orderly domestic routines that included work, religious observance, and a wide variety of diverting social activities, all with the ultimate objective of resocializing the insane patients into the behavior expected outside the asylum (see A. Digby, 1985, S. Tuke, 1813).

The advances of the York Retreat lent impetus to a parliamentary committee on the state of insane hospitals in Britain and, so ghastly were the reports, that the Bedlams, at least in their very worst aspects, were altered, and the English Lunacy Acts of 1828 and 1844 were passed. With the advent of lunacy reform in the early nineteenth century, the asylum was endorsed as the sole approved response to the problems posed by all forms of mental illness (see Scull, 1975, 1976; Walton, 1979). In Great Britain public asylums for the insane poor were established after 1845.

Another typical sequence in special education—the treatment of the insane precedes and illuminates the treatment and education of mentally handicapped individuals—is apparent in the case of Britain: schooling for mentally defective students arose later. The education of mentally retarded children began with the establishment of a school in Bath in 1846.

The period of the Enlightenment in the history of special education opened on a speculative and theoretical note, but it closed on a decidedly practical one. As the intense focus on rationalism wound down, it left in its wake many new institutions for the treatment and management of all kinds of exceptionality. The age of the asylum had begun.

Part 2

Into the Light of a More Modern World

Introduction

Ever since the discovery of the New World by the Old, there has been a steady exchange of people, ideas, and goods. The Old World contributed culture, religion, political dissension, smallpox, scarlet fever, and gunpowder; the New World reciprocated with tobacco and perhaps syphilis (see Zinsser, 1935). Material items were only part of the steady trade across the Atlantic; the New World imported ideologies and philosophies and altered them to suit the uniquely American experience.

By the middle decades of the eighteenth century, a spirit of reform was abroad in both Europe and North America. The influence of the European Enlightenment was pervasive, especially in the political literature of the time. The writings of the leading secular thinkers of the European Enlightenment were quoted everywhere in the colonies (Bailyn, 1967). But it is important to remember that in its goals and outcomes, America's revolution differed sharply from the turmoil that altered the French social and political order. The underlying quest for freedom may have been the same, but America's revolution entailed not the disruption of society but the realization (for some of the American population, at least) of the inheritance of liberty.

One manifestation of the influence of the glittering generalities of the European Enlightenment on American eighteenth-century thought was the unequivocal declaration that something must be done for the weak, the dependent, the disabled—for all those who could not earn a living in competition with the fit. Americans readily responded to the challenge; urged on by a humanitarian philosophy, evangelical commitment, and unbounded philanthrophy, they established a growing number of institutions designed to cater to the unique needs of exceptional individuals. Schooling in the New World did not become the norm for exceptional children any more than it was for other nineteenth-century youngsters, but enormous social, economic, and political alterations in American society assured an increasing commitment to the requirements of exceptional populations.

Many factors contributing to the development of special education in North America were different than those in Europe, factors that were neither temporary nor superficial. Although the vitality of French educational endeavors undoubtedly laid the basis of North American ventures, pedagogy and administrative structures were quickly adapted to the peculiarly American conditions. American institutions tended to adopt the organizational structures of the British charity enterprises and the pedagogy of the French.

Special schooling in British North America (Canada) developed later, about forty years after special education was firmly entrenched on American soil. Nevertheless, Canada and the United States share a common heritage in special education. "Geographically, we may be two peoples," commented a 1906 writer. "In aim and heart, we are one" (Ontario, Dept. of Ed. 1906, p. 12). Developments in Canadian special education were tightly bound to those in all of North America; Canada reiterated American advances as it spread the essential tenets of education and social emancipation for its own disabled populations. The basic features of Canadian special education were painted in the same colors as the American, with modifications determined by factors such as the size and distribution of the population, changing demands, and economic variables. Canadians saw no problems in reconciling their determination to remain British with the mass importation of American ideas; they placed great faith in the American system of special education. Not only were American initiatives used as guides to assess Canadian progress, but favorable comparison was necessary to gain the support of legislatures and the general public for the expansion of special education.

Canadian special education institutions adopted American pedagogical techniques; personnel were recruited from American institutions; teachers were trained at American centers; and the annual reports of Canadian schools were larded with excerpts from the writings of American educators, accompanied by detailed explanations of their philosophies and practices. Canadian schools became an integral part of the North American institutional complex, and Canadian educators were important contributors to a North American enterprise. "We always include the Canadian schools with the American schools," said Alexander Graham Bell, they being "about the same" and "employing the same methods" (quoted by J. C. Gordon, ed., 1892a, p. 65).

Early nineteenth-century Americans saw special training as a prime means of uplifting disabled individuals, of bringing them to the sacred text of the Bible, and of instilling in them patriotic notions of duty to class and country. These goals were remarkably similar to those expounded for the development of a public system of free education for all children. Indeed, common elements were apparent in the growth of facilities for special education and for regular education, but most conspicious was the similar rhetoric advanced for the elaboration of both systems.

Articulate educational reformers, directing their efforts to the reform of society through the school system, included special education under their evangelical umbrellas. Men such as Henry Barnard and Horace Mann in the United States and Adolphus Egerton Ryerson in Upper Canada were insightful commentators on learning environments in general and involved themselves in the campaign for the establishment of institutions to serve the special needs of deaf, blind, and mentally retarded children as well as those designated as confirmed or potential delinquents.

The institutional developments that began in the second decade of the nineteenth century are particularly noteworthy because they advanced alongside the extension of the common schools, embodied what can be considered the three major principles of nineteenth-century child rescue—protection, separation, and dependence—and led to the emergence of forms that are still present, although finally disappearing, today. Moreover, the emergence of specialized institutions marked a significant shift in attitudes toward, and treatment of, disabled individuals, and their development illuminates rapidly changing perceptions of the role of disabled persons in an industrializing society.

Institutional development for exceptional populations was therefore intrinsically associated with changing social, economic, political, and religious determiners in American society in the nineteenth century. Moreover, the perception of the social roles of disabled individuals changed over the course of the century. Initially seen as supplicants depending on private philanthropy, they were next viewed as dependents on official charity, and, finally, by the opening decades of the twentieth century, as individuals deserving of educational rights similar to those ceded their nonexceptional counterparts.

At another level, the rapid development of institutions may be viewed as a mechanism for ordering society, for fostering a more sophisticated control, especially of the lower classes, that worrisome and fractious stratum of society from which many special children came. Reformers directed moral disapproval of the poor and chided them for their supposed spiritual and moral inferiority. Part of the reformer's litany about the disorders of working-class life centered on the pernicious effects of unsavory surroundings and their brutal contamination of developing children. Lower-class youngsters required protection from the harsher elements of society. For those with disabling conditions and those slipping toward social deviance, protection entailed segregation in settings where children could be trained in the values held dear by the middle class.

Throughout the nineteenth century increasing numbers of exceptional students—specifically, those labeled in the traditional parlance as deaf and dumb, blind, and feeble minded—received their education and training within this institutional complex. As the institutions drew more students within their orbit, components that would eventually characterize all educational enterprises appeared. Throughout the century there were gradual increases in daily average attendance, in the length of the school year, in the consolidation of control at the state level, in the standardization and classification of students, and in the increased differentiation of programs. Yet although increased and expanded educational opportunities to develop a more highly skilled work force were seen as desirable by reformers, large numbers of special children were still not in school. Many factors contributed to depressed enrollment and attendance figures, not the least of which was parents' poverty, lack of understanding of the aims of the institutions, and fear of allowing their special child away from their care.

Unique to special education was the "medicalization" of the enterprise. To be sure, medical aspects had historically been paramount, but now, as special education expanded and became a permanent venture, the etiology and the definitions of disabilities and the classification of disabled persons attained greater importance. This was true for blind and deaf students but even more so for the ever-broadening category of feebleminded (mentally retarded), for whom physicians played a central role in institutional development, management, and curriculum. By the close of the nineteenth century medicine and the newly emerging scientific method in psychology combined to forge even closer links between special education, mental retardation, and etiological considerations.

A medical model justified the expansion of institutional facilities to serve the needs of exceptional students. Under a medical or disability model, problems of learning, behavior, and socialization were seen as located within the individual. Such problems then explained school and social failure. Given that the failure was believed to inhere in the individual, it was appropriate to assign such children to a segregated system with training provided by specialists (see Gelzheiser, 1987).

Schools and institutions acquire life only with their chief constituents—the pupils and the teachers. But about these individuals, history is relatively silent. Schooling for exceptional individuals in North America arose not at the prompting of disabled groups themselves, but in response to the advocacy of parents, reformers, and the clergy. Leaders emerged who identified and elaborated the methods, principles, and philosophy of the emerging field of special education; they then further inspired reformers as well as public, government, and corporate bodies to invest financially and socially in the creation of a system of local institutions.

Nineteenth-century institutions owe much to their architects, both structural and pedagogical, and history has been kind to these pioneers and innovators. Whatever deficiencies the nineteenth-century pioneers may have had, reticence was not one of them. They wrote amply, and their journals were crowded with institutional reports, delineations of methodologies, extracts of speeches and sermons, and sometimes debate and counterdebate. In these exchanges may be found the essential lines of conflict that plagued nineteenth-century special education and that, to some extent, remain issues of intense debate. Placement issues, curriculum, vocational training, early intervention, and the status of teachers with disabilities are only a sampling of the nineteenth-century concerns that remain unresolved today.

But although superintendents and school principals provided voluminous statements of educational intent, these are far from trustworthy guides to what children actually experienced in school or of actual classroom practice and the daily lives of classroom teachers. Details about the teachers are relatively scarce in the field of special education. It can be said that, as reform efforts gathered momentum, the stress on structure spilled over into pleas for greater professional expertise. The nature of teaching and teachers changed: it became important to train teachers in approved methods, to provide them with a sense of vocational identity and spirit, and to appoint officials to supervise them. But of their daily experiences in the classroom, history tells us little.

'History tends to be as silent about the children who filled the special schools. We know relatively little about the students themselves or their families, responses to their institutionalization; the prism of time permits only surmise pulled from dry reports about institutional life and its impact on developing children. Finding detailed information about disabled adults in society proves to be an equally arduous task. Writings are sparse, and almost nothing is known about their occupations, marriage patterns, family life, child rearing, mobility and transiency, and recreation.

Chapter 3

The Rise of Institutions, Asylums, and Public Charities

Chronology of Early Landmarks in North American Special Education

1783   Benjamin Rush consolidates his career at Pennsylvania Hospital

1803   Francis Green attempts a census of the deaf population of Massachusetts

1812   John Braidwood arrives in the United States

1817   The Connecticut Asylum for the Education and Instruction of Deaf and Dumb Persons (subsequently, the American Asylum) opens in Hartford, Connecticut

1818   The New York Institution for the Deaf and Dumb is established

1822   Kentucky opens the first state school for deaf children

1829   Ronald McDonald trains at the American Asylum

1831   McDonald later opens the first special school in Canada

1832   The Massachusetts Asylum for the Blind (or Perkins Institution for the Blind) opens under Samuel Gridley Howe

1837   Horace Mann begins the revival of the common schools

1848   Howe establishes his experimental school for feebleminded youth; Édouard Seguin arrives in the United States; the first permanent Canadian schools for deaf children are established

1850   The Massachusetts School for Idiotic and Feeble-Minded Children is permanently established by the state legislature

1854   New York State funds the state's first school for mentally retarded children

In August 1816 the brig *Mary Augusta* sailed into New York harbor. On its deck stood Thomas Hopkins Gallaudet, a native of Hartford, Connecticut, and a young Frenchman, Laurent Clerc. To the teeming crowds on the New York dock, the elegant Frenchman and his bespectacled little American companion were, in all likelihood, worthy of little more than a passing glance. But the arrival of Gallaudet and Clerc signaled the opening of a new and more positive era for the disabled population of North America.

When Laurent Clerc (1785–1869) first stepped onto American shores, no public special institutions existed in the young nation except for a small hospital for the insane in Virginia. By the time of Clerc's death a flourishing complex of institutions reached across North America. To Clerc, the term *special education* would not have been familiar; it would not emerge until 1884. But Clerc was intimately associated with efforts to assist exceptional students with settings and programs designed to cater to their unique needs.

The initiation of the education and training of handicapped persons in North America coincided with a period of widely ranging social reform and rapidly expanding education, a movement impelled by the general recognition of the need for organized social responsibility. Widespread support for social legislation was first apparent in demands for expansion of the common schools. The opening half of the nineteenth century also witnessed the rise of new theories and practices in penal discipline, more imaginative efforts in the treatment of insanity, advanced work with the criminally insane, and rational schemes for the support of indigent and dependent populations (Splane, 1965).

Designs for separate child-care facilities and special schooling were urged on the grounds of expediency, charity, and imperative duty. During the first half of the nineteenth century schools for deaf and for blind persons began to emerge, by midcentury schools for mentally retarded individuals were being instituted as well. Much energy was also directed toward the special problems of neglected, delinquent, and vagrant children, which led to the establishment of reformatories, houses of correction, and industrial schools. Progress continued apace in the latter half of the nineteenth century, with schooling for exceptional students becoming more sophisticated and systematic, embracing ever greater numbers of children. However, though training was provided for socially at-risk and sensorily and intellectually disabled children, other disabled youngsters fared less well. Large numbers of those who were crippled, emotionally disturbed, multiply handicapped, or suffering a range of undetected or low-incidence conditions were simply excluded from the special institutions. (There are reports, however, of training for children with orthopedic handicaps in Boston in the mid-1860s.)

Deaf students, as usual, were the first to receive education. Success with these first ventures lent a note of optimism that extended new opportunities first to the blind and then to those labeled as feebleminded (see Table 3-1).

A graph of institutional development in North America after 1817 would show a steep rise until the 1860s, a flattening out during the Civil War period, and then another rise as special schools for blacks were established in the South. By the 1880s day schools and day classes became a scattered feature of urban special education (see Chapter 10).

Institutional reform refers to both the setting and the bureaucratization of education. We can distinguish three phases of institutional development. The formal care and training of disabled individuals was initially viewed as a

Table 3-1

The Typical Progression of Special Education

Nation	*Year Schooling First Provided*		
	Deaf Students	Blind Students	Mentally Retarded Students
France	1748	1782	1832
Great Britain	1760	1802	1832
United States	1817	1832	1848
Canada	1848	1872	1873

philanthropic exercise; institutions were funded as charities, often headed and staffed by fiercely evangelical reformers who were motivated by a desire to enlist their clients into the legions of the pure. Social reform or benevolence tended to become bureaucratic; as the novelty of special education wore off, the Christian philanthropist was supplanted by the official, the work motivated by statute rather than by the dictates of conscience. Special institutions became a part of the social-welfare complex administered by state boards of charity in the United States and by the inspectors of prisons, asylums, and public charities in Canada. But once their fragile enterprises were embedded as vital components of the social-welfare complex, the promoters of special education directed their energies toward altering public perceptions. By the opening decades of the twentieth century, the instruction of many exceptional students was viewed as a purely educational venture.

Advances in special education and institutional development cannot be viewed in isolation. Institutions have always been more than simply places that offered education and training for disabled populations. Developments in special education illustrate the way in which a society handled problems of disease, dependency, and disability, and they demonstrate how intervention is governed by a society's structures and values. Many of the issues in nineteenth-century special education transcended strictly educational considerations—the definition of handicaps, the criteria for institutionalization, the administrative structures governing schools, the financial responsibility for exceptional persons, and the differential treatment of various socioeconomic groups, to mention a few. These issues and their solutions link the structure and functions of the institutions with a variety of external economic, political, social, and intellectual forces.

It is not possible to detail the openings and rationales for every institution for exceptional persons in the United States and Canada during the nineteenth century nor to introduce all the innovators and reformers who lent their efforts to the cause. Demographic, economic, cultural, and ethnic factors all had a hand in the rapid openings (and closings) of schools. Although most of the state-sponsored institutions survived and became permanent, they were regarded as merely peripheral to education, not a central responsibility of government. Private schools fared less well: balanced precariously on an economic precipice, many schools fell victim to government indifference, public apathy or even hostility, parental prejudice, and managerial ineptitude.

THE PHILANTHROPIC THRUST

The Colonial Period

Recognition of the propriety of training or educating exceptional individuals emerged slowly and haltingly in North America. In the beginning, people could not turn from their intense preoccupation with survival and material development to handle the problems of those unable to earn a living, although sporadic pleas on the behalf of disabled persons were heard. Deaf children were the first to receive attention. Calls for the education of blind children soon followed, to be echoed by suggestions about the care of adult insane persons and the training of mentally retarded children, as well as the establishment of special training outside the public schools for socially deviant children described as neglected, vagrant, and delinquent.

Colonial America offered minimal official support to its dependent and disabled populations. Frontier conditions placed a premium upon self-reliance and implied that one was free of social controls. Independence was a matter of pride, and there was little inclination to look to the state for assistance in matters of social welfare. Poverty was considered an unavoidable part of society ordained by God, and it was the burden of community charity to support those families unable to make their own way (Demos, 1970). Poor and dependent members were kept from starving by the efforts of relatives, friends, and a burgeoning structure of private charitable organizations (Taylor and Searl, 1987).

Disability was a subcategory of poverty—a disabling condition caused the poverty and was often viewed as inevitable, an instance of God's will at work. If an entire family was disabled, the colonists found it only natural to try to maintain the family as a unit (Taylor and Searl, 1987). This was done either through direct provision by the community fathers of food and other necessities or through a pension of straight cash. Relatives were usually expected to help (Taylor and Searl, 1987).

Even though poverty and disability were viewed as the natural concerns of the family, the local community, or the church rather than the state, dependent groups were not totally ignored in colonial and revolutionary America. The first code of laws adopted by the Massachusetts General Court in December 1641 protected those of "greatness of age, defect of minde, fayling of sences, or impotencie of Lymbes" as well as "Children, Idiots, Distracted persons" (Eliot, 1938, pp. 67–68). The earliest attempt at special education on North American soil comes from Rowley, Massachusetts, where in 1679 Philip Nelson attempted to teach a deaf child. However, "the local church quickly took alarm, and, by denouncing, suspended the blasphemy of attempting a miracle which the Lord Jesus alone could perform" (G. O. Fay, 1899, p. 420).

As cities and young industries began to emerge in the late eighteenth century, poverty and dependence became increasingly visible, and communities in the United States instigated systems of both indoor (almshouses) and outdoor (charitable organizations) relief for dependent and indigent populations. British

North America largely opted for outdoor relief; only the Maritime Provinces developed a fairly close approximation of the British poor laws with the accompanying poorhouses and overseers of the poor. Both the British and the Americans distinguished between the deserving and the undeserving poor. The former were those "Who have been ancient Housekeepers and lived in good reputation and Credit and are reduced by Misfortunes." Conversely, the undeserving poor were "become so by Vice and Idleness" (Mohl, 1971, pp. 22–23).

The almshouse movement in the United States grew vigorously after 1800 (Wallin, 1914); in fact, Michael B. Katz (1986) described poorhouses as "the cutting edge of poor relief policy in the late eighteenth and early nineteenth centuries" (p. 4). In Massachusetts sixty towns constructed new facilities between 1820 and 1840; in New York the number of people in almshouses grew from 4,500 in 1830 to 10,000 in 1859 (Rothman, 1971). As they spread through the states, almshouses came to be used as ramshackle warehouses for the poor, the aged, and the disabled. In 1795, for example, the commissioners of the New York Almshouse found that the house was full of blind, lunatic, and aged paupers and many others "subject to Rheumatisms, Ulcers and Palsies and to Fits which impair their reason and elude all the force of Medicine" (Mohl, 1970, p. 93). When physically and mentally disturbed children of the poor were admitted, the desire to keep the family intact gave way to the familiar cry of cost efficiency. Families either went their way without the child or joined the child in the almshouse (Taylor and Searl, 1987).

American hospitals for the insane arose in the late eighteenth century. Generally, facilities for children formed no part of these institutions, in part because emotional disturbance was not thought to occur in children. (See also Chapter 11.) Nevertheless, care of the mentally ill and the mentally retarded remained closely intertwined on the American scene in the opening half of the nineteenth century.

William Thornton, more famous as the architect of the original National Capitol building in Washington, presented eloquent appeals on behalf of the deaf. In 1793 Thornton published *Cadmus: A Treatise on the Elements of Written Language,* to which he appended an essay "On the mode of teaching the surd or deaf, and consequently dumb, to speak," the first work on the topic published in America. An even larger influence in special education in Revolutionary times was exerted by Francis Green, an educational reformer claimed by both the United States and Canada (A. G. Bell, 1900b) (see Box 3-1).

The Early Nineteenth Century

Even though Green, Thornton, and others made isolated attempts at instituting special schools, real progress in special education in the United States and Canada did not occur until the opening of the nineteenth century. Through the transatlantic community of reformers, Americans had learned of French successes and hearkened to the news of the initiation of the British charity schools. Americans rapidly imported the precedents, sentiments, and attitudes of child saving or "child save" (essentially, the provision of specialized conditions, legislation, and institutions for children founded on new concepts about childhood), begun in England and parts of Europe in the eighteenth century, and

Box 3-1
Francis Green (1742–1809)

Boston-born Francis Green (or Greene; both spellings appear in the literature) was admitted to Harvard in 1756 when he was fourteen years of age. However, the following year his father purchased him an ensign's commission in the British army, and young Green joined a regiment that saw action in Jamaica, British North America, and Quebec. In 1760 Green returned to Boston, received his degree from Harvard, and married his cousin Susanna. He went into the importing business with his father, who lived in Halifax, Nova Scotia, and entered a partnership in a Boston business as well with a trading vessel he named *Susanna*. Francis Green went to England in 1765 and sold out of the army in 1766. Green held political views quite at odds with those of John Hancock and John Adams; his unwavering loyalist sentiments prompted a mob to attack him in Connecticut in 1774. Still, Green sided and served with the British and moved to Halifax in 1776 (see A. G. Bell, 1900b, 1900c; Blakeley, 1945, 1979).

With Susanna, Green had five children; only Charles and Susanna survived infancy. Charles, described as "an extraordinary genius (peculiarly circumstanced)" (Blakeley, n.d.), was found at six months of age to be deaf. In 1780, when he was eight, Charles was sent to the Braidwood Academy in Edinburgh, where he "acquired the facility of speech and almost perfect knowledge of Language, both oral and written" (Blakeley, n.d.). Green accompanied his son to Britain; his experience with the Braidwoods led him to write *"Vox Oculis Subjecta": A dissertation on the most curious art of imparting speech, and the knowledge of language, to the naturally deaf, and (consequently) dumb, with a particular account of the Academy of Mrrs. Braidwood of Edinburgh in 1783.*

When Francis Green returned to North America in 1784, he was appointed sheriff of Halifax County in Nova Scotia. Tragedy struck when Charles drowned in August 1787. Green resigned his office in November of that year. In England again in 1790, Green conceived the idea of beginning a charitable school for the deaf in London but, as his notions proved anathema to the grasping Braidwoods, Green united with John Townshend and the Clapham sect in formulating plans for the Bermondsey Institution, which opened in 1792 for indigent deaf children.

In 1793 Green became first joint treasurer of the province of Nova Scotia and in 1794 was appointed a justice of the Court of Pleas. In 1796 his lands were appropriated to make way for an army contingent newly arrived from Jamaica, and Green returned to the United States and settled in Medford, near Boston (Blakeley, 1979). He worked as an insurance underwriter but lost his money in the venture, so he turned to the education of deaf persons. He "appears to have devoted his leisure hours to advocating in the journals the importance of educating the deaf and dumb, and endeavouring to enlist public sympathy on their behalf" (Halifax Institution for the Deaf, 1892, p. 4).

Green wrote about the Braidwood school and, under the pseudonym Philocophos, the Friend of the Deaf and Dumb, translated the Abbé Charles Michel de l'Épée's work into English. Beginning on June 14, 1803, Philocophos had printed three times in the Boston *Palladium* a card addressed "to the Reverend of the Clergy (of every persuasion and denomination) of the State of Massachusetts," asking for details of deaf individuals within their knowledge in order to obtain statistics that would bolster his contentions regarding the necessity for an American institution. Although the census indicated the presence of "seventy-five deaf mutes in Massachusetts" (De Land, 1931, p. 92), Green inspired little enthusiasm for the project, being successful in obtaining only a census of the deaf. Pricked by failure, Green pointed out the unlovely aspects of burgeoning trade: "The *philanthrophy and charity* of the present era seem to be elbowed off the stage by the predominant speculations of the *banking mania,* and the universal *lust of lucre*" (original italics; A. G. Bell, 1900c, p. 12).

Though Francis Green ultimately saw his advocacy as a failure, he is still remembered as the first man in America to advocate the oral method of instruction for deaf children (Numbers, 1974). As well, he wielded deep influence on the later formation of the New York Institution for the Deaf and Dumb (H. P. Peet, 1857).

---

translated them into plans for the elaboration of an institutional complex that would cater to orphans, indigent children, and those with disabilities.

When American special education began, the newly formed United States was a relatively homogeneous agrarian and isolated nation. Spain, France, and England together still controlled much of what is now part of the continental United States (Moores, 1987). About three million people lived chiefly on the Atlantic seaboard. Those of English descent formed about half of the population; blacks were about one-quarter, with Germans and Scotch-Irish composing the only other identifiable groups (Moores, 1987). Although blacks made up an estimated 20 to 25 percent of the population, they were almost totally subjugated (Bloch and Dworkin, 1976; Moores, 1987).

British North America was even more sparsely settled, with its few large towns clustered along the border with the United States. No more than 200,000 souls inhabited British North America in 1800. The two founding nations, the French and the English, existed in an uneasy alliance, and between the United States and British North America, sovereignty over large tracts of land was in dispute.

With the birth of the new century, vast alterations in the fabric of American society were set in motion. Industrialization, an irreversible and seemingly inevitable process, brought the most profound changes in the nature of daily life seen in human history since the establishment of stable agricultural societies. The accompanying demographic changes during the nineteenth century—the growth of the towns, increasing immigration, and a soaring birthrate—dramatically transformed the United States from a relatively homogeneous society to one of almost overwhelming ethnic, linguistic, cultural, racial, and religious diversity (Moores, 1987). Manufacturing and commercial development led to exponential growth of the urban areas of the eastern seaboard and in the upper

Midwest. The percentage of the American population living in urban areas rose from 6.1 percent in 1800 to 25.7 percent in 1870 and 51.2 percent by 1920 (Stockwell, 1968).

The natural growth in America was supplemented by substantial influxes of immigrants from the British Isles and Europe. America became the refuge of Europe, the hope of depressed millions. During the 1820s, 151,000 persons emigrated to the United States; between 1846 and 1855 the numbers soared, to 2.3 million immigrants from Great Britain and Ireland (Coleman, 1973). In the next hundred years more than 38 million foreign-born persons came to the United States, a tide that reached a peak of more than 8 million in the period 1900 to 1909, an average of 800,000 per year (Stockwell, 1968).

The 1840s witnessed the beginning of the great immigration of the Irish, which peaked in the decade 1850–1860. Masses of unskilled and impoverished people crowded into the cities, bringing with them typhus and dysentary. Their presence contributed to the growth of ghettos and urban blight; their welcome soon soured when their poverty and high disease rate became apparent. Irish immigrants consequently became a highly visible unemployed and feared minority.

Immigration and urbanization created large-scale social problems—slums, unemployment, vagrancy among children, cultural conflict, crime, and delinquency—which then engendered new roles for the traditional social institutions, home, church, and school. Perceptions about the new industrialized society were polarized along class lines; the middle class created a view of the poor (and the disabled) best suited to its own emotional and economic needs. Reformers pointed to the spiritual and moral inferiority of the poor; they betrayed the characteristic middle-class opinion that poverty was somehow socially subversive. As "poverty in the lower classes" was recognized as "very generally the parent of every deviation from right and order" (Canada, *Journals*, 1854, app. DD), many adopted the notion that destitution, vice, and crime are inevitably linked.

The experiences of children changed dramatically in the transition to an industrializing society. For one thing, work itself changed. Certainly, the industrial revolution did not invent child labor—in colonial America, children labored in mills, mines, and factories—but industrialization did expand and systemize the exploitation of the young and of women. Many urban working-class families, like their counterparts on the farm, depended on the labor of several members of the family, including the children, to survive. Children often went to work after their sixth birthday in enterprises that were no longer home centered but contained in factories and workshops. Or homes became sweatshops where families on the economic margin worked on clothing, sometimes in a converted living room or bedroom. Women and children took their places on the lowest rungs of the manufacturing enterprises, often suffering long hours and horrendous conditions. It was not until the middle of the nineteenth century that children in the United States were given at least minimal protection through child labor laws and other reforms. By that time, an expanding concept of childhood had developed that entailed the criteria of protection, segregation, dependence, and the delay of responsibilities. Although a fully developed notion did not emerge until the close of the century, new opinions meant new ways of treating children.

Urbanization not only altered traditional economic and labor patterns, it changed the activities open to children and made them dependent on street play groups and gangs. Middle-class fears concerning the deterioration of the social order were fueled by the visible increase in the numbers of street children, said to "graduate in vice with awful rapidity" (Machar, 1881, p. 329).

The new economic creed, which focused on trade and investment and the technological boom, found few answers to the subsequent social dislocations and economic inequalities. Social and economic conditions were especially stressful for the less competent. In an agrarian society disabled persons were often useful in an undemanding work regime and supported by an extended social network. But for many, their limitations prevented their functioning in anything even marginally more sophisticated than simple agrarian labor, and industrializing society ceded little sympathy to those who could not compete with the nondisabled. In early nineteenth-century North America, problems of physical and mental health were increasingly visible, and mounting problems in the maintenance of public order brought the incompetent person much more frequently to the attention of the courts.

Child Save and the Public Schools

By the opening decades of the nineteenth century, social and economic conditions had so altered that public opinion was demanding philanthropic and governmental action on matters previously held to be personal and of little concern to the state. Widespread movement targeting the staples of nineteenth-century reform—ignorance, vice, crime, drunkenness, poverty, and lunacy—began to permeate American life. Imbued with an optimistic sense of mission, reformers established a bewildering array of charities and relief organizations for every imaginable purpose, supported by those who "looked forward to that delightful day, when the earth shall be filled with righteousness and peace" (T. H. Gallaudet, 1817, p. 12). Richard Mohl (1970) lists charities that came to the aid of orphans and widows, aged females and young prostitutes, immigrants, imprisoned debtors, and blacks. Organizations sprang up to educate the children of the poor in charity schools, Sunday schools, and free schools; to promote religion and morality among the destitute; to supply medical care for the indigent; to create and provide employment for the poor; to reform juvenile delinquents and sinful seaman; and to study the causes of pauperism (Mohl, 1970). Others called for the abolition of war, agitated for women's rights, and demanded the extension of the common school system and the establishment of facilities for disabled people.

The development of principles and methods of social welfare was a slow and almost unconscious evolution in both the United States and Canada. (*Social welfare* is a widely used but ill-defined twentieth-century term, perhaps best defined as a broad field of human endeavor based on "values rooted in convictions about individual worth and dignity and social interdependence and responsibility" [Weisman, 1959, p. 29].) Work specifically for the benefit of children paralleled other social-welfare efforts and mirrored changing conceptions of children and childhood in American society. In the broadest sense child-welfare work included all possible provisions for children in the home, the schools, the churches, all sorts of institutions, and society at large. At the outset child-care work was individualistic, then it was crudely organized; by midcentury it assumed a far more definite form and obtained general recognition. By the close of the nineteenth century child welfare related to all the formal agencies of the community, states, and nation (see Splane, 1965).

, Urbanization and industrialization brought new child-rearing practices. Nineteenth-century social and educational reformers conceptualized childhood in a new way, and so they interpreted children's needs in a new way. The discipline of child psychology slowly evolved, and educators adopted the notion that children as learners need carefully constructed environments (Finkelstein, 1985). This conviction contributed to the widespread support of the demand for social legislation that would expand the common schools.

Although colonial America boasted a hodgepodge of private, church, and state schools, these were chiefly for the gentry, and only a few children received more than the barest minimum of schooling. Moreover, schooling for girls was generally not a possibility beyond a few years at the elementary levels. For most girls, learning took place around the hearth at mother's knee and was directly related to their future roles. In a rapidly advancing nation a primary concern had to be the building of a self-reliant, diligent population that would create a stable, industrious, and morally upright society. As well, schools that were to educate immigrant children would perform the function that Michael B. Katz calls "cultural standardization" (1983, p. 373). Not only was an educated citizenry essential to the survival of the American republic, but reformers saw the school as the appropriate mechanism to deal with social problems.

The common-school revival of nineteenth-century North America owes much of its development to the reforming instincts and organizational genius of Horace Mann (1796–1859), an ardent reformer involved in a diversity of ventures designed to improve society. Acting on the basis of strong moral convictions, Mann became a leader in the antislavery movement and a strong advocate for a range of issues, from temperance to the establishment of asylums for insane persons and those with disabilities.

In 1837, when Massachusetts became the first state to establish a board to oversee public education, Mann assumed the post of the secretary of the state board of education. Under his tutelage Massachusetts developed centralized public schooling—a popular system of free public schools with compulsory attendance, all supported by public taxes. Simultaneously in Upper Canada (Ontario) a similar process motivated by the same considerations underlay the impetus for free public schooling. Egerton Ryerson (1803–1882), a Methodist minister, was appointed superintendent of education for Upper Canada in 1844. He brought about the Common School Act of 1848, which established a system of common schools; in 1850 Ryerson introduced the principle of free schooling in Upper Canada, later embodied in the School Act of 1870 (see Putnam, 1912; Sissons, 1937).

As a result of Mann's reorganization of the Massachusetts school system, American schools functioned for the first time as state vehicles, with their primary object being the socialization of all children into a common cultural world view. No doubt, without Horace Mann, the people of the United States would have devised a good school system, as would have Upper Canadians without

Egerton Ryerson. But to a considerable extent Mann and Ryerson created the public sentiment that made the advances possible. Both eloquently articulated the prevailing ideology, tempered it with European educational experiences, added the needs of an industrializing society and the problems of massive immigration, and wrapped the whole in a mantle of evangelical reform.

In 1843 Mann and Samuel Gridley Howe, principal of the Massachusetts Asylum for the Blind, toured educational institutions in Europe. Mann was impressed by the work of the schools in France in fostering French nationalism, but he was more influenced by the Prussian two-track system of education, which was free, universal, and compulsory (Moores, 1987). Upper-class children attended a gymnasium and later perhaps a university or a military academy. Children from the masses attended a common school, with some males matriculating at technical schools and some females matriculating at normal schools to be trained as teachers (Moores, 1987).

To the European imperatives, Mann added evangelical models. Evangelism was the hallmark of nineteenth-century Protestantism, a blend of Reformation doctrine, exuberance for the democratic ethos, and hope that people and societies could change for the better under God's will. Salvation was increasingly portrayed in secular terms; it was as much a matter of happiness in this world as of peace in the next (Prentice, 1977b).

The evangelical belief that, despite the persistence of sin in the world, all people are capable of being saved was fundamental to the crusade for educational reform. Educational promoters increasingly saw their mission as being one of converting the population to the cause of salvation through the common schools. Schoolmen explicitly asserted that the family and the church were insufficient for the formation of upright and patriotic character in children and argued that instilling moral and social virtues rested upon the school's assumption of responsibility. Then, blending the religious with the secular, Mann and other evangelical reformers stressed the need for the common schools to develop an educated and patriotic citizenry and to promote character development in a class deemed a potential threat to the stability of American society.

The task of Americanizing the foreigner fell chiefly to the school system. Mann realized that the schools would have to play an increasingly important role if the growing numbers of newcomers were to be "civilized" and Americanized (Lee and Stevens, 1981). The self-appointed guardians of the American way worked with fervor to make over the foreigner in their own image. The Boston School Committee, describing its task, made it clear that the school's expanded responsibility included acculturation, which it described as "taking children at random from a great city, undisciplined, uninstructed, often with inveterate forwardness and obstinancy, and with the inherited stupidity of centuries of ignorant ancestors; forming them from animals into intellectual beings, and ... from intellectual beings into spiritual beings" (quoted by M. Katz, 1968, p. 120).

Inherent in the notion of Americanization was the adoption of a work ethic that would contribute to an expanding industrial nation. Work discipline was essential to economic growth. A functional school system would maximize working-class involvement in the years just before employment and stress regular attendance and attitudes deemed appropriate by those who controlled the workplace (Kaestle and Vinovskis, 1980). Therefore, public schooling would serve as "a preventative of pauperism and vice," as well as "a benefit to the industrial pursuits of life" ("Review," 1848, p. 175).

THE ROLE OF THE INSTITUTION IN SPECIAL EDUCATION

The Establishment of Special Institutions

Children who could not be easily accommodated by the public schools were not forgotten by educational reformers. Horace Mann, Henry Barnard, Egerton Ryerson, and other public school promoters rapidly embraced the disabled population, advancing similar rhetoric for the education and training of exceptional students. Reformers and philanthropists chafed about the condition and treatment of disabled persons in early nineteenth-century society and the pernicious results of lack of schooling. Private special education, obtainable in Great Britain or Europe, was within the reach of only a favored few; the great mass of disabled individuals were left to "their ancient doom of wretchedness and degregation" (H. P. Peet, [1846], 1847, p. 9).

The horrors experienced by exceptional children who were denied education were expressed in lurid hyperbole. It was pointed out that the deaf individual's "moral and intellectual condition before instruction is little above that of the more intelligent brutes and lower than that of the most enlightened savages" (McGann, 1888, p. 43). Other claims stated that a deaf person lacking education inevitably became "a grief and shame to his relatives; a burden to society" (W. W. Turner, 1858); deaf people were "irresponsible and in many cases dangerous to the community" (McGann, 1888, p. 5). Uneducated blind persons adopted their ancient trade of begging and were "generally paupers" (Dunscombe, 1836, p. 98).

One trope invariably forwarded to promote special schooling equated disability and dependency. Inevitably, it was argued, schooling for blind children would remove from society "so many dead weights" and prevent them from becoming "taxes on the community" (Dunscombe, 1836, p. 97). Education would emancipate deaf children from "the fetters imposed . . . by their deafness" (OSD, 1895, p. 12) so that "the old ignorance, the old animism, the old brutishness are passed away" (W. W. Turner, 1858). In like vein, schooling for mentally retarded youngsters would serve to teach "such habits as to render possible for them, life in a domestic relation" (Ontario, Inspector, 1876, p. 3).

School promoters also brought to early special education a burning concern for the states of the souls of their clients; their rhetoric was permeated by cultural and moral values carrying Protestant overtones. Not only were many special children thought to be unaware of the existence of God or a future life, but reformers viewed them as possessing no innate potential for good; rather, they were thought to be open, in the Lockean sense, to the pernicious effects of environmental influence. The standard constellation of educational influences in society—the family, the community, and the church—were not viewed as appropriate socializing agencies for disabled persons, for whom education was judged to be even more completely dependent on schooling than it was for normal children.

If special education had been inserted into the stable framework of an existing school system, it might have evolved quite differently than it in fact did.

The pervasive stress on isolated institutions might not have developed, and the notion of special education as a discrete enterprise separate from regular education might not have evolved. Given the lack of an existing framework and given the increasing emphasis on a medical model, special children were simply excluded from the public schools, which had neither the desire nor the trained personnel to handle these youngsters. Rather, large institutions to serve exceptional populations sprang up as one facet of the reform movement sweeping the land.

Even though the more subtle possibilities of education were recognized by those seeking to promote self-reliance and independence among the disabled, these reformers also believed that exceptional children demanded different forms of organization. Schooling was fashioned in light of prevailing sentiments: the clients were viewed as special, discrete groups, quite different from the general school population, and their needs were thought to demand institutional isolation. Hence, the system that emerged reflected not an alignment with the common schools, but the traditional perceptions of disabled people as charity recipients. Institutionalization formed the educational milieu and, although the services were educational, they were presented wholly within the context of public charities.

Institutionalization in America

The provocative notions of the French Enlightenment, the romanticism of the era, new humanitarian instincts, evangelism, and a mounting distaste for traditional structures permeated early nineteenth-century society. Michael Katz (1973) observes that, within this climate, the creation of institutions preoccupied early Americans. He notes that whether they were building banks or railroads, political parties or factories, hospitals or schools, Americans confronted the inappropriateness of traditional organizational arrangements, and their attempts to find a suitable fit between the form and the content of social life stimulated a prolonged national debate (M. Katz, 1973).

Attention focused early on the enduring difficulties of the poor. Across the country almshouses, the earliest form of poor relief, flourished. A public hospital for the insane opened at Williamsburg, Virginia, in 1773. Orphan asylums, reformatories, state penitentiaries and, of course, county jails were in place at the opening of the nineteenth century.

Many of the institutions founded during the first half of the nineteenth century served many purposes. Almshouses provided work for the able bodied and shelter and refuge for the old and helpless poor and the disabled. Houses of refuge for orphans and other juveniles served some of the functions of the later industrial schools, providing moral and trade training. Many jails functioned more as poorhouses, insane asylums, and hospitals combined. At Barrie, Ontario, for example, the inspector in 1869 found that, of fourteen prisoners, only three were convicted of crime. Of the remainder, eight were labeled as dangerous lunatics, idiots, or imbeciles incapable of taking care of themselves. Another woman, of "weak intellect," had two illegitimate children, one born in the jail (Ontario, *Sessional Papers,* 1869, p. 11).

The pledge to ameliorate the problems of disabled persons in North America dates from 1817, when Thomas Hopkins Gallaudet (1788–1851) opened an institution for deaf students at Hartford, Connecticut. With one form of special education firmly entrenched in the public consciousness, schooling for other groups soon appeared. Although the institutions that arose after 1817 were administered in different ways and served different clienteles, they tended to be more specific in their orientation and purposes than were the almshouses. However, nineteenth-century institutional development was neither orderly nor particularly logical, and specialization developed erratically. Newly emerging states tended to borrow ideas from their longer established counterparts, but they often advanced more quickly, seeking alternate forms of administration and funding, so that organizational models differed across the country. In the absence of bureaucratic centralization, each school operated under a different administrative authority, ensuring at least some flexibility and adaptation to local circumstances.

Four models of institutional organization evolved in early nineteenth-century North America: paternalistic voluntarism, corporate voluntarism, democratic localism, and incipient bureaucracy (M. Katz, 1971). In their germinal stages the founding institutions for exceptional students adopted an organizational model most closely resembling corporate voluntarism, which Katz describes as "the conduct of single institutions as individual corporations operated by self-perpetuating boards of trustees and financed wholly through endownment and tuition" (1971, p. 22).

States preferred the corporate form of organization for special institutions and actively promoted its diffusion by granting land or money to individual institutions (M. Katz, 1973). The people selected to serve on corporate boards supported evangelical reform. Phyllis Valentine (1991) points out that many New England evangelical Protestants were former Federalists who became Whigs and then infused Whiggery with the concept that they, as "wealthy and educated stewards of society," had the God-given responsibility to tend to the spiritual and moral well-being of others (p. 4). Their once-private acts of charity they now channeled through corporations in order to lead the underclasses with stern but benevolent authority (Valentine, 1991).

Boards of directors functioned to raise money, hire teachers, and obtain incorporation from the state. They organized and managed separate institutions, kept the operations and the educators away from the rough and often unpredictable field of politics, but still offered disinterested, enlightened, and continuous management. The men elevated to the boards tended to be respectable, wealthy, and influential enough to carry weight in the legislatures. In New York City, for example, the care and control of the institution for deaf students was placed under a board of directors consisting of twenty-five citizens whose "social and political influence had much weight with the Legislature on its behalf" (H. Barnard [1861b] 1969, p. 243).

Schools under corporations often followed the model offered by the Connecticut Asylum for the Education and Instruction of Deaf and Dumb Persons at Hartford, Connecticut, the first institution in North America for exceptional persons. In Connecticut an act of incorporation was procured from the legislature in May 1816, and thirteen Hartford residents "formed into, constituted and made a body politic and corporate by the name of the Connecticut Asylum, for the education and instruction of deaf and dumb Persons." In 1819 the Congress of the United States granted the institution 23,000 acres of land in Alabama that were then sold to raise operating costs, which allowed the erection of a permanent building in 1821 (Weld, 1847). At the Connecticut Asylum, Thomas Hopkins Gallaudet, the principal, was not given undisputed power but shared it with the household manager, the superintendent. Faculty members went their own way with little coordination. The corporation considered themselves the final arbiters of management, although they were often more concerned with household matters than with academic problems (Tull Boatner, 1959).

As the institutional complex expanded, it rapidly became apparent that only those institutions financed by the community or state and directly controlled by its officers merited definition as public, and corporate voluntarism was doomed (M. Katz, 1973). By the middle of the century most states where institutions existed assumed full or partial responsibility for institutional costs and management. Bureaucracy replaced philanthropy as the organizational mode, and there developed an increasing conception of the schools as public enterprises—*public* implying service to a nonexclusive clientele with entrance determined solely by disabling condition. Schools were placed under elected rather than self-perpetuating boards, and they were usually administered by state boards of charity in the United States and by the Department of the Provincial Secretary (Prisons, Asylums and Public Charities) in Canada.

Although organizational structures and internal management differed, striking parallels are apparent among the institutions that arose to serve the special needs of the deaf, blind, and mentally retarded students. These are most readily observed in the philosophy underlying curriculum (see Chapter 6) and the general perceptions of exceptional persons, manifested clearly in the geography of institutional locations and fund-raising activities.

Institutional Finance

Perhaps the most striking feature of American special education in the early years was the philanthropy that financed all forms of work among exceptional children. Many school buildings were magnificent; in their lines they embodied reformist ideas for improved structures. If architecture is social art, then the speech of the buildings epitomized the facts of institutional life as well as generally held perceptions of disabled persons. The gothic architecture seen in many institutional buildings served to uplift and elevate the base spirits of the clients and to impress "the mind of the beholder with feelings of reverential grandeur and majestic sublimity" (McGann, 1869, p. 248).

Yet derisive names were attached to the institution, the central facet of nineteenth-century American special education, names that belied the capacities of the clientele. Labels reflected public perceptions as well as the underlying rationales of early special education. *Institution, asylum, training school,* and later *colony* were terms commonly applied within the institutional network.

Industrialization saw the demise of cherished rural values, to be supplanted by the urban horrors characteristic of large cities of the day. Still, well after urbanization and industrialization had transformed agrarian America, idealization of the countryside remained a powerful force; the nineteenth century still believed that nature could serve as a moral text for the betterment of humans.

Wordsworthian values were applied to special education, and many of the institutions were set well apart from urban areas. It was thought that exceptional children could be redeemed and regenerated by country living, and that it was vital that they be separated from the cities, which were feared as likely to ensnare, enfeeble, and corrupt their inhabitants. One survey in 1927, for example, showed only eight of twenty-nine schools for the deaf in or near a city (Day, Fusfeld, and Pinter, 1928).

Beginning with the first experiments with handicapped people by John Wallis and other members of the Royal Society, exhibitions of pupils—to display their attainments, prove their rationality, or procure funds—was a crucial aspect of the enterprise. Jacob Rodrigue Péreire and his French counterparts presented impressive public displays, and the Braidwood family in Britain was not averse to raising additional funding by such means.

The tradition of exhibiting pupils to garner private and official support became a common element in the development of institutions in North America throughout the nineteenth century. Demonstrations of pupil progress were instrumental in advocating the claims of the disabled and in maintaining the flow of benevolence (Mitchell, 1971). In the process, the humble exceptional child became a public figure displayed under the magnifying glass of the fashionable philanthropist (see Ramsland, 1989).

Profound ambivalence characterized public attitudes to special education, fostered by "the prejudices of many" and the "incredulity of others," as well as "the indifference with which the great bulk of mankind regards matters which no particular circumstances have pressed upon their personal notice" (Convention, 1851, p. 6). In order to inspire a credulous public in the belief that disabled people are both capable and worthy of education, teachers and students traveled to many towns and villages of the country. The *Halifax Morning Chronicle* for July 13, 1868, reported that "the annual public examination of the deaf and dumb institution which took place at Temperance Hall" had an audience "principally composed of ladies." The principal "asked by signs, questions in the branches of a common school education, the pupils writing the answers on slates or blackboards." The institution was commended to the public, and the day closed with a collection "in aid of the funds of the institution" (p. 2). At a Montreal exhibition by deaf students in 1872, the audience "was startled to hear some twenty of these unfortunate creatures speak out loudly, distinctly, without apparent effort, and quite intelligibly in both English and French." The audience was further inspired to donate funds following "the exhibition of reading, writing on the blackboard, and elocutionary and dramatic pantomime" (Lesperance, 1872, p. 506).

Most importantly, exhibitions were used to influence legislators. In 1832, only six months after opening his institution for the blind, Samuel Gridley Howe exhibited his blind children before the Massachusetts General Court (Perkins Inst., 1834) and thereafter made annual visits to the legislatures of the New England states soliciting funds. Deaf pupils of the American Asylum presented annual demonstrations before the legislatures of several New England states, in the halls of Congress, and in all the large cities of the northern and middle states (H. Barnard, [1861b] 1969). One student, Alice Cogswell, vividly described in a letter how all the ladies and gentlemen of the asylum went before the state house for an exhibition in 1817. After relating how many people watched the pupils write on the board, Alice confided that a Miss Gilbert was so timid that "her heart beat and trembled" (Cogswell, 1817).

Critics vehemently attacked the content, if not the purpose of these shows, questioning the disparity between performance and reality (e.g., Caldwell, 1888; Cheek, 1855). Only outstanding pupils took part, and spectators were "led to form a false estimate, by our presenting only a few choice examples as specimens of the advancement of which they are greatly suspectible" (Cheek, 1855, p. 173). Public expectations of phenomenal results led to fraud, and it was suggested that "benevolence would not be lacking if the truth of the 'humble' progress attained by educators was aired" (Cheek, 1855, p. 173). S. B. Cheek, a teacher of the deaf, advised giving the world "some specimens from that far more numerous class of their efforts in composition, where every sentence abounds in errors and deaf-mute idioms" (1855, p. 171).

The exhibitions also tended to perpetuate ancient stereotypes of defectiveness, deviance, and dependence. They may have held widespread appeal and brought approval and praise to the dedicated individuals engaged in the task, yet they also emphasized the different status of disabled persons (Mitchell, 1971). Isaac Lewis Peet, a respected practitioner, chided in 1872 that the pioneers in the education of the deaf seemed "to have been unconsciously influenced by a desire to exaggerate the sad condition of the uneducated deaf mute, so as to make a stronger appeal to public sympathy, and to set in a higher light the success of their own labors by contrast with the dark condition of the being whose education they had undertaken" (I. L. Peet, 1872, pp. 74–75).

SPECIALIZED INSTITUTIONS AND THE STATE

Education for Deaf Students

In American special education, education of the deaf entered first. William Thornton and Francis Green laid a tenuous groundwork that was solidified in the opening decades of the nineteenth century through a number of educational attempts that further stimulated interest in special education.

John Braidwood, a nephew of Thomas Braidwood of Edinburgh fame, married Thomas's daughter, an alliance that failed to save him from rapidly turning into the black sheep of that famous family. Young Braidwood became principal of the Braidwood Academy in Edinburgh in 1810 but, facing arrest in 1812 (A. G. Bell, 1918), he accepted a commission to come to the United States from Major Thomas Bolling of Virginia. Bolling had three deaf children and two deaf grandchildren and had originally sent three of the children to the Braidwood Academy in Edinburgh. But he decided to hire a teacher and keep the children at home, so offered John Braidwood $600 to open a school, first suggesting Baltimore and then Virginia (A. G. Bell, 1900a).

Braidwood was in the United States between 1812 and 1815 but proved "totally deficient in steadiness and moral principle" (H. P. Peet, 1857, p. 170) and actually accomplished little more than bringing the venture to the attention of contemporary reformers. He worked for Major Bolling in a little school in Virginia, but the venture was short-lived. Braidwood "squandered in dissipation and debauchery the funds entrusted to him" (H. P. Peet, 1857, p. 170) and soon left Bolling's employ and wandered to New York. There, he collected a few deaf children and opened another short-lived school which, though a failure in its day, significantly influenced the later founding of the New York Institution for the Deaf and Dumb.

There was also some correspondence with Thomas Jefferson on the subject of the education of deaf students. In 1816 Jefferson suggested that "the vicinity of the seat of government" was "most favorable" for a school for the deaf, although he felt that it should not be connected with a college, as the objects were different: "one is science, the other mere charity" ("Braidwood in America," 1897, p. 120). None of Braidwood's schemes succeeded, and he soon lapsed into habits of neglect, dissipation, and extravagance. Forced to leave the United States, he eventually returned to England, became a bookkeeper in Manchester, and finally died in 1820 "a victim to the bottle" (A. G. Bell, 1918, p. 463).

Major Bolling was not the only parent eager to obtain the services of a teacher of the deaf. Braidwood had also been invited to open a school in Hartford, Connecticut, by Mason Fitch Cogswell (1761–1830), a respected doctor and surgeon, the first person to perform cataract surgery in the United States. The emotional logic that underlay Cogswell's plea centered on his daughter, Alice, deafened at four years of age by spotted fever. Cogswell could not allow Alice to remain "in the deplorable state of an untaught deaf-mute" (Weld, 1847, p. 9), nor would he accept sending her to London or Edinburgh for instruction.

No American at that time was trained to teach a deaf child. Lydia Huntley Sigourney, the writer, tried to teach Alice with homemade signs (Lane, 1976), as did the next-door neighbor, Thomas Hopkins Gallaudet, who had read of the Abbé Roche Ambroise Cucurron Sicard's work and taught Alice many signs. Still, the results remained meager and impelled Cogswell toward establishing an American school. He began by ascertaining the number of deaf people in New England at that time. Through a circular addressed to all the Congregational clergymen in Connecticut, Cogswell discovered that there were at least eighty deaf persons in the state, many of them of school age; on this basis he estimated that "New England contains more than *four hundred persons* in this unhappy situation, and in the United States upwards of *two thousand*" (original italics, H. Barnard, 1852a, p. 92). The numbers encouraged Cogswell in his intention of forming an American institution for the education of deaf children.

Cogswell first wrote to John Braidwood but, receiving no reply, modified his plans. On a spring evening in April 1815 Cogswell called together to his own home a small group of men, the financial and social leaders of Hartford. The goals of the group were ambitious: they hoped to inspire public and private benevolence toward an American institution for the education of deaf children and youth. Cogswell's group discussed the practicality of sending an emissary to Europe to delve into methods of instruction for deaf persons. It was proposed that Thomas Hopkins Gallaudet "visit Europe for the sake of qualifying himself to become a teacher of the deaf and dumb" (H. Barnard, 1852a, p. 101). Gallaudet accepted the commission gratefully: "I informed Dr. F. Mason Cogswell and Mr. Ward Woodbridge of my willingness to undertake the employment," he noted in his diary of April 20, 1815 (E. M. Gallaudet, 1888, p. 51). Subscriptions raised more than two thousand dollars for expenses (Hodgson, [1952] 1973), and Gallaudet sailed from New York on the *Mexico* in May 1815.

In England, Gallaudet first presented a letter of introduction to John Townshend, founder of the Bermondsey Institution, who, Gallaudet wrote optimistically, "promised his strongest efforts for the accomplishment of my wishes" (T. H. Gallaudet, 1815c). Just as promising were the good auspices of the Scots philosopher Dugald Stewart. But optimism faded when Gallaudet confronted the Braidwood monopoly and the pervasive secrecy with which they guarded their methods. Joseph Watson, speaking for the Braidwoods, refused Gallaudet instruction at the London asylum, "except on the condition of his remaining *three years* an usher in the asylum, instructing one of the classes daily" and contracting "to be with the pupils from seven o'clock in the morning till eight in the evening, and also with pupils in the hour of recreation." Mr. Kinnsburgh of Braidwood's Edinburgh institution similarly informed Gallaudet that he "was bound not to communicate the art of teaching deaf mutes to any person intending to practice it, during a period of seven years" (original italics, "Institution," 1818, p. 129). Not only did Gallaudet voice his astonishment that "in Great Britain the benevolent and Christ-like work of teaching the deaf has been for two generations in the hands of a certain family" (T. H. Gallaudet, 1815b), but he complained that the suggestions of the Braidwoods "interfered a little with my right of private judgment, not to say with my feelings of delicacy and honour" (quoted in E. M. Gallaudet, 1888, p. 66).

In 1815 the Abbé Sicard fled Paris with two deaf men, Jean Massieu and Laurent Clerc (T. H. Gallaudet, 1815c). Sicard, as a secret monarchist, had corresponded with the Bourbons in exile, but with Napoleon sailing for France, Sicard quite wisely fled. By accident, Gallaudet happened on an advertisement for a speech to be given by Sicard in the south of England (Golladay, 1991). When Gallaudet met Sicard, he found that, unlike the secretive Braidwoods, Sicard held it "a duty and a privilege to impart his methods freely to all enquirers" (H. P. Peet, 1852b, p. 69). Sicard invited Gallaudet to Paris to train at the Institution Nationale des Sourds Muets, an opportunity the American seized, realizing that it was impossible to induce the Braidwoods to part with their secrets.

After waiting out the political upheavals that were shaking France in 1815—Waterloo and the demise of Napoleon's power—the trio returned to France, and Gallaudet commenced his instruction in February 1816. In a letter to Cogswell he described how he attended one of the classes at the institution for two hours daily, usually a class of fifteen or sixteen lads. For a further two hours Thomas received private instruction from the deaf Massieu at the cost of $15 a month (T. H. Gallaudet, 1816a).

During his time in Paris, Gallaudet discussed with Sicard his feelings of inadequacy in teaching the deaf and stated his need for an assistant (T. H. Gallaudet, 1816b). Soon, Gallaudet was approached by Laurent Clerc, the teacher of the highest class at the Paris school, who wished to travel to America with Gallaudet as an assistant if the Abbé Sicard would give his consent (E. A. Fay, 1879). Clerc's original plan was to stay in the United States for three years, but he eventually married one of his pupils and, except for visits to France, lived out his life in America. He taught at the American Asylum and promoted the ideals and methods of the education of deaf students, as begun by Épée, throughout North America (W. W. Turner, 1870).

While Gallaudet was away, Cogswell and others secured an act of incorporation from the legislature of Connecticut that allowed sixty-three Hartford residents to be formed into a corporation under the name of the Connecticut Asylum for the Education and Instruction of Deaf and Dumb Persons (Weld, 1847). To aid the fledgling institution, the legislature appropriated $5,000 of public money (Weld, 1847). The governor of Connecticut commended the work "to public sympathy by a special proclamation, and encouraged collections in the churches" (*History,* 1885, p. 10), and a further $12,000 was raised from private donations (D. Wright, 1969). Once back on American soil, Gallaudet and Clerc built on this base. They spent two years organizing a permanent association, raising funds, finding and training teachers, and disseminating the aims and objectives of the enterprise throughout the press, in public addresses, and in personal interviews.

On April 15, 1817, the Connecticut Asylum for the Education and Instruction of Deaf and Dumb Persons, the first school on the continent designed especially to serve a disabled group, "was opened for the reception of pupils and the course of instruction commenced" (De Land, 1931, pp. 103–104). The Hartford institution was established as a national school. "The number of deaf mute children in the country was so little known," commented Alexander Graham Bell in 1884, "that the idea was seriously entertained that one school would be sufficient to accommodate the deaf children of the United States" (A. G. Bell, 1885a, p. 14). To indicate its national character, the name was changed in May 1819 to the American Asylum at Hartford for the Education and Instruction of the Deaf and Dumb (Weld, 1847).

In spite of being branded by critics as a "useless extravagance . . . a quixotic undertaking" and "utterly impractical" ("Dr. T. H. Gallaudet's," 1886, p. 74), the venture gained wide public approval. Anne Newport Royall, a travel writer, described it as "the glory of Hartford and indeed that of America" (Tull Boatner, 1959, p. 7). Once planted, the seed grew quickly; New York, Pennsylvania, and Kentucky soon witnessed the formation of institutions for deaf children (Winzer, 1981a).

Following John Braidwood's sodden attempts to establish a school in New York, Mr. Gard, a deaf man from the Bordeaux school in France, offered to come to New York to open an institution (H. P. Peet, [1846] 1847). However, it was John Stafford, chaplain of the Human and Criminal Institutions of New York City, who finally established a small private school for impecunious deaf children. A forceful personality, drawing on charitable resources, Stafford obtained an act of incorporation in 1817 and opened the school in an old almshouse in May 1818 as the New York Institution for the Deaf and Dumb (H. P. Peet, [1846] 1847). Support came from private subscriptions, $10,000 from the city, and a moiety of the tax on the lotteries (Hodgson, [1952] 1973). The institution was founded as a charity for both students and teachers—two teachers were clothed and supported for their services but, because of the school's small size and limited funding, many indigent pupils were rejected in the early years (Akerley, 1826).

Many of the early institutions allowed an unrestricted clientele. Liberal sprinklings of children with mental retardation were found in schools for deaf and blind children. For example, the American Asylum admitted a few retarded children, as did the New York Institution for the Deaf and Dumb (Brockett, 1856). For these, and for orphans and abandoned children, the schools often functioned not so much to educate the children as to provide an asylum for them. By the 1860s schools for deaf and blind children balked at accepting children with mental retardation, as other facilities for these children were opening (see McIlvaine, 1909).

Closely paralleling the pattern of the New York institution was that of Pennsylvania, where David Seixas, a crockery dealer, opened a school in 1820 with ten pupils and one teacher (Domich, 1945). In 1822 the Kentucky Asylum for the Tuition of the Deaf and Dumb was created by an act of the Kentucky legislature; it was the first state school for deaf students in North America (McClure, 1923).

British North America was not hesitant in following Gallaudet's lead. In 1829 the training of a newspaperman, Ronald McDonald, was funded by the Education Committee of the House of Assembly of Lower Canada so that he could establish a school for deaf children (Denys, 1889; Rae, 1848b). McDonald trained for a year at the American Asylum under Clerc and Gallaudet (Clarke and Winzer, 1983). His small school staggered along but eventually proved too expensive for the province, and it closed after five years (Rae, 1848b). It was not until mid-century that permanent schools for Catholic deaf children opened in Lower Canada (later, Quebec) (Widd, 1877).

In Upper Canada (Ontario) sporadic and haphazard educational attempts were solidified by John Barrett McGann (1810–1880), the pivotal figure in early Canadian special education. McGann, a fiery Irishman, proved a vocal and effective educational reformer; the development of the education of the deaf and the blind is closely bound with his contributions (Winzer, 1983). After working as a writing clerk at the New York Institution for the Deaf and Dumb, McGann arrived in Toronto in 1858 and opened a small school for deaf children. Blind youngsters were admitted in 1861. By 1863 McGann was supported by government grants through the Department of Asylums and Miscellaneous Charities; by 1870 he persuaded the Ontario government to finance a permanent institution for deaf students; that school was followed by a provincially funded school for the blind in 1872 (Widd, 1880b; Winzer, 1983).

In the fifty years after 1817 twenty-four institutions for deaf students were established in the United States; by 1880 the country boasted fifty-five schools. In Canada four institutions that would become permanent existed by 1867; another two were added in 1870. By 1907 there were 131 schools for deaf students in the United States serving 11,259 pupils; in Canada six schools handled 735 children (Ontario, Dept. of Ed., 1907).[1] The sampling of schools and their opening dates in Table 3-2 illustrates how a number of schools were founded for deaf and blind students jointly. It also shows that separate schools or departments sprang up to serve black students in the post–Civil War period.

Although no bureaucratic centralization existed, the schools were strikingly similar in philosophy and practice: all took their cues from the American Asylum, considered the epicenter of the North American education of the deaf.

---

[1]On the development of other Canadian schools for deaf students, see Haworth, 1961; J. S. Hutton, 1869a; "Manitoba," 1924; Widd, 1880a; and Winzer, 1979–80.

Table 3-2

The Spread of Schools for Deaf and Blind
Students in North America

Locale	Year opened
United States	
Connecticut	1817
New York City	1818
Philadelphia	1820
Pennsylvania	1822
Kentucky	1822
New Jersey	1825
Ohio	1827
Virginia (deaf and blind)	1839
Indiana	1843
North Carolina (white only)	1845
South Carolina (white only)	1846
Louisiana (white only)	1852
Tennessee	1854
Massachusetts (Northampton)	1867
North Carolina (black, deaf and blind)	1868
Maryland (black)	1875
Western New York (Rochester)	1875
Georgia (black)	1881
Mississippi (black department)	1882
Washington Territory	1887
Texas (black, deaf and blind)	1887
Kentucky (black)	1885
Alabama (black)	1893
Canada	
Halifax	1856
Montreal (Catholic boys)	1848
Montreal (Catholic girls)	1851
Montreal (Protestant)	1870
Ontario	1870
Manitoba	1888
Saskatchewan	1931

Thomas Hopkins Gallaudet, whose views and prestige served to anoint him as unchallenged leader, propounded the philosophy of deaf education and delineated the route that educators of the deaf, as well as other special educators, could follow. Gallaudet must be viewed as a widely influential reformer of the ilk of Henry Barnard and Horace Mann: in his person he symbolized all that was good in special education (see Box 3-2).

Perhaps the most critically important point to make about the rise of the specialized institutions for deaf persons is that, more than for hearing children or even other disabled groups, schooling for deaf students became synonymous with education. The education of hearing children "begins and to a large extent is acquired outside and quite independent of schools and pedagogues," observed a school superintendent in 1900. "To the deaf, however, their alma mater is the true home of their minds, where their intellects were first awakened, where their first mental concepts were obtained, where their understanding was born into light and freedom" (OSD, 1900, p. 9).

Institutionalization, moreover, implied a distinctive set of social relations for exceptional students. The usual distinctions and circumscriptions based on class, ethnicity, and religion crumbled, as the students were defined primarily by their handicaps. Deaf students viewed their "common affliction" as cutting across social and religious lines and forming "a common bond, a binding strength" (Ontario Deaf-Mute Association, 1906, p. 439). Within their own institutions children failed to internalize the cultural symbols of the greater society; rather, they developed an identity more closely bound to the constraints of their handicaps. Education supplied the basis of culture—a living language—and the residential schools furnished maximal conditions for the acquisition of sign, so that signing rapidly became an indicator of one's identity as a deaf person.

Education for Blind Students

As French ideology and pedagogy underlay designs for the education of deaf students in the New World, a similar imperative guided early education of the blind in North America. Dr. John D. Fischer of Boston first brought the matter to public attention. As a medical student in Paris, Fischer often visited the school for blind students; he translated this interest into advocacy on the American scene after his return to Boston in 1826 (Perkins Inst., 1881). In 1827 Fischer and others collected money to underwrite the cost of ascertaining the number of blind persons and the ways to organize a school; their informal census estimated that there were 400 blind people in Massachusetts and 1,500 in all New England (H. Best, 1934). Fischer's proposals in aid of the blind population crystallized in 1829 when an association was formed and Fischer obtained an act of incorporation for the New England Asylum for the Blind.

Just at the time that Fischer was searching for a superintendent to manage the new institution, Thomas Hopkins Gallaudet resigned from Hartford and inevitably became Fischer's immediate choice as superintendent. When Gallaudet declined, the position went to Samuel Gridley Howe (1801–1876), although it was not until 1831 that Howe was appointed director of the new school.

Both in their physical and personal attributes, two men could not have been more different than Gallaudet and Howe. Gallaudet was described as "short in

Box 3-2
Thomas Hopkins Gallaudet (1788–1851)

Many of the advances witnessed in the care and training of exceptional persons in the first half of the nineteenth century sprang from the crusading work of Thomas Hopkins Gallaudet, one of America's paramount educational reformers. Gallaudet was not merely a schoolman; he attacked all the staples of nineteenth-century reform—crime, vice, drunkenness, lunacy, and slavery—with an emphasis on social change, chiefly through the medium of publicly funded charities and institutions.

Gallaudet began in a career in law but, forced out by poor health, attempted commercial selling, traveling through Ohio and Kentucky on horseback. He then accepted the position as a tutor at Yale for two years. In 1811 he turned to religion and entered the newly established Andover Seminary, from which he graduated as a congregational minister in 1814. Andover was the first seminary to train missionaries for foreign parts, and it was this missionary instinct, built on early nineteenth-century evangelical religion and fired by the conviction that God had ordained the middle and upper classes to oversee the welfare of the weak and dependent, that guided Gallaudet's thinking and underlay his designs for deaf students and a range of philanthropic enterprises (see Valentine, 1991).

When Thomas Hopkins Gallaudet assumed the principalship of the Connecticut Asylum in 1817, Hartford was a hub of benevolent activity. As an educational innovator, Gallaudet socialized on equal terms with the leaders of other schools, the pastors of churches, and educational reformers and advocates. He formed close social and professional ties with such people as Wilbur Fisk, the president of Wesleyan University; William Channing Woolbridge, the first hearing teacher at the Connecticut Asylum and an advocate of common-school reform and teacher training; William Russell, the editor of the *American Journal of Education* and the holder of liberal views of the education of women; Lydia Huntley Sigourney, a writer, leader of Hartford society, and the first teacher of Alice Cogswell; and Emma Willard, founder of the Troy Female Seminary (Winzer, 1981a).

In the early decades of the nineteenth century little difference was seen between different forms of deviance, and educators glided from one condition to another. When Gallaudet left the American Asylum in 1830, he was met by a flood of offers to work in special education, in the common schools, and in the promotion of a range of philanthropic activities. Gallaudet was invited to take the helm of the Oneida Institute of Science and Industry, to take charge of the Pittsfield Female Academy, and he was offered professorships at Cincinnati College and at New York University. He was asked to teach at Dartmouth College, the Utica Female Seminary, the Cincinnati Seminary, and other institutions, either as professor or principal. It was also suggested that Gallaudet head the New England Asylum for the Blind at twice the salary he had received at Hartford.

In 1838 Henry Barnard spoke for a bill that provided for the "better supervision of the common schools" in Connecticut. It was this bill that provided for a state supervisory board with an executive similar to the one formed shortly before in Massachusetts, which had ushered Horace Mann into office. Gallaudet, famous for his interest in the education of the deaf, was "so admired for his sound views" that he was "the only one contemplated to fill the office" (H. Barnard, [1861b] 1969, p. 107). Gallaudet refused on the grounds of "his unwillingness to absent himself as much from his family as the plan contemplated" (p. 107), and the position was offered to Henry Barnard himself (Brubacher, 1965; Steiner, 1919). Nevertheless, Gallaudet lent his assistance to the new secretary and accompanied Barnard on visits to every one of the eight counties of Connecticut.

Refusing all offers, Gallaudet chose to write and to dabble in diverse areas of education. As an efficient promoter of educational reform, Gallaudet was asked to assist in almost any public appeal of a benevolent or religious nature, and he lent his prestige and professional energies to a wide range of activities.

Gallaudet was an active member of the Connecticut Society for the Improvement of the Common Schools. In 1830 he was prominent in the organization of the first teachers' convention held in Hartford, presided over by Noah Webster. In 1833 he tried to begin a correctional manual labor school in Connecticut and became involved in infant schools in Hartford (*American Journal of Education,* 1827). He lent his name to, supported, and worked for Catharine Beecher of the Hartford Female Academy; in 1832 Gallaudet became acting principal of Beecher's Female Academy when poor health forced Beecher to resign (*American Annals of Education,* 1832). Later, Beecher's major appeal for the Western Female Institute was made in the name of Gallaudet (Sklar, 1973).

With Lyman Beecher, Catharine's father, Gallaudet shared concerns about the danger of an increasing Roman Catholic population. In 1835 he joined a scheme with the motto "Look up, Press onward," designed to prevent the spread of Roman Catholicism in the West (see E. M. Gallaudet, 1888). Gallaudet was asked to manage the Pennsylvania Colonization Society; he was an organizing member of the American Colonization Society as well as the African Repository Society, dedicated to abolishing American slavery and relocating blacks in Liberia.

Gallaudet also wrote schoolbooks and books for children; his children's books were extremely popular. Thousands of copies were circulated and translated into many languages. They were read as English reading books of the foreign missionary societies and through these channels made themselves felt in unexpected places. In 1848 the king of Siam, immortalized in the story of Anna Harriette Leonowens in the book *Anna and the King of Siam* (later made into the play "The King and I"), wrote to Gallaudet and thanked him for his easily read books.

By 1838 Gallaudet had decided to devote his time to the mentally ill. He undertook the role of chaplain at the asylum in Worcester, Massachusetts, that had been established by Horace Mann, and he worked there until his death in 1851.

stature, below the ordinary height but erect and dignified" (Sprague, 1857, p. 613). This kindly, bespectacled, and reticent man reformed through gentleness built on the precepts of evangelical religion. In contrast, Howe seemed to epitomize the spirit of romanticism with his tall figure, flowing beard, and passionate and fiery personality. Howe adopted the underdogs of society; he battled for blind, retarded, insane, deaf, enslaved, and oppressed people. His diverse philanthropic interests usually translated into definitive action and extended from supporting poor people in Greece, to leadership of the Emancipation League, to actively working with the Kansas Emigrant Aid Society and John Brown in attempting to abolish slavery. Howe fought in the Greek war of liberation against the Turks for six years; he joined the Polish revolutionaries, was imprisoned for a time in Berlin, and opened a school for refugees in Crete (see French, 1932; Richards, 1985; Sanborn, 1891; Schwartz, 1956).

Both Howe and Gallaudet were deeply influenced by evangelical religion and the emphasis of early nineteenth-century Protestantism on one's responsibility for the welfare of others. However, when Gallaudet began his work, his training as a Congregational minister offered him little background and experience in the unique problems of deafness. Similarly, Howe, as a physician, did not have the background of interest that had impelled Valentin Haüy into the work of educating the blind. He did not have a Maria Theresia von Paradis to inspire him, nor had he joined in discussions with philosophers such as Rousseau and Diderot. But, like Gallaudet, Howe readily adopted the humanitarian philosophy that was sweeping the world and finding fertile soil in Boston.

The New England Asylum for the Blind, with Howe at the helm, did not officially open until 1832. Before he undertook the task, Howe traveled to Europe to visit schools in Paris, Edinburgh, and Berlin and to "make himself fully acquainted with the mode of conducting such institutions; to procure one, or at most two, instructed blind as assistant teachers; also, the necessary apparatus" (Perkins Inst., 1881, p. 85). Howe actually hired two teachers, one from Paris and one from Edinburgh.

When the school finally opened in 1832 as the Massachusetts Asylum for the Blind, the first sessions for the original six indigent children were held at Howe's home on Pleasant Street in Boston. Later a Boston man provided his home on Pearl Street as a permanent residence; in his honor, the name was changed to the Perkins Institution and Massachusetts Asylum for the Blind. Again, the school moved to a hotel in South Boston and finally, in 1912, to Watertown, Massachusetts.

As Hartford had, Howe's enterprise began as a national school for the blind; other New England states provided appropriations to send pupils (Perkins Inst., 1834). Connecticut and New Hampshire began to send pupils in 1832, Vermont in 1833, and Maine in 1834. By 1872 pupils were coming from all over the United States and Canada.

To further finance the fledgling institution, the legislature allowed the institute to use the unexpended revenues of the Hartford school for the deaf (Perkins Inst., 1881). Under the pressures of both necessity and tradition, Howe then followed the time-honored exhibition trail. After the school had been operating six months, the pupils gave an exhibition before the Massachusetts legislature, which procured the new institution $6,000 on the condition that twenty poor children from Massachusetts be educated free (H. Best, 1934). Thereafter, Howe and his pupils presented exhibitions before the legislature of seventeen states. The public was not excluded; on weekends in Boston, visitors to the asylum could marvel at blind children reading, doing mathematics, and playing musical instruments. So that skeptics could be assured that the children could really not see, a green ribbon was bound over each child's eyes (Koestler, 1976). Pupils also presented vocal and instrumental concerts to raise money (Perkins Inst., 1836). Howe, however, discontinued exhibitions by the late 1840s, as they strengthened the idea that the blind were a class apart and the schools, charity schools (Perkins Inst., 1851).

New York founded a school for blind students at the same time under the advocacy of Dr. John D. Russ, who had been in Greece with Howe. In 1831 Russ found some boys in a New York almshouse; a year later the New York School for the Blind opened with three pupils, all from the almshouse, and Russ as principal. Russ appeared to have lacked administrative skills; even though James Boonan gave the school his mansion in 1837, the New York school was plagued by financial problems until 1863, and it managed to keep afloat only through pupil exhibitions (see Wait, 1892a, 1892b).

In 1833 a school for the blind opened in Philadelphia under the auspices of the Quakers. Joshua Fisher, a Quaker, had visited European schools for blind people in 1830. With the support of a recently arrived German teacher, Julius B. Friedlander, who had been giving private lessons to blind pupils in his own home, and Roberts Vaux, a leading Quaker, Fisher was instrumental in establishing the Pennsylvania Institution for the Instruction of the Blind. Friedlander was the principal (see Friedlander, 1833).

Schools for blind children slowly multiplied, there existed six schools in the United States by 1847, seventeen by 1854, and eighteen by the time of the Civil War. By 1875 there were thirty schools for blind persons serving 3,000 pupils (Halifax Institution for Blind, 1875). By 1900 thirty-seven schools were in existence. Many of these institutions began as multipurpose settings; by 1875 eleven states provided schools to jointly serve both deaf and blind children.

Canadian schooling for blind children developed more tardily. The Nazareth Institute in Montreal was founded by the Catholic Church in cooperation with the Grey Nuns in 1866 (Beggs, 1983; McLelland, 1934). In 1867 William Murdoch, a retired Halifax merchant, died in London but left a £5,000 endownment for a school for the blind. The Halifax Institution for the Blind opened in 1871 under the control of a board of management of sixteen men representing the Atlantic provinces (see Fogarty, 1960). Under pressure from Egerton Ryerson and John Barrett McGann, Ontario established a school for blind children at Brantford in 1872. By 1875 there were three Canadian institutions serving 150 students (Halifax Institution for Blind, 1875). A sampling of opening dates is shown in Table 3-3.

Institutions for Mentally Ill Persons

In France the education and training of mentally retarded children developed only after humane measures were initiated for the treatment of the insane population. A similar progression was seen in North America; subtle influences arising from the treatment of mentally ill patients wound around the care and

Table 3-3

The Spread of Schools for Blind Students in North America

Locale	Year Opened
United States	
Massachusetts	1832
New York	1832
Pennsylvania	1833
Ohio	1837
Tennessee	1838
Virginia (deaf and blind)	1839
North Carolina	1845
Kentucky	1847
Mississippi	1848
South Carolina	1849
Iowa	1853
Maryland	1853
New York (Batavia)	1866
California	1867
North Carolina (black, deaf and blind)	1869
Oregon	1873
Texas (black, deaf and blind)	1887
Western Pennsylvania (Pittsburgh)	1890
Canada	
Montreal	1866
Halifax	1868
Ontario	1872

training of mentally handicapped persons, and psychiatric theory and practice gradually developed perspectives on childhood emotional disturbance that emerged in mature form at the opening of the new century. In fact, as Rosen, Clark, and Kivitz (1976) point out, the parallels between the origins of the first state mental hospital in the United States and the first schools for retarded persons are remarkable.

American management and treatment of mental illness largely echoed the work of the Frenchmen Philippe Pinel and Jean Étienne Dominique Esquirol, who perceived the basic issue as being that of framing the political order so that human health would be fostered by good social institutions. On the other side of the Atlantic similar views were formulated and applied by Pinel's contemporary, Benjamin Rush (1745–1813), signer of the Declaration of Independence, remarkable exponent of the Enlightenment in America, and the most eminent American physician of his time (Gelb, 1989).

As a reformer, Rush proved a strong advocate of public education under more liberal conditions—he argued eloquently and vehemently for the abolition of corporal punishment in schools and worked to establish the first black college in Philadelphia. He campaigned against slavery, capital punishment, and the harmful use of liquor (see Goodman, 1934; Smith and Smith, 1989; Waserman, 1972). Rush was cofounder, secretary, and later president of America's first abolitionist society, in Pennsylvania. To his way of thinking, slavery violated the laws of nature and of God; advocates of the practice suffered a form of madness, "negromania," which Rush defined as "a want of perception, or an undue perception of truth, duty, or interest" (quoted by D'Elia, 1969). As well, Rush promoted asylums for the mentally ill and the mentally handicapped and a Quaker version of solitary confinement for criminals (Erikson, 1966).

Rush's enduring memory rests on his contributions as a physician at the Pennsylvania Hospital, which opened in Philadelphia in 1752. Rush was appointed to the Pennsylvania Hospital in 1783 and did much to alter contemporary attitudes toward the mentally ill (L. V. Bell, 1980). Before Rush, insane patients were handled with the same inhumane treatment employed for so long in Europe. Lunatic hospitals provided entertainment for the callous; at the Pennsylvania Hospital in the eighteenth century a small admission fee entitled sightseers to watch the patients (L. V. Bell, 1980).

Although more stringent and rigid than Pinel, Rush adopted aspects of the *traitement moral* and argued that insanity was largely due to life's difficulties rather than to any innate tendency. In *An Enquiry into the Natural History of Medicine among the Indians of North America,* which was read before the American Philosophical Society in 1774, Rush observed that disease, political institutions, and economic organization were so interrelated that any general social change produced accompanying changes in health (Rosen, 1968). Rush claimed that there was no difference between physical and mental illness, a belief that has led psychiatrist Thomas Szasz (1970) to attribute to Rush an ideological conversion from theology to science. In other words, what had previously been viewed as sin now became illness (Taylor and Searl, 1987).

Rush refused to allow the asylum to become a convenient place for inconvenient people. He selected his patients and offered the hope of curing mental illness. The moral management he envisioned meant removing patients to a quiet retreat under a system of human vigilance (Beck, 1811) and subjecting them to various forms of treatment, including work and strict discipline. Like Pinel's, Rush's treatment nevertheless involved downright Draconian rules. He demanded complete control over patients and insisted that respect and affection between himself and them emerge before treatment could proceed smoothly (Szasz, 1970). Rush also espoused bloodletting in the belief that insanity was seated primarily in the blood vessels of the brain. He bled patients vigorously, taking 20 to 40 ounces of blood a treatment.

A lack of consensus about psychiatry in nineteenth-century America led to a wide variety of asylum regimens (see Dwyer, 1987; Grob, 1973). Rush's seminal contributions notwithstanding, early nineteenth-century treatment of mentally ill patients was chiefly characterized by harshness and callousness. Some made earnest efforts to use Pinel's methods, but, in spite of their pious hopes, physical restraint remained the mainstay of treatment in public institutions.

Nevertheless, facilities expanded rapidly. The first state hospital opened in Virginia in 1773; Kentucky opened a public asylum for the insane in 1824. In the next few decades practically every state opened public facilities for the insane as "a cult of asylums swept the country" (Rothman, 1971, p. 130). By 1860 twenty-eight of thirty-three states had established public insane asylums. Ohio became the first to differentiate among types of mental illness by providing special institutions for dependent and insane epileptics (Vineland, 1895).

It was not until the 1850s that conditions within the asylums noticeably altered, largely because of the passionate arguments of Dorothea Lynde Dix (1802–1887), who adopted mental illness and the inhuman treatment of its victims as her main focus. Dorothea Dix, often confused with the newspaper columnist of the same name, was a retired teacher who directed her indignation on behalf of mentally ill people toward the Massachusetts legislature in the 1840s (Rosen, Clark, and Kivitz, 1976).

Dix, born in Maine, opened a small school in Worcester, Massachusetts, when she was only fourteen; she later started a school in Boston (Irvine, 1976a). After her retirement she taught part time and in the winter of 1841 agreed to teach a Sunday school class at the East Cambridge, Massachusetts, House of Correction (Irvine, 1976a). There she found mentally retarded and mentally ill people housed among the criminals. She protested to the jailer that no stoves were provided for the insane inmates on a blustery spring day. The jailer returned the stock answer that insane persons were insensible to the cold (Tiffany, 1890). Dix then vowed to investigate the situation; over the next two years she visited every jail and almshouse in Massachusetts.

Dorothea Dix took her findings to the Massachusetts legislature. She railed against "the present state of insane persons confined within this Commonwealth" (quoted by Rosen, Clark, and Kivitz, 1976, p. 6) and passionately described their plight: "More than 9,000 idiots, epileptics and insane in the United States, destitute of appropriate care and protection . . . [are] bound with galling chains, bowed beneath fetters and heavy, iron balls attached to drag chains, lacerated with ropes, scourged with rods, and terrified beneath storms of cruel blows, . . . abandoned to the most outrageous violations" (Dix, 1843, quoted by Abraham, 1976, p. 331). Dix's testimony produced a sensation in Boston. She made the legislature and the public aware of the deplorable conditions of the mentally ill and created the sympathy necessary to the success of her campaign to have the government cede public lands for their care.

Dix then traveled to New Jersey and other states investigating conditions at first hand and studying the care of patients in detail. By 1847 she had visited 128 penitentiaries, 300 county jails and houses of correction, and 500 almshouses (Bromberg, 1975).

Dix was soon joined by other reformers (Rothman, 1971; Scheerenberger, 1983). Their reports prompted improvements in both treatment and facilities. Dix was specifically responsible for improvements in hospitals in Rhode Island and New York and for the establishment of insane hospitals in thirteen other states as well as the District of Columbia, Ontario, and Nova Scotia (Irvine, 1976a).

Children were not generally considered as clients in mental hospitals; however, the psychotic child was an object of study in the first part of the nineteenth century, and a substantial body of knowledge on the subject accumulated during that period (MacMillan, 1960). Some early nineteenth-century descriptions of idiocy and its varieties resemble later pictures of children labeled as autistic or psychotic (Kauffman, 1976) (see Chapter 12). However, only sparse evidence of institutionalization or treatment for psychotic children remains (Winzer, 1989b). Stribling (1842) reported that, of 122 patients in one asylum in 1841, 9 were under age twenty and 2 under age fifteen. In 1844 Dorothea Dix reported finding in an asylum "a little girl, about nine or ten years of age, who suffered the fourfold calamity of being blind, deaf, dumb and insane" (Bremner, 1970, p. 777).

Institutions for Mentally Retarded Persons

As Dorothea Dix avidly promoted humane treatment for mentally ill persons, Samuel Gridley Howe turned his attention to the special needs of mentally retarded individuals. In 1846 Howe launched an exhaustive two-year inquiry into the treatment of mental retardation in Massachusetts. When he used the 1846 census to discover the number of idiots in specific localities in the state, he found at least 574 in a condition of hopeless idiocy "who are considered and treated as idiots by their neighbors, and left to their own brutishness" (Howe, 1848b, p. vii). Working from the census figures, he estimated that there were between 1,200 and 1,500 idiots in the entire state.

Always ready to assist the dependent and the disabled, Horace Mann added his influence to Howe's. Mann used his knowledge of the methods of Édouard Seguin in Paris to awaken American interest in the education of exceptional children generally (Hodgson [1952] 1973). On a trip with Howe in 1843 Mann visited several special schools in Britain and Europe. In the late 1840s Howe sent George Sumner to France to delve further into European methods. Sumner was a philanthropist and reformer long interested in such social problems as education and slavery. Sumner's thinking, colored as it was by the New England reform movements, held enormous interest for Howe. Sumner's letters expressed admiration for the theory, practice, and results at Bicêtre. Sumner reported the hospital program in detail and noted that the Bicêtre's organization, with some modifications, was the one Seguin had set up in 1843. In his letter to Howe in February 1847, Sumner expressed astonishment at the progress made by human beings previously thought uneducable (Talbot, 1964).

Spurred on by the obvious need in New England, Mann's support, and Sumner's glowing letters, Howe chaired a commission mandated by the Massachusetts legislature to report on the problem, and in his 1848 report to the legislature he demanded a school for idiots in Massachusetts. His report stirred the embers of established values—the moral and economic arguments he presented were precise echoes of those used in support of the education of deaf students. So persuasive was he that the legislature became convinced of the justice, or at least the feasibility, of his cause.

Couching his arguments in religious terms, Howe stated that it was a moral offense for society to allow "beings originally made in God's image [to sink] into brutishness" (Howe, 1848b, p. 4). "Indeed," he said, "the number of persons left in any society in a state of idiocy, is one test of the degree of advancement of that society in true and Christian civilization" (Howe, 1848b, pp. 16–17). The moral imperatives were crucial. Howe estimated that one-third of the mentally

retarded population could benefit from instruction and that, by inculcating habits of self-control, industry, and morality, the school could remove from the
community the moral blight of "an idiotic man" ignorant of the laws of conscience (Zainaldin and Tyor, 1979). Then, relying on the Whig notion of responsibility for others, Howe argued that the "home of the Pilgrims" could not allow
human beings "to sink into hopeless idiocy for want of a helping hand" (Howe,
1848b, p. 10).

Upon hearing the commission's findings concerning the prevalence and
treatment of mental retardation, the legislature passed a resolution allowing for
a sum of not more than $2,500 annually for the training for three years of ten
idiotic children (Howe, 1848b). Howe's experimental school was to test the capacity of idiots for instruction (Brockett, 1856, p. 76) as well as to serve as a
model for the rest of the country. Howe hoped to demonstrate "that no idiot
need be confined or restrained by force; that the young can be trained for industry, order, and self-respect; that they can be redeemed from odious and filthy
habits, and there is not one of any age who may not be made more of a man and
less of a brute by patience and kindness directed by energy and skill" (quoted by
Kanner, 1964, pp. 41–42).

On October 12, 1848, the experimental school for mentally retarded children
opened in a wing of the Perkins Institution for the Blind in Boston with James B.
Richards, previously sent to Paris to learn methods of instruction, as the
teacher. The school, not surprisingly, was modeled on the Perkins Institution,
designed as a "boarding school for idiots" (Perkins Inst., 1857, p. 9). Only individuals showing promise of improvement were admitted; the typical admission
age was eight years, and children were returned to their families within five to
seven years (Zainaldin and Tyor, 1979). Ten state and three private pupils, all
boys, made up the first class.

Howe's training school, although restricted by lack of space and a paucity of
funds, ran for three years. The results sufficed to prove Howe's contention "that
many idiots are capable of improvement in their bodily habits, in their mental
capabilities, and even in their spiritual natures; and almost all can be made less
burdensome to their friends and the community" (Howe, 1848b, p. 67). Success
prompted the legislature to found a permanent school in 1850, the Massachusetts School for Idiotic and Feeble-Minded Children (see F. E. Williams, 1917).

It is likely that Howe's successful experiment alone would have provided the
impetus for the elaboration of a chain of institutions dedicated to the needs of
mentally retarded children. Structure and pedagogy might have diverged more
sharply than they did from the French model, however, except for the propitious
entry of Édouard Seguin into the United States in 1848. Seguin first settled in
Cleveland and then ostensibly practiced medicine in New York City. But he also
assisted in the development of a number of early institutions, including Howe's
program, the institution for retarded youth at Barre, Massachusetts, and the experimental school at Albany, New York (Rosen, Clark, and Kivitz, 1976). Under
Seguin's influence, the residential training school (asylum) model, already conceptualized and operational in France, became the most usable option in the
United States.

Other states rapidly followed the Massachusetts precedent. In January 1846
the Honorable F. F. Bachus of Rochester, New York, a member of the Senate of

that state, referred to the portion of the state census concerning idiots and led an inquiry urging the necessity of an institution in New York (Brockett, 1856). New York appointed a commission to judge the status of mentally retarded persons in the state. But then the state dragged its feet until pupils from Howe's school presented an exhibition before the state legislature and Howe himself made an earnest appeal (Barr, [1904b] 1913). In 1851 the New York legislature finally acted and hired Hervey B. Wilbur (1820–1883) as superintendent. Wilbur had opened a private school for mentally retarded students at Barre, Massachusetts, in July 1848, which actually predated Howe's school by a few months, so he brought some experience to the enterprise in New York. (Dr. George Brown and his wife, Catherine, succeeded Wilbur at Barre.)

Under the auspices of the New York legislature, Wilbur established an experimental school at Albany, New York, which opened in September 1854; it was the first institution in the state expressly for mentally retarded students (Seguin, [1866] 1907). Before he began his first school, Wilbur, inspired by reports of the work at Bicêtre, sent to Paris for published materials and received copies of Seguin's writings. Now Édouard Seguin himself came to New York and contributed to the leadership of the new school by structuring it according to principles outlined in his 1843 *Hygiène et éducation des idiots* (Rosen, Clark, and Kivitz, 1976). In 1855 the school was moved to its permanent location in Syracuse as the State Asylum for Idiots.

The Elwyn Institution, founded in 1852 as the Pennsylvania Training School for Idiotic and Feeble-Minded Children, was the fourth such school established in the United States. Pennsylvania, like New York, received an impetus from Massachusetts, and again Seguin played a role (Rosen, Clark, and Kivitz, 1976). In 1852 James Richards, the teacher at Howe's experimental school, left Boston and opened a private school in Germantown, a section of Philadelphia. With the support of prominent citizens, he was able to generate public interest in the project (Barr, [1904b] 1913). An exhibition before the Pennsylvania legislature in Harrisburg resulted in an appropriation of $10,000 from the state, and the school was moved to larger quarters (Rosen, Clark, and Kivitz, 1976). Seguin became associated with the school but later left, along with Richards, when the establishment ran into financial difficulties and disputes arose concerning lines of authority. Dr. Joseph Parrish assumed leadership, saved the school from disaster, and made a move in 1859 to Media, Pennsylvania (see Kerlin, 1877, 1891). Dorothea Dix assisted in choosing the site, fifteen miles south of Philadelphia (Barr, [1904b] 1913; Rosen, Clark, and Kivitz, 1976). Following Parrish, Dr. Isaac N. Kerlin became superintendent.

In 1857 an institution was established at Columbus, Ohio, with Dr. G. A. Doren as superintendent. Again Seguin was influential in its development. Dr. Henry B. Knight (1827–1880) became superintendent of the first Connecticut School for Imbeciles at Lakeville in 1861, despite some public opposition to the endeavor. In 1860 similar progress was being made at Frankfort, Kentucky. In 1865 the State Asylum of Illinois was established under the leadership of C. T. Wilbur, Hervey Wilbur's brother (Rosen, Clark, and Kivitz, 1976). In Ontario the Orillia Asylum opened in 1873 "with the capacity of serving 150 idiots" (Ontario, Inspector, 1876, p. 2).

From 1848 to 1857, five North American institutions for mentally retarded children were established. By 1865 there were eight such schools; by 1890, four-

Table 3-4

The Spread of Institutions for Mentally
Retarded Persons in North America

Locale	Year Opened
United States	
Massachusetts (Boston)	1848
Massachusetts (Barre)	1848
Rhode Island	1850
New York City	1851
Pennsylvania	1852
New York (Albany)	1854
Ohio	1857
Kentucky	1860
Connecticut	1861
Illinois	1865
Iowa	1879
New Jersey	1888
Canada	
Ontario	1873

teen states had institutions for the mentally defective children (Davies, 1959). Most were on the colony plan and consisted of a custodial department, training school, industrial department, and farm. A sampling of institutions and their opening dates is shown in Table 3-4.

Education for Neglected, Vagrant, and Delinquent Students

Throughout the nineteenth century increasing numbers of sensorily hand-icapped and mentally retarded children were accommodated in special facili-ties. Less educational concern was directed toward children who might today be categorized as psychotic, pervasively developmentally disordered, or severely emotionally disturbed.

The recognition of severe and profound disturbance in children arose years before treatment was developed, and until the beginning of the twentieth cen-tury such afflicted children were simply categorized as mentally retarded. Work with adult mentally ill patients certainly wielded some influence. But it was not until mental retardation was viewed as a distinct category of handicap, with its own teaching and institutional approaches, that severe emotional disturbance could in turn emerge as a discrete entity.

In the schools and the courts less severe behavior disorders earned a pleth-ora of descriptions—unruly, truant, or incorrigible. In the interest of order and school harmony, educators largely ignored these children, preferring to expel or suspend them from school and leave their fate to the courts. In the com-munity such socially disruptive youngsters were officially termed as vagrant, neglected, and delinquent, and they rapidly gained the attention of reformers and child savers.

Neglect, vagrancy, delinquency, and crime in nineteenth-century North America were subject to the economic and social pressures of a young, evolving society. As American society became more industrial and urban, the mounting problems of disruptive and fractious elements became strikingly visible. When the simplicity of pioneer life ceded to the greater complexity of commercial civilization, the cities became the crucibles of delinquency. Children all too easily slid toward the cesspool into which the human refuse of an intensely competitive society drained. Many dangers stalked unwary youngsters: rootlessness, the harsh demands of premature adulthood for those whose families needed their earnings, loosened parental controls, the increased variety of activities in which children could indulge, and, for many, a growing dependence on street play groups and gangs.

Urban Americans became alarmed by the apparent upsurge in the numbers of vagrant and delinquent children, many of whom roved the streets in gangs to wage an unending assault on the mores and manners of the rest of the population. Not only did social planners object to the presence of so many rough youngsters on the public byways, but the increasing visibility, especially among the urban working class, of impoverished, delinquent, or recalcitrant children symbolized a breakdown of the family and a direct threat to the social order. Reformers further feared that constant exposure to the harsher elements of life would turn vulnerable children into vile and irresponsible adults. Moreover, the numbers appeared to be on the rise. The children who were arrested were sent to state reform schools, farm schools, nautical branches of state reform schools, and the houses of the Angel Guardian (E. Wright, 1865).

The hordes of clamorous scarecrows on the streets made the problem visible to such a degree that governmental failure to act was interpreted as contributing directly to social and economic dereliction. Reformers believed that the impending social disaster could be averted only through a concerted effort to change the child's environment. Reforms could take two forms—rebuilding working-class families or establishing alternate families in the form of institutions that would at least save some children.

The public schools, largely designed to improve and uplift working-class youth, proved unhappy environments to many potential clients, especially in urban areas. "Such children," observed Henry Barnard (1857), "cannot be safely gathered into the public schools; and if they are, their vagrant habits are chafed by the restraints of school discipline. They soon become irregular, play truant, are punished and expelled, and from that time their course is almost uniformly downward, until on earth there is no lower point to reach" (pp. 5–6). The failure of the public schools to prevent juvenile crime and vagrancy generated arguments in support of the establishment of more specialized institutions through which to attack the problem.

The first decades of the nineteenth century witnessed the expansion of correctional institutions. The focus rested on the correctional act, not the individual's social context; treatment was founded on the traditional goals of incarceration—isolating the criminal, preventing crime, and gaining retribution for past crime. The central idea of the Victorian penitentiary, as proposed by

Jeremy Bentham and first tried in Philadelphia, was that prison should be a place of isolation, discipline, and systematically used punishment alleviated by precise injections of hope.

Measures to control delinquent youth, following this same correctional pattern, were punitive and aversive, despite the fact that some children were committed to the common jails and the penitentiaries, not in response to any criminal activity, but in response to their highly visible need, destitution, and neglect. Few people gave credence to the notion that children differed substantially from their adult counterparts. Child offenders were dealt with in much the same way as adults—they were subjected to the same laws, their cases were heard in the same courts, and they suffered the same punishments (McGrath, 1962). Children were sentenced by judges of the police courts and could be sent to county jails (E. Wright, 1865) or even state prisons. In 1859, for example, the penitentiary and the common jails of the Canadas housed 585 persons under the age of sixteen years, a little more than 5 percent of the total prison population (Canada, *Sessional Papers,* 1860).

Reformers held grave concerns about children's subjection to the demoralizing influence of the harsh discipline and wanton malnourishment and the legal violence embedded in a penal system based on retribution rather than reformation. They fretted about the brutalization of youth by the criminal justice system and sought to change the notion that all these children were criminals who deserved the moral condemnation of the community. Instead, these reformers argued the special nature of children and contended that they should be cared for, educated, and protected (Orlando and Black, 1975).

As there slowly emerged a recognition of the increasing diversity among criminals, of the novel pattern of urban crime, and of the different status of youthful offenders, pleas for the inauguration of a more human, effective, and efficient system grew more urgent. Convinced that children in the formative years could be helped through training and education, reformers advocated freeing them from the odium of being labeled as prisoners and placing them instead in facilities separated from "a crowd of old and hardened offenders" (Halifax Protestant, 1861–62).

Although many children still found themselves in county jails, alternate dispositions emerged with the establishment of a string of reformatories for juveniles. Although reform schools differed in practice and philosophy from the adult institutions, their inmates still passed through the formal procedures of law. And because little differentiation was made between the enforcement of morals and the enforcement of welfare, the reformatories continued to cater to the victims of neglect as well as to the perpetrators of antisocial acts (see, e.g., Sutton, 1988). Critics vehemently denounced the stringent legalities, the tight security, the rigid discipline, the penal attributes, and the stress on retribution rather than rehabilitation that characterized early nineteenth-century reform institutions. The facilities may have sufficed, though barely, to "reform a boy who has become criminal," but they could not "train and instruct the pauper boy while yet innocent of crime" (Meredith, [1862] 1975).

It was no longer considered appropriate to make prevention subsidiary to repression. Fundamental to this credo of prevention was the maintenance and training of young children in a compensatory environment. With defensive foresight, reformers contended, the "volume of vice and crime may be greatly reduced and the number of criminals be greatly lessened by proper care of the young" (*Royal Commission,* 1891, p. 104). They proposed the establishment of facilities set at the juncture of educational and penal practices—the industrial school.

Industrial schools were not intended to replace public schools but "to be preparatory to them and to reach a class who are at present below the influence of public instruction" (New York, Children's Aid, 1855, p. 9). An imaginative solution to the mounting numbers of neglected and potentially troublesome children evident in urban society, the industrial school was visualized as "a combination of home, public school, and place of industry" (B.C. Boys Industrial School, 1923, p. 5).

Holding to the fervent belief that early exposure to work and discipline would guarantee the development of an industrious and moral citizenry, the promoters of industrial schools advanced designs that combined industrial training and moral imperatives in a compensatory environment. The proposed schools would provide strong sanctions to a child's failure to conform to social standards by allowing the institutionalization of relatively young children in an effort to halt their slide "from the nuisance to the criminal class" (Edminson, 1949). The exclusion of convicted offenders from the ranks of those eligible to attend the industrial schools distinguished the schools from the reformatories, and the clear delineation of the industrial schools' target groups as vagrant, destitute, neglected, or homeless children also distinguished these schools from the public schools (Morrison, 1974).

In the mid-nineteenth century, as part of a general child save movement, there was a flurry of activity on behalf of the neglected children on both sides of the Atlantic. Those served would be chiefly children between the ages of eight and fourteen "whose faults have been largely on account of improper home training" (Toronto, 1912)—those from pernicious environments but also those still relatively unscathed by the contradictory claims of adult society and childhood. Included would be children "found to be orphans, begging, vagrant or incorrigible, or those whose parents were neglectful, drunk or vicious, or who exposed the child to an idle and dissolute life" (Ontario, *Statutes,* 1874, chap. 29).

Boys engaged in more overtly antisocial acts were prime candidates. Nevertheless, many reformers fretted over the condition of young females and viewed them as desperately in need of protection from promiscuity and prostitution as well as care during unwanted pregnancies (see Sedlak, 1983). In New York, for example, industrial schools emerged in the 1850s; by 1854 there were six functioning industrial schools serving females (Gilman, 1984).

The dominant motifs of the industrial schools were education, evangelism, and industrial elevation ("Social vice," 1919), and thus the industrial schools saw the marriage of industrial education and cherished social values of the period. In concept and practice, the combination of practical training and character building was not new; such ventures date back to the sixteenth century.

In 1862 the Board of Inspectors of Prisons, Asylums, and Public Charities of Canada recommended "ragged schools," homes, or industrial farms for "neglected and perishing children" to "enable them to earn an honest living for themselves" (Meredith, [1862] 1975). Philanthropic agitation and funds initiated the British Industrial School and Reformatory Movement in 1849 (MacDonnell, 1897). Legislation in the following decade greatly extended the scope of the facilities, which rapidly "proved their worth for the 'Juvenile Vagrant Class' " (McMurrich, 1872, p. 424).

The birth of industrial schools implied official recognition of the existence of more suitable ways to deal with children who were creating a problem in the community than through correctional procedures that were essentially the same as those applied to adults. Different settings developed: some industrial schools served students on a daily basis; others became permanent shelters. Permanent settings tended to dispense with the congregate model of the prisons—and instead were generally based on a family plan, in an attempt to approach the ideals of a Christian family. Inmates at the Victoria Industrial School just outside Toronto, for example, lived in cottages of fifty boys; a surrogate mother, the matron, was in charge of each cottage and took responsibility for the moral and religious training of the boys, fostering the values of punctuality, self-restraint, regularity, piety, and respect for manual labor (Morrison, 1974).

Industrial schools were less punitive than reformatories; prevention, not cure, was the byword. Efforts focused on the provision of a compensatory environment in which to maintain and train young children in the moral, physical, and material standards that the middle class held dear. But aversive relations, to some extent, still reigned; although reformatory aspects were deemphasized, retributive and deterrent elements were not completely lacking. For one thing, adults had greater protection against the arbitrary and whimsical decisions of judges than did children. Children were often not sent to the industrial schools for a fixed period: "The length of time they stay in the school depends upon the boys," explained one superintendent. "With some, six months, a year or two years may be sufficient while with other boys who have been allowed to drift too much and so have become difficult to manage, it takes longer" (Ferrier, 1897). Moreover, superintendents possessed almost complete discretionary powers over the discharge of children from the industrial schools.

In the case of neglected, vagrant, and delinquent children, the relationship between the reformers' ideology and their style of reform is telling. Although the industrial school model represented a shift in law where authority no longer engaged in punishing antisocial behavior but instead sought to assist wayward children, it also interjected a new party into the basic relationship of parent and child. The state could intervene, not as a punitive force, but as a protector of the child.

Reformers often did not share delicate feelings about family integrity in their efforts to rescue children from pauperism and immorality. Child savers believed that, if children were to be nurtured and protected, in some cases at least the rescue mission could be accomplished only by removing youngsters from unsavory environments. When parents directly or indirectly contributed to dereliction and criminality by failing to provide for a child's physical, moral, and intellectual well-being, then the state, as *parens patriae,* had the right to mediate between parents and child. To ensure character regeneration, reformers argued, "it may, and often will, be necessary to remove the child from its natural parents" (Kelso, 1893–94).

The movement toward state intervention can be interpreted two ways. On the one hand, reformers can be seen as policing the morals of the underclasses and actively seeking to control the family life of the poor. Permanent regeneration was thought possible only through character regeneration, so the protection of children from the abuse of adult improvidence and vicious example would be most effectively ensured by segregation in institutions modeled on middle-class family life. Such thinking may reflect the Victorians' view of some families as a cause of delinquency and crime, but in tidying up the streets, the Victorians also ran the risk of driving the emotional bonds of the dependent lower classes out of existence. On the other hand, public involvement can be seen not as an attempt to undermine the influence of families but rather as an effort to provide substitute care when families were unable or unwilling to fulfill their responsibilities (see Brenzel, 1980).

Nevertheless, before this, the family was sacrosanct, and the incremental delimitation of parental rights in the interests of the socialization of unruly youth met "with a great deal of opposition" (*Royal Commission,* 1891, p. 297). Reformers countered that parents forfeited their natural rights by neglecting to teach their children the precepts of moral and upright living and lauded the industrial schools as the appropriate mechanisms to instill social and moral values. "The system of education and the habits of industry" to which they were trained would more than counter "the evil effects incident to the system" (*Royal Commission,* 1891, p. 280).

Alternate child-saving models rapidly followed the advent of state-augmented industrial schools, as there was a movement from a reliance on institutional mechanisms to a strategy that stressed deinstitutionalization. Howe (1854) was among the first to argue against congregate reform institutions and to advocate foster-home care instead. Hence, throughout the second half of the nineteenth century, three options were available to restrain and correct potentially socially disruptive elements. The reformatory, the industrial school, and foster-home care were each offered under a different jurisdiction, each with a distinct philosophy.

The industrial school model was advanced as the most effective institutional means for the handling of intractable working-class youth. The movement proved popular; by 1919 the United States had 135 industrial schools in operation (U.S. Bureau of Education, 1917–18). Nevertheless, as children and youth did "not confine themselves to petty crimes" but sometimes emulated "the graver offences of old and practised culprits" (E. Wright, 1865, p. 7), many industrial school promoters and home finders became reconciled to the idea that there would always be some children requiring institutional care. Government officials, as well as magistrates and judges, continued to believe that reform schools reformed delinquent boys and that they should be retained for that purpose (A. Jones, 1978).

Chapter 4

Education for Exceptional Students in North America after 1850

Landmarks in Late Nineteenth-Century Special Education

1859   Thomas Gallaudet establishes the first American church for the deaf

1864   The National Deaf Mute College is established

1867   Clarke Institution for Deaf Mutes opens

1870s   Schools for black children open in the South; institutions are established for special populations, such as mentally retarded women and epileptics

1880s   The kindergarten movement is revitalized, and kindergartens are formed in institutions and special schools; Manitoba and Nova Scotia provide free and compulsory schooling to deaf and blind students

1888   The New Jersey Training School for Feeble-Minded Boys and Girls opens at Vineland, New Jersey

1909   The first compulsory school laws in the United States for exceptional children are enacted

Institutional developments in special education in the latter half of the nineteenth century occurred during a period of profound social change. America may have slowly reconciled itself to industrialization and urbanization and their concomitant problems, but the country was now faced with new and greater problems engendered by mounting immigration, territorial expansion, and internal disharmony.

The population of the United States increased more than ten times between 1800 and 1860 and was to double again by 1890. Just after the Civil War large numbers of Jewish immigrants arrived from Poland and Russia. In the 1890s Poles, Slovaks, and Hungarians began to arrive in increasing numbers to work in the mines and factories; by 1900 Italians had replaced the Irish as the largest ethnic group in many northeastern cities (Bloch and Dworkin, 1976; Kamin, 1974; Moores, 1987). A bitter civil war had been fought and slavery had been abolished, and by 1870 blacks were theoretically free. The need to educate newly freed blacks as well as the immigrants who were pouring into the country stimulated a parallel demand for the extension of facilities staffed by adequately trained personnel to serve disabled people. In the post–Civil War era the institutional complex expanded dramatically. By 1868 Pennsylvania, for example, had five hospitals for the insane, an institution for feebleminded children, an institution for deaf mutes, one for blind persons, two reformatories, and one home for friendless children (Pennsylvania Institution for the Feeble-Minded, 1868).

By midcentury most states were assuming at least some responsibility for the education and training of disabled children. But such schooling was generally not free; nowhere was it compulsory; and rarely were special schools part of the regular education system. Private philanthropy, so dominant in the first half of the century, ceded to bureaucratic social welfare; institutions were viewed as charitable ventures and the students, public beneficiaries. Late nineteenth-century educators directed much of their energy to altering these conditions—they agitated first for free schooling; then for altered designations that would separate educational institutions from prisons, asylums, and other public charities and place them under local boards of education; and finally for compulsory attendance (see Chapter 11).

Beginning in the 1860s enormous and divisive changes occurred in the education of deaf students. None of these changes were suddenly thrust upon the field; they had been simmering since the time of John Wallis, John Conrad Amman, and their contemporaries in the seventeenth century and fueled by Charles Michel de l'Épée and Samuel Heinicke in the next. In the mid–nineteenth century the shape of deaf education to come was most clearly evident in the formation of the National Deaf Mute College in 1864 and in the establishment of the Clarke Institution for Deaf Mutes in 1867. The Clarke Institution curriculum, more attuned to that of the public schools, is of vital importance in the saga of American deaf education and, indeed, in all special education. The brave new concepts of Clarke, together with the philosophical underpinnings of the National Deaf Mute College, began to clear the mists of prejudice that had long surrounded deaf individuals. The idea that deaf children were not deviant and dependent but rather worthy of educational rights identical to those allowed their hearing counterparts began to take root and grow.

The last half of the nineteenth century, then, was a time of enormous ferment in all fields in special education. A close look at the educational developments and issues of this time reveal the outlines of both the triumphs and the most persistent problems of modern special education.

THE EXPANSION OF THE INSTITUTIONAL COMPLEX

Institutions for Black Students

In the second half of the nineteenth century special institutions for deaf and blind students grew apace. Especially in the South, economy and convenience dictated placing both groups in the same facility, each with its own teaching personnel. The South also witnessed the growth of institutions for blacks.

During the Civil War many southern institutions either closed or suspended services. They reopened with separate departments for blacks or, more often, as separate facilities founded on principles drawn from contemporary medicine, psychology, and social mores. Educators argued, for example, that black and white deaf children developed differently. It was said that when learning language, black children seemed to "learn up to a certain age" but then "arrive at a point where further progress is difficult," a difference explained by the belief that "the cranial bones of the colored child knot together as a rule at an earlier age than do those of a white child" (Convention of Superintendants, 1913, pp. 443–44). A later writer asserted that "tradition, custom, political determination, as well as other economic and social practices, have set apart the colored people from whites." He argued, "It is considered a sound social philosophy and factual social psychology that this accepted demarcation and fairly definite preparation gives Negroes certain advantages, and at the same time, it assures the whites their sense of superiority and authority" (Whitten, 1937, quoted by Moores, 1987).

Francis Koestler (1976) stressed that many schools for black blind children' were inferior, with poorly trained teachers, ragged materials, and different curricula. As late as 1939 a survey of schools for the blind in the South showed that some of the schools for black students had to do with hand-me-downs from the sister schools for whites, not only worn furniture, chipped crockery, and threadbare towels, but also discarded classroom materials such as Braille books with the dots so worn down as to be all but useless (Koestler, 1976).

Higher Education for Deaf Students

Thomas Hopkins Gallaudet married one of his deaf pupils, Sophia Fowler, in June 1821; with her he had eight children, four sons and four daughters. As Thomas Hopkins dominated the education of the deaf in the first half of the nineteenth century, so his sons, Thomas, the eldest, and especially Edward Miner (1837–1917), the youngest, assumed leadership in the latter half. In fact, throughout the entire nineteenth century the Gallaudet family energized the movement to provide educational and social facilities for the deaf population. With other prominent families, such as the Fays, the Peets, the Clercs, and the McGanns in Canada, the Gallaudets dominated the profession; their influence significantly shaped the lives of deaf individuals. Family members were engaged not only in education but in welfare agencies, social groups, voluntary associations, and churches designed to cater to the special needs of the deaf population.

Thomas Gallaudet, the eldest son, first entered the ministry and then assumed teaching duties at the American Asylum and the New York Institution for the Deaf and Dumb (Draper, 1902). Long involvement led Thomas to recognize that "worship and religious instruction of the Sabbath, in their own language of signs, was a great need among the adult deaf" ("Church," 1852, p. 169) Consequently, Gallaudet launched a Bible class in St. Ann's Church in New York City in 1852 (T. Gallaudet, 1856, 1858). He founded the first American Church for the Deaf in 1859, the Church Mission for Deaf Mutes in 1872, and the Gallaudet Home for Aged and Infirm Deaf Mutes in 1875 (J. H. Kent, 1922).

Harvey P. Peet, longtime principal of the New York Institution for the Deaf and Dumb, had four sons, three of whom entered the education of the deaf. Laurent Clerc's daughter taught at the American Asylum, and his son became a pastor of a mission for deaf people in Philadelphia. In Canada no less than twelve members of the McGann family entered the profession and were responsible for founding schools for deaf and the blind persons in Canada and the United States (Dobyns, 1889; Winzer, 1983).

Though Edward Miner Gallaudet owed a great deal to his famous father, he was in no sense an educational reformer involved in a diverse range of activities: he was more strictly utilitarian than Thomas Hopkins Gallaudet and remained largely within the realm of deaf education, directing his energies to pedagogical issues and the concrete pressures inherent in guiding a rapidly expanding profession.

When only twenty years of age, Edward Miner Gallaudet undertook the superintendency of the Columbia Institution for the Deaf and Dumb and Blind, a facility established in Washington, D.C., in 1857 by Amos Kendall, postmaster general under Andrew Jackson and Martin Van Buren. A year earlier Kendall happened upon a charlatan who had gathered five deaf children from the streets of Washington, bound them to him legally as apprentices, and opened a school, soon collecting a dozen or more deaf and blind indigents. Kendall, horrified at the "cruel master," removed the children, had himself appointed as their legal guardian, offered his farm for a school, and donated funds and a house for a legitimate school (E. M. Gallaudet, 1870, p. 43). He first offered the position of superintendent to Isaac Lewis Peet, then settled on young Gallaudet (Tull Boatner, 1959).

Both Edward Miner Gallaudet and Samuel Gridley Howe recognized the power of the college and the university. The subject of the higher education of deaf persons was thoroughly explored throughout the 1850s at the conventions and meetings of educators in the field and in their journals (see *AADD*, 1852; Carlin, 1854; W. W. Turner, 1851). Edward Miner Gallaudet became deeply embroiled in the agitation to provide college facilities to deaf persons.

For Gallaudet, the timing was propitious. The 1862 passage of the Morrill or Agricultural Colleges Act provided for the granting of public lands within each state for the establishment of colleges for the agricultural and technical education of students in the "several pursuits and professions of life." Its effect was to establish the current system of state-supported higher educational institutions in the United States with its diversity of types of schools—special-purpose institutions, land-grant universities, and elite research universities (Armstrong, 1987).

In 1864 the directors of the Columbia Institution prevailed on Congress for degree-granting privileges. They argued that a college for deaf people would function "to afford a class of persons in the community . . . an opportunity to secure the advantages of a rigid and thorough course of intellectual training in the higher walks of literature and the liberal arts" (*Announcement*, 1866, p. 4). Just as importantly, it would demonstrate that persons deprived of hearing could "still engage successfully in advanced studies" (Ryerson, 1868, p. 21). Still, Gallaudet's campaign was tinged with a little doubt. "I can regard my course in asking for it," he said later, "as nothing else than an illustration of *monumental cheek.* Pardon my slang—for polite language is inadequate" (original italics, quoted by Armstrong, 1987, p. 14). Nevertheless, on April 8, 1864, degree-granting rights were conferred under an act to authorize the Columbia Institution for the Deaf and Dumb and the Blind to confer degrees (P. Hall, n.d.). The National Deaf Mute College became the highest department of the Columbia Institution, under the care of the national government, with Gallaudet at the helm and Abraham Lincoln as *ex officio* patron. In honor of Thomas Hopkins, the name was changed to Gallaudet College in 1894 and is today known as Gallaudet University.

Courses at the National Deaf Mute College leading to collegiate degrees occupied five years and embraced instruction in ancient and modern languages, mathematics, social sciences, history, philosophy, and political science (Ontario, Dept. of Ed., 1907). Of primary importance were the efforts focused on teacher training: clearly reflecting the precedents established by his father, Edward Miner Gallaudet viewed "the furnishing of young men well fitted to teach the deaf and dumb" as "one of the most important results of our college enterprise" (E. M. Gallaudet, quoted by Tull Boatner, 1959, p. 66).

Sophisticated teacher training was to be not only a factor in dispelling the myth of the intellectual inferiority of deaf persons but also a major concession in that it would allow deaf adults a voice in determining the structure and course of the institutions designed specifically to serve their discrete needs. The emphasis on the education of the deaf teacher reflected the National Deaf Mute College goal of placing deaf individuals "more nearly on a level with their speaking and hearing brethren" so as to "exert a wider influence" (*AADD*, 1871, p. 59).

Blind students were transferred away from the Columbia Institution in 1865. Following Gallaudet's success in founding an institution for advanced training for deaf students, Samuel Gridley Howe in 1869 called, unsuccessfully, for a national collegiate institute for blind persons. Nothing more of a substantial nature was done for the blind in higher education; they were admitted to and were successful in the regular universities. It could be surmised that the advent of materials in special alphabets and then Braille in 1892 accelerated this process.

The Clarke Institution and Oral Methodology

In the fifty years following the 1817 establishment of the American Asylum by Thomas Hopkins Gallaudet, the manual methods of Épée were used exclusively in American schools for deaf students. Energies in this period were directed to the development of established schools, the affirmation of support of social and financial leaders, and the consolidation of gains. Ideology, passed from one generation to the next, tended toward stratification, assertively resistant to change. The early educators exhibited an entrenched conservatism with regard to methodology, and they insistently promoted moral development as the essential tenet of instruction (see Chapter 6).

But even at this early period, when the policy of Thomas Hopkins Gallaudet was to pursue a single method at the expense of competing oral interests, deep tensions within the profession were making themselves felt. These tensions, though expressed in terms of communication, were in fact rooted in the ineradicable antagonisms between two divergent philosophies and their class bases.

The pedagogical issues were pertinent to wider social values; they implied the differing viewpoints held by oralists and manualists concerning the role of deaf persons in society.

Manualists perceived deafness as a human difference best accommodated through a unique language of signs; oralists, in contrast, viewed deafness as a handicap to be overcome and held that skill in speech and lipreading allowed deaf persons full access to normal society. The controversy consequently precipitated a debate not only over the techniques but also the purposes and content of education. As oral advocates challenged the traditional diligent adherence to manual modes of communication, the argument spilled over into diverse areas encompassing curriculum, teacher training, teacher associations, the freedom of those afflicted with deafness to marry and procreate, the status of deaf teachers of the deaf, and the gender of teachers.

The French methods of instruction, introduced by Thomas Hopkins Gallaudet in 1817, "remained undisturbed for fifty years" (A. G. Bell, 1897, p. 12). When oral advocates assaulted the ramparts of this entrenched pedagogical conservatism, they came not from the ranks of the profession, but from without. Attempting to demythologize the figure of Épée and explode the myth of manualism, the oralists faced a concerted and consolidated opposition that led inexorably to rising partisan passions and the bitter divisiveness that characterized the education of deaf people after 1867 (Winzer, 1991).

In 1844 Horace Mann and Samuel Gridley Howe toured European schools for the deaf. Mann's contentious *Seventh Annual Report,* written when he was secretary of the Massachusetts State Board of Education, lashed common-school education (see M. Katz, 1968, 1971) and included the barb that "institutions for the Deaf and Dumb in Prussia, Saxony and Holland are decidedly superior to any in this country" (H. Barnard, [1861b] 1969, p. 244). Mann and Howe thereafter diligently stirred up educational and public opposition to the manual methods, speaking consistently in support of the superior advantages of oralism. Not surprisingly, manualists resented the criticism, seeing it as a personal attack on their own characters and competence, and they resented the surrender of the manual autonomy to the pleas of those who would initiate oral education and oral schools. Thomas Hopkins Gallaudet, among many others, was prompted to reply with a spirited defense of the system adopted in 1817 (T. H. Gallaudet, 1844). Harvey Peet and other educators of the deaf themselves toured European schools and essentially denied Mann's contentions (Burnet, 1873; Currier, 1894).

Sporadic and haphazard calls for alternative schools employing oral approaches for deaf children crystallized in the person of Gardiner Greene Hubbard, a wealthy and influential Bostonian. When his four-year-old daughter Mabel was deafened by scarlet fever in 1862, Hubbard contacted Samuel Gridley Howe and Mrs. Horace Mann regarding Mabel's education by oral modes. At the same time Hubbard joined with Howe and Mann to disparage manual modes of communication and decry the mediocre intellectual products of manual education.

The agitation for an oral school was propelled not only by the urge to advance the philosophy of oralism but by the demands of Hubbard and other parents like him who held more than an intellectual stake in the ideology of educational reform. These parents were naturally concerned that their deaf children acquire the social graces and be able to speak and understand the speech of others in hearing society; it was equally undesirable, from these parents' point of view, that their children be able to converse manually with other deaf persons.

Deeply disturbed at the narrow social organizations that manualism allowed the deaf person to enter, Hubbard devised a solution based not only on an alternate communication methodology but on the creation of a distinct educational setting, patterned on middle-class family life (see Winzer, 1981b). The manifestations of respectability—social mobility, refined manners and taste, respectable religions, proper speech, and literacy—could be attained only through an education that paralleled, as far as possible, that of hearing children of the same social class. Hence, for Hubbard, the making of an oral school was intimately joined not only to the promotion of oral pedagogy but to a school population delineated clearly along class lines.

In pursuit of their goal, oral adherents devoted their energies to opposing fiercely the system of Gallaudet and to promoting ideals antithetical to his aims. Of those who were hostile to the manual system, none expressed their stance with more detail and clarity than Hubbard. When speaking of oralism, Hubbard equated oral approaches with emancipation for hearing-impaired children, or for some of them at least. He drew sharp distinctions between those who should be educated manually and those who should be taught orally, between those children who were deaf and those hard of hearing.

In response, manualists contended that "the logic of facts was entirely against the system of articulation" (Hubbard, 1876, p. 179) and that "the instruction of the deaf by articulation was a theory of visionary enthusiasts, which has been repeatedly tried and abandoned as impractical" (p. 179). William Wolcott Turner, principal of the American Asylum, stated flatly: "We can never make hearing and speaking persons of these deaf mutes" (De Land, 1906, p. 7).

Hubbard went before the Massachusetts legislature numerous times over a three-year period pleading for the establishment of an alternative school (Hubbard, 1876; "Dr. Gordon's report," 1899). Each time, he was defeated by the powerful opposition of the sign teachers. The manual schools, entrenched behind a rampart of vested interests, looked with suspicion and fear upon the advances of the oralists and, for a time, possessed sufficient determination to express and reinforce their will in respect to the crucial question of communication modes.

Until 1864 the advocates of sign controlled every avenue in Massachusetts leading to legislative or municipal action. When a bill regarding an oral school was defeated in that year, Hubbard suggested that taxes were being diverted; the charge was openly made that government funds given to the cause of deaf education were used to prevent the establishment of what would possibly become rival schools (De Land, 1905b). He failed to take into consideration an 1860 proposal by a group of deaf Bostonians for a Massachusetts school, undoubtedly manual, that was also rejected by the Massachusetts legislature ("The project," 1860).

Before Hubbard could obtain his oral school, it was necessary that the legislature be induced to abandon its support of a single manual method and be prepared to accept other pedagogies. What inspired legislative acceptance was an alliance of rich and powerful spokesmen, joined to provide proof of the successful results of oral instruction. It was the voice of Horace Mann, with his report of the achievements of European institutions tucked under his arm; of Gardiner Greene Hubbard, dismayed by the mediocre intellectual products of American schools for the deaf; of Samuel Gridley Howe, peddling the notion that oralism held the key to extended opportunities for the deaf (Howe, 1866c); and Harriet Burbank Rogers and her inspired and innovative instruction that finally persuaded the state's officialdom to invest financially and socially in the elaboration of a novel institution for deaf children.

In 1864 Harriet Rogers (1834–1919) opened a small private oral school in Chelmsford, Massachusetts. In this school Hubbard finally found a convincing argument in favor of his plan. Hubbard and Rogers met in 1865 and Hubbard arranged further funds to underwrite the school at Chelmsford. Still seeking official support, Hubbard then sponsored demonstrations for Miss Rogers, to which she invited the mayor, the governor, members of the legislature, and the press. By far the most telling exhibitions were those presented before the Special Joint Committee on Oral Schools ("Proceedings" 1899, p. 55). In 1867 eight-year-old Mabel Hubbard appeared before the committee and "confounded the doubters" (R. Bruce, 1973, p. 86). At the same time, John Clarke, a wealthy Northampton merchant, gave a $50,000 endowment and, in his will, made the institution his residuary legatee (Clarke Institution, 1870). In June 1867 two bills passed the House, one allowing the incorporation of the Clarke Institution for Deaf Mutes, the other the provision of state funds to educate deaf children from five years of age, for ten years (Numbers, 1974).

From the outset the officers and directors of the Clarke Institution constituted a distinguished succession. Alexander Graham Bell, for example, was elected a trustee and later the fifth president of the board of directors. Other members of the board included Franklin Benjamin Sanborn, one of the Concord group of philosophers; Samuel Gridley Howe; Horace Mann; and G. Stanley Hall, president of Clark University and first president of the American Psychological Association.

Not only would the Clarke Institution teach deaf children exclusively by oral methods but it was more aligned to the public schools. Whereas the manual schools generally restricted admittance to children over the age of ten, Clarke took children between five and ten years of age. It also lengthened the time of instruction to ten years, and the school was placed directly under the direction of the Massachusetts Board of Education (Clarke Institution, 1868).

Hubbard envisoned a school for children who had lost their hearing after the age of three; originally the Clarke Institution "was adapted for the instruction of semi-deaf and semi-mute pupils, although others may be admitted" (Clarke Institution, 1873, p. 8). To provide hard-of-hearing children with extended auditory skills would have served Hubbard's unwritten goal of emancipation; it was the application of oral methodologies for deaf children that proved such a contentious issue.

Wittingly or unwittingly, Hubbard also defined a class base for oral education. Certainly, his prejudices were genteel: his opinions of the poor reflected widely held views. When addressing the Massachusetts Special Joint Committee on Oral Schools in 1867, Hubbard commented that "if a child were of poor parents, I should not attempt articulation," suggesting that indigent pupils be sent to the American Asylum at Hartford (J. Williams, 1891, p. 119).

The Clarke Institution brought a new dogma to the education of deaf children. Pedagogy was the cornerstone on which philosophy rested: speech and lipreading skills were intended to emancipate deaf children from the linguistic and social shackles of deafness and made them as like normally hearing individuals as possible. Setting also distinguished Clarke from the traditional institutions. Clarke was conceived on a familial model; familial metaphors were used to describe it. In the belief that the ideals of a Christian family could never be approximated in a large residential institution, Clarke attempted to provide a model environment in which teachers would assume the roles of surrogate mothers as they exercised their skills as pedagogues. Clarke became female oriented and matriarchial in tone, appropriately analogous to middle-class family life (Winzer, 1981b). Institutional characteristics were deemphasized, replaced by a familial ambience; the whole was conceived as a model family where "the domestic regime resembled that of a large, well-regulated private family" (Numbers, 1974, p. 311). In contrast, the manual schools were masculine, strictly regimented, and institutionalized; as late as 1936, "pupils went around like prisoners in striped clothes" (Pollack, 1970, p. iv).

The formation of the Clarke Institution and the National Deaf Mute College precipitated a debate not only on the techniques but also on the progress and content of the education of deaf children. From their founding onward, partisan passions divided the profession of deaf education. Educators were forced to confront their ideas critically, to rationalize the advantages of their preferred system of communication. Pursuing different avenues toward the general goal of the intellectual and social development of deaf persons, teachers divided themselves into opposing camps of oralists and manualists. Each side in the debate asserted that the techniques of the other would not produce the development necessary to allow the full moral, social, and intellectual development of deaf individuals. Yet, though many educators rejected the tenet that speech was vital to the increased social mobility of a deaf person, all enlisted in the mounting campaign to redesignate schools under departments of education and to divorce them from the pejorative connotations of their being categorized as schools for paupers and charity recipients.

The Clarke school became a convincing argument in favor of oralism. The institution of other oral schools rapidly followed. In 1864 the Lexington School for the Deaf, a private oral school, opened in New York, clearly delineating its mandate by renaming itself the Institution for the Improved Instruction of the Deaf and Dumb three years later. Boston in 1869 witnessed the opening of the Boston Day School, renamed the Horace Mann School in 1877.

Oralists propounded views that decisively altered the views of legislators. Those flying the oral banner rapidly came to dominate the profession. By 1880 eleven oral schools were in operation, and in 1882, 9 percent of American deaf children were being taught by oral methods (Bell and Gillett, 1884). By 1893 the ratio rose to 24.7 percent, and ten years later it was 48.4 percent (Ontario, Dept. of Ed., 1907).

Institutions for Mentally Retarded Persons, 1860 to 1900

The field of mental retardation witnessed extraordinary institutional expansion in the latter half of the nineteenth century. Diverse facilities serving

Box 4-1

Caroline Ardelia Yale (1848–1933)

Oralism was an educational reform initiated and brought to dominance by female teachers. Women teachers played significant roles in shaping the lives of deaf persons, as organizers and supporters of the campaign for the adoption of the oral system. Within the institutional network and in the public sphere, women ventured to dispute the traditional pedagogical practices of experienced male educators, the ferment on communication modes revealing most clearly their differing aspirations and anxieties concerning their pupils. Women spoke out widely, challenging the trenchant conservatism of the manualists not only with regard to pedagogy but concerning the entire value and content of the education of the deaf. Every aspect of schooling, from administration to pedagogy, from finance to the sex of teachers, was examined and transformed by the oralists; everything that was explicitly related to the myth that deaf children could learn the elements of language only by manual means came under fire.

As they formed a community of articulate educational innovators, women became the carriers of a new professional ideal. Oral teachers placed an unprecedented emphasis on academic claims; in their view intellectual development superseded the inculcation of moral values. Attempting to win elite status for their students, the oral teachers defined their status claims in such a way as to place more emphasis upon academic achievement and institutional affiliation, less upon defining deafness as a characteristic, and almost none on industrial training. The oralists' reforms in curriculum led to the imposition of rigorous standards and greatly heightened expectations of the intellectual capacities of deaf students. Not only did the oralist women teach academic skills, they emphasized values that encouraged and enabled students to attempt public roles not previously thought consonant with their handicaps.

Although Harriet Rogers actually founded the Clarke Institution (Yale, 1920), the woman who emerged as the institutional leader of the oral movement was Caroline Yale. She was only twenty-two years old when she came to Clarke, after having spent two years at Mount Holyoke Seminary and some time teaching in her native Vermont (Nielson, 1934). For sixteen years Yale taught under Harriet B. Rogers, the first principal; for thirty-six years she was herself principal. For another eleven years she was principal emeritus and director of the Normal Department.

Yale approached each child as a unique individual. Although she herself was a staunch Congregationalist, for example, Yale prepared Roman Catholic children for their first communion, she taught Jewish students about their prophets and the Psalms, and she taught Protestants about their religion ("Caroline," 1934).

In addition to her work at the Clarke Institution, Caroline Yale served on the executive board of the American Association to Promote the Teaching of Speech to the Deaf. She was a part-time lecturer in phonetics at Smith College, was for twenty-five years a member of the Northampton school board, for thirty-one years a trustee of the Northampton Hospital for the Insane, and for several years a trustee of the Massachusetts Institution for the Feeble-Minded ("Caroline," 1934).

Three institutions conferred honorary degrees on Yale. She received a doctorate of laws from Illinois Wesleyan University in 1896, a doctorate of humane letters from Smith College in 1910, and a doctorate of laws from Mount Holyoke in 1927 ("Caroline," 1934).

---

different clienteles arose; some were devoted to adult males, others to adult females or epileptic patients, and some to children only.

By the 1870s custodial facilities were being built. The new institutions would function not only to protect the mentally retarded but also to control them in order to protect the community. States also began to provide specialized facilities for epileptics and women, where residents were given useful and remunerative occupations (U.S., Dept. of Labor, 1915). In 1879, for example, New York created an experimental custodial asylum for feebleminded women of childbearing age at Newark as a colony of the Syracuse Asylum. The purpose was twofold: to determine whether there were feebleminded women in county poorhouses or elsewhere who needed care and protection to prevent them from bearing children and so increasing the number of dependent classes in the state, and to discover if they could be maintained without undue cost (New York State Asylum for Feeble-Minded Women, 1893; see Taylor and Searl, 1987). Because in asylums for the insane, epileptics "steadily deteriorated in moral and mental condition" (Vineland, 1896, p. 34), by the 1890s many states began to establish hospitals and homes specifically for sufferers of epilepsy (Vineland, 1896).

Residential institutions to accommodate adult retarded persons grew apace: by 1876 thirty-four states had institutions for retarded adults accommodating approximately twenty-five thousand persons (Thurston, 1876; U.S. Dept of Labor, 1915). In that year, for example, there were more than three thousand inmates in both the New York and the Pennsylvania institutions. By 1888 fourteen states had institutions that admitted mentally defective children (Davies, 1959), and Hervey P. Wilbur estimated that there were four thousand minors who were residents of state and private institutions for retarded children (Rosen, Clark, and Kivitz, 1976). The buildings and grounds in use for all institutionalized persons with mental retardation cost, in round figures, more than $3 million, and more than a thousand persons were employed as officers, teachers, domestics, and in other occupations connected with the care of the buildings and grounds. The annual expense of their tuition, shelter, support, and maintenance was about $800,000 (Rosen, Clark, and Kivitz, 1976).

Of course, not the entire population of persons considered to be mentally retarded was institutionalized; they were still often committed to state institutions such as prisons, reformatories, county training schools, and city and town almshouses (League, 1916). As late as 1915, for example, of 1,338 inmates in 160 Massachusetts almshouses, 138 were blind and 9 were blind and mentally retarded (League, 1916).

Mid-nineteenth-century Americans imported, along with Édouard Seguin's training-school model, a general optimism regarding the rehabilitative prospects for mentally retarded persons. However, as the century drew to a close, rigid thinking about retardation in mental development became more and more apparent, and, as it did, institutional conditions declined (Tyor, 1977). The training-school or asylum model, which came to the United States along with a host of European educators, gradually ceded to the custodial institution. Promoters now asserted that "those who were mentally subnormal must be guarded and cared for as children" (Vineland, 1903, p. 15), and care predominated over education.

Public support diminished. A commission sent out to check into the condition of the feebleminded in Connecticut found that the majority of citizens thought the work to be "a waste of time" (Barr, [1904b] 1913, p. 70). At the Orillia Institution in Ontario the school program almost closed in 1896 as a result of public criticisms regarding the cost and futility of "education for idiots" (Hackett, 1969).

The advocates of institutionalization called for separate asylums for idiots that could be run on a more economical basis than could be accomplished within institutions that combined people with many different needs and disorders. They also suggested the use of farm colonies, a concept pioneered by Walter E. Fernald in Massachusetts, who established Templeton Colony in 1900 for forty-seven boys, where workers trained in another institution could maintain themselves productively and relieve the overcrowding at the institutions from which they came.

The institution for mentally retarded persons founded by Samuel Gridley Howe in 1848 illustrates the trend. The school was made a permanent enterprise in 1851 and incorporated in 1858 as the Massachusetts Institution for Idiots and moved to Waverley, Massachusetts. In 1883 the name was changed to the Massachusetts School for the Feeble-Minded. In that year a custodial wing was added. At the outset Howe, who was able to create a school that matched his philosophy, set strict parameters on clientele and expectations. He demanded that the original enterprise be a small school, with minimal regimentation and admission initiated by parents or guardians. Students older than sixteen were not admitted, nor were those who showed no promise of improvement. All students were to return home in the summer, and the full course of schooling would be six or seven years.

By the early 1880s parents and public officials were demanding wider access in terms of client age and condition. At the same time the state's appropriations ceased (Zainaldin and Tyor, 1979). Inevitably the trustees bowed to political and financial pressures, altering the mandate of the institution to such an extent that in 1885 they ruefully admitted: "The character of our institution is rapidly changing from that of a school to that of an asylum" (Massachusetts Institution, 1885, p. 23).

Walter Fernald, who assumed the superintendency in 1887, ratified the process even if he did not accelerate it. Fernald, a physician, came to the Massachusetts Institution at Waverley after five years as assistant superintendent of a Wisconsin mental hospital and brought with him philosophical underpinnings at odds with those of Howe. Whereas Howe viewed the failure to uplift and educate mentally retarded persons as morally offensive, Fernald held it to be dangerous. Subtly, the service clientele changed: now it was society, not the mentally retarded individual, who was being served (Zainaldin and Tyor, 1979). Under Fernald's tutelage numbers increased dramatically; by 1913 the Massachusetts Institution at Waverley and the associated Templeton Farm Colony served 1,500 inmates (see Fernald, 1903, 1919b, 1919c).

As schools for the mentally retarded generally assumed a more custodial character, daily routines became more regimented and a stress on manual training superseded any academic curriculum. There was a move to finance these institutions through inmate labor (see Chapter 6). With client labor, institutions became self-sufficient, with their own power plants, gardens, and farms. Uniforms were instituted for staff and residents, and there had been successful attempts to abolish the annual vacation in June and July and to extend the mandatory school-leaving age of sixteen or eighteen (Tyor, 1977). From school programs, inmates could move into adult institutions where lifelong segregation was often promoted. Once the inmates were committed to an institution, discharge became problematic; some inmates were allowed to return to conscientious parents; others ran away. When institutional staff disputed a discharge, cases would be brought before the courts for settlement.

By the turn of the century the institutions for mentally handicapped persons typically were divided into two departments—educational and custodial. The latter departments included idiots, the juvenile insane, and epileptics. Some of the children here were described as "helpless as infants"; others were "excitable and noisy with marked destructive tendencies" (Vineland, 1893).

The Institution at Vineland

In terms of the future course of special education, one of the most important institutions to develop in the later nineteenth century was the New Jersey Training School for Feeble-Minded Boys and Girls at Vineland. The schools provided leadership in programming and especially in teacher training. Vineland staff members included such leaders in the field as Henry Herbert Goddard and Edgar A. Doll. Among its many contributions to special education were the very important Vineland Social Maturity Scale, the first measurement of adaptive behavior (Doll, 1965), and the *Training School Bulletin,* a small but excellent journal. The school, founded by Professor S. Ohn Garrison (1853–1900), was incorporated on June 6, 1888, as an institution for white children only. Garrison modeled the facility after the organization of the Pennsylvania School for the Feeble-Minded at Elwyn, which by the mid-1880s had nearly a thousand inmates (Vineland, 1895).

Garrison started his school on $2,000 in a private home in Millville, New Jersey. Because it was founded as a private school, Vineland originally functioned on cash donations; Garrison worked without salary for the first six months, while the first teacher received $8 a month (Vernon, 1942). Until 1942 clients were charged $100 a month. Garrison opened with a school, kindergarten, and industrial department. Children lived in cottages; the Seguin and Itard cottages opened in 1890, the same year as a new building for epileptic and custodial children.

From Vineland grew the State Home for Feeble-Minded Women and the State Village for Epileptics. At the same time Garrison's work lent impetus to the emergence of similar institutions in Colorado, Oregon, and California (Vineland, 1908).

THE ISSUES SURROUNDING INSTITUTIONS AND INSTITUTIONALIZATION

The Burdens of Institutionalization

Throughout the nineteenth century increasing numbers of exceptional students were being educated within an institutional milieu. The educational efficiency and the ability to control costs that institutionalization made possible were clear gains that encouraged the spread of the institutions for exceptional persons. Moreover, as the curricula and pedagogical methods of the special schools developed, their divergence from those of the general public schools became increasingly apparent. This in turn reinforced the public perception of the qualitative differences between the normal and the handicapped or exceptional individual, a process that made the special schools and institutions seem all the more necessary. However, increased institutionalization also increased the isolation from the rest of society of those who were served by the institutions. Thus, ironically, they posed new problems even as they solved others.

Originally philanthropic enterprises, many institutions came under official control by midcentury; states began to assume partial or full responsibility for institutional costs and management, bureaucracy replaced philanthropy as the organizational mode, and there developed an increasing conception of the institutions as public enterprises—*public* implying service to a nonexclusive clientele with entrance dictated solely by disability.

As components of the complex of charity institutions, not part of the regular school system, the institutions were administered by state boards of charity in the United States and by departments of prisons, asylums, and public charities in Canada. Superintendents, especially those of institutions designed to serve deaf and blind students, fought the charity designation. Deaf and blind students, they complained bitterly, were "officially classed, and therefore always associated in the public mind, with the criminal incorrigibles and mentally defective classes" (OSD, 1895, p. 234). This, together with the connotations of charity, constituted severe detriments to the future status of the pupils: they instilled in the public mind the notion that people handicapped in these ways are deviant and dependent, an idea that educators were trying so hard to eradicate.

In the final three decades of the nineteenth century the issue of institutional designation became a major issue. It was an obsessive concern at which superintendents hammered away week after week and year after year, denouncing the pernicious effects of such discrimination.

Lobbying for Universal Education for Exceptional Students

In the United States school law has been centered on local school districts from the early days. The original federal Constitution delegated all school matters to the states. Subsequent amendments to the Constitution also avoided any direct federal assumption of school authority or responsibility; this obligation was left to the states and whatever school entity they chose to provide for public

education (Melcher, 1976). Constitutions in each of the states provided the
mechanisms under which free public education would be provided, although
the states varied markedly in the manner in which they carried out this prerog-
ative (Melcher, 1976). In Canada the British North America Act of 1867 assigned
the responsibility for education solely to the provinces, with no federal centralization (see McHenry, 1881).

Many of the early state constitutions in the United States spoke freely and
somewhat loosely about guaranteeing free public education to all children
(Melcher, 1976), but as far as exceptional children were concerned, the ethic of
universal provision was an elusive dream. The same could be said for Canada.
In both countries the drive toward universal education for exceptional youngsters began in about 1880; promoters of the idea mounted increasing pressure
on public officials to provide free and compulsory education for deaf, blind, and
mentally retarded students under educational, rather than charitable, designations (see H. Best, 1930).

The superintendents of the existing institutions, under pressure to use public funds parsimoniously, battling the negative connotations of running charities, and coping with the difficulties inherent in an abbreviated length of
schooling, became constantly preoccupied by enrollment and attendance. Professional educators denounced the social-welfare mentality and mode of operations. They viewed the categorizing of "destitute orphans, abandoned children,
vagrant and vicious children and youth; the blind ... paupers" (Massachusetts
State Board of Charities, 1886, p. 29), and other handicapped groups as charity
recipients as being incongruous with the goals of education. In one of the earliest attacks on the system Samuel Gridley Howe wrote in 1839: "We do not consider blind children as mere objects of charity, but as members of the rising
generation, whose claims upon us for an education are the strongest of nature,
and not to be resisted upon the ground of difficulty or expense. We have too
great confidence in the faculties of the human mind—too much reliance on the
powers of the human intellect—to admit that the deprivation of a bodily organ
can destroy or repress them" (Perkins Inst., 1839, p. 80). Howe further believed
that blind children deserved "equal participation in the blessing of education
with seeing children."

Others haltingly adopted Howe's stance; by the 1880s issues concerning new
designations for the institutions, increased length of school time, increased enrollment and attendance, and free and compulsory education for all exceptional
children were widely articulated. School officials asked for power to seek municipal and state conformity to fees for institutionalized children, that is, that
municipalities and states not be allowed to change or withhold appropriations.
The school officials also made vigorous efforts to interpret the work for the public and embarked on campaigns to round up pupils. They used their annual
reports to express their views unequivocally, to present their growing disillusionment, and to explore the weaknesses of the system (Winzer, 1981a).

The high cost of educating institutionalized populations was the leading
concern of those who resisted the efforts of the institutions' proponents; the
concept of compulsory attendance was a closely allied issue the educators repeatedly had to defend. On the whole, the special educators fought for altered
designations in the belief that once the negative connotations were swept away

Table 4-1

The Costs of Attendance and the Number of State-Supported
Students at Selected Schools for Deaf Persons, 1866

School	Cost $	Total Enrollment	State-Supported Students
Connecticut (American Asylum)	100	228	211
New York	150	315	225
Pennsylvania	140	173	143
Kentucky	105	75	67
Ohio	100	155	153
Virginia	130	41	—
Indiana	100	153	147
Tennessee	130	61	60
North Carolina	—	45	—
Illinois	100	115	115
Georgia	175	45	35
South Carolina	150	24	21
Mississippi	100	84	75
Wisconsin	100	41	41

SOURCES: various reports in AADD, OSD.

and exceptional pupils were viewed simply as school children, resistance to the provision of free and compulsory education for them would be much reduced.

Free Schooling for Exceptional Students

At the outset the institutions for exceptional students were generally not free, as were the common schools, nor was institutional life cheap. At the Catholic Institution for the Deaf and Dumb in Montreal, for example, tuition and board in the 1880s came to $200, with washing, bed and bedding, and physician's fees accounting for another $17 for one year (Montreal Catholic, [1885]). During the same period the MacKay Institution in the same city charged children from Quebec $250 and those from other provinces $300 a year (MacKay, [1880]). In the United States in the 1860s schools for the deaf charged annual fees of $100 to $200, although states were increasingly assuming the costs for individual pupils (see Table 4-1).

Because many potential students for these institutions came from middle- or low-income families, and attendance was not always free, school administrators first attacked the legislative ramparts in quest of free education, a key part of their effort to gain equal educational rights for exceptional students. From 1817 on there was a gradual, albeit halting, advance toward official sponsorship of special institutions and away from private benevolence. Yet unanticipated subversions of reform promises to accommodate all special students ensued, often the result simply of lack of financial aid. At the state level, funding remained woefully inadequate throughout the century; although some states responded liberally, others were less generous.

In 1857, for example, the Virginia Institution for the Deaf and Dumb and Blind was "utterly unequal to the education of more than half of those for whom it was intended" ("Notices," 1857, p. 123); in Ohio "not more than one-half of the deaf-mutes of suitable age in the State" could gain an education (p. 124) The Indiana legislature adjourned in 1857 without passing the appropriation bills for the institution for the deaf, which consequently had to suspend services for six months (p. 125). By 1872, of the forty schools for deaf persons in the United States, twenty-five were free to all the pupils who resided in the state, eleven were free to parents who were certified unable to pay, and in four students were supported by their home counties (OSD, 1872). As of 1880 schooling for the deaf and the blind was not free in Massachusetts, although it was in Illinois, Ohio, Kentucky, and Nova Scotia (Dudley, 1880).

The promoters of special schools recognized that full support would come only after the effectiveness of the schools was proven. Officialdom required evidence of the success of a venture before guaranteeing aid, so the schools' hopes for survival rested on their ability to clarify their purposes, identify potential students, and use any success, however modest, to reinforce their image.

To identify and locate potential clients, the schools' officials sent out streams of letters, circulars, and questionnaires to public school inspectors, county clerks, newspapers, religious leaders, members of congresses, wardens and clerks, and other interested persons. Occasionally they tried to canvass census reports to locate potential students. Principals and teachers spent their summers visiting the parents of pupils, identifying prospective places of employment for graduates, and locating new students. They were often accompanied by current pupils, who presented exhibitions and demonstrations in small towns and villages. J. Scott Hutton of Halifax, for example, traveled 11,000 miles over a period of twenty years, held between three hundred and four hundred public meetings, and collected $9,000 (McGann, 1888). During the summer of 1875 Mr. Brown, a teacher of the blind in Ontario, traveled more than two thousand miles throughout the eastern part of the province, including eight hundred miles on foot, visiting the families of blind children. On his return to the school Mr. Brown, quite understandably, felt "jaded and emaciated" and after only two weeks "fell an easy victim to typhoid fever" (Ontario, *Sessional Papers,* 1875, pp. 257–58).

Some promoters argued that many parents would not send their children to an institution "if it were entirely free, and had the character of a pauper establishment" (OSD, 1875, p. 6). "No degredation attaches to a free education by the State" (p. 6) countered others, who demanded that sufficient funds be made available to allow people of all classes to avail themselves of education and called for the enactment of legislation requiring public payment of the costs.

As free schooling became the norm for nonexceptional children, many jurisdictions also assumed the costs of housing and educating their institutionalized blind, deaf, and mentally retarded populations. By the turn of the century fiscal considerations were no longer a source of controversy. The abatement of the free education issue did not, however, hinder the desire of special educators to duplicate for special children the range of educational privileges available to the nonhandicapped (see Chapter 11).

Who Went to School?

A key criterion for the success of schooling is the percentage of school-age children enrolled and in classes, for clearly, if schools are to work, everyone has to attend. School enrollment indicates the recognition by parents or guardians that schooling is socially, economically, or intellectually advantageous; rates of attendance indicate how determined parents are to pursue it.

Throughout much of the nineteenth century only the middle class responded to the public schools. Even though all the states gradually enacted compulsory attendance laws and were legally empowered to compel all children to attend, attendance rates were often distressingly low. Public apathy, parental recalcitrance, and the general laissez-faire attitude of society all contributed to the low rates. Irregular attendance in the public schools remained a persistent feature long after enrollments of school-age children approached universality and attendance was made compulsory.

It was not until the 1880s that the truancy laws began to be seriously enforced (see Chapter 11). Pressures on children to attend school and families to send them gained impetus from legislation in the area of child welfare and protection, new labor codes, and the emergence of the nemesis of all recalcitrant students—the attendance or truant officer (see Tyack and Berkowitz, 1977).

Depressed enrollments and nonattendance problems were not confined to the regular child population; they plagued the institutions for exceptional children as well. Although the numbers of pupils attending these institutions increased steadily after 1817, nowhere were all children who required assistance actually enrolled in some form of schooling. Even when students enrolled in the institutions, school officials were appalled when each session witnessed a substantial number of nonreturnees, a high number because of poverty. Economic trends consistently affected institutional enrollments; in periods when the United States and Canada had a shortage of labor and high wages, for example, the rates of nonreturnees rose alarmingly (OSD, 1905).

When the Ohio Institution for the Deaf opened in 1829, for example, only three pupils from the immediate vicinity attended, despite the fact that a circular "stating the objects of the school, had been published for some months previously in the principal papers of the State" (Stone, 1853, p. 229). In 1859 in Wisconsin only about half of the eligible students enrolled for instruction ("Reports," 1860, p. 175). Similarly, school officials in Indiana mourned that there were "a large number of suitable subjects for admission to the Institution, females particularly, who have not yet availed themselves of the privilege" (p. 173). By 1880 only about 33 percent of all eligible deaf children had attended school; even by 1907 the U.S. census showed a deaf population of 89,287, of whom only 33 percent had never been to school (Ontario, Dept. of Ed., 1905). The Oregon School for the Blind opened in 1873 but soon shut down and remained closed for four years because of the lack of both pupils and funds (Koestler, 1976). In 1883 there were 2,314 feebleminded children reported in Iowa, of whom 960, more than one-third, were kept at home (Iowa Inst., 1883).

The relative ubiquity of irregular attendance and low enrollments of children from all social and economic backgrounds cannot be explained simply by illness or the presence of a disabling condition. Rather, a complex of demographic, cultural, and economic variables combined to determine school enrollment and subsequent attendance for both normal children and those with special needs. Persistent irregular attendance went hand-in-hand with industrialization, urbanization, transience, and the periodic economic dislocations that pushed many families into destitution. Noncompliance with attendance laws must be viewed in light of the contemporary demands of the labor market, the ages and genders of members of the family, and the strongly asserted rights of parents to maintain their customary control over their children's time.

Moreover, contemporary medical and etiological emphases affected school attendance for exceptional pupils in two ways. First, they were generally excluded from the public schools because of their disabilities, and, second, handicaps were often equated with illness, in which case compulsory attendance laws did not apply (see Chapter 10). Still, the economic status of the family, its need for the child's economic contribution, and parents' decisions and protectiveness must not be discounted.

In many families the distance between the demands of childhood and the demands of poverty were often unbridgeable. In a setting where the survival of many poorer families depended on the labor of all members, including the children, the nature and availability of employment for children became one of the most important factors determining school attendance. Lower-class families often depended not only on the wages the children might earn but also on the chores they commonly performed: gathering coal, wood, or water, tending animals, or working in the home or garden. Sometimes children were needed to watch over younger siblings, thus freeing mothers for wage work. Many youngsters labored in sweatshops—tiny workplaces, sometimes in a converted living room or bedroom, where a predominantly female and child labor force worked long hours producing materials for large retail or wholesale outlets such as the ready-made clothing industry. In addition, some children preferred work to school. Finally, in the cases of disabled children, some parents simply would not part with their special child.

For many nineteenth-century children, disabled or not, being a pupil was part of growing up, but it was not the primary goal. School was something to be fitted in with the other needs of the family—the work of the farm, the workshop, or the home. No amount of legislation could improve this situation as long as school inspectors and lawmakers failed to recognize the importance of children's work in the home and beyond it.

Such subtle points were lost on the promoters of the special schools, who railed against what they interpreted as parental perfidy. Nineteenth-century educators and reformers pointed to the spiritual and moral inferiority of the poor, and they rained a veritable storm of criticism on the heads of parents who would not, or could not, conform to middle-class notions of education, morality, and hygiene. Those who were not only poor but also parents of a disabled child were even more likely to be castigated as immoral and uncaring (Taylor and Searl, 1987). Institutional officers maintained an evangelical ideal of moral and spiritual regeneration for their pupils and disparaged the "criminal cupidity" of parents who, they said, seemed to attach a higher value to the manual labor of their children than they did to their education and moral improvement. In attempting to raise school enrollments, institutional educators focused on the child's needs as separate from the pressing needs of the family. "The only question that enlightened parental love should ask," chided one commentator, "is, what will be the most agreeable to my unfortunate child, what will be best for him?" (Keep, 1867, p. 13).

When educators did look at the family as a whole, they tended to assume that home care for a disabled child was inimical to parental serenity. Walter Fernald, superintendent of the Massachusetts Institution for the Feeble-Minded and Idiotic, spoke feelingly of "countless loving mothers [who] have been worried into nervous breakdowns or insanity, or an untimely grave by the ceaseless anxiety and sorrow caused by the presence of a blighted child in the home. Many fathers have been driven to drink, sons to the 'gang' and daughters to the streets to get away from the unnatural and intolerable home conditions caused by the defective one" (1904, p. 27).

Probably few of the students had the degraded and uncaring parents portrayed by social reformers. But many potential institutional pupils did come from poorer families, and, apart from the necessity of children's work, many parents could not defray the costs of schooling. At the opening of the Tennessee Institution for the Deaf and Dumb in 1854, not a single pupil appeared on opening day because "the parents of such pupils were generally in such indigent circumstances, that they were unable to bear even the small expense necessary for the board and tuition of their unfortunate children" (Scott, 1857, p. 118). Similarly, Ontario officials reported that about half of the parents of deaf children were in such poor circumstances that they could not afford the costs of board and travel (OSD, 1871).

Nevertheless, given that disabled students were seen as charity recipients, the route to state sponsorship was often humiliating to parents already stigmatized by their poverty and the official and public perceptions of their disabled offspring. Parents who could not afford the annual fee levied by many of the institutions found that they could enroll their child in an institution only if they obtained a certificate of poverty (_AADD_, 1859, p. 123). Many parents, whether from pride or from sensitivity to their condition, were reluctant to approach welfare agencies for support and were then labeled as irresponsible for shunning the special schools.

Public parsimony and the needs of the family were not the sole factors contributing to low enrollments and depressed attendance rates; parental apathy and recalcitrance also contributed to the problem. Often, parents regarded the special child as requiring the utmost watchfulness and care, and they could not be persuaded to let it out of their sight (OSD, 1880, p. 29). "Parents," chided Howe, "absolutely smother the facilities of a blind child in kindnesses" (Perkins Inst., 1836). Some parents would not part with their children in the belief they would be subjected to neglect or treated cruelly (Scott, 1857); others viewed institutional promoters as suspicious characters "trying to spirit away their child for some mercenary motive" (Pybas, 1909, pp. 358–59). One teacher of blind youngsters ruefully reported, "Some mothers seem to imagine me a sort of sharper who only needed the assistance of their sightless children to complete my fortune" (Ontario, *Sessional Papers,* 1874, pp. 200–201).

Parents often looked for a flaw in the diagnosis (Vineland, 1912); others refused to accept the possibility that their child was defective. Workers were advised to gloss over the terms and "call him 'atypical'" but to persuade the parents that "the weaklings require special care" ("Defective," 1915, p. 4).

The handicapped children who were kept at home were more often the girls (Hollingworth, 1913). As Edward Fay (1890) explained, there existed "a degree of popular indifference to female education; the greater sensitiveness of the sex itself, and a greater parental solicitude for the security of daughters away from home" (pp. 230–31). Further, women were said to "belong to a non-competitive and dependent class" and therefore "are not so readily recognized as defective since they do not have to compete mentally to maintain themselves in the social milieu" (Hollingworth, 1913, p. 753). Hesitancy about institutionalization more often affected deaf or blind girls. Girls suffering mental retardation tended to enter the institutions earlier and be retained longer than girls with other handicaps (Tyor, 1977), largely because of the fears for their sexual safety at large in the community.

The Length of Schooling

Even when they attended institutions, nineteenth-century exceptional students experienced an abbreviated length of schooling. At the outset, the American Asylum at Hartford admitted students for four years which, given the temper of the times and the public ambivalence that surrounded the enterprise, was, as one commentator observed, "as much, perhaps, as they ought to expect from the public bounty" (*American Journal of Education,* 1826, p. 631). Education for blind persons lasted at first only for three or four years, sometimes only two. By midcentury, as institutional arrangements proved their effectiveness, the length of schooling was extended so that institutions offered programs of five to seven years. Length gradually increased, and most institutions for deaf and for blind students provided as much as ten to twelve years of schooling by 1900. For mentally retarded students institutionalization often implied an almost permanent placement, with graduates of the school venue simply moving to an adult institutional milieu.

Early special education catered to discrete age groups. Schooling was not designed for young children. The public schools catered to children from seven or eight years of age and up; disabled youngsters, because of the perceived dangers in sending them from home and the demands of the curriculum, were admitted much later.

In the schools for blind children the lower limit on admittance was frequently set at ten or twelve years of age (H. Best, 1934). It was generally the same for deaf students. However, owing to the difference that was thought to exist between the sexes as to the development of intellect, it was suggested that boys be admitted at twelve years of age, girls at ten (Convention of Instructors, 1850; W. W. Turner, 1852b). For mentally retarded students, admission seemed to come later. The average admission age between 1851 and 1919 was 15.1 years

(Tyor, 1977). The mean age of admission between 1850 and 1860 was 10.8 years; by 1910 this had risen to 15.8 years (Tyor, 1977).

Because schooling for special populations was a new enterprise, institutions in their early years took in a relatively large number of adult clients. The American Asylum opened in 1817 and in the beginning the average age of pupils was twenty-two. The Ontario Institution, established in 1870, recorded similar statistics in 1879: about 7 percent of the student population was between the ages of twenty-one and forty. In the schools for blind students, people were allowed to remain up to their thirtieth birthday (H. Best, 1934).

The adults' attendance at school was voluntary and is a fair indicator of the most pressing need of disabled lads—getting a job and keeping it. Some adults were early school leavers who wanted more skills for the workplace; others had never before been offered the opportunity for education and training. When students were admitted for upgrading in the trades, they received no wages for their work but were given free room and board.

On the other hand, education of very young children was incompatible with the usual school program. Educators saw early adolescence, not early childhood, as the formative years for both normal and exceptional populations. It should be noted that this philosophy followed an initial period of growth in early childhood education. Infant schools were introduced in the 1820s (Hewes, 1989), and by the late 1820s infant schools could be found in "all principal cities and towns" of the North American seaboard as well as in Halifax and Montreal (W. Russell, 1829). By 1842 most of these were closed or had been phased into primary classes (Hewes, 1989). Early childhood education returned in the 1870s and 1880s with a widening of the original mission (Taylor Allen, 1986). Development of preschool programs tended to be independent of the public schools and arose out of the work of individual teachers, mostly women (Hewes, 1989).

Barbara Finkelstein (1985) reports that between 1830 and 1860 a veritable outpouring of opposition to premature mental exertion suffused the literature of domestic advice, the reports of educational administrators, the rhetoric of reformers, and the pages of professional educational journals (Finkelstein, 1985). Most agreed that a commitment to mental discipline was inappropriate for children under the ages of six or seven. Parents who taught young children exposed them to developing "a fatal langor resulting from premature mental exertion" (Finkelstein, 1985, pp. 6–7). State officials, medical spokesmen, and school officials were thus led to discourage the attendance of very young children at school in the belief that school was physically, psychologically, and intellectually harmful to children younger than five or six years of age. By 1860 the assumption that very young children, from birth to six or thereabouts, should be enclosed in domestic and private rather than impersonal environments became codified both in law and practice: school laws excluded children under the age of five (Finkelstein, 1985).

Such philosophies were readily applied to special education. "It is well understood," said one teacher, "that hearing and speaking pupils acquire information more readily between the ages of 10 and 19 than at any other period, and the same conclusions may by arrived at in regard to deaf and dumb children" (OSD, 1882, p. 11) and, for that matter, blind and mentally retarded youngsters.

"The childish brain is very vulnerable at all times," they argued, and "very much mental stimulus is always hurtful" (Vineland, 1894, p. 38).

Not all educators derided mental stimulation for young children. Some educators suggested that young children could be more profitably taught at home, with the institutional staff acting as advisors to the mothers (Talbot, 1964). Donald Moores (1987) points out that many schools for deaf children developed instructions and procedures for parents to use with their young children (J. C. Gordon, 1885), and professional journals were sprinkled with suggestions for parents of young children (see Arrowsmith, Ayres, 1849; Bartlett, 1852; Woodruff, 1848).

In the final three decades of the nineteenth century the view of the incapacity of young children was revised as part of the emerging child-study movement. Infancy was distinguished from childhood as a discrete period of development. Educators such as Édouard Seguin described young children as "on the war-path of curiosity" (Thurston, 1876, p. 10) and began to suggest major changes in childhood training methods; they proposed that training ought to follow "the inherent nature of children's minds" (De Guimps, 1906). Children from birth to about six years of age were now seen to be essentially under the control of animal impulses, and, as active beings, they required play rather than formal lessons (Finkelstein, 1985).

G. Stanley Hall, who established the study of child development as a legitimate academic field, influenced nurture writers (those who believed in the primacy of the environment over heredity) and educational reformers, who began to consciously conceptualize young children as learners and promote their instruction in special environments. As well, reformers presented a new view of parents, not as overseers or teachers, but as moral and psychological midwives, gently molding the growth of children (Finkelstein, 1985).

Kindergarten care, together with day care and nursery education, became a feature of American education in the 1880s (Taylor Allen, 1986). Institutions for exceptional children rapidly adapted, and in some cases even anticipated, the new thinking in child rearing. Since its 1867 establishment, for example, the Clarke Institution accepted deaf children at the age of five because an oral methodology demanded early intervention. This imperative was rapidly adopted by subsequent oral schools. Michael Anagnos, Howe's son-in-law, assumed leadership of the Perkins Institution for the Blind in 1865. In 1877 he established a kindergarten at Perkins for ten five-year-olds using Friedrich Froebel's methods of physical, mental, and moral development (Perkins Inst., 1893). In 1888 a proper school was organized at the Orillia Asylum in Ontario that included a kindergarten program (Hackett, 1969).

By the end of the nineteenth century the institutions for exceptional children had become well established, and the social, educational, and psychological philosophies that propelled the institutional movement in special education were well developed. As the thinking of the professionals continued to evolve, their opinions sometimes diverged, and distinct schools of thought emerged. One thinks instantly of the manualists and the oralists in deaf education. Sometimes, conventional wisdom in a given field alternated between two points of view; this was the case in early childhood education, which passed in, out, and then back into fashion once again.

But despite the proliferation of theories and methods, institutionalized special education in the second half of the nineteenth century shared two basic qualities with many other broad social movements of the time: a highly progressive and reformist zeal on the part of its leaders, and an increasing reliance on the expertise of a scientific and professionalized officialdom. The impact of the sciences on special education during the later nineteenth century was particularly critical, as the next chapter will show.

Chapter 5

Physicians, Pedagogues, and Pupils: Defining the Institutionalized Population

Key Developments in the Scientific Understanding of Disabilities

1838	Jean Étienne Dominique Esquirol distinguishes between mental retardation and mental illness
1840s	Distinctions between deaf and hard-of-hearing persons are begun
1850	The term *feebleminded* is widely adopted
1862	Herman Snellen designs the Snellen charts for testing visual acuity
1866	John Langdon Haydon Down makes the first clear differentiations among types of mental retardation
1870s	Information on the etiology of different types of mental retardation proliferates
1871	Successful aural surgery is performed
1880s	John Hughlings Jackson throws light on the nature of epilepsy
1880	Dr. Isaac N. Kerlin uses the term *moral imbecile;* Alexander Graham Bell becomes involved in the U.S. census
1884	Bell's *Memoir upon the Formation of a Deaf Variety of the Human Race* is published
1886	Bell uses an audiometer to assess the hearing of children in Washington, D.C.
1905	The term *moron* is introduced
1906	Henry Herbert Goddard becomes director of research at the New Jersey Training School for Feeble-Minded Boys and Girls at Vineland
1920	The term *mentally retarded* is introduced

Beginning in 1817, the builders of special schools cobbled together a complex of institutions designed to accommodate the special needs of discrete groups—those traditionally labeled the deaf and dumb, the blind, the feeble-minded, and the neglected, vagrant, and delinquent. Efficiency in reform demanded institutional isolation and, throughout most of the nineteenth century, institutionalization formed the educational milieu for disabled children. By the close of the century the United States and Canada boasted a complex of institutions, asylums, colonies, and training schools to serve the unique needs of disabled and exceptional individuals. Within the regular school system a small number of day schools, usually for deaf children, developed after 1870, and segregated classes in public schools were established in some cities.

Any question of schooling for exceptional groups must deal with several questions, the most basic being, who attended school and why? Simply, students became institutional clients because they suffered hindrances to learning that could not, or would not, be accommodated by the public schools. The early institutions in special education accepted the child who "by deficient intellect is unable to acquire an education in the common schools" (Powell, 1882, p. 268), as well as those impaired by defective hearing or vision.

About the middle of the nineteenth century there appeared in all branches of science, and especially in medicine, a growing demand for greater precision and accuracy, which ultimately translated into more cogent definitions and classifications for exceptional conditions. The medical orientation and the disability model, always prevalent in the field of special education, became even more pronounced by the middle decades of the century. Children were classified within medical parameters, labeled with a specific disability status, viewed as failing in school and society because of inherent disability, and then directed toward certain types of special schooling. But even as a medical orientation came to dominate, the primary need was for functional differentiations for educational purposes. These would not appear until structured methods of assessment emerged at the opening of the twentieth century.

The causes of disabling conditions that propelled children toward special schooling in the previous century are difficult to determine. Neither medicine nor technology was sophisticated enough to define with any accuracy many handicaps. It is entirely possible that disabling conditions were more prevalent in the nineteenth century than they are today. Rapid urbanization and industrialization, with their squalor, close living quarters, and lack of sanitation, would have made diseases and epidemics more acute. Childhood mortality and morbidity rates were high. One contemporary physician (J. L. Smith, 1869) estimated that 53 percent of all deaths in New York City occurred in children under the age of five and, of these, 26 percent were infants under one year. Many deaths were due to congenital conditions and the ravages of syphilis. Postnatal causes included infections such as scarlet fever, unhygienic living conditions, careless or ignorant management of young children, the widespread use of artificial feeding techniques for infants, and the provision of indigestible food that led to diarrhea, emaciation, and death. By the close of the century mortality remained high (Abt, [1944] 1965), estimated at 10 percent for newborns (Shapiro, Schlesinger, and Nesbit, 1968). Modern medicine has largely eliminated many of these destructive diseases and conditions; others may have simply lost potency. For example, scarlet fever, once a major cause of childhood handicapping conditions, became much more mild throughout western Europe, England, and America after about 1880 (Zinsser, 1935).

Accidents caused large numbers of disabilities—children lost arms, legs, and hands in factory and domestic mishaps. Employers, looking for cheap labor, hired untrained children and, even if they did not put them on machines, placed them close enough to saws and other dangerous implements for accidents to occur. Unsanitary and unhealthy working conditions accentuated the problems by spreading diseases and exposing workers to hazards such as hot metals and sawdust, potent causes of burns and blindness. It is also entirely possible that the massive immigration of the nineteenth century increased the number of disabled persons. Precautions were supposed to be taken against the entrance of "undesirables" under the terms of the Passenger Acts, which controlled the flow of immigrants. An American immigration act of 1837 was used after 1847 to turn away idiots, lunatics, maimed or infirm persons, and others (Coleman, 1973). All passengers entering at New York were examined for possible quarantine, and there were explicit instructions to inspectors to watch for disabled persons. But although these measures were supposed to ensure against the entry of persons who clearly were disabled, migration was a business and, in truth, many disabled persons passed inspection and entered the United States and Canada (see Coleman, 1973).

Many institutionalized students had been handicapped by the massive epidemics that raged across North America, caused by forces completely beyond the control of medicine and public health. Scarlet fever, typhoid fever, and measles were great villains; whooping cough (sometimes known as chincough) was a continuing problem that frequently proved fatal. As well, there was spotted fever—a first cousin of typhus—meningitis, and brain fever (A. G. Bell, 1907b, 1908b).

The actual numbers of children and youth who required special schooling are difficult even to estimate. The annual reports of the institutions indicated the number of students each had enrolled or had in attendance, but the educational net did not scoop up all children needing assistance. In fact, even among the children handicapped by conditions for which special schooling already existed, only a small proportion attended school, although numbers increased steadily throughout the century. The ethic of universal provision was applied haltingly.

, Moreover, children who were severely or multiply handicapped, seriously crippled, not toilet trained, or considered to be ineducable were not provided with schooling. Those with handicapping conditions such as epilepsy or paralysis (cerebral palsy) were seen as potential hindrances to the existing programs because of the individual care they needed. When discussing the student population of his Massachusetts experimental school for feebleminded and idiotic children, for example, Samuel Gridley Howe was quick to point out that "the institution is not intended for epileptic or insane children, nor for those who are incurably hydrocephalic or paralytic." Moreover, asserted Howe, "any such shall not be retained, to the exclusion of more improvable subjects" (quoted by Wolfensberger, 1975, p. 25).

As discussed in the preceding chapter, the markedly low rates of school attendance by many exceptional children reflected fundamental social values: often, school was something to be measured in the light of the other needs of the family and was only one relatively minor aspect of growing up. Institutional enrollments similarly reflected the age restrictions characteristic of nineteenth-century schooling.

In their germinal years most institutions operated below capacity. As the validity of institutional training was slowly established, average daily attendance gradually increased, the school year lengthened, the time of schooling increased, control became more consolidated at the state level, standardization increased, and the classification of students was refined. But it was not until free and compulsory schooling within the educational establishment became prevalent in the early twentieth century that special education became an option for the majority of exceptional children (see Chapter 10). Even then, those suffering severe and multiple handicaps pushed the limits, and schools accommodated them only tenuously.

The other major question surrounding schooling must concern the social status of graduates. If schooling essentially serves to prepare students for successful negotiation of the adult world of work, community, and relationships, then the transition of graduates and their ultimate fates are important matters to examine.

LABELING EXCEPTIONAL POPULATIONS

In the nineteenth century Americans embarked on the quest for labels that was (and is) so characteristic of special education. Labels would not sanitize the disabled population and make it either normal or invisible, but labels would identify disabled people as different. And, with the difference specified, they could be treated differently and provided different education and training.

Before today's children can be slotted into appropriate educational programs, stringent medical and academic assessment is necessary in order to confirm the existence of a problem, determine the etiology, define its developmental consequences and educational implications, and predict future functioning. None of these procedures was available to our predecessors. In the nineteenth century contemporary medical knowledge provided few accurate descriptions of disabling conditions or their precursors; there was an almost total lack of the medical evidence necessary for comprehensive and accurate diagnoses. Lacking complex and sophisticated medical information and technology, the professional educators and physicians tended to be, at best, imprecise about etiologies, severity levels, and prognostic implications; at worst, they made mere educated guesses. The lack of understanding translated into diagnoses and classifications that tended to reflect social and medical judgments more than any verifiable hierarchy of mental or severity level. Superstition, myth, and prejudice still surrounded handicapping conditions, and these added their own subtle tinge to diagnostic and prognostic directions.

Psychoeducational diagnosis was virgin territory; without IQ tests or any other formalized assessment procedures, educators had no means to assess cognitive functioning and academic standards. They relied on personal direct observation of an individual's mental and social capabilities. It was not until the early twentieth century that innovations in psychological and medical diagnosis allowed more accurate identification, differentiation, and categorization of exceptional students.

Certainly, as the nineteenth century progressed, both technical innovations and medical discoveries allowed for progress in the education and training of disabled people. Interestingly, some of the experimentation in aid of disabled individuals developed into unexpected and unanticipated advantages for the nondisabled population. Typewriters, for example, grew from efforts to make writing machines for the blind; the telephone arose from Alexander Graham Bell's experiments to make speech visible to deaf children. When Thomas Edison applied for a patent for his Tin-Foil Phonograph in 1877, the second of ten potential uses was "phonograph books, which will speak to blind people without effort on their part" (Koestler, 1976, p. 130). By the 1930s talking books for the blind were recorded on records that ran for twenty to twenty-five minutes a side and eventually gave rise to long-playing records used by everyone (Koestler, 1976).

ADVANCES IN THE CLASSIFICATION OF SENSORY IMPAIRMENTS

Blindness

Among the conditions warranting special attention in the nineteenth century, blindness tended to be easiest to identify and diagnose, if not to classify etiologically, and it engendered the most optimistic responses. "Of all the defective classes," workers averred, "the blind give the largest and most hopeful returns for the efforts made on their behalf" (Willis, 1879, p. 11). Persons with some residual vision, termed *the purblind,* were generally believed to be greatly inferior in moral and intellectual functioning to those who were totally blind (Perkins Inst., 1851).

More cogent and descriptive classifications of visual impairment developed after Herman Snellen, a Dutch ophthalmologist, in 1862 created the Snellen chart to assess visual acuity. The chart, still widely used, consists of a series of letters, numbers, or symbols to be read at a distance of 20 feet. Each line of the Snellen chart is a different size that corresponds to a standard distance at which it can be distinguished by a person with normal vision. Snellen's original equation, $V = d/D$, where V is visual acuity, d is distance, and D is the distance at which the letters can be clearly read, allows the measure of 20/20 normal vision (see Winzer, 1992).

It was not, however, until the 1930s, with the establishment of state and federal aid for the blind and the institution of the Social Security Act in 1935, that the need for a definition of blindness came to national attention. North American definitions generally described blindness as 20/200 visual acuity in the better eye, with a severely restricted visual field (Koestler, 1976).

Figures regarding the number of handicapped persons requiring special education in the nineteenth century are unreliable at best. Census reports throughout the century asked citizens to report the presence of handicapping conditions. Enumerations of the blind took place in New England from 1819 on. From 1830 until 1930, the U.S. federal government required citizens to report the presence of deafness or blindness in census reports (H. Best, 1934). For both these conditions, however, early census returns provide prevalence figures that one must view with suspicion.

For example, Francis Koestler (1976) explains that the census of 1880 reported 48,929 blind persons, which was double the number provided in the report of ten years earlier, 20,220. Workers with the blind were concerned that blindness might have doubled in a decade; however, a more plausible explanation for the rapid increase was the fact that the census enumerators in 1880 received a bonus of five cents for each case of blindness reported (Koestler, 1976).

Nevertheless, the prevalence of blindness was strikingly high: in the early nineteenth century it was calculated that blindness struck one in every 300 persons (Dunscombe, 1836). Among children, scarlet fever was a major villain: measles and scarlet fever accounted for the majority of the children enrolled at the Perkins Institution for the Blind in Massachusetts. Syphilis, said to infect up to 10 percent of the population (Lincoln, 1918), was a major cause of blindness, as was smallpox, although its impact was lessened after Edward Jenner's discovery of a vaccine against smallpox in 1798.

Early twentieth-century physicians fretted about the devastating effects of gonorrhea, which began to outrank scarlet fever, smallpox, diphtheria, and tuberculosis as a cause of disabling conditions, especially blindness, for which it became "the largest single cause" (Lincoln, 1918, p. 31). One physician went so far as to assert that this form of venereal disease accounted for "practically 100 per cent. of blindness in children" (Koestler, 1976). Infant blindness from gonorrhea, called ophthalmia neonatorum, was caused by inflammation of the eyes resulting from contamination from mucus carrying gonorrheal infection found in the mother's birth canal. The condition had been known from the dawn of recorded history; throughout the ages physicians have administered various kinds of treatments to newborns to alleviate the condition. High infection rates were slashed in the 1920s when physicians began to routinely use an effective prophylactic, silver nitrate, in the eyes of newborns. The prevalence of congenital blindness continued to spiral downward until the retrolental fibroplasia (retinopathy of prematurity) scare of the mid-1940s.

Deafness

When the ancient Greeks confronted deafness, they used the same word to signify "deaf and dumb" and "dull of mind." Early nineteenth-century Americans, notwithstanding Charles Michel de l'Épée and Thomas Hopkins Gallaudet, harked back to ancient prescriptions and lumped together all nonspeaking persons, ostensibly hearing impaired, under the pejorative appellations of *deaf and dumb* or *deaf mute.* They then classified the hearing-impaired population with an infinity of detail that echoed—even mirrored—the system devised centuries earlier by the Roman jurists who created the sixth-century Code of Justinian. Legally labeled and classified as deaf and dumb in the last century, and precluded by their disabilities from attending the public schools, were those individuals variously described as "deaf-mutes, the speaking deaf, the semi-speaking deaf, the speaking semi-mute, the mute semi-deaf, the hearing mute, and the hearing semi-mute, the latter two groups usually being persons of limited mental powers" (J. C. Gordon, ed., 1892a, pp. 30–31).

As the century progressed clearer differentiations between deaf and hard-of-hearing persons slowly emerged, built on knowledge rooted in discoveries dating from as long ago as the late Renaissance period. Capivacci (1580) made one of the first differentiations between conductive and inner-ear deafness. In the next century Thomas Willis (1672) identified the cochlea as the primary structure in hearing, and Georges Louis Duvernoy (1777–1855) focused on aspects of bone conduction and conductive hearing losses. Antonio Maria Valsalva in the early eighteenth century separated the ear into three distinct regions, which led to great strides in the treatment of conductive hearing loss, such as the development of myringotomy (surgical incision of the eardrum) and the use of the tuning fork (French St. George, 1981). Julius Robert von Mayer's scientific work in 1842 suggested ideas concerning the conservation of energy that were then developed in an orderly fashion by Hermann Helmholtz (1821–1894). It was Helmholtz's resonance theory that heavily contributed to a scientific distinction between deaf and hard-of-hearing cases. Helmholtz suggested that the basilar membrane of the organ of Corti is like a piano or harp, resonating to frequencies of sound according to the lengths of the fibers.

In educational circles it was not until after 1867, when American oral schools for hearing-impaired children were established, that the term *hard of hearing* entered popular and educational jargon. Successful training in speech and lipreading for many hearing-impaired students persuaded educators to abandon the terms *deaf mute* and *deaf and dumb* in 1887. But even though educators, knowledgeable about the potential for speech for many deaf children, embraced new terminology, the old pejorative terms lingered and are sometimes used even today.

Nineteenth-century medicine lacked even basic audiological equipment; apart from the ubiquitous hand clap, slammed door, or ticking watch, only the tuning fork, originally developed in 1711 as a test of the refinement in the making of steel, was available for diagnosis. Tuning forks could be used to assess auditory acuity by "hearing through the air"; they could also be used to check bone conduction by direct application "to the bones of the head" ("Deafness," 1894, p. 20). To carry out a diagnosis, the examiner struck the tuning fork lightly, then placed it on top of the patient's forehead in the midline. It was held that normally the bones of the skull transmitted the vibrations of the tuning fork to each ear equally and so the sound should appear to originate at the midline; if it did not so appear, if one ear seemed to hear better than the other, a hearing loss in the other ear was indicated ("Deafness," 1894).

It was not until 1886, when Alexander Graham Bell used an audiometer of his own invention to test school children in Washington and New York (De Land, 1923; *Science,* 1885), that a crude beginning in mechanical assessment of hearing was made. A true audiometer, providing accurate parameters of hearing loss across frequencies and intensity levels, did not emerge until the 1920s, at about the same time that the first mechanical hearing aids were developed. In 1900 Ferdinald Alt in Vienna produced the first electrical amplification device, but not until the 1920s did they become compact enough to be commercially viable. Audiometric testing began in the United States in 1924 and in Great Britain in 1928. With technological advances, consistent definitions emerged. Generally, hard-of-hearing persons are described as those who can obtain information through auditory means; deaf individuals, on the other hand, are defined as those who are unable to employ the auditory channel.

Alexander Graham Bell surfaces again and again in the story of the development of special education. Details of some of his contributions in the scientific and technological areas are described in Box 5-1.

Beginning in 1830 special censuses of the deaf were taken by the U.S. Federal government. They continued until 1930. After 1930, no such census was taken until 1970, when a research grant from the Department of Health, Education, and Welfare to the National Association of the Deaf enabled it to undertake a national census of the deaf population of the United States (Adler, 1991). Data gleaned from early census reports is suspect, especially those facts regarding the black population. Far from being a neutral report of numbers, the census helped create history by upholding the validity of slavery. For example, census returns in the 1840s and 1850s revealed that "the colored race is less disposed to deaf-mutism than the white" ("Statistics," 1859, p. 117). The 1860 census provided a ratio of one deaf-mute person among every 1,892 whites, one among every 16,782 southern blacks, and one among every 3,470 border-state blacks (De Hearne, 1877, p. 150). But contemporary commentators quickly pointed out that it was likely that early census reports, particularly that of 1840, were perverted "in the interest of slavery as falsely to show that a far greater proportion of the free blacks of the North suffered with various physical infirmities than the states of the South." For this purpose "many white deaf mutes were recorded in the census as colored, and afflicted with divers calamaties besides deafness" ("The census," 1872, p. 63). Slavery was justified as a preventative of handicapping conditions because masters "rarely allowed them to intermarry with near kin for fear of weaker progeny." On the other hand, freedmen, able to marry at will, were more likely to reproduce hereditary infirmities such as deafness (De Hearne, 1877, p. 150). After inquiry, Alexander Graham Bell later discovered that the congenital deafness was very much greater among black persons than among whites (Bell, 1884a, p. 244). The census and Bell's findings also indicated that epilepsy had a somewhat higher incidence among blacks. Bell (1884a, 1884b) reported that 9.2 blacks, as compared with 8.5 whites, per 100,000 were afflicted with epilepsy.

In about 1829 an epidemic of scarlet fever appears to have "entered a cycle of unusual activity and virulence" (Style, 1873, p. 140); it effectively deafened and blinded large numbers of children in both the United States and Canada. In fact, scarlet fever was accounted the most frequent cause of deafness in the United States in the opening half of the nineteenth century (J. S. Hutton, 1869b; New York Inst., 1854), being responsible, for example, for 20 percent of all deaf students at the American Asylum for the Education and Instruction of Deaf and Dumb Persons up to 1854 (Style, 1873). From 1863 until 1873, cerebrospinal meningitis emerged as the major cause of childhood handicapping conditions as an epidemic raged across the North, Midwest, and New England ("Institutional reports," 1872). By the later decades of the century scarlet fever reappeared—the 1890 census of the United States indicated that scarlet fever was the leading cause of deafness among the population as a whole (E. A. Fay, 1898a). Etiological trends for one school for deaf persons are detailed in Table 5-1.

Box 5-1

Alexander Graham Bell (1847–1922), Scientist

In the second half of the nineteenth century a phalanx of school-men (and a very few women) directed the course of special education. Many of the forms, methodologies, terminologies, classification schemes, and even attitudes and perceptions they designed and practiced came to dominate the field, and even now the precedents they set still tinge today's special education.

None was more influential than Alexander Graham Bell, not only in the education of deaf students but in the entire field of special education. Bell, for example, was the first to give popular use to the term *special education*. He advanced the cause of day classes for exceptional students, promoted kindergartens and preschool training using Maria Montessori's methods, directed an integrated kindergarten in the 1880s, and trained teachers to work with deaf children. In the late 1870s Bell embarked on complex investigations of hereditary deafness and blindness and over the next two decades became an expert advisor and evaluator of the U.S. census returns (Winzer, 1981a).

Bell, said a friend, had "given the subject of the education and the welfare of the deaf and dumb more study than any other living man" (De Land, 1905a). To separate Bell's invention of the telephone and his work in deaf education is not feasible; each illuminated and enforced the other. It was from Bell's experiments to obtain a more effective way to reproduce speech visibly for deaf children that the telephone ultimately evolved, and it was the enormous royalties and influence accruing to him from his invention that allowed Bell to dominate the field of deaf education and to spend lavishly on his favorite projects and schools.

Bell's work, his character, and his ideas were influenced by his father and grandfather, both also named Alexander Bell (R. Bruce, 1973). Grandfather Bell began the family elocution business in the early nineteenth century, and his son, Alexander Melville, ultimately joined the venture, as did Alexander Melville's three sons (Mayne, 1929). When tuberculosis claimed two of his sons, Alexander Melville Bell emigrated to the healthier climate of Brantford, Ontario, in 1870. As Alexander Graham Bell remarked later, the telephone "was conceived in Brantford in 1874 and born in Boston in 1875" (quoted in R. Bruce, 1973, p. 483).

In Boston in 1872 Alexander Graham Bell first opened a school; the next year he joined the faculty of Boston University. Mabel Hubbard, now sixteen years old, enrolled with Bell in 1872 for help with her speech and was soon immersed in the complexities of Visible Speech (see Chapter 6), a technique she found odd and not very interesting (Silver, 1971). Through Mabel, Bell became friendly with Gardiner Greene Hubbard.

While Bell taught elocution and feverishly promoted Visible Speech, he courted Mabel and worked untiringly on electrical experiments for the telephone and the harmonic telegraph. "Pecuniary considerations had considerable influence in my mind," Bell confided later, "as I was desirous of making sufficient money to enable me to marry" (Claudy, 1916, p. 5).

As early as 1865 young Bell, using his own voice and vocal mechanisms, had made an elaborate series of experiments to determine the resonance pitches of the mouth cavities in uttering different vowel sounds (*The Bell Telephone,* 1908). He found that these experiments paralleled those of the German scientist Hermann Helmoltz, although on a less sophisticated level. Along with his involvement in the mechanisms of speech, Bell grew fascinated by the simplicity of the Morse code of reading by sound, and in 1867 he strung a telegraph wire between his room and that of a friend to experiment with sending messages (R. Bruce, 1973).

In Boston, Bell continued his experiments with sound and with electricity. Bell claimed he was not an electrician at all but a "specialist in voice production, in the mechanics of sound making" (Claudy, 1916, p. 5). He was determined to discover "a definite shape of each sound" as "an assistance in teaching the deaf and dumb" (De Land, 1906, p. 7). The telephone arose from methods of exhibiting optically the vibrations of sound (*AADD,* 1878). Bell tried a "momometric flame" in which the "changing flame shapes were reflected in ribbon-like, serrated-edge wave forms" that became "visualized speech sounds" (De Land, 1906, pp. 21–22). He created a phonoautograph with a mouthpiece that guided sounds against a membrane. When words were spoken, the membrane vibrated and moved a lever that made a wave pattern on a piece of smoked glass. Although the experiments were rich in scientific interest, they failed to achieve the desired end, which, said Bell, was to create "an apparatus by which the deaf child could look and see vibrations of speech recorded as to enable him to see the elements of speech" (Bell, 1896, p. 45). The apparatus, however, ultimately became the telephone.

Throughout his experimentation Bell refused financial assistance from Hubbard but was not loath to accept aid from Thomas Sanders, the father of one of Bell's deaf pupils. With the $10,000 that Sanders eventually forwarded, Bell conceived, reduced to practice, and patented the basic form of the telephone before anyone else (R. Bruce, 1973). The Bell Patent Company of Bell, Hubbard, and Sanders was formed in February 1875; in April of that year Bell received the patent for the predecessor of the telephone. On January 30, 1877, Bell received one of the two fundamental telephone patents (R. Bruce, 1973).

Gardiner Greene Hubbard was slow to appreciate the possibilities of the telephone, although it was he who eventually "launched Dr. Bell's electrical-speaking telephone on its marvellous commercial career" (De Land, 1906, p. 414). By August 1877 there were 600 telephones in operation; by 1922 there were fewer than 10 million in the system; fifty years later, 100 million (R. Bruce, 1973). A friend of Bell's reported later that the inventor hated telephones. Once, when they were chatting at Bell's house, the friend asked to use the telephone, to which Bell replied: "There is a telephone in the house but the pesky thing is as far from here as I could possibly get it" (*Volta Review,* 1923, p. 49).

Bell's experimentation did not stop with the invention of the telephone. He was interested in flight and experimented with giant man-lifting kites. He made an experimental boat driven by aerial propellers, experimented with an x-ray device, invented a system of air conditioning, produced an electrical probe for surgeons, and suggested the iron lung. He became interested in breeding and carried on experiments to develop a strain of six-nippled, twin-bearing sheep (see, e.g., A. G. Bell, 1883, 1885, 1906; Castle, 1924; Dr. Bell's, 1907, 1908).

Medical theory grappled unsuccessfully with etiologies of deafness and failed to appreciate the connection between hearing impairment and an inability to speak; it was still widely held that deafness arose from a common organic lesion of the lingual and auditory nerves (H. P. Peet, 1851). "To be born deaf, or to lose the hearing at an early age, before the habit of speaking is so confirmed, or the stock of language so copious, as very powerfully to impress the memory," was believed to be "invariably followed by *Dumbness*" (original italics, J. Watson, [1806] 1809, p. 3).

As a diagnostic category, hearing impairment challenged the ingenuity of physicians and educators, especially when it was combined with other handicapping conditions. The anatomy was more clearly comprehended than the physiology of the hearing mechanism or the psychology of hearing loss. Nevertheless, because otology was a late-developing specialization, the ear was accurately studied long after some other organs (Gile, 1916). Problems of the middle ear were far better understood early on than were those of the inner ear, and nascent attempts at aural surgery centered on the middle ear. Kessel of Jena in 1871 removed the drum and the first two bones of the ossicular chain with permanent restoration of hearing. Miot in 1891 removed the stapes in an attempt to relieve the deafness caused by its being fixed in position by bony outgrowths (Bender, 1970). In Boston a Dr. Black undertook identical surgery (J. C. Gordon, 1894). At the time the surgery was condemned by leading authorities;

Table 5-1

Etiologies of Deafness for Selected Years
among Students at the Ontario Institution for the Deaf and Dumb

Etiology	1870–80	1883	1890	1900
Infections: colds measles, mumps, fits	13.40%	9.10%	18.20%	12.60%
Accidents	2.31	2.36	3.40	4.07
Meningitis	8.82	10.28	9.98	2.31
Congenital	45.16	42.15	38.81	42.26
Scarlet fever	13.02	19.70	14.75	25.20
Unknown	17.22	16.35	14.75	13.53

SOURCES: OSD 1881, 1884, 1891, 1901.

indeed, to perform such delicate work without antibiotics, proper lighting, and magnification was a very risky undertaking.

The etiology of the ubiquitous otitis media baffled physicians. Inflammation of middle-ear tissues was attributed to "violent efforts, vivid emotions, fatigue, work of mind, digestive troubles, but especially genital troubles," all viewed as "capable of producing almost instantly turgescence of the mucous membrane of the middle ear" ("Perron," 1888, p. 402).

Perhaps it was the lack of overt and obvious physical manifestations associated with deafness that persuaded reputable physicians as well as many charlatans to peddle a range of cures and hearing devices. Some were merely placebos; others fell into the realm of the weird; still others were downright dangerous. In fact, British schools in the 1880s barred medical experimentation on pupils; by 1915 the American Medical Association had banned a number of cures, including Actina, Branaman Remedy, Coutant's Cure, Gardener's Cure, Dr. Grain's Company, Help-to-Hear Company, the Morley Earphone, the Way Ear-Drum, and the Wilson Ear-Drum ("Deafness cure-fakes," 1916).

ATTEMPTS TO DISTINGUISH MENTAL ILLNESS AND RETARDATION

Views of Insanity

The organic movement of the late eighteenth century identified insanity as an illness based on bodily dysfunction. After Philippe Pinel, Esquirol, and Benjamin Rush, insanity was no longer viewed as a product of an individual's inborn nature but as a disorder generally unrelated to innate tendencies. Perceptions of insanity further changed in the first half of the nineteenth century, as the hazy boundary between sane and insane was constantly redefined (Walton, 1979).

What remained relatively resistant to change was the masturbatory hypothesis. Although the understanding of the etiologies of physical disorders greatly improved, not so for mental disorder. Masturbation remained prominent among the causes of mental illness in the beliefs of nineteenth-century physicians, just as it had during the seventeenth and eighteenth centuries. These beliefs formed a dominant part of American sexual ideology, which stressed moderation and self-control and supported assertions that sexual sins—masturbation, incest, consanguinous marriages, and overindulgence—were at once causes and effects of hereditary disabilities (Tyor, 1977). Holding aloft the moral banner of their predecessors, nineteenth-century physicians linked the masturbatory hypothesis and moral law. To a pious medical mind, the wickedness of masturbation was sufficient to explain its harmfulness (Hare, 1962).

Nineteenth-century physicians issued strictures against the dangers of masturbation, although, in comparison with eighteenth-century practitioners, they placed less credence in the masturbatory hypothesis. American doctors also claimed to have discovered a particular type of insanity caused by masturbation, most often diagnosed in young men between the ages of fifteen and twenty-five (Neuman, 1975). Hare (1962) notes that this "masturbatory insanity" stood for the same syndrome that later became known as the hebephrenic type of dementia praecox or of schizophrenia (see Chapter 11).

By the middle decades of the nineteenth century two interpretations of mental illness emerged, one functional and one organic. The organic orientation assumed that mental illness is rooted in some defect of the brain and the illness can be alleviated only by dealing with the physical causes. Mental derangement, still viewed as a condition occurring almost entirely among adults, was believed to be caused in manifold ways—"through overwork, disease of body, oversinning, overdrinking, or inheritance" (Vineland, 1903, p. 15).

Within the organic school, new medical data concerning the progress and prognosis of mental illness softened the stance against masturbation. One commentator referred to the practice as a "detestable vice" but was "induced to think [it] is often much exaggerated" as a cause of insanity (Stribling, 1842, pp. 22–23). More potent causes of mental illness, it was thought, include idleness and ennui, pecuniary embarrassment, sedentary and studious habits, inhaling tobacco fumes, gold fever, or indulgence in temper. One practitioner pointed to the psychiatric dangers arising from a kick on the stomach, bathing in cold water, sleeping in a barn filled with new hay, the study of metaphysics, reading vile books, preaching sixteen days and nights, celibacy, sudden joy, Mormonism, or the struggle between the religious principle and power of passion (Jarvis, 1852; Kauffman, 1985).

Commitment to the patient's well-being hastened the acceptance of a variety of medications and techniques to treat mental ills (Dwyer, 1987). Emetics, tartrite of antimony, venaesection, camphor, digitalis, opium, bark and wine, setons and blisters, purgatives such as calomel, blood letting, and cathartics such as jalap and senna were all used (Beck, 1811). Physicians experimented with hashish but were disappointed. "[O]n the stupid and demented it had no effect," complained Galt; "on others none that was permanent" (Galt, [1842] 1846, p. 561). Patients who suffered auditory hallucinations were treated with cotton dipped in laudanum, sprinkled with caustic potash, and applied to the ear or the mastoid bone. For visual hallucinations physicians used belladonna or large bleedings, then leeches down the spine if the symptoms did not improve (Galt, [1842] 1846).

A functional interpretation of mental illness assumed that social and psychological stresses warped an individual's development and that with humane treatment personality disturbances could be corrected. Functional advocates employed variations of Pinel's moral therapy, consisting of constructive activity, kindness, minimal restraint, structure, routine, and consistency in treatment (A. Brigham, 1847). Soon the process expanded to include recreational, occupational, musical, and play therapies (Bockoven, 1956).

Classifying Mental Retardation

No human difference was as much researched and discussed as the complex and often contradictory condition of mental retardation. Throughout the nineteenth century the field witnessed drastic alterations in conception, rapidly changing terminology, and increasingly sophisticated classification and etiological understanding.

The term *idiot* is derived from the Greek; the opposite of *citizen*, it denoted a person who did not take part in public life, one who did not have a place in the *polis*. At first, *idiot* was applied to the whole class of exceptionalities; however, in the nineteenth century the word acquired a quasi-scientific meaning. It came to specifically describe mental retardation, although it was used both generically and as a subcategory.

For many centuries mentally ill and mentally retarded people were lumped into one encompassing category—all were regarded as deranged because their behavior was considered too divergent from socially accepted norms. Madness was viewed widely as a cause of mental retardation, and discussions of real differences between dementia (mental illness) and defect (mental retardation) did not emerge until the end of the eighteenth century.

As a discrete condition, mental retardation had not been wholly ignored by philosophers, pioneer educators, law makers, and physicians. In Alcibiades 2, a document of unknown origin usually attributed to the Platonic school, the writer observed that "kinds of unsoundness of mind differ from one another as diseases of the body do." Subtle differences were described: "Those who are affected by it in the highest degree are called mad. Those in whom it is less pronounced are called wrong-headed, crotchety, or—as persons fond of smooth words would say—enthusiastic or excitable. Others are eccentric, others are known as innocents, incapables, dummies" (quoted in Scheerenberger, 1983, p. 35).

Roman legal thought, most fully articulated in the Code of Justinian, made some distinction between those who were mad and fools, granting both guardianships. During the reign of Edward II (1307–1327), laws were enacted that granted the king custody of the land of natural fools, although the heirs were promised a return of the property and "the idiot would be provided with life's necessities" (Barr, [1904b], 1913, p. 25). Later British common law provided a distinction between defect and insanity when it drew a line between the "natural fool" and the lunatic who "hath the use of his reason" (Lewis, 1960).

Building on this, the British jurist Sir Edward Coke later defined idiots as *non compos mentis*. Sir William Blackstone (1723–1780), the chronicler of English law, observed, "An idiot, or natural fool, is one that hath no understanding for his nativity, and . . . is by law presumed never likely to attain any" (Barr, [1904b] 1913). Nevertheless, legal distinctions lagged far behind medical and educational classification. It was not until 1886 that England produced a legal distinction between mental retardation and insanity (Hayman, 1939).

John Locke was able to arrive at a representative definition of insanity as distinct from idiocy. "Madman," he observed, "having joined together some Ideas very wrongly . . . mistake them for Truth. [And] the difference between Idiots and mad Men [is] that mad Men put wrong Ideas together, and so make wrong Propositions, but argue and reason right from them: But Idiots make very few or no Propositions, but argue and reason scarce at all" (quoted by Doermer, [1969] 1981).

In the early nineteenth century, accompanied by advances in psychiatry and in special education, more acute classifications of the retarded population surfaced. In 1838 Étienne Esquirol noted the difference between mental retardation (amentia) and mental illness (dementia). Early nineteenth-century physicians often employed the term *ideational insanity,* or sometimes *amentia,* for a condition considered to be "the expression of a continuous neurotic vice" (Spitzka, 1883, p. 124). Within this framework, retardation was not always viewed as a permanently disabling condition. Beck (1811) reported, "Many of them after remaining in this state for years, are attacked with paroxyms of acute mania, and the symptom is favourable, since in some areas it is succeeded by a resort to reason" (p. 21).

Samuel Gridley Howe defined three grades of retardation—low grade or idiots, middle grade or fools, and high grade or simpletons (Howe, [1848a] 1972). Édouard Seguin expanded the simple classification schemes of Esquirol and Howe. Seguin used the word *idiot* to describe mental retardation both generically and as a category. He then divided the generic category of idiocy into broad groupings, with idiots at the bottom of the hierarchy.

Idiot as a generic term disappeared during the 1850s when Americans adopted the concept and definition of feeblemindedness originated by the Royal College of Physicians in London (Vineland, 1893). In the United States and Canada *feebleminded* became the generic term for those thought to be unable to develop normally "because of some defect in the brain" (League, 1916–17). *Feebleminded* was seen as a less harsh expression than *idiot* and appeared to satisfactorily cover the whole range of retardation. As such, the term was sanctioned to encompass all degrees and types of congenital defect, from that of the simply backward child a little below the normal standard of intelligence to the profoundly retarded (see Barr, 1904a).

Idiots, the bottom grade of the retarded population, were the most accurately classified and the most fully described. These were likely to have been severely and profoundly retarded individuals, probably those with IQs of 25 or 30 and below (Talbot, 1964). To Seguin, an idiot was an individual "who knows nothing, can do nothing, and wishes nothing; and every idiot approaches more or less to this minimum of incapacity" (Brockett, 1856). "The appearances of idiots," observed a contemporary (Beck, 1811), "are marked by looks devoid of animation, and motion slow and mechanical. The senses are imperfectly developed, and the train of ideas (if any exist), are very slow and feeble" (p. 21). Others described idiots as "the lowest type of humanity" (Pennsylvania Institution, 1868, p. 6). To Howe ([1848a] 1972), these "idiots of the lowest class" were "mere organisms, masses of flesh and none in human shape" (p. 7). Howe believed idiots to be unteachable and firmly excluded them from the experimental schools in Massachusetts and New York. Edward Spitzka (1883) pointed out the likelihood of multiple handicaps in idiots; generally included were individuals suffering from overt physical conditions such as Down syndrome, cretinism, and microcephaly.

The next category, imbecility, included mildly and some moderately retarded persons who showed severe defects in moral (social) development. Imbeciles were capable of simple accomplishments but were sometimes described as "human animals" (Vineland, 1893), unable to exercise reasoning power beyond the extent of which a child was able.

As a generic term, *feebleminded,* as adopted in the 1850s, had legal connotations. Individuals were so adjudged on the basis of behavior that, because of low intelligence, was seen as nonadaptable and dangerous. The term also came to denote the highest grade and largest class of mental retardation. This final group within the broad feebleminded category were those described as *simpletons* in England: persons with simpleness or superficial retardation, evidenced by the slowing down of development (Scheerenberger, 1983). Americans described feebleminded persons as "those who were defective as to judgment and in whom the defect was of similar origin to, though not as intense as, that of imbecile and idiot" (Spitzka, 1883, p. 275).

As more was learned about mental retardation—its etiologies, developmental consequences, and prognoses—more specific classifications emerged. Alfred Binet and Théodore Simon (1908), formulators of the first commercially viable intelligence test (see Chapter 8), developed a classification system for retardation based on mental ages. According to the scheme, idiots are those with a mental age of one to two years; imbeciles attain a mental age of three to seven years; and the group Binet termed "de debile" have mental ages above eight years.

In 1910, just as IQ tests erupted onto the North American educational scene, Henry Goddard, director of the Research Institute at the New Jersey Training School for Feeble-Minded Boys and Girls at Vineland, appropriated Binet's divisions as his own without citing the source (Gelb, 1989; Goddard, 1910). Under Goddard, the American Association for the Study of the Feeble-Minded Committee on Classification assigned mental ages to its triparite classification system for mental retardation. Idiots were held to have a mental development of two years or less; imbeciles function between the ages of two and seven. Goddard also coined the term *moron,* from the Greek *moros* meaning "foolish," to designate the simpleton class. Morons achieve mental ages of between seven and twelve.

By 1912 the term *mental subnormality* had surfaced in the United Kingdom, the equivalent of the categorical term *mental retardation* in the United States. It was in 1955 that Sloan and Birch offered today's classification system organized by the severity levels of mild, moderate, severe, and profound. This system, which included a mention of adaptive behavior, was adopted by the American Association on Mental Deficiency in 1959 and formally accepted in 1961 (see Heber, 1961; Winzer, 1992).

The Etiology of Retardation and Its Management

Jean Marc Gaspard Itard's work with Victor and the subsequent contributions of Édouard Seguin, Philippe Pinel, and others moved mental retardation into the realm of special education. However, in this early period, retardation was conceptualized almost solely in medical terms; the social ramifications remained relatively unintegrated, causing some awkwardnesses in definitions and classifications until the notion of adaptive behavior surfaced in the 1930s.

The early workers also struggled with the diagnostic criteria for determining just who was or was not mentally retarded. Esquirol (1838/1845) first used anthrometric measures (the assessment of physical characteristics assumed to affect or predict psychology or behavior) but soon abandoned these in favor of a judgment based on the development of speech. In his *Mental Maladies: A Treatise on Insanity* ([1838] 1845) Esquirol divided the mentally retarded population on the basis of speech development into two levels—imbeciles and idiots—with a recognition of degrees within each category. Esquirol's classification, although not sophisticated, provided some consistency in terminology. It was the first to use the character of the behavior of an individual rather than the point

of origin or etiology of the condition as the means of distinguishing mental disorder from mental defect (Goodenough, 1949).

The use of speech development as the criterion for classifying retarded persons persisted throughout the nineteenth century (Blanton, 1976); it was the
cause of the subsequent confusion that arose over the distinctions among mental retardation, deafness, and severe emotional disorders. Alexander Graham
Bell observed that there exist "two classes of persons who do not normally
speak." There are "those who are dumb on account of defective hearing and
those who are dumb on account of defective minds." Bell stressed that "all idiots
are dumb" (Bell, 1884c, p. 50) and that most deaf children possess normal mental capacity, but no measures existed to offer irrefutable proof or even clear indications regarding developmental domains.

Many workers followed Esquirol's original thread and focused on phreno-
logic and later anthrometric measures that centered on appearance and physical stigma. Phrenology, most clearly explicated in the work of Franz Joseph Gall
(see Chapter 8), was essentially the science of reading the skull and interpreting
its shape and bumps. Phrenologists held that the mind consisted of thirty-seven
separate faculties that could be read in the shape and size of the skull. Faculties
could be strengthened by exercise or weakened by disuse or improper or unnatural use (Gelb, 1989). Mental retardation was thus understood as a state in
which the faculties lay dormant and underused. Idiots and other feebleminded
persons often also showed bodily anomalies. Howe, a founding member of the
Boston Phrenological Society and committed to the principles of phrenology
(Schwartz, 1952), pointed out that the physical anomalies of mentally retarded
persons were "the fingermarks of the Creator, by which we learn to read His
works" (Howe, [1848a] 1972, p. ix).

John Langdon Haydon Down (1826–1896), medical superintendent of the
Asylum for Idiots at Earlswood, England, from 1858 to 1868, is credited with one
of the first attempts to classify specific types of retardation. Classifying types of
mental retardation represented but one of Down's interests. He was equally concerned with the prevention of the condition through the temperate use of alcohol, the promotion of good mental and physical health among parents, sound
practices of prenatal care, and the proper rearing of children. In 1868 John Down
opened a private home for the mentally retarded youngsters from wealthy families (Scheerenberger, 1983).

After studying groups of patients, Down distinguished three etiological
groups: the cause he identified were congenital (idiots), accidental (idiots or
feebleminded persons), and developmental (feeblemindedness). Imbecility,
which Down closely associated with mental illness, was eliminated in his
scheme of severity levels. Down also suggested that the physiological features of
congenital idiots could be arranged according to ethnic phenotypes—Ethiopian,
Malay, Negroid, Aztec, and Mongolian (Down, 1866). These were later trimmed
down to four—Mongolian, Ethiopian, Caucasian, and American Indian (Tredgold,
1929). Of these, the Mongoloid classification endured and passed into common
usage to describe an identifiable group of mentally retarded individuals.

Although Down's comprehensive descriptive etiology of the so-called
Mongoloid individual illuminated a specific type of mental retardation, his terminology was unfortunate and his etiology incorrect. His notion that children

with what is now known as Down syndrome were throwbacks to a particular human variety was so long accepted that a 1924 publication, *The Mongol in Our Midst,* readvanced the theory of the Mongoloid ancestry of these children (Crookshank, 1924). However, later researchers generally attributed the condition to abnormal conditions of the ductless glands (W. E. Fernald, 1924). Following Down's etiological classifications, later researchers identified further specific forms of retardation. Scheerenberger (1983) lists these as von Recklinghausen's disease (neurofibromatosis), 1963; Laurence-Moon syndrome (cataracts, optic atrophy, hypogonadism, and polydactyly), 1866; Sturge-Weber syndrome (port-wine stain), 1879; Bourneville's disease (tuberous sclerosis), 1880; Tay-Sachs disease (amaurotic familial idiocy) 1881; Gaucher's disease (cerebroside lipoidosis), 1882; Pelizaeus-Merzbacher disease (familial diffuse degeneration of cerebral white matter), 1885; and Marfan's syndrome (skeletal and connective tissue disorder with structural eye problems), 1896. Owing to the efforts of Thomas Curling in 1860 and Charles Fagge in 1870, cretinism was identified as related to hypothyroidism (Scheerenberger, 1983).

It is not possible to estimate the number of retarded individuals in nineteenth-century American society, given the changing definitions and the varied social reactions to the condition. Nor is there any way to establish if the majority of the individuals institutionalized were actually retarded, or if they suffered from some other developmental disability not then diagnosable, or if they simply violated societal norms for other reasons and were institutionalized as a consequence (Tyor, 1977). However, of the institutionalized retarded population from 1850 to 1920, contemporary reports indicate that idiots constituted about 30 percent. Generally included in the lower grades were individuals suffering overt physical lesions—cretins, microcephalics, and children with Down syndrome (Tyor, 1977).

CONGENITAL VERSUS HEREDITARY CAUSES OF IMPAIRMENT

The etiology of most cases of mental retardation eluded physicians, apart from those instances where causes were obvious: epidemics, diseases, and inflammations. Many physicians still held on to medieval notions of anatomy and physiology. Moreover, both the medical profession and the public held that "the emotions of the mother affect the child and may mark it physically, mentally and morally" (Vineland, 1903, p. 15). In times of stress and war, it was believed, this problem became more acute, for "the nervous systems of females" were rendered "more than usually excitable" and shocks that could have a deleterious influence on the fetus were "more common" (H. P. Peet, 1852a, p. 11). Down wrote that "in no fewer than thirty-two percent of my cases was there a well-founded history of great physical disturbance in the mother by fright, intense anxiety, or great emotional excitement" (quoted by Scheerenberger, 1983, p. 58). The harmful affects of the mother's mental impressions on the fetus were thought to be particularly pronounced in cases of deafness. In a small town in Massachusetts, for example, four women with eleven deaf children among them were discovered, all reportedly proving the point. One mother related seeing a deaf and dumb woman at a funeral while carrying her second child, who was consequently born deaf, as were three subsequent children. A neighbor was so astonished by these events that she also produced two deaf children. A third woman who saw these deaf children subsequently had three deaf children of her own, and another neighbor bore two deaf children (W. W. Turner, 1847). In another instance, a woman whose husband refused to allow her to go to confession was said to have given birth to a deaf child, a consequence of the "hereditary transmission of moral turpitude" (D. Peet, 1856, pp. 136–38).

Although many sophisticated educators and physicians derided such ideas (e.g., W. W. Turner, 1847), others did not view the uterine environment as secure against outside disturbances. Expectant mothers were routinely cautioned by their elders about the dangers of fetal marking resulting from certain experiences: common superstition said that a child could be born with a harelip if a rabbit crossed mother's path or with a strawberry mark if she ate that fruit while pregnant (e.g., Ackers, 1878; Buxton, 1859; W. W. Turner, 1847).

Édouard Seguin presented a general explanation for mental retardation. The condition resulted, he said, from "an infirmity of the body which prevents, to a greater or less extent, the development of the physical, moral and intellectual powers" (Brockett, 1856). John Langdon Down, in addition to his "throwback" theory, held that "tuberculosis (consumption) must be accounted as one important cause of idiocy"; conversely, "idiocy of a nontubercular origin leads to tuberculosis" (Vineland, 1894, p. 36). Other writers mentioned mental underdevelopment and imbecility as stemming from "weakness of the parents, from parental sin or from drink, by some fright or nervous excitement of the mother at a certain stage of gestation, or by wounds after birth" (Vineland, 1903, p. 15). In the 1880s, Isaac N. Kerlin identified three primary forms of sexual dissipation that could cause mental retardation—masturbation, prostitution, and overindulgence (Tyor, 1977). Later writers attributed defective conditions in children to the subversion of women's natural functions in the interests of paid work. When a woman's energy was diverted by work, her childbearing organs underwent "a change comparable to rust" and were no longer capable of performing "their special tasks as easily or as successfully" (Schlepp, 1923, p. 391).

Although the philosophy of the early nineteenth century stressed the importance of environmental forces in determining the fate of an individual, the conjunction between deleterious environments and disabling conditions was not well conceptualized. Brockett (1856) was one of the few to point out the association of poverty and disabilities: "When poverty, filth, recklessness, and intemperance are united, and the half-starved inebriate, maddened with woe, drinks that he may forget his wretchedness, we have a combination of circumstances which can hardly fail to produce idiocy in the offspring."

Only the glimmerings of ideas about hereditary causes of disabilities were apparent in the opening half of the nineteenth century, for the process of the transmission of hereditary traits was not understood. Charles Robert Darwin's 1859 publication of *On The Origin of Species* sparked furor, controversy, and interest in the entire question of evolution and heredity, although Darwin, despite his stress on genetic mechanisms, emphasized the importance of environments in producing changes in organisms. The rediscovery of Gregor Johann Mendel's work in 1900 in an obscure local scientific journal added impetus to the study of the transmission of traits, but it was not until James Dewey Watson and

Francis H. C. Crick unraveled the complexities of the DNA helix in 1953 that the mechanisms of hereditary transmissions were more clearly understood.

Samuel Gridley Howe was one of the first to air concerns about the hereditary nature of disabilities. As he became more deeply immersed in the education of blind and mentally retarded students, Howe began to view disabilities as having both social and genetic origins; however, he almost completely overlooked the inadequacies haunting the lives of some of the children and ignored the malignant effects of poverty, slum life, and disorganized families on mental and physical health.

In 1848 Howe listed the major causes of blindness as low physical condition of the parents, intemperance, masturbation, consanguinous marriages, attempts to procure abortion, and the "hereditary transmission of certain morbid tendencies" (Perkins Inst., 1848, p. 2). By 1853 Howe was asserting that disabled children come from distinct, generally pernicious, backgrounds. "Now in all such cases the parents or progenitors must have offended against the laws of nature in some way or other," he declared, "and though it may have been without intent or knowledge, the consequences are more or less sure to follow; —their offspring are physically blind, because they were intellectually or morally blind" (Perkins Inst., 1853, p. 12). Even those cases where blindness is caused by disease could be explained in genetic terms—those so blinded hold an innate disposition to handicap. "Almost all who become blind by disease," Howe argued, "are made so in consequence of congenital feebleness of structures of the organs of sight, or inherited tendency for blindness; in some cases from both causes" (Perkins Inst., 1852, p. 10). Similarly, Howe largely blamed mental retardation on parents who, he said, "have so far violated the natural laws, so far marred the beautiful organism of the body, that it is an unfit instrument for the manifestations of the powers of the soul" (Perkins Inst., 1848, p. 2). Intermarriage among kin was particularly abhorrent, a "leading cause of perpetuation of peculiarities of body and character, from the parent to the offspring" (Howe, 1874, p. 103).

MORAL INSANITY AND MORAL IMBECILITY

In the late nineteenth century American morality was far more absolutist than it is today. The present orthodoxy is to look for environmental causes for crime and delinquency; in the past it was assumed that adults elected a life of crime or did nothing to halt their slide once on a downward path. Criminals were born to be criminals; will power was important only to the extent that it was acknowledged that children did not actually inherit will power, only the capacity for the development of will power (Goddard, [1914a] 1972).

As physicians wrestled with the problem of etiological classifications of mental retardation, reformers and educators forged strong links between morality and intelligence. Such thinking permeated the field of special education for mentally retarded persons well into the opening decades of the twentieth century. The boundaries of mental retardation were expanded, to embrace those in both "mental and . . . moral night" (Vineland, 1903, p. 15), the latter first labeled *moral insanity* and subsequently *moral imbecility.* As the notion evolved in the nineteenth century, moral disability was carefully separated from intellectual disability, for mental capacity and moral capacity were held to be quite separate faculties of the mind (Gelb, 1989).

The concept of moral imbecility can be traced to eighteenth-century ideas. Benjamin Rush, who held that humans possess an innate moral sense that guides them in distinguishing right from wrong, laid the groundwork for the field of mental deficiency to incorporate morality as part of its focus (Gelb, 1989). For Rush, the moral sense is an inner organ comparable to the eye or the ear, one that is wholly separable from other faculties of the mind (Gelb, 1989). When used as an adjective accompanying *idiot* or *imbecile,* the term *moral* was used to refer to all the nonphysical aspects of human life. At other times it referred more specifically to the emotions, and it was also used in the modern sense of ethical (Gelb, 1989). According to Walton (1979), the term *moral insanity* was first used in England during the 1850s.

Samuel Gridley Howe understood the difficulties of separating emotionally disturbed children from mentally retarded children. Howe, citing Rush, spoke of "moral idiocy," a condition in which "the sentiments, the conscience, the religious feeling, the love of neighbor, the sense of beauty" are defective, even though intellectual capacities are normal (Howe, [1848a] 1972, p. 21). He used the term "simulative idiocy" (Howe, 1852) to describe the appearance of mental retardation in a nonretarded person.

It was not until the 1880s, however, that the narrowing bounds of conduct acceptable to society in late nineteenth-century America wrought a moral revolution that conditioned attitudes toward moral imbecility, which became a well-defined construct. The primness of the era, evangelical religion, and the pseudo-science of phrenology widened the boundaries of mental retardation to include a moral dimension.

Moral imbecility was made real in the 1880s by Dr. Isaac N. Kerlin, superintendent of the Elwyn Institution for the Feeble-Minded. Kerlin found young moral imbeciles to be those displaying a perverted moral nature that frequently manifests itself in juvenile crime (Kerlin, 1879). He then identified four classes or moral imbecile—alcoholic inebriates, tramps, prostitutes, and habitual criminals (Kerlin, 1887).

Although workers found that moral perversions were difficult to separate from merely evil and vicious tendencies (see Carlson and Dain, 1962), they held that moral imbeciles suffer an irreparable defect of the moral faculties that compares to the intellectual damage suffered by the truly retarded. The moral imbecile was viewed as bad and practically incurable: "an instinctive liar and thief, cunning and skillful in mischief making" (Vineland, 1894, p. 41). This is the youngster who "lights a bon-fire on the carpet of the living-room of his home and accuses his younger brother or, perhaps, the cat for overturning a lamp. He has only two interests—one, to see a good big blaze with the resulting confusion and terror on the part of the family, and the other, to escape the personal consequences of discovery" (Pratt, 1920, p. 263).

At the outset the diagnosis of moral imbecility relied on the impressions of observers, an unscientific project given the broadness of the concept of moral imbecility. Numerous unsavory traits were heaped on the unsuspecting heads of moral imbeciles. They were variously described as childish in adult life; boast-

ful, ungenerous and ungrateful, cowardly, morally insensible, and lacking re-
morse; cunning and cruel, showing little sympathy for suffering or distress;
troublemakers and tattle-tales; indifferent to cleanliness; egotistical, selfish,
covetous; liars and thieves; and possibly obsessed with some form of religion
(after Rosen, Clark, and Kivitz, 1976).

By the closing decades of the nineteenth century mental and moral incapacity merged, as moral imbecility was wedded to the doctrines of criminal anthropology. Anthrometrics, the measurement of physical characteristics and
speculation about their effects on an individual's psychology, was essentially the
creation of Cesare Lombroso in Italy. Arthur MacDonald led an American movement that equated specific physical traits—such as the shape of ear lobes or
cranial protrusions—with a criminal type (MacDonald, 1902). MacDonald, never
as adamant as Lombroso, preached that traits such as genius, insanity, pauperism, and criminality seem to be associated with specific physical stigmata
(Gilbert, 1977).

Closely allied to the whole concept of moral perversity or amoral behavior
was the vaguely emerging taxonomy that would lead, in the next century, to a
precise classification of childhood emotional disturbance. Just as intricately
intertwined were concepts concerning neglected, vagrant, and delinquent children. The closing decades of the century witnessed the development of thinking
that saw strong relationships among ethnicity, delinquency, and feeblemindedness (see Chapter 9).

THE TREATMENT OF EPILEPSY

Probably no other exceptional group was as misunderstood and inappropriately handled during the nineteenth century as those suffering from epilepsy.
The word *epilepsy* is derived from the Greek, "to be seized." John Hughlings
Jackson, a pioneer neurologist, defined the condition in the 1880s as caused by
a sudden violent electrical discharge of brain cells (see Winzer, 1992). Still, no
drugs to control the condition or technical devices to trace its etiology existed,
and seizures engendered such fear in beholders that they retreated into the
myth that epilepsy and insanity are inextricably joined.

Institutionalization was imperative. It was widely held that epileptics become temporarily deranged following seizures, or fall into an "insane furor" that
could lead to crime or even homicide (Vineland, 1896, p. 34). Researchers asserted that probably more than two-fifths of epileptics are, at least part of the
time, insane and that many perpetrate lawless actions (Vineland, 1896, p. 33).
Even the sufferer in "fortunate circumstances" cannot be prevented "from injurious brooding over his hopeless misery" nor stopped "from gratifying his often
morbidly excessive appetite for injurious food or depraving himself by vicious
practices" (Vineland, 1896, p. 32). Physicians argued, "While the majority of
cases are incurable so far as complete immunity from subsequent attacks is
concerned, nearly all improve under enlightened treatment, cojoined with hygienic, dietetic and moral influences which, however, are possible only in properly constituted and wisely-managed institutions" (Vineland, 1896, p. 32).

Early in the century epileptics were sent either to hospitals for the insane or to almshouses. With the expansion of institutions for mentally retarded individuals in the 1880s, many were institutionalized alongside retarded clients, often in the custodial departments with idiots and the juvenile insane (Vineland, 1893). In some states separate facilities for epileptics emerged. Moreover, epileptics were viewed as chronic, incurable invalids affected with a disease that was described as "hereditary in a high degree" (Vineland, 1896, p. 32).

Epilepsy was viewed as simply one manifestation of weakened constitutionality, as affecting an individual "not only directly but as an alternate for certain other forms of nervous disease, inherited drunkenness and insanity" (Vineland, 1896, p. 32). Others who leaned toward hereditary explanations for disabilities advanced similar explanations. After studying congenital deafness, Alexander Graham Bell concluded, "All round the point where the deafness occurs you find evidence of something generally affecting the nervous system in connection with the brain . . . something to indicate that the thing intensified might be in the brain and not in the ears at all" (De Land, 1925, p. 142). Similarly, Howe viewed congenital blindness as a mark of vitiated constitutionality that could be manifested in many ways, blindness being only one (Perkins Inst., 1835).

Medically misdiagnosed and legally stigmatized, epileptics were "shunned, neglected, if not roughly treated" in society (Vineland, 1896, p. 32). Adults were prevented from attending church and social gatherings, and "no one wishes to employ them" (Vineland, 1896, p. 34). Children were generally not received into schools, public or private. Even after compulsory attendance laws went into effect, a seizure during school was deemed sufficient cause for removal. After a seizure it was "considered advisable to suspend him for a while for his own safety as serious accidents may arise, not only to himself but to others" (Vineland, 1912, p. 417). A child could return to school if free from seizures for a year. If the seizures were chronic, the child was provided home instruction (Vineland, 1912).

CLASSIFYING DELINQUENT, VAGRANT, AND NEGLECTED CHILDREN

Industrialized society, characterized as it was by social unrest, economic vicissitudes, and migratory habits, was particularly pernicious to children. Large numbers took to the streets, to be labeled by reformers in that elastic category of neglected, vagrant, and delinquent.

Social deviance was even more resistant to qualification than sensory and intellectual handicaps; through much of the nineteenth century the discrimination between neglect and delinquency was murky, more speculative than scientific. The opaque classification of juvenile delinquency depended "upon the statements of a few persons" who formed "their conclusions from a field of observations, limited by their own casual experience" (Mavor, 1893). Investigators, betraying the characteristic Victorian opinion that poverty is somehow socially subversive, saw little difference between areas of deviance and held the notion that destitution, vice, and crime are inevitably tied. Hence, neglected children became unwitting escorts to the confirmed delinquents who sallied forth from the tenements and slums; all were subsumed under the category of delinquent, whether present, potential, or problematic.

Practitioners saw juvenile delinquency as an enigma, a grave social problem disturbingly resistant to understanding, and their attempts to account for its motivational sources failed. Socially deviant behavior seemed to stem from a complex of causes. It resulted, noted one early twentieth-century writer succinctly, from a "poor home, mother working, lack of proper home training, suppression of legitimate freedom, or being placed at too early an age on the labor market" (Bench, 1919).

Moreover, attributions of delinquent behavior were heaped onto certain groups of children who, when exposed to the demands of adult society, seemed sure to flounder. Young street hawkers, pursuing occupations "most prolific in turning out delinquent boys" (Bench, 1919), attracted the attention of urban reformers and self-styled child savers. Most especially, "the profession of selling newspapers" was "pernicious right through," an occupation in which "children are systematically manufactured into criminals" (*Royal Commission,* 1891, pp. 723–28). In one study in 1919 the delinquency rate was led by newsboys, who accounted for nearly 22 percent of the total group under study; they were followed by errand boys at 18 percent (Bench, 1919). Truancy was inevitably associated with delinquency, or with adult perceptions of antisocial behavior. Membership in gangs was well nigh synonymous with delinquent behavior, and lads who fell under "the baleful influence of cigarette smoking" were preeminently suspect (Wyatt, 1919). Smoking was thought to be symptomatic of greater evil; it was demonstrated that, among delinquents, "eighty five per cent smoke cigarettes" (Henderson, 1919). Of all those whose behavior was antisocial or problematic, young girls paid "the highest price, the great sacrifice of morality" (Whitton, 1919); domestic service was "the commonest occupation of girls who go wrong" (*Report of the Social Survey,* 1915, pp. 41–42).

Nor did children and youth "confine themselves to petty crimes." All too often they emulated "the graver offences of old and practised culprits" (E. Wright, 1865, p. 7). For their diverse offenses, petty and criminal, popular wisdom held that juveniles required sanctions, as they "ought not, whether for their own sakes, or for that of justice, to be dismissed unpunished" (Halifax Protestant, 1861–62). Theft and incorrigibility accounted for the highest number of committals to houses of protection, houses of refuge, reformatories, industrial schools, and other dispositions.

Youngsters who drank, swore, pilfered orchards, played with catapults, harassed Salvation Army cadets, or broke into letter boxes were routinely disciplined (Houston, 1982). Those who appeared to be neglected or vagrant or sliding toward crime were similarly sanctioned. The Halifax *Morning Chronicle* reported that, of a group of youngsters committed to the Halifax Industrial School in 1870, "4 came from the police office, 4 others were known to be falling into bad habits, and the rest were vagrant or destitute, and on the high road to evil" (April 6, 1870, p. 2)

Complaints by citizens, peace officers, school officials, investigators for children's bureaus, and parents were deemed sufficient cause for committal. Of the first fifty boys admitted to the Victoria Industrial School just outside Toronto, twenty-five were sent on the specific request of parents and guardians and twenty-five were sentenced by magistrates under the categories of vagrancy, drunkenness, and theft (Morrison, 1974). Complaints by citizens were most often associated with offenses against property; those by parents concerned truancy and incorrigibility. One mother committed her son to the Victoria Industrial School in 1887 because "we can't get him to go to school and he won't stay at home; he beats the streets, steals . . . [and is a] bad boy generally" (Victoria, applications, 1887). Another wanted her thirteen-year-old in "a good Strict School" because "I Can Not Keep him out of Pool Rooms & playing Pool & I have just been told today that he even play's poker" (Victoria, applications, 1912). On the other hand, three citizens sent a lad to the Victoria Industrial School when they swore they "saw him . . . in Mrs. J's strawberry patch and tramping through them" (Victoria, committals, 1920). In Halifax a boy named Ashe was sent to the industrial school because he was "a source of great annoyance to this town" (Clerk, 1907).

The distinctions among the various types of disabilities gradually evolved over the nineteenth century, as medical science developed increasingly sophisticated means of diagnosing and treating them. Despite the increasingly scientific understanding of etiologies, however, the thinking of physicians and educators alike was still greatly influenced by the religious and moral preoccupations of the times. Thus, science and morality together shaped the development of the institutional complex that emerged, dictating not only who was institutionalized, where, and for how long, but also what life in the institution was like. The next two chapters examine that way of life, for the students and inmates, on the one hand, and for the teachers and administrators, on the other.

Chapter 6

More Than Three *R*s: Life in Nineteenth-Century Institutions

Key Dates in Institutional Life and Learning

1782	Valentin Haüy begins industrial training with blind pupils in Paris
1792	William Wilberforce introduces trade teaching in the British charity schools
1817	Thomas Hopkins Gallaudet introduces manual methods of communication for deaf students
1822	The American Asylum at Hartford, Connecticut, institutes industrial training
1830s	Claude Montal in Paris develops piano tuning as a trade for blind persons
1834	The Braille code is first published
1836	Perkins Institution opens a shop for the sale of pupil-produced goods; Samuel Gridley Howe builds a printing press at the Perkins Institution
1837	Howe finds Laura Dewey Bridgman
1850s	Printing becomes the most important trade for deaf students
1858	The American Printing House for the Blind is established
1864	Alexander Melville Bell devises Visible Speech
1866	Édouard Seguin publishes *Idiocy and Its Treatment by the Physiological Method*
1867	The campaign for the oral method of instructing deaf students in North America is born
1868	Dr. William Bell Wait develops New York point, a type for the use of blind persons
1870s	Institutions for the mentally retarded begin to depend on client labor
1872	Alexander Graham Bell begins to teach Visible Speech in Boston

1880   The Second International Congress for the Amelioration of the Condi-
        tion of Deaf-Mutes is held in Milan; oralism becomes the dominant ide-
        ology in the education of deaf students

1892   Braille is accepted in most North American schools for the blind

1900   Maria Montessori begins work in Italy with mentally retarded children

North American special education drew heavily on British and European
experience, especially in philosophy and pedagogy developed in France in the
mid-eighteenth century under the influence of Enlightenment thought (Winzer,
1986b). Underlying the philosophy of the French pioneer educators—Jacob
Rodrigue Péreire, Charles Michel de l'Épée, Valentin Haüy, Jean Marc Gaspard
Itard, Seguin, and many others—was the premise that disabled persons could
be educated through the astute application of alternate sensory stimuli—sign
language for the deaf, raised print for the blind, and in another vein, the physiological method for the mentally retarded. Charles Michel de l'Épée was one of
the most astute in translating these aims into practice. With his deaf students,
Épée made intellectual pursuits paramount. His main objective lay in awakening
the intellectual proclivities of his students to enable them "to think with order,
and to combine their ideas" (Épée, [1784] 1860, p. 3) through the "natural language of the deaf and dumb," the language of signs (Épée, [1784] 1860, p. 127).

The vitality of the French educational endeavors undoubtedly laid the basis
of North American ventures, which were motivated by a humanitarian philosophy, an evangelical commitment, and the unbounded philanthropy characteristic of early nineteenth-century North American society. Yet even as French
pedagogy and administrative structures were borrowed, they were changed, as
Americans adapted them to fit the essential tenets of their own educational
thought.

Throughout the nineteenth century the belief that disabled persons are biologically and morally inferior persisted. Those labeled as deaf and dumb, blind,
or feebleminded, as well as those in the elastic category of neglected, vagrant,
and delinquent, were seen to be both qualitatively and quantitatively different
from the normal person, endowed with strange, unsavory characteristics. "The
poor, the lame, the blind, the deaf, the insane, and the idiotic," may, it was said,
"be in general considered as proper objects of charity"; nevertheless, they were
"by the mass of mankind held in derision," or "looked upon as degraded and
inferior beings" (Jacobs, 1869, p. 20). Viewed as deviant, dependent, and delinquent, disabled individuals were assumed to be unable to attain the levels of
intelligence and competence of the general population.

Nineteenth-century reformers agreed that special students needed the min-
istering of a school in order to "elevate them to the mental and moral standards
of human beings" (Stone, 1848, p. 133) and assure them their places "as respectable members of society and law-abiding citizens" (OSD, 1874, p. 6). However,
the educational system that emerged was not aligned with the public schools; it
clearly reflected the traditional perceptions of disabled persons as charity recipients. Though the institutions provided educational services, they clearly
were administered wholly as public charities.

The institutional network was not centralized; each school developed au-
tonomously under different administrative structures, different organization
and funding, and in response to different social and political pressures. Nevertheless, most institutions functioned as variations on a consistent theme, and
educators in North American institutions, even while responding to the unique
needs of each disabling condition, tended to present remarkably similar curricula to exceptional students.

INSTITUTIONAL GOALS AND THE CURRICULA

The two tropes that were invariably used to promote special schooling
largely determined institutional curricula. First, there was the linking of disability and dependency as opposed to educatability and productivity. Second, educators decried the lack of spiritual values and moral imperatives that appeared
to inhere in disabling conditions. Schooling for exceptional students fashioned
under the sway of these sentiments was built largely to meet three objectives: to
educate, evangelize, and elevate industrially.

The insistence on useful employment and religious training as fundamental to the training of special children permeated institutional reports throughout the century. But although we know that the schools taught the ethics of
the workplace and stressed uniformity, conformity, and acceptance, we cannot
know how well the pupils adjusted to the discipline of machines and factories.
What is clear is that a growing number of graduates gravitated toward the cities,
where they could engage in school-taught trades (Winzer, 1989c).

It was not until the final decades of the nineteenth century that intellectual
aspirations overtook moral imperatives and industrial training as the central focus of special education. The development of religion, reason, and a work ethic
in the child remained important, but it eventually became equally important to
provide higher levels of academic skills. The greatest changes were seen in the
curriculum: under the aegis of Progressive educational reform, specialized instructional programs were introduced for various groups of exceptional pupils
(see Chapter 11). But, with instructional routine not as secure as it has become
today, experimentation remained the watchword of many special educators.

Public School and Institutional Curricula

The promoters of public schools who saw America in the throes of cultural
and material transformation brought on by the increasing tides of immigrants
were faced with the challenge of transmitting Anglo-American virtues to children often raised according to different customs and mores. Hence, Horace
Mann's crusade for the expansion and improvement of public schooling was
built on three goals—to teach students the common principles of Christianity,
to teach them the common principles of republicanism, and to avoid controversy (Johanningmeier, 1989). Even as they sought to inculcate the newcomers
with the religious and moral values that were held dear by the dominant society,
public school promoters simultaneously imparted the values of an urbanizing
and industrializing society. The implicit mandate of the public schools was to

provide an increasingly diverse school-age population the skills they needed to contribute to a complex, rapidly changing society. The advent of urban industrialized societies meant a change in educational emphasis. Technological society required trained and educated workers, and it also needed to be able to identify those individuals who might not be capable of benefiting from mass training and educational techniques. Barbara Finkelstein (1988) observes that public schools became places designed to complete a transition from agrarian to industrial modes of production, to ready people for contractual relationships, for impersonal rather than personal modes of association, for labor in factory and line rather than field and craft. In order to accomplish these goals, the five Rs—reading, 'riting, 'rithmetic, religion, and rules of conduct were stressed (Lee and Stevens, 1981).

Rhetoric identical to that advanced for the revival of the public schools was used to promote education for exceptional students, with one difference—the needs and goals were greater. If public school attendees required moral and spiritual training, then disabled children needed it even more; if regular students needed the skills for living in an industrializing society, then these were more imperative for exceptional persons to save them from their traditional fates as beggars, paupers, mendicants (Winzer, 1989c).

Educators saw disabled individuals as carrying a meager baggage of moral and spiritual values. As "it was felt that many children entered the institutions whose moral lives did not fit them to withstand the struggles and temptations of actual life" (Kelso, 1910, p. 3), their training was intended to carry strong moral and evangelical emphasis. Dedicated to the task of bringing exceptional children to the sacred text of the Bible, teachers rained on them a torrent of moral and religious precepts.

Then, blending their concerns for the everlasting with attention to temporal pursuits, school officials developed a noticeable preoccupation with their pupils' vocational destiny. A literary curriculum was not emphasized; educators argued that "intellectual education unless accompanied with industrial training and qualifications to obtain a livelihood, is not a benefaction" (OSD, 1871, p. 31). The main goal envisioned was to qualify handicapped persons to act as useful parts of society (Perkins Inst., 1832). The factory emerged as the governing model of institutional life; students were socialized to the work experience, and education became an increasingly refined training mechanism for the workplace. Literary accomplishments were restricted, deemed unnecessary and inappropriate for the disabled, tangential to the goal of instilling traits of character and technical skills needed for upright living in an industrialized society (Winzer, 1989c).

It was the devotion to industrial training that separated institutional and public school curricula so sharply. Manual training formed part of the public school curriculum, but students there were provided only basic precepts, more in manual crafts than in trades, and certainly not enough to move into paid skilled work without further instruction. It was not until the twentieth century that more specific trade teaching was introduced for public school boys and domestic training was offered to girls, both in an effort to improve the squalor and poverty often found in working-class homes. Institutional vocational training was from the outset far more sophisticated; special school educators viewed the process as "converting ... the learner into an accomplished workman able to compete successfully with the most skillful and ingenious of those with whom he is hereafter to run the race of life" (U.S. National Conference of Charities, 1883, p. 411).

Once the religious and industrial underpinnings were in place, educators embarked on a search for instructional approaches and techniques. Not that this search was always amicable or the results universally accepted. A variety of approaches emerged, and too often educators assumed irreconcilable stances. The education of deaf students was riven by the controversy concerning the most appropriate communication modes and that of blind students by the battle over suitable types of raised print. Even Seguin's physiological method, fully accepted in most institutions training mentally retarded students, came under attack at the close of the century by advocates of a more skill-based approach to training.

Religious and Moral Education

In the early nineteenth century those advocating special education came from neither business nor the military, but from evangelical religion. Pious activism motivated their efforts, and moral development was their central purpose. Many special children knew little of the existence of God or of a future life; such an ominous lack of learning created in reformers a burning concern for the state of their students' souls, a desire to bring them to the sacred text of the Bible. Education was characterized by an overpowering moral and evangelical emphasis (see H. P. Peet, 1855; Terrill, 1884). Instruction included examination of both testaments of the Bible as well as teaching about traditional values such as honesty, thrift, and toleration. As the century wore on, character education assumed greater importance, as standards of behavior and self-control became the equivalents of religious piety in interdenominational environments (see Valentine, 1991).

The pious activism associated with the education of disabled persons in the first half of the nineteenth century found its fullest expression in the work of Thomas Hopkins Gallaudet. He articulated the evangelical ideal of a moral and spiritual regeneration for disabled persons, bringing to the endeavor a missionary zeal. To a Hartford church congregation, Gallaudet defined the deaf population as "ignorant, isolated and unhappy," dwelling in a "moral desert" (quoted by H. Barnard, 1852a, p. 102). For these souls, Gallaudet craved "only the cup of consolation ... from the same fountain at which the Hindoo, the African and the savage are beginning to draw the water of eternal life" (quoted by H. Barnard, 1852b, p. 185).

Gallaudet and other early special educators defined their roles within a missionary context, holding themselves responsible for the character formation of their pupils and seeing themselves as entrusted, by God, as private stewards for the students' public welfare (Valentine, 1991). These educators stressed that as uneducated deaf persons possessed "no true idea of the Divinity" (H. P. Peet, 1851, p. 212), they were excluded "like the heathen, from the hopes, the consolations, the knowledge even, of Christianity" (Weld, 1847, pp. 98–99). So glaring were the spiritual and moral failings of exceptional students that teachers required "the enthusiasm and the devotion of a missionary to the heathen" (H. P. Peet, 1870, p. 215).

Those so passionately described rapidly adopted the rhetoric of hearing educators. John Carlin, perhaps the most eminent alumnus of the American Asylum, asserted that, before Gallaudet, "*all* the deaf mutes of the country were *ignorant heathens*" (original italics, Ceremonies, 1854, p. 33). A female student at the American Asylum saw herself "without light, like an idiot" (Stone, 1848, p. 135), while another described the deaf population as an "excommunicated class" (Ceremonies, 1854, p. 29).

Gallaudet was trained at Andover College, the first seminary in the United States and one with a curriculum focused on missionary work, so it is little wonder that he brought a missionary point of view to the education of disabled persons. Equally, it is unsurprising that throughout the American Asylum, religious instruction was "made a subject of special attention," allowing "the moral influence of the truth of the gospel" to render an "important and salutory effect upon its purely intellectual and temporal departments" (T. H. Gallaudet, 1821, p. 8). Pupils at the American Asylum participated in services in the chapel every morning and afternoon and every Sabbath (Ceremonies, 1854, p. 39).

Gallaudet's influence was pervasive; adherence to his moral and religious precepts characterized special education throughout the nineteenth century. A school for the deaf in 1882 reported that every school day opened and closed with prayers in the chapel and a brief moral lecture. Sundays at this same school were crowded with a nine o'clock Bible class, ten o'clock chapel, a sermon in the chapel at three, and further Bible classes and readings at four-forty. Grace was said at every meal (OSD, 1882).

The emphasis on moral training, though pervasive, seemed somewhat less intrusive in the early education of blind students. Perhaps this was because Samuel Gridley Howe came from medicine, not the clergy, or perhaps because of different perceptions of the innate capacities of blind persons. From the time of Aristotle, it was believed that the lack of sight was more deleterious to intellect than to moral nature (Bowen, 1847). Howe himself attributed more positive innate traits to blind persons: "Indeed," Howe said, "in all that regards his moral nature and his social affections, he has capacities far higher than the deaf mute" (Perkins Inst., 1850, p. 25).

Nevertheless, in the education of blind students religious and moral instruction was not neglected. Howe held to the belief that the moral and intellectual faculties were different and developed separately in humans. In special education he believed that the development of the moral faculty was the most important goal (Gelb, 1989), and he strove to impart to his blind students "a knowledge of the principles of Christianity" (Perkins Inst., 1838, p. 5). In fact, schooling for blind children was lauded as a means to "enable them to read the scriptures themselves" (Dunscombe, 1836, p. 97).

With only some lessening of emphasis but much in content, religious education was duly presented to mentally retarded pupils. Education and training of the mentally retarded pupil served "above all, to awaken the consciousness of his responsibility to God, and of his duties toward his fellow man" (Brockett,

1856). Because the comprehension of abstract ideas was difficult for mentally retarded persons, educators faced enormous challenges in bringing them to the Bible. Example was more important than lectures, love than services (Vineland, 1893). Music was an imperative in religious training: teachers were advised to "select songs with sound religious truths in them and drill and drill some more until many songs find a permanent lodgement" (Spilman, 1925, p. 251).

In the industrial schools religious education was considered a very important branch of training. Clients were "moulded according to the teachings and after the image of our dear Lord and Master" (Halifax *Morning Chronicle,* April 6, 1870, p. 2). Such shaping and molding demanded intense training, for permanent regeneration was possible only through character regeneration. At the Halifax Boys Industrial School, for example, there was worship morning and evening, Bible class on Wednesday evenings, and on Friday evenings recitation of verses from a passage of Scripture. On Sunday afternoons there was church school followed on Sunday evenings by church services (Halifax Protestant, 1890).

THE RISE OF TRADE TEACHING

Trade Teaching in Institutional Settings

Given the equations that countered ignorance, dependence, and consumerism with independence, education, and productivity, prominent themes in the arguments for special schooling, it is not surprising that institutional educators displayed a genuine, almost passionate, devotion to the interests of their students in the matter of industrial training. Believing that dependency was odious and that charity only encouraged pauperism, they saw the teaching of trades as the only way to break the cycle. Not only would early exposure to work build in students a work ethic that would contribute to an expanding nation, but industrial education could ease a student's move from the institution to industry and thereby prevent the needless public expense of caring for those unable to negotiate adult life.

The costs of educating the exceptional students were no longer viewed simply as expenditures, but also as down payments on future benefits for their full citizenship; it was a simple matter of economy to teach the young students trades to allow them later independence. "After their education is completed," argued promoters, "their reliance for self-support and independence must be on trades and occupations learned while at school" (OSD, 1873, p. 24). Otherwise they would become "a burden and care to their families and friends" (OSD, 1873, p. 24), doomed "to eventually become pensioners upon the community" (OSD, 1882, p. 10).

Schooling for blind children removed from society "so many dead weights" and prevented their becoming "taxes on the community" (Dunscombe, 1836, p. 97). For deaf students, Edward Miner Gallaudet pointed out that it was simply "a matter of selfish interest that we take these deaf people out of the condition of ignorant dependence, and, by the expenditure of an amount of money easily calculated, we turn them over into the other side, the producers and self-supporters, and gainers of wealth to the community; and the gain to the State is simply enormous by the change effected by education" (quoted by J. C. Gordon, ed., 1892a, p. 18). Similarly, industrial schools would provide an unruly lad with such skills that in later life he would be "placed in a position in which crime on his part is unnecessary and a loss" (McMurrich, 1872).

The prognosis for children with sensory impairments or those deemed so-cially deviant differed sharply from that anticipated for the intellectually hand-icapped. Still, schooling for the so-called feebleminded offered training in the hope that affected individuals would be at least partially self-sustaining (Barr, [1904b] 1913).

Rationales for Trade Teaching

Early nineteenth-century special schooling combined direct moral training with simulated factory conditions. In many institutions the questions of orga-nization, management, discipline, and efficient use of staff and pupil time over-shadowed concerns about creating a family atmosphere or presenting more than the rudiments of a literary education. Convinced that a work ethic could be created by self-control and the systematic inculcation of habit, the special schools attempted to socialize students to the work experience and industrial labor. As they stressed obedience and respect for authority, the factory emerged as the governing model. So prominent did this model become that many of the characteristics of the factory were present in school-based industrial training— standardized work patterns, reward systems related to production tasks, and competition in the quantity of production.

The stress on training in manual trades for nineteenth-century exceptional students may be viewed in a number of ways. These measures suggest a series of basic shifts in the definitions of work, and by implication, childhood, as it was perceived throughout the nineteenth century. Indubitably, earlier generations of Americans had reared their children to acquire a clear sense of adult duties but, even where legacies of diligent upbringing persisted, the inculcation of respect for work often fell short of sustained, systematic training.

The nineteenth century was a period of major industrial development, and a pronounced valuation of work characterized nineteenth-century North Amer-ican social thought. To ensure the continuing vitality of an industrial nation, fi-nancial, social, and educational leaders deemed a work ethic crucial. Not only did the nation require an intense work ethic, it needed workers who could adapt to the new conditions—to new modes of production, new roles for workers, ur-banization, the imposition of new schedules and new types of labor. In other words, society demanded workers who could contribute to an expanding Amer-ica and who would tolerate the drastic changes in work itself inherent in devel-oping technology.

The early years of special education coincided with this period of intense urbanization and industrial development. Clearly reflecting the needs of factory employment, special educators created a system that maximized working-class children's involvement in manual pursuits in the years just preceding their ac-tual employment and that stressed regular attendance and the attitudes decreed appropriate by those who controlled the workplace.

Institutional training also reflected an acute recognition of the social reali-ties of industrializing American society. In fact, others besides disabled groups

used industrial training as a vehicle for economic redemption. Lenkey (1991) explains that in the African-American community under the leadership of Booker
T. Washington the value of vocational training came to be highly stressed in the
years following the Civil War. Through programs of vocational education, Washington believed that African Americans could advance within the American
socioeconomic structure. Realizing that whites were not willing to give blacks
much more than jobs in manual trades, the African-American community pursued the economic avenue of industrial training.

America's social and economic changes challenged older cultural patterns
and expectations; the advent of large-scale manufacturing heightened differences in experiences and forged divisions between classes. The educators' consciousness of poverty was shown in the curricula they devised to provide their
students later with remunerative positions in trade; they viewed the skills taught
at school as the only means of providing their pupils opportunities for paid and
steady employment. Pragmatically, the brevity of schooling meant that instruction was necessarily limited, and subjects taught had to be "most useful in the
stern struggle for the necessities of life" (*Association Review,* 1901, p. 262).

On a more subtle note, industrial work was often viewed as the sole pursuit
appropriate for disabled persons. For special children education was narrowly
defined as role training, and educators rationalized and justified educational
settings, curricula, and child-training modes that reflected and complemented
contemporary perceptions of disabling conditions and the current economic requirements. From this, a language of class emerged. Students' future statuses
were thought to be bound by their disabilities, and educators played important
roles in assigning students to their future social and economic roles.

Educators' own perceptions of the capabilities and needs of disabled students shaped the objectives of the institutions, while their obsession with the
work ethic and belief in a self-regulating economy prevented them from seeing
wider vistas for their pupils. The identity of the disabled population looked simple; they were viewed in a one-dimensional way and ascribed traditional roles.
School officials perceived disabled persons as isolated within their handicaps,
capable of only limited scholastic achievement. It was said, for example, that
inherent limitations existed even for a well-educated deaf person, so that "a
man deprived of one important sense is not as valuable as one who has the use
of all" (Carlin, 1859, p. 63). Three deaf lads who approached the school inspector in Ontario in 1880 for financial assistance to attend the National Deaf Mute
College in Washington to become teachers were turned down, and it was suggested instead that they "learn the trades of shoemaking or carpentering or the
occupation of farm and garden work as . . . the best means of earning a living
after the institution" (Ont., Inspector of Prisons, 1880). Already, the inspector
noted, there were too many deaf teachers.

Hidden in the rhetoric of nondependence, production, and individual uplift
that permeated the industrial training notion nestled a confident hope that such
education would condition exceptional persons to a grateful acceptance of their
lot in society (Mitchell, 1973). Deaf people were counseled to keep their aspirations low, told to accept their subordinate role, and warned not to seek "to intrude themselves into stations for which they are unnaturally fitted" (Samuel
Porter, 1858, p. 137).

At the same time, appropriate schooling would serve to improve the lot, whether directly or implicitly, of some families. Many exceptional pupils came from society's poorer ranks, and child savers observed a fundamental discrepancy between lower-class mores and their own notions of correctness. Within the institutions children could be exposed to middle-class values; in turn, the children's new attitudes would have a salutary effect on the moral and social mores of the parents.

Finally, the elevation of industrial training to such important status can be seen as the establishment of controls over the character, behavior, and occupational future of children. Terry Morrison (1974) suggests that the manual training presented in the industrial schools served to stifle potential sources of social disorder and to regulate labor as it instilled the traits of character necessary for the factory.

The Nature of Trade Teaching

At the outset industrial education was a combination of practical training and character building provided for poor and delinquent children in an industrial school. It soon became synonymous with manual training and trade teaching. As such, it was developed for blind students by Valentin Haüy, who earned the criticism of his contemporaries because he stressed employment opportunities rather than intellectual stimulation. The utilitarian British evangelists held no such qualms; William Wilberforce introduced tailoring, shoemaking, and stay making into the British charity schools (Hodgson, [1952] 1973). Trade teaching was introduced at the first North American special institution, the American Asylum for the Education and Instruction of Deaf and Dumb Persons at Hartford in 1822. Boys were employed from four to five hours a day in carpentry and shoemaking, while females were engaged in bonding shoes, for which "they received a compensation equal to their labors" (American Asylum, 1822, p. 5). Subsequent American institutions all took their cues unerringly from this school, long considered the epicenter of North American special education.

How much emphasis educators placed on industrial training varied according to a number of factors, the most potent being commonly held perceptions of certain categories of disability and measures of social class. Reformers believed fervently that work discipline for poor children was essential to economic growth, and they brought a striking class bias to the training process. Schools were not designed to challenge the integrity of the class system nor to advance the social standing of graduates. Woven in and around the notion of trade teaching was the nineteenth-century moral and social precept that viewed the disabled as a special and discernible class that not only differed, by virtue of exceptionality, from the rest of the population but would fill the lower rungs of the social ladder by virtue of their general impoverishment.

The intellectual capacity of blind children was considered to be much greater than the capacities of deaf, mentally retarded, and socially deviant children. Samuel Gridley Howe argued that "the original capacity of the intellect is precisely the same in the blind, as in seeing children" (Perkins Inst., 1837, p. 5), and he reiterated three educational themes: each child was to be considered an individual and trained for personal ability; the curriculum of the school would follow that of the common schools, but with greater stress on music and crafts; and blind children were to be helped to become contributing members of society (Perkins Inst., 1834).

Still, for most blind children industrial training formed the central face of instruction; only those from the upper echelons of society were exempt. In the early days the Perkins Institution for the Blind had one class of children from rich parents who learned geography, history, English, French, and arithmetic—a curriculum almost parallel with that of the common schools. Another class, for children who needed to earn their living, focused solely on learning handicraft work and music (Perkins Inst., 1834). Institutionalized blind students from the poorer ranks manufactured doormats from Manila hemp in looms, produced various kinds of basketwork, made mattresses, and fabricated moccasins (Perkins Inst., 1834). Piano tuning, developed by Claude Montal, a student at the Paris Institution in the 1830s, soon developed as a lucrative employment for blind persons, "offering better remuneration than any other calling" (Perkins Inst., 1893).

From the time of Aristotle deafness had been viewed as a handicap severely debilitating to both intellectual and social development, more akin to mental retardation than blindness. It was consistently argued, for example, that "deaf mutes cannot, except in rare instances, enter any of the learned professions and comparatively few develop that peculiar talent necessary to enable them to engage in any of the fine arts" (Ontario, Inspector of Prisons, 1870, p. 16). For these students, trade teaching was considered particularly appropriate.

A whole range of activities, carefully attuned to the workplace and commercial possibilities, thus was put in place. At first, schools for the deaf generally taught carpentry and shoemaking. When educators foresaw that technological innovations would drastically reduce the demand for workers in such areas, trades more appropriate for an industrializing society were introduced. Shoemaking, originally seen as "particularly adapted for deaf mutes" (OSD, 1879, p. 27), became mechanized by midcentury and was superseded by printing, which soon became "the most universally taught of all trades in schools for the deaf" (Underhill, 1923, p. 318). Printing shops were found in fifty-five of the sixty-nine residential schools for deaf students in 1923 (Underhill, 1923). *Sloyd* (from the Swedish *slög* meaning "general dexterity," especially hand skill) soon became synonymous with woodwork and was widely taught to deaf (and to blind) students. By the turn of the century deaf boys were being taught cabinetmaking, joinering, shoemaking, tailoring, printing, bookbinding, and gardening. Girls learned domestic and ornamental sewing, dress and shirt making, tailoring, and millinery (U.S. National Conference of Charities, 1883). By 1907 sixty-five different industries were being taught in American schools for the deaf (*Proceedings,* 1907).

In the facilities designed for mentally retarded persons, educational treatment, largely founded on Édouard Seguin's physiological method, was designed to be both "hygienic and moral" in order "to develop the functions and aptitudes of the faculties and of the instinctive and moral tendencies" (Barr, [1904b] 1913, p. 34). One of the most prominent features of educational training was the attention paid to instruction in industrial occupations and manual labor. "Education by doing" was lauded as a "very valuable means of exercising and developing the dormant faculties and defective bodies of our pupils," as well as "training them to become capable and useful men and women" (Vineland, 1903).

Walter E. Fernald (1859–1924), principal of the school established by Howe for mentally retarded children now located at Waverley, Massachusetts, promoted manual training as the one route whereby mentally retarded adults could gain independence. Fernald stressed that from the age of twelve manual training should form the greater component of the child's education (W. E. Fernald, 1912a). The Waverley institution had industrial training for every branch of manual work. While boys in the institutions were engaged in more manual pursuits, the institutionalized females performed all the chores for the inmates and made and repaired the clothes of the pupils. Laundering and cooking seemed to make the children especially happy and contented, observed one writer (Mundie, 1919).

To Seguin's way of thinking, as soon as mentally retarded children could grasp and handle things, they had to be made to work. Even the simplest of work, such as wiping dishes or picking stones in the field, was considered better than idleness (Ball, 1971). Therefore, for those at the lower levels of the spectrum of mental retardation, there was laundering and gardening for the girls and hard, rough manual labor for the boys (Mundie, 1919). Land that seemed "to be absolutely unfit for cultivation" could "be made highly productive under the work of able bodied imbeciles and idiots" (Mundie, 1919). For his "low grade" pupils at Waverley, Fernald maintained a rock pile. Each day the children would move the pile to a different spot nearby, only to move it back again the following day.

Other training facilities for mentally retarded pupils followed Fernald's theme. At the New Jersey Training School for Feeble-Minded Boys and Girls at Vineland, for example, pupils were trained in basketry and brass work, with needlework for girls and knitting for boys. By 1903 Vineland was teaching tailoring, shoemaking, dressmaking, laundering, painting and drawing, carpentry, netting and chair caning, mattress making, farming, and dairying (Vineland, 1903); by 1911 the training school possessed a thriving tailor shop and woodworking facility (Vineland, 1911). Inmates at the Orillia Asylum in Ontario worked on the farm and learned manual work. Some left the asylum with skills that made them economically independent; the work of resident inmates reduced institutional costs for food and clothing (Hackett, 1969).

For the fractious elements of society, the children categorized as neglected, vagrant, and delinquent, confinement alone was viewed as an inadequate means of reformation. Operating within their mandate to stress trades, the industrial schools supplied a restricted literary curriculum supplemented with training and the ethics deemed appropriate for commercial activities in order to instil values consistent with middle-class standards of education, morality, hygiene, and work. "All work is honourable," preached school superintendents, "and no one has the right to live as a non-producer or sponger on others" (B.C. Boys Industrial School, 1930, p. 5).

Industrial school pupils were taught shoemaking, printing, and laboring (B.C. Boys Industrial School, 1905). At the Victoria Industrial School near Toronto boys made their own clothes, grew potatoes for sale, worked in the greenhouse or engine room, and learned tailoring, shoemaking, printing, carpentering, baking, farming, and floristry (Victoria Industrial School, 1896). Since marriage was "the greatest trade open to women," industrial school girls were provided "training in home efficiency, in the preparation and value of plain wholesome food," and "in household cleanliness" (B.C. Girls Industrial School, 1928, p. 7). Reformatory boys produced matches, furniture, and clothing (A. Jones, 1978).

The Critics of Trade Teaching

Many viewed with suspicion the emphasis on the teaching of various trades and industries in the institutions, seeing this as a deviation from more important literary pursuits and a subversion of the latent talents of deaf and blind students as well as an enterprise accruing few long-term gains. Alexander Graham Bell, for example, argued that "comparatively few of the deaf pursued in after life the occupations they were taught at school" (A. G. Bell, 1893b, p. 6). The critics in the deaf community, like their counterparts in the African-American community, also recognized the underlying significance of the emphasis on vocational education for members of their communities. Critics for the deaf community proposed the establishment of institutions of higher education and additions to the residential school curriculum that would allow deaf persons opportunities and access more like those available to the hearing majority (Lenkey, 1991). Similar calls arose from the black community.

Data on graduates are so scattered and imprecise that definitive assertions are not possible. Moreover, occupational categories were not as clear as they are today; slotting nineteenth-century jobs into groupings of skilled, semiskilled, and unskilled is a risky undertaking. However, the occasional analyses of occupations of graduates published in institutional reports and professional journals offer provocative glimpses and seem to indicate that deaf graduates were more likely than not to pursue the trades they were taught in school. Table 6-1 indicates the occupational categories of graduates of five institutions for deaf students in the latter decades of the nineteenth century.

A study of graduates of the Ontario Institution for the Deaf and Dumb (Winzer, 1986c) found that many pursued school-taught trades. In 1883 only two trades—carpentering and shoemaking—were taught at the Ontario Institution. Yet, of 47 male graduates, 53.3 percent were employed in these businesses. A more comprehensive survey in 1893, listing the work of 580 male and female graduates, indicated a similar pattern. Among the males, 25.4 percent were involved in trades directly taught at school, such as carpentry, shoemaking, printing, and tailoring. The fact that fewer occupational options were open to women was also indicated: 68 percent held school-taught occupations such as dressmaking and domestic service; a further 31.4 percent were noted as married and unemployed. Later figures in 1906, covering 145 graduates, revealed that 30 percent of females and 17 percent of males were engaged in work directly relevant to their earlier training.

Walter Fernald's 1919 study of the social lives of discharged mentally retarded clients formed one of the first comprehensive samplings of the status of mentally retarded people in society. In 1916 Fernald sent 1,537 letters to the

Table 6-1

Types of Occupations Held by the Late-Nineteenth-Century Graduates of
North American Institutions for Deaf Persons

School	Profes- sional	White collar	Skilled	Semi- skilled	Un- skilled	Agricul- tural	Other	Unknown	Married, unemployed
American Asylum, 1881	32	16	69	185	58	70	—	—	—
Kansas Institution, 1881	2	10	4	84	25	72	—	—	—
Ontario Institution, 1893	3	3	9	75	11	—	—	105	49
New York Institution, 1892	2	6	7	18	7	—	—	—	—
Clarke Institution, 1892	5	5	6	5	36	3	14	63	—

SOURCES: *AADD*, various years; OSD, various years.

relatives and friends of all the patients discharged from the Waverley Institution during the twenty-five years inclusive of 1890 to 1914. He inquired where graduates were living, how they were occupying themselves, whether they were useful and helpful at home, whether they were able to wholly or partially support themselves, what the benefits of school seemed to be, and which part was most beneficial—industrial education or school work (W. E. Fernald, 1919a). Initial letters were followed by visits from social workers who interviewed the family, the pastor, local officials, the police, and others who might have had contact with the retarded individual.

Fernald obtained information on 470 males and 176 females in the community. As far as the advantages of industrial education were concerned, results proved unpromising. Of the 176 women in Fernald's survey, 8, apart from 11 married women, were fully and independently supporting themselves with jobs. Another 32 helped with housework and, although they did not receive wages as such, were not a burden (W. E. Fernald, 1919a). Of the 470 males, 86 were steadily working, living at home, closely supervised by their relatives. They worked at diverse occupations—teamster, elevator man, city laborer, soda clerk, in factories, and on farms—in various semiskilled and unskilled occupations. Many were following the trades they learned in school (W. E. Fernald, 1919a). A further 77 of the men were working at home but receiving no wages; 8 were attending public school "not keeping up, but learning a little slowly" (W. E. Fernald, 1919a, p. 5).

Often, the educators's view of the vocational destination of pupils was tinged with ambivalence. On the one hand, the quest for economic independence through remunerative employment was vital if graduates were to rise above their traditional roles as beggars and mendicants. On the other, they were, as far as possible, to remain removed from the snares of the corrupting cities. Educators feared "the pernicious and debasing influences which prevail in large cities" (OSD, 1873, p. 24), predicting that the purity instilled by institutional training would be sullied in commerce with the wider world. Deaf adults, it was believed, were incapable of coping with urban living and were easily led into vicious habits. In the cities they were "exposed to the corruption of the evil influence which there congregate" and were, moreover, "little affected by the restraining influences, moral, social and religious, which exert so much power over others" (Stone, 1859, p. 133).

Pupil Upkeep of the Institutions

Industrial training did not simply serve to teach students remunerative trades; it also served to train them to assist in the upkeep of the schools. Pupil upkeep of the facilities was seen as both a desirable and a necessary goal of institutional operation. The motive was to make the institutions self-sustaining and to allow pupils, in some measure, to compensate governments "for the liberal provisions made for their intellectual improvement" (OSD, 1873, p. 23). With "a judicious selection of trades and careful management," explained one administrator, "they can in ordinary cases be made to pay their way" (Gillett, 1870, p. 207). In this manner institutionalized children could not only lessen the state costs of their support but, in some cases, erase it entirely.

Institutional reports show in detail the large variety and amount of work done by children. Students made clothing and articles for other government departments, did outdoor building, cleared the land, and engaged in dairy and poultry work. Boys built henneries and piggeries, raised fences and enclosures, tended the animals, and grew much of their own fruit and vegetables. Girls performed laundry and sewing chores. At the Elwyn Institution for the Feeble-Minded the boys worked on the farm and the girls were laundresses for the entire institution. At Vineland the girls darned and sewed, mended, and washed and ironed for the boys as well as themselves (Vineland, 1893).

Many annual institutional reports are larded with financial statements on the sale of pupil-made materials, which provided income that supplemented private and government grants and pupil fees. The Perkins Institution for the Blind, for example, opened a shop in 1836 for the sale of school goods and to serve as a depot where students could send goods for sale after they had left the institution (Perkins Inst., 1836). Howe reported in 1838 that manufactured goods in schools for the blind were not intended as a source of much revenue for, by the time the students became expert, they were ready to graduate (Perkins Inst., 1838). However, in the same year, the blind students at Perkins produced 100 mattresses, 80 cushions, 60 feet of rugs, 1,500 feet of mats, and 225 fancy baskets. Sewing was done by the girls, and the heckling, dressing, and spinning of the hemp for the mats was done by the boys (Perkins Inst., 1838). At the sister school for the blind in Halifax, students recaned old chairs; they cost 50 to 60 cents each and were advertised to the public as "giving employment and means to support a deserving class, and themselves a chair, perhaps equal to new, at one third of the cost" (Halifax Institution for the Blind, 1874).

Similar sales were seen in many schools for deaf students and in the industrial schools. One group of deaf boys in 1875 earned $1,591.18 for their school from the sale of brogans, slippers, boots, shoes, and from shoe repairs (OSD, 1875). For the New York industrial schools that opened in the 1850s, work was provided by many of the city's merchants and manufacturers. Girls learned all branches of sewing, straw banding, and paper bag manufacture (Gilman, 1984); in the early 1850s one New York industrial school made 150 pairs of shoes and as many as 50,000 paper bags (Gilman, 1984). Industrial school boys were sometimes let out for farm labor. The farmer provided schooling, board, clothing, mending, and costs for a doctor if needed. The $5 a month wages for the lad went into the coffers of the parent school (Victoria Industrial School, 1899).

The commercial value of pupil-produced products was important for the many institutions whose coffers were depleted. A poor sale of goods could place an institution in serious financial straits. Annual reports often lamented or bragged about what the pupils had produced in the previous year, and success or failure was sometimes judged by the number of sales (see Gilman, 1984). The managers of the Halifax Protestant Industrial School in 1884 bemoaned their estimated loss of $300 because there was no employment for the boys because of a depression in the shoe trade. To add to their woes, they did not make much bundling kindling wood because of "the coloured people bringing large quantities into the City and underselling us"; their carpet-cleaning trade also showed a small decrease (Halifax Protestant, 1884, p. 50).

The Changes in Trade Teaching

As they increasingly saw themselves as workshops or farming enterprises employing children, the institutions altered the thrust of industrial training, although the changes in schools for deaf and for blind students tended in different directions than the changes in schools for mentally retarded students. Institutional training for deaf and for blind students gradually swung toward a more literary curriculum, whereas training for mentally retarded pupils became more restricted and trade oriented.

The curriculum for blind students developed along more academic lines as the schools gained enough official support to abrogate the need for pupil sales. To be sure, industrial training and pupil service remained important, but no longer were they crucial. Like the exhibitions of pupil attainments that had been so vital in raising funds and demonstrating the viability of educational intervention, they soon became unnecessary.

The same can be said for schools for deaf students. Here, however, it was not just a gradual movement toward a more literary curriculum that determined changes. By the close of the nineteenth century a new mode of instruction—the oral method—was widely employed and brought new ways of teaching, new uses of school time, and new views of the intellectual abilities of deaf persons.

In addition, the note of optimism that had surrounded industrial training for deaf and blind students faded. Institutions now saw themselves as able to provide students with training "sufficient to enable them to qualify as apprentices . . . , but not enough to make them competent workmen" (Ontario, Dept. of Ed., 1911), a striking contrast to the earlier perceptions that saw trade teaching as the means for students to achieve ultimate independence.

Various other factors produced mounting pessimism. Forces included the growing demand for specialization in the industrial workplace and the lack of sophisticated appliances available in the institution. By 1890 the labor market, saturated with recent immigrants, was vigorously resisting the industrial training that formed part of the educational process. In the workplace the new worker's compensation laws placed restraints on the employment of handicapped persons—employers were loath to hire an individual who might be more prone to accidents (Winzer, 1981a).

The trend was quite different in institutions for mentally retarded persons, partly for demographic reasons. By the close of the nineteenth century vastly expanded populations were seen in the institutions designed for mentally retarded individuals. Schooling was not possible, nor was it seen as feasible, for all. Moreover, institutional costs had to be paid in some way, and the judicious use of client labor met that need.

Institutional settings solely for mentally retarded students first emerged in the 1850s and were largely founded on the pedagogical methods of Édouard Seguin. As schools became more confident of their survival, more acquainted with their clientele, more willing to use inmate labor, and more deeply influenced by social and political issues, many gradually assumed a more custodial character.

As these institutions began to productively employ the inmates' labor, they shifted their educational emphasis away from academic achievement to vocational training (Tyor, 1977). Daily routines became more regimented, and institutional life more inwardly focused. As pointed out by the trustees of the New York Asylum in 1862: "The school exercises, in the early days of the asylum its most prominent feature, still fulfill their proper function, but now are superordinated to the more practical objects of the institution" (New York Asylum, 1862, p. 13).

ACADEMIC INSTRUCTION IN THE INSTITUTIONS

By the middle decades of the nineteenth century the acquisition of literary skills was becoming the principal developmental task for children between the ages of six and twelve, and indeed universal literacy became an important mission of the public schools, alongside the teaching of skills in writing and arithmetic. Education was geared mainly to the three Rs, although the range of subjects taught was wide and the level attained by students depended upon their frequency and duration of attendance.

Because of the stress in institutions for exceptional students on trade teaching and the deeply ingrained belief in the intellectual incapacity of their students, they offered only a limited literary curriculum. Another reason for the emphasis on trades rather than academies lay in the abbreviated length of schooling for exceptional students. In many schools where children could attend for only seven or eight years, even as late as the close of the nineteenth century, it was felt that the school course was too short, and often the classes were too large, for anything more than the production of wage earners (Love, 1906).

As a general rule the pupils in the institutions for deaf and for blind persons devoted four hours daily to classroom work and the remainder of their time to manual trades and the upkeep of the institutions. At the Perkins Institution for the Blind pupils were slotted into four hours daily of intellectual work, four of vocal and instrumental music, four of recreation and eating, four of manual labor, plus eight for sleep (Perkins Inst., 1837). Generally, for older deaf students the academic work filled the morning session, and work in trades or in the upkeep of the institutions the afternoon. Younger deaf children received more direct classroom instruction time. The daily schedule for beginning students at the school for deaf pupils in Ontario in 1889 designated school hours from nine to twelve o'clock and from one-thirty to three; drawing class from three-twenty to five on Tuesday and Thursday; girls were in fancy-work class on Monday and Wednesday.

In the institutions for mentally retarded students, those designated as "high grade feeble-minded" were provided up to three hours a day of elementary work in reading, writing, arithmetic, and spelling. Trades and institutional upkeep filled the students' remaining time.

Industrial schools, designed to impart trade skills to youngsters, devoted relatively little attention to intellectual pursuits. At the Victoria Industrial School in Toronto only three hours a day were given to classroom work (Splane, 1965). The Halifax Protestant Industrial School employed a teacher for two hours on four evenings a week to teach reading, writing, arithmetic, and a little drawing, geography, and other subjects (Halifax Protestant, 1884). Literary instruction for reformatory inmates were even more restricted; until 1878 inmates at the Penatanguishene Reformatory in Ontario received only one daily school session of one hour before breakfast (Ontario, Inspector of Prisons, 1878).

Education for Deaf Students

It is doubtful that any issue in education has generated more heat and shed less light than the issue of the best way to communicate with and to educate deaf students (Kyle, 1980). The debate over sign language as opposed to speech and lipreading—the oral-manual controversy—has formed the core of one of the longest-running educational arguments of all time.

When Thomas Hopkins Gallaudet traveled to Europe and England in 1816 to learn the methods of educating deaf students, he originally hoped "to combine the peculiar advantages of both the French and the English modes of instruction" (quoted by De Land, 1906, p. 101). When Gallaudet found it impossible to persuade the Braidwoods to part with their secrets, lucky coincidence opened the French methods of Épée and Sicard to him. With Laurent Clerc, Gallaudet introduced the French silent methods of instruction into North America, which then "remained undisturbed for fifty years" (A. G. Bell, 1897, p. 12).

In the early years of deaf education, Thomas Hopkins Gallaudet, whose views and prestige served to anoint him as unchallenged leader, propounded philosophy. Laurent Clerc, dubbed "the apostle the deaf-mutes of the New World" by Roche Ambroise Cucurron Sicard (McGann, 1888, p. 13), guided methodology. Under Clerc, the sign language brought from France was adapted, refined, and extended until it matched the flexibility and nuances of any verbal language. Clerc brought with him Sicard's as yet unpublished *Théorie des signes* (1818), a grammar and dictionary of sign language that consisted of descriptions of the gestures used by deaf persons and the teachers instead of the words of conventional speech. It was set out, not in alphabetical order, but in word families (Knowlson, 1965). Soon after his arrival in the United States, Clerc "employed an artist for the purpose of having the letters accurately drawn, and he took advantage of the opportunity to make some slight improvements in the arrangement of the fingers" (McGann, 1888, p. 16). Mr. Stansbury, a teacher at the New York Institution for the Deaf and Dumb, between 1818 and 1826 devised the signs for numbers, as those of the Abbé Sicard were far from complete (Akerley, 1826, p. 27).

The French pedagogical imperatives concerning communication modes were accepted largely without question. In the tradition of Épée, the sign language was viewed as the sole effective means to stimulate the deaf student's intellectual capacities; articulation teaching was considered a mere accessory. A brief excursion into speech teaching at the American Asylum ceased in 1831: the *Annual Report* noted that "all efforts to accomplish articulation are now considered useless and are wholly abandoned" (Wheeler, 1920, p. 370). Harvey P. Peet, principal of the New York Institution for the Deaf and Dumb, mentioned in 1840 that "*if practicable* ... the deaf-mute should be taught to articulate" (original italics, Currier, 1894, p. 9) but failed to carry the thought into action. It should be noted that during the 1850s, even before the formation of the Clarke Institution, a slight surge toward teaching articulation was seen. For example, the American Asylum employed a teacher of articulation beginning in 1856 to provide short daily lessons to selected pupils (American Asylum, 1855, p. 245).

Indeed, it would have been extremely difficult for isolated individuals to effect any change in the established format; the reverence for Thomas Hopkins Gallaudet would have exposed any reformer to a charge of pedagogical heresy (Winzer, 1981a). Gallaudet was not a mere theorist who inculcated principles he had not already tested in practice; he was a working teacher and, as such, wielded profound influence on others who would follow.

It was not until 1867 that oral advocates began to batter down the ramparts of manualism. As they attempted to demythologize Épée and questioned the ideology of manualism, they faced concerted opposition from the manual educators. The reformers and the entrenched interests faced off, and deep division with its partisan passions became characteristic of deaf education after 1867.

Gardiner Greene Hubbard introduced a first unsuccessful bill for an oral school in Massachusetts in 1864; a second bill in 1867, sponsored by Horace Mann and President Thomas Hill of Harvard, also seemed doomed, for legislators believed that deaf children could not speak. However, just before the introduction of the 1867 bill, Harriet Burbank Rogers opened a small oral school in Chelmsford, Massachusetts, where she taught eight pupils. When legislators and others were called to the Boston mansion of Mrs. Josiah Quincy, they met Mabel Hubbard, among other Rogers pupils. The speech of these deaf children convinced the decision makers, and the success of Hubbard's enterprise was assured (see R. Bruce, 1973; also Chapter 4 above).

Hubbard's agitation for an oral school in Massachusetts was directed toward the education of "semi-mute" children. "I am not wedded to the idea of teaching articulation to deaf-mutes," said Hubbard; "I doubt very much whether it can be taught to congenital deaf-mutes" (J. Williams, 1891, p. 119). In this, Hubbard articulated the widely held belief that oralism could be applied to only a small segment of the deaf population—those partly deaf and from the right social class. In fact, in deaf education in North America oralism might very well have remained simply an alternate method, while its essential tenet—that deaf persons can reasonably be expected to assume less restricted educational and social roles than had previously been assumed possible—was adopted generally by all educators (Winzer, 1981a). Moreover, the vigorous debate between oral and manual proponents should have stimulated them all to reexamine their own pedagogy and to refine, improve, and broaden their theories.

Some redefining of theories and practice did occur; in 1868, for example, Edward Miner Gallaudet proposed the use of a "Combined Method," implicitly, a combination of teaching in sign language with additional speech training for students who demonstrated speech aptitude. Despite the experimentation, however, oralism did not remain an alternate mode of communication, but rapidly achieved dominance. No matter how hard manual proponents fought—and their numbers included many contemporary teachers, deaf teachers, and most deaf adults—they could not stem the rising tide of oralism. By the 1880s oral advocates were devising strategies designed to abolish sign language and put manualism to rout and to allow those of the oral conviction to control the profession. Rival facilities for teacher training, competing professional associations, and alternative school placements for deaf children formed major planks of the platform. Two important factors elevated oralism to the dominant philosophy: the advocacy of Alexander Graham Bell (1847–1922), and the resolutions of the Second International Congress for the Amelioration of the Condition of Deaf-Mutes, held in Milan in 1880.

Alexander Graham Bell and the Oral Campaign

In the final three decades of the nineteenth century Edward Miner Gallaudet and Alexander Graham Bell became the champions for the manual and oral stances, respectively. Gallaudet contended that "speech is not the matter of paramount importance in the education of the deaf"; Bell saw articulation as the "greatest of all objects" (E. M. Gallaudet, 1884). At the outset each of the protagonists seemed to respect, if not fully accept, the views of the other. Gallaudet promoted articulation instruction for selected deaf students as part of the Combined Method; Bell conceded the grave difficulties inherent in speech acquisition and lipreading for many deaf children and favored both writing and fingerspelling in the early years of learning, especially for those who were congenitally deaf. As oralism gained greater favor, the air of friendly rivalry soured, and by the 1880s Bell and Gallaudet were arguing with increasing animosity (R. Bruce, 1973).

Although revered as the inventor of the telephone, Bell was wont to assert that his work was the teaching of speech to the deaf, and to the end of his life he proudly described himself as a teacher of deaf persons (*AAD*, 1922, p. 185). Many professional educators of deaf persons resented his adamant stances in regard to communication modes and his tampering in instructional and professional domains that they considered their exclusive territory. In the 1880s Bell and Gallaudet clashed on many issues, including oralism, teacher training, and professional associations. Although by the middle of the next decade Gallaudet could note in his diary that "The hatchet is buried," he also commented: "I know where it is" (quoted by R. Bruce, 1973, p. 338).

Even with the Clarke Institution at the head of the oral movement in America, it still needed a prominent spokesperson to mount a concerted attack on manualism. None was as ready to take up the oral cause as Alexander Graham Bell. "His magnetic personality, and the prestige of his name as inventor of the telephone," noted his friend John Wright, "gave him great influence and made him the most powerful single force that made the cause of oralism successful" (*Volta Review*, 1923, p. 49).

Various interwoven threads in Bell's personal and professional life formed the fabric of his adamant stance with regard to oral training for all deaf children. First of all, his wife was deaf and his mother hard of hearing, so his interest in deafness was deeply rooted in his personal life, and very early on. Second, Bell had gained intimate knowledge of phonetics and the mechanism of speech and sound from his family's elocution business and his own experimentation with Morse code and the telephone. His pragmatic and personal knowledge then coupled with his notions of acculturation and heredity: Bell held to what may be simply termed the "melting pot" idea and believed speaking the majority language to be synonymous with acculturation.

In nineteenth-century North America the official goal of Americanizing and Canadianizing newcomers fell chiefly to the school system. The mandate of the schools was thus to absorb foreigners into national life and assist them in acquiring a general knowledge and appreciation of the language, laws, institutions, and ideals of their new land. Teachers became cultural initiators, guardians of the American or Canadian way, who served to introduce children to American life, American heroes, American culture, and the English language.

One fundamental tenet—that the goal of education is to produce cultural homogeneity—permeated Bell's thought and translated into his ideals for deaf persons. Bell viewed language as synonymous with acculturation; he deemed it "important for the preservation of our national existence" that Americans should "speak one tongue" (A. G. Bell, 1920, p. 340). Related aspirations for deaf children molded his oral advocacy and his perception of sign as "a foreign language" (E. A. Fay, 1891, p. 122). Bell held that deaf children "must be taught to communicate readily and freely by means of the language in common use among the people in whose midst they live" (A. G. Bell, 1910, p. 14), and he opposed all manifestations of sign language, viewing manual systems as ideographic rather than phonetic, limited in scope, flexibility, and precision. To Bell, sign was "not a language, but a vernacular" (A. G. Bell, 1898b, p. 6), a communication mode distinct and different from that of the larger society. "In an English speaking country, like the United States," Bell argued persuasively, "the English language, and the *English language* alone, should be used as a means of communication and instruction—at least in all schools supported by appropriations of public money" (original italics, A. G. Bell, 1913).

These beliefs about the importance of Americanization and acculturation combined in Bell's thinking with a general emphasis on the importance of heredity. The idea that hereditary endowments and traits define a human is apparent in his writings from the early 1870s, and he became progressively more adamant in these beliefs during his public career, which may be said to span from 1877 when the first telephone went into commercial use until his death in 1922. Along with many of his contemporaries, Bell was deeply influenced by new findings in human evolution and genetics, in anthropology, and in archeology (see Chapter 9). One manifestation of these influences was Bell's horror of inbreeding among deaf persons; another was his characterization of sign language.

The idea that gesture preceded speech in human development and is actually more sublime, as proposed by Étienne Bonnot de Condillac and Denis Diderot, held little appeal for Bell. Nor did he adhere to the conception of Thomas Hopkins Gallaudet that the possession of an immortal soul is the defining characteristic of the human race (Baynton, 1991). Rather, the defining characteristic for post-Darwinian oralists is the possession of language and speech. Moreover, if speech is distinctly human, then sign is lower in evolution and therefore more brutish (Baynton, 1991).

In addition, Bell misapprehended the impact of congenital deafness. He held that "all deaf-mutes could acquire an intelligible articulation" ("Discussion," 1884, p. 317). He thought it a fallacy to assert that gesture language "is the only language natural to the congenitally deaf," and that "such children must acquire this language as their vernacular before learning the English language, and must be taught the meaning of the latter through its means" (A. G. Bell, 1884c, p. 64). Those who failed to acquire speech Bell held to be somehow inherently inferior, their characteristics and leanings slightly subversive. Increasingly, Bell and his oral cohorts exhibited contempt for those who would not, or could not, dispense with the sign language.

Bell elucidated his views on heredity in his 1884 *Memoir upon the Formation of a Deaf Variety of the Human Race,* in which he contended that sign language and special schooling drew deaf individuals together in associations that often ended in marriage. "The constant selection of the deaf in marriage," he cried, "is fraught with dangers to the community" (A. G. Bell, [1884d] 1969, p. 74). He believed that the best way to prevent such marriages was to teach deaf children orally so that they would be made as like their hearing counterparts as possible (E. A. Fay, 1877). (See also Chapter 9.)

At the outset Bell's ideas were implicit in a teaching methodology for deaf children founded on his father's system of Visible Speech. Onto this base Bell then slowly erected not only an oral methodology but an oral philosophy that wove together the diverse threads of his thought.

Visible Speech

Alexander Bell (1790–1865) began as a shoemaker in St. Andrews, Scotland, and later went to London, first on the stage and then as a teacher of elocution (A. Bell, 1836; Mayne, 1829). His son Alexander Melville Bell (1819–1905) joined in the family elocution business. (So, too, in the 1860s, did Melville Bell's son, Alexander Graham Bell.)

The concept of a universal alphabet had engaged the interest of phoneticians for centuries, and Melville Bell became enthralled with the subject. However, in 1854 a conference of Europe's leading philologists and phoneticians met in London to search for a universal alphabet but adjourned, concluding that "it would be useless and impossible to attempt to find for each possible variety of sound a different graphic sign" (A. M. Bell, 1883a). Undaunted, Melville Bell continued the quest, with two main imperatives underlying his design. First, Bell visualized English as the most suitable universal language of the future and saw a universal alphabet as a ready vehicle for a universal language (A. M. Bell, 1883b). He also believed that the alphabet used to express speech in English, French, Spanish, and other Western languages was imperfect and did not reconcile the sounds and letters with speech; therefore, he concluded, a universal alphabet was needed, to remove anomalies in orthography (A. M. Bell, 1883b).

In 1864, Melville Bell claimed to have invented a universal alphabet (A. M. Bell, 1864, 1865), which he called Visible Speech. To accomplish this, he studied vocal physiology, including all the positions and actions made by the organs of speech (A. M. Bell, 1864, 1865). He did not arrange the sounds and then analyze the way they were produced; rather, Bell placed his own vocal organs in systematically varied positions in order to distinguish the precise sound made in each case (R. Bruce, 1973).

Visible Speech was not intended to replace established letters. It was designed as a key to their pronunciation, and therefore it bears no relation to the existing letter alphabet; the symbols depict the positions of the speech mechanisms and the actions that produce the sounds of the symbols (see Figure 6-1).

ALPHABETIC VOCABULARY OF TEST WORDS.—*Initial Vowels.*

(The vocabulary consists of Visible Speech phonetic symbols with language annotations in parentheses: (Sc.), (F.), (Ga.), (Am.), (Ir.), (Pro.), (Prov.), (Port.), (Cock.), (Colloq.), (Ge.), (It.), (Manx).)

* The accent is on the first syllable, unless otherwise expressed.

A page from Bell's *Visible Speech*

Figure 6-1. In its complete form, Visible Speech employs 29 symbols called *modifiers* and *tones*, 52 *consonants*, 36 *vowels*, and 12 *diphthongs*. All consonants have a horse-shoe curve standing for the tongue and facing down, right, or left according to the part of the tongue employed. Vowels are shown by a vertical line, standing for the breath aperture. A new class of sounds, *glides*, halfway between vowels and consonants, are also given a set of symbols. Modifying symbols, such as hooks and crossbars, are combined with the root symbols to specify certain vowel positions. A few small symbols stand for actions, like sucking or trilling, and for tones and inflections (A. M. Bell, 1883a, R. Bruce, 1973). SOURCE: Reprinted by permission of the publisher, from R. V. Bruce, *Bell: Alexander Graham Bell and the Conquest of Solitude* (1973): 41. Boston: Little, Brown and Co. © 1973 by Robert V. Bruce.

For easier writing, Bell produced two abbreviated forms of his alphabet: World English, a written pronunciation system similar to the International Phonetic Alphabet, and line writing, a shorthand system for use by stenographers (M. Gardiner, 1910).

Alexander Melville Bell is credited with ninety-three works in all, most of them on Visible Speech and its offshoots, as well as elocution and orthography (see *A Biography,* 1898; Fuller, 1907; Hitz, 1905). His Visible Speech became a classic in the world of phonetics. Édouard Seguin described the physiological symbols of Alexander Melville Bell as "a greater invention than the telephone of his son, Alexander Graham Bell" (quoted by De Land, 1919a, p. 618). Visible Speech was seriously considered as the pronunciation mode for the Oxford Dictionary. George Bernard Shaw even saw fit to have Henry Higgins promise to teach Eliza using Bell's Visible Speech symbols, and one of Shaw's dedications of *Pygmalion* was to Alexander Melville Bell. Visible Speech obviously never became the people's alphabet, but it did become the direct ancestor of the present International Phonetic Alphabet by way of Henry Sweet's adaptation of it in to what he called Broad Romic (R. Bruce, 1973).

Melville Bell himself saw Visible Speech as open to a wide range of applications. It could be used to teach illiterate persons to read their native tongues, "to teach the blind to read," to teach deaf persons to speak, to communicate the sounds of foreign languages to learners, to establish a standard of native pronunciation, to prevent and remove defects of speech, to telegraphically communicate messages in any language, to study fast-disappearing dialects, to spread the language of the mother country to the colonies, and to establish a universal language (A. M. Bell, 1867b).

Alexander Melville Bell offered the system to Queen Victoria for "the British Nation, and the World, for the common weal" (A. M. Bell, 1866) and his services to the president of the United States to teach Indians, train teachers, and set up an experiment wherein Bell himself would pioneer the teaching in one district (A. M. Bell, 1867a). Lacking encouragement from queen and president, Melville Bell published his findings in 1867 and arranged exhibitions with his three sons, who demonstrated how the sounds of any language could be pronounced correctly once the Visible Speech symbols were known and understood (A. M. Bell, 1867b).

Melville Bell's second son, Alexander Graham Bell, experimented with Visible Speech in teaching articulation to young deaf children at Susannah Hull's private school in London. (Hull was one of the first oral leaders in London). In 1871 he accepted an invitation originally offered to his father by the Boston school board to teach Visible Speech for three months at selected schools. Bell brought his experience and knowledge of Visible Speech with him as well as his ingenious ideas about the production of a harmonic multiple telegraph system.

Avidly promoting his father's system, Bell contended that Visible Speech was a concrete method that enabled deaf persons to teach themselves to speak, and that its use would give articulation in less time that it took to produce the same results without its use (A. G. Bell, 1872b, 1872c; "Professor," 1890). This hypothesis, coinciding with the growing impact of oralism, made Bell a rising star in Boston and Visible Speech "a sort of craze," with "teachers of the art ... everywhere in demand" ("Professor," 1890, p. 118).

Box 6-1

Alexander Graham Bell (1847–1922), Educator

Alexander Graham Bell's influence on the lives of deaf people was to be singular and far-reaching (Mitchell, 1973). Bell, the chief architect of oral deaf education in North America, looked askance at what he considered to be the mediocre efforts of manualism. With his intimate knowledge of the mechanisms of speech and his invaluable contacts and influence, he was able to orchestrate the movement toward oralism that shaped the lives of most deaf people in North America for more than half a century.

Bell elevated oralism to the dominant ideology, but his actions, attitudes, and philosophy offended and alienated deaf persons. He relegated sign language to inferior status as ghetto slang. By controlling the language of deaf persons, he sought to control their culture, their social network, and their aspirations as teachers. More, he ventured in many ways to intrude even on their choice of marriage partners. By advocating education for deaf children, oralism, and integration of deaf children into the public school system, Bell was in fact devising ways to prevent the consequences of marriages of deaf persons to each other.

Bell characterized the sign and the oral methods as irreconcilably opposed (A. G. Bell, 1890b; 1897) and ceded no value to the language of signs or to the diligent opposition of deaf persons themselves to his educational and social prescriptions. Deaf persons discovered Bell's advocacy to be inimical to their best interests (see Draper, 1895). One dubbed him "Alexander the Aggressor" and described him in unflattering terms: as possessing a personality combined of "a ponderous intellect," an "equally ponderous egotism," and "the stubborness of a Scotchman" so that "no evidence as to the falsity of a belief once accepted will induce him to abandon it" (quoted by Mitchell, 1971, p. 356).

Bell, a tireless proselytizer, donated nearly half a million dollars, about half the fortune of the telephone, to the Clarke Institution for Deaf Children, the Horace Mann School for the Deaf, and the American Association to Promote the Teaching of Speech to the Deaf (AAPTSD) (Lane, 1976). While many conceded that Bell was willing to spend lavishly, the generosity was too often directed to "crushing those who refuse to accept his word as law in the education of the deaf" (quoted by Mitchell, 1971, pp. 355–56).

Nevertheless, Bell's oral advocacy was pervasive and his influence profound. He promoted his ideas and experiments through ownership of, or interest in, various journals, specifically *Science,* the *Association Review* (later, the *Volta Review*), the *National Geographic Magazine,* and the magazine of the American Breeders Association (later, the *Journal of Heredity*).

By the beginning of the twentieth century the success of the oral campaign was unquestionable. When Bell arrived in Boston in 1872, only a handful of deaf children were instructed by oral methods. By 1884 the numbers being taught some articulation had risen to 27 percent; by the time he officially organized the AAPTSD in 1890, about 40 percent of deaf children were receiving at least some training in speech. By 1919 there were sixty-six schools for deaf persons in North America, of which all but six taught some speech (Numbers, 1974). By the time of Bell's death in 1922 the proportion had risen to more than 80 percent.

Bell formally introduced Visible Speech into North American instruction of deaf persons in 1871; he taught at the Sarah Fuller School and the Clarke Institution for Deaf Children, and for two months at the American School; he was also offered an appointment at the National Deaf Mute College, which he refused (R. Bruce, 1973). Bell opened a private school in Boston in 1872 to train teachers of deaf persons in the oral method and the complexities of Visible Speech but, in the face of stern opposition from the manual faction, altered the designation from teacher training to the School of Vocal Physiology and Elocution (A. G. Bell, 1872a). Then in 1873 Bell obtained an appointment at Boston University on the School of Oratory as professor of vocal physiology and elocution. Teachers flocked to Bell's lectures on vocal physiology to receive instruction on teaching articulation to deaf children; his classes were mostly filled with young women hopeful of entering the work of deaf education.

Approbation of the method was immediate. After hearing Bell's paper on the virtues of Visible Speech, delegates at the 1872 Conference of American Instructors of the Deaf and Dumb resolved that "the system of Visible Speech impressed the members of the Conference as being philosophical and that it promises great aid in the instruction to the deaf in articulation" (OSD, 1872, p. 26). By 1874 "the inestimable value of Visible Speech was generally recognized" (De Land, 1906), and the system was introduced at the American Asylum, the Clarke School, both schools for deaf persons in Pennsylvania, and at the institutions in Wisconsin, Minnesota, Missouri, Ohio, Kansas, Tennessee, and Ontario ("Professor," 1890).

The instruction of deaf children through the Visible Speech symbols seemed deceptively simple. To introduce the symbols, "the teacher would place some chalk dust on the back of her hand and then press her lips tightly together and part them with an explosive effect, producing the sound for 'p.' " The pupil then "performed the same action which was then written by the teacher as a Visible Speech symbol" (OSD, 1879, p. 25).

But Visible Speech was far from simple, a fact that rapidly became glaringly obvious. While some educators described Visible Speech as "ingenious and scientific," others called it "showy and absurd" (Garrett, 1882, p. 106). David Greenberger, principal of the New York Institution for Improved Instruction of the Deaf and Dumb, was one of the most scathing critics. "The symbols of Visible Speech can no more assist a mute in his attempts at vocal utterances than the signs of the zodiac," snapped Greenberger (1874, p. 67). "Mr. Bell," he continued, "with entire disregard of the nature and conditions of his scholars, is aiming at accomplishments which are beyond the reach of not only every deaf mute, but also the majority of hearing persons" (p. 73). Although a number of schools briefly experimented with Visible Speech as the basis of articulation instruction, most rapidly abandoned the system. In fact, after only a decade of experimentation, Visible Speech was almost entirely abandoned as a method to teach deaf children.

Alice Worcester, the teacher in charge of speech training at the Clarke Institution, observed that the use of Visible Speech symbols to teach articulation was "a hindrance rather than a help at every point" (Worcester, 1885, p. 11). It was feared that as the children began to write their communication in the air, using the symbols, their "habit of voluntary speech" would be delayed (Numbers, 1974). In the 1880s Worcester converted the Visible Speech symbols into the Northampton Charts (Yale, 1931). Worcester based her phonetic work on the principles underlying Visible Speech. She retained the order of the Visible Speech symbols but substituted English letters of the alphabet for the Visible Speech symbols (Numbers, 1974; Yale, 1889, 1931). Worcester's adaptation of the Visible Speech charts became a highly popular mode to assist in the teaching of speech to deaf children for more than half a century (see fig. 6-2).

The Milan Congress

With Bell orchestrating firmer adherence to oral communication modes, an additional factor elevated oralism to the status of the dominant communication ideology. The resolutions taken at the Second International Congress for the Amelioration of the Condition of Deaf Mutes, held in Milan in 1880, thrust oralism to the preeminent position it was to hold for nearly three-quarters of a century.

In 1878 delegates to the First International Congress for the Improvement of the Condition of Deaf-Mutes in Paris voted a preference for speech and lipreading, though they still advocated the retention of natural signs as an auxiliary, arguing that the oral method was unsuitable for all deaf persons ("Resolutions," 1900). Milan two years later witnessed an uncompromising avowal of the oral methods. The participants resolved that all deaf people could and should be educated solely by oral methods. Speech, hearing educators asserted, not only "restores the deaf-mute to society" but "places the deaf on the same platform that we ourselves occupy" (Sarah Porter, 1883, p. 186).

The conference in Milan probably did not change the minds of most European practitioners—it merely ratified their practice. It was only the American delegates, led by Edward Miner Gallaudet, who dissented when the Milan congress asserted "the incontestable superiority of speech over signs" and declared that "the oral method should be preferred to that of gestures for the education and instruction of the deaf and dumb" (Ontario, Inspector, 1881, p. 480). At Milan only the Americans disagreed. E. M. Gallaudet and others later asserted that the enthusiasm of the moment generated by vocal oral advocates swept many along. Many delegates who were uncommitted to either system eventually voted for oralism, and many manual exponents changed their stances to conform to what seemed to be a general consensus (see Kinsey, 1881; E. M. Gallaudet, 1881). So persuasive were the Milan resolutions and so promising the methods there advertised, that the London correspondent for *The Times* enthusiastically declared, "deafness is practically abolished" (*The Times,* Sept. 9, 1880, quoted by Kyle, 1980–81).

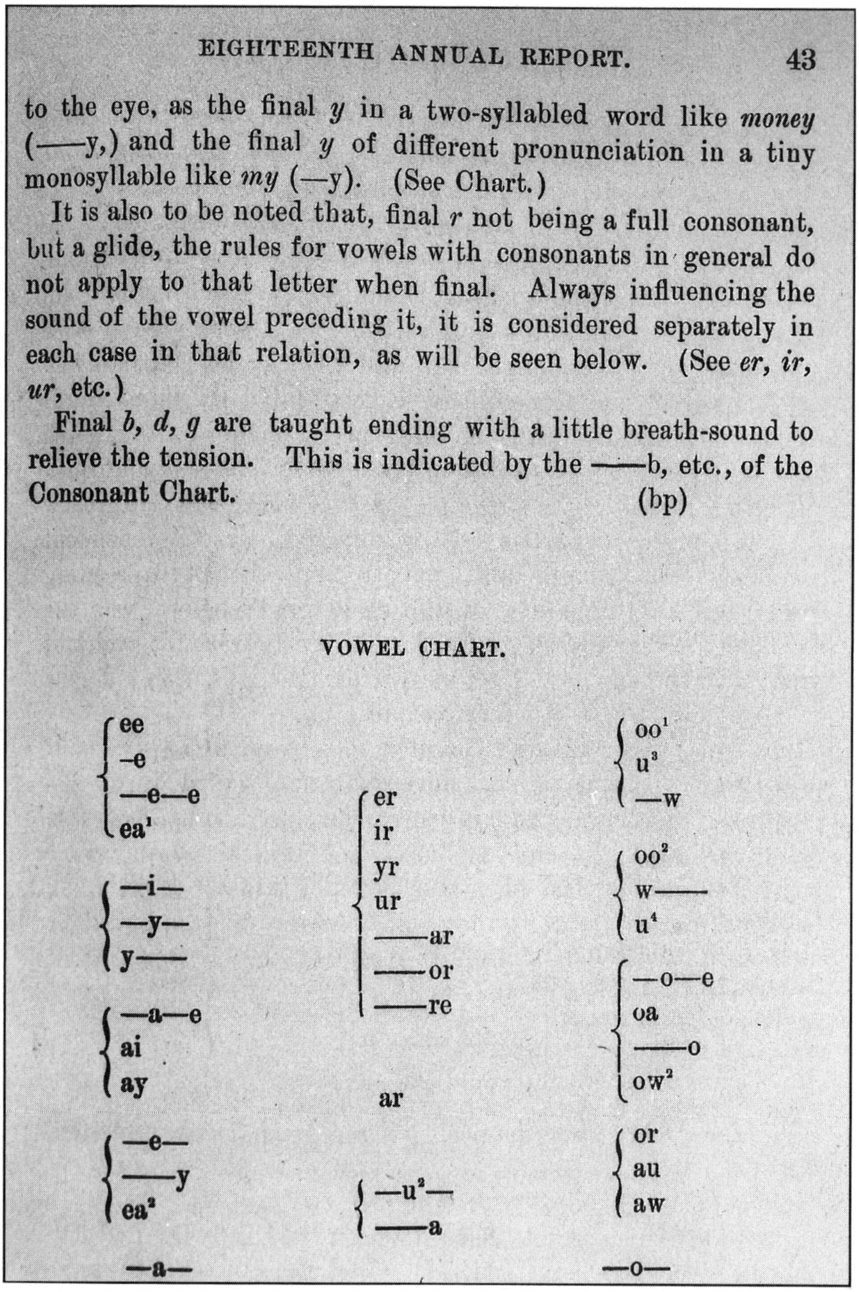

to the eye, as the final *y* in a two-syllabled word like *money* (——y,) and the final *y* of different pronunciation in a tiny monosyllable like *my* (—y). (See Chart.)

It is also to be noted that, final *r* not being a full consonant, but a glide, the rules for vowels with consonants in general do not apply to that letter when final. Always influencing the sound of the vowel preceding it, it is considered separately in each case in that relation, as will be seen below. (See *er, ir, ur,* etc.)

Final *b, d, g* are taught ending with a little breath-sound to relieve the tension. This is indicated by the ——b, etc., of the Consonant Chart.   (bp)

VOWEL CHART.

Figure 6-2. Consonant chart from the Northhampton chart. Photograph courtesy of the Gallaudet University Archives.

{ you
{ u'

{ —i—e
{ —y—e
{ igh
{ —y

{ ou
{ ow'

{ oi
{ oy

Key to Vowel Chart.

{ see
{ me
{ these
{ meat

{ sit
{ hymn
{ yard

{ came
{ tail
{ day

{ ten
{ sorry
{ head

cat

{ her
{ sir
{ martyr
{ fur
{ dollar
{ doctor
{ fire

cart

{ cup
{ sofa

{ boot
{ rude
{ screw

{ book
{ put
{ want

{ home
{ coat
{ potato
{ throw

{ corn
{ because
{ saw

not

. . . .

{ youth
{ use

{ mine
{ scythe
{ right
{ my

{ out
{ cow

{ oil
{ boy

CONSONANT CHART.

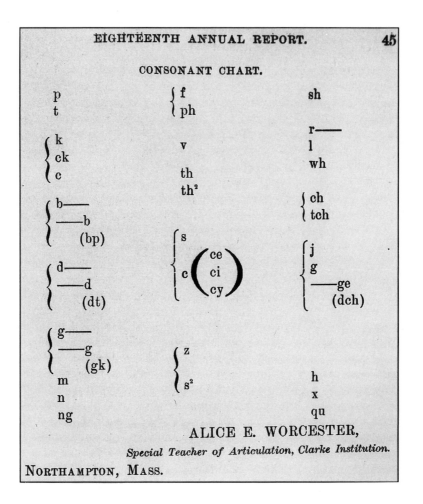

ALICE E. WORCESTER,

Special Teacher of Articulation, Clarke Institution.

NORTHAMPTON, MASS.

Oral Domination

The Milan resolutions legitimized oralism within the professional domain. At the same time Bell's work crystallized thinking on methodology by dramatically enhancing the contentions of the oral promoters.

As a method for teaching articulation painlessly and simply to deaf children, Visible Speech failed utterly; as the catalyst that irrevocably influenced the profession of the education of deaf students, the system achieved enormous success. Not only was Visible Speech the vehicle whereby Alexander Graham Bell met Mabel Hubbard, his future wife, and her father, Gardiner Green Hubbard, the major promoter of the commercial journey of the telephone, but it underlay all speech teaching in North America and led to the foundation of more practical articulation aids for deaf children. Moreover, the system emphasized, in both professional and public domains, Bell's expertise in the mechanics of speech and his willingness to lead an oral crusade.

Visible Speech precipitated a bitter debate not only on techniques but on the content and purpose of the education of deaf children. Teachers, caught in the cross-fire of powerful pedagogical issues, were swept by partisan emotions. Pursuing different avenues toward the common goal of the intellectual development of the deaf child, teachers adopted uncompromising stances and divided themselves into opposing camps of oralists and manualists.

Exaggerated claims and unjust deprecation characterized both sides of the debate. From the manual faction arose a "continual criticism of the oral method," and in response oral advocates directed "a continual avalanche of sneers and jeers at the so-called old-fogyism of the manual methods" (A. Wright, 1915, p. 219). Many of the arguments were founded on philosophy or a pronounced pedagogical orientation; just as often, the reasoning was rooted in personal prejudice, illogical assumptions, quackery, and occasionally outright charlatanism.

Oral advocates proclaimed the salutary effects of speech and derided the brutishness of sign. One teacher admonished the pupils: "If you make signs, you behave like monkeys; do you want to be monkeys?" (E. A. Fay, 1883, p. 238). In contrast, nobility of countenance was attributed to orally taught pupils, who were seen as much more likely to rise in status ("Dr. Gordon's," 1899; Fay, 1877, p. 115). Celebrated physicians declared that the health of deaf children improved under oral methods (Garrett, 1883, p. 17). Speech exercises for deaf pupils were "the true hygienic gymnastic exercises" ("The hygienic," 1892, p. 81); speech was said to stimulate the brain, making "the cerebral structure of the speaking deaf correspond more closely with normally developing brain-structure" ("Dr. Gordon's," 1899, p. 211). When children were taught speech early, it was claimed, their lungs expanded and their general health improved (Lesperance, 1872, p. 510). Moreover, a lack of such respiratory exercise was "apt to produce chilblains" (Chilblains, 1889, p. 311). From the Glasgow School for the Deaf came a report that chilblains were formerly common in all students; it was later found that chilblains attacked only "those taught by the silent system" (Sarah Porter, 1883, p. 187), a contention, however, that was derided by oralists and manualists alike.

While oral educators waxed effusive about the advantages of their system, manual advocates mustered a phalanx of counterarguments. Manualists viewed articulation training as only a branch of instruction, not a means. They contended that oralism was adaptable to only a small percentage of pupils; that it was costly, requiring smaller classes; that it was difficult and disagreeable to the pupils; that it could not be used as a means of imparting religious knowledge (Yale, 1931); and that it was an imperfect and unreliable means of communication (Monroe, 1926). The great advantage of sign language was the ease and rapidity with which it could be taught, the way in which it presented a group of ideas at once so that "the eye, the hand, the whole body, speaks simultaneously on one subject" (E. J. Mann, 1836, p. 26).

Articulation was denounced as being both disagreeable and unhealthy for deaf students. Speech was embarrassing and difficult and "almost always very *painful, harsh, discordant* and *comparatively useless*" (original italics, "Institution," 1818, p. 132). Moreover, speech could be dangerous, rasping and tearing the throat and producing "violent and unnatural straining on the lungs" (Keep, 1867, p. 13). Lesperance (1872) explained that when articulation was begun after the age of twelve, the efforts it required "often lead to the ruin of health, and to untimely death" (p. 510).

Deaf people themselves largely rejected the faddism and dreamy idealisms of the oralists in favor of sign language. They viewed oralism as an implausible ideology, surrounded by failures. Over and over they stated that "signs are the proper instrument of their intercourse" (Kitto, 1852, p. 110). Teaching "the Deaf and Dumb to articulate sounds" was characterized by Laurent Clerc as a "useless task" (p. 112); other deaf people argued that "oral speech is of little, if any, use to them, and not worth the labor which the acquisition has cost" (p. 110). But persuasive and eloquent though the arguments in favor of sign language may have been, they were all too often ignored or derided by oral adherents, especially if they were forwarded by deaf persons.

To those of the oral persuasion, only one method could be used. Oralism was promoted to "the exclusion of a purely conventional language of signs" ("Report of Bell's," 1884, p. 85) and the manual alphabet abandoned as "a hindrance to speech and speech-reading" (Stewart, 1892, p. 151). Nor would oralists contemplate any halfway measures such as the Combined System proposed by Edward Miner Gallaudet, in which students received their basic instruction in sign and selected children who demonstrated oral aptitude were provided with additional articulation training (E. M. Gallaudet, 1895).

Rapidly, oralism became the preferred mode for the instruction of deaf children. Delegates to the Milan congress in 1880 formulated the resolutions regarding the supremacy of speech; those at the Paris congress in 1900 confirmed the supremacy of oralism (Nordin, 1901). The only dissidents were deaf people themselves. In Paris deaf and hearing educators formed different sections, and the president of the hearing section refused to allow motions passed by deaf educators to be reported to his delegates. A visitor could hear in one place, reported deaf Amos Draper (1901), "of the wondrous things oralism can do, and see the triumphant votes in its favor," but would be confused by finding "in an adjacent room some hundreds of deaf men, evidently intelligent . . . earnestly opposing the sweeping claims heard in the first hall" (p. 200). Indeed, the "resolutions adopted by the Deaf Section on the question of methods of instruction were almost identical to those that were rejected by the Hearing section" (E. A.

Table 6-2

Communication Modes Used with Deaf Students

Manual methods	Sign language, with much writing
Combined method	Sign language for instruction, with articulation taught to pupils who show aptitude
Pure oral method	Speech, lipreading, and writing; no gestures
Oral method	Speech, lipreading, writing, natural gestures
Rochester Method	Fingerspelling, with speech, speechreading, and amplification
Acoupedic method	An oral approach; develops intelligible speech through the maximum development of listening skills
Oral/aural method	Stresses speech, speechreading, amplification, and auditory training
Cued Speech	Primarily oral; uses eight hand configurations and four hand positions to supplement the visible manifestations of speech
Total Communication	Speech, speechreading, amplification, and an English-based manual system
American Sign Language	A true language; quite different from spoken language

Fay, 1900, p. 415). Bell, the official delegate of the U.S. government, brushed criticism aside: "The members of the *Hearing section,*" he said, "were hardly prepared to admit that the opinions of deaf-mutes were entitled to the same weight as those of professional educators of the deaf . . . in an international congress for the study of educational questions" (original italics, E. M. Gallaudet, 1900, p. 479).

It is hardly surprising, though ironic, that the ideology and style of the oralists under Bell could not have been better designed to alienate the very people they sought to serve. Deaf individuals, seeing oral objectives as inimical to their social and intellectual security, aligned themselves with promoters of manual education. Implicit in the criticisms of deaf people was the perception that Bell and the oralists were contributing significantly to the social restrictions experienced by deaf persons, restrictions based on inaccurate evaluations of the impact of deafness (Mitchell, 1973). Not only did the advent of oralism relegate sign language to the status of a ghetto dialect, but it closed a ready route of professionalism to deaf adults, altered the character of the teaching personnel in American schools for deaf students (see Chapter 7), and promoted the notion that deaf persons lacking speech were deviant and defective, if not also prone to un-American and unpatriotic instincts.

To further cloud the communication issue, two alternate modes of communication emerged in the 1870s. The Rochester School in New York perfected a method that incorporated speech, speechreading, and fingerspelling, which was dubbed, not surprisingly, the Rochester Method (see McLaughlin, 1920). An aural method, concentrating on the stimulation of residual hearing, already seen in Jacob Rodrigue Péreire's work in France, reappeared (see Gillespie, 1884).

The late nineteenth-century fascination with the wonders of technology made itself felt throughout the profession, and not just in Bell's work. Many in the profession tried to combine new machines with new methods to find a solution to their students' communication problems. To compensate for a missing or defective sense, schools experimented with a range of technical devices. Some tried rooms with telephones connecting the pupils' desks with the teacher (Ontario, Dept. of Ed., 1907); others, Forchlammer's Phonoscope and Maloney's Otophone, types of hearing aids (*ADD*, 1888), or Verrier's Hearing Tube, which used a fitted ear mold (*ADD*, 1891). Still others experimented with the Currier Duplex Conical Conversational Tube (Currier, 1894). However, they all found that the audiophone, dentaphone, and electrophone were utterly useless (Ontario, Inspector, 1883), as unfortunately were most other contemporary devices touted to improve the hearing of deaf students.

The Academic Programs for Deaf Students

In schools for deaf students that adhered to the manual modes (especially in the first half of the nineteenth century), instruction was generally presented in four compartments—physical education, intellectual education, mechanical education, and religion and morality (Dunscombe, 1836). The heavy emphasis on morals and character development meant that intellectual education, although not ranking "in importance with that of morals and religion," still required "the exercises of talent, industry and perseverance, in a higher degree than any other" (p. 202).

Within "intellectual education," the great object was communication through sign language and written English. The overriding goal was the development of sufficient literacy to allow deaf persons to communicate through reading and writing, not to build up an elaborate and complex system of signs. Students were familiarized with written language and its common colloquial forms, "the only medium through which the deaf and dumb can communicate with the world" (Dunscombe, 1836, p. 194).

Students learned the names of familiar objects and the construction of phrases and sentences, beginning with the present tense (J. A. Ayres, 1852). Young learners were exposed to language by means of such subjects as a history of all domestic animals and fowls; they were read simple stories on slates, and teachers explained puzzling phrases in familiar language (OSD, 1884). To structure students' language learning, teachers employed a grammatical key, "syntax painted to the eye," a visual system representing all the complexities of English grammar—nouns and pronouns, all the forms of verbs, comparatives and superlatives, and so on (Dunscombe, 1836, p. 195).

Only after students had mastered basic communication skills were they instructed in geography, history, and arithmetic. Deaf students often studied from Harvey Peet's elementary work, *A Vocabulary and Elementary Exercise for the Deaf and Dumb* ([1844], 1882), which contained sections of "Scripture history for the deaf and dumb," large vocabularies of familiar phrases, and language exercises (J. A. Ayres, 1852).

Oralists were more optimistic about the intellectual abilities of their deaf clients. They disregarded the flow of manual school graduates to the National

Summary of the Art of Instructing Deaf and Dumb.

GENERAL SYSTEM.

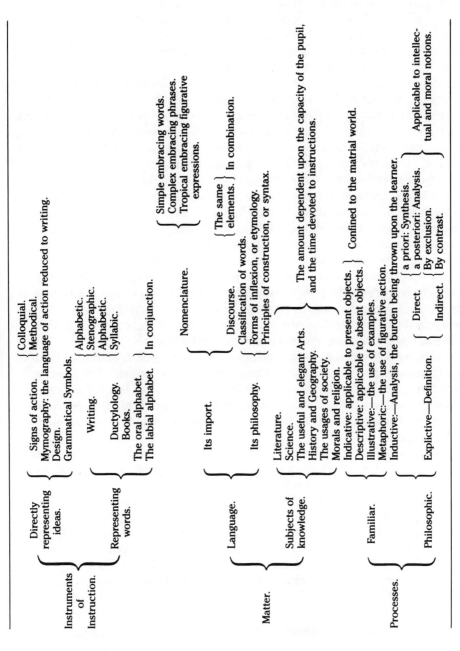

Figure 6-3. General System of Instruction, New York Institution for the Deaf and Dumb.
Source: Dunscombe, 1836.

Deaf Mute College and ridiculed what they perceived as the mediocre intellectual products of manual schools; moreover, they expressed dismay at the narrow social organizations that manualism allowed the deaf person to enter. Oral teachers placed an unprecedented emphasis on academic work, intellectual development superseding the inculcation of moral values. Attempting to win elite status for their students, the oral teachers defined their status claims in such a way as to place more emphasis upon academic achievement and institutional affiliation, less upon defining deafness as a characteristic, and almost none on industrial training. Their curricular reforms led to the imposition of rigorous standards and greatly heightened expectations of the intellectual capacities of deaf students. Not only were students taught academic skills, they were taught values that encouraged them to attempt public roles not previously thought consonant with their handicaps (Winzer, 1981b). Students were persuaded to mingle only with the hearing and to disavow any association with the deaf community. Graduates were groomed to enter the regular universities and discouraged from attending the National Deaf Mute College (Yale, 1931).

Bell was "inclined to think that the more nearly we can pattern our method of teaching after the method adopted by nature in teaching speech to hearing children, the better should be our results" (A. G. Bell, 1911, p. 113). Especially for young children learning under methods that stressed speech and lipreading, natural approaches to language learning, based on the stages of normal language development as they were then understood, emerged. Children were introduced early to reading, with many pictures used to aid comprehension (A. G. Bell, 1890a). Sense training, in the mode of Seguin and Jean Marc Gaspard Itard, was introduced by Caroline Ardelia Yale at the Clarke Institution in 1883, concurrently with other major curricular reforms (Numbers, 1974).

Oral schools stressed the acquisition and use of speech both in and out of the classroom. Specific articulation training began with sessions of fifteen minutes a day, gradually increasing to an hour (Lesperance, 1872). Children first learned to analyze the sounds of a word and to read words of one syllable when arranged in sentences. Then they moved on to read short sentences in colloquial language.

The manual institutions exhibited a passionate devotion to the interests of pupils with regard to industrial training, but the oral schools, holding different aspirations for their pupils, eschewed manual teaching. They taught sewing and cooking to the girls and simple tool work to the boys—the skills the children would probably have learned at home—but made no attempt to teach them a trade (Yale, 1931). In 1898 Caroline Yale reported that, of the latest twenty-five graduates of the Clarke school, nineteen successfully pursued courses in regular high schools and institutions of higher learning to become printers, publishers, engravers, teachers, draftsmen, architects, and other professionals (Numbers, 1974).

Education for Blind Students

Blind children also required special modes of instruction. "Their intellects," noted Samuel Gridley Howe in 1837, "cannot be developed by the common mode of education and it is to supply peculiar processes of instruction that our Insti-

tution is established" (Perkins Inst., 1837, p. 5). Yet Howe saw no contradiction
in aligning the education of blind children as closely as possible with that of
other children. Because "the blind must live among those who see," educators
argued that "we should endeavour to make them, in their habits and temperament, as like the seeing as possible, in order to spare them . . . painful reflection
upon their deprivation" (Duglison, 1854, p. 21). Education aimed at self-reliance,
self-respect, and self-maintenance, although there was a class bias discernible
in specific curricula, especially in the early days.

What was really unique to the instruction in schools for blind students was
the emphasis on oral teaching, communication, religious instruction, and the
materials used (see Bond, 1897; Wait, 1892a). Pupils were exposed to reading by
raised letters and were taught to write by special methods; arithmetic was
taught by the use of tangible figures or types (Perkins Inst., 1858, p. 9). Geography was presented through raised maps and globes, which were made "with
infinite pain and expense" by glueing strings onto another map pasted on a
board (*Address,* 1833, p. 109). Music was seen as fundamental and vital—teachers stressed vocal and instrumental music as well as theory (Perkins Inst., 1893).
There are indications that Howe's wife, Julia Ward Howe, provided singing instruction for both blind and mentally retarded pupils at the Perkins Institution
(Graham and Beer, 1980).

Howe's medical orientation led him to stress physical aspects of the curriculum: he was wont to correlate the restricted mobility associated with blindness
with lowered vitality and robustness in his pupils, and he consequently elevated
physical health and exercise to a major concern. Every day when the pupils at
the Perkins Institution rose, they opened the flues and windows, and they hung
their bed clothes on wooden frames in the open air for two hours "to get rid of
the humid exhalations of the body" (Perkins Inst. 1837, p. 4). Daily, pupils were
placed outside the school buildings with the doors locked to ensure their getting
enough fresh air (Koestler, 1976). And because a lack of physical mobility was
equated with lack of mental stimulation, regular and hearty physical education
was used to enhance bodily health and vigor (Perkins Inst., 1894).

The Battle of the Types

The divisive issue of communication modes that permeated deaf education
had its counterpart in the education of blind students, the so-called Battle of the
Types, though it was marked by less intensity and antagonism. By 1890 teachers
of blind students in Europe, Britain, and North America were hopelessly divided
over reading methods. They failed to agree on the question of whether Braille,
Roman print, New York point, or even Moon's type was the most suitable (Perkins Inst., 1895). In fact, when the American Printing House for the Blind began
printing library books, they issued proportionate numbers in Roman, Braille,
and New York point (Perkins Inst., 1895).

Following Valentin Haüy, early educators of blind pupils stressed the advisability of students' learning to read and write in modes analogous to those employed by sighted persons. Blind children, educators argued, should be
educated by means of the common alphabet so that others could read and communicate with them (Duglison, 1854, p. 20). Haüy used a type of raised print;

Table 6-3

Reading Systems Used with Blind Students

Early methods	Raised print; letters cut out of wooden blocks or cardboard, letters carved in relief or incised into wood or wax that simulated the normal alphabet
Boston line type	Howe's modified version of Haüy's raised print; angular modifications of upper- and lower-case Roman letters
Roman print	Raised letters in Roman print
Moon's type	Raised capitals of Roman letters reduced to the simplest forms, giving nine characters in different formations readable by touch or sight
New York point	Dot system using the fewest dots to code the most frequently used letters
Braille	Alphabetic dot system employing combinations of six dots

other used letters cut out of wooden blocks or cardboard, or letters carved in relief or incised into wood or wax that simulated the normal alphabet.

Boston line type, the predominant print used with blind pupils in the United States at the outset, was Howe's modified version of Haüy's raised print. It was not composed of arbitrary characters, but of angular modifications of upper- and lower-case Roman letters. At the Perkins Institution Howe built a press for Boston line type in 1836 in order to print materials for blind persons in English. In addition to schoolbooks, the press printed the *Acts of the Apostles,* a book of psalms, and the whole *New Testament.* Its first nonreligious text, *The Old Curiosity Shop,* took $1,700 to produce, costs fully covered by Charles Dickens himself (Koestler, 1976).

Other methods soon emerged. Roman print was particularly popular; it was regarded by blind persons as the print of their ancestors, of parents, and of the general population (Perkins Inst., 1895). Moon's type, named after its originator, Dr. William Moon, was first produced in England in 1847 and introduced into the United States in 1880 (Koestler, 1976). Moon's type consisted of raised letters; it used capitals of Roman letters reduced to the simplest forms, which gave nine characters in different formations that could be read by touch or sight. In these stripped-down and simplified versions of Roman capital letters, for example, the *A* had no crossbar, the *D* lacked its vertical line (Koestler, 1976).

There also was New York point, a dot system devised in 1868 by William Bell Wait, superintendent of the New York Institution for the Blind, as an improvement over the Braille code. New York point differed from Braille in that Wait took into account the frequency of certain letters such as *a* and *e* and made the fewest dots code the most frequently used letters. The code was only two dots high, although the width of the base could be one, two, three, or four dots. The American Printing House for the Blind, which was formally established in 1858 but could begin printing only after funds were finally available in 1866, did all music notations in New York point until 1892. An Act to Promote the Education of the Blind, passed by Congress in 1879, gave financial support for books for blind persons. Nearly all schoolbooks produced under this federal subsidiary were in New York point until 1890. Braille books were available but were not free (see Koestler, 1976).

As a system to assist blind persons read and write, the Braille code failed for many decades to find a niche in North America. The system arose from the work of Charles Barbiere, engineer, inventor, philanthropist, and officer in Napoleon's army, who devised a code he called *écriture nocturne*—night writing. These were not tracings of the ordinary alphabet but a secret code based on a twelve-dot unit or cell two dots wide and six high. Each dot or combination of dots stood for a letter or a phonetic sound.

In 1808, when Barbiere's system was presented to the Académie des Sciences in France, it was hailed as a brilliant invention. Various adaptations of the system were undertaken by Barbiere and duly submitted to the academy. One report found its way to the school for blind students in Paris, where the twelve-dot system was tried but rejected as impractical in 1820: the cells were simply too large to be read by a single fingertip. At the time when blind people rejected Barbiere's system, Louis Braille (1809–1852) was only eleven years old, but he would, less than two decades later, create a way to overcome the problems of Barbiere's code (Koestler, 1976).

Louis Braille was the son of a harness maker. He slit an eye at age three while playing with a sharp knife, and the resulting infection destroyed vision in both the injured and his other eye. In 1819 Braille went to the Paris school and later became an instructor there. Disconcerted by the raised-point method of teaching reading to blind pupils, Braille embarked on a search for a more efficient means. When he discovered Barbiere's military code, he set out to adapt it to meet the needs of blind readers.

When Braille undertook the adaptation of the Barbiere system, he first determined that the cell of twelve dots, two vertical rows six dots high, was too tall to be comprehended with a fingertip. After halving the number of dots, Braille then devised a new code, alphabetic rather than phonetic, employing combinations of six dots. Because the new code was arbitrary, the symbols could stand for anything the users wanted to code. Braille's alphabetic code was published in 1834; his music notations, in 1839. The Braille system for reading and writing was officially adopted at the Paris school for the blind in 1854.

Dr. Simon Pollak, one of the founders of the Missouri School for the Blind, brought the Braille system from Europe. From the 1850s on, Americans experimented with the use of Braille, although the transition was neither tranquil nor universal. In fact, American schools preferred New York point over Braille; many believed that New York point, Boston line type, and Roman type were better because Braille is not easily read by the sighted and its use would sever blind people from the seeing world altogether (Perkins Inst., 1895).

In the late 1850s Braille was introduced at Pollak's St. Louis school for blind persons. At first, students used it for surreptitious notes; music teachers were the first to use it in instruction (Koestler, 1976). The Perkins Institution adopted the Braille code in 1879. In some schools students selected their own mode. At the Halifax Institution for the Blind students were taught to read using Haüy's raised print in the Howe modified version; those over the age of sixteen could choose Braille (Halifax Inst. for the Blind, 1875). However, Halifax also experimented with the Moon system of raised print in 1877; it was not until 1892 that Halifax began using Braille with all students, at about the same time the code gained general acceptance in North American schools for the blind.

By 1892 most schools for blind students in North America opted for the Braille dot system. The fundamental reason for its adoption was that it was good for writing as well as for reading. Another potent factor leading to the acceptance of Braille was the 1890 invention of the Brailler by Frank Hall, superintendent of the Illinois Institution for the Education of the Blind (see Irvine, 1976b). Hall's Braille writer, a modification of the standard typewriter, used Braille rather than New York point because of the consistency of the Braille code; the usefulness of the new machine elevated Braille to the paramount position in the education of the blind. Hall also developed a motorized version and a comparable writing device for New York point, but by the time the latter was available, Braille had achieved dominance. The American Printing House for the Blind was then allowed subsidies for Braille printing.

The production of publications using dot codes, whether New York point or Braille, was cumbersome and laborious. Methods were slow, requiring hand composition. With Braille, a single sheet could be produced by the use of a Braille slate and a stylus. The production of more than one copy required duplicating machinery of some sort. Early efforts used adaptations of standard printing techniques and equipment. Moveable type set up the dot pattern in high relief; the type was then locked into a frame, placed in a flat press, and applied to heavy paper with sufficient pressure to make dents in the paper without piercing it. Sometimes the moveable type was cast in metal bars, one for each line, before being put in the press. Another method was to punch dots in a metal plate by means of a heavy stylus and a hammer. The hand-punched plate then served as a stereotype with a pattern that could be transferred to paper by a flat or rotary printing press. Then, once the heavy Braille sheets were embossed, they had to be varnished and dried to preserve the dots (Koestler, 1976).

Even though schools accepted the Braille code, the argument about which system was best teetered on. A commission on uniform type was established in 1915 to seek a solution to the question of standardized tactual forms. By 1917 a newly modified Braille code was accepted as the universal American standard for the printed word (Koestler, 1976), and it was decided that all literature would be done in that medium.

Deaf-blind Students

In a burst of nineteenth-century hyperbole, a newspaper reporter wrote, "Dr. Howe's wise, devoted work in the education of the blind and deaf-blind was not enlightened for his own time merely, but will outlast even the cherished memory of his name" (*Boston Evening Transcript,* Nov. 12, 1901). Certainly, Howe's contributions were not restricted to promoting special schooling; he proved a thoughtful commentator on learning environments in general and anticipated future conventions in special education. Howe took an interest in the daily operations of the Perkins Institution and personally sought out and enrolled many pupils. He advised the parents of blind children on the values of very early training and on exploration and mobility. He suggested that parents not be overprotective of their children and stressed the need for the development of courage, self-reliance, generosity of character, and much exercise (Perkins Inst., 1874).

Apart from his magnificent contributions as an educational reformer and founder, Howe is probably best remembered for his work with Laura Dewey Bridgman, a girl whom scarlet fever at the age of two had robbed of sight, hearing, taste, and smell. In 1837 Howe was escorted to a New Hampshire farmhouse where he met seven-year-old Laura. Howe enrolled the child in the Perkins school and there embarked on a structured series of lessons and exercises. He first took common objects, attached labels to them that spelled the names in raised letters, and trained Laura to associate the name with the object touched. Once she knew that letters were single entities that could be rearranged into words, Laura advanced quickly. Howe then taught her the manual alphabet, and eventually Laura read embossed books, did simple arithmetic, and mastered needlework and other kinds of handicrafts. She never became fully independent and remained at Perkins until her death in 1889 (see E. M. Gallaudet, 1876; Gleason, 1938; Howe and Hall, 1903; Lamson, 1878).

Howe's extensive reports of Laura Bridgman's education and development left an outstanding legacy to the entire field of special education, and to teachers of the deaf-blind in particular (Hallahan and Kauffman, 1982). His son-in-law, Michael Anagnos, used Howe's directives when Helen Keller became a pupil at the Perkins Institution.

Helen Keller, deafened and blinded by disease at the age of nineteen months, was until the age of seven an untutored, half-wild child, unable to perform the simplest tasks. Her father took six-year-old Helen to see Alexander Graham Bell in Washington in November 1888, and Bell contacted the Perkins Institution for the family (A. G. Bell, 1891b). Subsequently, Helen's father hired Anne Mansfield Sullivan, a pupil of Perkins, who taught Helen. Once she overcame the behavioral obstacles, Sullivan found Helen an amazingly apt pupil. In less than three months, for example, Helen learned to spell about four hundred words and to write a letter unaided. It took the child only six weeks to master Braille (see Blatt, 1985). Reports of Helen Keller's education (Farrell, 1956a) and her own advocacy and writings (e.g., Keller, 1903, 1929) illustrated the potential of persons with multiple handicapping conditions. Nevertheless, so daunting to educators did multiple handicaps appear that consistent educational approaches for affected children would have to wait until the 1960s (see Winzer, 1993).

Instruction for Mentally Retarded Students

Schools for mentally retarded children tended to adhere to the sense-training techniques developed by Péreire, Jean Jacques Rousseau, and Itard (Vineland, 1904). Physiological instruction, healthful exercise, and household employment constituted the core of the daily routine.

Rousseau's ideas, which tended toward the isolation and manipulation of the child, were adapted by Édouard Seguin; he expanded the techniques of Péreire and Itard into a complex systematic sequence of training that he called the "physiological method" and brought Rousseau's child into the warm reality of life, home, play, and learning. Seguin's efforts contributed much to the public awareness of special education for mentally retarded children in North America: his 1866 *Idiocy and Its Treatment by the Physiological Method* formed the basis for training programs in most institutions for the mentally retarded. Under his direction programs were founded on individual assessment; they tended to be highly structured, systematic, directional, and multisensory; emphasized training in self-help skills and daily living skills; and frequently used games, songs, and positive reinforcement (Kauffman, 1989).

In developing his methodology, Seguin readily adapted materials and techniques from education, philosophy, and medicine, and he modified his methods on the basis of work with normal children. Given his early medical training and his experiences with Jean Étienne Dominique Esquirol at Bicêtre and Salpêtrière, it is not surprising that a physiological point of view permeated Seguin's efforts.

Echoing Jacob Péreire, Seguin's early work was founded on the idea that the five senses are all variations of the sense of touch. Seguin believed that mentally retarded children can learn if taught through specific sensory motor exercises. His approach to training consisted of a number of interrelated steps: training the muscular system, training the nervous system, educating the senses, acquiring general ideas, developing the ability to think in abstract terms, and acquiring a strong understanding and practice of moral and social precepts (Barr, [1904b] 1913). Seguin's program developed the functions in order: the senses first, then intellectual functions, and finally the emotional faculties. All were to be undertaken in an institutional setting, which Seguin viewed as an educational facility whose main objective is to make children responsible members of society.

The physiological approach used a sequence of movement training, discrimination training, classification, object association, and logical operations (Seguin, 1846). Various techniques were applied to the training of the senses, especially the visual and the auditory. For example, visual sense training was accomplished by the use of blocks of various sizes and forms and colors.

Physical exercise was crucial to training. Howe, who used Seguin's methods in his Massachusetts experimental school, related in his 1851 *Annual Report* the tale of a six-year-old-boy who seemed severely retarded (Kauffman, 1989). The child could not walk, talk, or feed himself, and he functioned like an infant of three months. Howe's treatment consisted of daily cold baths, rubbing the child's limbs, moving him about outdoors in a wagon pulled by the other boys, and exercising his muscles and making him use them. After a year Howe reported that the child could walk alone, though cautiously, could sit at table and use a knife and fork, and could feed himself (Kauffman, 1989).

Institutional teachers similarly stressed physical aspects both in explicit exercises and training and as part of other subject areas. Often, the day began with children assembling for singing and marching exercises (Doren, 1878). Gymnasiums came equipped with ladders, swings, steps, and dumbbells to develop and invigorate the muscular system (Brockett, 1856). Children would be trained, for example, to walk along a plank ten inches wide or to step between the rungs of a ladder laid on the floor to learn balance and direction.

Music, a particularly important branch of training, was used to stimulate and improve listening ability, to assist in speech training, and for band and choir

work. Some superintendents pointed with considerable pride to the performance ensembles developed at their institutions. "One hour of the forenoon is
spent with those who seem to have a taste for vocal music in teaching them to
sing," explained the superintendent of the Illinois Asylum for Feeble-Minded
Children. "The singing of the pupils of this special music class," he said, "will
compare with that of any school in the land" (Wilbur, 1876, p. 240, cited in Graham and Beer, 1980).

Deborah Kallikak (1889–1978), who was to attain a certain sort of fame
through Henry Herbert Goddard's writings (see Chapter 9), was a prominent
member of the musical groups at the institution at Vineland. Deborah was institutionalized at the age of eight. Edgar Doll (1983) observed that whatever her
intelligence, the child showed a certain grace and facility in movement, in rote
memory, and in music. She was featured in many of the entertainments, playing
the cornet in the band and as the star of many plays (Doll, 1983).

The institutional music groups became recognized for their musical prow-
ess and in many cases gave regular concerts for their fellow students and for
visitors as well as exhibitions resembling those that deaf and blind students had
engaged in earlier. Toward the end of the nineteenth century it was common
practice to have institutional bands perform at horse shows, regional fairs, carnivals, and picnics (Graham and Beer, 1980). The individuals who participated in
these lucrative, at least for the institution, exercises, were selected on the basis
of interest and talent and in most cases were taught to perform. Some institutional children spent most of their lifetime "assigned to the band" (p. 8). The
schedule of the Iowa Institution for Feeble Minded Children (Figure 6-4) shows
explicitly the amount of time devoted to music.

Of particular importance in the instruction of mentally retarded children
was the acquisition of speech, which was difficult to teach and often required
"one or two years of patient labor before the enunciation of the first word"
(Brockett, 1856). Again music proved invaluable; often, children would hum
tunes before they were able to articulate words (Tredgold, [1908] 1922). To teach
the mechanisms of speech, teachers would shape and mold the student's lips
with their fingers, or put blocks of various sizes and shapes in their mouths
(Brockett, 1856). Teachers taught single sounds first and then joined these in
blends and diphthongs.

Children were taught to read by what we would today call a whole-word
method, which is based on the notion that words and not letters can be associated with objects. Geography was taught by outline maps and the elementary
principles of grammar through highly structured exercises in which the teacher
would give a sentence and the children would repeat it. Even basic mathematics
was particularly difficult for mentally retarded pupils, but with patient and repeated exercises and slow and painful practice, "the mysteries of numeration,
addition, subtraction, multiplication, and division [were] unravelled" (Brockett,
1856), for some at least.

In institutions adopting Seguin's principles, structure reigned. The day began with the teachers leading all the children in singing and marching exercises,
after which children went to their respective classrooms and followed a formalized program. Each teacher had a set of lessons, and the children rotated
through teachers in groups so that two successive lessons would not use "the

#		Grammar and Writing.	Arithmetic.	Arithmetic.	Reading and Spelling.		Geography and Physiology.	Numbers, Reading and Writing.
1	Morning exercises in Assembly Hall.	Grammar and Writing.	Arithmetic.	Arithmetic.	Reading and Spelling.	Recess.	Geography and Physiology.	Numbers, Reading and Writing.
2		Spelling.	Arithmetic.	Reading, Physiology.	Spelling and Arithmetic.		Reading and Geography	Spelling and Arithmetic.
3		Chart and Word Method	Numbers Word Method	Reading Language.	Spelling and Numbers.		Writing.	Second Singing Class.
4		Arithmetic.	Printing work and Reading	Reading.	Primary Arithmetic.		Arithmetic.	
5		Chart.	Chart.	Word Method	Word Method		Reading.	Geography.
6		Writing.		Reading.	Chart.		Reading.	Numbers.
7		Spelling.	Numbers and Reading.	Word Drill.	General.		Writing.	Word Method.
7		Form Drill.	Chart and Word Drill.	Numbers.	Word Method		Piano Instruction.	Second Singing Class.
8		Reading.	Word Method	Charts.	Individual Work.		Writing.	Form and Color.
9		1st K.G. Circle Work.	Reading.	Chart and Word Method	Spelling.		Numbers.	Numbers.
10		Color and Form.	Words and Chart.	Word Method	Writing.		Numbers.	Counting.
11	1st Division March Drill and Reading	Form Drill.	Attention Exercise.	Numbers.	Industrial Work.	2d. Division Attention Exercise.	Form Drill and Marching.	Noon intermission.
12	Band.	8:00-9:00.	9:00-10:00	10:00-11:00.	11:00-12:00.			
			Turning.	Carving.	Bench Work.			
			Cornets.	Trombone.	Alto Horm.			

2:00-2:30.	2:30-3:00.	3:00-3:30.	3:30-4:00.	
Second K.G. Story and Gift Work.	Angles and Lines.	Occupations.	Games.	Miss Dean.
Second Drawing Class.	1st Drawing Class		Calisthenics.	Miss Powell.
First Sewing Class.	Industrial Work.			Miss Waynick.
				Miss Irwin.
Reading.	Spelling.	Writing.	Industrial Work.	Miss Gene Sartelle.
Writing		Hand Sewing		
Word Method.	Reading Numbers,	Individual Work.	Industrial Work	Miss Inseare.
Fancy Needle Work.		Response.		Miss Clift.
First Singing Class	Piano Instruction.		Calisthenics.	Miss Shulters.
Number.	Number.	Industrial Work.		Miss Maywood.
Writing	Gift Work.	Occupation Work.	Games.	Miss Seelye.
First Sewing Class.				Mrs. Wahl.
Third Division Attention Drill.	Form.	Color and Reading.	Manual Drill.	Miss Sartelle.

(Dismission. — spanning the 3:30-4:00 period)

2:00-2:40	2:40-3:20.	3:20-4:00.	4:00-4:45	
Carving.	Turning.	Benchwork.	Band.	Mr. Bicknell.
Drums.	Bass.	Trombone.		

Figure 6-4. Schedule of the Iowa Institution for the Feeble Minded.
SOURCE: Annual Report of the Iowa Institution for the Feeble-minded, 1883.

same set of organs, nor exact the same intellectual functions." The rotation also prevented "the moral fatigue which results from protracted and often unsuccessful contacts of obedience and understanding" (Seguin, [1866] 1907, p. 277).

Seguin seemed to prefer to work with children at the lower end of the scale, those who unaided would make no progress. After bringing the "idiot" to a recognition and appreciation of the environment and those in it, his next objective was to "overcome the filthy and degrading habits in which the idiot has hitherto indulged; to transform this gluttonous, beastly creature into a man, capable of observing all the properties of life" (Brockett, 1856). Only through patience, intelligence, and love would such a laudable objective be assured.

Brockett and others were quick to point out that not more than a quarter of the retarded population acquired the hoped-for skills and competencies through Seguin's physiological method. In school, girls tended to outstrip boys in academic and vocational endeavors. "The natural gentleness of the sex," educators observed, "makes them more submissive, more docile, more ready to renounce bad habits, while they are more imitative and more desirous of pleasing." Moreover, "their greater fitness for sedentary and household life and duties qualifies them for usefulness in a sphere which boys cannot fill" (Howe, 1848b, p. 72).

Some children were deemed to be beyond the reach of education: those who were "helpless as infants" or "excitable and noisy with marked destructive tendencies" (Vineland, 1893) were more often placed in custodial rather than educational departments. Too, Seguin's techniques came under attack as not being readily adaptable to the full range of mentally retarded persons. "Seguin impresses us as an emperor endowed with great personal talent, which he has not succeeded in embodying clearly in his work," carped Alfred Binet. To Binet, Seguin's writings contained "some pages of good sense, with many obscurities, and many absurdities." Binet felt that the time devoted to sensory training would be better spent on learning to read street signs (Binet and Simon, 1914, pp. 3–4). Even though a more functional skills approach later did become prevalent in the training of retarded learners, sense training did not fade. In fact, the entire notion of remediating subskill deficits through specific sense-training activities underlay early instructional techniques for children labeled as learning disabled (see Chapter 11).

Seguin's influence on the education and training of mentally retarded children remained pervasive and profound, both in his own era and later. At the beginning of the twentieth century Maria Montessori (1870–1951) in Italy and Ovide Decroly (1871–1932) in Belgium, both psychiatrists and influenced by Seguin's ideas, opened new educational avenues (Rosen, Clark, and Kivitz, 1976).

Montessori was instrumental in establishing educational and rehabilitation programs for retarded children. Her methods grew directly from Seguin's work; she combined the physiological approach of Seguin with the newer approaches based on child development advocated by Friedrich Froebel. She demonstrated how these children could be helped to live fuller, more meaningful lives. Throughout this work, she insisted that mental retardation was an educational, not a medical problem (Montessori, 1912; 1917). When she began to work with retarded children in Italy, Montessori established a prepared environment in which children were free to use materials of their own choice and at their own pace. Montessori wanted each of the materials, which provided experiences with length, breadth, height, color, texture, weight, size, and form, to be used in a specific manner to provide a portion of the self-education that she envisioned.

Montessori's work was lent impetus in North America through the efforts of Alexander and Mabel Bell, who were instrumental in launching the method and assisting Montessori to visit the United States. The Bells became conspicuous leaders in the Montessori movement: each served as president of the Washington Montessori Association (M. H. Bell, 1914; R. Bruce, 1973).

Industrial School Training

The common schools' failure to prevent juvenile crime and vagrancy generated arguments in support of the establishment of more specialized institutions. The protection of children from the contamination of adult improvidence and vicious example would be effectively ensured by their segregation in specialized institutions where they could be instructed in the morality and mores of the middle class. The thrust of industrial, reform, and preventive schools centered first on identifying deviant children and then on providing them with a better place to live while they were in custody.

The controllers and participants in the surveillance network of these settings filled interlocking roles: matrons, nurses, clergy, attendants, teachers, domestic and trade supervisors, physicians, and official visitors. All came from middle-class backgrounds and held distinct sets of values, and together they created in the industrial schools the marriage of industrial education and cherished social values. The type of education supplied was a judicious mixture of humane amelioration and rational objectives intended to diminish the urban nuisance of beggars and paupers while providing society with additional skilled workers.

The Lockean principle of a working school, advocated as far back as 1697, was practiced enthusiastically in these schools. Dedicated to the task of "directing the life [*sic*] of the boys in the paths of usefullness" (Ferrier, 1923), industrial schools demonstrated a genuine devotion to the interests of their pupils in the matter of trade teaching. Literacy was taught but, as the essential tenet was industrial education to provide future remunerative employment, intellectual pursuits were minimal.

INSTITUTIONAL LIFE

Information on the actual classroom practices that were employed and the curricula that were presented to nineteenth-century exceptional pupils is scant. Even less detail is available about institutional life or the way in which children responded to it. In some ways, at least, institutional living was a negation of normal family life. Deaf and blind children were separated from home or family for ten months a year; mentally retarded children, sometimes completely.

It goes beyond the purview of the historian to describe the children's perception of their existence in the institutions, but we can imagine how frightening and intimidating the first encounter with schooling and educational authorities must have been for young children. Take, for example, one eight-year-old deaf child from northern Saskatchewan who had to travel the more than three thousand miles to school. She came by canoe from Cumberland House to The Pas to meet a train at Yorkton, where a social worker gathered all the children, neatly tagged them with their names and destinations, and traveled with them on a three- or four-day journey, during which they ate food from home and one daily meal supplied by the railroad (MacDonald et al., 1984).

Once in school, a student would find institutional life to be routine and regimented, both in the classroom and in living arrangements. Here, programs and routines were even more highly regimented than they were in the common schools. In their zeal to organize the common schools into an efficient system, Horace Mann and his fellow educators promoted an authoritarian structure. Rote learning remained the rule despite the pleas of some reformers; classroom procedures were formal and intensely structured, with sequenced textbooks for students to memorize. Physical activity and creativity were routine suppressed; conformity was the norm and, except for structured classroom lessons, there was no such expressive outlet as clay modeling or painting, nor was there direct or experiential nature study.

Institutional records are relatively silent about punishment, but they are bound to have been as severe as that used in the common schools if not more severe. Retributive and deterrent elements, of course, were not lacking in the common schools. Harsh discipline and strict punishment prevailed, one reason being that teachers handled large numbers of students. Corporal punishment was condoned, justified by the necessity to maintain adult authority. However, the use of corporal punishment declined rapidly as the century progressed. Horace Mann and other educational reformers repudiated the rod because it evoked a passionate reaction both in those whipping and in those being whipped. The recognition by the medical profession that children could be injured by physical discipline both drew on and reinforced opinions fostered in campaigns against corporal punishment. According to special educators, the good behavior among institutionalized children seemed remarkable when one considered the fact that "the early moral training of many of them has been entirely neglected at home" (OSD, 1873, p. 24). In special education few cases of corporal punishment are evident from school records; in fact, in some institutions corporal punishment was forbidden (see Vineland, 1902). More often children seemed to be deprived of privileges or committed to "reflection chambers" (OSD, 1888, p. 9).

Most of the early institutions were established on a congregate plan; children slept in communal dormitories and played and ate in large common rooms. Cottage plans and colonies developed first in the schools for retarded children; these were based on Seguin's colony model, which was planned as a home-like reunion for children.

The question of coeducation or single-sex schools was hotly debated. Indeed, separation of the sexes was not unique to the institutions for exceptional children; the boys and girls in many grammar and secondary schools in the public school system were segregated as recently as the 1930s, and many private schools exclusively for boys or for girls thrive today. Samuel Gridley Howe, who had a word on everything related to special education, unequivocally asserted,

"Co-education of the sexes among the abnormal and defective classes such as the blind and the mutes, is undesirable, unfavorable, and sometimes leads to lamentable consequences" (Howe, 1874, p. 102).

Schools for exceptional children went to extraordinary lengths to prevent boy-girl social relations, and students could be punished for mingling with members of the opposite sex. In some institutions for blind persons, a student found openly conversing with one of the opposite sex was subject to peremptory expulsion. Even in class, children were divided by sex. At the Perkins Institution for the Blind, boys' and girls' departments opened and closed on different days to prevent the children's becoming acquainted with one other on the trains (Koestler, 1976).

By the 1890s there were suggestions to separate boys and girls in the institutions for the feebleminded. Many educators, however, felt that efforts to separate the sexes would result in nothing less than disaster; others argued for different models for different groups. They did not feel there was as much danger in mixing the feebleminded as there was in coeducation for blind or deaf students, chiefly because "the feeble-minded generally lack the intelligence which the deaf and dumb and the blind have for laying out plans and schemes for clandestine meetings" (Vineland, 1893, pp. 34–35). In fact, the superintendent of the Vineland Institution, E. R. Johnstone, wrote that separating boys and girls would be "like locking the door on a crazy man. He can beat it until he gets out, when, if the door be left open, he may not care to go out" (p. 33). Not only did superintendents believe that separation was unnecessary for these youngsters, but they saw social advantages in integration. From each other, children learned lessons of politeness, gentleness, and courtesy, and they gained insight into the customs and manners of everyday life (p. 37). Teachers were not so sanguine. At the Elwyn Institution in Pennsylvania teachers as a unit declared that there was nothing gained in coeducation, even in convenience, while the nervous strain of disciplining the students would be greatly increased. A rearrangement of classes according to sex rather than grade was deemed advisable (Rosen, Clark, and Kivitz, 1976).

Food, largely raised or grown by pupils, was a constant area of concern. Superintendents promoted good dietary habits; pupils often complained about the food. "Abundant and suitable nutrition" was a necessity to "build up a constitution originally enfeebled by the physical causes which gave rise to their misfortune" (I. L. Peet, 1883, p. 414). At one school a Sunday menu included hash, bread, butter, coffee, and milk for breakfast, roast beef and mutton, gravy, potatoes, corn, butter, bread, apple and tapioca pudding for dinner, and grapes, bread, butter and tea for tea. On a weekday breakfast might consist of porridge, milk, syrup, bread, butter, and tea. Dinner, the large meal, might be roast beef and mutton again, gravy, potatoes, cabbage, and bread, with a supper of apples, bread, butter, tea, and milk (OSD, 1892, p. 19).

THE PROSPECTS FACING GRADUATES OF THE INSTITUTIONS

Little is known about the experiences of disabled adults in nineteenth-century society. A few overcame their handicaps to attain positions of prominence; a few suffered the indignity of stardom as freaks in circus sideshows. But history tells us little about the living experiences, occupations, marriage patterns, child-rearing practices, and recreational activities of the average disabled adult. Only sparse and scattered data exist—institutional records offer little information, the vagaries of the public record even less. Exceptional people themselves left little in writing. Although their silence may be attributable to their disabilities, we must not overlook the possibility that, by and large, they simply melded into the general community.

The Blind Graduates

Throughout history, blind persons have been viewed somewhat more favorably than have persons who are mentally retarded, deaf, or disabled in other ways (Anagnos, [1882] 1904; H. Best, 1919; French, 1932). Aristotle thought blindness to be more physically debilitating but deafness, more intellectually devastating. Moreover, it was said that blind people elicited more sympathy from others; "the blind have probably have had less of positive suffering from cold, nakedness, and hunger than other dependent classes. Neither the deaf-mute, nor the lunatics, nor the idiots, nor the halt, nor the crippled, excite so much compassion, nor receive such ready aid, as do the blind" (Perkins Inst., 1873, p. 31).

John Kitto, deaf himself, concluded that with regard to "the culture of the mind," deaf individuals were more deprived than blind persons (Kitto, 1852, p. 8). Samuel Gridley Howe agreed, observing that deafness "does necessarily lessen the amount of human pleasure and enjoyment more than blindness" (Howe, 1875). Blindness was a handicap, he said, but not one of the most devastating; it constituted "a mere bodily infirmity or imperfection, which deprives a man of the perception of light, and limits the freedom of his locomotion, but which impairs not his health, which dwarfs not his mind, which affects not his soul, which crushes not his affections, and which puts him off from none of the high and essential sources of human happiness" (Perkins Inst., 1850, p. 34). Further, said Howe, "in all that regards his moral nature and his social affections, he has capacities far higher than the deaf mute" (Perkins Inst., 1850, p. 25). Blind people, said Howe, "are cheerful, hopeful, sociable and confiding, while deaf mutes are inclined to melancholy, to be uncommunicative, unsocial, jealous, suspicious and dissatisfied with their lot in life" (Howe, 1875).

Despite its supposed advantages over other disabilities, blindness has been perceived as social liability, as punishment for sin, or as uselessness to self and others. And whether blind persons are protected or harassed, their disability arouses special responses from the sighted (Farrell, 1956b; French, 1932; I. Ross, 1951). Seeing persons tend to be ambivalent toward anyone who is blind—contradictory and paradoxical beliefs abound. Along with overprotectiveness and the expectation that blind people are innately dependent on charity, there exists the naive belief in the blind person's special powers. It has long been believed that blind people have the capacity to compensate for their loss by the development of special acuity in the other senses and of some magical inner vision (see Koestler, 1976).

Myths, stereotypes, and prejudices that have traditionally surrounded blind persons have forced them into roles of dependency. As beggars, mendicants, paupers, they were throughout the ages "thrown upon the charity of their more favored fellows" (Dunscombe, 1836, p. 96). The begging concessions allowed blind persons right through to the late nineteenth century had their beginnings in early Christianity. The tin cup, still common, emphasizes the helplessness of the blind person. Until the early decades of the twentieth century, blind persons were allowed to peddle without licenses; laws respecting vagrants and tramps did not apply to blind people, as begging was still seen as their natural way (H. Best, 1934).

The reformers in special education of nineteenth-century North America focused on the need to lift blind adults out of these stereotypical, dependent roles. To break the begging cycle and provide paid employment, for example, Howe opened an adult workshop for blind persons in 1840, and the Perkins Institution began a work department for blind adults a decade later (Perkins Inst., 1864). By 1908 there were sixteen workshops in North America for blind men and women, with 583 blind workers; broom making and chair caning were the major industries (Koestler, 1976).

The Deaf Graduates

The lack of a common mode of communication and similar ways of expressing thought sharply separated the deaf population from the larger hearing world. Once in general society, deaf persons "found few associates capable of interesting them in general conversation and this greatly retarded their material prosperity and happiness" (OSD, 1893, p. 18). A widely held belief in the moral and biological inferiority of deaf persons compounded the problems arising from restricted interaction and enhanced the derogatory evaluations of deaf persons. Most could contemplate only a subordinate social status, one that hearing educators urged them to accept with equanimity (Mitchell, 1973).

Nevertheless, increasing numbers of deaf graduates, trained in the urban trades, were drawn toward the cities in search of remunerative employment, although the movement was a trickle, not a flow. They formed a small part of the general urban migration of the nineteenth century, which arose from a number of factors. The city attracted new immigrants in search of work; other forces impelling North Americans toward the cities included the rise of school-taught trades, growing alienation from farm life and work, and the presence of an enticing urban support system (Winzer, 1986c). Once in the cities, many deaf graduates faced meager prospects and limited opportunities for social mobility. Education was crucial in determining who was to become a professional and what one's class status was to be. One's level of schooling increasingly dictated entry into certain occupations. Any real opportunities for white-collar clerical employment existed at a higher social level that was closely linked to secondary schooling (Houston, 1982). Only those rare deaf persons with the appropriately sophisticated education could hope for better employment opportunities.

As we have seen in the earlier section on trade teaching, deaf people tended to cluster in manual laboring enterprises, with a decreasing number going to farming (Winzer, 1981a, 1986c). As well, deaf people had to contend with the enduring stigma that "tended to prejudice them in the opinion of the public, and still further handicapped them in their efforts to obtain a livelihood in competition with hearing people" (Ontario, Dept. of Ed., 1905, p. 234). Compounding the problems created by prejudice was a widespread concern about the competence of deaf workers; many employers distrusted their capacity to operate machinery (*ADD*, 1907), and the advent of compensation laws placed many of these same employers in precarious positions (Perry, 1943). Deaf people were refused work by employers who were fearful that "they were especially liable to accidents which could entail upon their employers the payment of compensation" (*ADD*, 1907, p. 116). Later, several states passed laws prohibiting deaf persons from operating motor vehicles on the public highways (*ADD*, 1923, p. 245).

Deaf persons emerging from the institutions thus found "great difficulty in finding employment, in making friends, and in finding entertainment of any kind" (Perry, 1943, p. v). Letters from deaf adults provide a sad commentary of living conditions and the availability of urban work in the late nineteenth century. One deaf man wrote in 1897, "I am out of work for some months. It is hard times." The complaint was echoed over and over—by the Torontonian who did "not have steady work," and the one who had "not been doing anything since I left school," and by the deaf worker displaced by the introduction of typesetting machines (OSD, 1897, pp. 39–40).

The deaf population's response was to make an effort to equalize the status relationship. Not content to remain passive and isolated alongside the structures of an alien society, the deaf population developed its own system. Deaf individuals drew together into cohesive groups, and many confined their social relations to other deaf people. They formed their own communities in order to break down the isolation, relieve the monotony, ease the harshness of life, and establish a deaf system of values and priorities. Shared school experiences, a shared language, friendships, and marriages also operated "to attract together into the large cities large numbers of deaf persons, who form a sort of deaf community or society" (A. G. Bell, 1884c, p. 53). In other words, forces both internal and external to their own world prompted deaf persons to view themselves as "a distinct class" (S. Smith, 1876, p. 140). They moved rapidly to establish their own social networks. The deaf communities they formed were structures of social relationships resting on emotional and linguistic bases that emerged from common qualities, situations, and sentiments. The men and women who formed the community developed a culture that provided them a firm basis for resilience and continuity (Winzer, 1986c).

The deaf community catered to the special needs and sustained a unique way of life for an emerging deaf urban group. It provided for its members' identification with others sharing similar experiences, a social network, support in adapting to urbanization, and links to the countryside. Churches became involved in the "social, literary, and charitable work" with the deaf population (Whildon, 1926; see Van Cleve and Crouch, 1989).

Nineteenth-century sources provide implicit, if not explicit, evidence of the existence of deaf communities (Bell, [1884d] 1969; Draper, 1902; Extremist, 1873; Jenkins, 1890; S. Smith, 1876; J. Williams, 1891). Undoubtedly, a blind subculture, stimulated by segregated education and shared experiences, also existed (see Kim, 1970; Lukoff and Whiteman, 1961). But historical sources offer only tantalizing glimpses; there is no evidence of the existence of blind communities that had the longevity, resilience, political acumen, and the social cohesiveness of the deaf communities.

The Mentally Retarded Graduates

For the deinstitutionalized mentally retarded population, many jurisdictions imposed increasingly restrictive laws and regulations. Apart from the ubiquitous eugenic laws that arose in the 1920s, nine states passed laws forbidding the sale of alcohol and one forbade the sale of firearms to mentally retarded persons. Eighteen states refused them the right to vote, and nine refused them admission to the state National Guard (Scheerenberger, 1983). New Jersey in 1904 forbade anyone who was confined to a public asylum or institution as an epileptic, insane, or feebleminded person to marry in the state unless a cure had been certified (New Jersey Ch. 137–1).

Throughout the nineteenth century circuses, big and small, were a popular pastime in North America. In the first half of the century clergymen railed against such entertainment, but to little avail; the circuses remained powerfully appealing for all classes (see M. I. West, 1981). In the latter half of the nineteenth century exhibitions of mentally retarded people were popular, widely accepted, and lucrative. Circuses and carnivals also employed people with overt physical anomalies, displaying them as human freaks and throwbacks to an earlier human state (Bogdan, 1986). By 1850 many human curiosities had joined the circuses. P. T. Barnum's American Museum, a New York establishment that featured curiosities, became the Disneyland of Victorian America (Bogdan, 1986). The Barnam and Bailey circus featured microcephalic adults and advertised their appearances under various tantalizing labels. Microcephalics were exhibited with shaved heads and the other trappings the showmen gave them, an exotic presentation that was part and parcel of the flamboyant humbug of the world of amusement (Bogdan, 1986).

The images that promoters used emphasized the strangeness of these showings, and promoters were readily believed because the exhibits seemed to fit in with current scientific theory. For example, people with Down syndrome were readily presented as evolutionary throwbacks. Scientists and medical practitioners all too often aided and abetted such exhibitions by visiting, examining, and commenting on exhibits (Gould and Pyle, 1986; J. M. Warren, 1851). Barnam and Bailey's "Show of Life" raised some community concern and was partly instrumental in the passage of protective laws for handicapped people. But the main offense remained, as hundreds of circuses and carnivals displayed preserved abnormal fetuses, which in the rather macabre language of the circus world were known as "pickled punks" (Scheerenberger, 1983).

The nineteenth century saw enormous improvement in the care, training, and education of exceptional persons in all groups. Scientific advances, technological developments, and reforming zeal combined to change institutional approaches as the understanding of the nature of human handicaps improved and techniques for coping with them or even overcoming them became more sophisticated. But though progress was forward, it was also uneven, often marred by conflict and deep divisions. Moreover, the larger world remained for the most part unenlightened about the capabilities and the needs of the blind, deaf, mentally retarded, or behaviorly deviant child. Much remained to be done before such persons could look forward to reasonably productive and satisfying lives, and one area that needed particular attention was education. The teaching profession held many of the keys. The next chapter examines in detail the nineteenth-century roots of the modern profession of special education.

Chapter 7

Teaching Exceptional Students in the Nineteenth Century

Landmarks in the Professionalization of Special Education

1825   Thomas Hopkins Gallaudet publishes his series, "Plan for a Seminary for the Education of the Instructors of Youth"

1839   The Massachusetts Normal School is established

1844   The Association of Medical Superintendents of American Institutions for the Insane is formed

1850   The Convention of American Instructors of the Deaf and Dumb is founded

1853   The first meeting of teachers of blind students is held

1857   The National Teachers Association (later, the National Education Association) is formed

1858   The American Printing House for the Blind is established

1864   The National Deaf Mute College is established

1871   The American Association of Instructors of the Blind is formally established

1876   The Association of Medical Officers of American Institutions for Idiots and Feeble-Minded Persons is formed

1878   The National Conference of Charities and Corrections is established

1884   Formal training for teachers of blind persons begins at Columbia University; Alexander Graham Bell introduces the term *special education*

1890   The American Association to Promote the Teaching of Speech to the Deaf (AAPTSD) is formally organized as an independent organization

1891   The AAPTSD holds its first meeting at Lake George, New York

1897   The Department of Deaf, Blind and Feeble Minded of the NEA is formed

1917   The Canadian National Institute for the Blind is established

1921   The American Foundation for the Blind is established

Over the course of the nineteenth century, as the public schools accommodated increasing numbers of diverse students, teachers and teaching changed. The teaching profession became one vehicle by which society could achieve not only educational but also politically determined social ends. As the school system expanded, as teacher training increased, and as teachers joined together in professional bodies, teachers gained extraordinary cultural power, and their authority acquired new forms and possibilities. Teachers acquired the capacity to transform and stabilize the aspirations of their students; they oversaw the habits and lives of young people, directed students into roles thought consonant with their social class and ability, and became jealous guardians of specialized teaching approaches and techniques. Professional groups and associations, with their own journals and publications, evolved to both validate and enhance professionalism. These professional associations provided members with, among other things, a sense of professional community.

The values of those with the power established the system; those organizing it reiterated the values and translated them into practical instructional approaches; those being served were allowed little input into the system. Early special education, noted an 1847 commentator, "stands very much by itself, and embraces but a limited number of individuals." As the profession was "less interlinked with society at large than any other" (Rae, 1847), it was rarely open to effective criticism by the public. Students were literally shaped like clay in a system devised, organized, and regulated by a small group of specialists. Deaf people, for example, were allowed "practically no voice in directing matters" (Tillinghast, 1910, p. 466); blind persons, "the best judges of all," were "not sufficiently consulted" about their needs and aspirations (Duglison, 1854, p. 20).

Special education arose, not at the prompting of the disabled population, but at the urging of reformers and philanthropists. In early nineteenth-century North America the clergy regarded themselves, and were regarded by the people, as men of real ability, sound knowledge, and impeccable character. As such, they were the natural guardians of education; the schools and their teachers were rightly under their supervision. Thus, at the outset the model for educational administration of institutions of special education came from neither business nor the military but instead from evangelical religion. Pious activism motivated their efforts; the moral development of the student was the central purpose of special education. A missionary impulse was evident: so glaring were the spiritual and moral failings of exceptional students, that teachers required "the enthusiasm and the devotion of a missionary to the heathen" (H. P. Peet, 1870, p. 215).

By midcentury the work of educating and training disabled children was motivated by statute rather than the dictates of conscience, and, as the clergy withdrew, the system was left open for capture by professional educators. The Christian philanthropist was supplanted by officials who quickly saw the advantages of bureaucracies and acted with dispatch to erect large and rigid organizations. Professional educators, often members of the founding families that established schools for blind and deaf students, assumed leadership in the facilities designed for children with sensory impairments. Physicians moved into the institutions formed for mentally retarded persons to form a powerful alliance of medicine and psychology.

It was during the nineteenth century that teaching became a woman's profession. During the 1830s the economy and the population were both expanding rapidly, and women began to be attracted into teaching in ever larger numbers. According to popular wisdom, women were naturally gifted in the domestic virtues and had an innate piety; they were thought to be generally kinder and more gentle than men, more efficient for the work, and so preferable for the instruction of young children. But overriding all the perceptions of women as "natural" teachers because of their supposed maternal instincts and untiring patience were economic considerations. The notion that inefficiency that raised expenses produced poor education underlay the feminization of education that began in the 1830s in both the public schools and the special institutions. School promoters and legislators assumed that economy and improvement went hand-in-hand, and they avidly sought means by which to lessen expenditures—and women could be hired more cheaply than men, at perhaps one-third of the cost. Within a mere twenty years the numerical dominance of women in teaching was apparent, although equality with male counterparts in salaries and opportunities would wait for a much later period.

THE PROFESSIONALIZATION OF TEACHING

Over the years the very meaning of the term *profession* has changed. The term has become an honorific, covering a multitude of meanings. In precise usage, *profession* refers to "an occupation whose activities are subject to theoretical analysis and scientific study and improvable by knowledge derived therefrom. This knowledge and the process of discovering it are what distinguishes a profession from a craft" (J. D. Smith, 1985). The adjective *professional* therefore implies certain specific attributes—the existence of a systematic body of specialized knowledge; authority derived from the possession of specialized knowledge not understood by lay people; community sanction; a definable clientele; an implicit or explicit code of ethics; and a sense of unity and corporateness in the membership (Greenwood, 1957). An occupation becomes professionalized when people systematize the knowledge needed to perform it; they draw generalizations from the specific knowledge of individual practitioners and publish these generalizations so that those wishing to become practitioners may learn from them and become qualified for the occupation. (On professionalism see M. L. Larson, 1977.)

The development of teaching as a distinct profession in the nineteenth century was neither clear-cut nor simple. In the 1820s few occupations were professionalized, although the general outline of professionalization as it applied to the content of a field was established. After 1830 the term *professional* as applied to teaching underwent change because of the emergence of new techniques, changing social perceptions of the teacher's role, new avenues of recruitment, and the creation of a system of teacher education. Professionalism evolved as teachers increasingly viewed themselves as a discrete occupation and saw their contributions as valuable and, in turn, valued by officialdom and the public.

However, as Herbst (1988) observes, during the middle nineteenth century normal school officials in Massachusetts and elsewhere began to despair of ever being able to create a corps of professional elementary school teachers. A profession required rigorous training and lifelong commitment to a chosen task, and the growing number of young women in the field, many of them using teaching as a stopgap between common school and marriage, were unready to render such commitment. Genuine professionalism in teaching emerged gradually and far more unevenly than it did in other fields, especially in those dominated by men. The feminization and the professionalization of teaching were interrelated, and in complex ways.

Teachers' associations, with their journals, conventions, and meetings, became important components of the mounting professional spirit. The associations encouraged their members to consider themselves as experts and to improve their expertise. They also promoted the development of the members as a social group with a distinctive style and distinctive values, through which they could demonstrate their commitment to a professional ideal that stressed the merits of expertise.

Within the public school system the professionalism of teachers was enhanced through the development of professional associations such as the National Teachers Association (which later became the National Education Association, or NEA), formed in 1857 by forty-three educators from a dozen states and the District of Columbia. The purpose of the organization was "to elevate the character and advance the interests of the profession of teaching, and to promote the cause of popular education in the United States" (A. M. West, 1984). Until 1866 membership in the National Teachers Association was open only to men. Although membership opened to women in that year, women who were eligible for honorary membership were granted only one concession: they were permitted to write speeches for presentation at conventions, but not to deliver them. Women received no elevation in status until 1917 when they were fully welcomed as equal participating members.

In their quest for authority and status, the teachers of special children assiduously developed a sense of professionalism. Their needs and priorities were inevitably somewhat different from those of their colleagues in the public school system. Institutional instructors banded together in separate groups, shored up by professional journals and associations and annual conventions or meetings. All of these provided a forum to discuss ideas, allowed a much-needed source of legitimacy, and promoted the notion of membership in a respected group. They succeeded, in large part, in establishing the expertise of their members: Legislatures called upon these groups for counsel and looked to them for leadership; generations of exceptional children and their parents dared not question their authority (Koestler, 1976).

Professional Organizations for Teachers of Deaf Students

Being first on the scene in American special education, teachers of deaf persons were the first to form a permanent professional organization. The Convention of American Instructors of the Deaf and Dumb, founded in 1850 at a meeting at the New York Institution for the Deaf and Dumb, was the first formal national group of special education teachers in North America and is among the four oldest national educational organizations in the United States. A complementary group, the Convention of Principals of American Institutions for the Deaf and Dumb, was established in 1868 at the prompting of Edward Miner Gallaudet to discuss "the articulation controversy" and "other more important subjects" (cited in Tull Boatner, 1959, p. 66).

Prior to the inauguration of the Convention of American Instructors of the Deaf and Dumb in 1850, a group of teachers at the American Asylum at Hartford decided to publish a journal. The 1847 inaugural edition of the *American Annals of the Deaf and Dumb* was published in order to provide "a perfect treasury of information upon all questions and subjects related, either immediately or remotely, to the deaf and dumb" and thereby "dissipate this ignorance" of the work of the education of deaf persons. Luzerne Rae, the founding editor, observed that the *Annals* would "materially contribute to raise our institutions in the *intelligent* regard of the people at large and to give us a still firmer hold on their patronage" (original italics, Rae, 1847b, p. 2). The *Annals* was adopted as the official publication by the 1850 convention as "the common property of all the American institutions for the Deaf and Dumb" (Convention of Instructors, 1850, p. 32). Except for its suspension during the Civil War, 1861 to 1865, the *American Annals of the Deaf* has been continuously published, to become the longest-running educational journal in North America. (The word *Dumb* was dropped from the title in 1877.)

Professional Organizations for Teachers of Blind Students

The first convention of instructors of blind students was held in August 1853 in New York City. Calls for studies on the causes of blindness and ways to ameliorate the condition resounded at the first convention. Resolutions were adopted that called for demonstrations to public officials of the capacity of blind persons; approved of Boston line type as the standard embossed print but called for research into other codes for an improved system; pointed to the need for a periodical on blindness; called for a standard system of musical notation; asserted that the discipline of blind children be as exacting as that of the sighted; called for the employment of graduates of schools for blind persons; and pointed to the question of ideal architecture (Andrews and Bledstoe, 1972). A resolution also called for a national policy for printing embossed books (Koestler, 1976), which later gave rise to the American Printing House for the Blind.

Samuel Gridley Howe was elected president of the as-yet unnamed body of instructors of blind students in 1853. However, the group did not meet again until 1871, when it became the American Association of Instructors of the Blind, today the Association for Educators of the Visually Handicapped. To serve adults, the American Association of Workers for the Blind emerged in 1905 from a casual group formed earlier (Koestler, 1976).

The idea for an American Printing House for the Blind arose from the first convention. However, due to fiscal and other difficulties, printing did not actually begin until 1866 (Willis, 1879). Originally an offshoot of the Kentucky School for the Blind, the American Printing House was officially founded in 1858 by action of the legislature of Kentucky. Since 1879, when Congress passed An Act to Promote the Education of the Blind, the American Printing House for the Blind has been the agency through which the federal government provides Braille textbooks and other materials for education (Koestler, 1976).

In Canada the education of blind students began in the 1860s. Like their counterparts in the Canadian institutions for deaf students, teachers of blind students joined the professional groups formed in the United States. Their numbers were too small and they were too scattered to form their own national organizations at this early stage. The care and education of the blind made rapid advances in Canada with the return of blinded soldiers after World War I. In 1917 a representative group of blinded soldiers and civilians met with women's organizations and businessmen and set about forming the Canadian National Institute for the Blind (Canadian War Blinded, 1942).

Professional Organizations in Mental Retardation and Mental Illness

One of the first professional groups dealing with disabled persons was the Association of Medical Superintendents of American Institutions for the Insane, created in 1844 (McGovern, 1986). At the same time the *American Journal of Insanity* was founded to provide a forum for scientific discussions and an impetus for scientific research (Goodenough, 1949). The association evolved into the American Medico-Psychological Association from 1892 until 1921, when it was succeeded by the American Psychiatric Association. The *American Journal of Insanity* became the *American Journal of Psychiatry* in that year.

In 1876, when there existed only five state and three private schools for mentally retarded children in the United States (A. S. Hill, 1951b), Édouard Seguin encouraged the establishment of the first American association devoted solely to mentally retarded persons. He called upon his fellow superintendents to meet annually to share their experiences and lent his influence to form the Association of Medical Officers of American Institutions for Idiots and Feeble-Minded Persons. Dr. Isaac N. Kerlin, prominent in the foundation of the new group, advocated an abbreviated title, the American Association for the Study of the Feeble-Minded, in 1907. In 1933 the group became the American Association on Mental Deficiency; in 1988, the American Association on Mental Retardation (See Milligan, 1961).

The National Conference of Charities and Corrections, a blanket group that included institutions for deaf, blind, and mentally retarded students, was established in the United States in 1878 by members of state boards of charities dedicated to scientific charity. Its formation led directly to the formation of the Canadian Conference of Charities and Corrections (Hareven, 1969). The National Council of Social Work and the American Public Health Association were also formed in the 1870s, both of them blanket groups whose missions included disabled people.

Teacher Education

The earliest public schools in North America were relatively undeveloped; during the colonial period, children entered the public grammar schools at seven, after having learned to read fluently at home or in private dame schools. The work of teachers was occasional and their authority limited. In colonial America and in British North America, teaching was an untrained or temporary job, "a mere matter of convenience to transient persons, or common idlers, who often teach school one season and leave it vacant until it accommodates some other person" (G. J. Hodgins, 1889, p. 47). Americans at the time of the Revolution were wont to complain that the country suffered a lack of good schoolmasters, and teachers were as often distrusted as they were respected. It was even said that some districts were "obliged to employ in their schools, vicious imported servants, or concealed Papists, who by their bad Examples and Instructions often deprave the Morals or corrupt the Principles of the Children under their Care" (quoted by Knight and Hall, 1951, p. 31).

After the Revolution schooling slowly expanded. By the 1820s public concern over illiteracy and the failure of families to provide reading instruction led to the beginnings of agitation for education laws (Hewes, 1989). Despite the enthusiasm for improvement, not all views of the profession were idealistic. Catharine Beecher, a reformer advocating the greater involvement of women in teaching, described the job as "the most wearying drudgery" (quoted by Sklar, 1973, p. 173). Her friend and supporter, Thomas Hopkins Gallaudet, concurred. "The teacher's life is not all Elysium," asserted Gallaudet, and the teacher's work "not more highly appreciated than the common domestic" (T. H. Gallaudet, 1837).

Certainly the rewards and conditions of early teaching militated against the recruitment of good candidates. Prospects for income were meager; those for advancement, even less. Training was almost nonexistent. In the 1820s a few private academies in the United States began offering a modicum of teacher education (Woodring, 1975), but few candidates were accommodated. Even up to the Civil War many elementary teachers had little or no training.

Teacher education through normal schools had its origins in the French schools of the seventeenth century. Much of the impetus and organization that underlay designs for teacher training and professionalism in North America arose from the crusading efforts of Thomas Hopkins Gallaudet. Throughout his career in education, spanning the years from 1816 until his death in 1851, Gallaudet sought to raise standards and to elevate teaching to the status of "a *distinct profession* or calling" (original italics, T. H. Gallaudet, 1831, p. 26).

Gallaudet recognized the special requirements of good teaching and saw the need to select teachers with care, educate them for the work, and pay them appropriate salaries. Teacher training and professionalism became paramount concerns for him. Building on the idea of professional teachers as holders of unique expertise, Gallaudet called for the training of current teachers to expand and enhance their expertise. One of his goals was to develop ways to pass on the values and ideals of the teaching profession to potential candidates; the formation of professional associations was an important factor in his pursuit of those goals.

Gallaudet was an effective advocate of more substantive courses of instruction for those aspiring to teach; in fact, it is to Gallaudet that America owes the idea of normal schools (Clarke, 1900). From its opening days, Gallaudet had used the resources of the American Asylum in Hartford to train young hearing and deaf men to enter the profession of educating deaf students (Clarke, 1900). From 1817 on, teachers of deaf pupils from Canada and the United States applied, almost exclusively, to the American Asylum for training. This meant that teachers and alumni of the American Asylum, thoroughly immersed in Gallaudet's practical methodology and philosophical orientation, disseminated his views widely. It also meant that Gallaudet's influence in the future route of American teacher training would be pervasive.

Seeing that special training of teachers of deaf students was so successful, Gallaudet felt that systematic training would be equally advantageous for teachers in other schools (Clarke, 1900). In 1825, under the pseudonym "A Father," Gallaudet published in Lyman Beecher's *Observer* his "Plan for a Seminary for the Education of the Instructors of Youth," a series of fourteen educational articles that examined the curriculum, textbooks, economics, and the needs of children in the classroom. Gallaudet's fundamental assumption was that "the present modes of instructing youth are susceptible of great improvement" (T. H. Gallaudet, 1831, p. 51); he therefore proposed that "an institution should be established in every state for the purpose of training candidates for work of teaching the common branches of English education" (*Horace Mann,* 1900, p. 51).

Gallaudet's advocacy of the establishment of special institutions to provide professional training for teachers was widely influential. The essays attracted much attention at the time and were republished, more or less abridged, in leading educational journals (*Horace Mann,* 1900). Although many of the concepts Gallaudet articulated in his "Plan for a Seminary" sprang from his immediate experience with training teachers of one group of exceptional children, he wielded profound influence on the training of teachers in all fields. Horace Mann consulted with him in Hartford about the original plan for the Massachusetts Normal School, which opened in Lexington in 1839 (Steiner, 1919); he then offered Gallaudet the principalship.

The Board of Education for Massachusetts had encouraged Mann in his quest for a normal school, although many thought the idea too ambitious or impractical. It was felt that the remoteness of rural school districts, the capriciousness of supervision, the meager pay, and the seasonal employment would make it unlikely that normal schools would ever attract a sufficient number of would-be teachers (Herbst, 1988). To be sure, young men, enticed by the economic opportunities offered by an expanding industrial sector and uninspired by the unattractive working conditions in and the low pay of rural schools, shunned employment in education. But young women were more attracted to the idea of becoming teachers; indeed, the majority of seventeen- and eighteen-year-old girls who contemplated paid employment preferred teaching over their other options (Herbst, 1988).

Following the founding of Mann's normal school in Massachusetts, normal schools opened in Connecticut, New York, Rhode Island, Pennsylvania, Michigan, Illinois, and Minnesota. By 1874, 67 state and 54 private normal schools were serving prospective teachers; by 1898 the number had risen to 166 and 165, respectively (L. E. Connor, 1951).

Teacher training could not alleviate all the problems of American education in the nineteenth century. The most severe problems had little to do with the functioning and curriculum of normal schools; they were the consequence of the American insistence on the control over hiring, pay, and working conditions of teachers by local school boards and superintendents (Herbst, 1988). Typically, layman or perhaps a minister, someone without any teaching experience, hired young men and women who gladly consented to teach school for a season or two until some better opportunity or marriage beckoned. For much of the nineteenth century, but especially the first half, elementary school teaching remained a virtually unskilled and temporary job (Herbst, 1988).

This situation began to find a solution when, in the 1870s, normal school educators began to add training courses for high school teachers that stressed academic subject matter and what was termed as "professional" work. *Professional* now came to mean that students were being prepared for special subjects or for careers as school administrators or faculty members at other normal schools (Herbst, 1988).

Training Teachers for the Institutions

The preparation of teachers of disabled children emerged in the late eighteenth century when experimenters like Valentin Haüy, Charles Michel de l'Épée, and Seguin shared their pedagogical methods with other teachers. Gallaudet's American model of in-service training was adapted in many other institutions for deaf, blind, and mentally retarded students. Many candidates for teaching positions had only basic school education; some were graduates of the institutions; a few came from normal schools; even fewer from colleges. Teaching was learned basically through an apprenticeship. Motivation and adaptability were the main criteria set out by superintendents.

On-site training was deemed most suitable for those aspiring to teach deaf or blind students. It was not until the founding of the National Deaf Mute College in 1864 that any other kind of teacher training was available, and there the effort focused on training deaf individuals for the work. Howe developed in-service training for teachers of blind students at the Perkins Institution, although he did suggest that teachers go out for a few years to "take lessons of life in the actual world" (Perkins Inst., 1858, p. 23).

Later in the century, as normal schools expanded, it became common practice to recruit teachers from among those training in either kindergarten (which was preferred) or primary education. Some experience in a residential setting was also desired. Occasionally, teachers were sent to other institutions to train. Some of those opting to work with mentally retarded students, for example, were sent to Elwyn Institution to study for a period of three months.

In the education of deaf and blind students, higher qualification were deemed a prerequisite for teaching at the upper levels. Those preparing to teach deaf students attended the National Deaf Mute College in Washington, D.C. Throughout his career, Samuel Gridley Howe made calls for a similar institute of higher education for blind persons, but with little success. Blind individuals seeking higher degrees attended colleges and universities with their sighted counterparts. Special education training for teachers of blind students began at the Teachers College of Columbia University in 1884. By 1903 the Perkins School for the Blind had eighteen instructors in the literary department: six were college or university graduates; three-quarters of the remainder had been trained in normal schools (Perkins Inst., 1904).

The Duties of the Teacher

Few detailed descriptions of teachers' practice and duties in the special institutions of the nineteenth century exist, but the scattered evidence we do have clearly indicates that the work was arduous, difficult, and all-consuming. When, for example, Thomas Hopkins Gallaudet tried to learn the Braidwoods' methods in England, he was offered a position as an usher (beginning teacher) "instructing one of the classes daily" and contracting "to be with the pupils from seven o'clock in the morning till eight in the evening, and also with pupils in the hour of recreation" (Institution, 1818, p. 129). George Sumner's day-by-day account of the Bicêtre that so vividly influenced Samuel Gridley Howe indicated that one of the teachers supervised a school day that began at five-thirty in the morning and ended at eight-fifteen at night (Talbot, 1964).

The Elwyn Institution for Feeble-Minded Children in Illinois was explicit about the duties of teachers, which included scheduling classes, conducting lessons, controlling the students, and taking care of the classroom; even the after-hour studies of the teacher were prescribed. Before the school term began, teachers were to "harmonize" their schedules "so that there be no intrusion on each other in passing from room to room for material, and so that noisy exercises such as free gymnastics, concert recitations, and marching, shall be held in adjoining rooms at concurrent hours." Teachers were instructed to be in their classrooms "at least fifteen minutes in advance of the children so that you may make timely preparation of the material used in the work of the session." School rooms were cleaned daily, but during the course of a day it was the teacher's responsibility to "see that the floors are kept free from litter, bits, blocks, etc, having them carefully picked up before the adjournment of each session." Orders to students were to be "energetic, prompt, and decisive—'Arms fold!' 'Into line!' 'Dress line!' 'Quiet!' 'Order!' etc." Finally, teachers were advised to "read and study at least one good book a year on education" (quoted by Rosen, Clark, and Kivitz, 1976, p. 318).

A teacher's duties did not end with the final school bell. Most single teachers boarded on the school property, and a host of chores besides actual classroom teaching were assigned. The instructors usually took their meals at the same tables with the pupils. They organized excursions and supervised "evening pleasures" (Seguin, [1866] 1907) as well as the weekly parties, picnics, and the observation of many holidays (Vineland, 1893). "We sometimes play a game of whist," reported a Montreal teacher in 1886, "and sometimes we have an impromptu debate on women's rights or upon some equally debatable subject" (Montreal Institution, 1886, p. 59). Daily, after hours, teachers made notes about the students (Seguin, [1866] 1907).

THE FEMINIZATION OF TEACHING

In the early nineteenth century teaching was not a woman's profession. To be sure, women had long been involved in the education of very young children. Monoghan (1989) identified three types of female teachers in colonial New England, all of whom taught reading but not (except on the rarest of occasions) writing. Penmanship, as the name implies, was a male skill reserved for those with the expertise to teach it.

One group of female teachers were the "dames" who taught reading privately to small children in "dame schools" conducted in their own homes. A second group was the "school dames," employed and paid by New England townships. Mention of these begins in the 1680s, and their employment by townships seems to have become a fairly general practice from the 1730s on. The third group was the entrepreneurs who offered advanced sewing and embroidery along with reading instruction; women in this category often provided the equivalent of a secondary education to older girls (Monoghan, 1989).

The acceptance of women as teachers in the common schools was universal by the middle decades of the nineteenth century, although only a few decades before the notion of women as professionals was rarely entertained. Even when they were employed and self-supporting, women had few rights and little power; their role in society was passive and sharply limited. Women's station in life was to be morally useful; their proper sphere was thought to be the home. They were viewed as the helpmate of men, the keeper of the lamp of domestic piety (T. H. Gallaudet, 1819), their universes bounded by their homes and the career of father and husband. In general, females were denied formal education above the minimum required by a literate early-industrial society. After the age of ten years, females were rarely placed in the common schools (Senex, 1831). (See, e.g., Smith-Rosenberg, 1971).

Catharine Beecher was one of the first to envision teaching as a profession dominated by—indeed, exclusively belonging to—women (Sklar, 1973). Her colleague, Thomas Hopkins Gallaudet, involved in many educational and social reforms, was an early advocate of education of and by women. As he became increasingly conscious of women and their special roles, Gallaudet began to visualize teaching as a viable and honorable profession for women, a respectable alternative to marriage that would allow a woman independence and extensive usefulness while not stepping beyond the commonly prescribed boundaries of feminine modesty (Winzer, 1981b). He "was among the most earnest to call attention in conversation, through the press, and in educational meetings to the whole subject of female education, and especially to the more extensive employment of women as teachers" (H. Barnard, 1861b, p. 108).

To Gallaudet, the home and the school were the most potent molders of human character and needed to function in harmony. In concert with Catharine Beecher, Emma Willard, and other advocates of female education, Gallaudet viewed teaching as a natural extension for women's nurturing propensities, maternal instinct, and untiring patience. "Her influence upon the child," he said, "is inferior only to that of God" (T. H. Gallaudet, 1828, p. 183).

Gallaudet was right about the important role women would fill in professional education. During the 1830s women began to move into teaching; the midcentury witnessed an influx of women to the extent that their numbers came to dominate the profession. Approximately one out of every five white women in pre–Civil War Massachusetts was a teacher at some time in her life (Bernard and Vinovskis, 1977). By 1837, 60 percent of all Massachusetts teachers were women; the number rose to 88 percent by 1870 (Herbst, 1988). In Ontario 42 percent of teachers were females in 1867; by 1903 the proportion had risen to 77 percent (Ontario, Dept. of Ed., 1904).

Women brought to teaching the domestic virtues and piety that had previously made them the teachers of their own children in their own homes. They were thought to innately possess "a well grounded religious sense, which finds its best expression in self-sacrifice, conscientious duty, and instinctive kind-ness" (quoted by Rosen, 1968, p. 318). Women teachers were thought to be "kinder and more gentle than men, more efficient in the work and, for the first ten or twelve years of a child's life, preferable" (Blackburn, 1883, p. 591).

Nevertheless, the belief in a maternal instinct effectively limited women's roles. For one thing, they were generally restricted to the teaching of young chil-dren in the common schools. For another, the belief that motherhood was a woman's fulfillment and parenthood her only creative and challenging activity meant that nineteenth-century women, for economic and social reasons, needed marriage more than men did.

In the United States economic and demographic factors, and not just an im-pulse toward social reform, opened the profession of teaching to women. A rap-idly developing population created the need for more teachers at a time when a swiftly expanding economy was attracting the men to jobs in industry and com-merce. The growing numbers of tax-supported common schools and institu-tions for deaf, blind, and mentally retarded students offered many new positions for women. The feminization of the teaching force was in fact inevitable, as men were abandoning teaching for more lucrative opportunities.

Of course, few occupational options were open to women. Factory and piece work was arduous and restrictive and paid even less than teaching. In fact, com-pared to the jobs in other sectors of the economy, teaching was a lucrative oc-cupation (K. C. Berkeley, 1984). Not only that, it was far more acceptable than factory work to middle-class women with some education.

However, the major reason for hiring women lay "in the comparative cheap-ness of the terms on which they may be employed" (*American Annals of Edu-cation,* 1835, p. 83). As Henry Barnard observed, women were cheaper than men, and that was the sole reason that by the 1850s they had replaced nine-tenths of the men in American public schools (in Sklar, 1973). Women accepted less pay than men; they were compensated for their work at one-third to one-half the rate of male teachers. In most states teachers were paid by the month, and then only for the actual time of work. In Massachusetts in 1865 men earned $59.53 a month, women $24.36. In the same year, Pennsylvania male teachers received $35.87; their female counterparts, $27.51 (Ryerson, 1865). In Memphis between 1855 and 1869 women constituted between two-thirds and three-quarters of the city's teaching corps. However, in 1868–1869 men earned an av-erage of $111.25 a month, women $80.12 (K. C. Berkeley, 1984).

The rising costs of the expanding school system made every economy vital. Low pay for women was also justified on the grounds that the purposes of the public schools was limited: although the schools may have been necessary institutions, their programs did not require the extensive skills or great train-ing on the part of the teacher that were required in the colleges, for example. (Sklar, 1973).

But lower salaries for women were justified on more than just economic and educational grounds. Lower status for nineteenth-century female teachers was rooted in the assumption of female inferiority, not only as teachers but as par-ticipants anywhere in the traditionally male marketplace. The world of wage earning was considered foreign to females; the school officials who hired them explicitly assumed responsibility for protecting women from the full impact of marketplace pressures.

Women were paid less, finally, because females did not have families to support. Women were not expected to have job-related aspirations, but were expected to look ultimately to marriage. Teaching was viewed as a viable job for women: not a career, but a remunerative way of filling in the time before marriage. For some, it provided an alternative to marriage, "one means of providing a respectable and useful occupation" (Seminary, 1831, p. 341).

Nor could women receive advanced training; few facilities were available for the higher education of women. There were probably only several thousand women studying in colleges, normal schools, and women's seminaries in the United States in the nineteenth century, less than one-fifth of the total enrollment in higher education (Rury and Harper, 1986). Many colleges excluded women and blacks; most colleges open to women at the time were in the Midwest. Antioch, founded in 1852 with Horace Mann as the first president, admitted women; Oberlin admitted women with its first class, the class of 1837. Some universities did admit women but many found pitting young men and women against each other in examinations repugnant. Too, there were the problems of moral development: daily contact with the opposite sex raised the terrible specter of promiscuity (Rury and Harper, 1986). Nor could male administrators and faculty members (and occasionally male students) agree with women about what their college courses should contain.

It was a misogynous ideology that was rooted in very old ideas. Many physicians and educators, arguing from supposed medical evidence and from the Bible, agreed that the female brain and nervous system were inadequate for sustained intellectual effort. Charles Darwin (1874) did not make this proposition but he seemed to confirm it when he said that the male was the more "variable" sex. Because variation from the norm was considered a primary evolutionary mechanism, the alleged greater variation among males seemed a distinct advantage and a sign of the superiority of the male sex (Shields, 1990). The variability hypothesis continued to find support right into the twentieth century.

So although women rapidly achieved numerical dominance in the teaching profession, they filled the bottom rungs of the educational ladder. In the normal schools their instructors were chiefly men; later, once the women were installed in classrooms, they found themselves working under the direction of male principals and supervisors. Women quickly discovered that, as women, they would be perceived and treated as inferior to their male counterparts.

The Feminization of the Institutional Complex

Women teachers within the network of schools designed to serve deaf, blind, and mentally retarded students encountered treatment identical to that of their female counterparts in the common schools. Institutional life found men at the administrative and research levels; women were left to put the men's principles and policies into practice. In fact, the institutions overtly functioned as a special form of household, dependent largely upon male leadership and female domestic employment. The administrative structures were carefully designed to direct females into positions where they would be subordinate to male bosses.

Éduoard Seguin, a strong advocate of extended roles for women, decried the structure that inevitably placed female teachers under male supervision. Too often he discovered the institutions to be "a machine run by men-power, instead of an organization resting on women's tenderness and quick perceptions" (quoted by Thurston, 1876, p. 83). Seguin may have disliked the role of the women in institutional settings, he could not find fault with their numbers. As in the common schools, women rapidly formed the majority of the teaching corps. In 1892, for example, the New Jersey Institution for Feeble-Minded Boys and Girls at Vineland was staffed by five female teachers and a male superintendent. In the next year the *Annual Report* of the Iowa Institution for the Feeble-Minded showed a staff of fourteen—thirteen females and one male.

The increasing numerical dominance of women in the institutions (as well as the common schools) was a subject of grave concern to male teachers; they "disapproved of the preponderance of women teachers" (Ontario, Dept. of Ed., 1904, p. 37). They objected that the work was too arduous and that the frail women might more appropriately seek occupations in other fields than special education; they also cited the pernicious effect of the women's pampering on students, especially the boys. Because of the "essential difference between the mind of man and the mind of woman," it was argued that extended exposure to women teachers would "simply develop the female mind in the male body" (J. C. Howard, 1902, p. 279). Young men required "daily contact with the sterner attributes of human nature, the more logical facilities, and the stricter sense of justice that are masculine characteristics" (Draper, 1904, p. 359). "One good man teacher," said another, "is worth more in preparing these boys for their life work than ten or a dozen women teachers" (J. C. Howard, 1902, pp. 279–80).

Women's acceptance as instructors in the institutions for exceptional students rested on a number of factors. Not the least was the influence of Édouard Seguin. He pointed out that the educational capacities of women with young children were generally "recognized to be far above those of men" (Seguin, 1876a, p. 48) and lauded American teaching as "feminine—that is to say, gentle, breeding more gentleness in the pupils" (Seguin, [1866] 1907, p. 88). He viewed women as particularly suitable "to the work of training idiots" and argued, "The American idea of the better fitness of women than of men to educate children received an unrefutable demonstration from its adaptation to the work of training idiots" (Seguin, [1866] 1907, p. 94). In his eyes, the woman who was the ideal teacher was "well educated, refined, intensely interested in her pupils and has a professional zeal to grow in her work; she is original, striving to introduce new and bright methods, but not passing hastily from subject to subject before the child has grasped the first. She is patient but energetic, sweet-tempered but persistent, and to the influence of her education and character she adds the charms of personal neatness and attractive manners" (quoted by Rosen, Clark, and Kivitz, 1976, p. 318).

Another important reason for using women with no special training related to methodology. Save in the area of reading systems, the instruction of blind and mentally retarded students required no specialized skills on the part of the teacher. Print methods for use with blind students and the physiological method of sense training for mentally retarded children were taught on the job.

The Feminization of the Education of Deaf Students

The women were not as readily welcomed into the schools for deaf students. "As all privileged bodies are apt to make one mistake," wrote Fred de Land, a commentator in the field, so did the school officials: they "omitted women from their system" (De Land, 1906, p. 3). Several factors contributed to their omission from the institutions designed for deaf students. The early schools were staffed by a male elite, predominantly members of the clergy, who expected the profession to follow their image. Another reason was the advanced ages of the pupils; in the early years of the American Asylum, for example, the students averaged twenty-two years of age (J. W. Jones, 1918).

It was not until 1852 that Henry Barnard, seeking greater cost efficiency, began to promote the employment of women. "The appropriations now made for the institutions of the deaf and dumb," prompted Barnard, "could be ... more economically" and "more wisely applied, by the employment of well educated and properly trained female teachers" (H. Barnard, 1852b, pp. 196–97). In this same vein, the New York Institution for the Deaf and Dumb in that year opened its doors to female teachers for various reasons, "of which the *necessity of economy* was not the least" (original italics, E. M. Gallaudet, 1892, p. 5). Thereafter, the number of women in schools for deaf students increased rapidly, "for the sole reason that their services can be had at low rates" (E. M. Gallaudet, 1892, p. 7).

In 1852 there were fourteen schools for deaf students in North America, only two of them employing women, for a total of three. By 1868 there were fifty-one women teachers, or 34 percent of the total teaching corps; by 1895 women constituted 68 percent of the teachers. The rapid increases were partly attributable to demographic and economic factors, but in the case of deaf education, female numerical dominance was more directly related to the rapid rise of oral modes of instruction, first introduced in 1867. The use of an oral methodology created a need for more teachers, and women elected, in large numbers, to staff the oral schools or to teach articulation in the traditional institutions.

The controversy over communication modes in deaf education reached its most divisive pitch in the second half of the nineteenth century. The fiercest debates concerned the medium and environment of teaching: Each side argued that the techniques and approaches of the other would not produce the intellectual, social, and moral development of deaf students. The fissure in the profession over communication modes deepened into a chasm that followed gender lines (Winzer, 1981b).

Divisions were exacerbated by the two leading protagonists: Alexander Graham Bell found his chief allies in women, while Edward Miner Gallaudet deplored the feminization of the profession. Bell supported equal rights for women and worked for the suffragist cause (R. Bruce, 1973); his father-in-law, Gardiner Greene Hubbard, the inspiration behind the Clarke Institution, consistently advocated "the employment of women as teachers of the deaf" (De Land, 1906, p. 417). In contrast, Edward Miner Gallaudet was cool, if not downright hostile, to the mounting numbers of women entering the profession. "I do not wish to be understood as condemning the employment of women in schools for the deaf," said Edward in 1892. "What I do condemn," he explained, "is the regression ... of the college graduates in the corps of instructors." Because the proportion of highly educated men among the teachers had shrunk, Gallaudet concluded that "the standard of efficiency in the profession has been correspondingly lowered." Women would be satisfactory in the lower classes, but for more advanced pupils "success can only be obtained by instructors who have secured the acquisitions and mental discipline in a collegiate course of training." And, he maintained, even if there were highly educated women available, "in no corps of instructors, should women be in the majority" (E. M. Gallaudet, 1892, p. 7).

Economic forces brought women into the profession; other factors induced them to make the oral schools their particular domain. The tender ages of the pupils, the barriers raised against occupational mobility in the manual institutions, and, most importantly, the perceived special fitness of women for oral teaching effectively feminized those schools founded on or adhering to oral philosophies.

The deployment of women in the oral schools rose largely from a perception of sex-based expertise in the teaching of speech. Not only did women possess a "fondness and tact in communicating knowledge, especially by means of oral methods" (Seguin, 1876a), but, as one commentator noted: "Their lips are more easily read,—they have more practice, perhaps, and women do not wear beards" (H. Taylor, 1900, p. 365). Views about women's skill in speech teaching echoed notions expressed by Épée a century earlier. The abbé described the process of speech teaching as "tedious and oppressive," engendering and "intolerable weariness for both pupil and instructor." Seeing the work as a merely mechanical part of education, in which "patience was the great desideratum, learning superfluous," the abbé assigned it to "simple females" (Épée, [1784] 1860, p. 6).

Moreover, traditional notions about women and men abounded. "No man," wrote a male educator, "has the patience to teach little children, deaf or hearing" (Wheeler, 1920, p. 375). Women, however, were naturally endowed with "the maternal instinct, the untiring patience," so "characteristic of the sex" (Seminary, 1831, p. 341). Deaf children floundered without their "natural teachers— who are female, of course, particularly as teachers of speech" (Seguin, 1876a, p. 71).

Equally important was women's exclusion from schools of higher learning and their subsequent status in the traditional institutions. Unlike his father, Edward Miner Gallaudet did not profess a strong commitment to the cause of female education and the professionalization of women teachers. Rather, he appears, from both his personal and professional dealings with women, to have assigned them a decidedly secondary position in society (see Tull Boatner, 1959). Consonant with traditional employment patterns in schools for the deaf, Gallaudet demanded that the faculty of the National Deaf Mute College be drawn from the most prestigious universities, preferably Yale ("Yale graduates," 1879). In turn, schools for deaf students throughout North America were to be staffed with graduates of his all-male college (Winzer, 1981b).

When the National Deaf Mute College opened in 1864, only male students were admitted. In 1867 Gallaudet requested that the directors of the college consider admitting hearing young men and women to train as teachers of deaf people (Tull Boatner, 1959, p. 66). However, he later adamantly opposed the admission of women students. When the subject was broached in 1881, Gallaudet rejoined, "I oppose co-education" and observed that "the Faculty showed no disposition to change the policy of the College which declines to admit ladies" (E. M. Gallaudet, 1881, quoted by Tull Boatner, 1959, p. 114).

By denying them college training, Gallaudet effectively closed the avenues of advancement in the manual institutions to women. Within the manual schools, status became directly linked to academic achievement; advanced education became a prerequisite for upward mobility, and the pool of candidates was limited to those who could obtain the proper training (Winzer, 1981b). Women could not; apart from academic expertise, the lack of access to the National Deaf Mute College meant that women failed to gain the full advantage of a structured and stringent training in the sign language, a system with semantic and syntactic structures quite different from English. Manualism became the province of male teachers. A contemporary of Gallaudet's visualized the ideal institution for deaf persons as having "each class . . . under the charge of a zealous and faithful female instructor who would teach . . . written language . . . , and spoken language." But the male principal and vice principal, men of liberal education and accomplished sign makers, would "lecture daily to the pupils in the language of signs" (Pettengill, 1872, pp. 32–33).

When in 1886 the board of directors of the National Deaf Mute College proposed that women be admitted on an experimental basis, Gallaudet, perhaps sensing the inevitable, acquiesced gracefully (E. M. Gallaudet, 1886), conditional on his taking a leave of absence in that year. It was not until 1887 that the first woman was admitted, and the first females graduated in 1893 (Alumnis, 1900, p. 45; see also J. C. Gordon, 1892; Sheridan, 1875).

Teachers in the oral schools became professionally qualified and certified through a practical knowledge of the oral methods, refined by in-service training programs that were unrelated to the university. In 1889, for example, Caroline Ardelia Yale, the school principal, organized normal classes at the Clarke school but apparently admitted ladies only (E. P. Clarke, 1900; E. M. Gallaudet, 1907, p. 21). Nearly all women choosing deaf education as an occupation during the final three decades of the nineteenth century took positions in the oral schools. Here, despite their exclusion from specific universities and their denial of status in the manual institutions, they could receive training and achieve certified expertise. In fact, in many schools it became an unwritten policy to hire only women.

Because of the oral methodology she adopted and the young age of her children, Harriet Burbank Rogers chose to employ only women teachers at the Clarke Institution. When Rogers retired from the principalship of Clarke, Caroline Yale (1848–1933), the associate principal, was offered the position. Yale knew that most of the schools in the country were under the charge of men and so "urged upon the Board the possible wisdom of appointing a man to the vacant principalship." The suggestion was roundly rejected, as the trustees felt strongly that it was "wiser to continue the policy of the school without change" (Yale, 1931, p. 163).

In 1873 the faculty of the Jacksonville, Mississippi, institution was, except for the trade teachers, all women. The Boston Day School for the Deaf employed only women, and there was a high percentage of female staff at the MacKay Institution in Montreal under Harriet McGann. Women were not only employed in the schools but filled the highest administrative positions. In 1884 such prestigious institutions as the Chicago Voice and Hearing School, the Portland Day School, the Rhode Island School for the Deaf, and the oral branch of the

Table 7-1

The Distribution of Men and Women on the Faculties
of Schools for Deaf Students, by Instructional Method, 1890

School	Men	Women
Combined Method		
American School	7	9
New York	7	7
Pennsylvania	10	27
Kentucky	9	5
Ohio	12	15
Virginia	8	2
Indiana	9	10
Tennessee	5	4
Manual Method		
Georgia	11	22
National Deaf Mute College	9	0
Maryland Colored	2	0
New Orleans Public	1	0
Cincinnati	0	1
St. Louis Day	1	1
Evansville	1	1
Texas Colored	1	2
Georgia Colored	5	2
Oral Method		
Chicago Voice and Hearing	0	5
Sarah Fuller	0	3
New York Institute for Improved Instruction	5	10
Clarke	0	14
Horace Mann	0	10
St. Joseph's	1	20
Portland Day	0	6
Rhode Island	0	5
Milwaukee Day	1	5

SOURCE: Winzer, 1981b.

Pennsylvania Institution for the Deaf and Dumb were all under the leadership
of women. In the same year manual institutions such as those in New York,
Hartford, and Halifax and the National Deaf Mute College were not only administered by men but employed a majority of male teachers. Table 7-1 reveals the
large numbers of women in the oral schools and their considerably smaller

ratios in the manual institutions. In schools employing a combined method—manual with articulation taught to selected pupils—the numbers are more even, with women teaching the oral components and men assuming administrative positions.

Advances in Oral Education for Deaf Students

Because oralism was an educational reform initiated and brought to dominance by female teachers, women played a significant role in shaping the lives of late nineteenth-century deaf students. Within the institutional network and in the public sphere, women ventured to dispute the traditional practices of experienced male educators; the ferment on communication modes revealed most clearly the differing aspirations and anxieties concerning their pupils held by men and women. Women became major spokespersons, disseminating and articulating their ideas widely, challenging the entrenched conservatism of the manualists, not only in regard to pedagogy but concerning the entire value and content of the education of deaf people. Every aspect of schooling, from administration to teaching methods, from finance to the sex of teachers, was examined and transformed by the oralists, all explicitly in relation to the myth that deaf children could learn the elements of language only by the manual method (Winzer, 1981b).

As they formed a community of articulate educational innovators, women became the carriers of a new professional ideal, demanding academic respectability for their programs and professional mobility for themselves. They assumed public roles and won not only public attention but acclaim. For example, Caroline Yale, principal of the Clarke Institution, was awarded honorary degrees by Wesleyan in 1896 and Mount Holyoke in 1927.

Oral teachers placed an unprecedented emphasis on the academic, the intellectual development of their students superseding the inculcation of moral values. Attempting to win elite status for their students, the oral teachers defined their status claims in such a way as to place more emphasis upon academic achievement and institutional affiliation, less upon defining deafness as a characteristic, and almost none on industrial training. Reforms in curriculum led to the imposition of rigorous standards and greatly heightened expectations of the intellectual capacities of deaf students. Not only academic skills but values were taught, values that encouraged and enabled students to attempt public roles not previously thought consonant with their handicaps.

It was this articulate and dedicated group of women teachers who put manualism to rout and finally convinced legislators, parents, and other educators that the oral modes were the most suitable for the instruction of all deaf students. By 1897 articulation teachers became the majority among all instructors of deaf students, including superintendents and principals (American Association, 1899, p. 75). So pervasive was the feminine influence that by the opening decades of the twentieth century the great majority of deaf children in North America were educated by speech and lipreading alone. By 1905, 96 percent of American schools for deaf students were designated as oral schools (Crouter, 1907); the use of sign language, now considered a lower-class dialect, was forbidden in the schools.

As an educational philosophy and approach for deaf students, oralism would reign for the next half-century. Women teachers, still viewed as holders of extraordinary expertise, gradually ceded their dominant status, as men enlisted in the oral cause once the fate of manual methods was sealed.

Professional Organizations and Oralism

Oralists formed a distinct group within the profession. They saw themselves as experts, separate from the manualists, with their own professional ideals and values. In devising different schools, different philosophies, and different pedagogies, oral adherents also created a parallel profession, almost entirely the domain of females.

In a blatant use of political power in the 1880s, Alexander Graham Bell set out not only to elevate oralism to the paramount ideology but also to dominate the entire profession of deaf education. His chief route was building a conception of oralists as a discrete group that inevitably led to the formation of a different professional association. Participation in a professional organization would enhance the oralists's conception of themselves as a distinct group.

Bell considered forming a national society to promote articulation teaching in the mid-1870s. By 1880 he decided to move cautiously and to lay the groundwork by first organizing a section of speech teaching within the Convention of American Instructors of the Deaf and Dumb (R. Bruce, 1973; De Land, 1919b). The 1884 meeting of his group, the American Association to Promote the Teaching of Speech to the Deaf (AAPTSD), adopted a resolution "that the Convention of American Instructors of the Deaf and Dumb be requested to organize a section of the Convention for the promotion of articulation teaching" (*AADD*, 1884, p. 256). But at the 1886 convention the unexpectedly enthusiastic resolutions in favor of speech teaching led Bell and his allies to put off their move for a separate section (R. Bruce, 1973). But at the August 1890 Convention of American Instructors of the Deaf not only was an oral section organized but the Bell forces also announced their independent organization, the AAPTSD (R. Bruce, 1973).

The convention and the AASPD met at fairly regular intervals but, chided a 1919 observer, "both organizations, instead of devoting their time to an open forum for scientific and pedagogic discussion, occupy a large part of their energies in presenting and developing political, factional, personal, and sectional differences" (Goldstein, 1919, p. 339). At one stage there were serious discussions about a union of the two groups. In fact, commented Gallaudet, "We not only debated it very seriously, but we went to war over it" (*Proceedings*, 1907, p. 91; see E. M. Gallaudet, 1894). The groups did not unite, and the AAPTSD became a leading force in the promotion of oral teaching with its own journal, the *Association Review*, later the *Volta Review*. The AAPTSD became the Alexander Graham Bell Association for the Deaf in 1956.

DEAF TEACHERS

An unwritten goal of nineteenth-century education for both deaf students and blind students was the training of a very few of the most promising for roles in the teaching profession. From 1832 on, Howe promoted in-service teacher training for blind students, but to some extent his hopes were disappointed. During the 1850s fewer blind graduates got jobs as teachers than was hoped (Perkins Inst., 1851); blind teachers were unable to teach in the common schools because they could not supervise (Perkins Inst., 1856). Nonetheless, by 1861 the Perkins Institution had employed four adult blind teachers (Perkins Inst., 1861).

Institutions serving the unique needs of deaf students were the first to emerge, although the last to welcome women as teachers. In these schools women were assigned to subordinate roles, and their salaries and advancement opportunities were unequal to those available to hearing male educators. The status of deaf male teachers was curiously analogous. To be female or disabled was to be powerless, dependent, less well paid, stuck on the lower rungs; to be male and nonhandicapped assured power, independence, higher salaries, and opportunities for professional and social mobility.

As hearing men abandoned teaching for more lucrative opportunities in the commercial sphere, both a feminization of the profession and an influx of young, deaf male teachers occurred; both groups took positions subordinate to hearing male teachers (e.g. Canage, 1859; Carlin, 1859). Ironically, as women slowly gained recognition in the profession, their increasing dominance and advocacy of oral methodologies served to eliminate deaf teachers from the schools, thus closing off one of the few professional pursuits available to nineteenth-century deaf men.

Being deaf was a social role as well as linguistic deprivation. Despite public awareness of outstanding deaf individuals, the conventional view was that deafness meant inferiority, and the social mobility of deaf people was severely restricted. Like women, deaf men were perceived to have a proper sphere and were subjected to differential treatment with regard to responsibility, occupational mobility, and economic remuneration. But unlike many nineteenth-century women aspiring to become special educators, deaf men were admitted into courses of higher training.

In the early schools deaf men constituted a large proportion of the teaching staffs. In 1852, the year that women began to enter the ranks of teachers of deaf persons, deaf males formed about 40 percent of the staffs (J. W. Jones, 1918); by 1870 deaf men accounted for about 42 percent of the teaching personnel in North America. Deaf teachers were paid less and generally "treated unjustly" (Carlin, 1858, p. 196). Little opportunity existed for promotion: deaf teachers often taught classes "composed of the dregs of the others" (OSD, 1876, p. 11), and "only in rare cases were deaf-mute teachers qualified to instruct the higher classes" (Carlin, 1858, p. 196). Never were they allowed charge of pupils who possessed any residual hearing (Convention of Principals, 1884).

In an assembly of deaf and hearing teachers in 1858 the superintendents of major institutions were quick to justify the lower status of deaf teachers. Few hearing educators could "subscribe to the doctrine that a deaf and dumb teacher can become as useful as a speaking teacher" (quoted by Carlin, 1859, p. 74). It was said that even a well-educated deaf person had inherent limitations; " a man deprived of one important sense is not as valuable as one who has the use of all" (quoted by Carlin, 1859, p. 63). As one leading educator observed: "There is a kink, as it were, in the mind and action of the individual that can never be overcome" (quoted by Carlin, 1859, p. 63).

Table 7-2

The Gender and Hearing Status of Teachers
of Deaf Students, 1851–1920

Year	Male	Female	Deaf
1851	97%	3%	—
1860	88	12	—
1865	66	34	41%
1870	61	42	—
1875	56	43	—
1880	47	53	29
1885	42	58	—
1890	40	60	26
1895	32	68	—
1900	35	65	18
1905	32	68	17
1910	27	73	—
1915	25	75	—
1920	23	77	—

Sources: I.S.F., 1921; J. W. Jones, 1918; H. Taylor, 1900; Wheeler, 1920.

Deaf teachers protested with spirit to the stereotyping and simplistic generalizations. "By this CASTE," they vehemently argued, "the mute is degraded and given to understand that he belongs to a lower order of beings" (original punctuation, "Fair deaf-mute salaries," 1862, p. 15). To little avail: they were counseled to keep their aspirations low, told to accept their subordinate role, cautioned against aspiring to social or occupational mobility, and warned not to seek "to intrude themselves into stations for which they are unnaturally fitted" (Samuel Porter, 1858, p. 137). The deaf man was advised that he would "do well to submit as gracefully as he can, and with a quiet resignation, to the will of providence" (p. 137) rather than rebel against social strictures.

Deaf teachers bitterly resented their lower status and meager salaries, but arguments for equal pay for equal services won little sympathy. Harvey P. Peet, principal of the New York Institution for the Deaf and Dumb, observed that the argument for equal pay for equal services was also used in all women's rights conventions. Peet pointed out that the lower wage rate for women were based on the fact that they could live on less, expected less, and were content with less (Carlin, 1859). Similarly, deaf male teachers were paid less on the assumption that hearing males had greater social expenses, and the salary of any educator had to take into consideration the position he should maintain in his social circle (Carlin, 1859).

Few willingly acceded to the comparison. One deaf man did maintain that a comparison of the salary scales of deaf and hearing teachers had no validity and that discussion only engendered a "suspicious and discontented spirit" ("Fair deaf-mute salaries," 1862, p. 11) The only valid comparison was to ask if another equally qualified deaf person would accept the position at that same salary. If the answer was yes, then a deaf man should be thankful that he was even employed. Only one reservation should be upheld—a qualified deaf teacher should receive preference over hearing men in hiring since employment was limited for deaf men (see Mitchell, 1973).

Despite the unfair employment practices of the schools for deaf persons, teaching, one of the few professional pursuits to which deaf persons could aspire, drew large numbers. By 1898 there were 171 graduates of the National Deaf Mute College, of whom 86, or just over half, chose teaching careers (Alumnis, 1900, p. 63). Deaf men were said to be among the best teachers, bound to their pupils "by ties of sympathy" and serving as examples by reason of their "own experience of the difficulties the deaf have to overcome" (Convention of Principals, 1884, p. 307).

Oral advocates were ambigious in their aims: their ideology was belied by their professional prescriptions for deaf graduates. On the one hand, oralists denied the manualists' contention that deafness was a human difference; on the other, they tacitly accepted the manualist view that deaf persons rarely attained the oral skills of hearing individuals. They therefore excluded deaf people from teaching deaf children. In their eagerness to obtain intellectual results and prove the validity of their method, oralists made it a rule not to employ any deaf person in any school for the deaf in any capacity whatsoever (Draper, 1889). Oralists considered deaf individuals with their linguistic difficulties to be unfit to teach deaf children, especially in speech and language.

In pursuit of this policy, Alexander Graham Bell addressed the Committee on Appropriations of the House of Representatives in 1885 and "clearly proved his contention that any increase in the numbers of deaf teachers of the deaf would work injury to the cause of articulation teaching, for the reason that deaf persons cannot teach articulation to the deaf or to anybody, no matter how competent they may be mentally" (De Land, 1905b). A little earlier Bell had pointed out that nearly one-third of the teachers of the deaf were deaf themselves. "This," he said, "must be considered as another interest favorable to the formation of a deaf race—to be therefore avoided" (A. G. Bell, 1884c, p. 48). In pointed opposition, Edward Miner Gallaudet contended that the oral schools could not legitimately oppose the employment of deaf teachers (Ferrari, 1908, p. 82). However, Bell's stand foreshadowed the eventual closing of the teaching profession to deaf persons in all North American schools.

Part 3

Into the New Century

Introduction

As the nineteenth century drew to a close, a host of social and political problems beset North America. The decay engendered by urbanization, industrialization, and immigration was made manifest by labor unrest and by rising rates of vagabondage, divorce, suicide, and crime. The apparent increase in deviant behavior, made more tangible by the statistical scrutiny of the tenth and eleventh United States censuses (Billings, 1890; E. A. Fay, 1898a; Gilbert, 1977; Wines, 1888), prompted unexpectedly strong reactions to those who were different by reason of ethnic background, disability, or social status.

A new breed of moral entrepreneurs emerged. Citing an equal concern for the preservation of society and the well-being of the poor and the disabled, they directed the nation's social thought and action toward an acceptance of a state in which the individual would be scientifically shaped and controlled to fill the nation's destiny. Under the banners of Social Darwinism and eugenics, they sought to explain the successes of the establishment and the failures of misfits through a theory of inherited intellectual potential. Scientists embarked on a campaign to seek the roots of feeblemindedness, devise ways to stamp it out, and warn the public of the impending threat to America.

Over and over, North Americans were warned of the problems raised by feebleminded individuals in society. Not only would they become criminals, prostitutes, and paupers, but in addition they would pass on their defective genes to future generations. The startling fusion of feeblemindedness, delinquency, crime, and vice stimulated the establishment of new institutions and the proposal of legislation to segregate and sterilize the misfits to prevent their passing their handicaps on to future generations.

The mainstay of the crusade for a genetically and socially pure America was the IQ test, which not only introduced scientific method into a field where previously only subjective judgment was possible but also purported to demonstrate the superiority of specific groups and upheld the popular bias about unassimilable and inferior European stocks. In the schools unprecedented numbers of students were subjected to IQ tests, examinations, and medical inspections. The resulting statistics then lent a specious scientific validity to often dubious judgments regarding individual cases. School-aged children who met the new standards were declared normal; those who failed were labeled as inadequate, delinquent, laggard, feebleminded, to name just a few of the unsavory labels. In the wider society results of tests of immigrants, as well as tests the Army used on new recruits, were used to lobby for immigration restrictions.

The study of intelligence and mental retardation challenged psychologists and educators not only because of the theoretical concepts involved but also because of the implications relating to child care and education. If intelligence was found to be a fixed entity, relatively unmodifiable by changes in the environment, then changes in living conditions and the amount and kind of education could be expected to have little influence on the mental level of individuals. With a mounting conviction that many disabled persons could never truly attain normalcy, many educators adopted the principles of hereditary determinism. Believing that human development and competence were not malleable but predetermined and inevitable—the result of a biological master plan—they came to also believe that education and therapy for exceptional individuals could, at best, only ameliorate or contain the unfortunate conditions that frustrated development. It was not that educational and scientific constituencies embarked on separate paths with different or conflicting goals. Scientists and educators sought to understand, identify, and control mental retardation, the scientific community through sterilization, the educational through segregation.

The period that matches the growth of scientific racism—from approximately the last quarter of the nineteenth century to the early 1920s—was also the most critical in developing public school programs for children and youth perceived as exceptional. School districts, under pressure to maintain increasing numbers of unruly, disabled, low-functioning, and immigrant children, created the community equivalent of institutions—special segregated classes. Exceptional pupils were not isolated in institutions but instead were separated in special classes that were labeled many different ways as ungraded classes, opportunity classes, auxiliary classes, and classes for particular conditions.

Reform may have been prompted externally, but it was shaped from within the schools themselves. Of the matrix of reasons that underlay the establishment of special classes, compulsory attendance laws were the most important. Once these laws were enacted, schools could no longer ignore exceptional students and were challenged to find solutions to their problems within the system. Teachers were generally unwilling to handle these children in regular classes, and officials, seeking to establish order, discipline, and high standards in the schools, were adverse to placing them in regular classrooms. Segregated classes were an obvious way to satisfy the requirements of the law and meet the needs of the schools. Problem children, removed from the mainstream, could not contaminate the learning of normal children or lower the standards of a school. Further, compulsory education laws were bolstered by new legislation governing child and female labor and creating children's and family courts. An interwoven bureaucracy of court officers, social workers, public health nurses, attendance officers, and others circled the educational core and ensured the attendance at school of large numbers of children. As well, state and federal support for special classes was on the rise.

With the advent of more sophisticated assessment procedures and a burgeoning of special classes, new categories of students requiring attention emerged. Not only did schools now identify and provide programs for children with a wide range of physical and health difficulties, but they assumed responsibility for discovering and labeling children as autistic, schizophrenic, emotionally disturbed, gifted, and learning disabled. Special services were added to those already offered by the schools, services provided by psychologists, public health nurses, social workers, and counselors. Teacher training expanded and became more associated with postsecondary education as teachers' colleges ceded to university or college training. Inevitably, new teacher associations were formed in the wake of the increasing specialization in education.

Chapter 8

Measures and Mismeasures:
The IQ Myth

Important Dates in the Rise of Intelligence Testing

1802	Franz Joseph Gall relates functions to specific parts of the brain
1861	Paul Broca identifies speech centers in the left frontal lobe
1879	Wilhelm Wundt's Leipzig laboratory for experimental psychology is founded
1890	James McKeen Cattell coins the term *mental test*
1892	G. Stanley Hall initiates the American Psychological Association
1895	Alfred Binet begins publishing on mental measurement
1905	Alfred Binet and Théodore Simon publish their intelligence test
1906	The laboratory at the New Jersey Training School for Feeble-Minded Boys and Girls at Vineland is established
1908	The Binet scale by Binet and Simon undergoes its first revision
1910	Henry Herbert Goddard translates the Binet scale for use in America
1911	The Binet scale is revised by Binet and Simon a second time
1911	William Stern uses term *intelligence quotient*
1913	John Broadus Watson outlines the essential tenets of behaviorism
1917	Goddard publishes Ellis Island data; Alpha and Beta tests are formulated and used by the U.S. Army
1930	Behaviorism is well accepted

In 1900 psychology was a young science, determined to conquer the complexities of the human mind through the astute application of experimental science. Modern scientific psychology is often dated from the founding of Wilhelm Wundt's (1832–1920) laboratory for experimental psychology in Leipzig in 1879

(Hilgard, 1987). The development of scientific research methods in educational psychology is attributed to Edward Lee Thorndike, who began his work before World War I (Winzer and Grigg, 1992). As a modern discipline, separate but arising from philosophy, psychology had first emerged during the era of the French Enlightenment. The *ideologues,* led by Pierre Jean Georges Cabanis and Philippe Pinel, and later by Jean Étienne Dominique Esquirol, G. M. A. Ferrus, and Édouard Seguin, attempted to treat mentally ill and mentally handicapped individuals, to promote better understanding of the conditions, and to insti-tute more humane treatment for patients. By the opening of the nineteenth cen-tury the essential outlines of the fields of psychiatry and psychology were apparent. Research efforts accelerated, albeit slowly and haltingly, throughout the century.

Psychology is the science of behavior; psychologists systematically inves-tigate behavioral phenomena—that is, they develop a systematic body of knowl-edge dealing with behavior and with the principles by which it can be predicted, modified, and sustained (see Atkinson et al., 1990; Salkind, 1990). Early psychol-ogy was essentially the study of groups; the goal of scientific psychology was to discover the laws of the normal human mind, which would allow generalizations about human behavior to be drawn. The qualities that constitute each person's individuality were slow to be accepted as legitimate objects of scientific psy-chology so long as the primary interest was the discovery of the universal laws of the human mind (Hilgard, 1987).

Attention to individuality and variability was considered to be more within the purview of anatomists, physicians, and special educators. Those who were abnormal—an obvious reference to the concept of the normal—reaped a har-vest of attention from these disciplines; those classed as feebleminded attracted special attention. Only after researchers began to develop the tools, the mea-sures, and the methods of statistical analyses to enable them to systematically study the ways that thinking develops (Winzer and Grigg, 1992) did psycholo-gists, grudgingly, turn to the study of individual differences. By the 1890s interest peaked as the interrelationships of the biological, social, and educational un-derstandings of mental retardation became matters of serious study and debate. Here was the beginning of psychoeducational research, initially associated more with schools and clinics in the community than with the institutions, and often directed by persons not well accepted by the influential medical superinten-dents of institutions (Rosen, Clark, and Kivitz, 1976).

Historically, human intelligence has been studied in a number of closely re-lated ways. The central focuses have been to define intelligence; to identify the influences on intelligence, specifically the relative influences of heredity and en-vironment; to devise ways to measure intelligence; and to discover how humans use intelligence in their learning. Notions about human intelligence are closely linked to the controversy about nature and nurture—about how much heredity or environment contributes to the total human being. Notions of intelligence also greatly affect the measurement of intelligence, the tools that are used for assessment, and the uses to which the data are put (Winzer and Grigg, 1992).

No psychological construct has engendered more controversy than intelli-gence (Winzer and Grigg, 1992). Given its complexity, it is little wonder that in-telligence has been defined in so many ways. Alfred Binet thought intelligence to be "the tendency to make and maintain a definite direction; the capacity to make adaptations for the purpose of attaining a desired end; and the power of autocriticism" (Binet and Simon, 1916, p. 45). Researcher Floyd Allport viewed intelligence as "the capacity for solving the problems of life" (Allport, 1924, p. 104); psychologist E. G. Boring remarked that "intelligence is what the tests test" (Boring, 1923, p. 35).

The way humans think and process knowledge has been of perennial interest to philosophers and educators. Intelligence seems to be more complicated than any other variable and, because it underlies so much of human functioning, has generated interest at least since the time of classical Greece. The relative contributions of environment and heredity have been seriously debated since that time, too. Early twentieth-century psychologists directed their energies to determining the answer to the nature-nurture conundrum and to devising and using tools that would scientifically measure a person's IQ, predict that person's social role, and ultimately decide on that person's value to society.

Many arguments were provided to justify the assertion that no feature was as important as heredity. And, with the introduction of the scales to measure intelligence objectively, the involvement of psychologists with disabled persons centered on establishing their mental status.

Various models to explain human learning—how intelligence was used— emerged, most notably in the second decade of the twentieth century when John Broadus Watson put forward his provocative and controversial model of the behavioristic view of learning. (See Box 8-1 for descriptions of the common models of learning.)

The sociopolitical atmosphere of Europe and the United States in the late nineteenth and early twentieth centuries nurtured the spread of a concept that linked intelligence to the possession of biological "goodness." In other words, intelligence is innate and found more in some groups than others. Science then inevitably used the concepts and measures relating to intelligence to link delinquency, crime, and feeblemindedness. Advocates of the testing movement, scientists, eugenicists, and others shifted the testing emphasis from the needs of the individual to the needs of society. As it became acceptable to stratify society on the basis of test results, they called for policies to counter a specter of their own making, "the threat of the feebleminded."

It was easy for the established population in North America to see immigrants as the source of many of society's problems. From about 1915 on, assimilation and Americanization became popular crusades that gained momentum from the xenophobic and political reaction of the postwar period. The restriction of immigration was seen as necessary to foster the moral, economic, political, and racial health of the United States and Canada. Of the many arguments forwarded for restricting immigration, one of the most telling was that based on the data gathered on immigrants through IQ testing. The test results were used to prove irrefutably that certain areas of Europe produced genetically inferior stock.

Following the widespread application of standardized testing during World War I, Americans adopted tests and accepted test data that perpetuated myths involving genetic inheritance and strengthened latent racist views. So great was public credulity that few questioned the accuracy of the testing procedures.

Box 8-1

Models of Human Learning

Models and theories of learning arising through the years from the work of philosophers and psychologists continue to influence our practices and beliefs. Most of the early theories about how humans develop and learn can be assigned to one of two schools—the associationalist and the nativistic. These have been called different names over the centuries and have taken on different emphases, but their essential tenets revolve around that old and still controversial question, the relative importance of nature and nurture in human development.

The associationalist theory is the traditional theory of knowledge against which all others argue. Associationalist theories see learning as the result of connections (associations) between stimuli (sense impressions) and responses. A fundamental principle of associationalism is that every event is caused by other events.

Two basic principles are common to most associationalist theories (see Eckler and Weininger, 1988). The first is empiricism, the belief that all knowledge arises from experience. The assumption is that babies at birth hold no preconceived notions; they know nothing; they are what John Locke called a *tabula rasa,* a blank slate. In other words, the mind has form but not content. The second basic principle, which gives associationalism its name, is that the only innate mental ability is the ability to receive sense impressions and to form associations among them (Rosenblith and Sims-Knight, 1985). Humans learn such things as who mother is, what time is, and how to reason logically by associating sense impressions.

Locke was not the first to use the analogy of the white paper. Aristotle (384–322 B.C.) first formulated the associationalist view when he conceptualized the infant's mind as a blank slate and emphasized the role of experience in the development of the child. Aristotle argued for three principles of association: contiguity—things are associated because they are experienced at the same time and place; similarity—things are associated because they are alike; and contrast—things are associated because they are opposites (Eckler and Weininger, 1988).

Associationalism flowered again among the British philosophers of the seventeenth and eighteenth centuries. John Locke (1632–1704), David Hume (1711–1776), James Mill (1773–1836), and John Stuart Mill (1806–1873) belonged to the associationalist school. Empiricists such as Thomas Hobbes (1588–1679) and George Berkeley (1685–1753) also emphasized the impact of experience upon the passive mind. Associationalism (sensationalism) was adopted by the major philosophers of the French Enlightenment—Étienne Bonnot de Condillac, Denis Diderot, and, at least to some extent, Jean Jacques Rousseau. Nineteenth-century associationalists were deeply influenced by such founding fathers of philosophy as Aristotle and Locke, whereas the British philosophers provided the foundation for American behaviorism that flourished in the first half of the twentieth century.

Philosophers who did not subscribe to associationalism searched for internal determiners of behavior. The heart, lungs, liver, kidneys, spleen, not to mention the humors and the brain, all became promising candidates (Skinner, 1989). The result was nativism. Proponents of nativistic theories do not see learning as an association between two events—a stimulus and a response. Rather, they hold that humans are born with innate abilities, that certain structures of knowledge exist independently of sensations and thus of experience.

Arising from a nativistic philosophy of innate structures is rationalism, which identifies reason as the primary source of knowledge, prior to, superior to, and independent of sense perception. This position has a long past, starting with Plato (428–347 B.C.), who expressed the view that individual differences in traits such as intelligence, talents, and aptitudes are inborn. (However, aware as well of environmental influences, he also argued that children should be separated from their parents early in life, and the state should control their rearing and education.) René Descartes (1596–1650) held that knowledge is derived from ideas with which we are born, rather than from experience. Immanuel Kant (1724–1804) held that the highest functions of the mind are knowing, feeling, and willing. He believed that the concepts of objects, space and time, and casuality are given *a priori,* that is, they do not have to be learned. We know reality independently of observation, experience, and the use of empirical methods. Kant suggested that knowledge is acquired by a process in which order is imposed on the data that the senses provide and is not merely a quality detected in these data.

A third theory, called historico-cultural, may be traced to the writings of Johann Wolfgang von Goethe (1749–1832), Georg Wilhelm Friedrich Hegel (1770–1831), and Karl Marx (1818–1883). According to this view, knowledge is always acquired in a social context as a function of the unique historical circumstances in which the group finds itself. Intellectual development cannot be separated from cultural and social experiences, from the social and physical environment, from the tools that have been developed for coping with environments, and from the ways in which these tools are passed from one generation to the next (see Eckler and Weininger, 1988).

The associationalist, rationalist, and historico-cultural models may be seen as precursors to current theories of learning, specifically, behaviorism, social learning theory, cognitive processing, and humanism. As the discipline of psychology emerged in the nineteenth century, associationalist and rationalist views of learning developed alongside each other. In the twentieth century associationalism, manifested in the behavioral movement, was dominant until the so-called cognitive revolution of the 1960s.

The empirical psychology of John Locke, as interpreted by philosophers of the European Enlightenment, held that humans learn primarily by association. Charles Darwin's publications of the mid-nineteenth century strengthened the concept. His theory of natural selection as basic to evolution provided the intellectual basis for perceiving continuity between the animal species and humans, which is basic to an associationalist or behavioral stance. At first, in *On the Origin of*

Species (1859) Darwin was reticent on the matter of human evolution. Later, in *The Descent of Man* (1874) he made clear his view that humans shared a common ancestor with the apes. He concluded, "The difference in mind between man and the higher animals, great as it is, certainly is one of degree and not of kind" (p. 193). Darwinian theory focused attention on the functional significance of different constellations of characteristics, including behavior, as both the products and determinants of a species' evolution (Bell and Harper, 1977).

However, in the late nineteenth century the dominant nonbiological approach in psychology was Wilhelm Wundt's cognitive perspective, with its stress on introspection. The experimental psychology conceived by Wundt owed little to Darwinian evolutionary theory; it was conceived as the science of the human mind, to be studied through introspection. There was little place for animal psychology in such an approach, although Wundt (1894) did later argue that animal consciousness might be established through comparisons with human introspection (Corballis, 1989).

Wundt's view held sway until the first enunciation of behavioral principles in 1913. American behavioral theory was first advanced by John Broadus Watson, an aggressive, controversial figure whose position was inspired by associationalist theory, given credence by the identification of classical conditioning by the Russian physiologist Ivan Petrovich Pavlov, and lent direction by laboratory experiments with animals (see Winzer and Grigg, 1992). Watson rejected introspection as a means to study human behavior. To Watson, introspection has a private quality that distinguishes it from observations in other fields of science. He saw introspection as a futile approach and argued that if psychology is to be a science, its data has to be observable by any qualified scientist. Watson held that observable behaviors should form the sole subject matter of psychology and that the goal of psychology is to control and predict behavior through the manipulation of environmental stimuli.

Behavioral research has played a pivotal role in the study of learning, and it is easy to see how learning psychology fits in with the traditional philosophical view of associationalism. According to that view, human learning is essentially responses to stimuli in the environment. Conditioning occurs when two events, not previously associated by the organism, become associated. Imitation also fits into associationalism if an imitation is assumed to be an association of another's behavior with one's own.

Watson set the stage for the work of B. F. Skinner and the proponents of the use of behavior modification in the classroom. Not long after Watson first enunciated the principles of behaviorism, B. F. Skinner embarked on a course of research that was to have a profound impact on psychology and educational practice. Though Skinner also pointed to the importance of the environment, he departed from the research direction outlined by Watson by turning his attention away from study of the reflexive behaviors that are elicited by preceding stimuli. Skinner identified a second type of behavior—operant behaviors, which are not elicited by a particular stimuli but are affected by the consequences that follow the behavior.

Major transformations in views of human learning occurred in the 1950s and 1960s. The English translation of Jean Piaget's work, Noam Chomsky's notions of language acquisition and development, new ideas about innate learning structures, and a reaction against rigid behavioral theories, all contributed to a sharp swing toward cognitive views of learning. The late twentieth-century cognitive theories have expanded to include many diverse formulations, but one important assumption underlying all cognitive theory is the belief that human beings develop increasingly differentiated and integrated cognitive structures that represent and organize their knowledge. Cognitive theorists view learning as a reorganization of a number of perceptions that allows the learner to see new relationships, solve new problems, and gain a basic understanding of a subject area. Change occurs in a person's ability to respond to particular situations. According to these theorists, the change in behavior that strict behaviorists call learning is only a reflection of an internal change. Jean Piaget's rich and detailed descriptive theory of cognitive development, sometimes called genetic epistemology, is the foremost example of this tradition (Case, 1984). Piaget describes how the human mind develops by gradually constructing knowledge about the world from the feedback received through interactions with it.

The cognitive aspect of the nativistic tradition is currently represented by Gestalt psychologists, ethologists, and those linguists and cognitive psychologists who follow Noam Chomsky's views about language (Rosenblith and Sims-Knight, 1985).

In the sociocultural tradition the theories of Vygotsky and Bruner are the best known (Case, 1984). Jerome Bruner (1965), for example, stated that growth of the mind is always assisted from the outside. He stressed the importance of understanding the structures of the social context in which the transmission of knowledge takes place in order to understand the nature of the mental structures that result. L. Vygotsky offers a picture of human development that insists that development is inseparable from human social and cultural activities.

Certainly, some cried out against the abuse of the measures, the narrow univariate conceptions of intelligence, and the notion that everything about a human was ordained at birth, but for the most part the critics were not heeded. It was not until the mid-1930s that serious doubts about the IQ tests finally surfaced.

THE STUDY OF HUMAN INTELLIGENCE

The study of human intelligence did not begin with the nineteenth-century psychologists. Ancient and medieval philosophers endeavored to understand the unique spark that gives humans intelligence—their ability to think, learn, and reason.

The Greeks considered both functional and structural aspects of intelligence. It was the Greeks who first localized the mind in the brain and clearly identified sensory perception as a major source of knowledge (Mann, 1979). Pythagoras in the sixth century B.C. divided the soul into two parts—the rational and the emotional, the first located in the brain, the second in the heart (L. Mann, 1979). Hippocrates identified the brain as the seat of intelligence but believed it to be a gland that secreted thought. Alcmaeon, a follower of Pythagoras, identified lower and higher cognitive capacities, or sense perception and intelligence, a distinction repeated by later Greek theorists, especially Plato and Aristotle (L. Mann, 1979). Thomas Aquinas (1225–1274) followed Aristotle and believed in two types of mind—the *intellectus* and the *ratio* (L. Mann, 1979). Later, René Descartes assumed that nerve tubes that conduct "animal spirits" are responsible for mental functions; Baruch Spinoza regarded mind and matter as one substance.

The Greeks held that intelligence allows humans to reason and that it is this reason that separates humans from animals. Aristotle posited the *nous* (intellect) as a characteristic of the human species; *nous* serves to differentiate humans from animals but contains no notion of individual differences (L. Mann, 1979). The Greeks attributed "higher ability" to a personal factor that is part of a human's endowment.

During many centuries following the Greeks, philosophers and theologians linked the intellect to the soul. This religious conception, coupled with a distaste for violating the human body, the crucible of the soul, by dissection, erected a metaphysical barrier that allowed unhampered philosophical speculation but not physical exploration. Serious anatomical studies of brain structure and function began only with the Renaissance, although the complexity of the human brain baffled early physicians.

An advance in knowledge about brain function occurred when, for example, searches for brain lesions revealed that they caused aphasia, the loss of the power to use or comprehend words, and other language disorders. Modern interest in localization of cerebral function and experimental studies related to it began with the work of Franz Joseph Gall (1758–1828), a Viennese physician and anatomist who embarked on a search to trace aphasia. In Gall's time the brain was considered to be a formless pulpy mass, but his anatomical searches led to an unfolding of the complexities of gray matter. Gall demonstrated that the nervous system has a design and presumably a meaning. In 1802 he published a description of a theoretical construct in which he related specific mental activities to identified parts of the brain.

Gall lost his strictly scientific orientation and much of his research reputation when he became obsessed with phrenology after making the chance observation that fellow students at the University of Vienna who had prominent eyes proved to be better students with the best memories. Gall began to lecture on his theories of phrenology in Germany about 1800 (Temkin, 1947). His reputation deteriorated when he entered into an academic argument with Philippe Pinel concerning the seat of insanity and was bested by the master. Regardless of the impact of later criticisms, however, Gall's work had a strong influence on American psychology. Phrenology became a large part of early psychology; it became a pragmatic psychology in America, lacking academic acceptance. Phrenology played a prominent role in the identification of mentally retarded persons and can be seen as the beginning of the modern testing movement.

The essence of phrenology was the belief that various parts of the brain, specialized for various functions, can be identified by tissue prominences and that the type and density of prominences (bumps) reveal the character and personality of the subject. These psychological characteristics, called *faculties* by the phrenologists, fall into two broad orders. The first order, feelings, are divided into two subcategories—*propensities* and *sentiments*. Propensities, located in the back of the brain, are those faculties that humans share with all animals, such as combativeness, destructiveness, and secretiveness. Sentiments, located on the top of the brain, are those faculties exclusive to humans and include veneration, firmness, and hope (Passinen, 1974). The second order consists of *intellectual faculties* and includes external senses, such as taste and smell, as well as perceptive faculties—language, comparison, and causality. These were said to be located in the front of the skull, roughly from the hairline to just below the eyes (Passinen, 1974).

The French scientist and anthropologist Paul Broca (1824–1880) also explored the brain in his quest for the site of aphasia. Although Broca's craniometry was eventually discounted (S. Gould, 1981), his autopsies provided one of the first discourses on the separation of the functions of the right and left hemispheres and a further indication that specific brain functions exist in particular locales of the brain. After conducting postmortem examinations of four stroke victims, Broca identified the left temporal lobe as prime in speech production; he identified the speech center (Broca's area) in 1861 (see Hilgard, 1987; Sagan, 1979).

Anthrometrics, most closely identified with Cesare Lombroso in Italy and Arthur MacDonald in the United States, swung the precepts of phrenology into the field of criminality. Specific physical attributes or stigmata were associated with antisocial traits such as criminality, insanity, and poverty. By classifying such things as ear lobes, cranial protrusions, tatooing, asymmetries, lefthandedness, and the like, Lombroso claimed to have discovered a criminal typology (Gilbert, 1977). MacDonald, less adamant than Lombroso, also studied physical typology as a means of identifying an individual's tendencies, criminal and otherwise (MacDonald, 1902). MacDonald's questionnaire study of Washington school children, published in 1897, and his statistical work on abnormality and its causes were at least temporarily reputable competitors of the child-study works inspired by G. Stanley Hall (Gilbert, 1977), the crowned leader of the early child-study movement (see Winzer and Grigg, 1992).

THE TESTING MOVEMENT

Not only were early philosophers concerned about what intelligence actually is, they were also interested in ways to measure human intelligence. The first formal attempts at developing tests are attributed to the Chinese. As early as 2200 B.C. they implemented an extensive system of civil service examinations that lasted almost 3,000 years (Dubois, 1966). Anna Anastasi (1968) points out that the ancient Greeks also used testing as part of the Socratic method of teaching.

From time to time English legal writers attempted to formulate measures for determining the mental status of persons either charged with crime or under observation of the law. In the sixteenth century one writer suggested as a test of mentality that a person should be examined to see whether he could measure a yard of cloth or name the days in the week (Linden and Linden, 1968). In the same century a Spanish physician, Juan Huarte, may have been the first to suggest formal testing. Huarte examined the concept of intelligence and its characteristics, such as docility in learning from a master, understanding and independence of judgment, and inspiration without extravagance. His 1575 work *Examen de ingenios* provided a guide to youth and advice to parents on the aptitudes of their children (Linden and Linden, 1968). Achievement testing had been used as early as the thirteenth century in France, where oral exams were used at the Sorbonne; later, Louvain University tested students for educational competencies. In the sixteenth century a system of written examinations was used for students at Jesuit universities for the dual purposes of testing learning and deciding educational placement. Such examinations were used at Oxford in 1636 for degree certification; written questions were adopted at Cambridge in 1828 (Luftig, 1989). Standardized testing in North America may have begun with Joseph Rice's spelling surveys in the 1890s (Resnick, 1981).

The foundations of modern methods to measure mental ability were laid in Germany at the time of the rise of experimental psychology. Wilhelm Wundt, working in his laboratories at Leipzig in 1875, formulated general descriptions of human behavior. Wundt conceived of psychology as the science of the human mind, to be studied through introspection; he studied sensory phenomena by measuring reaction times and made qualitative checks of introspection. Wundt did not devise a mental test per se; his contribution to the testing movement was the methodology he used in his experimental studies. Wundt's emphasis on standardized conditions and procedures formed an important legacy for modern psychology and measurement (Goodenough, 1949; Linden and Linden, 1968, Young, 1923).

Although uniformities rather than differences in behavior were the focus of Wundt's research, some of his students and colleagues turned to the study of individual differences. In England, Sir Francis Galton (1822–1911), a scion of a leading British family, the Wedgwoods, and a second cousin of Charles Darwin, became interested in the study of human differences as the basis for his eugenic models, which first appeared in the 1860s.

Galton's work in Britain's leading families essentially confirmed society's traditional ranking of persons on the basis of family—on social rather than biological factors. Galton demonstrated that members of leading families were far more likely to attain eminence than members of other classes. When he attributed such phenomena to distinguished breeding and good "germ plasm," he tacitly argued that among the ruling classes differences or deviations could then be blamed on defects in character rather than defects in ability and overlooked the obvious environmental advantages of adequate nutrition, good medical care, stimulating environments, and exclusive schooling (Galton, [1869], 1870–1883).

Galton attempted to define intelligence in terms of its behavioral correlates. To accomplish this, and to measure individual ability and achievement, Galton created a test method that was brief and useful for sampling large numbers of people. He did not distinguish between potential capacity and actual academic or social success and considered repetition to be an accurate measure of ability. Galton's measures involved activities such as discrimination between weights, colors, and sounds; the speed and accuracy with which a subject could cancel all the *A*s on a page of printed material; color naming; and word association (Linden and Linden, 1968).

Galton's work did not translate into specific measures of intelligence, but he did introduce the idea of the intelligence tests and made their development an important research problem for the future (Fancher, 1985). Galton ([1869] 1870) suggested distributing intelligence, like other human characteristics, on a linear metrical scale ranging from idiocy to genius. His biometrics gave the underlying statistical laws that made measurement possible, and he was the first to use correlation to represent the degree of agreement between pairs of measurements on the same individual (Hilgard, 1987). To statisticians he also willed the concepts of regression and the normal curve and centile ranks. Galton developed methods for measuring abilities and for statistically analyzing the data obtained; he discovered the law of regression, expressing the relationship between the abilities of parents and offspring in what he called the regression or correlation coefficient. His student Karl Pearson (1857–1936) carried on the work with considerable ingenuity, developing what has been come to be called *biometrics,* including most of the basic methods of modern statistical analysis (Blanton, 1976, p. 175). Pearson proved the exact mathematical formulation of the theory of correlation in 1884, still known as the Pearson product moment correlation, described by the coefficient r. With these tools psychologists could express their findings in statistical terms, averages, measures of dispersion, and correlations.

One of the pioneers in the modern study of intelligence was the British psychologist Charles Spearman (1863–1945), who had become interested in the theory and practice of IQ testing even before the first report of the Binet tests (Spearman, 1904). Spearman viewed intelligence as a mental capacity that underlies all cognitive performance and saw levels of intelligence as related to levels of cognitive performance.

When presenting children with batteries of tests, Spearman noticed two trends. Some children showed a strong tendency to rank consistently from test to test; children who scored high on one test such as memory tended to score high on the other tests. Other children scored well on some tests, poorly on others. Spearman ascribed the tendency to do well over all the measures as a general, or *g,* factor. The differential rankings for individuals he ascribed to specific, or *s,* factors, which referred to particular abilities. Spearman (1904) proposed that all individuals possess the general intelligence factor, *g,* in varying amounts, so a person can be described as bright or dull depending on the amount of *g* he or she possessed. Further, the *g* factor is the driving force that powers the set of special skills unique to specific situations (Hilgard, 1987). The *g* factor, therefore, was seen to be a form of dynamic brain energy. Spearman also determined that any test of mental performance would reflect greater or less amounts of the *g* factor (Winzer and Grigg, 1992).

Spearman wanted to define intelligence objectively, which to him meant developing a quantitative description. His two-tier view of intelligence is intuitively understandable—two persons might be of equal intellectual competence, though one might possess special aptitude such as musical ability or skill in acquiring a foreign language (Hilgard, 1987). However, critics of Spearman's position refused to accept the existence of a general intelligence. Instead, they suggested that intelligence is composed of several "primary mental abilities."

Lewis L. Thurstone (1887–1935) worked diligently to refine Spearman's ideas but could find not evidence to support the *g* concept. Ultimately, he denied the existence of a general factor for intelligence (Thurstone, 1938) and instead suggested that intelligence is a composite of special factors, each peculiar to a particular task. He believed that intelligence is constituted of a number of primary abilities: verbal comprehension, word fluency, number fluency, space perceptiveness, memory, perceptual speed, and reasoning.

Other early psychologists, specifically Joseph Jastrow, Hugo Münsterberg, and Hermann Ebbinghaus, developed achievement and mental tests for use with diverse populations. Ebbinghaus ([1885] 1913) one of the pioneers in memory research (Colson and Mehring, 1990), believed that the combining activity of the mind is the highest; his Ebbinghaus sentence-completion test, which appeared in 1897, was the only test of the time to demonstrate a clear relationship with later school achievement (see Hilgard, 1987).

Credit for establishing the foundation of mental measurement in North America goes to James McKeen Cattell (1860–1944), a student of both Wilhelm Wundt and Francis Galton. Although Wundt was unsympathetic to the study of individual differences, Cattell studied higher processes, focusing on individual deviations. When Cattell met Galton in England, the two recognized their common interest in individual differences. Cattell took Galton's ideas on mental tests and his correlation formulae back to America and used them as the foundation of his psychological experimentation in the laboratory he founded at Columbia University. Further influenced by Galton's ideas about eugenics and the heritability of intelligence, Cattell as early as 1898 also suggested the use of mental tests to identify the feebleminded (Kamin, 1974).

Cattell was primarily interested in individual differences and careful quantitative methods. He sought to formulate mental tests that were simple, reliable, and easy to analyze statistically. In pursuit of this goal Cattell set out to test a large sample of the population in order to discover "the constancy of the mental processes, their independence, and their variation under different circumstances" (quoted by Linden and Linden, 1968, p. 10). Cattell studied variables such as perception and sensory acuteness, "sense of effort," mental time, and mental intensity, convinced that these were correlated with mental capacity and academic success. He studied freshman students to predict academic success but, after four years, Cattell's correlations of psychological measures with future achievement were poor, an outcome that caused the testing movement to lose some credibility.

However, Cattell's claim to distinction rests more on his leadership and initiative than on any system or theory (Hilgard, 1987). Cattell insisted that the study of psychology requires the rigor of physical science, that it should rest on a foundation of experimentation and measurement. He hoped to stimulate psychologists to devise sets of tests that would measure separate mental processes; Cattell favored uncomplicated, physiologically and sensory oriented tests that were easy to administer and quantify (see Cattell, 1890). His approach was adopted as official policy by the fledgling American Psychological Association in 1897 (although the policy was largely abandoned by 1900). Nevertheless, like Francis Galton, Cattell successfully promoted the idea of mental testing as a desirable pursuit for scientific psychology but left the productive implementation of the idea for later generations. His students included Edward Lee Thorndike, Edward K. Strong, and Robert Sessions Woodworth, all of whom ultimately greatly influenced psychological testing (Luftig, 1989).

The Beginnings of Widespread Testing

One of the first studies of the assessment of exceptional students in North America was conducted by David Greenberger, principal of the New York Institution for Improved Instruction of Deaf-Mutes. Because he could not assess a deaf child's mental condition merely by observation or interviews, Greenberger devised a battery of measures to distinguish the children who would benefit from instruction from those who should be directed into institutions for the mentally retarded (Slusarczyk, 1986). The assessment began when the child was asked to pronounce some of "the principal elements of speech and their combinations, and required to repeat them" (Greenberger, 1889, p. 96). The child was then presented with colored pictures, books, and numbers, and the child's reactions were closely observed. As part of the testing procedures, Greenberger interviewed the parents and questioned them about the applicant's behavior, daily routine, and success in communicating. Children who remained apathetic or inattentive during a testing session would not seem to Greenberger to be promising candidates for education in his school. He favored children who tended to become embarrassed; he believed that "a real imbecile or low grade idiot does not know enough to show embarrassment or bashfulness" (Greenberger, 1889, p. 96). He defined dull children as the "doubtful cases" and found differentiating among them to be very difficult (p. 93).

At this same time other instruments were available to assess such skills as spelling, memory, strength of grip, tapping, sensory acuity, and perception of size and weight (Mott, 1899, 1900; R. Taylor, 1897, 1898). Athletic tests involved running, jumping, pushing, pulling, throwing, and judging distances and direction (Mott, 1899). Manual dexterity was assessed by having children string sets of beads, pile sets of dominoes, sort by size, and turn the pages of a blank book and write their initials on each page (Mott, 1900). Observation and memory were tested by asking children to observe objects, by having them write their names after a wait, or by asking them to observe a collection of letters and then write them the next day. A spelling test that used unconnected words such as *rhinoceros, schoolhouse, anxious,* and *fog* was also used as part of the battery (Mott, 1900). Seguin created the Seguin formboard (Seguin, 1856) (much like the wooden puzzles that children put together today), which was much later standardized as a test item (Sylvester, 1913). Rudolph Pintner and his colleagues, who devised tests in the 1920s, used it in evaluating exceptional students (see Pintner, 1920, [1923] 1931).

Most of the early tools were single tests that assessed quite specific functions. Tests were not organized into scales, they were not standardized, and no methods for ascertaining reliability or validity existed (Freeman, 1926). As a consequence, the early measures had limited application. The prime test was the cancellation of *As*, as used by Galton and others. The tests all dealt with sensory and motor processes, and even when a battery of tests was used, the results were not combined. The early measures failed to make much impression and were even viewed negatively (Freeman, 1926); educators at the time saw little value in mental tests in the schools (Linden and Linden, 1968; Young, 1923).

But as compulsory education laws propelled increasing numbers of children into the public schools and the formation of special day classes for exceptional students drew more special children into their orbit, the need to standardize the psychological protocols became evident. In 1901 the Committee on Psychological Research of the American Association for the Study of the Feeble-Minded provided a format for an appropriate psychological examination that included physical, mental, and emotional measurements (Report of Committee, 1901). In 1906 the American Psychological Association, founded under the auspices of G. Stanley Hall in 1892, appointed a committee on tests to undertake the task of standardizing the existing tests of motor and sensory skills (Freeman, 1926).

The Binet Tests

It is generally conceded that Alfred Binet (1867–1911), aided by his young assistant Théodore Simon (1873–1961), devised the first widely acceptable test of mental ability. Binet's initial psychological work, experimentation with the psychological measures used by Cattell, Wundt, and Galton, was at the Salpêtrière, where he also became acquainted with hypnosis and parapsychology. By the time he began publishing his work on mental tests in 1895, Binet was considered a leader in experimental psychology and experimental pedagogy and had acquired substantial experience in the measurement of individual differences.

In 1904 the French government asked Binet to produce a measure that would identify those children who did not possess the potential to achieve in regular classrooms under regular school instruction. To avoid injustice, officials wanted the selection to be based on objective diagnostic procedures. With these goals in mind, Binet devised a way to measure the intellectual capacity of school-aged children, specifically to assess the level of their development of various mental processes.

Binet considered intelligence to be an entity founded on judgment and reasoning, not a grouping of separate components. "To judge well, to comprehend well, to reason well," observed Binet, "are the essentials of intelligence. A person may be a moron or an imbecile if he lacks judgment, but with good judgments he could not be either" (Binet and Simon, 1905). Like Galton, Binet subscribed to the belief that individual differences consist of deviations from a population average, but he also thought that mental tests should yield both quantitative and qualitative information about mental differences (Young, 1923). Binet and Simon sought to create a single scale in which samples of different aspects of mental ability could be combined in order to provide a rough but serviceable means of appraising general intelligence. They recognized the need to sample complex mental processes such as judging, remembering, and imagining, so their test encompassed diverse activities, from reasoning to reading.

Binet devised thirty subtests that could be objectively scored and used to differentiate mentally retarded from normal children. The tests required children to carry out simple verbal commands, coordinate actions, recognize and use common objects, define words, and complete sentences (Luftig, 1989). After presenting the items to a group of fifty normal children ranging in age from three to eleven and a number of subnormal and retarded children, Binet assigned each item to the age level at which 60 to 90 percent of children in that age group passed the item. Children who passed were considered normal or above average. The result was Simon and Binet's intelligence test, first made public in 1905. The Measuring Scale of Intelligence comprised thirty items arranged in order of increasing difficulty, scored simply by the number of items passed correctly.

Binet soon recognized the weaknesses of the 1905 scale, produced as it was under time constraints. Binet and Simon's 1908 revision was more statistically representative; they generated its standardization norm from a sample of 203 children. On the 1908 scale Binet and Simon added some items, eliminated others, and made a significant advance: items were grouped according to age (Binet and Simon, 1908), and the concept of mental age was introduced. Binet and Simon revised their scale again in 1911. Since that time the Stanford-Binet has been revised four more times, in 1937, 1960, and 1972, most recently in 1986 (Thorndike, Hagan and Sattler, 1986). The 1960 revision used a different method of computing IQ.

Parenthetically, it should be mentioned that in 1920, after the death of Binet, a young Jean Piaget worked at the Binet laboratory in Paris. Piaget assumed a different stance than Binet—rather than assessing how children performed correctly on the tests, he was more concerned with what they did, how they arrived at their answers, and how they reached incorrect conclusions. Later, Piaget formulated his model of cognitive development and its stages from what he called sensory-motor development through to the level of formal operations.

Binet's Scale in America

Much of the impetus for the promotion and direction of the early testing movement in America arose from initiatives taken at the New Jersey Institution for Feeble-Minded Boys and Girls at Vineland, most specifically by Henry Goddard, director of the Psychological Laboratory at Vineland. Records of the Vineland Training School trace the origins of Goddard's laboratory to the formation of the Feeble Minded Club in March 1902, which undertook the discussion of the problems of mental retardation. E. R. Johnstone, director of the training school, was committed to the idea that public institutions should be considered human laboratories where problems of human growth and development could be studied under controlled conditions. In his annual report of 1906 Johnstone translated notion into policy when he recommended the establishment of a scientific laboratory.

Henry Goddard became director of the research department that opened in September 1906, with the primary purpose of finding the causes of mental retardation and eradicating the condition. Goddard had earned his doctoral degree in 1899 under G. Stanley Hall at Clark University. Goddard's early psychological studies and experiments with psychomotor tests stimulated his interest in the 1905 Binet scale, which Goddard introduced to North America in 1908 when it was translated by Elizabeth Kite, his assistant and field worker.

In 1910 Goddard adapted Binet and Simon's 1908 revision. In 1911 he standardized this revision on 2,000 school-aged children in the Vineland public schools; he discovered at least 2 percent of the sample to be mentally retarded, unable to achieve in traditional classrooms (Goddard, 1910, 1911).

The Goddard revision of 1910 became one of the most commonly used versions of the Binet scale in the United States (Sattler, 1982), although not the only one (e.g., Huey, 1910). In 1911 Lewis Madison Terman, who had also studied under Hall, became interested in the intelligence testing of school-aged children. Terman began his work on the American version of the Binet test in Los Angeles and continued the project when he went to Stanford University in 1910. With his coworker H. G. Childs, Terman published the Terman and Childs Revision of the Binet-Simon scale in 1912 (Terman and Childs, 1912). In the next four years this revision was further modified, extended, and standardized, and finally in 1916 published as the Stanford Revision and Extension of the Binet-Simon Intelligence Scale (Sattler, 1974). Terman expanded the number of tests given at each age and standardized the scale on what he believed to be a typical American sample. This first edition of the scale generated a standardized norm from a sample of 2,300 Caucasian children from California (expanded to 3,184 in 1937).

Terman linked Stanford's name with the Binet to provide the most widely known English title for the test, the Stanford-Binet Individual Test of Intelligence. The Stanford-Binet provided the model for future IQ tests and later achievement measures. Terman's other contributions are described in Box 8-2.

The practical value of the Binet type of scale, as translated by Goddard and further developed by Terman to fit American conditions, was immediately obvious to educators and psychologists. They were enthralled with the new tools, which would allow them to compare the mental and physical attributes of students and to understand the thinking of disabled children. With the careful use of "modern psychometric tests," educators were confident that the intelligence of a child could be "accurately measured and a very close estimate made as to what his mental development will be when he reaches adult life" (W. E. Fernald, 1924, p. 966). Educational usage could become universal. The 1916 revision of the Binet scale by Terman made possible the use of the test by any schoolteacher who could afford to buy the book.

Sweeping claims and theoretical bases are, however, far removed from the rank and file of classroom teachers. Not all teachers, of course, accepted the IQ tests as unambiguous instruments, and not all administrators viewed the measures as the revolutionary educational and diagnostic tools of the new century (see Raftery, 1988). Some remained skeptical, although many educators continued to place an unwavering faith in the new measures through the 1920s and beyond.

MENTAL AGE AND IQ TESTS

More often than not, educational ideas follow rather than create social trends. New conceptions, whether philosophical, pedagogical, or psychological, are shaped and molded on the currents of contemporary social, political, economic, and even religious tides. With the coming of the twentieth century,

Box 8-2

Lewis Madison Terman (1877–1956)

Lewis Madison Terman is the single person in American education most clearly associated with IQ testing. He was born the twelfth of fourteen children of an Indiana farmer. He was a student in a country school, attended a normal school, taught for a time, and then graduated from Indiana University with a bachelor's degree in 1902 and a master's in 1903. He sought and received a fellowship to Clark University and borrowed enough money to attend, even though he had a wife and two infant children to support.

Under the leadership of G. Stanley Hall, Clark University was the center for psychological study, and as a student of the renowned psychologist Terman acquired his lifelong interest in testing. Terman investigated the psychology of genius, the measurement of intelligence, and the phenomenon of individual differences. In 1905 Terman presented his doctoral dissertation to the faculty at Clark University; it was entitled "Genius and Stupidity: A Study of Some of the Intellectual Processes of Seven 'Bright' and Seven 'Stupid' Boys" (Terman, [1906] 1975).

Terman contracted tuberculosis and like many other health seekers, subsequently traveled to southern California. After a year in San Bernardino he accepted a position at the state normal school in Los Angeles, where his enthusiasm and innovative theories of intelligence measurement influenced many students (Hilgard, 1957, 1987). In 1910 Terman moved to Stanford University and continued his studies on testing. His 1916 production of the Stanford-Binet Individual Test of Intelligence became the most widely accepted version of the Binet measures and elevated Terman to leader of the testing movement.

With Henry Goddard, Terman was a leading innovator in devising the army tests, which led Terman, Robert Mearns Yerkes, Edward Lee Thorndike, and others in 1920 to publish the National Intelligence Tests for use in public schools (P. D. Chapman, 1981). In 1921 Terman began his study of the gifted, for which he designed the Stanford Achievement Tests. In 1923 Terman published the Terman Group Test of Mental Ability for grades seven to twelve, which sold more than half a million copies (P. D. Chapman, 1981). In 1936 Terman and Catherine Cox issued an Attitude-Interest Analysis Test designed to measure masculinity and femininity; in 1937 Terman had a new version of the Stanford-Binet (Krugman, 1939).

Terman used IQ tests to assess the efficiency of California's state welfare institutions by surveying the mental status of boys in reform schools, of prisoners in San Quentin prison, of residents in an orphanage, and of students in the schools of an entire county. Finding that "the children of subnormal mental endowment undoubtedly constitute one of our gravest social problems" (Terman, 1912, p. 132), Terman became an advocate of eugenics as the solution to crime, poverty, prostitution, and feeblemindedness. For many years this emphasis on heredity was the chief motif of Terman's thought; however, he grew less sure of his notions of heredity as he grew older (Hilgard, 1957).

According to Michael Sokal (1984), Terman's most important work was as a leader of the mental testing movement and as a proponent of heredity more than environment as the main determinant of mental ability. He also crusaded against the experimentalists who believed that testing was not a legitimate part of their science. Terman himself believed that his longitudinal study of a gifted population was his greatest achievement (see Seagoe, 1975; Sokal, 1984; see Chapter 11, below).

America spawned a new breed of moralists who sought to scientifically shape and control the individual. IQ tests became one of the mainstays of their crusade. Advocates of a better America used these measures to search out those who would not, or could not, contribute to their vision of the future.

The bright prospects envisioned for mental tests rapidly tarnished as the original conception of the testing movement was subverted by the simmering realities of America as it entered the new century. Binet's revolutionary attempt to measure intelligence focused on the benefits for individual children, but as the testing movement developed in North America, social control and a pseudo-scientific movement to cleanse society of its deviants and defectives emerged as the dominant ideology.

Practically, the individual tests developed by Binet to be administered to one child at a time by a trained tester ceded, under pressure to assess large numbers quickly, to a reliance on measures designed for group testing. Philosophically, the focus shifted from individual benefits to social concerns, and the promise of IQ tests broadened perceptibly as the IQ became the password to the inner mysteries of human behavior. Binet was aware that the tests measured not only innate ability but knowledge gained from school (Binet and Simon, 1916). In America the tests and their users, all social products of the middle class, confused innate intelligence with an appreciation of bourgeois norms (McLaren, 1986).

To Henry Goddard and his followers, tests of mental ability did not measure conscious learning but actually gauged underlying mental processes. Moreover, Goddard and a host of American scientists and psychologists produced seemingly overwhelming proof that those mental processes, and indeed everything else about a human, are due to hereditary factors, and that environment possesses little or no impact. Conflicting opinions about the nature versus nurture controversy came to haunt the study of individual differences.

As test promotion and usage continued apace, a lexicon of terms developed to describe the new measures. James McKeen Cattell coined the term *mental test*, which appeared in 1890, the year he published the seminal work "Mental Tests and Measurements." Binet did not use the term *intelligence quotient* to describe the results of his measure—it was first used in 1911 by William Stern (1871–1938), a German psychologist interested in the characteristics of prominent men (Stern, 1914). Terman gave full expression to the concept of IQ originated by Stern (Stern, 1914) when he adopted Stern's formula of the IQ to make possible an apparently exact measurement of an individual's mental inventory. Terman transformed Binet's concept of age to mentality and was one of the first to use the term *intelligence quotient* to express the numerical relationship of an individual's mental age to chronological age. On the Binet tests anyone who scored more than three mental ages (MA) below their chronological age (CA) was judged as mentally retarded. In other words, if eight-year-old Jimmy scores a mental age of four, he is assigned an IQ of 50 (MA/CA × 100 = IQ) and is considered mentally retarded.

The concept of mental age led to the emergence of new classifications of retardation and a new scheme adopted in 1914 by the American Association for the Study of Feeble-Mindedness. Idiots were now those with a mental age up to and including two years; imbeciles included those with mental ages from three to seven years. IQ testing also revealed a new grade of mental defect, the moron. Equivalent to the English term *feebleminded, moron* was employed for those with tested mental ages of seven to twelve years (Vineland, 1914). Morons constituted the largest number of the mentally retarded population and were seen as the ones chiefly responsible for the antisocial behavior attributed to the group as a whole (Hincks, 1918). Backward children, said by Goddard to account for 14 percent of the general school population, were those with tested IQs of 75 to 90 (Tredgold, 1929).

TESTING THE IMMIGRANT

Through the early part of the twentieth century the massive immigration that started with the influx of Germans and Irish-Catholics to North America continued, together with waves of immigration from central, eastern, and southern Europe (Bloch and Dworkin, 1976; Kamin, 1974). By 1900 approximately half the American population was foreign born or the children of foreign-born parents. When the U.S. Immigration Commission conducted a large-scale study in 1909, 57.8 percent of children in the public schools of the thirty-seven largest American cities were of foreign-born parentage (Cremin, 1961). The roots of the newcomers had changed from northern to southern Europe: by 1910 immigrants from southern and eastern Europe made up 77 percent of the whole immigrant population (Phelps, 1924).

Changes in the ethnicity of immigrants stirred the embers of long-held prejudices. According to the dominant racist mythology, cooler climates and virtue are connected; northern climes are clear, fresh, and morally salubrious, whereas hot southern winds supposedly sap energy and induce idleness, crime, vice, and a constellation of similar deviant traits. Hence, northerners were thought to be vigorous and healthy and southerners were seen as cowardly, sly, and lazy (see Orwell, 1934). Many early twentieth-century North Americans clung to this mythology as they pondered the impact of immigrants on the nation. To their way of thinking, the desirable immigrant was Anglo-Saxon, easily assimilated, and unmarked by the sharp physical and cultural differences of the southern and eastern newcomer.

Americans seemed to find discussions of racial questions irresistible; the debate combined unresolved issues in science with contentious disputes in politics. Henry Goddard and others of his ilk, intent on portraying the underside of immigration at its most lurid, brought the issues sharply into focus. They forged a link between ethnicity, crime, and feeblemindedness, using the new measures of intelligence to bolster their contentions. The biological theory of innate criminal tendencies, joined to concerns over mounting immigration, excited already frayed nerves: the "threat of the feebleminded" was elevated to the status of a national concern and inevitably accelerated misgivings regarding the tide of immigrants then flooding into North America (see P. H. Bryce, 1913; Winzer and O'Connor, 1982).

In 1910 the Immigration Commission recommended an English literacy test for immigrants, a requirement that was enacted by the House and Senate in 1917. In the meantime, although doctors at Ellis Island were examining 29,000 newcomers a week by 1913, Goddard speculated that many feebleminded persons were passing through. Planning to formulate suggestions for a more thorough culling of potential immigrants, Goddard and his associates visited Ellis Island in the fall of 1912 and selected immigrants they suspected of feeblemindedness (Goddard, 1913). On a return to the immigrant sheds in 1913, Goddard used interpreters to administer the Binet tests and some performance scales to selected immigrants, all of them steerage passengers. When Goddard published his findings in 1917, he announced that 83 percent of the Jews, 80 percent of the Hungarians, 79 percent of the Italians, and 87 percent of the Russians were feebleminded (Goddard, 1917), below the age of twelve on the Binet scale. A new scale, consisting of questions passed by 75 percent of the original group, was devised, but still 40 percent of the immigrants failed (see Knox, 1914). Goddard insisted that his results applied only to immigrants traveling in steerage and not to those in the first or second class (Goddard, 1917).

Such devastating assessments of immigrants' intelligence offered Americans little confidence in the ability of the newcomers to Americanize rapidly and contribute to the nation (e.g., Cance et al., 1914; H. Fairchild, 1917, 1924; Garis, 1927; Gulik, 1916; Knox, 1914; Winkler, 1917). Latent racism was strengthened and the misgivings about unrestricted immigration was translated into stringent quotas imposed by both the United States and Canada (see Chapter 9).

THE ARMY TESTS

As America was inexorably drawn into World War I, those stoking the war machine felt that they needed a structured method by which to assess the capabilities of draftees. Government testing of some sort was deemed necessary "in order to weed out the inefficients and to be sure that there are none to clog the great war machine or to endanger the lives of others by their weakness" (Vineland, 1918, p. 19).

Robert Yerkes, then president of the American Psychological Association, offered its services to the United States Army as America prepared to enter the war in 1917. A seven-man committee led by Henry Goddard and Lewis Terman and including the behaviorist John Watson was selected by the chairman of the Eugenics Section of the American Breeder's Association's Committee on the Inheritance of Mental Traits. The committee formulated two tests in six weeks. The Alpha test, based largely on a group IQ test developed by Arthur Otis, a Terman graduate student, was for literates (P. D. Chapman, 1981); the Beta test served for nonliterates. Both were group examinations given by one examiner and marked by enlisted men ("The Psychological," 1917).

In less than two years the group-administered tests were given to 1.7 million recruits (Haney, 1981). Yerkes acquired data on 81,000 native-born whites, 12,000 foreign-born whites, and 23,000 native-born blacks. Assessment of the results was discouraging: data indicated that 4 to 5 percent of the recruits were very superior, 13 to 28 percent were superior or high average, 25 percent scored as low, while the remaining 42 percent showed as very inferior with an estimated mental age of ten to eleven years. In fact, overall, the United States Army found six feebleminded men per thousand ("Two Out of Five," 1917; Yerkes, 1921).

The army Alpha and Beta tests were not mental age scales of the Binet school; nevertheless, the data were later compared to the Stanford-Binet, and the conclusions were devastating. According to these data, 47 percent of the white sample and 89 percent of the black had mental ages of twelve years or less, which slotted them into the category of feeblemindedness invented by Goddard, that of moron. Goddard then fudged and claimed that the term *moron* was applicable only to those obviously feebleminded and not to others with a tested mental age of twelve or under. To little avail; a large section of the public believed the data and believed that America was sinking into a morass of illiteracy, crime, and feeblemindedness.

As if to compound their fears, Carl Brigham in his *Study of American Intelligence* (1923) marshaled data to demonstrate the reliability of the army tests and then presented the results according to nationality. Analysis of the data along racial lines showed that eastern and southern Europeans scored only slightly higher than blacks. Researchers concluded that the U.S. population was on a mental decline and there was no need to add more of the inferior races to already poor stock. The general public trembled at the thought of a democracy that would allow morons to vote.

THE EXPANDING USES OF TESTING

Testing advocates, delighted with what they saw as the usefulness of the army tests even if appalled at the results, rapidly moved onto the domestic front, to be met with a ready welcome. Americans developed an almost passionate regard for IQ tests; the possibilities of measuring an individual's capacity with short and simple tests captured the imagination of the American public. Few questioned the infallibility accorded the results, the specious statistics, or the worrisome conclusions.

For the first time, the nebulous phenomenon of intelligence could be measured, and society was armed with a technological innovation that provided scientific ground for making difficult, socially relevant decisions. The testing movement helped meet the need for "continuous measurement" and "accountability" (Karier, 1972) and stressed the importance of a larger and more orderly corporate state, one that would use experts to ameliorate the many varied problems of that state. Large corporate structures, themselves the products of the twentieth century, moved to finance and support the testing movement. Lewis

Terman, for example, was supported by the Carnegie Foundation and the Commonwealth Fund (see Karier, 1972).

With the new testing procedures, classification of mental retardation proceeded apace, for the measures allowed a scientific definition of mental retardation by the use of systems that could define the population with an infinity of detail. The abuse of the tests, the eagerness to categorize and label, and the lack of awareness of social factors in behavior all contributed to a clinical test-related concept of mental deficiency. The intelligence of a child, it was believed, depended almost completely on the IQ as measured by some sort of scale.

Henry Goddard, one of the most devoted advocates of testing, tested all the children at the Vineland Institution with the Binet measuring scale and detailed their genealogies. Children were tested upon entrance, when going home for vacations, and on their return (Vineland, 1911). Giving a nod to environmental variables, Goddard also embarked on a series of studies into the children's height and weight, as well as experiments in feeding. Twelve children were selected and placed on especially nourishing diets, with the object of discovering whether physical growth could be stimulated and a concomitant advance in mental growth be observed (Vineland, 1908).

Lewis Terman coined the slogan "A mental test for every child" (P. D. Chapman, 1981). He stressed the use of IQ tests for precise tracking in schools and suggested a system of vocational and educational guidance based on the results. An IQ below 70, observed Terman, "rarely permits anything better than skilled labor," whereas scores above 115 "permit one to enter the professions or the larger fields of business" (Terman, 1920).

The tests were not restricted to school children or to those in institutions. Many viewed the measures in terms of social control. Not every American in every nook and cranny of every ghetto and red-light district could be assessed, but the predictive powers of the tests were employed to socially indict many problematic groups in early twentieth-century society. Researchers used the data already generated to produce sweeping claims about feeblemindedness and its threat to social stability and progress. Goddard (1914), for example, estimated that 25 to 50 percent of the nation's prisoners were mentally defective and incapable of managing their affairs with ordinary prudence. At least 50 percent of prostitutes were feebleminded, he said, as were 50 percent of the inmates of almshouses (Vineland, 1914).

RISING DOUBTS ABOUT IQ TESTING

From the start some researchers and workers involved in psychological measurement stressed that the tests were delicate instruments, that testers required specialized training and skills, and that assistance to individual children, rather than tracking and segregation, should be the aim of all testing. Robert Yerkes and a very few others questioned the supposed infallibility of IQ measures, the use of the tests, and the interpretation of the results. They called for structured professional guidelines and judicious use. Edgar Doll (1913), who was to follow Goddard at the Vineland institution, carped about "inexpert Binet users," and psychologist J. E. W. Wallin (1911) tried to get psychologists to adopt uniform standards. Further, they begged that psychological testing become a positive component in "the great task of better suiting educational treatment to the needs of the individual" (Yerkes, 1917, p. 252). The tests were seen as being capable of distinguishing 10 to 15 percent of children needing special help: "those intellectually superior or supernormal; intellectually inferior or subnormal; intellectually dependent; and affectively or instinctively defective" (Yerkes, 1917, p. 252).

None of the cautions, however cogent and timely, could stem the rush for testing in the schools. Moderate voices were drowned out in the tumult created by those who employed the measures not for the betterment of individual children but for social control. Most testers and testing advocates could not admit to the possibility that the testing movement had a social agenda or that they were serving the interest of privilege, power, and status (Karier, 1972). They preferred instead to believe that what they were measuring was, in fact, true merit (Karier, 1972). Classification errors, they claimed, were a product of inexact use of the instruments and not inappropriate application or interpretation of the results of the tests.

Educational testing grew rapidly in the period between the two world wars. Following World War I, Terman and a committee of psychologists involved in the original army tests formulated the National Intelligence Test. Within less than a year of the issuance of the test, more than 575,000 copies were sold; during the years 1922–1923, 800,000 copies were sold (Freeman, 1926). By 1926 there were thirty group tests on the market for use in schools (Freeman, 1926); a 1939 list of mental tests reported 4,279 measures as well as six printed pages of bibliographies on testing (Cohen and Lazeron, 1972). When Oscar Buros began his long career as the preeminent bibliographer of testing, his first bibliography in 1934 was only forty-four pages long; by the 1938 edition, it had grown to more than four hundred pages listing the 4,000 tests available for use (Haney, 1981). Further, between 1921 and 1936 more than 5,000 articles on testing appeared in print.

Although the 1930s were characterized by an even greater proliferation of standardized testing, sounds of discord also increased. Criticism of IQ tests accelerated, and the use of IQ test results alone was shaken, the unerring faith in the scientific method was broken, and the belief in the technology daunted. A professional reaction to the univariate conception of intelligence as being what the tests tested began to form. The IQ tests, psychologists now stressed, should be viewed as measures of acquired knowledge and the ability to handle language (Curti, 1938).

Researchers who reexamined the army data castigated the technical inadequacy of the measures as well as the interpretation of the data that subverted the design of the tests. The army tests, for example, had not been designed to provide mental ages, but these were the data that were presented to an unknowing public. Others stressed the hereditary emphasis of the IQ measures in general, a criticism largely directed toward Lewis Terman (Hilgard, 1987). Others, less concerned with ideology, held simply that the tests were untrustworthy evaluators of intelligence.

One of the most impassioned critics was Walter Lippmann, the journalist, who during much of his career was identified as a left-wing socialist. In six articles in the *New Republic* Lippmann damned the army tests and castigated Terman (see Bloch and Dworkin, 1976; Pastore, 1978; Terman, 1922). Lippmann's essential question concerned the early training opportunities available to children of different abilities and whether people could attain similar abilities if they were provided with similar training (Lippmann, 1920, 1922a, 1922b, 1922c, 1922d, 1922e, 1923).

Lippmann, in turn, was accused of being too emotional about standardized testing. Lewis Terman (1922) responded to Lippmann with a sarcastic piece, which spoke to Lippmann's lack of rationality and supported his own arguments with research and academic credentials of the leaders of the testing movement. To this charge Lippmann answered, "I admit it. I hate the impudence of the claim that in fifty minutes you can judge and classify a human being's predestined fitness for life. I hate the pretentiousness of the claim. I hate the abuse of the scientific method which it involves. I hate the sense of superiority which it creates, and the sense of inferiority which it imposes" (Lippmann, 1923, p. 146). Michael Sokal (1984) observes that many psychologists of the early 1920s believed that Terman bested Lippmann. However, many others did not and even saw Terman's responses in the *New Republic* as embarrassingly hysterical.

During the early 1930s psychologists began to assess the importance of both heredity and environment in shaping behavior. As methods for studying and understanding human behavior became more refined and reliable, it grew clear that environment interacted closely with an individual's biological makeup to form a total human being.

The notion of adaptive behavior as an important component to consider in defining mental retardation emerged. By 1929 mental retardation was defined as not solely "a state of incomplete mental development" but as incomplete mental development "of such a kind and degree that the individual is incapable of adapting himself to the normal environment of his fellows in such a way as to maintain existence independently of supervision, control, or extended support" (Tredgold, 1929 p. 4). The construct of adaptive behavior—simply, an individual's adaptation to the environment depending on age and situation—was crystallized by Edgar A. Doll, who was director of the research laboratory at Vineland from 1925 to 1949. Doll advanced the concept of parole and community care of the mentally deficient (Doll, 1941). However, he is best known for his efforts to develop criteria for assessing social functioning to supplement the intelligence test used to diagnose mental retardation, the Vineland Social Maturity Scale (Doll, 1965).

THE DEVELOPMENT OF EDUCATIONAL AND SCHOOL PSYCHOLOGY

With objective methods for testing intelligence in place, the discipline of psychology grew rapidly; the public role of psychologists came to the fore as soon as IQ tests became embroiled in the social problems of the day. As new professions, educational psychology and clinical psychology became part of graduate training programs, and distinct departments emerged in normal schools. Ultimately, new academic degrees and professional journals also emerged.

Although the discipline of educational psychology can be said to have developed about 1910, the subcategory of school psychology arrived later. The term *school psychologist* first appeared in print in 1923 (Hutt, 1923), but it took almost three more decades for the American Psychological Association to recognize school psychology as a specialty within the field.

The term *school psychology* was derived from the work of William Stern (Fagan and Delugach, 1984), who advocated the study of, and educational services for, gifted children in Germany. School psychology in North America emanated from Lightner Witmer's work in the first psychological clinic and in connection with Hall's child-study movement (Fagan, 1990). Clinics sprang up, and school districts began to constructively employ the skills of the new discipline (see Chapter 11). In 1915 the Connecticut Board of Education became the first to appoint a psychologist to help plan education for backward and defective children. New York City had employed psychological examiners for its schools from the early 1900s, but few were employed in the schools until the 1920s (Fagan, 1985).

The issues raised by the growing controversy over IQ tests and the meaning and use of their results could not be settled without a better understanding of the role of inheritance in human functioning. However, the study of heredity would itself give rise to further controversy, centered mostly on the concept of eugenics. The issues related to the management of human heredity are explored in the chapter that follows.

Chapter 9

The "Threat of the Feebleminded"

Landmark Events in the Understanding of Heredity and Intelligence

1798   Thomas Robert Malthus publishes *"An Essay on the principle of population"*

1859   Charles Robert Darwin publishes *The Origin of Species*

1865   Sir Francis Galton publishes *Hereditary Talent and Character,* the first public presentation of what would become eugenics; Gregor Johann Mendel publishes his work in an obscure journal

1869   Galton publishes *Hereditary Genius*

1870   Galton founds the Eugenics Society

1877   Richard Louis Dugdale publishes his genealogical study of the Jukes

1883   Galton coins the word *eugenics* and publishes *Enquiries into Human Faculty*

1884   Alexander Graham Bell publishes *Memoir upon the Formation of a Deaf Variety of the Human Race*

1889   Galton publishes *Natural Inheritance*

1891   Galton addresses the Seventh International Congress of Hygiene and Demography and calls for new means of checking fertility

1900   Mendel's work is rediscovered

1905   Albert Binet and Théodore Simon publish the first IQ test; the American Breeder's Association Committee on Eugenics is established

1907   Indiana passes first sterilization law in the United States

1910   Henry Herbert Goddard imports and translates the Binet tests

1912   The First International Congress on Eugenics is held; Goddard publishes his study on the Kallikaks

1913   Goddard begins testing immigrants at Ellis Island

1917   The U.S. Army uses the Alpha and Beta tests on draftees

1921   The Second International Conference of Eugenics is held

1922   Harry Laughlin presents an analysis of America's melting pot to Congress

1924   Laughlin publishes *Eugenical Sterilization,* the first American book on the subject; the Johnson Act (Immigration Restriction Act) is passed, restricting immigration to 2 percent of the 1890 census

1925   Serious questioning of the tenets of eugenics begins

1931   The Third International Congress on Eugenics is held

1933   Adolf Hitler's Eugenics Sterilization Law is enacted in Germany

1940   The Eugenics Record Office in Cold Springs Harbor, New York, closed

1965   U.S. Congress lifts national quotas and permits immigrants to enter in the order they applied

In the early 1900s both public and professional views of disabled persons began to change. Special education lost much of its momentum in North America. Public opinion, professional dissension, and new scientific notions about heredity and environment, all shaped by the social realities of the new century, contributed to the declining support for the education of disabled persons.

Public assumptions, particularly about mental retardation, shifted: in the belief that disabilities are genetically determined, people increasingly assumed them to be unamenable to improvement through education. Perceptions of disabled individuals were clouded by pessimism and fear, and coercive methods were developed to control deviant behavior. The enthusiasm generated by Seguin's training-school model faded; mentally retarded individuals were herded into institutions that were little more than warehouses for the storage of human beings (Hallahan and Kauffman, 1986). Public commitment waned: in Connecticut, for example, a commission sent to check into the condition of the feebleminded found that the majority of citizens thought their work was "a waste of time" (Barr, [1904b] 1913, p. 70). The Orillia Institution in Ontario almost closed the school program in 1896 as a result of public criticisms regarding the cost and futility of education for idiots (Hackett, 1969).

Accentuating the problems were overzealous professionals who bickered among themselves and led the public to expect miraculous cures that never happened (Hallahan and Kauffman, 1986). Industrialization, urbanization, and immigration placed increasing strain on social services. But perhaps the most important cause of the darkening mood was the convergence of the eugenics movement, science's increasing belief in heredity as the only significant force in human development, and Social Darwinism—a theory that ranked people, cultures, and society in a hierarchy narrowly constructed from ethnocentric perspectives (Rogers, 1972). Moreover, all this drew support from the new quantitative methods for assessing intelligence.

The conflicting claims of nature and heredity versus nurture and environment were not new to educational reform. Before 1800 disabilities were believed to be imprinted on one's soul by nature, God, or the devil, and, as we have seen; amelioration was rarely tried. After John Locke, sensationalist (nurture) theories were widely accepted, and the nurture side of the old debate came to dominate, lending a distinctly optimistic tone to the education and training of disabled people. The nurture side remained ascendant until about 1880. However, as Darwinian thinking became well accepted, the evolutionary theories and the new biological doctrines inevitably drew attention to differences within the species and to the selective significance of inborn differences in human beings. During the 1880s heredity once again superseded environment as the explanation for educational failure and social dereliction.

In attempting to understand and explain the social problems of their times, social theorists began to apply Darwin's vision of the evolution of the animal world to the development of society (Rogers, 1972). Moreover, the public came to believe that the application of science to society—most notably in the pseudo-science of eugenics—would improve existing social conditions. Procreation began to be viewed as a social, not an individual, issue: life and sex were to be regulated by the laws of business and industrialization. Some advocates envisaged utopias populated by perfect human stocks. They maintained that only society's superior classes should procreate, and they campaigned for increased reproduction among the fittest and the best. Others accepted a scientific point of view that socially indicted the mentally retarded and other disabled groups and directed moral opprobrium at the poor.

It was generally believed that in the evolutionary process only the more competent would survive, that the physiological, cultural, and economic woes of the poor, the immigrants, and the disabled are ordained by nature and therefore neither preventable nor reversible. Philanthropic ideas about education and training were cast aside as sentiment, and only limited improvement of the disabled, it was now believed, could be achieved. Larger institutions to corral the offending classes for life, restrictive immigration laws to bar offensive hordes of inferior foreign stock from North American shores, and sterilization laws to curtail the further procreation of the socially and mentally unfit were established.

Many held that, to maintain the status of the species, society should halt uncontrolled breeding among the less competent. Professionals and politicians began to agree that the only way to save the world from hereditary defects was to isolate all defectives and prevent them from procreating. Society was "fully justified in using close supervision, segregation or sterilization whenever necessary to prevent reproduction among the markedly unfit" (Pollock, 1922, p. 138).

Civilized society in North America, threatened by the intrusion of immigrants seen to carry virulent, genetically defective strains, was hostile and repressive. The results of tests given to immigrants, combined with data from army tests, were used to lobby for immigration restrictions. The ideas of the eugenics movement, along with the xenophobic and political reaction of the postwar period, contributed to the movement to slam the door on immigration in the mid-1920s.

There emerged a handful of influential leaders who elaborated the principles of Social Darwinism and eugenics as they sponsored public legislation and scientific investigation directed toward the eradication from society of the delinquent, the defective, and the diseased. Their aim was to stem the tide of racially inferior stocks and to prevent the spread of degeneracy and immorality.

Although they were neither fascist nor communist, their quest for orderly change in a managed society led some to wax enthusiastic about certain characteristics of emerging totalitarian societies abroad (e.g., Lietz, 1934; Poponoe, 1922, 1934).

Special education, its teachers, and its clients were all caught up, to some extent, in this broad philosophical swing. Samuel Gridley Howe's disappointment with his blind students translated into pronounced leanings toward a belief in immutable hereditary causes; Alexander Graham Bell became a leading advocate of hereditary principles, which sprang from his own fears concerning the formation of a deaf variety of the human race. But it was mental retardation that attracted the most worried attention from scientists and others. They accepted the myth of the "threat of the feebleminded" and saw hereditary determinism as scientific dogma.

The changing temper of the late 1920s ushered in a period of more tempered conflict and a greater reliance on research findings to settle issues relating to human intelligence (Hilgard, 1987). A scientific front emerged, to challenge the contentions of the hard-line eugenicists. Extravagant claims fell before an onslaught of criticism and new research. Critics shouted that results in genetics, IQ testing, and family studies were in actuality inconclusive and that the pursuit of improved racial stock was not only ineffective but scientifically invalid.

THE MENTAL HYGIENE MOVEMENT

As the nineteenth century drew to an end, a broad social movement known as mental hygiene emerged. Its simple but commendable purpose was to make people "think better, feel better and act better" (Hincks, 1919b, p. 130). (Mental hygiene for a fitter society was interwoven with but was not the same as the mental health movement, which emerged from psychiatry.) Under the general rubric of mental hygiene and its subcategories of family culture and eugenics, a general public awareness of the concepts of breeding and stock developed. In 1897 a women's congress in Paris resolved that all their intended sons-in-law should provide certificates of health prior to marriage so as to protect any future offspring (Bullock, 1897). American physicians promoted the notion that young men about to be married should be obliged to produce health books (Saleeby, 1911). In America whole families entered Fitter Families competitions, sponsored by eugenics societies, where they competed for trophies on the basis of "heredity, physique and mentality" (A Eugenics Catechism, 1927, pp. 10–11; see "Familyculture," 1927; Osborn, 1974).

Promotion of fitness and good breeding was but one facet of the mental hygiene picture; within the school system mental hygiene epitomized the idea of the schools' responsibility for personality development (Cohen, 1983). In fact, Cohen states that "few intellectual and social movements of the century have had so deep and pervasive an influence on the theory and practice of American education as the mental hygiene movement" (p. 124).

For persons with disabilities, it was the pseudo-scientific branch of mental hygiene, eugenics, that, translated into public policy, not only altered conceptions about disabled persons and their status in society but created new ways of limiting their numbers and new methods of segregating them. Eugenics essentially sought the eradication or suppression of tainted or inferior human stock, a goal that resulted in startling new methods to control those who differed from the norm, whether socially, intellectually, or physically.

The Eugenics Movement

The eugenics movement can be traced to the 1860s and more generally to the reaction that followed the 1859 publication of Darwin's *Origin of Species* (Field, 1911–12). Darwin's controversial publication (see Herbert, 1971; Levin, 1966; Vorzimmer, 1969), with its theory of natural selection as the basis for evolution, supported by geological and archeological discoveries, unseated the accepted explanations of the origin and development of humans and signaled a return to a view of human development that put nature over nurture.

Scientists increasingly disputed the contention that the environment was important in human development. The evolutionary mechanism was seen to be natural selection, operating, of course, through heredity. Great attention was focused on inborn instincts, which were seen as unfolding at certain predetermined points in an individual's development. Psychologists held the notion of fixed intelligence and predetermined development; individual differences were dismissed as inconsequential variations of instinctual patterns. Adaptability was viewed as an inherited characteristic, and the most adaptable were the most likely to survive.

Sir Francis Galton was the modern founder of the eugenics movement. He was born near Birmingham, England, and in 1838 took up the study of medicine at Birmingham General Hospital and later at King's College in London. In 1840 he transferred to Trinity College, where he majored in mathematics. An inventor, researcher, psychologist, statistician, and leader of the eugenics movement, Galton shaped many of the notions of the assessment of mentality circulating in the second half of the nineteenth century. The literature of eugenics began with his studies of hereditary talent or "genius" and character (Galton, [1869] 1870, 1883). In these studies Galton revealed that eminence followed a few family lines (of which his was one). Galton coined the phrase *nature versus nurture* but stressed heredity. He overlooked the role that wealth, leisure, health care, nutrition, and family tradition played in making possible the achievements of many members of the British upper class. Galton supported his propositions through intense psychological research. His findings greatly influenced the contemporary study of individual differences and the mathematical formulae used to quantify them.

In his *Enquiries into Human Faculty* (1883) Galton elucidated the term *eugenics;* coined from the Greek word *eugenes,* meaning "good in stock" *eugenics* designates the improvement of a race through purposeful breeding. Essentially, he said, eugenics is "the study of those agencies under social control which could improve or impair the inborn qualities of future generations of humans, either physically or mentally" (*A Eugenics Catechism,* 1927, p. 2). (*Euthenists,* on the other hand, hold to the notion that the environment is the essential factor contributing to the makeup of a human being.) The function of eugenics lay "chiefly in the sweeping away of a legion of ineffectives, and in the introduction in very much greater proportion the number of men of independent and original thought" (Galton, 1873, p. 121).

Galton argued that the struggle for survival had been reversed by medical advances that allowed the unfit to survive and multiply and by the use of birth control that permitted the able to restrict their fertility (Galton, 1883). Hence, eugenics had two fundamental aims—*positive eugenics* encouraged the best human stock to reproduce, while *negative eugenics* sought to restrict matings of the unfit. The ultimate goal was the evolution of human beings who would "have larger thinking brains than average and the moral good to accompany their intellectual greatness" (D. Fairchild, 1922).

Eugenicists divided society into five basic groups: "the men of great talent and genius; the normal class of individuals; the dependent class as represented in hospitals, asylums, almshouses, and similar institutions; the delinquent class inhabiting the penal and reformatory institutions; and the defective class, including the feeble-minded, the insane, the idiotic, the deaf and dumb, and the blind" (*A Eugenics Catechism,* 1927, p. 31). It was on the dyseugenic consequences of allowing the unrestricted breeding of the dependent, delinquent, and defective classes that eugenicists constructed their platform. Strident eugenicists denied that unemployment and poverty were the products of an emerging capitalism. Having adopted the idea that everything about a person's condition—from socioeconomic status to life span—is inherited and immutable from the moment of conception, they could argue that human society, like nature, must be harsh to its weaklings or it would foster within itself destructive social ills. Eugenicists sought to prevent procreation among "inferior people, in inferior places" (*A Eugenics Catechism,* 1927, p. 5) so that they would be finally rendered harmless to the community. Social ineptitude and its carriers were to be stamped out by all available means: education, legislation, segregation, and even sterilization.

Social Darwinism

Galton defined the essential tenets of the eugenics movement and gave it a sense of moral purpose. His British contemporary Herbert Spencer (1820–1903) emerged as the philosopher for the new credo. Spencer combined Galton's notions with Darwinist theory and social racism to develop a philosophy of social selection deftly summarized in his phrase "survival of the fittest." Spencer proposed that only the most fit of the human species should be permitted to survive so that humanity as a whole might advance; he said that the weaker members hinder the biological process of the race and pose a threat to the future of humanity. Spencer condemned not only poor laws but also public health and public educational facilities, since these institutions sustained many innately inferior individuals. Eventually, his philosophy ran, nature would weed out through natural selection all such undesirables, and social problems would be eliminated. Consequently, a program of public aid for such individuals was ridiculous as well as grossly unscientific (see Spencer, 1851, 1852).

Spencer echoed sentiments articulated earlier by Thomas Robert Malthus (1766–1834), the first professor of political economy in a British university. In his 1798 *Essay on the Principle of Population* ([1798] 1963), Malthus denounced social welfare schemes aimed at improving the living standards of the poor as a futile waste of public money. As one later Malthusian chided: "We absolutely refuse to let the poor, the incapable, or the diseased die; we enable or allow them, if we do not actually encourage them, to propagate their incapacity, poverty and constitutional disorders" (Gregg, 1868, p. 362). Many scoffed at Malthus and derided the suggestion that workers could improve their situation by limiting their numbers. Nevertheless, in the following decades the ideas were articulated again and again. Henry Herbert Goddard, the chief architect of the American eugenics movement, observed in 1920, "Much money has been wasted and is continually being wasted by would-be philanthropists who give liberally for alleviating conditions that are to them intolerable . . . it is being wasted because the people who receive it have not sufficient intelligence to appreciate it and to use it wisely" (p. 103).

The central dogma of eugenics and Social Darwinism was that intelligence and nearly all other human characteristics are inherited. Social Darwinists and eugenicists saw every aspect of a person's life, from socioeconomic status to health and educational achievement, as predetermined by the genes they received from their parents (Chase, 1977). "Heredity," said Martin Barr ([1904b] 1913), superintendent of the Pennsylvania Training School for feebleminded children, "is herein proven law, as inexorable in the descending as it is beneficial in the ascending scale; heredity—whether it be direct from parent to child, collateral as from other relatives, or reversional, appearing ever and anon through generations—which none can escape" (p. 123).

Not only were the qualities of the mind said to be subject to the laws of heredity, but so, too, were acquired accidental deformities ("Heredity," 1876). Scientists increasingly disputed the contention that ignorance and poverty are the fundamental causes of many of society's problems; a good environment was seen as merely a means of allowing good heredity to express itself. It was deemed useless to improve environmental conditions for individuals who lacked good heredity (Editor, 1915, pp. 228–34). The so-called dangerous classes have received their qualities and tendencies from "a vicious ancestry" and are powerless to escape that heritage (Cobb, 1911, p. 254).

Darwinism, in assuming that characteristics acquired through adaptation are inherited (although the mechanism was not identified until the reappearance of Mendel's work in 1900), suggested that a progressive society should not preserve the unfit. By looking after the poor and the deviant, society would be subverting the "cruel but biologically salutary laws of natural selection" (E. M. Best, 1935, p. 118). Naturally operating social forces should have the effect of limiting the reproduction of the unfit and facilitating that of the naturally superior. But as, in fact, the poor seemed to be producing more prolifically than the wealthy, other solutions had to be found.

Eugenics in North America

The eugenics movement was rooted in Europe, but it quickly crossed the Atlantic, where it profoundly influenced the thinking of Progressives and other social reformers in the United States and Social Gospellers in the Canadian West (T. Chapman, 1977). Late nineteenth-century North America, it is true, gave only

chary support to the demographic theories of Malthus or to the sociological notions of Spencer, but it did become intellectually respectable to maintain that
society could be cleansed and improved through the astute application of the
breeding principles of eugenics.

Carried forward on converging currents of Darwinism, elitism, racism, and
social reform, and given added impetus by Mendelian genetics, eugenics played
on the fears and prejudices of the American middle class. In a rapidly expanding
and competitive society, some saw the principles of social evolution as enhancing the traditional American values of equality and natural rights. They synthe-
sized Darwinian theory with traditional Protestant values to argue that social
and biological inferiority is an inevitable law of nature and that, lacking the law,
survival could have no meaning.

The findings of scientists seemed to prove the importance of heredity in human makeup. Influential disciples sponsored and "signed into law policies
aimed at the ultimate extinction of humanity's least suitable races or strains"
(Chase, 1977, p. 15). For example, the "divine cause of race-culture" (Saleeby,
1911, p. 24) was embraced by Alexander Graham Bell, who attempted "the rec-
tification of public practice in accordance with scientific theory" (*Science*, 1885,
p. 207). James McKeen Cattell, influenced by Galton's ideas about eugenics and
the hereditability of intelligence, advocated as early as 1898 the use of mental
tests to identify the feebleminded in the United States (Kamin, 1974). Lewis Madison Terman believed that heredity was the prime determiner of intelligence. He
attributed mental retardation to "inferior mental endowment" (Terman, 1919,
p. 73) and discounted any role for such factors as irregular school attendance,
the use of a foreign language in the home, malnutrition, bad teeth, and adenoids
in causing poor performance on IQ tests. Psychologist Edward Lee Thorndike,
after conducting studies of twins in New York schools, concluded with others
that nine-tenths of an individual's make up is attributable to heredity (Editor,
1915). Psychology's grand doyen G. Stanley Hall was the president of Clark University, editor of four psychological journals, first president of the American Psychological Association, pioneer in the study of developmental psychology, and
creator of the modern concept of adolescence (see G. S. Hall, 1904; D. Ross,
1972). Hall despaired about the possibility of educating the so-called unfit, noting that "the ascendent individual, family, or stock, is the one that refuses to
yield in excess to the temptations of the flesh, and the descendent are those
whose instincts for selfish gratification preponderate over those of race conservation" (Hall, 1906).

The eugenics cause was quickly taken up by charitable organizations, the
Congress of the United States, and state legislatures. Large corporations, in their
quest for a larger and more orderly corporate state, financed the eugenics
movement, just as they did the testing movement (Karier, 1972). Charles Benedict Davenport, a geneticist, secured the support of the new Carnegie Institute of
Washington in 1904 for a biological experimental center. He opened the Eugenics
Record Office in Cold Springs Harbor, New York, and became director of the
Station for Experimental Evolution in 1904 (see Karier, 1972). The Race Betterment Foundation at Battle Creek, Michigan, was established in 1906 with substantial endowments from John Harvey Kellogg. Prominent members of various
professions joined the campaign, and eugenics became a science taught at col-

leges and universities between 1914 and 1944. Respected authorities presented graphs, tables, and statistics to further the notion of inbred differences. Francis Galton, Karl Pearson, Edward Thorndike, and others devised mathematical means (coefficients of correlation) to statistically measure data (Blanton, 1976).

Theories centering on eugenics and possible solutions to the problems of dependent and handicapped people in society did not remain the bailiwick of scientists and physicians alone. As advances in genetics stimulated wide public interest in human heredity, there was a great increase in eugenics promotions. By about 1913 "eugenics was turned from a fad to a fashion," said the English writer G. K. Chesterton. "It was not only a science, not only an art, but also a national creed amounting to an almost religious faith" (1922, p. 180).

Not everyone, of course, accepted the eugenics manifesto; reactions varied all the way from boundless enthusiasm to the most bitter antipathy. Eugenics became the credo of many Americans of the Gilded Age, but the British largely rejected their intellectual offspring (at least as it was translated into public policy). G. K. Chesterton, one of its most scathing critics, related with wicked irony how one set of parents, having devoted themselves to the establishment of perfect prenatal conditions, produced a superwoman whom they duly named Eugenette. When the father was later arraigned in court for keeping his flat in conditions of filth and neglect, Chesterton observed that it "cast but a slight and momentary shadow upon the splendid dawn of science" (Chesterton, 1922, p. 181).

SPECIAL EDUCATION AND EUGENICS

Some of the most vigorous proponents of the new hereditary determinism were found among prominent special educators; their influence upon contemporary opinion was critical, for they were instrumental in hardening the attitudes of their contemporaries. Although their views may not have been representative of the more tolerant teachers in institutions and special schools, they were far more visible. However, their intolerance must not be placed on a black-white interpretive grid but must be viewed within the social context in which it developed. They acted on the basis of strong moral convictions and of their vision of a modern America.

Among the earliest to articulate hereditary principles was Samuel Gridley Howe. As he became increasingly discouraged by the results achieved at the Perkins Institution, Howe grew to believe that at least some blind persons were inherently mentally inferior. Throughout his tenure as principal of the Perkins Institution, Howe's reports reveal his mounting pessimism, and a general emphasis on the importance of heredity became more characteristic of his thought. By the time he assumed the position of secretary of the Massachusetts State Board of Charities in 1864, Howe was devoting his reports to the depressing results of the inheritance of characteristics and warning against the dangers of consanguineous marriages. In his 1866 *Second Report of the State Board of Charities* Howe openly contended that "inherited organic imperfection,— vitiated constitution, or poor stock," were the chief causes of failure, and these were most manifest in the less affluent, the immigrant, and the deviant, who passed on to their offspring socially unacceptable characteristics (Howe, 1866a, pp. 12–13). Howe used statistics of mortality to demonstrate the "vital force," the "differences in stock," and the "modifying influences" (Perkins Inst., 1860, pp. 8–9).

Alexander Graham Bell was convinced that heredity was among the greatest of all life forces (A. G. Bell, 1923). Coupled to this was Bell's mounting apprehension about the effects of the environment to which institutionalization subjected exceptional children. For deaf students, Bell adamantly espoused the oral orthodoxy, was hostile to all manifestations of sign language, and accused the manual schools of subverting the talents of the deaf. He argued persuasively that because institutionalization isolated deaf students, it led to the use of a special language, the formation of deaf communities, to marriages of deaf with deaf, and ultimately to the production of more deaf children. The fear that the country was faced with the formation of a deaf variety of the human race, first voiced by Gardiner Greene Hubbard (Mitchell, 1971), was provided substance and science by Alexander Graham Bell.

From the time when he first publicly mentioned hereditary principles in 1874 until his death in 1922, Alexander Graham Bell assumed a paramount and influential position in the American eugenics movement. He leaned toward the positive eugenicists, those who believed that "the improvement of the human race will only come from the mating of the desirables, and that to stop the mating of the undesirables will not advance the race unless it is accompanied by the mating of the desirables" (D. Fairchild, 1922, p. 198).

Their national prominence and their contributions to general and special education allowed Howe and especially Bell to wield great influence. Nevertheless, the translation of the principles of eugenics into public policy owes more to Henry Goddard, director of the research department at the New Jersey Training School for Feeble-Minded Boys and Girls, which opened in September 1906. As director of psychological research at Vineland, Goddard profoundly influenced the American eugenics and mental testing movements. At Vineland, Goddard plunged into the work of not only testing and classifying mentally retarded individuals but seeking the roots of the condition and finding solutions that would lead to its eradication.

Even before the formation of the psychological laboratory, ongoing study at Vineland focused on epilepsy and cretinism (Vineland, 1903). By 1911 Goddard was involved in a range of research, including a special study of the "Mongolian type of feeble-mindedness" (Down syndrome). By 1912 Goddard had established three divisions in the research department in order to study biochemistry, neuropathology, and clinical psychology.

As Goddard was drawn more deeply into the study of etiology a distinctly medical view of mental retardation began to color his thoughts. In assuming this stance, he explicitly sided with institutional superintendents, most of whom were physicians who viewed retardation from a physiological viewpoint. Goddard, an experimental psychologist, owned a different background, yet his psychological understandings were influenced by the medical atmosphere. Medicine provided a natural (if inappropriate) model for many of the social interventionalist policies he endorsed in his campaign against the pollution of American society by the feebleminded (see Zenderland, 1987).

GENEALOGICAL STUDIES OF MENTAL RETARDATION

Debates about feeblemindedness, its causes, and its social and moral consequences surfaced in the 1870s and 1880s. The hereditary nature of feeblemindedness was given spurious support by Richard Louis Dugdale's 1877 retrospective studies on the Jukes. Dugdale (1841–1883), a member of the New York Prison Association, conducted a genealogical survey on a family he named the Jukes, a fictitious surname derived from a generic term of reproach. Dugdale collected information on 709 of the 1,200 descendents of the original Jukes, an American backwoodsman; he found that 140 had been imprisoned for various crimes, 200 were paupers dependent on public support, 18 kept brothels, 120 were prostitutes, and most of the others displayed inferior mental and physical abilities, at least partly attributable to poor and unhealthy environments (Dugdale, 1877).

In contrast to later researchers, Dugdale could not make a total commitment to heredity as the explanation. Although he believed that crime, idiocy, intemperance, and the like are related to the genetic heritage of a person, Dugdale also held that "where the moral conduct depends on the knowledge of moral obligation, the environment has more influence that the heredity" (Dugdale, 1877, p. 57). He solved his dilemma by surmising that a hereditary trait such as intemperance could be affected by the environment (Dugdale, 1877).

The use of genealogical studies as decisive proof of the hereditary nature of feeblemindedness and "the threat of the feebleminded" gained credence with the publication of Henry Goddard's companion study in 1912 (see Box 9-1). Goddard followed Dugdale's theme but made heredity the central factor in a variety of unacceptable behaviors.

One of Goddard's earliest discoveries in his studies at Vineland was a girl named Deborah, a feebleminded child who had been born in an almshouse and entered the Training School in October 1888 at the age of eight years (Doll, 1983). Goddard quickly saw Deborah's story as worthy of an entire book and embarked on the tale of the Kallikaks. Like "Jukes," the name "Kallikak" was invented. Goddard created it by combining two Greek words—*kalos,* meaning "attractive," and *kakes,* meaning "evil." The name symbolized both branches of the family—one made up of worthy members of society, and the other composed of criminals and deviants (Goddard, 1912).

In his 1912 account of the Kallikaks, Goddard told the story of Martin, a Revolutionary soldier who impregnated a feebleminded tavern girl. Of the 480 descendents of this union, Goddard claimed that 143 were feebleminded, 46 were normal, and the rest were undetermined. After leaving the army, Martin married a respectable girl. Through this second union came another line of descendents of a radically different nature. In this family were found none but respectable citizens, men and women prominent in every phase of social life (Kanner, 1964).

The flimsy character of Goddard's findings were not questioned; the public accepted the feeblemindedness of the mistress and the intelligence of the wife and the conclusion that heredity was the sole differentiating variable (see J. D. Smith, 1985). The Kallikaks, said Goddard (1912) "were feeble-minded, and no amount of education or good environment can change a feeble-minded individual into a normal one, any more than it can change a red-headed stock into a black-haired stock" (p. 188).

Henry Herbert Goddard (1866–1957)

Of all the exponents and researchers in the field of eugenics and mental testing, none held a more prestigious position than Henry Herbert Goddard. Born in Vassalboro, Maine, Goddard earned his bachelor's degree at Haverford College and began his career as an instructor in Latin, botany, and mathematics at the University of Southern California. In 1899 he entered Clark University to study with G. Stanley Hall. With a doctorate in hand, Goddard became a professor of psychology at Pennsylvania State Normal School and then served as a consultant to E. R. Johnstone, superintendent of the New Jersey Training School for Feeble-Minded Boys and Girls at Vineland. After Goddard accepted the post of director of the Research Institute at Vineland, he stayed there for twelve years and then moved to become director of the Ohio State Bureau of Juvenile Research. In 1922 he became a professor of abnormal and clinical psychology at Ohio State University.

Goddard's influence on both the early testing movement and the eugenics movement was profound. He documented and popularized the theses that crime, pauperism, prostitution, and alcoholism are attributable to heredity, with mental retardation being the principle factor in such socially repugnant conditions. He successfully introduced the Binet tests to America and, championing a simplistic hereditarian theory of the origin of feeblemindedness, used the measures to bolster his ideas. He applied test measures to normal school children, disabled children, and immigrants entering at Ellis Island, and he was deeply involved in devising the army tests.

Goddard published prolifically: among his works are *The Kallikak Family: A Study in the Hereditary of Feeble-Mindedness* (1912); *Feeble-Mindedness: Its Causes and Consequences* ([1914a] 1973); *School Training for Defective Children* (1915b); *The Criminal Imbecile: An Analysis of Three Remarkable Murder Cases* ([1915a] 1986); *The Psychology of the Normal and the Subnormal* (1919); *Human Efficiency and Levels of Intelligence* (1920); *Juvenile Delinquency* (1921); *School Training of Gifted Children* (1927a); *Two Souls in One Body?* (1927b); *How to Raise Children in the Atomic Age* (1948).

Although originally fashionable and popular, Goddard's writings have since been dismissed as poor science, and Goddard has been portrayed as one of the prime pseudo-scientists or even villains of the blackest period of special education. Goddard may be seen as a moral whitewasher, too zealous in the interpretation of flimsy data. At the same time he represented and articulated the opinions of contemporary researchers in psychology. He attempted to explain the societal difficulties of particular groups and construct solutions, though these were based on insufficient evidence and naive constructs. (See Burtt and Pessey, 1957; Irvine, 1971.)

Goddard's book on the Kallikak family became a classic and served to bolster Dugdale's earlier work on the Jukes, which was republished by Arthur Estabrook in 1916. Although Dugdale had reported only one case of idiocy and had largely attributed the generations of criminal behavior to bad environments, Arthur Estabrook reanalyzed the Dugdale data and concluded that half of the Jukes were feebleminded and that all of the Jukes criminals were feebleminded (Estabrook, 1916).

Following his tale of the Kallikaks, Goddard (1914a) published a book of case studies of 327 families in which he wrote about the feebleminded, ne'er-do-wells, and truants. Later he published *Feeble-mindedness* (1916a), in which he identified as genetic traits all instances of tuberculosis, stroke or apoplexy, cancer, epilepsy, goiter, and speech defects among the ancestors of his cases. Consistently, Goddard brushed aside the possibility of environmental etiologies for disabling conditions. When confronted, for example, with the use of forceps as a cause of brain injury during the birth process, he responded: "Since many normal children are delivered by the use of instruments with more or less temporary deformity to the head but without any effect upon the mentality, it is unreasonable to conclude, in those cases where there is both hereditary feeblemindedness and . . . instrument delivery, that the latter is the cause of mental deficiency. It is only logical to conclude that the hereditary condition is the causal one, and the other a mere accident superimposed upon the first condition and probably without any special effect upon it" (Goddard, 1916a, pp. 447–48).

All the studies of defective families (e.g., Danielson and Davenport, 1912; Estabrook and Davenport, 1912; Goddard, [1914a] 1973) included long genealogical charts, complete with abbreviations for the individual features and shortcomings of family members. These tables and their accompanying explanations (see Figures 9-1 and 9-2) demonstrate clearly the crude sort of Mendelian determinism that these researchers used to support their contentions about the hereditary nature of the traits on which they focused concern.

INTELLIGENCE AND DELINQUENCY

Most modern psychologists agree that intelligence is not a thing; it is a hypothetical construct, an abstraction inferred from assorted behaviors that a given culture happens to value. In the hands of Goddard, however, intelligence became extremely concrete, something that was genetically transmitted. Not only did Goddard see intelligence in concrete and measurable terms, but his work clearly explicated intelligence as a sociopolitical concept. American liberal tradition had long assumed a positive relationship between talent and virtue, so it is not surprising to find people assuming that those with less talent had less virtue (Karier, 1972). The fact that individuals could not meet the demands of civilization was taken to be indicative of their mental degeneracy.

Goddard, a moralist, was convinced that "good" genetic construction was totally identifiable with the "good" of his white, Protestant, capitalistic value system. With such puritan ethics coloring his thinking, Goddard, together with Walter E. Fernald, Martin Barr, and others, revived concern over the moral im-

"Case 8: Nannie D. 30 years old. Mentality 10. Has been here 21 years. American born, American parentage. It is reported that opium and spirits have been used by the whole family for generations. The child had whooping cough at the age of 12 and grip at 15.

"Upon admission at the age of 9, she knew the alphabet, but could not read, write nor count. Although she tried for a number of years, was never able to get very far in these lines. Industrially she did better, as they usually do. Now sews very well and takes charge of a dormitory, does some good woodwork. Is somewhat queer, goes to school, when she is able—is somewhat sickly. She is sober, silent, and sometimes stubborn; generally obedient and good tempered; is truthful, excitable and very sensitive.

"The chart shows at a glance the large amount of alcoholism throughout the different generations. Immorality and illegitimacy, together with mental defect, show a low grade family throughout. The father and mother of this girl were both feeble-minded and alcoholic and the mother was immoral.

"Section II of the chart shows the result of the marriage of the paternal grandfather's sister with the paternal grandmother's brother, said sister being feeble-minded and alcoholic. At least one of their children was feeble-minded and two others alcoholic and the descendents from these are alcoholic and several are inmates of public institutions. On the entire chart we find nine people, besides our girl, who are inmates of such institutions. This is surely a heavy expense to the community which should be prevented"

Figure 9-1. Case history of Nannie D.
SOURCE: Goddard, [1914a] 1973, pp. 76–77.

becile, as reintroduced by Dr. Isaac N. Kerlin in the 1880s. Goddard's diagnostic category of moron matched that of moral imbecile (although *moron* could also designate those below the mean intellectually).

Goddard was preoccupied by vice and crime in society, holding that prostitution and intemperance were among the greatest social dangers. He was among the most militant of those who attempted to document the thesis that crime, pauperism, prostitution, and alcoholism were due to heredity, with mental retardation being the principal factor. He believed that there was a close relationship between mental retardation and delinquency, and a genetic basis for the two conditions (also see Crofts, 1916; Gordon, 1921; Otis, 1916).

Goddard and the other eugenicists estimated that 25 to 75 percent of prisoners were mentally retarded and incapable of managing their affairs (Barss, 1920; Goddard, [1914a] 1972). Statistics demonstrated, they claimed, an intimate "relationship between illegitimacy and mental abnormality" ("Mental survey," 1921). They also asserted that at least 50 percent of the inmates of almshouses were feebleminded, as were 50 percent of prostitutes (Goddard, [1914a] 1972). Harboring moral degeneration and physical infection, these girls then bred children, often mentally retarded, who drifted "into a life of drunkenness, prostitution or criminality" (Lincoln, 1918). Unsupervised mentally retarded children were said to account for probably 40 percent of the cases appearing in juvenile courts (Hincks, 1918).

"Case 102: Grant T. 37 years old. Mentality 6. Has been here 19 years. American born, of American parents. Had whooping cough.

"At the age of twenty-two years Grant could print, A, P, and B. He knew "A" when he saw it; has partial hemiplegia, on the right side so that he does not walk well, but he is a rather agreeable, pleasant fellow, talks freely and is trained to do simple work; sweeps, scrubs, washes dishes; does good work in the laundry.

"Grant is the second child in a family of six. Three died in infancy; one was drowned at the age of nine; one is married. There seems to be nothing wrong with the father's family. The mother was feeble-minded and had a feeble-minded sister; also three brothers, condition unknown. The defect breaks out again in the descendents of the maternal grandfather's sister. She had two feeble-minded children; four others are undetermined. In still another branch, the maternal grandmother had a feeble-minded brother who was sexually immoral, spoken of as a 'good-for-naught.' He had five children, one of whom was normal, two died in infancy, one was feeble-minded, another one, undetermined, married twice, her first husband giving her a feeble-minded child. The normal son of the old man had eight children, one of whom died in infancy, four were normal and three were feeble-minded."

Figure 9-2. Case history of Grant T.
SOURCE: Goddard, [1914a] 1973, pp. 218–219.

Charles Benedict Davenport (1866–1944), incorporating ideas similar to Goddard's, focused on those regarded as moral imbeciles—the tramps, the prostitutes, and the criminals. For example, Davenport found a common association between nomadism and "well-known aberrant errors and mental state" (1915b, p. 24). Nomadism, Davenport claimed to have discovered, occurs more often among males, is probably a sex-linked recessive monohybrid trait, a fundamental human instinct that is typically inhibited in intelligent adults of civilized peoples (Davenport, 1915b). "All the evidence," said Davenport, "supports the hypothesis that the nomadic impulse depends upon the absence of a simple sex-linked gene that 'determines' domesticity" (Davenport, 1915b, p. 23). As nomadic men tend to marry women with like impulses, all the offspring tend to be nomadic.

Others quickly joined the cause. Scientists, physicians, legislators, and not a few educators made sweeping claims. They argued that "the feeble-minded are irresponsible mortals; that without supervision they cannot be trusted; that, unless special provisions are made for them, some will undoubtedly burn down buildings; others will spread venereal disease; others will bear illegitimate feeble-minded children; others will steal; others will become chronic paupers; others will retard whole classes in public schools and will poison morals; and others will commit murder" (Hincks, 1919a).

Moreover, scientists demonstrated that feeblemindedness was on the increase and the American way of life was at risk of being overthrown by the hordes. Advances in medicine had reversed the struggle for survival, and scientists argued that the mentally retarded and other disabled groups were increasing at a prolific rate. W. L. Hutton, president of the Canadian Eugenics

Society, asserted, for example, that statistics drawn from records of the asylum at Orillia, Ontario, suggested that the families of the feebleminded had an average of eight children whereas the normal had only three (W. L. Hutton, 1936). Alexander Graham Bell suggested that a deaf variety of humans was about to emerge.

The supposed increase was the consequence of an increased awareness of the problem of mental deficiencies. The widespread use of IQ tests provided detailed classifications based on scores, and the data from mass testing seemed to indicate that increasing numbers of Americans were indeed feebleminded. Moreover, compulsory education laws propelled huge numbers of children into the public schools, children heretofore overlooked or excluded from formal education. As the community's demands on children increased, so did the apparent prevalence of feeblemindedness. Once youngsters—many speaking a different language, many from different cultures, and many from impoverished environments—were seated in classrooms, they were exposed to a specific form of education, expected to perform and behave in very specific ways, and subjected to achievement and IQ tests designed by, and based on norms of the white middle class. Teachers thus unwittingly added impetus to the idea that the prevalence of feeblemindedness was increasing (McLaren, 1986). If test and examination results did not serve to single out problem learners, deviant behavior did, and teachers tended to attribute behavior problems to retardation rather than to the child's environment (McLaren, 1986). It is little wonder that feeblemindedness appeared to be on the increase.

CONTROLLING THE DISABLED POPULATION

Education and Legislation

Goddard's campaign to alert the public to the dangers of feeblemindedness spread alarm throughout North American society. The 2 percent of the population judged as feebleminded were seen to be the cause of much misery and concern, the chief offenders in such realms as crime, prostitution, illegitimacy, the spread of venereal disease, pauperism, chronic alcoholism, and public school inefficiency (Goddard, 1916b; Hincks, 1919a).

The fear of social threat translated into exaggerations of criminality: at its most extreme, the fear saw deviant persons as a distinct threat, a sort of magma that would flow through any crack to engulf middle-class society. Many late Victorians contemptuously rejected the past humanitarian and educational efforts of special educators and investigators and instead adopted a viewpoint that judged disabled people to be innately and perpetually inferior.

With dire social problems directly attributable to individuals who, because of their innate mental deficiency or other disabilities, were unable to cope with the complexities of modern life, it was incumbent upon scientists to devise solutions to restrict those disabled persons already in existence and to hinder the production of even more such individuals. Ever more stringent practices, beginning with education and ranging through legislation, segregation, and sterilization, were put forward as not only desirable but necessary.

Goddard asserted, "No feeble-minded person should ever be allowed to marry or become a parent" (Goddard, [1914a] 1972, p. 565), and he recommended education, segregation, or sterilization. Martin Barr ([1904b] 1913), invoking the purity of society and the well-being of disabled individuals, called for new institutional structures and for rigid segregation of the sexes and asexualization procedures, or sterilization (Rosen, Clark, and Kivitz, 1976). Alexander Graham Bell made deafness the first trait to be studied from the standpoint of scientific eugenics (Tinkle, 1933, p. 17). He was "among the ranks of the earliest explorers in the field of eugenics" (D. Fairchild, 1922, p. 198) and was drawn into the movement as it entered its period of greatest influence on American thought. Bell wrote widely on eugenics, funded the *American Breeder's Magazine,* and was honorary president of the first and second congresses on eugenics, in 1912 and 1921. Bell's *Memoir* was favorably reviewed by British eugenicist Sir Francis Galton in *Nature* (Draper, 1888).

Bell first enunciated his basic creed of heredity in a lecture on Visible Speech in 1874, in which, reported a correspondent for the *Silent World,* Bell promoted his father's system as lessening the tendency of the deaf to intermarry, "thus perpetuating a race of deaf mutes" (quoted by R. Bruce, 1973, p. 381).

Bell was drawn into elaborate investigations of hereditary deafness and blindness in the late 1870s when he accepted a commission from the Massachusetts State Board of Health "to collect statistics upon which can be based an investigation of the laws governing the inheritance of pathological conditions, abnormal characteristics of all kinds" ("Inherited deafness," 1879, p. 126). In the belief that detailed accounts of the families of the ancestors of a large number of unrelated deaf-mute families would throw light upon the origins of deafness, Bell constructed genealogical charts showing the ancestry of about one hundred New England families with traits of hereditary deafness. He charted, for example, the Lovejoy family of Massachusetts from 1644, illustrating the descent through the generations of twenty-seven deaf persons as well as the deaf of Martha's Vineyard (A. G. Bell, 1877; "The deaf mutes," 1886). After compiling the genealogies, Bell then entered upon a detailed assessment of 22,473 cases of the disability from census reports from 1770 to 1880, and a separate analysis of 3,726 incidents of deafness from selected American institutions (Bell, 1886, 1888, 1917). Bell reinforced his findings with purportedly scientific evidence, using statistical analysis of the records of two schools for deaf students. On the assumption that pupils with the same surname belonged to the same family, he used names such as Smith, Brown, Anderson, and Miller, which appeared numerous times, as evidence of the hereditary nature of deafness. When the study was complete, Bell made graphical representations of the families so that "the dysgenic effect of the marriages of deaf persons can therefore be seen at a glance" ("Review of Bell's," 1917, p. 214).

His extensive research on 26,199 cases of hereditary deafness led Bell to conclude that grave differences existed between persons congenitally deaf and those adventitiously deafened. Earlier, Howe had surmised that blindness was simply one manifestation of aberrant heredity. Bell arrived at a similar conclusion: congenital deafness was one manifestation only of a generalized mental incapacity. "All round the point where the deafness occurs," wrote Bell, "you find evidence of something generally affecting the nervous system in connection with the brain . . . something to indicate that the thing intensified might be in the brain and not in the ears at all" (De Land, 1925, p. 142). Because of this, Bell saw an undoubted correlation of deafness, blindness, and idiocy, (A. G. Bell, 1885c). Further, Bell believed that the innate inferiority of congenitally deaf persons was exacerbated by the separate environments provided for the education of deaf children and youth.

Bell's work led to a number of influential papers, including a preliminary report on hereditary deafness presented to the National Academy of Sciences in 1885, a paper on the ancestry of deaf persons presented to the same body in 1886, and testimony before the British Royal Commission examining deafness in 1888 (De Land, 1925). By far the most sensational and controversial result of Bell's studies into the ancestry of American deaf people was his *Memoir Upon the Formation of a Deaf Variety of the Human Race* ([1884d] 1969), first presented to the National Academy of Sciences at New Haven in 1883.

Six main findings surfaced in the *Memoir.* Bell discovered that there were marked groupings of deaf persons into families; that the proportion and number of deaf individuals was increasing; that deaf persons married one another in 80 percent of cases in the latter half of the century, whereas in the early half the proportion had been smaller; that children with deaf relatives were more likely to be deaf than the population at large; that the congenitally deaf were increasing at a greater rate than the general population; and that intermarriage was promoted by institutionalization (A. G. Bell, [1884d] 1969). Bell warned, "Something striking and abnormal was going on among deaf mutes" (E. A. Fay, 1884, p. 73), and he concluded that, as the "special character" of deafness in time becomes fixed by heredity and probably becomes intensified by selection, there was growing "in our midst . . . a distinct race" (A. G. Bell, [1884d] 1969, p. 75). To counteract such a dire possibility as the propagation of a deaf race, Bell proposed "a law forbidding congenitally deaf persons from intermarrying" and further legislation "forbidding the intermarriage of persons belonging to families containing more than one deaf-mute" (A. G. Bell, [1884d] 1969, p. 45). (See Box 9-2).

Bell's restrictive proposals were contained within the covers of his *Memoir,* but the idea that a deaf race was growing within American society plucked the already taut strings of public anxiety. Then, in 1884 a bill, the first of a number on the subject, was brought before the Congress of the United States proposing that the marriages of deaf individuals be restricted by law (Mitchell, 1971). Bell had no knowledge of the bill, but his name was linked to it when an overzealous newspaperman saw a copy of the *Memoir* and assumed that Bell had written the bill (De Land, 1912, p. 186).

Bell was not the first to visualize dangers in the marriages of congenitally deaf individuals; his arguments echoed earlier concerns expressed by Thomas Hopkins Gallaudet and Edward Miner Gallaudet, both of whom spoke against unrestricted marriages of the deaf; by Harvey P. Peet, who investigated deaf marriages; and by Edward Allen Fay, who stressed the importance of heredity (Draper, 1888, p. 40; E. M. Gallaudet, 1890). Nevertheless, Bell was the first to articulate his fears in the public forum and to document the subject, and his

Box 9-2

Marriages of Deaf Persons

Bell, Howe, Gallaudet father and son, and many others associated with deaf education in the nineteenth century warned of the dangers of deaf persons' marrying other deaf individuals. Nevertheless, it appears that marriages of deaf persons did not occur at the same rate as did marriages of hearing persons.

Before the establishment of schools for the deaf, it appears that comparatively few deaf people married one another (De Land, 1905b), probably because they were so widely dispersed. In Ontario, for example, marriages of deaf persons seem to have been rather rare before the opening of the provincial institution in 1870. An examination of the marriage patterns of 262 deaf Ontario residents in 1871 indicated that only 40 percent above the age of nineteen were married, 37 percent of the males and 48 percent of the females (Winzer, 1981a).

But even after schooling provided deaf individuals with a wider choice of marriage partners, low marriage rates remained a characteristic of Ontario's deaf population. In 1891 Ontario's census showed 1,563 deaf persons, 54.2 percent males and 45.8 percent females. Of the males, only 25.6 percent were married; of the females, only 21 percent (OSD, 1893). By 1902 approximately 50 percent of marriages of deaf persons were to others with the same disability. Marriage patterns in the United States resemble those reported in Ontario. Almost 73 percent of deaf males and 69 percent of deaf females were single at the time of the twelfth census, taken in 1900 ("The Twelfth," 1907).

Doubtless, many factors contributed to decisions as to whether to marry. One of the most potent was the economic resources required to furnish a household and raise a family. Many disabled persons found it difficult to obtain and retain a job; others were underemployed, if not unemployed. Lack of occupational stability and mobility translated into straitened resources that could not bear the costs of marriage.

---

claims fed middle-class fears. At the same time, he propounded the theory that acceptable speech in the English language was synonymous with Americanization and usefulness to the country.

Immediate reaction to Bell's conclusions and restrictive proposals was sharp. "It is only natural," said Fred De Land of the Volta Bureau in a masterful understatement, "that some among the deaf, and even some among their instructors, should jump to the conclusion that Dr. Bell's views were erroneous" (De Land, 1925, p. 142). Opponents disparaged both the man and his methodology. They argued that the *Memoir* was based on census figures that Bell had "arranged to show that deafness was increasing" (Jenkins, 1890) and perceived his fears "as having little foundation" (E. A. Fay, 1884, p. 70). Too, they saw the power of the work lying in the "weighty names by which the theory is endorsed, rather than by any thing of value contributed to the discussion" (Jenkins, 1890,

p. 85). Dr. Edward Allen Fay, a leading authority on the deaf, chided, "Dr. Bell had gone to the extreme" (E. A. Fay, 1884, p. 70), and he suggested that "it would have been better if our friend had obtained his statistics first and presented his conclusions afterwards" (p. 70). Teachers, though acknowledging many of Bell's contentions regarding oralism, dismissed his underlying rationale. A letter of 1888 directed to the heads of all institutions for deaf persons in the United States and Canada and requesting comments on the theory drew responses pointedly in opposition—only 14 percent of those replying agreed that deaf persons should be prevented from marrying (OSD, 1889).

Not surprisingly, the most antagonized and insulted were deaf people themselves, who saw the *Memoir* as degrading them to the level of incapables, implying that they were the forerunners of an inferior species. Bell's restrictive proposals were viewed as "a cold blooded and heartless proposition" (Arms, 1887, intro.). So irate were deaf people that in Boston a large number publicly protested against Bell (E. M. Gallaudet, 1890).

Bell confessed that his statistics were "very imperfect" but only in underestimating the true number of deaf children (A. G. Bell, 1891a). However, pressed by the spirited opposition, Bell initiated a second study, undertaken by Dr. Fay and funded by the Volta Bureau. Fay based his work on 4,471 marriage records of 7,277 deaf persons, using 3,078 marriages. He found that deaf marriages produced about 10 percent of deaf children; that there appeared to be no greater risk when both partners were deaf than when one partner was deaf; and that having deaf relatives increased the risk of having deaf children (E. A. Fay, 1896; OSD, 1900). Although Fay's findings substantiated Bell's concerning the prevalence of deafness, Fay disagreed sharply regarding the pernicious effects of institutional environments. Fay reported that the marriage of deaf people were far more common in the United States than in Europe (OSD, 1888, p. 16) and that deaf persons in North America were about as likely to marry other deaf individuals whether they attended day, boarding, oral, or combined method schools. "The deep feeling of fellowship, affinity, kinship, sympathy" bonded them "regardless of school type or mode of communication" (E. A. Fay, 1896, p. 176). So, concluded Fay, "I can see no valid reason why deaf persons should not marry as the marital relation is calculated to afford them as much, if not more, happiness and protection than it does hearing people" (Mitchell, 1973; OSD, 1888, p. 16).

Bell tried to strike a fragile balance between advocacy of the well-being of the deaf and eugenical commitment. He described matings of deaf couples as "the marriages of the inferior" (A. G. Bell, 1908a, p. 119) but still advanced to the deaf themselves a policy of education rather than compulsion. "I am sure," he said in an address to a deaf audience in 1891, "that there is no one among the deaf who desires to have his affliction handed down to his children" (A. G. Bell, 1898a, p. 12). Therefore, he promoted marriage with a hearing partner so that the undesirable "blood is diluted" by "admixture with normal blood" (A. G. Bell, 1914, p. 7).

Still, the 1884 draft bill in Congress set the tone for many subsequent bills aimed at restricting the marriage of deaf persons. For example, in 1895 Job Williams of the American School halted the passage of a Connecticut bill recommended by the Committee of Humane Institutions that would have prevented all deaf men and all deaf women under the age of forty-five from marrying and forbidden any man from having carnal knowledge of a deaf woman younger than forty-five ("Marriage," 1895, p. 310). In 1918 reference was made to prohibiting the marriages of the congenitally deaf, even to the point of enforcing this by segregating those ruled to be congenitally hearing handicapped (R. H. Johnson, 1918, p. 77). In 1922 some researchers deemed deaf persons to be "socially inadequate" and among those in need of special restraint, direction, or care ("The Socially Inadequate," 1922, p. 339)

Eugenics faded from the American scene before sterilization of the deaf or compulsory enactments against deaf marriages became a reality. But some deaf persons, in reaction to Bell's predictions, either did not marry or sought sterilization for themselves or their children voluntarily (Mitchell, 1971). Paul Poponoe reported in 1929 that marriages among deaf persons were rare "because it is generally recognized that they are undesirable, although there would be no objection to them eugenically if one of the partners were sterilized prior to marriage" (p. 63).

Segregation

To overcome the profileration of unsavory elements in society, Bell in his *Memoir* advanced solutions centered on education and legislation. However, neither was seen as a viable alternative: not only was "the desire for offspring" believed to be "an inheritable characteristic," but it was thought futile "to expect that the worst would take vows of celibacy or keep them" (A. G. Bell, 1920, p. 339).

Alternative proposals centered on segregation rapidly followed. One writer suggested transporting the unfit ones to islands in the sea, each sex by itself ("Compulsory Childlessness," 1891); another contended that "every imbecile of reproductive age should be held in such restraint that reproduction is out of the question" (Jordan, 1913, pp. 78–79). Further attempts would bar defective immigrants from the country and segregate the feebleminded in farm colonies so they could not reproduce their own kinds (Hincks, 1919a).

In the face of high rates of recidivism (return to an institution) and an increasing institutionalized population, special educators grew skeptical about attaining their initial goal—solving the problems of feeblemindedness. Believing that mental retardation was a hereditary characteristic, subject to Mendelian law, they too held that custodial segregation was necessary to halt the perpetuation of intellectually inferior people. Institutional superintendents and educators promoted "permanent custodial care" for the feebleminded to prevent their increase (Vineland, 1903, p. 24).

Much of the campaign was waged against those from impoverished backgrounds. Although it was believed that mental retardation was inherited and not due to poor living conditions, mentally retarded individuals from the middle class were perceived and treated differently. Middle-class feebleminded children were not seen as a great threat to society; they were treated as individual deviants and, as long as they did not become involved in delinquent acts, were left for their parents to handle (Mercer and Richardson, 1975).

Feebleminded persons were often committed to state institutions such as prisons, reformatories, asylums, county training schools, and city and town almshouses (League, 1916). Institutional building proceeded apace, propelled by fears about the threat of the feebleminded. Martin Barr called for separate asylums for idiots that could be run on a more economical basis than could be accomplished within the general institution, and he suggested the extension of the farm colony idea.

Before the late nineteenth century few persons were actually institutional-ized, but by 1890 fourteen states had opened separate public institutions for the mentally retarded (Davies, 1959). The 1890 census showed 95,571 idiots in the United States, of whom 6,315 or 6 percent were cared for in institutions (Vine-land, 1893). Numbers had risen to 9,334 institutionalized by 1900; by 1923, of the 500,000 to 1 million feebleminded persons believed in need of segregation, 43,349 were incarcerated in state institutions for the feebleminded (*A Eugenics Catechism*, 1927, p. 6); there were 68,035 inmates by 1930 (Scheerenberger, 1983). Put another way, the number of residents of public institutions for the mentally retarded per 100,000 of the general population grew from 4.8 in 1880 to 47.8 in 1926 (Lakin, n.d.).

Sterilization

The value of education in controlling the feebleminded proved question-able; segregation was too costly, and social sanctions untenable. More aggres-sive measures had to be undertaken if defective elements were to be eliminated from society. Eugenicists maintained that human society, like nature, must be harsh in its treatment of its weaklings, and they directed their energies to con-trolling "the crop of feeble-minded which our misguided indifference has per-mitted to grow" (W. L. Hutton, 1936, p. 3). By the late nineteenth century feeblemindedness had come to be defined in terms of amorality, so social policy had to substitute something for the missing restraints of moral compunction. And, since advances in medical science had kept the markedly unfit alive, it was thought that medicine should then assume a responsibility for curbing the surge of feeblemindedness.

At the Seventh International Conference on Hygiene and Demography in 1891 Sir Francis Galton called for the sterilization of the world's less affluent and fortunate people (see Field, 1911–12; Pendell, 1924). Americans, seeking radical solutions to the presumed social problems of mental retardation, readily adopted the supposition that by practicing sterilization, society would be greatly helped in ridding itself of those likely to pass on unacceptable traits. Moreover, the sterilization of certain persons would reduce taxes, alleviate misery and suf-fering, and actually do "what nature would do under natural conditions" (*A Eu-genics Catechism*, 1927, p. 7). "The whole matter," Barr asserted, "might be simplified and the nervous atmosphere relieved by early invoking the aid of sur-gical interference to secure at once safety to society, less tension to community life, and greater liberty, therefore greater happiness, to the individual" (Barr, [1904b] 1913).

Goddard, Davenport, Bell, David Starr Jordan, and a host of other eugenical promoters saw the improvement of the race as a breeder's problem, not one of education or environment (A. G. Bell, 1908a). Bell, for example, began animal breeding experiments in 1886 in efforts to develop a strain of multi-nippled sheep (see A. G. Bell, 1923). Holding that "the laws of heredity that apply to animals also apply to man" (A. G. Bell, 1908a, p. 120), he assumed the right to publicly air his contentions because "the breeder of animals is fitted to guide public opinion on questions relating to human heredity" (A. G. Bell, 1914, p. 2). From the animal world, Bell cited the English sparrow and the mongoose as noxious pests and the thoroughbred horse as a desirable animal (A. G. Bell, 1908a, pp. 118–19); for humanity, he used paupers and criminals as examples of the horrors of inbreeding (*AADD,* 1884, p. 75).

In 1907 the American Breeder's Association (ABA) became the first American group to use the term *eugenics* when it established a eugenics section to promote both positive and negative eugenics. The ABA sought, on the one hand, to improve society by helping people to "a better selection of marriage mates" and, on the other, "to control the reproduction of the defective classes" (*American Breeders Magazine,* 1909, p. 235). Nine committees fell under the Eugenics Section, dealing with, respectively, the heredity of feeblemindedness, insanity, epilepsy, criminality, eye defects, deafness, mental traits, immigration, and sterilization (Davenport, 1910). Bell was offered the full chairmanship but deferred to David Starr Jordan and instead chaired the committee on hereditary deafness.

The Eugenics Section preached that "where the life of the state is threatened extreme measures must and may be taken, the defective, the dependent, and delinquent classes restrained either by segregation during the reproductive period or even by sterilization" (Jordan, 1913, pp. 78–79). Proposals for sterilization were based on the contention that certain persons would be certain to bear children who "would be a liability rather than an asset to future generations, because of their inherited natures" (Poponoe, 1928, p. 405). These included the mentally retarded and the mentally ill, the physically defective, the 75,000 blind individuals, and the 100,000 deaf persons in the United States (Poponoe, 1928).

Objections to involuntary sterilization based on the argument that it violated individual freedoms were quashed with arguments that it was criminal to intentionally spread disease and degeneracy. If the crime of inferior breeding could not be punished by the courts, then it could at least be prevented. Moreover, segregation was an abrogation of liberty, but sterilization would allow greater freedom because the sterilized feebleminded could leave the institutions and marry without the fear of reproduction. Still others (e.g., F. E. Hodgins, 1919) promoted sterilization for the benefit of the disabled population. They believed that many mentally retarded persons would be relieved of the dread of unwanted pregnancies and provided an escape from the burdens of recurrent parenthood.

Explicit cautions went relatively unheeded. Walter Fernald, for example, argued that "sterilization would not be a safe and effective substitute for permanent segregation and control" because "the presence of these sterile people in the community, with unimpaired sexual desire and capacity would be a direct encouragement of vice and a prolific source of venereal disease" (1912a, pp. 95–96). Similarly, others saw the sterilization of delinquent girls as simply "a licence for active immorality" (Ordahl, 1917, p. 8). To these arguments, proponents simply responded that the practice of sterilization would result in greater order and increased self-control.

Sterilization Practices

Dr. Harry Sharp of the Indiana State Reformatory in Jacksonville performed the first sterilization on a human inmate in 1899. At that time Indiana had no law to deal with such contingencies, and Sharp proceeded merely on the assent of the inmates. Nevertheless, far-reaching implications attended the work: Sharp's reports of hundreds of sterilizations performed provided a substantial basis for future legislation to allow sterilization and underlay Indiana's later laws. Pennsylvania in 1905 passed the first sterilization law, but it was vetoed by Governor Samuel Whitaker Pennypacker (Poponoe, 1923). Indiana, then, in 1907 became the first state to vote itself the authority to use compulsory sterilization with any confined criminal, rapist, and imbecile in state institutions (Chase, 1977). Washington and California both adopted sterilization laws in 1909, although the Washington law went unused (Bogarth, 1910).

Given the mounds of apparently irrefutable evidence demonstrating that heredity is the source of two-thirds of feeblemindedness (C. Russell, 1920), it is not surprising that sterilization efforts largely focused on this population. Dr. Isaac N. Kerlin, superintendent of the Elwyn Institution and founder of the Society for the Study of Feeble-Mindedness, promoted sterilization procedures. At the Elwyn Institution about six patients a year were sterilized; in one ten-year period 98 operations were performed—59 males and 39 females. Of these, 58 were of the middle- and high-grade groups. Of the females, 70 percent were said to have shown improvement in habits and 35 percent, improvement in mentality. Of 38 males on whom operations were performed, 78 percent showed improvement in habits and 42 percent, improvement in mentality (Rosen, Clark, and Kivitz, 1976).

The groups subject to sterilization expanded sharply in 1915 when Harry Laughlin, a fervent promoter of eugenics and the author of the first American book on sterilization (Laughlin, [1924] 1930), formulated his "model law." Laughlin called for the sterilization of all those in society who might produce socially inadequate offspring. Ten categories were included—"the feeble-minded, the insane, the criminalistic, the inebriate, the epileptic, the diseased, the blind, the deaf, the deformed, and the dependent" ("The Socially," 1922, p. 348), in all, 10 million or more Americans. The sterilization fervor reached the point where laws were introduced that called for its use as punishment for such crimes as chicken stealing, car theft, and prostitution (Karier, 1972).

By 1921 fifteen states had enacted laws that allowed for 3,233 eugenical operations of insane, feebleminded, and criminal persons (Poponoe, 1923). However, many state laws were found to be unconstitutional and were overturned or never used. It was not until the 1927 Supreme Court decision of Justice Oliver Wendell Holmes in the case of *Buck vs. Bell* that sterilization was ruled by the high court to be constitutional.

In 1924 Virginia adopted a sterilization measure. Under this law Dr. A. S. Priddy filed a suit against Carrie Buck, and when Priddy died, the suit was taken over by J. H. Bell, superintendent of the Virginia State Colony for Epileptics and the Feeble-Minded. Bell filed a petition in September 1924 to sterilize Carrie Buck, an eighteen-year-old institutional inmate described as having a mental age of nine. Buck had given birth to an illegitimate feebleminded child; her mother, then fifty-two years old, was also characterized as feebleminded, having a mental age of less than eight years and a long history of immorality, prostitution, and dependency.

Buck vs. Bell culminated with the May 1927 decision in which Justice Holmes upheld the constitutionality of the Virginia sterilization law. Given that Carrie Buck was the probable potential parent of socially inadequate offspring, she could be sexually sterilized without detriment to her health or her welfare. Holmes's opinion declared, "It is better for all the world, if instead of waiting to execute degenerate offspring for crime, or to let them starve for their imbecility, society can prevent those who are manifestly unfit from continuing their kind ... three generations of imbeciles are enough" ("Three Generations," 1927, p. 495). The negative eugenicists had won an important victory: The Supreme Court denied that sterilization was unconstitutional under the Fourteenth Amendment of the Constitution and upheld the rights of states to enact such laws.

The entire question of eugenics was once again aired in the courts in the 1931 case of *Eugenics vs. Troutman* in Idaho. Albert Troutman, a twenty-six-year-old man, had normal sexual desires but the intelligence of a five- or six-year-old. His mother, father, and five siblings were all feebleminded and had at times been institutionalized. Again, the Supreme Court upheld the decision of *Buck vs. Bell.*

By 1930 twenty-eight states had enacted sterilization laws, and 12,057 persons had been legally sterilized (Laughlin, 1930, p. 77); by 1932 these states had performed some 16,000 sterilizations. Of these, 8,504 were in California, where inmates of asylums and institutions were, as a matter of course, sterilized before discharge (Holmes, 1933, p. 155). Although thirty states had eugenical laws on the books from 1907 to 1958, only 30,038 mentally retarded persons were ultimately sterilized (Davies, 1959).

Canada rapidly followed the same route (H. H. Bruce, 1936). Alberta passed a eugenics law in 1928, and the 1933 Sexual Sterilization Act in British Columbia allowed a eugenics board to decide on the sterilization of persons in mental hospitals, industrial homes for girls, and the industrial schools (Winzer and O'Connor, 1982). Manitoba's 1933 Act to Provide for Mentally Defective Persons contained a clause that provided for voluntary sterilization, although this was quickly deleted (Atkinson, 1935). Ontario seriously debated the question but, despite the urgings of prominent physicians, no legislation was enacted (see W. L. Hutton, 1936).

EUGENICS AND IMMIGRANTS

During the nineteenth century Canada and the United States adopted, with the approbation of business and government, lax and largely nonrestrictive immigration policies that were intended to promote economic growth. Until the 1890s most newcomers to the United States came from England, Ireland, Germany, and the Scandinavian countries. After 1890 Italians, Poles, Bohemians, Russians, eastern European Jews, and others from southern and eastern Europe came in ever greater numbers. By 1910 the southern and eastern Europeans were making up nearly 77 percent of the total immigration to the United States

(Phelps, 1924). In Canada the traditional Protestant British-Canadian milieu altered radically. In the period from 1901 to the start of World War I, more people emigrated to Canada from Europe, especially from the eastern and southern part, than had ever done before (Pennachio, 1986).

At the outset, "the practical exponents of eugenics always had their faces turned to the slums and instinctively thought in terms of them" (Chesterton, 1922, pp. 141–42). The original enemies list of scientific racism consisted solely of people who were white, nonaffluent, deviant, defective, and delinquent (Chase, 1977). Accompanying the political philosophy of Social Darwinism that encouraged the public to reject the needs of the helpless was the creation of a new pseudo-science or mythology based on race and heredity.

As the eugenics promotions swelled, one faction tenaciously pursued legislation aimed at restricting immigration. Their xenophobic racism focused on racial, religious, geographic, linguistic, and cultural differences (see Chase, 1977); their goals were "preserving the white race in the United States, as well as . . . protecting American standards of living" (Ward, 1927, p. 17).

American eugenicists were quick to assert that feeblemindedness was linked with race. As feeblemindedness, social deviance, and ethnicity were linked and placed in opposition to educated Anglo-Saxon quality, the problems of the immigrants assumed sinister proportions. At the feet of immigrants was laid much of the blame for the consequences of rapid industrialization and urbanization, and the rise of ethnic ghettos. Immigrants drew further opprobrium by their failure to Americanize or Canadianize rapidly enough. By 1900 there was a growing sentiment among the American people that the influx of immigrants threatened the stability of the nation's institutions and its racial purity. Perceptions of the inferiority of many immigrant groups were lent spurious support from IQ tests.

Goddard, Madison Grant, Bell, and others warned people of the impending self-destruction of America as they had known it. The native American, warned Bell, was "surrounded by prolific immigrant races ready to take its place," and there appeared "a serious danger" that the native race would be "displaced by the immigrants" (A. G. Bell, 1920, p. 340). By no means a militant xenophobe, Bell yielded to the assumption that ethnic groups differed in temperament and intelligence, as well as in superficial characteristics. He looked askance at the lowered birthrate of the American people and the tides of new immigrants. When Bell asked himself "Is race suicide possible?" he drew the conclusion that "the only hope for a truly American race is the restriction of immigration" (A. G. Bell, 1920, p. 341). Before any immigration restrictions were imposed, however, Bell proposed "an ethical survey" to determine which foreign elements were beneficial and which harmful (A. G. Bell, 1908a, p. 123).

In 1910 the Immigration Commission recommended that a literacy test be given to all immigrants, a measure that passed the House and Senate in 1917 (H. Fairchild, 1917). In 1912 and again in 1913 Henry Goddard tested representative samples of immigrants at Ellis Island in order to develop suggestions for a more thorough culling of potential immigrants (Goddard, 1913, 1917). Results of his tests and the army's Alpha and Beta tests were used to bolster arguments about the intellectual inferiority of the new immigrants. The tests purportedly demonstrated how European immigrants could be graded by their country of origin (S. Gould, 1981, p. 196). Further analysis of the data showed that eastern and southern Europeans scored only slightly higher than American blacks. In Canada advocates of restrictive immigration argued that "50 per cent. of our insane and feeble-minded in Canada have come to us from countries outside the Dominion" (Hincks, 1919a).

Increasing support for the restriction of immigration followed World War I, as Americans fretted about massive immigration from the ravaged countries of Europe. Under the Harding administration a temporary immigration restriction bill was passed, limiting the number of aliens from Europe to 5 percent of each nationality resident in the United States according to the 1910 census. By the second decade of the twentieth century poor economic conditions stimulated anti-alien sentiment further. The majority of Americans came to believe that regulations against the flood of immigrants from southern and eastern Europe were necessary.

When Harry Laughlin was appointed expert eugenics agent of the House Committee on Immigration and Naturalization in 1920, he testified before the House at great length on three occasions on the scientific basis and implications of immigration restrictions. In 1922 Laughlin presented his analysis of America's modern melting pot to Congress and promoted the idea that inferior new immigrants were threatening to wipe out native American stock. His arguments aided in the development of laws that imposed quotas on the basis of national origin. By 1923 the formerly lax immigration laws had been replaced by more restrictive regulations. Permanent restrictive policies were enacted in Canada and the United States, and by 1924 the flow of immigrants from eastern and southern Europe to the United States was reduced to 2 percent from each nation on the basis of the 1890 census. The use of this census, rather than the one from 1910 or 1920, made it possible to keep the numbers to a minimum (H. Fairchild, 1924).

With the enactment of the national origins basis for immigration, the United States and Canada adopted policies that were no longer based on economic or charitable principles. Many factors contributed to the shift, but the imposition of harsh quotas might never have been implemented without the army data and the pressure from the eugenicists.

OPPOSITION TO EUGENICS

The results of mass IQ testing and genealogical studies, inconclusive as they were, nonetheless appeared at the time to be factual and authoritative and, above all, scientific. As such, they perpetuated myths involving genetic inheritance and strengthened fears about the feebleminded and the immigrant. Notions of the hereditary transmission of innate and acquired traits reigned; environmental etiologies were barely given a nod. Scientists, physicians, psychologists, and the general public increasingly accepted the notion that criminality, pauperism, alcoholism, and a range of other human conditions are hereditary. By the end of the World War I the heredity-environment debate had heated up once again; biologists, sociologists, and psychologists entered the arena, and all brought the tools of their separate disciplines to the debate.

Scientists' success in persuading the public of the truths of eugenics and Social Darwinism owed less to the power of their arguments than to the social and political context in which they labored. As the simmering social problems of the first decade of the century abated and the euphoria following the war became manifest, public, scientific, and educational reaction against eugenics emerged. By the mid-1920s advocates of eugenics faced stern intellectual opposition from geneticists, educators, and psychologists.

For one thing, eugenicists needed the continuing respect of scientific leaders to maintain status and respectability and to receive ongoing support from influential leaders. But the notoriety of some of the more radical eugenical positions and the outspoken views of blatant racists (e.g., Grant, 1921) ultimately made it unlikely that they could continue to hold the confidence of leading scientists.

Scientific criticism of eugenics came from scholars and researchers such as the sociologist Franz Boas (1858–1942). He argued that human behavior could not be explained by immutable laws of biology (Boas, 1916). Eugenics came now to be sharply criticized for being not science, but propaganda directed toward class and racial prejudices (Pearl, 1927, p. 260). Proponents were accused of allowing political opinions rather than specific scientific theories to shape their thinking. Criticism tended to focus on the poor or even complete lack of scientific method in earlier studies, on the fact that eugenicists had used questionable tests administered under questionable conditions and subjected to questionable statistical analysis and interpretation. Researchers urged the abandonment of the absolute conclusions drawn about feeblemindedness. They questioned the conclusions drawn from early IQ tests, called for more research, and saw the need to conceptualize and study feeblemindedness in terms of social competence.

The more geneticists learned about the importance of recessive hereditary characteristics, the more skeptical they became of the crude social engineering sought by the eugenicists (McLaren, 1986). Charles Davenport had assumed that retardation was the result of the absence of some definite simple factor so that two imbecile parents were certain to produce only imbecile offspring (Davenport, 1915a, p. 77). New genetic research demonstrated that mental deficiency is caused by not only a recessive gene, but a rare recessive gene. Clinical studies also demonstrated the significance of other sources of mental retardation—infection, trauma, and endocrine disturbance.

Ongoing scientific research also forged a new scientific truth: like did not produce like, but a wide variety of new and different combinations of genes could occur in virtually every mating of human beings (Pearl, 1927, p. 266). Science rejected the notion that a single gene causes a single identifiable trait; studies suggested that if both parents had IQs of less than 70, 40 percent of the offspring would be retarded; if only one parent had the low IQ, then 15 percent of the children would be affected. But if both parents were normal, then only 1 percent of the children would suffer retardation. In other words, 83 percent of mentally retarded children were born to parents with normal IQs (*Canadian Medical Assoc. Journal*, 1933, p. 260). To eliminate mental retardation, it would be necessary to do something other than sterilize parents having low IQs.

Other researchers reported that the purported growth in numbers of and the high fertility of the feebleminded were myths (*Canadian Journal of Public Health,* 1937, p. 152). Then the entire notion of moral imbecility came under attack. Estimated numbers were clearly aberrations; it seemed that less that 5 percent of retarded persons living in institutions could be so classified (Rosen, Clark, and Kivitz, 1976). Goddard's 1914 estimation that 55 percent of criminals were defective was undermined by a 1940 study establishing the rate at 2.4 percent (Penrose, [1949] 1966).

Psychologists discarded the idea that it was possible to obtain precise ratios for the contributions of heredity and environment to the human makeup and proposed instead that each plays a role in influencing the process of development. But extremism was not easily vanquished, and the controversy surfaced again in 1940. This time, however, the ensuing debate ushered in a significant breakthrough for psychologists concerned with the development of intelligence. There was a radical movement away from the previously held notion of fixed intelligence and predetermined development.

In 1940 a Year Book of the National Society for the Study of Education appeared in two parts (Stoddard, 1940). In this, researchers from Stanford University, following the lead of Lewis Terman, tended to favor heredity, over environment. Other researchers came to the opposite conclusion, claiming that environment is the primary determinant of intellectual ability (Skodak, 1939; Stoddard & Wellman, 1940). Researchers working at the Iowa Child Welfare Research Station attempted to produce evidence that intelligence, especially that measured by intelligence tests, is a product of the environment. They tried to show that manipulations in the environment produce variations in intelligence and that intelligence tests were not really measuring native intelligence. This work, which has come to be known collectively as the Iowa studies, came out strongly in favor of nurture (Winzer and Grigg, 1922).

Even though the California and Iowa researchers held different views about whether intelligence was determined more by genetics or by environmental influences, the stances were not as irreconcilable as they had tended to be earlier. By this time researchers were beginning to agree that both genes and the environment contribute to the intelligence of a human being. They discarded the idea that it is possible to obtain precise ratios for the discrete contributions of heredity and environment, but rather proposed that both nature and nurture operate all of the time (see Anastasi, 1958; Hebb, 1942).

Hereditary principles further wavered under the impact of the new theories of behaviorism. Behaviorism was the work of several psychologists although it was John Broadus Watson who defined it, shaped it, promoted it, coined the terminology, and gave American psychology its behavioral footing after he announced his platform in 1913 (see Box 9-3). Behaviorism focused exclusively on the impact of the environment on behaviors, not on the influence of hereditary or innate traits and characteristics. American psychology was not immediately converted to behaviorism or to Watson's approach, with its emphasis on habits and conditioned reflexes to replace instincts. However, during the 1920s there was a strong trend toward objectivism among American psychologists and other social scientists and biologists, including those who felt no formal allegiance to

Box 9-3

John Broadus Watson (1878–1958)

John Watson burst onto the field of psychology in 1913 and eventually made himself champion of the behavioral movement that made such a significant impression on psychology. Behaviorism had a wide appeal to students at that time, for many had begun to react strongly to the stringency of the testing movement.

Born in Greenville, South Carolina, Watson had an unpromising early career. His mother was a religious woman who wished him to become a Baptist minister; his father was a notoriously violent man who abandoned the family when Watson was thirteen. At the age of sixteen Watson reached Furman University, where he earned his way as a laboratory assistant in chemistry. After graduating, he taught in a one-room school.

Eventually Watson traveled to Chicago to obtain his doctoral degree from the new department of psychology in Chicago. He was then offered several academic positions but chose to remain in the department at Chicago. In his classes in experimental psychology Watson adhered to traditional psychological methods, teaching students to use introspection to analyze their own minds. However, he felt more comfortable with experimentation using rats and other animals, and he veered sharply in this new direction.

Watson married in 1903 and then, after repeated offers, accepted a position at Johns Hopkins, where he remained from 1908 to 1920, except for a few months of military service. The new position allowed him to work out his ideas about behaviorism, which he first aired in 1913.

Watson's behavioral position was inspired by associationalist theory drawn from John Locke, given credence by the identification of classical conditioning by the Russian physiologist Ivan Petrovich Pavlov, and lent direction by his own laboratory experiments with animals. Watson's theories owed much to the concepts of classical conditioning, a process by which reflexive responses come to be triggered by new cues, first identified by Pavlov in his work on the salivation of dogs. In classical conditioning an organism learns that one event follows another—Pavlov's dogs learned that the sound of a bell was always associated with food so became conditioned to salivate at the sound of the bell even when food was not present (e.g., J. B. Watson, 1927).

Quite aside from his contributions to psychology and the emerging school of behaviorism, Watson's personal life became the focus of great public interest and abruptly terminated his academic career. Watson became involved with a graduate assistant, Rosalie Raynor, and wrote her compromising letters that were eventually obtained by his wife and found their way into print. His divorce was a sensation, played up particularly by the Hearst press; it was page-one copy all across the country. Watson married Rosalie on the New Year's Eve following his divorce. He was also asked to resign his teaching position, not so much because he had become divorced but because he violated the unwritten code about faculty and student liaisons (C. A. Larson, 1972). Before 1920 was ended, Watson was employed by the J. Walter Thompson company, became vice president in 1924, and remained with them until 1936, when he joined the William Coty Company as vice president and continued until his retirement in 1945 (E.A.B., 1958; C. A. Larson, 1972).

Much of Watson's reputation is colored by this affair. However, he has also often been denigrated by professional debunkers and unfriendly psychologists (Weyent, 1968). On a positive note, Bergmann (1956) suggested that Watson was second only to Freud as "the most important figure in the history of psychological thought during the first half of the century." On the other hand, others such as Roback (1937, 1964) dismissed Watsonian behaviorism as a "rah-rah technique" that "made a big noise" that was "not substantiated by deeds." Nevertheless, Watson contributed enormously to the field of psychology. He won acceptance for animal psychology, gave impetus to the field of child study and observation, and demonstrated that psychological experimentation can be as important in the marketplace as in the laboratory (E.A.B., 1958).

---

a radical behaviorism (Hilgard, 1987). In education, behaviorism spread on a wave of revolutionary fervor. Progressive schools, adopting the tenets of John Dewey and other exponents of American progressivism in education, embraced behavioristic concepts. The three Rs were considered less important, as emotional training became an integral part of the new education.

Under a barrage of criticism and in light of new findings, geneticists, psychologists, physicians, and educators tempered their imperious stances or reiterated their former unpopular liberal positions. In 1922 J. E. W. Wallin (1922a, 1922b), a leading psychologist and never a eugenics advocate, reviewed his experiences over the preceding decade. He concluded that many persons with mental ages in the eight- to twelve-year range were self-supporting and that the eugenicists were probably mistaken in their claims that mental retardation is a hereditary trait. Moreover, he believed that claims that feebleminded people are vicious or criminal were untrue; he also thought that mental retardation has different implications for the sexes, with higher levels expected for males.

Walter Fernald, who in 1912 had asserted, "Every feeble-minded person, especially the high-grade imbecile, is a potential criminal" (1912a, p. 6), by 1924 admitted, "We have begun to recognize that there are good morons and bad morons" (quoted by Wolfensberger, 1975, p. 54). Much of the change in Fernald's stance may be attributed to the results of his longitudinal study of 646 discharged mentally retarded clients from the Waverley Institution. Fernald's study did far more than provide a close look at mentally retarded adults in society and indicate the strength of institutional training; it signaled a change in attitudes toward mentally retarded people. Previously Fernald had recommended full custody of the mentally retarded population in order to protect society, but his 1919 survey indicated that he had erred in seeing all such individuals as dangerous to society.

Fernald found that thirteen men of his sample married, of whom eleven made good husbands; two were sentenced to the reformatory for larceny. Of the

Table 9-1

Results of Fernald's Study of Discharged Mentally Retarded Adults

	Male (N = 470)	Female (N = 176)
Married		27
Married, sex offenses		16
Self-supporting, unmarried	114	8
Unmarried mothers		11
At home under supervision, some work	77	32
At home, little work	59	23
Committed to other institutions	43	29
Died	54	24
Readmitted to Waverley	68	33
Arrested, not sentenced	23	
Sentenced to penal institutions	32	

Source: W. E. Fernald, 1919a.

females, twenty-seven were married; all but one of the married women were designated as morons. Eleven of the married women led "useful and blameless lives; had neat and attractive homes, bore good reputations in the community; went to church, and apparently were making good in every way" (W. E. Fernald, 1919a, p. 2). There were fifty children; seventeen children had died and thirty-three were living at home. None of the children was found to be defective.

From 1850 to 1920 institutions for the mentally retarded could neither initiate admissions nor hinder removal—they could only reject unsuitable cases (Tyor, 1977) and advise about the suitability of discharge. In Fernald's study workers found sixteen married women, all of whom had been discharged against the advice of institutional staff, to be behaving badly, with records of sexual promiscuity, alcoholism, thievery, and syphilis. There were eleven unmarried mothers among the discharges, with thirteen children among them. Fourteen women were subsequently committed to other institutions. Five women were returned to Waverley and another three were known to be occasional prostitutes. Fernald's results are summarized in Table 9-1. Cases counted in two or more categories account for the discrepancies in the totals.

These findings, joined to limited custodial resources and the cost of institutionalization, caused Fernald and others to advocate a different approach to the care of mentally retarded people. Fernald suggested a comprehensive plan of statewide registration, outpatient clinics, special school classes, intensive public community education, extra-institutional supervision by trained social workers, and coordination by a central state authority (Fernald, 1918, 1919b; Zainaldin and Tyor, 1979).

In 1940 Dr. W. R. Baller published a twenty-seven-year longitudinal study of mentally retarded people in general society that provides an interesting contrast with Fernald's study. Baller found their homes to be characterized by poor economic standards, unskilled labor, and frequent geographical and occupational moves. The people in Baller's sample displayed antisocial conduct to a greater extent than persons of normal intelligence and seemed to have larger families; the women seemed to marry at an earlier age than women of normal intelligence. Baller found the death rate to be seven times higher than among normal people and the marriage rates to be lower, but divorce rates were about the same (Baller, 1936; Baller, Charles, and Miller 1967; "How Do," 1940).

Even Goddard recanted his extreme position on the dangers, etiology, and prevalence of feeblemindedness in America. While new findings in psychology and genetics probably underlay Goddard's liberalization, it is also likely that his observation of different clientele in a different setting served to soften his previously adamant position. In 1913 Ohio governor James Cox commissioned Goddard to design a juvenile bureau for dealing with the growing problem of delinquency; Goddard was appointed the clinic's director in 1918. Besides encountering considerable administrative and political difficulties in his new post, Goddard also learned at first hand that most juvenile offenders were not simply hereditarily feebleminded, as he previously held; rather, they required more comprehensive methods of diagnosis and treatment than could be afforded by intelligence tests alone (see Cravens, 1987).

As a new appreciation of the effects of environment surfaced, the "threat of the feebleminded" faded from the public mind. Although isolated voices continued to call for sterilization laws as late as the 1930s and a few were lauding the new German policies (e.g., Poponoe, 1934), the issue of sterilization for eugenic purposes had lost ground. Ultimately, it was concluded that selecting individuals for segregation or sterilization in pursuit of improved racial stock was not only ineffective but scientifically invalid.

GERMAN STERILIZATION LAWS

Mounting apprehension about German militancy throughout the 1930s rang the death knell for eugenics and sterilization as appropriate responses to social ills in North America. Hitler seized power in 1933; his obsession with *Lebensraum* (living space) and racial purity precluded the peaceful coexistence of Germans with many groups, including disabled persons. Power legitimized eugenics in Germany.

It was Friedrich Wilhelm Nietzsche's philosophy that set up the ideal of better breeding and prepared the way for the use of eugenic principles (Lenz, 1924). The German eugenics law, promulgated in 1933, allowed the sterilization of persons afflicted with feeblemindedness, insanity, epilepsy, Saint Vitus's dance, blindness, deafness, serious bodily deformity, and chronic alcoholism (*AAD*, 1933; Poponoe, 1934). Hitler's law was, observed a German writer with horrifying understatement, "extraordinarily harsh, but ... biologically necessary" (Lietz, 1934, p. 204). During the first year well over 50,000 sterilizations were ordered or performed (Siegel, 1939). Not only were disabled persons sterilized, but they were also denied the rights of full citizenship.

Many Americans, increasingly aghast at the implications of Germany's overt policies of *Rasenhygiene* (racial purity), grew uneasy about similar policies at home. Certainly, hereditary determinism was not totally abandoned in North America. But the period witnessed the declining importance of strict hereditarian theories of human behavior and a growing recognition of the importance of environment and the complex interplay of factors that shape behavior (McConnichie, 1983).

By 1940 most states had abandoned the notion of restricted marriages, sterilization, and institutionalization as primary means of controlling the growth of the mentally retarded population. The increasing numbers of mentally retarded individuals who were identified, the proliferation of special programs, revised expectations concerning the stability of IQ scores, new concepts about heredity, and lack of public and legislative support, all rendered such efforts impractical. There was also growing opposition to sterilization as a substitute for the adequate supervision of young adult retarded men and women.

Because of the discriminatory abuse implicit in the early mandates, some individual states changed their laws in an effort to move away from the racist eugenics movement and toward practices that would seem more humane. In 1942 the Supreme Court in *Skinner vs. Oklahoma* ruled against the sterilization of a man convicted of stealing chickens, rejecting the reasoning that had dominated the *Buck vs. Bell* case and establishing procreation as a fundamental constitutional right. The court stated that the power to sterilize could have far-reaching and devastating effects (see Winzer and O'Connor, 1982).

Nevertheless, the change in attitudes was not universal, and court cases continued to reflect society's inconsistency and ambivalence. Although *Buck vs. Bell* was the classic case justifying the state's use of compulsory sterilization, it was not used to support the constitutionality of a compulsory sterilization order until 1968, when the Nebraska sterilization law was challenged in the courts. Sterilization was upheld as a prerequisite to parole or discharge from institutions, and the court stated that the public good should be put above the constitutional rights of citizens, that the state could limit a class of citizens in their right to bear children. The claim was that it is the function of the state to "protect the public and preserve the race from known effects of . . . procreation . . . by the mentally deficient" (Vitello, 1980, p. 406).

Chapter 10

From Isolation to Segregation: The Emergence of Special Classes

Landmarks in the Rise of Special Classes in the Schools

1817   Thomas Hopkins Gallaudet begins teacher training at the Connecticut Asylum

1852   Massachusetts passes the first compulsory school attendance law

1864   The National Deaf Mute College establishes training for teachers of deaf students

1867   The Horace Mann day school for deaf children in Boston opens

1870s   Ungraded classes and classes for the unruly are established

1884   Training for teachers of blind persons is instituted at Columbia University; Alexander Graham Bell begins advocating day classes for deaf and blind children

1898   Collegiate training for teachers of mentally retarded students begins

1904   A training program for teachers of the mentally retarded begins at the New Jersey Institution for Feeble-Minded Boys and Girls at Vineland

1909   The first compulsory school attendance laws for deaf and blind children are enacted

1910   Segregated classes in the public schools are well established as a viable alternative for training exceptional children

1922   The International Council for the Education of Exceptional Children is founded

In the institutions for deaf, blind, and, to a lesser extent, mentally retarded students, resistance to charity designations crested in the 1880s; the push was on to create new modes of operation and administration that would replace the custodial and retrogressive modes so long established in public residential institutions. During the opening decades of the twentieth century free, compulsory education for deaf and blind children in the United States and Canada gained even wider acceptance. The charity connotation had been swept away, and institutions became schools, albeit separate and special, with strictly educational goals.

Altered views of the institutionalized population accompanied the development of special classes in the public school system. Segregated day classes seemed an inevitable next step as the concept of specialized programming expanded to embrace a wider range of children. Many who now were included exhibited problems that, although usually less devastating than those of the institutionalized clientele, still created insurmountable barriers to learning in regular classrooms.

School districts, under pressure to manage if not to educate increasing numbers of unruly, disabled, low-functioning, and immigrant children, could no longer ignore the needs of these pupils and were challenged to find solutions to their problems within the system. Teachers were generally unwilling to handle these students in regular classes, and officials, seeking to maintain order, discipline, and high standards in the schools, were adverse to placing them in regular classrooms. To satisfy the requirements of compulsory education laws and the wishes of the schools, school districts created the community equivalent of institutions—special segregated classes. Exceptional pupils were not isolated in institutions, but they were very much separated in special classes, which were given many different names: ungraded classes, opportunity classes, auxiliary classes, and classes for particular conditions. Problem children, thus removed from the mainstream, could not contaminate the learning of normal children or lower the standards of a school.

Advocacy for segregated classes in the public schools, begun in the 1880s, surged after about 1910; the persuasive arguments of promoters were bolstered by a matrix of legal, social, educational, and even medical advances and mandates. Classes developed as part of what Barry Franklin (1989) calls "the first stirrings of Progressive educational reform" (p. 571). Reformers used curriculum differentiation as a "bureaucratic strategy to respond to an array of external demands and pressures facing turn-of-the-century urban, centralized school systems" (Franklin, 1989, p. 572). Plans for program differentiation that called for special classes also pointed to the need for vocational education and guidance programs, for kindergartens, and for junior high schools (Franklin, 1989). Franklin (1989) observes that historians of education have interpreted the push for curriculum differentiation in various ways. Some stress the practical need for numerous courses of study. Others stress the way school reformers embraced the tenets of efficiency-oriented American business (e.g., Callahan, 1962; E. A. King, 1969). Still others see the school reformers as the agents of business elites (e.g., Conroy and Levin, 1985; Hogan, 1985).

The most potent among the many spurs for the establishment of segregated classes within the public schools were the laws compelling children to attend school, first directed toward the nondisabled population and later toward exceptional children. These laws emerged with the new century and were enforced with increasing vigor. Before the advent of compulsory education laws, issues relating to the education of exceptional children were fought outside the school arena. But with compulsory attendance, the issues moved into the public schools. No longer could they ignore exceptional children; they were forced to accommodate a much broader range of youngsters, many incapable of functioning in regular classrooms.

Compulsory education laws were bolstered by new legislation governing child and female labor and mandating the creation of family and children's courts, and by the establishment of children's aid societies. A bureaucracy of court officers, social workers, public health nurses, psychologists, attendance officers, and others circled the educational core and ensured the attendance of larger numbers of children. In addition, state funding to support special classes increased as the federal commitment mounted.

Cities took the lead in establishing day classes; rural districts possessed neither the facilities nor the funding for instituting special classes. By 1911 more than one hundred large city school systems had established special schools and special classes for disabled children, and a number of states had begun to subsidize special programs by paying the excess costs special classes entailed. Increased financial support for special classes and schools after World War I ushered in a period of rapid growth in services for mildly handicapped students (G. O. Johnson, 1962). By the 1920s two-thirds of large cities in the United States and many in Canada had special classes to serve a range of students.

With the burgeoning special classes, the professional paradigm that guided special education shifted and expanded. Special educators developed a distinct mission and a clear perception of the means to carry it out; they also established the credentials that qualified a person to enter the profession. In doing so, they generated new beliefs about educators' status and power in relation to clients, to parents, to allied disciplines, and to the world at large. New visions of teacher training emerged, as did new and more encompassing professional associations.

THE CHANGING INSTITUTIONS

During the final three decades of the nineteenth century institutional superintendents began to move away from the belief that disabled students would best attain their industrial training and moral development in segregated institutions founded on philanthropic commitment. Once again, Samuel Gridley Howe was among the first to articulate the new sentiment. As early as 1857 Howe denigrated public charitable institutions, which, he said, "like all prisons and penal establishments, are evils; and are maintained only to avoid greater ones" (quoted by Kirk and Lord, 1974, p. 5). Howe rejected the notion that the institutions were entirely separate from the rest of education; rather, he saw special facilities for blind students as "a link in the chain of common schools" (Perkins Inst., 1859).

By the 1870s institutional superintendents began to stress the advisability of education rather than trade teaching or mere maintenance for disabled students. The main object of institutions for exceptional populations, they now contended, was not punishment or restraint, treatment or cure, but education and training. The social welfare designation for the institutions, associated as it was with prisons, asylums, and charities, was pernicious to the exceptional population: such categorization emphasized the differential status of disabled persons, who were then seen to be inferior in judgment, in ability, and in moral responsibility. Some superintendents, however, made distinctions among the types of institutions, believing that the charity designation was inappropriate for deaf and blind institutions but applicable to those for the mentally retarded.

On the whole, then, at the turn of the century special education reformers were coming to see that disabled individuals were neither dependent nor delinquent, but worthy of the same educational rights and privileges accorded to regular children. Discounting the myth of the intellectual inferiority of deaf and blind people, they asserted that every child has the right to an education. They argued vehemently that the special schools trained pupils in scholastic and industrial pursuits and were by no means charitable institutions or asylums, and they envisioned the special schools as part of the total educational complex.

But commonly held ideas about disabled persons, based on centuries of superstition and myth, could not be quickly washed away by the argument however cogent, that the system was pernicious to the disabled. The perception was too deeply rooted to be undone by exhortation. The changes the reformers sought could occur only in an atmosphere of altered perceptions of the value, the clientele, and the essential purposes of the special institutions. An important step was made toward the accomplishment of this goal when the names applied to the institutions and also to the groups they served were changed. New labels forged new images of exceptional people and their schools.

In the beginning, the institutions adopted bluntly explicit names for themselves; these in turn affected both the public and the professional perceptions of the nature of disability. Name changes accompanied the late nineteenth-century agitation for altered roles for the institutions. Many now condemned the term *asylum,* finding it "altogether out of place when applied to establishments designed solely for educational purposes" (E. M. Gallaudet, 1888, p. 3). Schools for blind students dropped the word *asylum* in the 1877. In 1890 the New York School for the Blind was transferred from the Department of Welfare to the Department of Education. In 1895 the American Asylum for the Education of Deaf and Dumb Persons was renamed the American School for the Deaf at Hartford (*AAD,* 1895). In 1896 the Supreme Court of New York ruled that institutions for deaf and blind students are chiefly educational and are not properly classified as charitable institutions (*AAD,* 1898). The year 1896 also saw the Clarke Institution for Deaf-Mutes request the state legislature for a name change to the Clarke School for the Deaf (Clarke, 1896). In 1905 the New Jersey Institution for Feeble-Minded Boys and Girls at Vineland dropped the term *institution* in favor of *training school.*

By the opening decades of the twentieth century facilities for deaf and blind students were officially viewed as schools. Redesignation was no longer a matter of debate, and school personnel were referring with pride to the fact that attendance seemed to increase after the schools were separated from the system of charitable institutions.

THE DEVELOPMENT OF DAY SCHOOLS

Even as the institutions moved into a new, forthrightly educational mode, the isolation of institutional education came under mounting attack. As early as 1863 John Barrett McGann in Upper Canada was advocating "the practicability of giving to all the deaf-mutes of the Province at least two years primary instruction in the Common Schools situate in their respective districts" (McGann, 1863, p. 5). Though McGann failed to secure official support for this controversial scheme, he still placed sixteen deaf students in public school classes between 1860 and 1868 (McGann, 1863, 1888). Like McGann, many late nineteenth-century school officials grew increasingly confident that one of the great improvements of the future would be "the practice of training and teaching of blind and of mute children in the common schools" (Perkins Inst., 1874, p. 120).

Deaf children were the first to be served in the new settings. Blind students followed, and advocacy for programs for mentally retarded pupils arrived later. As they so often did, Alexander Graham Bell and Samuel Gridley Howe beat a new path, this time in the direction of increased public school involvement in the education of deaf and blind students. Both Howe and Bell consistently opposed the congregation of large numbers of persons subject to a common disability (A. G. Bell, [1884] 1969; Perkins Inst., 1859). To be sure, their opposition to institutional settings rested more on their fears concerning the perpetuation of disabilities than on their hopes for the educational progress of pupils. Both promoted day schools and special classes so as to remove their clients from sole contact with others with similar disabilities and thereby prevent exclusive association and marriages among disabled persons. Even if day schools and special classes grouped disabled children together, the argument ran, the children would still have much contact with their normal peers and not be separated from their families and communities.

Howe in 1866, in an address at the opening of the state institution for blind students in Batavia, New York, advocated the integration of persons with disabilities. "As much as may be," he said, "surround insane and excitable people with sane people, and ordinary influences; vicious children with virtuous people and virtuous influences; blind children with those who see; mute children with those who speak; and the like" (quoted by Wolfensberger, 1975, p. 65). The public school provided the prime milieu for surrounding exceptional children with normal peers. Almost from the time that he entered the field of the education of blind persons, Howe promoted the idea that blind children could receive public school education (Perkins Inst., 1856). Again and again he suggested that "blind children can attend common schools advantageously, and be instructed in classes with common children" (Howe, 1874, p. 119).

Howe recommended the establishment of small day schools if integration into public school proved untenable. In 1857, when Howe was called upon "to give advice about the establishment of an Institution for the Blind and the Deaf Mute in a new State," he began by noting that "I have counselled a course, different from the one I, myself, followed many years ago." Howe's new course was "to dispense with any great costly building, having common dormitories, dining-rooms, chapel, and the like. To make no preparation for any great common household at all; but to build a simple building, with all the conveniences for instructing classes, and make provision for boarding the pupils in private families. In a word, to reduce the Institution, as we would any machine, to the simplest possible form.... I would advise modification of several of our public institutions; curtailment of operation in some cases, and total discontinuance of the establishment in others" (quoted by Kirk and Lord, 1974, p. 5).

Bell adopted a similar stance. When he addressed the National Education Association (NEA) in 1898, he pointed out that disabled children had the right to an education through the public schools (Abraham, 1976). A complex of rationales, both tacit and articulated, underlay Alexander Graham Bell's promotion of day classes and day schools. If his fear of the growth of the deaf population was one, another was his belief that institutions were the breeding ground of manualism, deaf communities, and a deaf culture. "The collection of defective children exclusively together," Bell wrote to Helen Keller, "is a thing to be avoided as much as possible. Exclusive association with one another only aggravates the peculiarities that differentiate them from other people, whereas, it is our object by instruction, to do away with these differences, to the greatest extent possible" (quoted by Blatt, 1985, p. 407).

To provide deaf children with a normal language environment, Bell suggested that "the instruction of deaf children should go hand in hand with the education of those who can hear and speak in the public schools" (OSD, 1884, p. 10). In an 1884 speech Bell recommended supplementing the current schools and institutions "by an exhaustive development of day schools" (A. G. Bell and Gillett, 1884, p. 3). Although Bell's speech focused on day classes for deaf children, he also stressed that "all that I have said in relation to the deaf would be equally advantageous to the blind and to the feeble-minded" (A. G. Bell quoted in National Education Association, 1898, pp. 1057–59).

Like Howe, Bell anticipated future conventions when he suggested: "A small room in a public school can be set apart for the use of the deaf children of the neighborhood, and the board of education should supply a teacher who has been specially trained in the methods of teaching the deaf. In this room the deaf children can receive all the benefits of special education without the disadvantages that arise from exclusive association with deaf-mutes.... There is no reason in the world why a deaf child might not join a class of hearing children when instruction is given in such studies as map-drawing, writing, drawing, etc." (A. G. Bell and Gillett, 1884, p. 16).

Day schools, which would compel students to live and interact in the hearing world, would simultaneously raise children's incentive to read and use speech, widen their range of personal contacts and later employment, and lessen the likelihood of their eventually intermarrying and thereby perpetuating hereditary deafness. Children would not be taken from their home life, and day school teachers could advise and encourage parents (R. Bruce, 1973).

The fact that almost half of American deaf children were not attending school, whether because the schools could not take them or because their parents would not send them, served to bolster Bell's contentions. He argued as well on audiological principles, stating that many pupils in schools for the deaf were actually hard of hearing because they could hear the bell that summoned them to classes (A. G. Bell, 1884c). Among the many arguments marshaled in favor of day classes by Bell, economic necessity stood front and center; he asserted that day classes in public schools would be "the most practical, most useful, and most economical kind of school" and quoted average institutional per capita costs of $233 as compared with $100 in day classes (A. G. Bell and Gillett, 1884, p. 3). The day schools would be state supported but, to allow for freedom of experimentation, controlled by local educational authorities. Although he hoped to obtain teachers with at least one year of experience in deaf education, Bell was aware that the greatest difficulty would be in obtaining qualified personnel for the work (A. G. Bell and Gillett, 1884).

Bell advanced the cause of day schools most conspicuously as a lobbyist for state support. With Philip Gillett of Gallaudet College, he helped draft bills for day schools in Wisconsin, Michigan, Illinois, Maine, Connecticut, and California. Although their efforts in California and Minnesota were unsuccessful ("Day Schools," 1899), Michigan passed a day school act in 1899; the legislatures of Wisconsin, Illinois, and Ohio also passed laws by which the number of day schools could be increased indefinitely (A teacher, 1902). Wisconsin created the largest day school system; by 1910 there were twenty such schools, and at about this time blind pupils were included in the program and a few day classes for the blind were established (Bush, 1942).

Reaction to day classes and day schools for deaf and blind pupils ranged from vehement opposition through resigned acceptance to hearty enthusiasm. One advocate declared, "Small classes and special teachers could well manage the dull, the excitable, the wrongly made children" (F. Warren, 1884, p. 7). At the other end of the spectrum was Warring Wilkinson, then superintendent of the California School for the Deaf and Blind and one of the most antagonistic opponents of day classes for deaf and blind children. Even before Bell began his campaign, Wilkinson protested at the meeting of the American Association of Instructors of the Blind in 1872 against a resolution that recommended that schools for the blind "should be conducted as nearly as possible according to the manner and methods of seeing schools" (Lowenfeld, 1956, p. 53). With the day class movement under way a decade later, Wilkinson decried the fact that Bell's appeal was so strong that any interest group "who will get Dr. Bell to come out and appear before the legislature . . . is going to have a day-school law, and it is going to be drawn just according to Dr. Bell's dictates" (Wilkinson, 1905, p. 82).

Many experienced teachers and deaf adults characterized the day school experiments as "cruel" and "barren of good results" (Wing, 1886, p. 22). A manual educator in 1891 chided that the results achieved by day schools were "not worth criticizing" (*AAD*, 1891, pp. 156–57), while another pointed out that the chances of success "are far less favorable than in boarding schools" ("Mr. Stainer's," 1884, p. 252). When the legislature of Illinois passed an act for day classes, deaf adults in that state opposed its passage on the grounds that the institution at Jacksonville offered greater advantages than did public school classes ("Classes," 1897). Critics drew support from European experiences, where organized efforts to have deaf children instructed in the regular school system were said to have led invariably to failure (see Wing, 1886). In fact, most European efforts had been abandoned by this time, and European deaf education was confined to "trained specialists in organized institutions" (OSD, 1895, p. 15).

Only peripherally did Bell and Howe advance similar calls for public school training for mentally retarded students. Nevertheless, many believed that retarded children could reap benefits from day school instruction. By 1912 special educator Margaret Bancroft in New Jersey was advocating special training in the public schools for those with sensory or motor defects and restorative training (remediation) in small schools for retarded children with underdeveloped faculties.

EARLY PUBLIC SCHOOL SPECIAL CLASSES

Bell's advocacy of day schools and day classes for deaf students ultimately crumbled in the face of a lack of trained teachers, the negative attitudes of regular classroom teachers, a paucity of materials, and the vehement opposition of established educators (see Nix, 1981). Nevertheless, the scattered day school laws and the classes they spawned provided at least a partial model for the public school classes that emerged.

The first day classes were those offered by the Horace Mann School for the Deaf, established in Boston in 1867. After that, a smattering of special classes to serve children displaying varied disabilities appeared within the public schools, although they existed without legislative sanction, and in most places state reimbursements were negligible. As a contemporary writer observed, these classes were "not the result of any theory." Rather, most resembled the class in New York City that "grew out of conditions in a neighborhood which furnished many and serious problems in truancy and discipline" (Farrell, quoted by Sarason and Doris, 1979, p. 290).

Apart from the classes for deaf children, public school segregated classes essentially grew from the need to serve intellectually backward and recalcitrant children. Some of the first to emerge were the ungraded classes that served children and youths returning from the work force, incorrigibles, truants, and low achievers; these classes functioned as coaching or remedial classes to give individual attention to students but to present the content of the regular curriculum (Tropea, 1987a). New Haven, Connecticut, opened an ungraded class for truant, dull, and insubordinate children in 1871. "The ungraded classes," noted the New Haven superintendent of schools, "are an indispensible appendage to our graded system. They provide for a class of children, who, for any cause, must necessarily be irregular in their attendance.... Unreasonably disobedient and insubordinate youths, who are a detriment to the good order and instruction of the school, are separated from it and placed here where they can be controlled and taught, without disturbing others. Truants, also, are placed in these schools for special discipline" (quoted by Hoffman, 1975, p. 17).

Most importantly, perhaps, ungraded classes removed recalcitrant children from the regular classroom and allowed teacher and other pupils to proceed undisturbed. The New Haven superintendent explained how "the grade schools, relieved of these classes, move on with greater ease and rapidity, while both pupils and teachers perform their duties with pleasure, satisfaction, and profit that would be impossible in the presence of disturbers of good order" (quoted by Hoffman, 1975, p. 17). Wholly segregated settings for the instruction of unruly

Table 10-1

Founding Dates of a Sampling of Early Segregated Day Classes

Year	City	Type of Clientele or Class
1867	Boston	Deaf children
1871	New Haven	Ungraded class
1874	New York	Truant and refractory boys
1876	Cleveland	Incorrigible children
1879	Cleveland	Feebleminded children
1883	Detroit	Ungraded class
1896	Providence	Crippled children
1898	Boston	Feebleminded children
1898	Detroit	Ungraded School No. 1
1899	Chicago	Orthopedic classes
1900	Chicago	Blind children
1906	Quebec City	Health-impaired children
1906	Cleveland	Epileptic children
1911	Jersey City	Speech therapy
1913	Roxbury, Massachusetts	Sight-saving classes
1913	Boston	Sight-saving classes
1913	Cleveland	Sight-saving classes
1920	Lynn, Massachusetts	Lipreading classes
1920	Rochester, New York	Lipreading classes

students eventually emerged. Special schools for the training and discipline of refractory and truant boys were established in New York in 1874; Cleveland founded a day school for incorrigible children in 1876 (Heck, 1940).

Further subdivision of special classes created classes designed for backward children and those, labeled as "steamer classes," to serve immigrant children who did not know English. A newly arrived child might be assigned to a steamer class but just as often might be sent to the backward classes, "not because the backward class is the right place for him but rather because it furnishes an easy means of disposing of a pupil who, through no fault of his own, is an unsatisfactory member of a regular class" (quoted by Hoffman, 1975, p. 419). A class began in Cleveland in 1879 for the training of the feebleminded and in Providence in 1896 for crippled children. Chicago in 1900 and Roxbury, Massachusetts, in 1913 opened classes for blind and partially sighted children. (See Table 10–1.)

Many of the special classes formed before 1900 failed because of the lack of trained teachers, materials, official commitment, and funding. Many classes that sought to raise the pupils' standards to those of regular class members failed in their efforts at remediation. Too, many schools systems operated only one type of special class, which was often used merely to manage children who did not conform to a school's behavioral standards (Rhodes and Sagor, 1975). Little distinction existed between obstreperous or recalcitrant pupils and defective learners. Only small numbers attended, a condition perpetuated by attrition, for many of these pupils were early school leavers. "Few of them," observed a school superintendent, "remained long enough in school to attract serious attention or to hinder the instruction of the more tractable and capable" (quoted by Sarason and Doris, 1979, p. 263). The public schools were quite content to see unruly pupils leave. A school administrator in Philadelphia in 1909 observed that "the pupil who failed to keep step with his fellows, or who, because of physical or moral defect seriously interfered with the regular work of a class, tend [*sic*] to drop out, or be forced out, of school and the problem of the exceptional child disappeared with him" (quoted by Tropea, 1987a, p. 31).

In summary, then, early public school special education became the setting for children the schools could not or would not educate and just as often served as the transmission belt to move disabled children and youth and those displaying behavioral problems beyond the schools. Principles regarding the provision of education for all pupils floundered in the face of the need for schools to maintain order, discipline, and high standards. This fundamental divergence of the best interests of special learners and of the schools would continue to plague special education for years to come.

New Impetus for the Rise of Modern Special Classes

After Horace Mann's reorganization of the common schools of Massachusetts in the 1850s, the development of the American public school system was rapid. The period from 1852 to 1918 established the public school as an integral component of the newly industrialized society; it would become the public institution most responsible for the socialization of the American child (Cremin, 1961). The public school was transformed from a relatively minor social institution catering largely to the middle class to one that not only was available to all levels of society but that was legally empowered to compel all children to attend. Between 1852 and 1918 all the states passed compulsory school attendance laws. Massachusetts was first, and Mississippi, with a population that was more than 50 percent black, was last (Cremin, 1961). However, in the states that passed compulsory education laws before 1900, enforcement tended to be scattered and sporadic. Before the turn of the century, such legislation served more to symbolize the notion that all children should attend school and that parents had a responsibility to send them than to force actual practice.

During this same period American secondary education underwent a drastic reorganization, moving from the predominantly classical, elitist, semiprivate academy to the mass public high schools. In 1870 there were only about 80,000 students in all of the secondary schools in the United States, a figure that included only 2 percent of all seventeen-year-olds. In 1900, 8.5 percent of eligible students attended high school, and these students were almost entirely from the upper and middle classes (Boyer, 1983). By 1910, however, there were more than 1 million students, of whom 15 percent were seventeen-year-olds.

It is generally accepted that economic reasons dictated the pace of the transition to free, compulsory education for nondisabled students (Sigman, 1982). School in the nineteenth century was only part of a child's life, not the core, and many economic and social reasons militated against a family's and a community's compliance with compulsory education laws. With regard to special education, bringing families and schools into compliance with legislative mandates occurred very slowly (T. A. Turner, 1944). Although the logical corollary of free schooling was compulsory attendance, only a few states by the opening of the twentieth century had enacted laws compelling parents to send their exceptional children to school. "The more favored brother and sister, by the strong arm of the law are moved from careless indifferent supervision," cried one reformer in 1903, referring to the compulsory attendance laws affecting nondisabled youngsters, "while the less favored having no legal rights are compelled to remain where no authority can reach, no law protect" ("Compulsory Education," 1903, p. 181).

Many European jurisdictions provided both free and compulsory education for exceptional students. Denmark, for example, mandated compulsory education for children with sensory impairments in 1817 (Hansen, 1916). France passed legislation in 1882 enforcing primary instruction for disabled children (Belanger, 1907), and the British Elementary Education Act (Deaf and Blind Children) of 1893 placed the financial responsibility for compulsory education on departments of education. In North America, Manitoba and Nova Scotia both mandated free and compulsory education for deaf and blind children in the 1880s (Winzer, 1981a).

If the European prompts were the carrot, then the enforcement of the emerging compulsory education laws to nondisabled children was the stick. Yet, when it came to the education of disabled youngsters, school promoters had to contend with public indifference, parental apathy, and an ingrained belief in the moral and biological inferiority of disabled persons. In many places a disability was looked upon as a type of illness and deemed sufficient reason for nonenrollment in school. Parental irresponsibility and ignorance, especially among "the very lowest class," only made the problem worse. Many parents were "utterly incapable of estimating the value of education for their children" or were "utterly destitute of the firmness or the self denial of insisting on their regular attendance at school" (Machar, 1881, p. 327).

By about 1910 social pressures had created both a growing awareness that school attendance should be the norm for all children and a reconceptualization of disabling conditions. Handicaps were less likely to be seen as illness, more likely as disability. As this happened, states began to implement the compulsory attendance laws. Compulsory schooling for deaf and blind children was mandated in Washington, North Dakota, Utah, Ohio, Indiana, and North Carolina in 1909 (Pybas, 1909). Other states followed suit, albeit tardily: as late as 1930 nine states still had no compulsory education laws for blind students (Koestler, 1976), and for mentally retarded children no special laws or definite school regulations come into being until later (Haines, 1925; League for Preventative Work, 1916–17). Nor did free and compulsory education mean that all severely disabled children attended school; even by 1940 the United States census showed 5 million children still not in school.

By 1930 sixteen states had passed legislation authorizing special education. Of these, ten also set forth legal requirements for teacher certification, which in most instances was limited to an elementary degree plus supplemental training (see H. Best, 1930; Haines, 1925; Scheier, 1931).

Table 10-2

Early Special Education Legislation: A Sampling

State	Year	Legislation
Michigan	1900	Establishment of day classes for disabled students
Wisconsin	1900	Establishment of day classes for disabled students
Massachusetts	1911	Mandatory education for mentally retarded children
New Jersey	1911	Compulsory attendance laws for deaf, blind, retarded children
Minnesota	1915	Permissive legislation*
New York	1917	Mandatory education for mentally retarded children
Illinois	1917	Permissive legislation*
Iowa	1919	Statewide care for disabled children
Wyoming	1919	Permissive legislation*
Missouri	1919	Permissive legislation*
Massachusetts	1920	Mandatory education for mentally retarded children
Connecticut	1921	Permissive legislation*
Washington	1921	Permissive legislation*
Louisiana	1921	State aid for special education
Ohio	1921	State aid for special education
Oregon	1923	Permissive legislation*
Maryland	1930	State aid for special education

*Permissive legislation meant that local school boards might but were not required to provide special education.

Compulsory school laws meant that public schools were now required to handle all children who entered their doors. By bringing in a great number of children with varied abilities and diverse learning problems, the laws alone might have stimulated the development of special classes, but other social developments also spurred their growth. Special classes were part of the larger movement for curriculum differentation associated with Progressive educational reform. A new urgency became attached to the cause of special education, and not only because the institutions and the disabilities were reconceptualized; there also developed a greater awareness of the problems that could hinder learning and more confident educational and medical diagnosis. At the same time, the schools were confronted by the mounting numbers of immigrant children, who for many reasons were often seen as prime candidates for special settings.

Compulsory attendance laws were enforced by a body of professionals gradually added to the schools and the courts. These laws were bolstered by the proliferating legislation directed toward children and their families. Beginning in about the 1880s laws dealing with women, children, their labor, and the family led inevitably to the formalization of services and a routinization of procedures for bestowing of benefits.

In the first ungraded and unruly classes, the negative consequences of segregation and lowered standards were offset by the moderate level of their use and especially by the early exit of the pupils, who typically left school to go to work (Tropea, 1987b). However, in the new century the market's need for common labor decreased and its need for a more skilled and disciplined work force grew. Moreover, increasingly stringent labor laws governing the age of youngsters in the work force were enacted; under these laws and compulsory school attendance laws, under-age children were required to obtain work permits, and officialdom gained unprecedented control over young peoples' school and work lives. As a consequence, child labor decreased dramatically between 1900 and 1930, and the balance between the time spent at work and time at school shifted. Work had been the vocation of most mid-nineteenth-century youth; school became their vocation in the early twentieth century. No longer could jurisdictions abrogate their responsibilities by sending recalcitrant and unruly older students into the work force. Students stayed in schools later, and the schools were forced to accommodate them for longer periods (see Tropea, 1987a).

At the same time, the schools experienced an influx of immigrant children. In 1909, when the U.S. Immigration Commission conducted a massive survey, 57.8 percent of children in the public schools of the thirty-seven largest American cities were found to be of foreign-born parentage (Cremin, 1961). The presence of large numbers of immigrant children lacking the competencies to succeed in regular classrooms provided yet another catalyst for the formation of segregated classes. Immigrant children were perceived as posing a serious threat to the stability of school systems. One observer argued that "these southern and eastern Europeans are of a very different type from the northern Europeans who preceded them." Not only were they "illiterate, docile, lacking in self-reliance and initiative," but they also felt little allegiance to the "Anglo-Teutonic" ideas of law, order, and government (Cubberly, 1909, pp. 15–16). Lewis Madison Terman announced that, contrary to some "of the fuzzy theories of the progressives, educational reform may as well abandon, once and for all, all efforts to bring all children up to grade" (Terman, 1919, p. 73). Believing that there were genetically determined differences in intelligence across races and that mental subnormality was more common in Spanish, Indian, and black populations, Terman advocated the segregation of these children in special classes (Terman, 1916).

To compound the problems associated with an increased and more diverse clientele, child mortality and child morbidity decreased, and the schools were consequently faced with increasing numbers of students who had survived serious illness but at the cost of emerging with mild learning disabilities. The new century ushered in a developing concern over child health care that paralleled the child study movement and was supported by new psychological and medical findings, as well as significant advances in public health. Professionals, parents, and the public became more alert to the educational implications of physical handicaps. Professional writings on the effects of defects in sight, hearing, and mental acuity on learning began to motivate inquiry about and observation of pupils for possible physical and intellectual handicaps.

It came to be understood that minor handicaps to learning arose from a host of conditions, many stemming from poor living conditions and malnutrition. Paraprofessionals from the public health field, such as public health nurses, began to move into the schools after World War I to identify masses of children who were undernourished, tubercular, or suffering minor physical disorders that hindered learning. An examination of 13,000 children in 279 Ontario schools in 1918, for example, discovered 19 percent with defective eyesight, 35 percent with diseased tonsils, 10 percent with defective hearing, and 65 percent with defective teeth (MacMurchy, 1919).

THE SCHOOLS' RESPONSE

So long as they lacked compulsory school attendance laws, or hearty enforcement of the laws on the books, school districts could ignore exceptional children or simply direct them to the institutions. But once these laws were promulgated and enforced, the exclusionary practices in the public schools were challenged, not so much with regard to children with severe conditions, but to those with milder disabilities—the unruly, the recalcitrant, the incorrigible, the feebleminded, and the backward. Rigorous enforcement of attendance laws forced the schools to face some unforeseen problems related to issues of order, discipline, standards, accessibility, and logistics. Administrators lauded the ideal of equal access and universal education, but the numbers of children who functioned below the norm added to the pressures created by already overcrowded schools and large classes.

The large numbers of children knocking on their doors indeed posed logistical as well as philosophical problems for schools. For one thing, the expansion threatened to overwhelm the schools in some cities. As class sizes jumped, lack of space, lack of desks, and lack of trained teachers became an obvious focus of concern. From the beginnings of Atlanta's school system in 1872, for example, there were never enough classrooms for all the children who wanted to attend, and double sessions and class sizes of sixty students were a common feature for years in urban Atlanta schools (Franklin, 1989).

Not only were the schools compelled to maintain increasing numbers of children, but they had to find the most efficient means to provide for those children who could not be handled in regular classes. Educators in most communities realized that no special provisions were available for these youngsters. Further, legislation put teachers' classroom authority and bureaucratic organization in an increasingly uneasy relationship; administrators had to mediate between legal mandates, on the one hand, and the expectations of teachers, on the other (Tropea, 1987a).

Solutions had to be found that met the perceived needs of exceptional children, the school's desire for order, and the ideal of accessibility embodied in a public system—and they had to be devised within the school system. So, inauspicious as their beginnings may have been, special segregated classes within the public schools received renewed attention, as ability grouping became part of a broad series of reforms to make the schools more flexible and productive. Special classes provided the alternative that satisfied the law, the administrative quest for order, and the educational goal of high standards (Tropea, 1987b).

Exponents of segregated day classes, not the first to visualize the benefits of public school placement for exceptional pupils, built their persuasive arguments on the base of existing sentiment and experience. In 1899 the Educational Commission of the City of Chicago was authorized by the mayor and city council to conduct an in-depth study of the faltering Chicago school system. The report, which provided a model for many urban school systems in the United States, urged the establishment of "ungraded" classes and "parental" schools for children who could not be accommodated in the regular classes (Hoffman, 1975).

As leading educators articulated in practical terms the philosophical and pedagogical bases for the establishment of special segregated classes in the public schools, they argued that special education was a logical extension of regular education and demanded the extension of educational opportunities to exceptional students. They viewed the disabled population as a pool of potentially productive citizens whose problems most often stemmed from neglect, mistreatment, inadequate economic support, and inappropriate schooling. They saw special schooling as the only way to turn disabled dependents into productive, independent adults. Even though disabled children were unlikely to attain the academic standards of their normal peers, they could at least become contributing members of the community. E. R. Johnstone, superintendent of the New Jersey Training School at Vineland, captured the prevailing sentiment when he said in 1912: "I believe that the time has come for the commonwealth to recognize that every child is entitled to such education as is best suited to his needs. This means that special classes of various kinds must be established under the school authorities. The blind, the deaf, the cripples, the incorrigibles must some day take their place in the life of the commonwealth with normal people. Therefore they at least must have training in the public schools to keep them from becoming institutionalized and thus losing touch with normal community life" (Vineland, 1912, p. 22).

J. E. Wallace Wallin, a psychologist and leading spokesman for special education, wrote that it was time to acknowledge that many disabled children needed community-based facilities rather than institutional isolation (Wallin, 1924). Johnstone (Vineland, 1912) held only that those who lived in communities too small to support the formation of special classes should go to institutions. To Wallin, only those unable to care for themselves or who threatened society should be placed in custodial settings (Wallin, 1924).

Special children already in regular classrooms were also at issue. In the early 1900s approximately 20 percent of all students in U.S. public schools failed and were retained each year. More than half dropped out before completing elementary school; less than 10 percent graduated from high school (Doyle, 1989). The cost of these failing children within the schools, in terms of finances, teacher time, and classroom disruption, was a constant irritant. Reducing such failure rates became an important political and bureaucratic, if not pedagogical, indicator of efficiency (Tropea, 1987a).

When Leonard P. Ayres wrote one of the earliest books on special education, *Laggards in Our Schools* (1909), he provided the first account of the discrepancy between the goals of the public schools and the underachievement of many students. Ayres reported that 33.7 percent of all elementary school children demonstrated an age-to-grade retardation, thus creating a phenomenal financial burden on the schools as they repeated classes (Ayres, 1909). Ayres suggested that these children needed "a different kind of teaching and a different sort of treatment from the other children, and their presence renders the teacher's work harder and its results poorer" (L. Ayres, 1915, p. 40).

The concept of the standard grade was first introduced in Massachusetts in 1847 in response to the organizational needs of the evolving school system. Children of the same ages were expected to master the same curriculum in the same time. As Kozens (1990) says, the standard grade theory implied an eleventh commandment: Thou shalt progress at the same time as thy neighbor. Wallin discounted as myth the idea that all children should fit within a standard grade and that schools should assign children to the same grade level on the basis their ages. He pointed out that students with learning problems were "almost always irritated, disheartened, depressed or embittered by the progress and not infrequently jibes and ridicule of the normal pupils." They often exerted "an injurious influence upon the normal children" because "of their indolence, eccentricities, abnormalities, and not infrequent vicious, depraved or immoral practices." Even the "good natured ones," continued Wallin, became "the dupes and 'cat's paws' of their wiser but designing fellows." Others soon lapsed "into indifference" or became "chronic rebels" (Wallin, 1914, p. 390).

Wallin called for abandonment of the inflexible curricula that proved the undoing of children who did not conform to the common notion of normal. Instead, schools could include remedial, corrective, or differential instruction designed to meet the varying needs of all types of talents and all types of educational abnormality or deviation (Wallin, 1914, p. 382). He suggested these settings be called "special classes," although he preferred the terms "orthogenic" or "orthophrenic" for children clearly disabled—those at least two or three years over age for their grade levels, "the imbeciles, morons, and seriously backward" (Wallin, 1914).

Quick to recognize the difficulties inherent in segregated classes, Wallin, with amazing foresight, anticipated many of the arguments that would later be forwarded in defense of mainstreaming. He observed that grouping many abnormal children together threw their idiosyncracies and their abnormalities into conspicious relief; it made them feel they were a group apart and inferior or different; parents objected to the stigma of special class placement; students had no occasion to mingle with normal children and were robbed of the opportunities to learn imitatively by association with their normal fellows; and many had to travel long distances to special classes. However, he said, advantages outweighed these obvious drawbacks: segregated classrooms allowed closer grading of pupils and were altogether more economical and efficient (Wallin, 1914, p. 391).

Others observed that the deficient pupils themselves began to respond to the special class as they had never responded before, under the influence of individual attention and guidance, differential training adapted to individual needs, and the personal touch of a sympathetic, understanding, and properly trained teacher. When the first class for mentally retarded children opened in Atlanta in 1915, the school principal reported to the school board after one month of operation that the class instilled self-respect in "backward children," helped those with improvable retardation return to the regular classroom, and prepared the "worst cases" to be self-reliant (quoted by Franklin, 1989, p. 576).

Moreover, because in regular classrooms exceptional pupils "absorbed the energies and productive powers of other students," segregation in special classes was vital to allow the unhampered progress of normal children (Pratt, 1920). "Great relief" was afforded to the normal pupils and the regular grade teachers by the removal of the "flotsam and the jetsam," the "hold backs and the drags" (Wallin, 1914, p. 390), the "unassimilable accumulation of clinkers, ballast, driftwood, or derelicts" (Wallin, 1924, p. 94) who retarded the progress of the class and created discipline problems (Wallin, 1914).

The use of IQ tests was crucial to the advance of special segregated classes. Advocates of the mental hygiene movement in the schools were convinced, after their work of testing and classifying students, of the necessity for more special classes together with the early identification of problems. "The widespread employment of these tests," noted Wallin, "has indubitably done more than anything else to promote the organization of special classes and the introduction of differentiated courses of instruction in the public schools" (Wallin, 1914, p. 46). Lewis Terman explained that, in the "diagnosis and classification" of special class students, "our main reliance must always be on mental tests, properly used and properly interpreted." "Without scientific diagnosis and classification of these (feeble-minded, physically defective, backward, truants, incorrigibles ...) children," said Terman in 1916, "the educational work of the special class must blunder along in the dark" (Terman, 1916, p. 5). In the same year a clinical criterion was adopted for assigning children to classes for the retarded; in many states an IQ score became part of the legal basis for this assignment (Achenbach, 1975).

So successful was the movement for segregated classes that by 1925 workers were calling for the training of all exceptional children in the public schools, including the "psychopathic," the "psychoneurotic," and those who exhibited behavior problems. But little in special education gains universal acceptance. Even if special classes seemed logical extensions of the organizational, curricular, and pedagogical reforms of Progressive education, drawing exceptional students into the orbit of the public schools was novel. This reform encountered militant opposition that reflected the conflict between the humanitarian aims of accommodating all children in the schools, the legal mandates of compulsion, and concerns about the effects of deviant individuals in society.

During the height of public alarm over the "menace" of the feebleminded, many eugenicists advocated complete institutionalization and argued against the placement of disabled children, especially the mentally retarded, in the public schools. "Give them an asylum, with good and kind treatment," cried Governor Benjamin Franklin Butler of Massachusetts, "but not a school" (quoted by Wolfensberger, 1975, p. 28). Others promoted public school classes for children with mild handicapping conditions, institutional placement for more severe disabilities. E. R. Johnstone, appealing for public school placement for a diverse range of handicapped children, still noted that "with the mentally deficient, we have a slightly different problem" (Vineland, 1912, p. 22). Nevertheless, one of the arguments in favor of special classes still emanated from some of those advancing eugenic solutions to societal problems. The ultimate solution of institutionalization and sterilization of the huge mass of the mentally retarded was simply unfeasible in financial and human terms, but it was thought that the maintenance of feebleminded children and youth in school would at least stem some incipient truancy and delinquency.

It would be unwise to assume that schools always willingly opened their classrooms and their programs to disruptive, recalcitrant, and low-functioning pupils. In fact, the process was beset by hindrances: some districts refused to comply with the law; others hid behind work permits that encouraged underage children to enter the work force and abandon school. Legislation to reimburse school boards for the annual excess costs for educating some exceptional groups was a necessary stimulus for the establishment of special classes (T. A. Turner, 1944). To force compliance with the mandates of compulsory education laws, some states even had to threaten school districts with the loss of state funds if they did not enforce the law (Tropea, 1987a).

All balked at accepting seriously handicapped youngsters. The public schools made it clear that they did not want untrainables, and institutional placement remained a precarious compromise. Seriously handicapped children were not compelled to attend, or their parents could not afford the fee, or the institutions would not accommodate some of them. Institutions saw these children as further drains upon staff time and energies and as largely noncontributing to the maintenance of an institution.

THE GROWTH OF SPECIAL CLASSES

From 1910 to 1930 there was a huge spurt both in enrollment in the public schools and in the number and type of special classes that were formed. Boston, which established its first class for mentally retarded children in 1898, was encouraged to further the movement after the superintendent of schools observed in his annual report that "experience and observation of the matter thus far suggest that it will be desirable to multiply these special classes until there shall be one in each division of the City, say 9 or 10 in all" (quoted by Coveney, 1942, p. 57). His prediction was correct; his numbers, wrong. Boston, with 9 special classes in 1912, boasted 132 by 1930, 141 by 1941, as well as special classes for intellectually handicapped children within the public schools, the Disciplinary Day School for truant and emotionally disturbed children (*Report*, 1930), the Industrial School for Crippled and Deformed Children, and the Horace Mann School for the Deaf.

In Canada the first day classes opened to meet the special needs of health-disordered children. Quebec led the way with hospital classes for crippled and for epileptic children. The classes rapidly expanded. Toronto's 3 classes in 1910 were expanded to 240 by 1930 (e.g., Pennachio, 1986).

The categories of children served increased. In the schools children were tested, labeled, and slotted into ungraded, auxiliary, opportunity, open-air, steamer, welfare, and other types of classes. Special settings and teachers came into being to serve children variously labeled as deaf, blind, hard of hearing, near blind, undernourished, crippled, academically maladjusted, mentally retarded, gifted, speech defective, tubercular, and so on (Palen 1923). The most heavily funded programs in both the United States and Canada were in mental retardation, followed by speech and hearing disorders.

With its early commitment to day schools for deaf children, it is not surprising that in 1904 Wisconsin, in accord with a legislative enactment, appointed a state supervisor for the deaf, the first such appointment in the United States (Bush, 1942). Yet despite Bell's advocacy and an early proliferation of day classes, residential schools remained the most stable educational setting for deaf children. Public schools saw the establishment of special classes for hard-of-hearing youngsters.

Accurate audiometric assessment of hearing impairment was not available until the 1920s. However, screening for visual impairment was possible at an earlier date; screening programs for the blind began in 1899 when Connecticut used the Snellen chart as a test of visual functioning. Accurate screening and the relative ease with which blind and visually impaired children could be accommodated in the public schools contributed to the early establishment of special classes for these students. Even in 1910, 4.5 percent of blind children were in public school programs; by 1948 about 10 percent of blind children attended public schools. In 1913 visually impaired students were beginning to be cooperatively taught by specialists and regular classroom teachers (Abraham, 1976).

Credit for establishing day classes for visually impaired students goes to Frank Haven Hall and John B. Curtis, blind himself, both in Chicago. Frank Haven Hall (1843–1911) convinced school authorities in Chicago, then considering the establishment of a boarding school for the blind, that in order to provide a combination of special teaching and participation in regular classrooms, the school system should establish day classes instead. As a result, the first public school day class for blind students in the United States was established in Chicago in 1900, with one of Hall's teachers as supervisors (Irvine, 1976b, p. 120). John Curtis also pioneered day classes for the blind; the first Braille class opened in Chicago in 1900.

Additional day classes for visually impaired students opened in Cincinnati (1905), Milwaukee (1907), Boise (1909), Cleveland (1909), and New York (1909). Boston's day classes for blind students, established in 1909, were promoted by Edgar Allen who, as principal of the Perkins School for the Blind, used institutional funds to buy needed supplies for five blind day students (Koestler, 1976). As well as classes for children accepted as blind, sight-saving classes for those with less severe visual impairments came into the schools. By 1925 there existed 260 sight-saving classes in the United States; by 1935, 476 (Bush, 1942).

Classes for stammerers and other children with speech defects began in Detroit in 1912; by 1925 there were programs for children with speech defects, lisping, stammering, and stuttering. By the 1920s educational programs for crippled children were organized in the form of decentralized hospital-based facilities, diagnostic centers, and local clinics (Cruickshank, 1967). By 1944 twenty-one states had enacted legislation in aid of crippled children (T. A. Turner, 1944).

From the time of the formation of the first class specifically for the mentally retarded in 1879, special classes for children with intellectual impairments flourished rapidly. Increased financial support for special classes and schools after World War I ushered in a period of growth in services for the educable mentally retarded: there were 75 classes by 1919; by 1941 there were 141 classes with an enrollment of more than 22,000 (G. O. Johnson, 1962).

Cities took the lead in establishing segregated classes. To offset difficulties in rural areas and to educate children who could not attend school because of health difficulties, the visiting teacher movement began, first in Boston and Hartford in 1906 as a private organization. Home instruction in New York City was originated in 1913 by Adela Smith and 125 volunteer teachers. After a polio epidemic of 1916–1917, the increasing numbers of crippled children prompted the Board of Superintendents to recommend that home training be part of organized schooling for homebound crippled children. Rochester, New York, was the first district to join visiting teachers to its school board (F. E. Howard, 1935). By 1935 there were visiting teachers for emotionally disturbed and juvenile delinquent children (F. E. Howard, 1935), as well as those with severe physical and health handicaps.

THE SPECIAL CLASS CURRICULUM

The word *curriculum* derives from the Latin *currere*, which refers to a course, a track for a race. The implication, of course, is that students run through a course of study from a beginning point until they reach some designated finishing post. Special students, slower in negotiating the track, could, in a special class, be provided with a curriculum suited specifically to their needs. Their results could then be reported separately so that their poor academic levels and lowered promotional standards would not drag down the performance reputation of a school.

Nowhere were the links between residential schools and day classes stronger than in the early curricula presented in segregated classes. The expansion of special classes far exceeded the supply of trained teachers, and the school boards inevitably turned to the institutions to fill their staffing needs (see Fitts, 1916). The Boston school system, for example, during the first years of its operation sought teachers with some experience at the Barre Institution in Massachusetts or at Seguin's schools.

Institutionally oriented workers moved into public school service, and the training activities that dominated residential school programs, with their strong emphasis on "doing" and crafts and manual pursuits, were transplanted with them. A 1928 report of the Atlanta special classes noted that teachers provided activities that were concrete and practical, that students could enjoy, and at which they could succeed (Franklin, 1989). Special classes, most especially those that served mentally retarded pupils, found children engaged in making rugs, scrubbing brushes, raffia baskets, and Swiss lace (Stevens, 1954). In Atlanta younger children were given "daily lessons in all elementary book work subjects." By junior high school, students spent two periods daily on units that integrated social studies, English, and spelling and that were used to solve such concrete problems as obtaining shelter, saving money, transportation, and employment (Franklin, 1989). They spent another period each on mathematics, practical science, handicrafts, shop, home economics, and physical education or music (Franklin, 1989).

Social training became a hidden part of the special curriculum. The superintendent of the Pennsylvania Department of Public Education included among his list of "school values" "habits of industry, obedience, politeness, punctuality, regularity, silence, self-restraint." A colleague, the superintendent of Indianapolis schools, was also convinced that since the parent had "transferred his powers and duties to the teacher," the school should "nourish the germs of character and starve the tendencies to evil" (quoted by Issel, 1979, p. 573).

For mentally retarded children education formed only one of the essential elements of day classes. By instituting special classes within the public schools, educators could "ensure diagnosis and treatment at an early age" and use the classes admirably as "clearing houses for personnel segregation before adult life is reached" (W. E. Fernald, 1912b, p. 9). Diagnosis, identification, and data for future placement were important, and classes sometimes served as clearinghouses to eliminate low-grade children from the schools or as a conveyor belt to hasten their exit to more restrictive environments.

TEACHER TRAINING

The increasing numbers and more diverse categories of special children in the schools and institutions meant greater emphases on teacher education. As reform efforts gathered momentum, a new professionalism emerged. No longer would the poorly trained teacher do or the apprenticeship model serve; consistent and comprehensive teacher training was clearly mandatory.

By the close of the nineteenth century three models of teacher training were in place—the apprenticeship or internship model established by Thomas Hop-

kins Gallaudet, the normal school plus in-house training model, and a new departure that saw universities and colleges establish programs and courses
directed toward special education.

Apprenticeship programs were the first offered, modeled on the training devised by Gallaudet and Howe at the beginning of the nineteenth century. Training for teachers of the mentally retarded followed, somewhat tardily but in a
similar vein. At the New Jersey Training School at Vineland, for example, teacher
training was initially established on an internship basis. The later established
formal program became the prototype for professional training programs that
were introduced into other institutions in the following decades. In 1902 Vineland announced the first formal six-week summer seminar training program for
public school teachers (Vineland, 1914) and in 1904 first offered summer training
sessions for American and Canadian teachers of mentally retarded individuals
(H. F. Hill, 1945). By 1924, for example, there were five auxiliary classes in Halifax, run by teachers trained in summer courses at Harvard and Vineland.

College-based training for teachers of deaf students began in 1864 and for
those teaching blind students in 1884. By the final decades of the nineteenth
century normal schools, colleges, and universities all began to recognize the
mentally retarded student. Beginning in 1897 the University of Pennsylvania
offered a three-course sequence on mental retardation (Wallin, 1914). By 1929
thirty-seven teachers' colleges and eight normal schools in twenty-two states
and an additional fifty-four colleges and universities in thirty-eight states and
Washington, D.C., offered one to twelve courses for the preparation of teachers
and supervisors of mentally retarded pupils (Scheier, 1931). Special education departments opened in twelve institutions, three teachers' colleges, three
normal schools, and six universities and colleges (Scheier, 1931). The programs generally included curriculum and methods, practicum, and industrial,
manual, and domestic training. In addition, eighteen institutions offered courses
on physical handicaps, including ten on speech defects, four on sight saving,
three on the hearing impaired, two on crippled persons, and two on blind students (Scheier, 1931; see Burke, 1976; F. P. Connor, 1976; Lord and Kirk, 1950;
Tenny, 1954).

By 1930 sixteen states has passed legislation authorizing special education.
Of these, ten also set forth legal requirements for teacher certification, which, in
most instances, was limited to an elementary degree plus supplemental training
(Scheier, 1931). At the same time, many school supervisors were calling for a full
four-year degree program, the first two years devoted to elementary education
and the last two to special education. The 1930s saw forty-five teachers' colleges
and normal schools in twenty-two states as well as fifty-four colleges and universities in thirty states and the District of Columbia at least offering an introductory course on the exceptional child (Scheerenberger, 1983).

PROFESSIONAL ASSOCIATIONS

The term *special education* probably dates no earlier than 1884, apparently
arising from initiatives taken at a meeting of the NEA in Madison, Wisconsin, in

that year (National Education Association, 1898). Alexander Graham Bell mentioned the idea of special education; his was probably the first popular use of the term.

With the assistance of Joseph Gordon of Gallaudet College, Bell attempted to form a special education group. Gordon pointed out that although the new "special education" group was "primarily intended for educators of the deaf, it soon came to include the educators of the blind, and afterwards it took in those who are interested in the education of backward and feeble-minded children" (National Education Association, 1898, pp. 1031–33). However, the attempt to organize into a multidisciplinary organization failed because there were not twenty qualified NEA members petitioning for the department (Geer, 1977).

In 1897 Gordon and Bell again petitioned the NEA and were accepted for an organization named the Department of the Deaf, Blind, and the Feebleminded, although Bell wanted it named the Department for the Education of Classes Requiring Special Methods of Instruction. The new department held its first meeting in 1898; speakers included Bell, Gallaudet, Gordon, and Margaret Bancroft (see "The NEA meeting," 1899). Gordon was the first president, followed by Bell as the second. Through the years the name changed to the Department of Special Education. It existed until 1918 when, without a trace, it disappeared.

An association that could comfortably encompass all special education personnel but still allow very specialized groups their autonomy was epitomized by the International Council for the Education of Exceptional Children, established in 1922. Essentially the council evolved from two college courses, one on methods and one on organization of special classes, taught by Elizabeth Farrell (1870–1932), a supervisor of ungraded classes in New York City, at Columbia Teachers College. Henrietta Johnson of California sparked the notion and invited eleven of the special education summer students to a dinner meeting in the Women's City Club Building in New York City on August 10, 1922, to discuss the possibilities of organizing a national association for persons interested in the care and treatment of exceptional children (Warner, 1942, 1944). Warner (1942) noted that there was some reluctance to hold the initial meeting at the Women's Club in case the new organization should be seen as solely for women. Because the original participants came from both the United States and overseas, they called it the International Council for the Education of Exceptional Children.

Elizabeth Farrell was unanimously elected the first president for four years. At the first annual meeting in February, 1923, she addressed the needs of the embryonic organization and all the children it would serve. She was specific, including "the gifted, dull and defective, deaf, blind, feeble-minded, tubercular, undernourished, cardiac, idiot, dull normal and anti-social" (Abraham, 1976, p. 331). Early objectives of the council were to emphasize the education of special children rather than their identification and classification, to establish professional standards for teachers in the field of special education, and to unite those interested in the problems of the special child (A. S. Hill, 1951b; Warner, 1944). Farrell hoped that the council would be a clearinghouse of knowledge useful to teachers in their special fields, promote the ideas of special education and professional training, and sponsor conventions and journals (Geer, 1977).

During the first year a constitution was drawn up and by-laws were put into action by 1924. The movement spread rapidly. In 1923, when the organization held its first convention in Cleveland, fifty people attended, and the secretary reported a membership of 389 (Geer, 1977). By 1944 there were 4,134 members; by 1950, 6,500 members; by 1977 membership had expanded to 67,000 (Geer, 1977).

At Minneapolis in 1933 the word *education* was dropped, and the name was changed to the International Council for Exceptional Children, to reflect the notion that the problems of exceptional children more than simply educational. In 1958 *international* was dropped as being nonessential. In 1942 the council became a department of the NEA (Lord, 1976).

At the outset the group did not have an official publication, although in *Ungraded* Farrell offered a forum for members of the council to publish. The *Council News Letter* followed in 1923, superseded at the Toronto meeting in 1934 when the *Council Review* was launched as the official publication, with Harley Z. Wooden as first editor. The journal became the *Exceptional Children* one year later; it was at first privately owned but later bought by the council in 1942.

By the end of the 1920s the principle of segregating exceptional students in special classes in the same schools that normal children attended was well established, and special curricula designed to meet the needs of children in a growing number of different categories of exceptionality were being developed. Special education itself was becoming a distinct subspecialty of professional education, a fact reflected in the courses offered in collegiate education programs and in the journals and books devoted to the subject. As the system itself matured, so too did the enquiry into the nature and causes of exceptionality.

Chapter 11

New Categories, New Labels

Important Dates in the Rise of Modern Views of Exceptionality

1838	Jean Étienne Dominique Esquirol reports on insanity in children
1868	Henry Maudsley writes *Physiology and Pathology*
1869	Sir Francis Galton publishes *Hereditary Genius*
1891	Cesare Lombroso publishes *The Man of Genius*
1893	Children's Aid societies are established in Canada
1896	The psychological clinic opens at the University of Pennsylvania
1898	The first public school department of child study opens in Chicago
1899	Juvenile courts are established in Chicago and Denver
1905	Dr. Sante de Sanctus identifies dementia praecoxissima
1906	Eugen Blueler identifies autistic behaviors
1908	The first child guidance bureau in a public school opens in Boston; the Canadian federal Juvenile Delinquents Act goes into effect
1909	William Healy founds the Psychopathic Laboratory in Chicago
1910	The term *emotional disturbance* comes into use
1911	Blueler names schizophrenia
1912	The American Association of Social Workers is formed; the U.S. Children's Bureau is established
1917	James Hinshelwood writes *Congenital Word-Blindness*
1920	The term *gifted* appears in the literature
1922	Lewis Madison Terman begins his longitudinal study of gifted children
1926	Samuel T. Orton begins to publish on strephosymbolia
1943	Leo Kanner identifies the syndrome of autism
1963	Samuel A. Kirk introduces the term *learning disabilities*

In the opening decades of the twentieth century the focus of special education changed from isolated institutional settings to segregated classrooms within the public schools. Children with mild handicapping conditions were served in the new settings, and, as the century progressed, special education expanded to embrace more children, to redesignate others, to adopt new philosophies, and to implement more sophisticated diagnostic and instructional approaches. The special classes did not exist in a vacuum: around them developed clinics and courts, a host of paraprofessionals, professional disciplines, and related services.

Compulsory school attendance laws led to more rigorous tracing, sorting, and categorizing of children; the labeling of special children, begun in earnest in the 1850s, grew more common as well. Increases in the numbers of children identified as poor performers yet displaying no clear-cut etiologies resulted in the creation of new labels such as *orthogenic, dyslexic, brain damaged,* and *learning disabled.*

On one level the new labels were intended to remove stigmas attached to traditional labeling systems. *Idiot* became *feebleminded,* and by about 1920 the term *mentally defective* or *mentally retarded* came into popular use. In 1877 the terms *deaf mute* and *deaf and dumb* were altered to *deaf* to reflect changing notions about the intellectual and speaking capacities of hearing-impaired individuals.

On a less positive note the categorical definitions of exceptional children that emerged served to maintain the purity of each population by focusing on discrepant attributes, the unique and often elusive characteristics that distinguished one defined population from the others. Exceptional children were thought not to share common etiological factors and behavioral characteristics and to differ in performance levels in certain areas. Differences were said to exist in levels of cognitive ability, in academic achievement, in patterns of cognitive performance, in degree of underachievement, and in adaptiveness of social and emotional development. Educators judged exceptional individuals to be qualitatively different and tended to focus on their handicaps, disadvantages, and weaknesses. Children were categorized on the basis of medical orientations; around each category there emerged professional groups and programs responsible for conducting programs tailored to the specific needs of the exceptional children in that category (see Winzer, 1993).

Labeling encouraged educators to discover new groups of children needing attention and to assign large numbers of children to segregated classes. With segregated classrooms in place, they became more discerning about the types of children who could be expected to function in regular classrooms. Those perceived as falling below the norm physically, mentally, or socially became prime candidates for segregation. And, like liquid seeking its own level, more and more children were identified as requiring special services as the administrative structures expanded to encompass more and more diverse categories of exceptionality. As increasing numbers of children with mild handicaps were identified for special education services, a variety of educational and social welfare roles were added to the functions of schools—public health and health care concerns, psychological and guidance counseling, and so on.

All the categories and subcategories of exceptionality that Americans labeled, diagnosed, and programmed for in the first half of the twentieth century cannot be addressed here. Rather, the stress herein is on students labeled as emotionally disturbed and as learning disabled, for the roots of these conditions lie deeply embedded in mental retardation. All the shades and levels of severity of emotional disturbance were revealed as more sophisticated assessment procedures were developed, as a more open attitude concerning disorders that could strike children emerged, and, most importantly, as clearer distinctions between mental retardation and emotional problems were detailed. The old, elastic category once labeled "incorrigible" now was characterized as mild emotional disturbance (behavior disorders), and it continued to be a concern of both the educational and the legal systems.

The early twentieth century also witnessed a more careful distinction between children with mental retardation and children who appeared to possess normal intellectual ability but still failed to achieve adequately. The etiologies seemed to lie in the realm of neurological dysfunction; such youngsters were saddled with a plethora of terms and names until Samuel Kirk in 1963 introduced the term *learning disabilities*. From that time on, this newest category in special education developed at such a phenomenal rate that today it forms the largest focus of special education in many school districts (Winzer, 1992).

The controversial category of the gifted owes much of its existence to the pioneering studies of Lewis Terman and can be traced to early eugenic imperatives as well as the testing movement. Of all the special classes formed, those for gifted students traveled the rockiest route. Roadblocks in the form of widely held myths about the gifted, the fear of abrogating the ethic of a democratic school system, and the enormous financial and moral resources directed toward the disabled lurked at every turn.

SEVERE EMOTIONAL DISTURBANCE

Insanity and madness have long been a grave concern to humanity. Cases of schizophrenia were recorded as early as 1400 B.C., and evidence remains of sophisticated discussions of mental illness by the Greek philosophers and educators. Generally, however, physicians were concerned with the effects of physical and neurotic ailments on adults, and only brief descriptions of children exhibiting serious emotional problems surface in the early literature.

It was not until the late 1800s that the mental health revolutions in America and in Europe began to encompass the study of disturbed children; however, the term *emotional disturbance* did not appear in the literature till about 1900, and then without being defined (Reinert, 1980). To some extent, at least, the psychotic child was an object of study in the first part of the nineteenth century, and a substantial body of knowledge on the subject was accumulated in that period (MacMillan, 1960). One eighteenth-century physician narrated the tale of a woman who gave birth to "a male child who was raving mad" (quoted by MacMillan, 1960, p. 1091). A physician at the Bicêtre in Paris described a fifteen-year-old idiot as "wholly an animal." "He was without attachment; overturned everything in his way; but without courage or intent; possessed no tact, intelligence, power of dissimulation, or sense of propriety; and was awkward to excess. His moral sentiments are described as null, except the love of approbation, and a noisy instinctive gaiety, independent of the external world. . . .

Devouring every thing, however disgusting, brutally sensual, passionate—breaking, tearing, and burning whatever he could lay his hand upon, and if prevented from doing so, punching, biting, scratching, and tearing himself, until he was covered with blood (Brigham, 1845, quoted by Kauffman, 1989).

Jean Étienne Dominique Esquirol, one of the first to differentiate between mental retardation and mental illness, directed attention to psychoses in children. James Kauffman (1976) observes that a perusal of Esquirol's work ([1838] 1845) reveals discussions of the influence of age on madness and the particular forms of insanity most common in childhood—behavior problems related to dentition, epilepsy, suicide, incendiarism, homicidal monomania, and idiocy. Esquirol, for example, reported the cases of children he described as "little homicidal monomaniacs." One was an eleven-year-old girl who pushed two infants into a well. Esquirol had nothing more to say than that she "was known for her evil habits." Another of Esquirol's cases was an eight-year-old girl who threatened to kill her brother and stepmother and was returned to her grandmother (Kanner, 1962).

After a brief early surge of interest, concern for the psychotic child waned until the close of the nineteenth century. Only a few brave souls wrestled with the diagnostic distinction between what would be later labeled childhood schizophrenia or infantile autism and mental retardation (e.g., H. M. Knight, 1872). Factors discouraging effort such as this included disillusionment with the results of work with adult mentally ill individuals, contradictory and confusing terminology and etiology, a distaste for ascribing severe mental disorders to children, and especially the conceptual confusion between mental retardation and mental illness. Even today mental retardation and behavior disorders are intertwined (Balthazar and Stevens, 1975; MacMillan, 1960; Walk, 1964), and the recognition of insanity in children seems generally to have been delayed until early training centers for the mentally retarded were established.

In 1867 Henry Maudsley (1835–1918), one of the few midcentury authoritative writers on the subject of the psychotic child, included a thirty-four-page chapter, "Insanity and Early Life," in his seminal work *The Physiology and Pathology of Mind.* Maudsley attempted to relate the type of psychosis to the level of a child's development and described sensorimotor insanities such as epilepsies and choreic movements associated with hallucinations, and delusions that were related to the development of stable ideas (Hare, 1962). Maudsley suggested a classification system for infant psychoses.

Like Maudsley, a few physicians and psychiatrists believed that both maniacal and melancholic forms of insanity—that is, the recognized range of adult forms—could be seen in children (Greisinger, [1867] 1882). Most nineteenth-century practitioners, however, disparaged the notion that emotional disturbance could affect children; they held that insanity is an adult disorder, whereas childhood manifestations are signs of mental deficiency. Many American psychiatrists and psychologists stubbornly clung to the belief that "insanity is rare in childhood" (Vineland, 1894, p. 37).

Nineteenth-century terminology and understanding of the etiologies of childhood insanity were varied and vague, confusing, and often contradictory. The scattered references to the disturbed child included such terms as *ideational insanity, amentia, simulative idiocy,* Seguin's *incipient insanity,* and *juve-*

nile insanity. Samuel Gridley Howe understood the difficulties of separating emotionally disturbed children from mentally retarded children; he used the term *simulative idiocy* to describe the appearance of mental retardation in a nonretarded person (Howe, 1852). Legal distinctions arrived tardily; it was not until 1886 that England produced a legal distinction between mental retardation and insanity (Hayman, 1939).

Disordered behavior was defined as illness, and those few children treated were primarily the responsibility of physicians who put forward a plethora of etiologies to account for bizarre and aberrant behavior. Some physicians pointed to the interaction of temperament and child rearing—overprotection, overindulgence, and inconsistency in discipline (Parkinson, [1807] 1963; C. West, [1848] 1963; both quoted by Kauffman, 1989).

The belief in the existence of masturbatory insanity was upheld almost to the end of the nineteenth century by some American physicians (Spitzka, 1883, 1887–88). Although masturbation was seen to be especially common among the insane of both sexes (Galt, [1842] 1846), close parallels were drawn between dementia praecox, the insanity of adolescence, and masturbation; physicians saw the typical age for masturbatory insanity as between thirteen and twenty years, and as being at least five times more common in males (see Hare, 1962; Neuman, 1975). Edward Spitzka (1883) noted a condition of periodic insanity, named (but not defined) *circular insanity,* which was generally seen to begin at about the age of puberty, was seen more frequently in females than males, and was intractable to treatment.

Credence was still ceded to causes of insanity such as overwhelming dread, religious teaching of a lurid hyperbolic type, and superstition (Spitzka, 1883). Any disease causing high fevers could be a villain in emotional problems. So could family conditions: alcohol, opium, or even tobacco use by the parents was thought to be able to engender mental ills in children. It was likewise believed that tubercular families and those of notably unstable nervous equilibrium were the explanation for cases of insanity. Environmental causes were then thought to act on the child "hyper-sensitive by heredity" (Vineland, 1894, p. 38).

Seriously affected children, the rarely mentioned *juvenile insane,* when institutionalized, were placed in settings with mentally retarded students. Little evidence of specific institutionalization or treatment for psychotic children separate from the mentally retarded remains. Stribling (1842) reported that, of 122 patients in the Western Lunatic Asylum in 1841, nine were under age twenty and two under age fifteen. In 1844 Dorothea Lynde Dix reported finding in an asylum "a little girl, about nine or ten years of age, who suffered the fourfold calamity of being blind, deaf, dumb and insane" (Bremner, 1970, p. 777).

Even if the concerns of the pioneer psychiatrists were not focused specifically on children, this does not mean that children were not affected by psychosis. Childhood psychosis may have been of so little concern to our predecessors for pragmatic reasons. The note of optimism that accompanied Philippe Pinel's *traitement moral* as interpreted by Benjamin Rush and others faded by midcentury. Private mental hospitals could devote the time and the personnel to individual therapy, but their cure rates were not duplicated in the large, state-funded institutions, which degenerated into dank custodial places (see Deutsch, 1949). The inauspicious results seen in the mass of adult mentally ill patients were unlikely to encourage psychiatrists to expand their clientele to include seriously disturbed youngsters.

It was not until the final decades of the nineteenth century that professionals finally confronted the notion that emotional disturbance constitutes a childhood disability different from the adult form and separate from mental retardation. The psychotic child again became an object of study, as psychiatrists and others initiated careful efforts to observe, describe, and classify the disordered behaviors exhibited by child patients (Kanner, 1962). Attempts were made to collect and organize the existing material in monographs on psychic disorders, mental diseases, and insanity in children, so that by 1900 there was an assortment of works asserting that children were known to display psychotic disorders (Kanner, 1962).

Two contrasting perspectives on emotional disturbance emerged. The functional approach, first seen in the seminal work of Pinel and lent substance by mid-nineteenth-century psychiatrists, emphasized the relationship between a patient's psychological personality and the development of mental illness. Devotees of this approach made careful observations of the patient's behavior, looking for clues to unlock the mysteries of causation. Physicians advocating a functional approach banded together to form schools of psychiatric treatment, ultimately developing the methods of psychotherapy. Sigmund Freud and others promoted the idea that deviant behavior could be explained in terms of subconscious phenomena and inner turmoil. They developed the psychodynamic view in which disturbance was seen as symptomatic, not of organic illness, but of conflict within the child, often associated with some breakdown of interpersonal relationships.

For children, the functional approach was clearly associated with the mental hygiene movement that, as one focus, concentrated on the promotion of mental health and the development of personality. Under the mental hygiene paradigm, mental illness referred to disorders of the personality confronting the stresses of life (Cohen, 1983). Childhood, so long overlooked as a crucial stage in development, became "the conditioning period of personality" (p. 127), and mental hygienists (divorced from the eugenicists by the early 1920s) turned to the schools.

The opposing organic viewpoint was based on the belief that all symptoms of mental disturbance could be attributed to specific brain malfunctions or physical disease. Emil Kraepelin (1856–1926) is the individual most often associated with the organic perspective. With James McKeen Cattell, Kraepelin studied under Wilhelm Wundt in Germany. Kraepelin's interest was not directed toward the new methods of measurement as much as to insanity, its etiology, path, and prognosis. In 1896 Kraepelin presented a classification system for emotional disturbance that clearly identified two major clusters of symptoms: manic depressive psychoses and dementia praecox (schizophrenia), the latter term to indicate the beginning of emotional disturbance in early life. Dementia praecox Kraepelin then subclassified as catatonic, hebephrenic, and paranoid. (Kraepelin, 1896).

Even though dementia praecox was sometimes called the insanity of adolescence, Kraepelin's work actually dealt only with adults. It was Sante de Sanctus who in 1905 applied the concepts to children, calling the entity observed in youngsters dementia praecoxissima. Eugen Blueler (1857–1939), a Swiss psychiatrist, christened dementia praecox *schizophrenia* in 1911. To Blueler, schizophrenia was a reflection of an underlying integrative dysfunction—a splitting of the mind, a break in the synthesis of thought, feeling, and activity (Blueler, [1911] 1950).

Psychodynamic and organic views of emotional disturbance vied with each other until the 1930s. At that time a radically different approach was developed by the behaviorist school of psychology, which postulated that disordered behavior has no innate or underlying cause, but is specific to situations and can be learned. Behavioral theorists such as John Broadus Watson and B. F. Skinner then emerged as the chief critics of the psychodynamic school of thought. Further supplementing studies of behavioral disorders in children was research into organic and genetic causes, the development of the humanistic model in psychology, and research into social psychology, with its emphasis on cultural influences on behavior (Newcomer, 1980). More recently, some theorists have attributed disturbed behavior to poor interactions between the child and the environment.

The work of de Sanctus, Blueler, and others contributed to the identification of a distinct condition known as childhood schizophrenia, and by 1935 schizophrenia in children was well documented (F. E. Howard, 1935; Potter, 1933). Credit for first identifying autistic behaviors in children and adults goes to Eugen Blueler who, in 1906, isolated specific nonverbal and nonrelating behaviors. Blueler used the word *autistic* as an adjective; it was not until Leo Kanner's major study in 1943 that an autistic syndrome, with *autism* as a noun, was identified in children (Blueler, [1911] 1950; Kanner, 1943, 1973). However, serious biomedical research on autism began only in the mid-1960s (Winzer, 1992).

Even after recognition of psychoses in children and the formulation of methods for identification, diagnosis, and treatment, severe childhood emotional disturbance remained largely the bailiwick of psychiatrists and psychologists, and not the school system. Severe handicap, however defined, was always a condition so removed from the norm that the meager chances of improvement muddied the success of any reforms. Even when the schools became relatively comfortable, or at least resigned, to children functioning below the norm in intellectual, physical, or social domains, they remained remarkably resistant to accepting students with severe and profound handicaps. Trained teachers, suitable facilities, and a range of support services were not available. Well into the twentieth century children with severe and multiple handicaps were excluded from public school segregated classes and often were not accepted even into institutional settings. Even when anxious parents could persuade school authorities to accept a severely handicapped child, it was usually only on a trial basis.

It was not until the 1960s that education assumed responsibility for seriously emotionally disturbed children (Csapo, 1984). There were strong attacks, both within and without psychiatry, on the legitimacy of the medical paradigm of illness as applied to children labeled severely emotionally disturbed (Paul and Warnock, 1980). A lack of personnel resources in the mental health field as well as the emerging humanistic concern about the inadequacy of institutional psychiatric services for children and the need to remove youngsters out of adult wards contributed to the controversy. In addition, Public Law 88–164, the Comprehensive Community Mental Health Centers Act (1963), as well as the move to more fully develop community services, evoked strong interest in returning many previously institutionalized children to the community. Seriously emotionally disturbed youngsters, previously in the purview of mental health clinics and the institutional milieu where the focus of treatment was on the pyschopathology of children, gradually moved into educational orbits.

BEHAVIOR DISORDERS

New Legal Imperatives

Severe and profound emotional disturbance in children remained largely the concern of medicine and psychology well into the twentieth century. Much more attention was paid to mild and moderate emotional disturbance, the "mental defects" described as "only too common" and those that "grow worse with startling rapidity unless most wisely handled" (Vineland, 1894, p. 37). Even though a specific classification for emotional disturbance (behavior disorders) remained unnamed until about 1910, a confusing array of terms for the various problems had emerged. Children were labeled as neglected, vagrant, delinquent, or truant, or as part of that category of matchless elasticity—incorrigible.

Children and youth displaying a wide range of behavior disorders came under intense scrutiny from the schools and the legal system: behavior disorders became an educational challenge, juvenile delinquency a legal problem. Segregated classes were established to handle the socially deviant, and the schools, not alone in their efforts, found ready allies in the court system, benevolent societies, and the child-rescue movement. New legal imperatives at the opening of the twentieth century focused on delinquency as a condition of children and youth. The term *juvenile delinquency,* originally designating children neglected and vagrant as well as delinquent, became ensconced in law and provided an operational definition of a particular group of children that was shared by a range of professionals as well as society at large (Achenbach, 1975).

American social conscience awoke slowly to the problems of delinquent, vagrant, and neglected children. Adherence to a pervasive laizzez-faire credo during the early nineteenth century had contributed to the general neglect of socially deviant younger citizens. Government intervention into the sacrosanct domains of the family or individual was strongly disapproved. As the century progressed the tendency was for society to enlarge its right to intervene in the affairs of individuals and their families. By midcentury the increasing visibility, especially among the urban poor, of impoverished, delinquent, and recalcitrant children seemed a sign of a breakdown of the family and a direct threat to social order. Society's obvious failure to deal with delinquency and neglect altered public and official opinions; government's nonintervention was interpreted as contributing directly to social and economic dereliction. The specter of disorder pushed reformers into establishing mechanisms to handle children that were based on an alliance between philanthropy and the state.

Child rescuers were confident of the rightness of their own values and unflinchingly asserted the combined power of the state and the reformer over the individual child and parent. They articulated the concept of *parens patriae,* the duty of the government to involve itself in the lives of all children who might become a community crime problem (Fox, 1972). The reformers made no distinction between neglected and delinquent children and often did not exhibit delicate feelings about family integrity in their efforts to rescue children from pauperism and immorality. The rescue mission could be accomplished in two ways—by removing the child or by improving the family. Because they interpreted delinquency as the product of pathological, crime-breeding environments, reformers saw their mission chiefly as one of removing the child from the pernicious environment. In order to provide an education "which cultivates the heart and the moral nature, which inculcates truthfullness and noblest instincts of humanity," noted one reformer, "it may, and often will, be necessary to remove the child from the parents" (Kelso, 1893–94, p. 213).

Not only could children be arbitrarily removed, but their misdemeanors and criminal activites could assign them to the criminal courts. There the focus rested on the overt act, not on the individual's social context; the class nature of crime mattered more than the specific causes. Nevertheless, even as children were assigned to adult courts, there developed an implicit assumption that the courts should protect children from bad influences to prevent them from becoming criminals and that the child need not be convicted of any crime to be placed under the court's jurisdiction. It was on this base that the courts built the machinery that enabled the government's removal of neglected children from their natural homes.

A great variety of offenses, minor and serious, propelled children toward the court system. One writer listed the crimes of children: "arson, assault with dangerous weapons, assault and battery, begging, breaking car seals, carnal knowledge, carrying concealed weapons, disorderly conduct, drunk, destruction of property, grand larceny, indecent conduct, incorrigibility, jumping on moving trains, petty larceny, reckless driving, rushing can, shooting craps, loitering, placing obstruction on railway tracks, trespass, truancy, vagrancy, violating bicycle, curfew and firearms ordinances, violating tobacco law, violating poolroom law" (Bench, 1919, p. 126).

A chain of dispositions for children emerged. Court officers were free to arrange for the protection of juveniles in a relatively informal manner, by placing them in the custody of welfare agencies, church groups, reform schools, industrial schools, or in foster care for an indeterminate time. Many youngsters still found themselves in county jails and almshouses, where they were subject to callous treatment. In Cook County, Illinois, for example, 575 children were in jail in 1898 (Hilgard, 1987). Other children were removed from their families and placed in reform schools, industrial schools, and foster care. Ostensibly modeled on family structures, many of the reform and industrial schools functioned under austere and regimented conditions. Systems showed a wide gap between enlightened theory and actual practice; retributive elements, cloaked in the mantle of well-meaning treatment, were not lacking. Institutionalized youngsters were subject to deprivation of food, bread-and-water diets, solitary confinement, corporal punishment, and, in extreme cases, fetters and handcuffs (Sanders, 1970; Toronto, 1912). Poor, vagrant, neglected, and misbehaving youngsters could also be sent to foster homes. The New York Children's Aid Society, for example, specialized in placing city children with families in distant parts of the country. By 1879 the society had placed 48,000 children outside New York (Achenbach, 1975).

Hitherto the family had been sacrosanct, "a sacred corporation" that the law treated "as the social unit for many purposes" (MacDonnell, 1897). When the state as *parens patriae* assumed the right to mediate between the child and the parents, the incremental limitation of parental rights in the interests of the socialization of unruly youth met with a great deal of opposition. Reformers countered with the argument that parents forfeited their natural rights "by neglecting to teach their children the moral precepts of leading pure and chaste lives" (*Royal Commission,* 1891, p. 297).

The state's mediation between parents and their children was challenged, and the presumptive rights of parents over their children were established by an 1870 decision of the Illinois Supreme Court, which ordered Daniel O'Connell, committed to the Chicago Reform School without being convicted of any crime, released to his father, on the grounds that the parent had a natural right to the child that was abrogated only if gross misconduct or almost total unfitness of the parents was proved (Achenbach, 1975). The 1870 decision established a new polarity between parents and the power of welfare agencies to remove children from their homes (Achenbach, 1975). Then vocal women's groups in Chicago reiterated objections to having children housed in the county and city jails (Hilgard, 1987). Joined to this was an implicit assumption of child rescue by the courts and a mounting pessimism concerning the coping abilities of benevolent societies. Moreover, in the final decades of the nineteenth century apprehension over crumbling family structures intensified as the new knowledge being generated about children's health and developmental patterns spread. Such information seemed only to widen the gap between what was possible in child rearing and what was happening in many families.

A reformist faction tenaciously pursued new legislation concerning children and the advancement of alternate child-saving models, all wrapped in the concept of *socialized justice.* An innovative judicial technique, socialized justice was predicated on assessment of the unique circumstances of each case, the use of administrative procedures, and the employment of experts such as social workers and probation officers, as opposed to the due process of an adversarial system.

The crescendo of rhetoric over socialized justice from the 1880s onward brought about the establishment of special procedures and personnel for children. The United States and Canada both effected a major reorganization of family law, particularly in relation to the dependent poor. In most jurisdictions the reordering of summary justice entailed the establishment of children's courts and the adaptation of other courts for the hearing of domestic cases. The courts were part of a system of law that began to reorganize family life. In the United States and Canada juvenile and family courts evolved as distinct entities.

Juvenile Courts

The rigid definitions that distinguished delinquency from crime and affected subsequent legislation throughout North America were formulated by the state of Illinois in 1899 (McGrath, 1965). A reform movement gained sufficient impetus to achieve unanimous approval of a state law for the establishment of a court whose sole function would be to act as a chancery court—a court charged with the responsibility of ensuring the welfare of those in its charge as opposed to adjudicating criminal responsibility. By 1893 Harvey B. Hurd was formulating legislation for Chicago's proposed juvenile court and became the first judge in 1899. The purpose of the Illinois juvenile court law was "to regulate the treatment and control of dependent, neglected, and delinquent children" (McGrath, 1965).

Enthusiasm greeted the advent of juvenile courts, which fit comfortably with the Progressive reforms embodied in child labor laws and other welfare policies. For the first time, delinquency was separated from adult crime and was given its own philosophy, legislation, courts, and treatment services (McGrath, 1962). Children's tribunals effectively blurred the civil-criminal distinction and emerged as the core of a tutelary complex of social agencies and the family courts (see McGill, 1919).

In Canada two statutes dealing with juveniles were enacted in Ontario in 1890—An Act Respecting the Custody of Juvenile Offenders and An Act Respecting the Commitment of Persons of Tender Years, each of which further restricted the use of reformatories and extended the use of industrial schools for children (Hagan and Leon, 1977). Ontario's Royal Commission into the Prison and Reformatory System in 1891 further stimulated child welfare proposals and investigated the causes of crime, the improvement of industrial schools, and the rescue of destitute children from criminal environments.

Denver in 1899 passed a law to establish juvenile courts; other states soon followed suit (Addams, 1925) and produced legislative systems and procedures to keep youngsters from entering the criminal court system. Canada passed the federal Juvenile Delinquent Act in 1908; the first effective juvenile court was established in Winnipeg in 1909.

Although many of the existing judicial procedures for juveniles were merely institutionalized by the acts, the creation of a separate court explicitly distinguished the juvenile and adult justice systems. A new terminology was employed to emphasize the noncriminal nature of juvenile court proceedings. The term *petition* was substituted for *complaint, hearing* for *arraignment, adjudication of involvement in delinquency* for *conviction* and *disposition* for *sentencing* (Achenbach, 1975). Placing children in jails was now forbidden; probation became a legally defined option for the first time, and the disposition of children to private welfare organizations was explicitly sanctioned, even for children who had committed criminal acts (Achenbach, 1975).

Juvenile courts were not designed to determine guilt or innocence of youngsters; they were a "first attempt by the state to make the aim of the law a protective rather than a punitive member of the body patriotic" (Henderson, 1919, p. 16). Courts were designed to oversee children's welfare either by placing them under the supervision of the courts, in foster homes, or in reform institutions. The court's responsibility was to assess a child physically, mentally, and morally and "then if it learns that he is treading the path that leads to criminality, to take him in charge not so much to punish as to reform, not to degrade but to uplift, not to crush but to develop, not to make him a criminal but a worthy citizen"

(Mack, 1909, p. 107). Reformers held the laudatory belief that "bad boys are merely good boys who have strayed into side paths and who may, in nearly every instance, be guided back to the main road if only the right person is leading" (Kelso, 1910, p. 4).

Social Work and Social Welfare

The advent of juvenile and family courts shifted the focus from the removal of the child from a pernicious environment to reconstruction of the nuclear family. "It is the neglected child that becomes the delinquent," observed one worker, "and it is the wrong conditions that should be dealt with, rather than the unfortunate victim" (Kelso, 1910, p. 15). Improving conditions in the child's own family would render arbitrary removal unnecessary; once a delinquency-generating environment was unmasked by the state's agents, the task of the family courts was to enforce conformity to middle-class standards of morality, hygiene, and education.

The new tribunals, characterized as they were by their adherence to the best interests of children and their families, emphasized the existence of a specialized apparatus run by specialized workers. Social work stood at the junction of the family and the various practices—education, medical-hygienic, judicial, and penal. Its personnel, lauded a 1920 writer, "recognises that the child fresh from the hand of God is the foundation of all the constructive work for human betterment" (P. Bryce, 1920, p. 255). Nevertheless, the interlocking structure of social agencies and officialdom created a huge potential, albeit mostly unrealized, for the surveillance of the poor. Social workers were enabled to scrutinize the morality and internal family relations of the dependent poor in a detail that was inconceivable within the bounds of earlier administrative structures.

Social workers focused on the reconstruction of the nuclear family; they attempted to resolve the tension between the preservation of family unity and the reality of dysfunctional families, and they stressed the need to help dependent people in their homes rather than punish them in large institutions or asylums (A. Jones, 1978). Social work gained new stature, and by 1920 social work was a well-established, growing profession. The American Association of Social Workers was formed in 1912; the American Association of Psychiatric Social Workers, more aligned with medical practice, in 1926. Social workers were one of the few groups to experience 100 percent employment during the Depression (Struthers, 1981).

Behavior Disorders and the Schools

Formalized procedures and professional services for problematic children and their families saw the emergence of new occupations—social workers and probation officers being but two—and new professional thrusts in the form of psychological clinics tied to the courts, the schools, or social agencies. The American Orthopsychiatric Association was founded in 1924 to encourage the dissemination of information on therapeutic and educational endeavors for emotionally disturbed children.

The mental hygiene movement, which soon ended its flirtation with the pessimistic eugenicists, led a campaign that began in the second decade of the twentieth century to focus on children's mental health and to designate the schools as its bailiwick. Advocates called attention to the public school system as a "fertile and untouched field of mental hygiene work" (Cohen, 1983, p. 127).

By the second decade of the twentieth century, mental hygienists were "convinced that psychiatry had identified a specific susceptibility to mental disorder, a specific symptomology, a specific constellation of personality traits: shyness, daydreaming, withdrawal, introversion, the 'shut-in' personality were psychiatric danger signals, an early warning system of serious mental illness, even of dementia praecox" (Cohen, 1983, p. 129). Stress brought on by schooling was thought to be a major factor and, because the school was considered a "uniquely stressful and pathogenic milieu" for children, mental hygienists focused their efforts there (Cohen, 1983, p. 130).

Guidance clinics, which were initiated as a means of identifying and managing behavioral problems, soon came to take a focus on the predelinquent or problem child, for hygienists soon concluded that by the time children came to the attention of psychiatrists and social workers, it was too late (Cohen, 1983). The "Program for the Prevention of Delinquency" financed by the Commonwealth Fund and begun in 1922 launched the child-guidance movement. It "greatly stimulated the school social work or visiting teacher movement as well as the development of child psychiatry and psychiatric social work and became the spearpoint for mental hygiene penetration in the school" (Cohen, 1983, p. 198).

Child-guidance clinics focused on any child displaying deviant or annoying behavior. Psychopathic clinics were established, wrote Wallin (1914), in order to assist in "the righting or correction of mental functions which are deviating or abnormal, either by removal of physical handicap or by proper mental and educational treatment; the stimulation by appropriate stimuli of functions which are slowed down or retarded, and the placing of the child in the right educational classification or environment, so that he may attain with the least expenditure of energy and the least amount of friction to his maximum potential" (p. 160).

Clinics, not always with the approbation of school personnel, opened first as private enterprises, sometimes associated with universities. With the advent of the juvenile courts, some became associated with the legal system; school boards then established their own offices of pupil services, as variations on the same theme.

The first psychological clinic in the United States, originated by Lightner Witmer at the University of Pennsylvania in 1896, was in continuous operation for sixty years. Witmer was the first to use the term *clinical psychology;* his was an enduring interest in studying the problems of mental retardation, and his was the first clinic to treat the retarded. It then served as a model for other clinics at universities and school systems throughout the country (Rosen, Clark, and Kivitz, 1976).

In 1909 Chicago's model juvenile court was enhanced by the adoption of a quasi-clinical approach, with the establishment of the Juvenile Psychopathic Laboratory for the clinical evaluation of delinquents. This clinic was established under the aegis of reformers of the Hull House Settlement and was directed by psychiatrist William Healy (1869–1963), assisted by Grace Fernald (1879–1950).

Healy's clinic looked at delinquency as a behavior problem of a neurotic nature (Healy, 1915a, 1915b; Healy and Bronner, [1926] 1969). It became a model for future clinics.

An Ohio clinic opened in 1915 under Henry Herbert Goddard. Samuel Orton was led to his interest in learning disabilities when, in organizing an experimental mobile mental hygiene clinic to serve outlying communities in 1925, he met a sixteen-year-old of average intelligence who could not read. A St. Louis clinic, following Healy's pattern but tied to the juvenile court, opened in 1921. In all, eight child clinics opened across the country in the period 1922 to 1927 under the Program for the Prevention of Delinquency (Horn, 1984).

The typical staff of the clinics consisted of a psychologist, a psychiatrist, and a social worker. Clinics could enforce behavioral standards and control potential deviants. A list of clients in 1928 included three groups of children. First, there were those displaying unacceptable behavior such as temper tantrums, fighting, teasing, bullying, disobedience, "show-off" behavior, truancy, lying, stealing, rebellion against authority, cruelty, sex difficulties, and the like, whether shown at home, school, or elsewhere. The second group of clients displayed problems chiefly manifested in personality reactions such as reclusiveness, timidity, fears, cowardliness, excessive imagination, fanciful lying, "nervousness," excessive unhappiness, and crying, stubbornness, selfishness, restlessness, overactivity, and unpopularity with other children. Finally, there were those youngsters who showed problems in habit formation, such as sleeping and eating difficulties, speech disturbances, thumb sucking, masturbation, and prolonged bedwetting (Horn, 1984; Stevenson and Smith, 1934).

Later the clinics tended to be tied to schools and social agencies. In the schools, offices of pupil personnel services, which followed the psycho-educational clinics, emerged. These offices usually offered guidance and counseling, group measurement, and child and youth study divisions. Teachers were provided a standardized form to request from these offices an evaluation of students they considered particularly troublesome in the classroom, behaviorally or academically (see Tropea, 1987b).

GIFTED STUDENTS

Cultural values have always influenced the attitudes of society toward its outstanding members. Throughout recorded history much honor has been paid to individuals who made significant contributions to their own or succeeding cultures, but different eras have valued achievement in different fields of endeavor: ancient Greece admired the philosopher, Rome the soldier and orator, and Renaissance Italy the artist. Nevertheless, the notion of precocity has been shrouded in myth and mysticism, and genius has often been misunderstood. Even in the late 1800s genius was still popularly viewed as directly related to insanity (Winzer, 1993).

As a descriptive term for a specific group of individuals, *gifted* was first used in the literature by Guy M. Henry in 1920, although investigations into the charactistics that produce high achievers were undertaken much earlier. The term was seen to encompass those who were highly intelligent and those who were high academic achievers.

Studies of gifted individuals and the precursors of giftedness arose largely out of the eugenics movement and, in fact, contributed to the spread of the philosophy. For his 1869 work *Hereditary genius* Sir Francis Galton took as subjects eminent British men who lived between 1768 and 1868; included in his sample were statesmen, soldiers, scientists, writers, poets, artists, and ministers. Galton investigated the close relatives of these subjects to determine the frequency of eminence among the related groups. Galton found that many of his group of 977 men had close relatives as eminent as themselves and, on the basis of these data, concluded that genius is largely a hereditary factor. Galton proposed that motivation to achieve is inborn and claimed that genius would actualize itself despite external circumstances (Galton, [1869] 1870), a position that led to the enduring and dangerous myth that "the cream will rise to the top" regardless of difficulties or lack of environmental support.

The contemporary Italian scientist Cesare Lombroso (1836–1909), interested in anthrometrics and aspects of individual differences that were much broader than intellectual functions, investigated the popular notion that genius is closely related to insanity. In 1891 Lombroso published *The Man of Genius* in which he concluded, using a case-study method, that genius is a marked aberration from the norm and akin to other mental aberrations. In 1926 Catherine Cox, one of Terman's coworkers, published a work on genius that used, as Galton had done, accounts of the lives of eminent men as sources of data. Cox estimated the IQs of the men and concluded that youthful genius has a superior hereditary and environmental advantage; that it is manifested at an early age; and that later eminence is a function of high IQ and persistence, motivation, effort, self-confidence, and great strength and force of character (Cox, 1926).

The Terman Studies

In one sense schools have always accommodated gifted students; early schools were designed for the rich, the very bright, and the very ambitious. In the late nineteenth century, with the passage of compulsory school attendance laws, gifted students, along with their average and below-average counterparts, flowed into the free public schools. Teachers were faced with the unpromising task of providing adequately for classes of children of the same age level but of vastly differing abilities. While attempting to follow a course adapted to the main group of students—the average—teachers found that their time was taken up with the below-average students who required extra help. Meanwhile, the above average were left to themselves. True, they could master the work in a much shorter time, but if they finished early, they were only given more of the same to keep them busy. Often, children became bored, resentful, or demanding, or they behaved in ways that disrupted the class and exhausted the teacher.

The provision of programs for gifted students has always been a complex and difficult undertaking, as well as one of the most controversial in special education. Myths and misunderstandings have served to make programming insecure, at best. For one thing, Galton's truism, "the cream will rise to the top," has been perpetuated, as educators have continued to debate whether special programming for individuals already well endowed violates the ethics of a democratic school system. Funding, willingly bestowed on children functioning below the norm, has been grudgingly allowed to those possessing superior abilities. The fear has been that the schools could create a meritocracy anti-thetical to the ideals of a democratic society. Another persistent stereotype por-trays the gifted individual as an "egghead"—physically weak, homely, socially inept, narrow in interests, and prone to emotional instability (Winzer, 1992).

Many stereotypes surrounding gifted students and their education were shattered by Lewis Terman, the educator and psychologist who expanded the concepts and procedures developed by Alfred Binet in France at the beginning of the twentieth century. Terman believed that the Binet scale assessed a wide range of performance and could be adapted for use with high-functioning chil-dren, and so he embarked on a longitudinal study of giftedness.

Terman's study, which ultimately included 1,528 children (with a mean IQ of 150), was intended not only to increase knowledge of the origin and traits of gifted children. Certainly, the study "was designed to discover what physical, mental, and personality traits are characteristic of gifted children as a class, and what sort of adult the typical gifted child becomes" (Terman and Oden, 1951, p. 21). More importantly, since it was widely believed that mental ability was scarce, it seemed vital that the few capable of high achievement and leadership be identified and trained. Terman's main goal was to "increase the supply" of giftedness by promoting educational programs "with better hope of success" (Terman, [1925] 1926, pp. 16–17).

Terman's belief was that intelligence is manifested essentially in the ability to acquire and manipulate concepts. He defined the gifted as those who score in the top 1 percent of general intellectual ability as measured by the Stanford-Binet scale or a comparable instrument (Terman, 1926). Terman carefully dis-tinguished giftedness from talent and creativity. He viewed talent as the potential for unusual achievement, but only when combined with high IQ scores. Creativity, he believed, is a personality factor and thus differs from both giftedness and talent (Wolf and Stephens, 1982).

To identify his gifted sample, Terman used teacher nominations and a group IQ test, either the National Intelligence Tests or the Terman Group Tests of Men-tal Ability, both devised by Terman in the 1920s. High-scoring students were ad-ministered the individual Stanford-Binet; students who scored 140 IQ or above on the Stanford-Binet were asked to serve as subjects in Terman's study (Sea-goe, 1975). His hereditarian leanings led Terman to an expectation that his sam-ple would come from a specific class and a specific racial group (which they did). "The racial stocks most prolific of gifted children," observed Terman, "are those from northern and western Europe, and the Jewish. The least prolific are the Mediterranean races, the Mexicans and the Negroes" (Terman, 1924, p. 363).

From his gifted sample Terman found that most came from a middle or higher socioeconomic group, with a low incidence of broken homes. Nearly half of the children could read before entering kindergarten; one in five children skipped part or all of the first grade; on average, the children finished school 14 percent faster than normal students; and the children averaged 40 percent higher than their age mates on achievement tests. In school, they preferred ab-stract subjects, such as literary debate and ancient history, and were less in-terested in such practical concerns as penmanship and manual training. They read more and better books, made numerous collections, and had many hob-bies; they were far superior to their age mates in general health, physique, mental health, and emotional adjustment. Samples were periodically retested; as adults, they were found to have retained their intellectual superiority and were ahead in terms of occupational status, earned incomes, publications, and patents (Terman and Oden, 1947, 1951, 1959). When checked in 1959, Terman's group had published more than two thousand scientific papers and taken out 230 patents (Sprinthall and Sprinthall, 1987).

In both historical and contemporary terms, the Terman studies (which continue, even though Terman died in 1956) contributed vastly to the enhancement of the field of the education of gifted students; in fact, the gifted movement began with Terman. Not only did Terman's work represent the first full-scale longitudinal study of the nature of giftedness, but it legitimized the field and presented a decidedly more positive image of gifted individuals (Winzer, 1992). Many of Terman's findings remain remarkably relevant; so far, his study is unsurpassed in the field of giftedness. On the other hand, Terman's work established for three decades the superiority of IQ tests as the sole measure of giftedness (see Seagoe, 1975). The identification of giftedness focused solely on intellectual attainments.

Education for Gifted Students

Although Terman's work defined the general characteristics of the gifted population, dispelled some traditional myths about the gifted, and supported special education for gifted students, the field remained relatively small and poorly funded, compared with the education of disabled children (e.g., Henry, 1920; Witty, 1965). However, some school systems instituted programs to meet the needs of the "pupils of more than average capability," "brilliant children," "pupils of supernormal ability," and a variety of other terms—all of which referred to individuals of high intelligence (Passow, 1990).

But, right from the start, class designation proved a difficulty. As a later writer observed: "To label it 'Special Opportunity Class for Superior Children' would be a good way to arouse hatred and envy among those not included" (Hollingworth, 1926, p. 304). *Special opportunity class* became a common term; later some classes were called *Terman classes.*

Acceleration models were the first vehicle to emerge. In 1868 William T. Harris instituted flexible promotion as a way of providing for able pupils in the St. Louis schools (Passow, 1990). The first such class opened in Elizabeth, New Jersey, in 1886 when an accelerated multiple-track system was established; in 1891 Cambridge, Massachusetts, promoted acceleration, allowing students to complete six grades in four years. Rapid-advancement classes for exceptionally bright children were started in New York City in 1900. By 1915, what eventually became known as the "SP" classes were designed to hasten the progress of bright children by enabling them to complete seventh, eighth, and ninth grades in two years (Henry, 1920, p. 31). In Los Angeles, Opportunity A rooms were established in 1915 for students two years ahead of their chronological age.

Leta Stetler Hollingworth, a clinical psychologist, was actively involved in studying the nature and needs of gifted students in New York City at the same time that Terman was studying his gifted students in California. In 1936 Hollingworth established the Speyer School in New York city. For further details of her work, see Box 11-1.

Box 11-1

Leta Stetler Hollingworth (1886–1939)

Leta Stetler Hollingworth was an educator, psychologist, researcher, and curriculum developer, as well as an early advocate of expanded roles for women in society and the rights of extremely gifted children. Although her career spanned only twenty-six years, her influence on the field of the education of the gifted was profound. She was one of the first to propose insights into the relationships between levels of intelligence and social development (Passow, 1990) and was probably the first educator to explore the social and emotional needs of gifted children and to provide guidance to parents, teachers, and the psychological community for dealing with the affective dimensions of gifts and talents (Passow, 1990). She taught the first course at the Columbia Teachers College on the education of the gifted; wrote the first textbook in the field; conducted dozens of significant studies dealing with gifted children; organized and operated one of the most celebrated experimental programs for the gifted at Speyer School; and developed curricula and counseling techniques. Her book *Children above 180 IQ, Stanford-Binet* remains the "most comprehensive longitudinal study ever conducted on children in this range of abilities" (Silverman, 1990, p. 123).

Fagan (1990) describes Hollingworth as "a data-oriented social reformer who preferred change on the basis of science and data to the status quo based on unscientific opinions held over from the advice and 'research' literature of the nineteenth century" (p. 157). Fagan also observes that the reform framework explains her research contributions, which concerned issues of equality, mental subnormality, professional regulations, the delivery of psychological services, special talents and defects, gifted children, nervous children, and the establishment of special education services for the gifted and children with very high ability (Fagan, 1990).

The eldest of three girls (Roweton, 1990), Leta Stetler was born in a small dugout in north Nebraska's White River Valley into geographic isolation, poverty, and domestic turmoil (R. Miller, 1989). She taught for one year in Sadine County, Nebraska; in 1902 she entered the University of Nebraska to study literature and poetry writing. She hoped for a career in writing but elected to teach so that she could support her two sisters (R. Miller, 1989). She moved to New York City in 1908 and married Henry C. Hollingworth, a university graduate from Nebraska, when she was twenty-two.

In New York, Leta Hollingworth could not teach because married women were not allowed to teach in New York schools. She wrote, but nothing was accepted. In 1913 she took a temporary position at the Clearing House for Mental Defectives in New York City in the mental testing program.

She earned an master's degree at Teachers College, Columbia University in psychology and earned a doctoral degree in 1916. Edward Lee Thorndike supervised her doctoral thesis on the relationship of the menstrual cycle to sex differences in performance (Hollingworth, 1914). During this time she assisted her husband in his research, conducted by the Coca-Cola company, on the effects of the caffeine contained in Coke (Passow, 1990).

Hollingworth was well aware of the arbitrary social restrictions placed upon women's achievement and their active participation in activities outside the household (Shields, 1990). She emerged as a leader in the psychology of women and the study of gender. She published papers on the psychology of women (Benjamin, 1975) and "was hailed as the scientific pillar of the women's movement for her work in the study of . . . women" (Kelley, 1976, p. 74). She challenged the notion that males are more intelligent than females. In opposition to Darwin, Cattell, Thorndike, and others, Hollingworth did not hold to the variability thesis, which attributes more variability and therefore more intelligence to males. She viewed differences in achievement as attributable to differences in opportunities (Passow, 1990).

In 1916, the year she received her Ph.D., Hollingworth became an instructor in educational psychology at Columbia Teachers College. (Carl Ransom Rogers was one of her students.) She also practiced clinical psychology at Bellevue Hospital and counseling psychology for the New York City Police Department (Passow, 1990).

In 1922 the Teachers College received a grant from the Carnegie Corporation to establish experimental classes for gifted students. In the same year Hollingworth formed two special opportunity classes at New York PS 165—one for children with IQs over 150 and one for children with IQs between 134 and 154. PS 500, the Speyer School, opened in 1936 with classes for slow learners and classes for gifted students (Passow, 1990).

The seventy-five classrooms with 1,834 gifted children in the United States in 1934 grew to ninety-three classrooms with 3,255 pupils by 1940 (Froelich et al., 1944). Still, as late as 1946 only a handful of states had any laws or legislation dealing with the gifted. By 1952 Kansas was the only state with laws that named the gifted among the exceptional population, although other state laws may have been interpreted as applying to gifted students.

In the many places where special classes were not available, other models developed. By 1934 both enrichment and acceleration models were in vogue, with acceleration the more popular. Enrichment, which placed more pressure on classroom teachers for differential programming, existed as an outshoot of Progressive education, which stressed development of the whole child and critical creative and thinking skills (Cremin, 1961; Osborn and Rohan, 1931; Stedman, 1924).

The enterprise method and the major work classes were other models used in the education of gifted pupils. The enterprise method trained students in learning and community-oriented group activities. The major work program, used in Cleveland, offered children with IQs of 125 and above greater intellectual stimulation, along with training in advanced creativity and problem solving (Bain, 1980).

LEARNING DISABILITIES

Defining Learning Disabilities

Learning-disabled students, as they are known in our school systems today, have probably always been in society. But wherever pushing a plow is more important than pushing a pen, the subtle learning problems exhibited by these children are little cause for concern. And whenever the quests for universal schooling and mass literacy face these children with the complexities of learning the three *R*s in traditional classrooms, they flounder and fail and soon come to the attention of educators and psychologists.

Early research into learning disabilities, conducted by physicians and psychologists who emphasized clinical investigation rather than practical application in the schools, began with the study of brain-injured adults, moved on to brain-injured and mentally retarded children, and then to children of normal intelligence. The initial investigations focused primarily on disorders in three areas—spoken language, written language, and motor and perceptual skills (Mercer, 1979).

The history of the field of learning disabilities reveals three main phases of development. During the foundations phase, between about 1800 and 1930, physicians investigated the etiology of specific learning disorders, classifying and categorizing them into different types. The transition phase took place from about 1930 to 1960, as psychologists and educators used many of their predecessors' theories to develop diagnostic procedures and remedial programming. The integration phase began in 1960 and is still continuing. During this time the field of learning disabilities took the form that we see today (Wiederholt, 1978).

Much of the pioneering research concerned children with reading problems. At the outset investigators regarded the condition as a form of imperception, sometimes called *agnosia,* sometimes *mind blindness, word blindness,* or *word deafness.* Word blindness was the most widely described (e.g., Hinshelwood 1900a, 1900b; Kussmaul, 1877; Tredgold, 1929). One Scottish physician, eye surgeon James Hinshelwood, investigated letter, word, and mind blindness (Hinshelwood, 1900a, 1900b). Hinshelwood published *Congenital Word Blindness,* the first true monograph on the unique problems of children we now refer to as learning disabled (Hinshelwood, 1917). In this work Hinshelwood outlined his belief that reading disabilities are due to the destruction or improper development of the memory centers of the left cerebral hemisphere of the brain (Park and Linden, 1968).

Later, Alfred Tredgold (1929) explained that in word blindness the problems concern only the printed word, which the person can see but not understand. Children afflicted are either totally unable to learn to read or they read with the greatest difficulty. The condition is more common in boys than girls, and although, Tredgold said, some children are of average intelligence, the majority are, although not legally mentally defective, of subnormal intelligence. Tredgold also suggested that there could exist a relationship between the condition and left-handedness and mirror writing. Affected children, said Tredgold, often suffer emotional and social difficulties—lack of interest, general indifference, lack of initiative, emotional instability, impulsive behavior, lack of attention, and incapacity for sustained mental application.

Sometimes word blindness is accompanied by *agraphia,* an inability in writing. Word deafness is analogous, but a much rarer condition. In cases of complete mind blindness there is an inability to interpret the meaning of any visual or auditory images, although the person can see and hear adequately (Tredgold, 1929).

J. E. Wallace Wallin, vitally interested in all facets of learning disorders, conducted orthophrenic research—"the righting or correction of the mental functions which are deviated or abnormal through either the removal of physical handicap or the stimulation by appropriate stimuli of functions which are slowed down or retarded" (Wallin, 1914, p. 160). Wallin worked with child prodigies and children with alexia (complete reading disabilities), agraphia (complete writing disabilities), and motor defects but no corresponding mental impairment.

In the early 1920s Samuel T. Orton, an American psychiatrist, refused to accept the notions of some of his colleagues that many learning problems are caused by emotional maladjustment. Orton noted that children with learning difficulties often display mixed laterality or come from families where there is evidence of mixed dominance. Orton (1937) proposed a theory that rested on the bilateral symmetry of the brain when he suggested that the failure of one hemisphere of the brain to become dominant causes learning and reading disorders. Orton coined the term *strephosymbolia* to designate individuals who see "mixed symbols" when they try to read (Orton, 1925). Orton's publications on strephosymbolia attracted considerable attention; they seemed to offer a starting point for learning more about these undoubted differences in manners of learning.

It was Alfred A. Strauss (1897–1957), a neurologist, and Heinz Werner (1890–1964), a developmental psychologist, who developed the modern category of learning disabilities; their work forms the basis for much of the research and theories in the field. Strauss, a pupil of Kurt Goldstein, renowned for his studies on the neurology and neuropsychology of brain-injured adults, earned his medical degree with special training in psychiatry and neurology from the University of Hiedelberg in 1922. Werner was a student of William Stern; he taught at the universities of Hiedelberg and Munich.

By the 1930s Strauss was applying the findings of brain neurology to the field of mental deficiency. With the first rumblings of Hitler, Strauss went to Spain and thence to the United States, where he joined the staff of the Wayne County Training School in Northville, Michigan, in 1937. His close associate Heinz Werner also emigrated, and the two began a program of training and research for brain-damaged children. In 1947 Strauss founded the Cove schools at Racine. In 1945 Werner joined the faculty of Clark University to resume his earlier career in developmental psychology.

Through his early research Strauss developed a number of tests to diagnose brain injury in children; he demonstrated the differences in mental organization between the brain-injured and the mentally retarded child, which resulted in a refinement of the differential diagnosis of the brain-injured, the neurotic, and the psychotic child (R. A. Gardiner, 1958; Strauss, 1939, 1941a, 1941b, 1943). Strauss and Werner also succeeded in laying the foundation for a psychopathological analysis of perceptual and conceptual differences among retarded children. They studied the impact of brain damage on children's behavior and psychological development and drew a distinction between the exogenous (largely from brain damage) and the endogenous (largely genetic) mental retardation. Such differentiation led Strauss to discredit the notion that mental retardation is a homogeneous entity characterized simply by slowness of development due to inherited defect (Gardiner, 1958).

To distinguish the organic syndrome of mental retardation from feeblemindedness, Strauss suggested characterizing children with exogenous retardation as mentally crippled, implying that these children were damaged in the mental sphere during development much as crippled children were in the physical. "The mentally crippled child," noted Strauss, "presents to the child neuropsychiatrist a problem analogous to that of the brain injured child" (Strauss and Lehtinem, 1947). Later, after he had left Northville, Werner depicted the thinking processes of brain-injured children as rigid and erratic, analogous to the mental functioning of primitive and savage people (Carrier, 1986).

Strauss then described an organic behavior syndrome diagnosable even in children in whom these residual isolated signs are absent. He outlined the characteristics of the minimally brain-damaged child, later known as the Strauss syndrome. This outline has five principal components: hyperactivity, hyperemotionalism, impulsiveness, distractibility, and perseveration, components that have been expanded, subdivided, and made more specific over the years but that still describe the core behavioral characteristics of children with learning disabilities.

After Strauss and Werner, the focus of research gradually shifted to encompass seemingly normal children who achieve poorly in school. Hinshelwood had largely established the neurological explanation for learning disabilities that was explicated and expanded by Strauss. Newell Kephart, Ray Barsch, Marianne Frostig, and many others carried on this line of research and claimed to have identified a similar pattern of neurologically based learning and behavior problems in children of average or above-average intelligence (see L. Mann, 1970, 1971).

Children exhibiting these subtle and contradictory learning difficulties have been labeled in many different ways. The labels arose chiefly from neurology and reflect a medical orientation that attributes disabilities to various types of brain damage. Common labels include *minimal brain dysfunction, brain crippled, cerebral disordered, neurologically impaired, dyslexic,* and *dysphasic.* In 1963 at a Chicago parents meeting of the Fund for Perceptually Handicapped Children, Samuel Kirk proposed the term *learning disabilities* as a standard description for children of normal intelligence with learning problems. Kirk defined his term carefully: "Recently, I have used the term 'learning disabilities' to describe a group of children who have disorders in development in language, speech, reading, and associated communication skills needed for social interaction. In this group, I do not include children who have sensory handicaps, such as blindness and deafness, because we have methods of managing and training the deaf and the blind. I also exclude from this group children who have generalized mental retardation" (Kirk, 1963, p. 3).

Kirk's speech had two important effects. First, it served as a catalyst to stimulate interest in the field. Second, it isolated the general characteristics of the population to be subsumed under the label of learning disabilities (Wiederholt, 1978). The new term implied an educational rather than a medical orientation; it was included in the definition suggested by the National Advisory Bureau on the Handicapped and adopted by the 91st U.S. Congress in 1969 (Paul and Warnock, 1980). Also, because *learning disabilities* is relatively nonstigmatizing, it appeals greatly to parents and educators; the term *learning disabilities* has been embraced by middle-class parents as a way to explain low achievement. Kirk's speech also precipitated a vote to reorganize diverse groups into the Association for Children with Learning Disabilities (ACLD). Primarily a forum for parents of learning-disabled children, the ACLD expanded rapidly.

Once the single category was established, increasing attention was paid to learning disabilities. In fact, the growth of interest in the area, the number of students identified and served as learning disabled, the growth of parental and professional organizations, and the contributions of allied disciplines has been little short of phenomenal. As it expanded, the field of learning disabilities brought changes and innovations to all of special education. Novel instructional approaches, new materials, and new types of tests and assessment measures all emerged. Then, too, there evolved new ways of conceptualizing special education, especially as it applies to mildly handicapped students (see Winzer, 1989a, 1993).

Education for Learning-Disabled Children

Throughout the history of the field that was to be called learning disabilities, all approaches were related to perceptual motor theory. Hinshelwood (1917) presented detailed instructional plans that followed three main steps—teaching a student to store the individual letters of the alphabet in the part of the brain that processes visual memory; teaching the student to spell words orally, thus developing auditory memory and the ability to retrieve words rapidly; and transferring the auditory retrieval to the visual memory centers of the brain. During the 1930s teachers discovered that, for word-blind children, the "look and say" word method of teaching reading was not suitable. Instead, children were taught to make the letters themselves by putting together pieces of wood, or by tracing letters in sand, or by handling larger models of the letters made of wood with the idea that the muscle memories would help in recognition and memory of the letters. Dyslexic children were taught to master the technique of reading through the alphabetic method, letter by letter, syllable by syllable, and sound unit by unit. The flash card system was seen as too difficult for them ("Excerpts," 1934).

Since that time dozens upon dozens of methods, procedures, and therapies have been developed. These include structured methods such as the Orton-Gillingham system and the Frostig method, the use of different settings such as engineered and stimulus-reduced classrooms, and different instructional models such as modality training, skills approaches, and perceptual-motor training. Therapies include the patterning of Doman and Delacato and the auditory program of Tomatis (see Cruickshank, 1976; Lerner, 1981; Winzer, 1993).

By the 1930s the world of special education had advanced far beyond the level of the field in the late nineteenth century. Specialists' understanding of the sources and nature of many of the handicapping conditions had advanced rapidly, educators' practices in the classroom were increasingly tailored to more well-defined problems and each child's unique needs, and parents' perceptions of their children's needs and their own roles in meeting those needs were far more sophisticated. The modern era in special education was well under way, but there remained much to be accomplished.

Part 4

Segregation to Integration

Introduction

World War I changed forever the face of Europe and the world balance of power. Dozens of grand monarchies disappeared, federal states emerged, borders were redrawn, tiny countries were swallowed up, national entities subjugated. Revolutionary Russia began its march to world prominence; the League of Nations was formed to ensure that such mayhem would never again violate humanity. The nations of the New World moved into new phases of political and economic growth and social responsibility. Across North America the expansion of industry brought soaring production, the concentration of capital, and the need for a more organized and skilled labor force. North American confidence transformed the 1920s into a decade of sparkling optimism. Joy in the new era filtered to all levels of society, and, not surprisingly, special education expanded and flourished.

In the post–World War I euphoria special education was no longer seen as a distant relative, remembered only occasionally with a few fiscal crumbs. Although it was not yet accepted as an equal member of the educational family, it was now at least invited to family functions.

Institutional settings remained important for serving a discrete population of disabled individuals. But from the firm establishment of segregated classes in about 1910 until well into the 1970s, the education of learning- and behaviorally disordered children was generally equated with special class models of service delivery. The reason for the continuity of special classes is fairly obvious: they both removed from regular classrooms children perceived as disruptive or unable to perform and ostensibly provided specialized instruction designed to remove or ameliorate their deficits in learning and behavior.

Which function, clientele, and type of segregated class might be best was still being worked out in practice during the 1920s. Generally, however, segregated instruction was viewed as a good thing. Calls for improvements focused on expansion, on making more special education available to more children affected by more varied types of disabling conditions. But with the 1930s came a steady evaporation of the optimism surrounding special education, especially segregated classes. In the wider social milieu the times brought the financial burdens of the Depression and later the fiscal focus on winning World War II. Within the school system the 1930s brought mounting dissatisfaction with inadequately planned special classes staffed by untrained or poorly trained teachers, the watered-down curriculum, the total segregation of exceptional students, and the misinterpretation of the ideology and practice of Progressive education. Under fiscal and philosophical pressures, school district involvement declined drastically. At the same time, professional and parental complaints mounted.

Both directly and indirectly, World War II encouraged important advances in special education, in social perceptions of disabled persons, and in their care and treatment. More liberal and flexible views emerged. New techniques were developed. In medicine great strides were accomplished in prevention, intervention, and care of disabling conditions. Technological advances improved the functioning of scores of disabled people. In educational circles apathy dissipated: the field became professionalized, and attention shifted to the technical problems of assessment, pedagogy, classroom management, and curriculum. Segregated classes were again promoted enthusiastically, with a strong impetus coming from parents, who combined forces to demand special facilities, outside the institutions, for their children. An upsurge of funding by the states and the federal government peaked during the late 1950s and 1960s (Reynolds, 1975).

The quality of life and education for disabled children and adults, especially those mentally retarded, improved greatly throughout the 1960s. Disabled persons found friends in the White House, and federal commitment expanded quickly. During the 1960s the problems of differential programming, along with some possible solutions, were mapped out in detail. Parents increased their demands that their exceptional children be provided with educational services in local school districts. Educators began to critically question the value of special classes; numerous efficacy studies delved into the justification for and effects of educational segregation.

By the 1970s a more humanistic movement had emerged; it represented a gradual but positive change in society's attitudes toward exceptional persons. The traditional notions that exceptional children should be educated separately from their peers or that mentally handicapped people should be herded into large institutional settings were now rejected. A key goal of society became the normalization of all exceptional individuals, which meant regarding exceptional people as individuals and treating them fairly and humanely. As segregated facilities that were once taken for granted were seriously challenged, many institutionalized people moved from large institutions into more normal living environments.

Educators came to agree that all children, exceptionality notwithstanding, had the right to an appropriate education at public expense. There was a powerful surge within the educational system toward the abandonment of many special classes and their replacement by regular class programs supported by special education services. The movement to mainstream exceptional students culminated in federal legislation when in 1975 the Education for All Handicapped Children Act, Public Law 94-142, was passed. Canadians closely observed the experiences of their American neighbors and rapidly followed suit, adopting the ideology and practice of normalization and mainstreaming but without enabling federal legislation.

The changes wrought in special education and the underlying practical and philosophical bases for these changes are diverse, numerous, and complex. Especially from the mid-1940s on, commitment, financing, and the involvement of government administrators, legislators, professional educators, parents, researchers, and those in allied disciplines increased dramatically. Special education, always closely allied with the medical and psychological disciplines, now cross-cut a wider swath that included medicine, neurology, genetics, pharmacology, psychology in all its many miens, linguistics, and psycholinguistics, to mention a few. It also included a range of paraprofessional fields such as audiology, public health, and social work. Legislation and litigation in a number of areas affected the schooling of exceptional pupils. Changing diagnoses, terminology, and definitions of exceptional people added to positive changes in the school system. All these fundamental alterations in special education that rescued it from a deeply ingrained dumping-ground mentality stemmed from the humanitarian principles that began circulating in society in the 1960s.

Students who were deaf, blind, or otherwise disabled were certainly not ignored in these advances. But it was to individuals with mental retardation that the greatest attention in educational, social, and vocational domains was directed. The enormous expansion of segregated classes in the 1940s mainly served mentally retarded pupils. The efficacy studies that challenged the school system in the 1960s and the challenges to institutionalization of the same period were similarly focused on the needs of the mentally retarded population.

One chapter could not adequately cover all the positive advances that have occurred in the past forty years. This section highlights only a few of the most important influences that propelled the humanitarian and social changes and briefly describes the way exceptional students came to enjoy the same rights allowed their nondisabled peers.

Chapter 12

Approaching Integration

Key Dates in the Recent History of Special Education

1910	The first White House Conference on Children is held
1919	The second White House Conference is held
1920s	John Dewey's Progressive educational principles are used in special education classrooms
1930	The White House Conference on Child Health and Protection is held; the Children's Charter is issued
1933	Cuyahoga County Ohio Council for the Retarded Child is established
1936	Blind persons are included under the Social Security Act (1935)
1940	The White House Conference on Children in a Democracy is held
1954	The U.S. Supreme Court hands down its decision in *Brown vs. Board of Education*
1958	Public Law 85-926 provides grants for training special education personnel
1959	The principle of normalization is incorporated into Danish law
1962	President John F. Kennedy's Panel on Mental Retardation is convened
1963	The Division of Handicapped Children and Youth is established within the U.S. Department of Health, Education and Welfare; Samuel Kirk first uses the term *learning disabilities*
1968	Lloyd Dunn publishes "Special Education for the Handicapped: Is Much of It Justified?"
1970	In Canada the Commission on Emotional and Learning Disorders in Children lays the groundwork for educational integration
1975	Public Law 94-142, the Education for All Handicapped Children Act, is passed by Congress

In the 1880s schooling, and compulsory school attendance for the handicapped or disadvantaged children were the leading subjects of theoretical discussion. By 1910 they had become imperatives. For nearly all children schooling became the social norm in the opening decades of the twentieth century. Schools sought to design programs and instruction for the average student; those above or below the mean required the ministrations of special classes, special programs, and special teachers.

The movement of disabled students from institutionalization to public school—from isolation to segregation—may be dated from about 1910 with the formation of permanent segregated classes in the public schools. The advent of segregated classes was greeted with enthusiasm, and until the end of the 1920s they seemed to meet the needs of students with behavior and learning disorders.

Undoubtedly, public expectations of the ability of the schools to handle and instruct "the school children who are crippled, deaf, suffering from speech or visual defects, the mentally deficient, the feeble-minded, the mentally disordered, and the moral delinquent" were hard to fulfill (Wallin, 1924). But special educators, perhaps more able at advocacy than prophecy, were sure that special classes were here to stay and would prove to be significantly advantageous for special students, especially when compared with regular classroom placement. Educators believed that segregated classes could offer disabled students the most benefits. A low student-teacher ratio could afford more individualized instruction for each child, while homogeneous groupings could enable the teacher to concentrate on fewer teaching strategies. Because the academic environment would be less competitive, the students' self-esteem would be improved. It was also thought that segregated classes could provide remedial instruction that could return some children to the regular classroom (although this rarely happened) (Winzer, 1992).

In the two decades spanning 1910 to 1930 segregated classes in the public schools grew at railroad rate and were accompanied by rapid increases in allied professions and services. State appropriations to support special education services expanded, and federal commitment became manifest with one of the most significant milestones in the field of special education, the 1930 White House Conference on Child Health and Protection.

The organizational planning for child rescue on a national level got a tentative start with the first White House Conference on Children in 1910, which was held to review management techniques used by big business, to consider what the government could do about children, to gather support for legislation (Bremner, 1956), and to define and establish remedial programs for special children. Although the 1910 White House conference began to take stock of children's needs, it was not until 1919, the year Woodrow Wilson declared the year of the child, that a more extensive view of special education was taken.

Now a tradition, the White House conferences sponsor studies every ten years to establish goals for improving the quality of life for children in the next decade. The White House conferences had enormous impact in advocacy for children's rights. They led indirectly but unquestionably to the adoption by the U.N. National Assembly (1959) of the Declaration of the Rights of the Child, which demanded the recognition of the rights of all children to develop to their full capacity.

The 1930 White House Conference on Child Health and Protection, called by President Herbert Hoover (who assumed a portion of the conference costs himself), was the largest conference on child welfare ever held in the United States to that time, actively involving 1,200 experts (Cohen, 1983). It gave birth to the Children's Charter, saw the presentation of an extensive report on special education, made important recommendations for exceptional children, and marked the first time that special education received national recognition as a legitimate part of the educational community.

The Children's Charter, a variation on a recurring theme, spoke to the therapeutic and educational needs of exceptional children. "For every child who is blind, deaf, crippled or otherwise physically handicapped, and for the child who is mentally handicapped," the charter recommended "such measures as will early discover and diagnose his handicap, provide care and treatment, and so train him that he may become an asset to society rather than a liability. Expenses for these services should be borne publicly where they cannot be privately met" (quoted by F. E. Howard, 1935, p. 277).

Further recommendations, ambitious and encompassing, arose from the conference. These centered on extending special education to greater numbers of children; making better efforts at diagnosis, treatment, and training; coordinating services; modifying the curriculum so that it conformed to abilities; increasing the vocational orientation of special education; overseeing job placement and follow-up; establishing a national council for handicapped children with state advisory councils; and engaging in more active campaigns to publicize the needs and advantages of special education (White House Conference, 1930, 1931). Further, the conference enunciated a basic outline for occupational education: vocational guidance, vocational training, occupational information, and vocational and social placement, most especially for mentally retarded persons.

DECLINE IN THE 1930s

In the general optimism of the gilded 1920s, only occasionally were concerns raised about special education, its rationale, its themes, its clientele, and its progress. But generally questions about what special education actually did were overwhelmed by the belief that special education's problems were quantitative—there simply was not enough of it. At the 1930 White House Conference the Committee on Special Classes presented "a study of conditions so obviously needing improvement that there should be no hesitation in effecting the recommendations of the various subcommittees" (White House Conference, 1931, p. 3). The committee acknowledged that special education was accepted in many urban school systems, that it had grown substantially since the early part of the century, and that a number of states provided financial aid, but members still fretted that the vast majority of potential clients did not receive special education.

During the Depression children stayed in school longer, the use of work permits declined, and the need for special education increased. The Committee on Special Classes estimated a total of 10 million students requiring special education to be present in the schools, of whom only 1 million were receiving additional aid (White House Conference, 1931). By 1934 special educators were still asserting that fully nine-tenths of exceptional children in the United States and Canada were floundering within the confines of regular classrooms and inappropriate curricula because their problems had not been identified ("Editorial," 1934). Many other potential students were out of school and beyond the reach of appropriate educational programs. Some of the most recalcitrant pupils were simply excluded or expelled; others dropped out or were considered unteachable.

Speakers at the 1930 conference echoed the sentiments of Samuel Gridley Howe, Alexander Graham Bell, and dozens of other nineteenth-century pioneers in special education when they announced, "Special education is not charity. It is good economy and sound public policy to provide medical treatment, special education, and rehabilitation for the disabled rather than leave them unemployed and dependent their lifetimes long" (White House Conference, 1930), pp. 6–7). Nevertheless, the White House Committee on Special Education and special educators believed that opposition to further expansion of special education was strong.

After the verve and expansion of special education in the 1920s, the 1930s witnessed a sharp decline. Special education may have been sound economy, but now educators, legislators, and other professionals turned away from the venture that had evoked such excitement a decade before. For example, Philadelphia, which in the 1920s had prominently featured special education, virtually ceased to acknowledge its existence in the next decade. New Jersey and California, states that passed special education legislation between 1910 and 1929, did almost nothing throughout the 1930s. As of 1935 New York City had only 500 teachers, psychologists, and social workers for 11,000 exceptional children (F. E. Howard, 1935).

Factors both within and without education generated an apathy that collapsed toward rejection. For one thing, all of North America, caught in the depths of the Great Depression, was struggling under straitened circumstances. Within the educational system poorly trained teachers, a lack of enthusiasm among other teachers in the schools, poor or ill-conceived curricula, and a low rate of success for disabled pupils, especially those labeled as mentally retarded, engendered deep pessimism about the progress and future of special classes.

At the opening of the twentieth century the school system was the object of a reform effort that hoped to cure all of education's ills. A public school system seemed an ideal organizational form for a democratic society, but the compulsory education laws led to a conflict between its democratic beliefs and its need to maintain order and high standards (Tropea, 1987a). Professional rhetoric combined with bureaucratic action to create special classes and special curricula for exceptional students (Tropea, 1987a). Public school special education offered school administrators a way to maintain the common school ideal of full accessibility in a changing society. Yet contradictions that would subvert the promises of special education were inherent in the plan. By the 1930s the contradictions had become pronounced, and reform ideology fell to practical necessity.

The development of special education and regular school programs had always progressed unevenly. Inevitably, there developed a sharp separation between regular and special education among both teachers and pupils. In the 1930s the social space between regular and special education widened into a chasm. Special education teachers and their exceptional pupils were isolated from the mainstream of education; special educators and regular classroom teachers lived in separate environments, each thinking the other used different methods and spoke a different language.

The democratic ideal of equal access was slowly eroded. Practices that seemed innocuous, even encouraging to the advancement of exceptional students, in truth subjected them to differential and, far too often, disparaging treatment (Tropea, 1987b). The advent of special classes raised the expectations of regular classroom teachers about the type and range of children they should accept in their classrooms and created a broad category of youngsters generically described as handicapped, defective, atypical, or exceptional. Then recalcitrant, backward, mentally retarded, and other exceptional students became subject to the selective use of exclusion and increasingly to indiscriminate segregation (see Tropea, 1987a, 1987b). Special classes too often served negatively, simply to eliminate unwanted students from the regular classrooms. By the 1930s many placements in the special classes thus became as restrictive and custodial as placements in the earlier institutions had been. Conditions were deplorable; children struggling with different conditions were lumped together, and no real effort was made to teach them. Special class students were stigmatized by their placements and taught by poorly trained personnel; placed in virtual isolation, they endured deplorable conditions. A self-contained special class became just another name for a lower track. "By relegating the less able and the nonconforming into the lower track, educators found a way of setting such children aside" (Dunn, 1973, pp. 45–46).

Disabled students, while not encountering the isolation of institutional settings, found that segregated classes led to another kind of isolation—public school classes in basements, down dark hallways, and in former closets or somewhere in the back of the main school building. Children were totally segregated—although in the same building, they entered and left school at different times and were kept apart at recess (Coveney, 1942).

Physical separation generated social rejection and stigmatization. Special classes were "so regarded that they cast a stigma on anyone who is assigned to them" (Chicago, 1932, p. 100). "If this attitude of mind were confined to teachers and principals alone it would be bad enough," the report noted, "but it inevitably spreads to the entire school community" (pp. 100–101). Regular pupils were "inevitably trained to look upon the more unfortunate members of the school community as persons to be avoided, ridiculed, or maliciously tormented" (p. 101).

Not only did the stigma associated with special placement foster negative attitudes in regular students, but it was used as a means of subtle coercion of assigned pupils. Optimism in special education had led to false hopes that the classes could greatly elevate the function of low-level pupils. Hence, the classes were "frequently used as a club over children who are not otherwise amenable in order to admonish them to renewed efforts in their studies" (Chicago, 1932, pp. 100–101). And, although educators asserted that "the immediate purpose of most of these special classes is, of course, to enable the pupils to mingle in due course with normal children" (Percival, 1947), this rarely happened although an inbuilt bribe was apparent. In Chicago (1932) "return to the regular class (and thus escape from the stigmas of the special class) is often held out as a prize to children who have been assigned to the special class, in order to stimulate them to learn facts which otherwise can mean little to them" (pp. 100–101).

THE SPECIAL CLASS CURRICULUM

The curriculum in special classes was no more settled than were the classes themselves. Oral approaches to communication were almost exclusively employed with deaf students; Braille was now used in the education of blind pupils. Sight-saving classes, as the name implies, were dedicated to assisting students to preserve their residual vision, not, as is the current practice, to use it fully. Special education experts in mental retardation advocated widely differing approaches to schooling. The field abounded in uncertainty and controversy over the direction it should take (Scheerenberger, 1983), which led to bickering among professionals.

The 1920s saw two main themes in Progressive education emerge: the developmental movement of John Dewey and others, and the scientific movement of Edward Lee Thorndike. Thorndike and Dewey both spoke in a Progressive idiom, but the differences that separated them were significant. The object of Progressive education was to provide a link between the school curriculum and the demands of adult life; to give society the capacities it needed at all levels to address the problems of twentieth-century urban industrial living through a scientifically based education more tailored to the individual. One important constituent was a child-centered curriculum that included practical subjects and the social and natural sciences. Dewey's and Thorndike's ideas vied for dominance in special education classrooms. In contrast to Dewey with his developmental approach to psychology stood Thorndike with his enormous emphasis on practice in the three *R*s and insistence on measurement in all aspects of education, supported by the importance assigned to the IQ tests.

Special education had a strong appeal as the logical extension of American Progressivism; in fact, some of what might be ascribed to Progressive education was already in place in the special schools. As the gospel of Progressive education, most clearly articulated in the work of Dewey, spread, its principles and practices were woven seamlessly into the goals of special education. The tenets of Progressive education found ready acceptance in special classes, as the more formal academic programs were recognized as inadequate and educators realized that the traditional structures of the regular classroom were inappropriate for disabled children (Stevens, 1954).

Teachers adopted the essential tenets of Dewey's Progressive education only to be disappointed, at least in some cases. The problem was rooted in a misinterpretation of the assumptions of Progressive education, typified by the notion that any basically good teacher could teach any group of special children (Robinson and Robinson, 1965). Moreover, "while we expounded progressive education theories," apologized a 1939 writer, "we did not practice them." The "older teachers were skeptical of the changes from formality to freedom," while "the young teachers were easily convinced of the value of progressive education, but did not know enough about exceptional children to adopt their techniques wisely" (Grave, 1939).

After a period of excitement and experimentation with Dewey's ideas, Thorndike's ideas became more influential. Even if it is allowed that Dewey had more influence across a greater range of scholarly domains—philosophy, sociology, politics, and social psychology—Thorndike's thought was more influential in education. It helped to shape public school practice as well as scholarship about education (Lagemann, 1989). Quantitative studies about the three Rs dominated special education classrooms. "At no other time in history," observed a later writer, "was so much learned about how we read, write, and spell," (Stevens, 1954, p. 60). Influenced by the scientific genre, teachers questioned the handwork-oriented curricula of traditional special education classrooms as well as the incidental learning of the activity method. By the 1930s drill had become the watchword of special education. Curricula were apt to be weakened versions of those used in the regular schools but lacking the stimulation and substituting the drab rigor of drill.

Postwar Developments

The 1940s may be considered a landmark decade in special education and the history of disability. The dearth of developments in the 1930s was forgotten as interest and involvement in the area was revitalized. The war and postwar period witnessed promising shifts in perceptions about and commitment to exceptional students and their education. The result was improved conditions for all disabled individuals, for their teachers, and for their parents. Not only did Canada and the United States seem to feel a profound need to heal their war wounded and assist the world's refugees; they seemed to be moved by a more humanitarian philosophy that impelled a renewed commitment to assisting those individuals with physical and mental disorders.

Prominent people in many fields began to lend a higher visibility and importance to the push for better education for disabled children. Professional knowledge in special education expanded rapidly, complemented by advances in medicine, psychology, and technology. Day classes were again promoted enthusiastically, with a strong impetus coming from parents who demanded special facilities for their children. Concurrently, children's centers, social services, coordinating councils, and a growing number of agencies flourished (Melcher, 1976).

Public perceptions changed in part because of an increased visibility of disabled persons in general society. The war effort propelled many exceptional persons into the mainstream to join the regular work force. By October 1942 it was estimated that 3 million disabled men and women were engaged in the war industry throughout the country (W. B. Miller, 1943). Simply the sight of disabled persons engaged in functional, integrated, and age-appropriate activities appears to have had a positive effect (Bates et al., 1984). Moreover, the war effort demonstrated that many mentally retarded persons could support themselves after the school years. In the next decade studies of the adjustment after their schooling was complete of moderately mentally retarded youths (those having IQs between about 40 and 55) (Delp and Lorenz, 1953; Saenger, 1957; Tisdall, 1958) found decreasing rates of institutionalization.

Public awareness of the ability of individuals with disabilities to pursue employment had risen steadily since the days following World War I, when thousands of physically disabled American veterans required assistance in returning to the work force. Federal legislation for vocational education was enacted in 1917, although it paid no attention to youth or adults with handicaps. In 1918 Congress enacted the first Vocational Rehabilitation Act to serve veterans, which also initiated translation services for blind individuals. Further federal funding was provided when Woodrow Wilson signed the Federal Civilian Rehabilitation Act on April 8, 1920; the act entitled veterans and all disabled citizens to a training that would enhance their economic independence. The Smith-Fess Act of 1918 authorized the expenditure of $750,000 for a joint federal-state program for the physically disabled. Throughout the 1920s and 1930s a few programs designed to serve the unemployed, (for example, the Civilian Conservation Corps,) benefited some youths with handicaps (Rusch and Phelps, 1987). The 1943 amendments to the Vocational Rehabilitation Act expanded services, including rehabilitation counseling for persons with mental disabilities (Rusch and Phelps, 1987).

Meager attempts to normalize a smattering of disabled individuals in the war period were accompanied by a flurry of major medical and technical breakthroughs that benefited the disabled population (Lee, 1944). Medical personnel studied diseases of the brain, mother-child blood incompatability, rubella, anoxia, endocrine chemistry as a cause of cretinism, and the effects of early nutrition on a child's development (Stevens, 1954). Dilantin for the control of epilepsy was developed in the 1940s, as was EEG technology (Miles, 1944). Antiobiotics effectively ended the reign of such childhood diseases as whooping cough and diphtheria; the etiologies of several handicapping conditions (for example, retinopathy of prematurity and rubella) were also discovered in the 1940s. Transparent incubators for infants began to be used in the 1940s (Hughes, 1980). Hearing aids became smaller and more sophisticated (Lee, 1944). Training for guide dogs, used by blind persons from the time of ancient China, received new impetus after World War I, and Dr. Richard Hoover developed techniques for using the long white cane more effectively following World War II. Improved hearing aids and mobility devices translated into improved methods and aids in teaching, particularly in the auditory and visual fields (Lee, 1944).

Special segregated classes were again promoted with the zeal of the 1920s. Although World War II provided brief respite to the schools by lowering enrollment rates and increasing work for youth, the numbers of students soon expanded again rapidly. In 1940 a total of 400,000 children in the United States were enrolled in some type of special school or special class, although conservative estimates placed the number actually needing attention as closer to 4 million. By 1947, 500,000 American and Canadian children in 7,000 city school systems were receiving special education from 1,600 teachers and supervisors (Dunlop, 1947). In 1920 only three states had directors or supervisors of special education; by 1946 twenty-five states had directors of special education (Martens,

1946). In the period between 1948 and 1953 the enrollment of children in special schools and classes increased 47 percent, and the number of school districts providing special education services increased 83 percent; the number of teachers in special programs grew by 48 percent. However, still only about 18 percent of all exceptional pupils were in specially adapted school programs (A. S. Hill, 1956).

The special class curriculum for mentally retarded pupils showed more sophistication. Educators abandoned at least some of the repetitious drill that had characterized earlier classes as well as the simplified curriculum that stressed manual training, sewing, drawing, nature study, and domestic arts (see Coveney, 1942). In Boston, for example, grave concerns about the reading standards of special class pupils led to changes in the reading program. Books were now to have "a content of an interest level two or three grades above the vocabulary level, . . . a vocabulary burden well controlled and characterized by simplicity and frequent repetition . . . print and illustrations—attractive to Special Class children" (Coveney, 1942, p. 58). There was greater emphasis on social participation and social contributions for mentally retarded students. They were provided a program of occupational education, and teachers were given the skills to help with specialized job placements and follow-up services.

Parents were now more willing to admit publicly to the presence and the needs of their exceptional children. Beginning in the early 1930s a few parents' groups began to form throughout the country: the first such group was the Cuyahoga County Ohio Council for the Retarded Child, established in 1933. Throughout the 1940s parents almost spontaneously began uniting to form strong, local, state, and national organizations. By 1954, for example, more than 30,000 people were actively involved in groups for retarded children (Stevens, 1954).

Professionals serving disabled individuals began to amalgamate their efforts and activities into both scholarly and political forces, which were reinforced by parental demands for services for the disabled (see Melcher, 1976). Often in uneasy alliance, the combined parental and professional groups became a potent force. They developed considerable local, state, and national prestige and added their voices to the call for carrying out fundamental mandates (Melcher, 1976).

Legislators, both at the state and national levels, decided that the disabled population was due their political consideration, and it became politically popular for legislators to fight for these people who had been avoided for so long (Melcher, 1976). In state after state lobbying organizations convinced key legislators to support more special education, fought the apathy and hostility of departments of education, and featured prominently in writing the legislation itself.

In the field of special education, permissive legislation is that which allows school boards to accept and instruct exceptional pupils; mandatory legislation says that they must and will do so. State efforts on behalf of permissive or mandatory legislation began with New Jersey in 1911, Minnesota in 1915, and Wisconsin, New York, and Illinois in 1917. The Depression slowed the process, but the effort accelerated again in the 1940s, when many states passed basic special education laws or broadened existing laws. Canada, where education is solely a provincial responsibility, began to acknowledge exceptional students in the various provincial school acts.

By 1946 there were well over a hundred laws in the United States dealing with the education of exceptional children. Thirty-three states had enacted legislation for the physically handicapped; sixteen, legislation for the mentally retarded (Martens, 1946). A total of thirty-nine states provided some form of mandatory or permissive legislation for their handicapped school-aged populations by 1951 (A. S. Hill, 1951–2). States in which legislative action was applied to the exceptionally gifted or to the socially and emotionally maladjusted, however, could be counted on one hand (Martens, 1946). Gifted students gained with the 1975 passage of Public Law 94-142. In Canada only Ontario specifically mentions gifted students in its legislation. Students defined as socially and emotionally maladjusted did not fare as well with Public Law 94-142, and debate continues as to whether social maladjustment can rightly be considered an exceptionality requiring special education.

THE 1950s

Although the late 1940s saw the public assume a substantially more sympathetic attitude toward mentally retarded persons, in many cases the new viewpoints failed to recognize their full humanity and citizenship. Many felt that protective treatment was owed to people with mental disabilities because they were perpetual children, forever innocent and lacking in significant abilities (Ellis, 1990, p. 264). However, the 1950s saw the development of a more optimistic view of the potential of disabled persons, particularly in the area of mental retardation.

For the first time, public concern and consciousness were directed toward providing mentally retarded individuals with the same opportunities available to ordinary citizens. Several landmark legal decisions designed to safeguard the basic human rights of mentally retarded individuals established as their constitutional right such principles as due process, equal protection under the law, and protection from cruel and unusual punishment (Rosen, Clark, and Kivitz, 1976). In addition, immense pressure was building to reverse the trend of institutionalization, to improve institutions, and to expand public school services for the mentally retarded.

In general, the 1950s saw an accelerating trend toward the recognition of the importance of disabled pupils and their rights to suitable educational facilities. The amount of special education increased and enrollments swelled; the preparation of personnel expanded, and state and financial commitment grew. Educational policy making moved from local school boards to state agencies, a redirection that increased opportunities for mentally retarded children (Scheerenberger, 1983).

The 1950s was an important decade in the legislative advocacy of parents of mentally retarded children. Parents banded together through the National Association for Retarded Children, which became a powerful legislative lobby. The association, for example, produced such position statements as the "Educational Bill of Rights for the Retarded Child," adopted in October 1953, which proclaimed the right of every mentally retarded child to a "program of education and training suited to his particular needs" (Zigler, Hoddap, and Edison, 1990, p. 4). Parent groups also set out to educate legislators to the needs of the disabled and to sensitize them to some of the problems involved in making adequate provisions for these children (Paul and Warnock, 1980).

By the early 1950s special classes had gained almost universal acceptance as a means for educating exceptional children. The most pronounced increases in newly developed special education services seemed to be in the field of mental retardation (A. S. Hill, 1951a).

By the 1950s the expulsion of pupils from public school systems in the United States was largely precluded by law; American school authorities thus were forced to resolve classroom problems within the organization of the school (Tropea, 1987b). The polio epidemic of the 1950s and the rubella epidemic of the 1960s generated still greater demand for special education. Moreover, advances in medicine meant that many disabled children simply lived longer and that many more high-risk infants were surviving. Not only that, but mental retardation, which had been defined to include children with IQs 85 and below (1 standard deviation below the mean), in 1972 was redefined to the 2 standard deviation below the mean. With this change, 80 percent of the mentally retarded population was eliminated (Zetlin and Murtaugh, 1990).

The net result of all these changes was huge expansions in numbers: between 1948 and 1968 the number of children in public school special education classes in the United States went from 357,000 to 2,252,000, or from 1.2 to 4.5 percent of the total enrollment in kindergarten to grade twelve.

THE 1960s

The fervent egalitarianism and humanism of the 1960s created a wholly new climate for exceptionality. The deprived and the oppressed, and those who saw themselves that way, became more militant, and the civil rights movement brought decisive action to improve the lot of blacks, of Chicanos, of women, and of the disabled.

During the late 1950s and the 1960s educators, parents, and professionals began to seriously question society's stereotypes about exceptional persons as well as the value of segregated classes. The 1960s ushered in a series of exposés about society's treatment of disabled persons, of studies of the efficacy of segregated classes, and a massive infusion of funding into and growth of professional and community interest in the problems of social disadvantage.

The Kennedy era marked a period of considerable federal interest in special education, vocational education, vocational rehabilitation, and other programs designed to assist unemployed disabled youths and adults (Rusch and Phelps, 1987). The federal government began to move slowly into a supportive role in both finance and research. Mentally retarded citizens especially benefited, for they finally had found their own spokespersons and advocates. John F. Kennedy's interest in the problems of mental retardation stemmed, at least in part, from his having a mentally retarded sister. Later, Vice President Hubert

Humphrey's granddaughter, who had Down syndrome, served to spur further sympathy and concern during the Lyndon B. Johnson administration.

In 1963 President Kennedy announced the formation of the Division of Handicapped Children and Youth, of which Samuel Kirk became director in 1964 (Burke, 1976). Especially encouraging was the development of a revitalized Bureau of Education for the Handicapped, which served as a rallying point in government for those concerned with the education of the disabled. The bureau also was a source of financial risk capital to fund creative programming in the education of children with exceptional needs at the state and local levels (Melcher, 1976).

President Kennedy's Panel on Mental Retardation in the early 1960s sent missions to study programs for the mentally retarded in Russia, the Netherlands, and Scandinavia. The panel's extensive report to the president in 1962, "A Proposed Program for National Action to Combat Mental Retardation," detailed the need for each state to establish a protective service for retarded individuals in an appropriate state agency (Melcher, 1976). Guardianship of the property of a retarded person was to be clearly differentiated from guardianship of the person; the court was to be provided with a comprehensive clinical evaluation by appropriate personnel drawn from the professions of medicine, psychology, education, and social work. A judicial review every two years regarding the need for continued institutional care of all retarded adults, whatever their type of admission, was recommended. Further, the whole body of law on mental retardation was to be reviewed periodically in each jurisdiction (Melcher, 1976).

The report adopted by the White House Conference on Children in a Democracy of January 1940 had stated, among other things: "Schools should give increased attention to the educational needs of individual children, including those who are physically handicapped, mentally retarded or socially handicapped" (*White House Conference,* 1940, p. 36). Until the 1960s, however, little federal commitment was expressed by way of legislation. Typically, attempts at federal legislation did not ask for specific appropriations for specific disabilities (T. A. Turner, 1944). The single traditional exception is the body of federal laws concerning blind persons. Indeed, no group among the physically handicapped has been as favored by special legislation as the legally blind. Their benefits have encompassed areas as diverse as tax exemptions or deductions, the privilege of operating vending machines in federal buildings, reduced postage rates for reading and writing materials, special appropriations for books and for Social Security, rehabilitation centers, and well-staffed and well-financed welfare agencies, both governmental and voluntary (Kim, 1970).

Throughout the 1960s federal and state assistance contributed to further expansion in special education. For example, in 1949 there were 175 institutions in the United States offering programs to prepare professionals in special education. In 1957 forty American colleges and universities offered course work on mental retardation, and in these schools there were only twenty-eight full-time and sixty-four part-time instructors (Burke, 1976). The first program in Canada was established in 1959 (Strothers, 1959). Thanks to enabling legislation, the period from 1958 to 1976 witnessed spectacular growth of such programs, which grew from fewer than forty to more than four hundred (Burke, 1976; see Harvey, 1978; Kirby, 1980). Public Law 85-926 (1959) provided federal grants to univer-

sities and colleges for training leaders in special education and to state education agencies for training teachers of the mentally retarded. In October 1963
President Kennedy signed Public Law 88-164, which broadened the earlier legislation to include most children with severe handicaps. The new law also defined the target population to include not only the mentally retarded but
children who were "hard of hearing, deaf, speech impaired, visually handicapped, seriously emotionally disturbed, crippled, or other health impaired children who by reason thereof require special education" (quoted by Burke, 1976,
p. 144).

Amendments to these early efforts followed. Public Law 90-170 authorized
programs in physical education and recreation and the training of personnel; in
1968 Public Law 90-576 provided for grants to other agencies in addition to colleges and universities and state agencies. Public Law 91-230 (1970), the initial
Education of the Handicapped Act, reinforced the federal commitment to the
preparation of personnel to educate special children, as did Public Law 93-380,
an amendment passed in 1974 (Burke, 1976; Martin, 1968).

CHALLENGES TO INSTITUTIONALIZATION

Even with the huge increases in the number and clientele of special segregated classes in the public schools, institutions continued to flourish, accepting
the most severely disabled children. Segregation was rationalized on numerous
grounds, that: the public school system could not provide for grossly deviant
children; the low incidence of certain disabilities in the population made it difficult to group children locally for educational purposes; teachers needed very
specialized training; certain categories of exceptional children were happier
with their own kind; specialized equipment, such as Braillers and hearing aids,
could not easily be provided by the regular school system; and some children,
such as the severely mentally retarded and the multiply handicapped, required
custodial care (Roberts and Lazure, 1970).

The 1950s brought a recognition of the need for standards in the institutions
for the mentally retarded; in 1959 the American Association on Mental Deficiency (AAMD) published a report on institutional standards (Sparr and Smith,
1990). However, in 1966 in the United States the per capita cost for mentally retarded persons in residential settings was less than five dollars a day (Holburn,
1990). Writers presented horrifying illustrated descriptions of conditions in institutions for mentally retarded persons and juvenile delinquents (Blatt and
Kaplan, 1960; Rivera, 1972; Vail, 1966). Photographs showed poorly clothed or
naked residents, residents in solitary rooms, and large, lonely day rooms
smeared with excrement on walls, floors, and even ceilings (Zigler, Hoddap, and
Edison, 1990). These "poignant exposés revealed the frequent tragedies in the
human condition" (Sparr and Smith, 1990, p. 95). Blatt described institutions for
the mentally retarded as a "land of the living dead" (Blatt and Kaplan, 1960,
p. v). When *Look* magazine published many of the photographs, the public response was greater than that drawn by any previous piece in the magazine
(Zigler, Hoddap, and Edison, 1990). Public scrutiny brought some improvements
to the deplorable conditions. By 1969 three-quarters of the institutions in the
country were observing AAMD standards (Sparr and Smith, 1990).

At the same time, advocates like Wolf Wolfensberger (1964a, 1964b, 1965) published their observations about the treatment of mentally retarded individuals in several countries; their work laid the groundwork for the movement of the 1970s to normalize and deinstitutionalize mentally retarded children and adults.

CHALLENGES TO THE SCHOOLS

Occasional questions about what special education was and what it actually did, articulated during the 1950s, grew more insistent in the next decade. Even though it was contended in 1965 that "the consensus of special educators today definitely favors special class placement for the mildly retarded" (Robinson and Robinson, 1965, p. 43), vexatious questioning of segregated classes mounted. Numerous studies that compared the progress of exceptional children in segregated and regular classes found that children performed no better in special classes (e.g., Bradfield et al., 1973; Bruininks, Rynders, and Gross, 1974; Dunn, 1968; Gallagher, 1972; Myers, 1976; Reynolds and Birch, 1977). Some claimed that special classes were too often used as dumping grounds; others pointed out that special education was often exclusionary rather than remedial and that special education did not appear to be returning a significant number of children to the regular classroom (Gallagher, 1972). Educators also argued that special education placement cast a stigma on exceptional children; children from special classes were barely tolerated by regular classroom teachers and administrators. Further, it was argued, segregated education provided low-quality education and was often allotted inferior facilities and untrained teachers (Winzer, 1992).

A serious concern was the apparently disproportionate number of minority group children placed in segregated classes, especially those for the mentally retarded. There was the suspicion that minority-group pupils were slotted into such programs more for the convenience of educators than for the good of the children.

Critical questioning of segregated placements and studies of their effectiveness led inevitably to a search for new solutions and the beginnings of integration. More strongly than ever, parents sought an increased involvement in the education of their children: they encouraged school boards to provide programs for their children or banded together to begin their own programs. Parents were successful in bringing litigation to establish the educational rights of exceptional learners, the results manifested in the formulation of policies and practices that allow parents more rights in the educational process. The formation of the Association for Children with Learning Disabilities in 1963, which became an important lobbying group in the United States and Canada, accelerated the agitation.

A growing feeling of urgency developed among parents and others who refused to let a good idea such as educational integration "walk rather than run" (Melcher, 1976). The reasoning of the Supreme Court in its *Brown vs. Board of Education* (1954) decision—that racially segregated classrooms could not be separate but equal—impinged on the thinking of special educators and parents (Blatt, Ozolins, and McNally, 1979). The activism of the professionals and the parents brought a torrent of legislation at the state level and a sharp increase in litigation calling states and school districts to task for violating statutes, constitutions, and the rights of children (Melcher, 1976).

From the mid-1960s on there was a series of cases in federal courts attacking special education on various fronts. The arguments presented to the courts focused on five points: that tests were inappropriate, that parental involvement was lacking, that special education itself was inadequate, that placement was inadequate, and that placement stigmatized children (Ross, De Young, and Cohen, 1971; Zelder, 1953). Important cases included *Diana vs. State Board of Education in California* (1970), *Pennsylvania Association for Retarded Citizens vs. the Commonwealth of Pennsylvania* (1971), *Mills vs. the Board of Education of the District of Columbia* (1972), *Colorado Association for Retarded Citizens vs. the State of Colorado* (1972), *Kentucky Association for Retarded Citizens vs. Kentucky* (1974), and *Panitch vs. the State of Wisconsin* (1974) (Melcher, 1976).

THE 1970s

Well into the 1970s many professionals held segregated classes to be the most promising option for exceptional students. Certainly, concerns about what special education actually did and about the inherent values of segregation increased throughout the 1930s and 1940s. But it was not until the late 1950s that moral and social philosophies moved in the direction of advocating the rights of individuals, specifically the mentally retarded, and these new focuses resulted in major advances.

The propitious educational and social climate that promoted equal opportunities for exceptional persons grew out of humanistic principles that began circulating in society in the early 1960s. Tentatively at first, and then with increasing conviction, professionals, parents, and the disabled themselves began to question the legitimacy of traditional perceptions and educational practices.

In general, society had shifted from qualitative to quantitative conceptions of exceptionality. The qualitative model holds that disabled individuals are different and deviant—they learn, perceive, and think in ways that are unlike the normal. The quantitative model views these differences as a matter of degree, not kind—exceptional people develop and function much as others do, but their progress may be slower and their achievements more restricted (Telford and Sawrey, 1981).

The 1970s saw the flowering of the ideologies of normalization and mainstreaming. The normalization principle, which advocates making available to mentally retarded and other disabled persons patterns and conditions of everyday life that are as close as possible to those of the mainstream society, was incorporated into Danish law in 1959. Beng Nirje, then secretary general of the Swedish Association for Retarded Children, began to apply this principle to retarded children and adults in 1967. In 1968 in the United States the President's Committee on Mental Retardation issued a monograph (Kugel and Wolfensberger, 1969) that outlined the theoretical and functional aspects of normalization and brought to public attention the ideas on normalization that had been used in Scandinavia (Juul, 1978).

Western society began to reject the policies that once subjected the severely handicapped to lifelong institutionalization. The normalization credo provides guidelines for the treatment of disabled people as well as concrete suggestions for action. The policy offers disabled people the chance of a normal life routine, normal developmental experiences, independent choices, and the right to live, work, and play in normal surroundings. Disabled persons are encouraged to remain in their own communities through the availability of foster homes, group homes, hostels, community training centers, day-care facilities, and community-based social services. Ultimately, normalization will have occurred when exceptional individuals live with members of the cultural group in a normal domicile within the community, and when they have access to all the privileges and services that are available to others (see Wolfensberger, 1972).

An obvious outgrowth of the philosophy of normalization is the process of deinstitutionalization. In the physical sense, deinstitutionalization implies the movement of individuals from large institutions into community-based living arrangements such as group homes and halfway houses. In the broader social context, deinstitutionalization means integrating exceptional individuals into the mainstream. The traditional obstacles raised by disabling conditions are overcome as exceptional people fill a variety of roles in general society (Winzer, 1993).

When the principle of normalization was extended to the school-aged child, it resulted in a parallel educational process known as mainstreaming. Underlying this movement is the belief that all children have individual differences that must be respected. Under a policy of mainstreaming special education stops functioning as a device for sorting exceptional children according to assigned labels. Instead, it offers a range of services to enable the tailoring of educational programs to meet individual needs.

As normalization principles became more manifest in practice, educators came to agree that all children, exceptionality notwithstanding, have the right to an appropriate education at public expense. Normalization prompted a powerful surge in the educational system toward abandoning many special classes and replacing them with regular class programs supported by special education services.

PUBLIC LAW 94-142

Three main reasons underlay the sudden transformation from segregated to integrated educational placement. One had to do with the gradual accumulation of empirical data on the effectiveness of special classes and concerns for the identification of minority-group children. A second reason revolved around the increasingly complex body of empirical knowledge concerning the learning of children in school and behavior problems. This research dissuaded educators and related professionals from the idea that homogeneous diagnostic categories exist for exceptional children. Rather, the research argued for individualized educational planning for each child receiving special education (Forness, 1981). Finally, emerging legislation and litigation supported the movement.

Although much of the federal legislation for the disabled was passed be-tween 1959 and 1967 (Chaves, 1977), none of it dealt with mainstreaming or compulsory attendance of handicapped children in local school systems (Sig-mon, 1982–83). Moreover, legislation for special education has long been of the permissive rather than the mandatory type. The case for mandatory special ed-ucation legislation was made primarily from what was wrong with education, or the lack of education, for the disabled, not from new knowledge and professional attitudes that needed a legitimate vehicle for delivery (Paul and Warnock, 1980). In the early 1970s reports in the United States indicated that 4 million of a total 7 million exceptional youngsters were being inappropriately or inadequately served (Meadow, 1980). Together with the empirical evidence of studies on seg-regated classes, parent activism, and professional pressure, these reports stim-ulated the passage of mandatory legislation.

A line of legislation that began in 1965 (J. A. C. Smith, 1980) culminated in Public Law 94-142, the Education for All Handicapped Children Act, signed into law by President Gerald R. Ford in November 1975. The new law was a legislative remedy for the failure of some schools to provide appropriate education for dis-abled students. It represented official recognition by the government of the United States of the growing dissatisfaction with the placement of exceptional students in segregated settings (Johnson and Cartwright, 1979). The law also al-tered the concept of special education, to bring it in line with the principles of normalization and the least restrictive environment (Karagianis and Nesbit, 1981).

With the passage of Public Law 94-142, the new philosophy became increas-ingly manifest in practice (Ballard and Zettel, 1978). The law defined the require-ments for reaching and enriching the lives of individuals not adequately served by traditional educational means. School systems could no longer exclude stu-dents suffering physical or intellectual handicaps, nor could they doom students to inappropriate placements and inadequate curricula. Under this legislation ex-ceptional children were, for the first time, accorded the right to a free and ap-propriate education in the least restrictive environment. Their parents or guardians were given the right of due process and confidentiality, and school boards were mandated to provide a range of educational services, an individual education plan for every exceptional student, and culturally fair testing.

This new educational and social philosophy meant that scores of excep-tional children now moved within the orbit of the public schools, and the numbers of students receiving special education and related services rose sig-nificantly. Special education services, especially for those students labeled mildly disabled, came to occupy a more central role and use a greater share of fiscal and human resources in the schools than ever before. Accompanying these mildly handicapped students were children with more severe impairments to learning (Cypher et al., 1984). By 1984 fewer than 7 percent of all disabled children in the United States were being educated in either separate schools or separate environments. Of those educated in regular schools, about two-thirds received at least part of their education in the regular classroom with nondis-abled peers (U.S. Department of Education, 1984).

In Canada special education also emerged as a key priority. The philosoph-ical underpinnings of desegregation appeared in the Hall-Dennis report (1968), the report of the Commission on Emotional and Learning Disorders in Children (Roberts and Lazure, 1970), the 1971 report on standards for the education of exceptional children in Canada (Hardy, et al., 1971), and the 1976 report on Canadian education prepared by the Organization for Economic Co-operation and Development (Csapo, 1984).

Each of the Canadian provinces has its own school system, which is based on provincial education legislation. Mandatory legislation for special education is found in Newfoundland, Nova Scotia, New Brunswick, Ontario, and Manitoba; the remaining provinces retain permissive legislation (Winzer, 1992). Canadian school jurisdictions have dealt with the integration of exceptional students in different ways. Some have adopted policies of full integration, which implies that all students, regardless of severity of handicap, are educated in regular classrooms with their age peers (Flynn and Kowalczyk-McPhee, 1989). A large number of school districts have chosen to maintain segregated educational options and typically approach integration on a case-by-case basis. In Canada in 1984 approximately 77 percent of the school-age population with disabilities were educated within the public schools (Canada, Council of Ministers, 1983).

PERENNIAL CONCERNS

Special education is now firmly established in American education; its evolution has been rooted essentially in the democratic ideal of equal opportunity for all people. Yet it is only recently that the creation of societies where exceptional persons can live productive and fulfilling lives has become an imperative, not just a dream. The passage from isolation to segregated settings to integrated education has been slow and halting, the route littered with problems and controversies.

Social attitudes concerning the care, education, and training of exceptional individuals reflect more general cultural attitudes concerning the obligations of a society to its individual citizens. The care and training of disabled individuals has followed historical trends, not created them. The ability of a society to provide services to help special people required not only the technical and scientific skills to do so, but also a social philosophy that recognized exceptionality as a human condition, not simplistically as deviance, dependence, or delinquency. The current philosophy underlying special education rejects the idea of merely caring for or maintaining persons with disabilities or simply helping them to adjust. Instead, it stresses correction and prevention and adheres to the notion that all children have the right to learn in the educational environment most suited to their academic and social needs.

Today's special education is a thriving enterprise, rich and varied in its topics, its theories, its practices, a vital component of the public school system. Special education is no longer a sanctuary for a few children separated from the rest of education. Now it is everybody's concern, from the specialist to the regular classroom teacher, from the parent of an exceptional child to a disabled adult, from the legislator to the advocate.

More than a century ago Alexander Graham Bell observed, "We are still engaged in discussing & rediscussing the questions that were discussed & rediscussed by other teachers before we were born. The experience of the past indicates that these discussions & controversies may continue ... to the end of time *without settlement* unless some new element can be introduced into the problem" (Bell, 1884, quoted by R. Bruce, 1973, p. 385, original italics). Bell's comments remain remarkably cogent today. Though some issues have been solved, many remain unsolved. Some are enduring, persistent problems that defy resolution. There are no easy answers today to questions of discipline, control, marriage, segregation, sterilization, any more than there were a century ago. Although the past decade has seen the number of institutionalized mentally retarded persons decline from 194,000 to 94,000 (White, Laki, and Bruininks, 1989), debate still surrounds the issue of institutionalization. Humanists and scientists still disagree, the former founding their arguments for deinstitutionalization on philosophical principles, the latter on empirical findings.

In many ways special education is still an experiment, a social and educational undertaking in which philosophical, legal, and humanistic principles are being worked out. As such, it is beset by problems at every level of practice. Great controversies continue to dominate the field, disagreements between proponents of different types of educational advances, different versions of development, and varied techniques of practice and pedagogy. Issues and concerns include the educational placement and instruction of exceptional students, unbiased and nondiscriminatory identification procedures, labeling and noncategorical approaches to students with mild handicaps, teacher training and the Regular Education Initiative, early childhood intervention, and transition programs for adolescents.

In an ideal world special education as a paradigm separate from regular education would disappear. The notion that there are two distinct sets of children—the disabled and the nondisabled—would be dispelled, as all children would come to be viewed as unique individuals with unique physical, intellectual, emotional, and psychological characteristics. To accomplish this, the Regular Education Initiative (REI) proposes that the regular education system assume the primary responsibility for educating all the students in the public schools, whether they be gifted, average, or disabled (Davis, 1989). Proponents of the REI call for the end of the dual system of education and its replacement by a unified, integrated approach and policy (Lowenthal, 1990).

The REI has kindled the flames of controversy in both regular and special education. Although the REI represents the ultimate object of mainstreaming principles, questions that revolve around the mainstreaming of exceptional students into the regular educational milieu remain the most controversial. In fact, the extent to which exceptional students can be profitably educated in association with their nondisabled peers is perhaps the dominant issue facing special education in North America.

Mainstreaming is a social experiment that continues to be more influenced by ideology and political and philosophical justifications than by empirical findings. In many ways the philosophical commitment is ahead of research and practice. Even as educators, legislators, parents, and others advance the notion, the manner in which the process will work most successfully has not yet been clearly delineated. Attempts to place philosophy into practice are not always successful.

Too often, ideal and reality part in face of pragmatic considerations that revolve around financial difficulties, adequacy of support services, legislative support, and public perceptions. There is not yet a quantitative measure of how great a disability must be to qualify for special services, nor are there definite numbers or types of characteristics that must be identified before a pupil can be diagnosed as exceptional.

Mainstreaming remains an unproven educational panacea; there seems to be no true answer as to whether regular class or special class settings are superior for exceptional students. Most of the zeal for the practice has stemmed from its anticipated effects in the social and emotional domain, which include removal of the stigma associated with special education classes, enhancement of the status of handicapped youngsters with their nonhandicapped peers, promotion of learning through the modeling of appropriate behavior by nonhandicapped, as well as the provision of a more realistic environment for learning (Kaufman et al., 1975). Nevertheless, investigators of the effects of mainstreaming have not yet found these benefits to accrue from mainstreaming in practice (Meyers, MacMillan, and Yoshida, 1980).

Discussions about where exceptional children should be instructed have received more attention, undergone more modifications, and generated more controversy than have discussions of what students are to be taught (Jenkins and Heinen, 1989). However, there remains widespread unease among teachers about the extent of support services available, their lack of training and exposure to exceptional pupils, and the extra demands that may be placed on them for program planning, delivery and evaluation (Winzer, 1989a). Problems also abound in such matters as resource rooms (Afflech et al., 1988; Anderson-Inman, 1986; Wang, Reynolds, and Walberg 1987), the stigma of pull-out or resource-room programs (Will, 1986), the responsibility of classroom teachers (Pugach and Lilly, 1984), and peer relations (De Apodaca et al., 1985).

Mainstreaming is not a universal policy. Senator Tom Harkin notes that one state educates 90 percent of mentally retarded pupils in separate classes; another instructs only 27 percent of mentally retarded students separately (Greer, 1990). But if historical precedent is any guide, the trend toward mainstreaming is likely to continue. A hundred years from now, when historians interpret the present, the fundamental debate will be whether social cultural, political, and economic factors provided force enough for normalization and mainstreaming to become appropriate realities for all persons with disabilities.

Bibliography

AAD. See American Annals of the Deaf.

AADD. See American Annals of the Deaf and Dumb.

Abraham, W. 1976. The early years: Prologue to tomorrow. *Exceptional Children* 42: 330–35.

Abt, I. A. [1944] 1965. *Baby doctor.* New York: McGraw-Hill.

Achenbach, T. M. 1975. The historical context of treatment for delinquent and maladjusted children: Past, present, and future. *Behavior Disorders* 1: 3–14.

Ackerknecht, E. H. 1959. *A short history of psychiatry.* London: Hafner.

Ackers, St. J. 1878. The causes of deafness: A lecture delivered Oct. 12th, 1873 before the Gloucester Literary and Scientific Institute. *American Annals of the Deaf and Dumb* 28: 10–17.

Addams, J., ed. 1925. *The child, the clinic, and the court.* New York: New Republic.

Address of Trustees of the New England Institution for the Education of the Blind to the public. 1833. Boston: Dutton and Wentworth.

Adler, E. 1991. History of rehabilitation research. Paper presented at the First International Conference on the History of Deafness, Washington, D.C., June.

Affleck, J. D., S. Madge, A. Adams, and S. Lowenbraum. 1988. Integrated classroom vs. resource model: Academic viability and effectiveness. *Exceptional Children* 54: 339–48.

Akerley, S. 1826. *Address delivered at Washington Hall in the City of New York on the 30th of May, 1826, as introductory exercises of the pupils of the New York Institution for the Deaf and Dumb, with an account of the exercises and notes and documents in relation to the subject.* New York: Published by order of the directors.

Alexander, F. G., and S. T. Selesnick. 1966. *The history of psychiatry: An evaluation of psychiatric thought and practice from prehistoric times to the present.* New York: Harper and Row.

Allport, F. H. 1924. *Social psychology.* Boston: Houghton Mifflin.

Alumni Association of Gallaudet College. 1900. *Minutes and proceedings of association meetings, 1889–1899.* Grinnell, Iowa: Waring Press.

American Annals of Education. 1832, 1835.

American Annals of the Deaf. 1888, 1891, 1895, 1898, 1907, 1922, 1923, 1933.

American Annals of the Deaf and Dumb. 1848, 1850, 1852, 1859, 1871, 1875, 1878, 1884.

American Association to Promote the Teaching of Speech to the Deaf. 1899. Proceedings (except papers and lectures) of the Sixth Summer Meeting of the AAPTSD, held at Clarke School for the Deaf, Northampton, Mass., June 22–28, 1899. *Association Review* 1: 53–106, 162–76.

American Asylum for the Education and Instruction of Deaf and Dumb Persons. 1822, 1855. *Annual Report.* Hartford, Conn.: Author, Hudson and Co.

American Breeders Magazine. 1909.

American Journal of Education. 1826, 1827.

Amman, J. C. [1694] 1972. *Surdus loquens* [The talking deaf man]. Amsterdam. Rpt. edited by R. C. Alston. English Linguistics Series, 1500–1800, no. 357. Menston, England: Scholar Press.

———. [1700] 1873. *Dissertatio de loquela, a dissertation on speech in which not only the Human Voice and the Art of Speaking are traced from their origin, but the Means are also described by which those who have been Deaf and Dumb from their birth may acquire Speech, and those who speak imperfectly may learn how to correct their impediments.* London: Sampson, Low, Marston, Low and Searle.

Anagnos, M. [1882] 1904. *The education of the blind in the United States of America: Its principles, development and results.* Boston: Geo. H. Ellis.

Anastasi, A. 1958. Heredity, environment, and the question "How"? *Psychological Review* 65: 197–208.

———. 1968. *Psychological testing.* New York: Macmillan.

Anderson-Inman, L. 1986. Bridging the gap: Student-centered strategies for promoting the transfer of learning. *Exceptional Children* 52: 562–72.

Andrews, M. and C. W. Bledstoe. 1972. Chronicle of the American Association of Instructors of the Blind. *Blindness* 5.

Anglo, S. 1977. Evident authority and authoritative evidence: "The Malleus Meleficarum." In S. Anglo, ed., *The damned art: Essays in the literature of witchcraft.* London: Routledge and Kegan Paul.

Announcement of a National Deaf Mute College, Washington, D.C. 1866. Washington, D.C.: Joseph L. Pearson.

Apter, S. J., and J. C. Conoley. 1984. *Childhood behavior disorders and emotional disturbance.* Englewood Cliffs, N.J.: Prentice-Hall.

Ariès, P. 1962 *Centuries of childhood: A social history of family life.* trans. R. Baldick. New York: Vintage Books.

Aristotle n.d. *Politics,* trans. B. Jewett. New York: Carleton House.

———. 1910. Historia Animalium. In J. A. Smith and W. D. Ross, trans., *The works of Aristotle,* vol. 4: *Historia animalium.* Oxford: Clarendon Press.

Arms, H. P. 1887. *The intermarriage of the deaf: Its mental, moral and social tendencies.* Philadelphia: Burk and McFetridge.

Armstrong, D. F. 1987. Deep roots: The historical context of Gallaudet's birth and growth. *Gallaudet Today* 17: 10–17.

Arrowsmith, J. P. 1822. The art of instructing the infant deaf and dumb. *Quarterly Review,* January, pp. 391–401.

Association Review. 1901.

Atkinson, H. S. 1935. The social control of the feebleminded. *Social Welfare* 15: 121–23.

Atkinson, R. L., R. C. Atkinson, E. E. Smith, and D. J. Bem. 1990. *Introduction to psychology.* 10th ed. New York: Harcourt Brace Jovanovich.

Ayres, J. A. 1849. Home instruction for the deaf and dumb. *American Annals of the Deaf and Dumb* 49: 177–87.

———. 1852. The responsibilities of officers of institutions for the deaf and dumb. *American Annals of the Deaf and Dumb* 5: 158–69.

Ayres, L. 1909. *Laggards in our schools: A study of retardation and its elimination in city school systems.* New York: Charities Publications Committee.

———. 1915. *Child accounting in the public schools.* Cleveland: Cleveland Education Survey.

Bailyn, B. 1967. *The ideological origins of the American Revolution.* Cambridge: Harvard University Press, Belknap Press.

Bain, D. A. 1980. Gifted and enriched education in Canada. In M. Csapo and L. Goguen, eds., *Special education across Canada: Issues and concerns for the '80s.* Vancouver: Centre for Human Development and Research.

Ball, T. S. 1971. *Itard, Seguin, and Kephart: Sensory education—a learning interpretation.* Columbus, Ohio: Merrill.

Ballard, J., and J. J. Zettel. 1978. Fiscal arrangements of Public Law 94-142. *Exceptional Children* 44: 333–37.

Baller, W. R. 1936. A study of the present social status of a group of adults, who, when they were in elementary schools, were classified as mentally deficient. *Genetic Psychology Monographs* 18: 165–244.

Baller, W. R., D. C. Charles, and E. L. Miller. 1967. Mid-life attainment of the mentally retarded. *Genetic Psychology Monographs* 75: 235–329.

Balthazar, E. E. and H. A. Stevens. 1975. *The emotionally disturbed mentally retarded.* Englewood Cliffs, N.J.: Prentice-Hall.

Barnard, H. 1852a. Eulogy: Thomas Hopkins Gallaudet. *American Annals of the Deaf and Dumb* 4: 81–136.

———. 1852b. *Tribute to Gallaudet: A discourse in commemoration of the life, character and services of Rev. Thomas H. Gallaudet, LL.D.* Hartford, Conn.: Brockett and Hutchinson.

———. (1857) *Reformatory education: Papers on preventative, correctional and reformatory institutions and agencies in different countries.* Hartford, Conn.: F. C. Brownell.

Barnard, H., ed. [1861a] 1969. Memoir of Harvey Prindle Peet, President of the New York Institution for the Deaf and Dumb. In *American education: Its men, ideas and institutions—Memoirs of teachers and educators and promoters and benefactors of education, literature and science,* pp. 232–48. 2d ed. New York: F. C. Brownell. Rpt., New York: Arno Press and New York Times.

———. [1861b] 1969. Thomas H. Gallaudet. In *American education: Its men, ideas and institutions—Memoirs of teachers and educators and promoters and benefactors of education, literature and science,* pp. 97–112. 2d ed. New York: F. C. Brownell. Rpt., New York: Arno Press and New York Times, 1969.

Barnard, H. C. 1922. *The French tradition in education: Ramus to Mme Necker de Saussure.* Cambridge: Oxford University Press.

Barr, M. W. 1904a. Classification of mental defectives. *Journal of Psycho-Asthenics* 9: 29–38.

———. [1904b] 1913. *Mental defectives: Their history, treatment and training.* Philadelphia: Blakiston.

Barss, J. N. 1920. The treatment of the delinquent as social service. *Social Welfare* 2: 188–90, 210–11.

Bartlett, D. 1852. Family education for young deaf-mute children. *American Annals of the Deaf and Dumb* 5: 32–35.

Bates, P., S. A. Morrow, E. Pancsafar, and R. Sedlak. 1984. The effect of functional vs. nonfunctional activities on the attitudes/expectations of nonhandicapped college students: What they see is what we get. *Journal of the Association for Persons with Severe Handicaps* 9: 73–78.

Baynton, D. C. 1991. Sign language. Paper presented at the First International Conference on the History of Deafness, Washington, D.C., June.

Beck, T. R. 1811. *An inaugural dissertation on insanity.* New York: J. Seymour.

Bede, the Venerable. 1849. *Ecclesiastical history of England, also the Anglo-Saxon chronicle,* edited by J. A. Giles. London: H. G. Bohm.

Beggs, R. 1983. A biographical history of education of the deaf in Canada. *ACEHI Journal* 9: 12–23.

Belanger, A. 1907. The education of deaf mutes in France. In *International Conference on the Education of the Deaf, proceedings of the conference held in the Training College buildings, Edinburgh, on 29th, 30th, and 31st July, and 1st and 2nd August, 1907,* pp. 50–52. Edinburgh: Darien Press.

Bell, A. 1836. *Stammering and other impediments of speech.* London: Sherwood, Gilbert and Piper.

Bell, A. G. 1872a. *Establishment for the study of vocal physiology, for the correction of stammering, and other defects of utterance; and for practical instruction in Visible Speech* (brochure). Boston: Rand Avery.

———. 1872b. *On the nature and uses of Visible Speech.* Boston: Rand, Avery.

———. 1872c. Visible speech as a means of communicating articulation to deaf mutes. *American Annals of the Deaf and Dumb* 17: 1–21.

———. 1877. Marriages of deaf mutes. *Island Reporter.* Reprinted from the *National Deaf Mute Gazette.* Located at Volta Bureau, Washington, D.C.

———. 1883. *Upon the electrical experiments to determine the location of the bullet in the body of President Garfield.* Washington, D.C.: Gibson Brothers.

———. 1884a. Deafness in white cats. *Science* 3: 170–72.

———. 1884b. Deafness in white cats, and statistics on deafness and epilepsy in America. *Science* 3: 243–44.

———. 1884c. Fallacies concerning the deaf. *American Annals of the Deaf and Dumb* 29: 32–69.

———. [1884d] 1969. *Memoir upon the formation of a deaf variety of the human race.* Washington, D.C. Rpt., Washington, D.C.: Alexander Graham Bell Association for the Deaf.

———. 1885a. Deaf mute instruction in relation to the work in public schools. In *National Education Report: Addresses and discussions relating to the education of the deaf, Madison, Wisconsin, 1884,* pp. 8–18. Washington, D.C.: Gibson Brothers.

———. 1885b. Echo soundings in the fog. *Science,* May, p. 354.

——. 1885c. Is there a correlation between defects of the senses? *Science* 5: 127–29.

——. 1886. On the ancestry of the deaf. *National Academy of Sciences,* April.

——. 1888. *Fact and opinions relating to the deaf from America.* London: Spottiswoode.

——. 1890a. *On reading as a means of teaching language to the deaf.* Washington, D.C.: Gibson Brothers.

——. 1890b. The question of sign language. *The Educator* 5: 3–7.

——. 1891a. Marriage. *Science* 17: 160–63.

——. 1891b. Letter to J. Hitz, December 7. Bell correspondence, Volta Bureau, Washington, D.C.

——. 1893a. *Address upon the condition of articulation teaching in American schools for the deaf.* Boston: Nathan Sawyer and Son.

——. 1893b. "Statistics of the deaf." An address delivered at the World's Congress of Instructors of the Deaf, July, 1893. Copied from a typed copy found at 1331 Connecticut Avenue, Washington, D.C., and showing some corrections. Volta Bureau, Washington, D.C.

——. 1896. *Growth of the oral method of instructing the deaf.* Boston: Press of Rockwell and Churchill.

——. 1897. *The Mystic Oral School: An argument in its favor.* Washington, D.C.: Gibson Brothers.

——. 1898a. *Marriage: An address delivered to members of the Literary Society of Kendall Green, Wash., D.C., March 16th, 1891, with an appendix on consanguineous marriages.* 3d ed. Washington, D.C.: Sanders Printing Office.

——. 1898b. *The question of sign language and the utility of signs in the instruction of the deaf.* Washington, D.C.: Sanders Printing Office.

——. 1900a. Historical notes concerning the teaching of speech to the deaf: Braidwood's institution for the education of the deaf and dumb, at Cobbs, Va. *Association Review* 2: 385–409.

——. 1900b. Historical notes concerning the teaching of speech to the deaf: Francis Green, 1781–1809. *Association Review* 2: 62–65.

——. 1900c. *A philanthropist of the last century identified as a Boston man.* Worcester, Mass.: Charles Hamilton.

——. 1906. Our heterogenous system of weights and measures. *National Geographic* 17: 158–69.

——. 1907a. Aerial locomotion: With a few notes of progress in the construction of an aerodrome. *National Geographic* 18: 8–21.

——. 1907b. The twelfth census. *Association Review* 9: 337–56, 427–44, 533–45.

——. 1908a. A few thoughts concerning eugenics. *National Geographic* 19: 118–23. Also *Association Review,* 9 (1908): 66–73.

——. 1908b. The twelfth census. *Association Review* 10: 138–47, 240–55, 349–64, 455–64.

——. 1910. The education of the deaf. *Beinn Bhreagh Recorder,* September 19, pp. 14–23.

——. 1911. *The mechanisms of speech.* New York: Funk and Wagnalls.

——. 1913. Letter to C. N. Kendall, Commissioner of Education for Trenton, N.J., August 27. Volta Bureau, Washington, D.C.

————. 1914. How to improve the race. *Journal of Heredity* 5: 1–7.

————. 1917. *Graphical studies of the marriages of the deaf in America.* Washington, D.C.: Judd and Detweiler.

————. 1918. John Braidwood in America. *American Annals of the Deaf* 63: 459–63.

————. 1920. Is race suicide possible? *Journal of Heredity* 11: 339–41.

————. 1923. Saving the six-nippled breed. *Journal of Heredity* 14: 98–111.

Bell, A. G., and J. L. Gillett. (1884) *Deaf classes in connection with the work in public schools.* Washington, D.C.: Gibson Brothers.

Bell, A. M. 1864. *Visible Speech: Every language universally legible, exactly as spoken; accomplished by means of self-interpreting physiological symbols, based on the discovery of the exact physiological relations of sounds.* Edinburgh.

————. 1865. *Class primer of English Visible Speech; for communicating the exact pronunciation of the language to native or foreign learners and for teaching children and illiterate adults to read in a few days.* London: Simpkin Marshall.

————. 1866. Letter to Queen Victoria. Bell correspondence, Volta Bureau, Washington, D.C.

————. 1867a. Letter to the President of the United States. Bell correspondence, Volta Bureau, Washington, D.C.

————. 1867b. *Visible Speech: The science of universal alphabetics.* London: Simpkin, Marshall.

————. 1883a. A primer for Visible Speech. *Science* 2: 204.

————. 1883b. A universal language and its vehicle—a universal alphabet. *Science* 2: 350–53.

Bell, L. V. 1980. *Treating the mentally ill from colonial times to the present.* New York: Praeger.

Bell, M. H. 1900. Sketch of the life of William Thornton. *Association Review* 2: 116–18.

————. 1914. What the Montessori method means to me. *Freedom for the Child* 1: 7–10.

Bell, R. Q., and L. V. Harper. 1977. *Child effects on adults.* Lincoln: University of Nebraska Press.

The Bell telephone: The deposition of Alexander Graham Bell in the suit brought by the United States to annul the Bell patents. 1908. Boston: American Telephone Company.

Bench, P. J. 1919. Juvenile delinquency—its causes. *Social Welfare* 1: 126–27.

Bender, R. E. 1970. *The conquest of deafness: A history of the long struggle to make normal living possible for those handicapped by lack of normal hearing.* Cleveland: Press of Case Western Reserve University.

Benjamin, L. T., Jr. 1975. The pioneering work of Letta Hollingworth in the psychology of women. *Nebraska History* 56: 493–505.

Bergmann, G. 1956. The contributions of John B. Watson. *Psychological Review* 63: 265–76.

Berkeley, G. [1709] 1901. Essay toward a new theory of vision. In A. C. Fraser, ed., *The works of George Berkeley.* Oxford: Oxford University Press.

Berkeley, K. C. 1984. "The ladies want to bring about reform in the public schools:" Public education and women's rights in the post-civil war South. *History of Education Quarterly* 24: 45–58.

Berlin, I., ed. 1956. *The age of enlightenment.* New York: Mentor Books.

Bernard, R. M., and Vinvovskis, M. A. 1977. The female school teacher in antebellum Massachusetts. *Journal of Social History* 10: 332–45.

Best, E. M. 1935. The exceptional child as a behavior problem in society. *Social Welfare* 15: 117–19.

Best, H. 1919. *The blind.* New York: Macmillan.

———. 1930. Educational provisions for the deaf, the blind, and the feeble-minded compared. *American Annals of the Deaf* 75: 239–40.

———. 1934. *Blindness and the blind in the United States.* New York: Macmillan.

Biklen, D. 1986. Framed: Journalism's treatment of disability. *Social Policy,* Winter, pp. 45–51.

Billings, B. 1890. *Report on the insane, feeble minded, deaf and dumb, and blind in the United States at the eleventh census.* Washington, D.C.: U.S. Department of the Interior.

Binet, A., and T. Simon. 1905. Application des méthodes nouvelles au diagnostic du niveau intellectuel chez des infants normaux et anormaux d'hospice et d'école primaire. *L'année psychologique* 11: 245–66.

———. 1908. Le développement de l'intelligence chez les enfants. *L'anée psychologique* 14: 1–94.

———. 1914. *Mentally defective children,* trans. W. B. Drummond. London: E. J. Arnold.

———. 1916. *The intelligence of the feeble-minded.* Baltimore: Williams and Whipple.

A biographical sketch of Alexander Melville Bell. 1898. New York: James T. White.

Blackburn, E. 1883. Our deaf and dumb. *Nineteenth Century,* October, pp. 575–98.

Blakeley, P. R. n.d. Eleven exiles: Accounts of loyalists of the American Revolution. Public Archives of Nova Scotia, Halifax.

———. 1945. Francis Greene. In W. S. Wallace, ed., *The dictionary of Canadian biography, 1801–1820,* p. 248. Toronto: Macmillan.

———. 1979. Francis Greene—a suffering Loyalist and friend to the British government. *Nova Scotia Historical Quarterly* 9: 11–14.

Blanton, R. L. 1976. Historical perspectives on the classification of mental retardation. In N. Hobbs, ed., *Issues in the classification of children,* 1, 164–93. San Francisco: Jossey-Bass.

Blatt, B. 1985. Friendly letters on the correspondence of Helen Keller, Anne Sullivan, and Alexander Graham Bell. *Exceptional Children* 51: 405–9.

Blatt, B., and F. Kaplan. 1960. *Christmas in purgatory.* Boston: Allyn and Bacon.

Blatt, B., A. Ozolins, and J. McNally. 1979. *The family papers: A return to purgatory.* New York: Longman.

Bloch, N. J., and D. Dworkin, eds. 1976. *The IQ controversy: Critical readings.* New York: Pantheon Books.

Blueler, E. [1911] 1950. *Dementia praecox, or the group of schizophrenias.* Leipzig: Deutiche. Trans. by J. Zinkin, New York: International University Press.

Boas, F. 1916. Eugenics. *Scientific Monthly* 3: 471–78.

Bockoven, J. S. 1956. Moral treatment in American psychiatry. *Nervous and Mental Disease* 124: 167–94, 292–321.

Bogarth, G. H. 1910. Sterilization of the unfit: The law in Indiana, Connecticut, Utah, Oregon, and Ontario, Canada. *Texas Medical Journal* 26: 279.

Bogdan, R. 1986. Exhibiting mentally retarded people for amusement and profit, 1850–1940. *American Journal of Mental Deficiency* 91: 120–26.

Bond, L. 1897. Education of the blind. *New England Magazine,* March. Reprint at the Volta Bureau, Washington, D.C.

Bonet, J. [1620] 1890. *Simplification of the letters of the alphabet, and a method of teaching deaf mutes to speak.* Madrid: Par Francisco Abarca de Angelo. Trans. by H. N. Dixon, Harrowgate: Farrar.

Boring, E. G. 1923. Intelligence as the tests test it. *New Republic* 36 (June 6): 35–36.

Boston *Evening Transcript.* November 12, 1901.

Bowen, B. B. 1847. *Blind man's offering.* 4th ed. New York: author.

Boyer, E. L. 1983. *High school.* New York: Harper and Row.

Bradfield, R. H., J. Brown, P. Kaplan, E. Rickert, and R. Stannard. 1973. The special child in the regular classroom. *Exceptional Children* 39: 384–90.

Braidwood in America. 1897. *American Annals of the Deaf* 42: 118–20.

Bremner, R. H. 1956. *From the depths: The discovery of poverty in the United States.* New York: New York University Press.

Bremner, R. H., ed. 1970. *Children and youth in America: A documentary history,* vol. 1: *1600–1865.* Cambridge: Harvard University Press.

Brenzel, B. 1980. Domestication as reform: A study of the socialization of wayward girls, 1856–1905. *Harvard Educational Review* 50: 196–213.

Brigham, A. 1845. Schools in lunatic asylums. *American Journal of Insanity* 2: 326–40.

———. 1847. The moral treatment of insanity. *American Journal of Insanity* 4: 1–15.

Brigham, C. 1923. *A study of American intelligence.* Princeton: Princeton University Press.

Brinton, C. 1965. *The anatomy of revolution.* New York: Vintage Books.

British Columbia Boys Industrial School. 1905, 1923, 1930. *Annual Report of the Provincial Industrial School for Boys in the province of British Columbia.* Vancouver, B.C.: author.

British Columbia Girls Industrial School. 1928. *Annual Report.* Vancouver, B.C.: author.

Brockett, L. P. 1856. Idiots and institutions for their training. *American Journal of Education* 1 (May): 601–13.

———. 1857. The founders of institutions for the instruction of the blind. *American Journal of Education* 3: 477–81 .

Bromberg, W. 1975. *From shaman to psychotherapist: A history of the treatment of mental illness.* Chicago: Henry Regnery.

Brubacher, J. S. 1965. *Henry Barnard on education.* New York: Russell and Russell.

Bruce, H. H. 1936. Sterilization and imbecility. *Social Welfare* 16: 95–97.

Bruce, R. 1973. *Alexander Graham Bell and the conquest of solitude.* Boston: Little Brown.

Bruininks, R. H., J. E. Rynders, and J. C. Gross. 1974. Social acceptance of mildly retarded pupils resource rooms and regular classes. *American Journal of Mental Deficiency* 78: 377–83.

Brulle, A. R., and T. Mihail. 1991. The dark side. Paper presented at the International Conference on Special Education, Milwaukee, May.

Bruner, J. S. 1965. Growth of mind. *American Psychologist* 20: 1007–17.

Bryce, P. 1920. Recent constructive developments in child welfare. *Social Welfare* 2: 255–56.

Bryce, P. H. 1913. Immigration and its effects upon the public health. *Public Health Journal* 4: 643.

Bullock, E. S. 1897. Social purity and marriage. *Dominion Medical Monthly and Ontario Medical Journal* 8: 146–47.

Bulwer, J. 1648. *Philocophus or the deafe and dumbe man's friend by J. B., surnamed the Chirosopher.* London: Humphrey Moseley.

———. [1654] 1975. *Chirologia, or, the naturall language of the hand, composed of the speaking of motions, and discoursing, whereunto is added Chironmia: or, the art of manual rhetoric, consisting of the naturall expressions, digested by art in the hand, as the chiefest instrument of eloquence, by historical manifesto, exemplified out of the authentic registers of common life, and civill conversation, with types of chyrograms, a long wish'd for illustration of this argument.* London: T. Harper. Rpt., New York: AMS Press.

Burdett, H. 1891. *Hospitals and asylums of the world.* London: J. and A. Churchill.

Burke, P. J. 1976. Personnel preparation: Historical perspectives. *Exceptional Children* 43: 144–47.

Burnet, J. R. 1873. Biographical sketch. *American Annals of the Deaf and Dumb* 18: 70–92.

Burtt, H. E., and S. L. Pessey, 1957. Henry Herbert Goddard, 1866–1957. *American Journal of Psychology* 70: 656–57.

Bush, M. G. 1942. The handicapped child helps all children in Wisconsin. *Exceptional Children* 9: 153–55.

Buxton, D. 1859. On the effect of mental impressions during gestation in producing deafness in children. *Liverpool Medico-Churgical Journal,* January, pp. 14–19.

Byrd, M. 1974. *Visits to Bedlam: Madness and literature in the eighteenth century.* Columbia: University of South Carolina Press.

Caldwell, W. A. 1888. Exhibitions. *American Annals of the Deaf* 33: 165–72.

Callahan, R. E. 1962. *Education and the cult of efficiency: A study of the social forces that have shaped the administration of the public schools.* Chicago: University of Chicago Press.

Canada, Council of Ministers of Education. 1983. *Survey of special education in Canada, 1982–83.* Winnipeg: Candid Research and Council of Ministers of Education, Canada.

Canada. 1854. *Journals,* app. DD. (Government publication)

Canada. 1860. *Sessional Papers,* no. 32. (Government publication)

Canadian Journal of Public Health. 1937.

Canadian Medical Association Journal. 1933.

Canadian war blinded. 1942. *Outlook for the Blind and the Teacher's Forum* 36: 281–86.

Canage, G. C. 1859. Letter to the Editor: The wages of deaf-mute instructors of deaf-mutes. *American Annals of the Deaf and Dumb* 11: 59–60.

Cance, E., J. Fireld, I. Fisher, P. Hall, and R. De C. Ward. 1914. Second report of the Committee on Immigration of the Eugenics Section of the American Genetic Association. *Journal of Heredity* 5: 297–300.

Carlin, J. 1854. The national college for mutes. *American Annals of the Deaf and Dumb* 6: 175–83.

———. 1858. The wages of deaf-mute instructors of deaf-mutes. *American Annals of the Deaf and Dumb* 10: 196.

———. 1859. Wages of deaf-mute instructors. In *Proceedings of the Fifth Convention of American Instructors of the Deaf and Dumb.* Alton, Ill.: Courier Steam and Job Printing House.

Carlson, E. T., and N. Dain, 1960. The psychotherapy that was moral treatment. *American Journal of Psychology* 117: 519–24.

———. 1962. The meaning of moral insanity. *Bulletin of the History of Medicine* 36: 130–40.

Carlyle, T. 1966. *The French Revolution.* London: Dent.

Caroline A. Yale, 1848–1933. 1934. *Council Review,* May, p. 19.

Carrier, J. G. 1986. *Learning disability: Social class and the construction of inequality in American education.* New York: Greenwood.

Case, R. 1984. The new stage theories in cognitive development. Why we need them, what they assert. Paper presented at the Minnesota Symposium on Child Development.

Castle, W. E. 1924. The genetics of multi-nippled sheep: An analysis of the sheep breeding experiments of Dr. and Mrs. Alexander Graham Bell at Beinnn Bhreagh, NS. *Journal of Heredity* 15: 75–85.

Cattell, J. Mc. 1890. Mental tests and measurements. *Mind* 15: 373–81.

The census of 1840. 1872. *American Annals of the Deaf and Dumb* 17: 63.

Ceremonies at the completion of the Gallaudet monument. 1854. *American Annals of the Deaf and Dumb* 7: 19–54.

Chapin, W. 1846. *Report on the benevolent institutions of Great Britain and Paris, including the schools and asylums for the Blind, Deaf and Dumb, and the Insane: being supplementary to the ninth annual report of the Ohio Institution for the education of the blind.* Columbus, Ohio: author.

Chapman, P. D. 1981. Schools as sorters: Testing and tracking in California, 1910–1925. *Journal of Social History* 14: 701–7.

Chapman, T. 1977. Early eugenics movement in Western Canada. *Alberta History* 25: 9–17.

Chase, A. 1977. *The legacy of Malthus: The social costs of the new scientific racism.* New York: Alfred A. Knopf.

Chaves, I. M. 1977. Historical overview of special education in the United States. In P. Bates, T. L. West, and R. B. Schmerl, eds., (pp. 25–41). *Mainstreaming: Problems, potentials, and perspectives.* Minneapolis: National Support Systems Project, 1977.

Cheek, S. B. 1855. Some suggestions in reference to the enterprise of deaf-mute instruction in the United States. *American Annals of the Deaf and Dumb* 7: 167–75.

Chesterton, G. K. 1922. *Eugenics and other evils.* London: Cassell.

Chicago. 1932. *Report of the survey of the schools of Chicago, Illinois.* New York: Teachers College, Columbia University Press.

Chilblains. 1889. To members of the Royal Commission. *American Annals of the Deaf* 34: 311.

Church, W. F. 1964. *The influence of the Enlightenment on the French Revolution: Creative, disastrous or non-existent.* Lexington, Mass.: D. C. Heath.

Church for the deaf and dumb. 1852. *American Annals of the Deaf and Dumb* 5: 169–81.

Clarke, B. R., and M. A. Winzer. 1983. A concise history of the education of the deaf in Canada. *ACEHI Journal* 9: 36–51.

Clarke, E. P. 1900. The training of teachers of the deaf in the United States. *American Annals of the Deaf* 45: 345–67.

Clarke Institution for the Deaf. 1868, 1870, 1873, 1896. *Annual Report.* Boston: author.

Classes in common schools. 1897. *American Annals of the Deaf* 42: 351–52.

Claudy, C. H. 1916. The young man and science. *Beinn Bhreagh Recorder* 19 (February): 5.

Cleland, J. 1965. *Fanny Hill.* New York: Signet Books.

Clerk, Letter to Provincial Secretary, Deputy, Halifax. July 13, 1907. Public Archives of Nova Scotia, Halifax.

Cobb, J. 1911. The influence of heredity. *American Annals of the Deaf* 56: 254–55.

Cogswell, Alice. 1817. Letter to Mrs. Philllipps. Gallaudet Archives, Gallaudet University, Washington, D.C.

Cohen, D. L., and M. Lazeron. 1972. Education and the corporate order. *Socialist Revolution* 2: 47–72.

Cohen, S. 1983. The mental hygiene movement, the development of personality and the school: The medicalization of American education. *History of Education Quarterly* 23: 123–49.

Coleman, T. 1973. *Going to America.* New York: Anchor Books.

Colson, S. E., and T. A. Mehring. 1990. Facilitating memory in students with learning disabilities. *LD Forum* 16: 75–79.

Compulsory childlessness. 1891. *Review of Reviews* 3: 263–64.

Compulsory education and its relation to the defective classes. 1903. *Association Review* 5: 115–17.

Condillac, E. B., Abbé. [1754] 1930. *Traité des sensations* [Treatise on the senses], trans. by G. Carr. Los Angeles: University of Southern California.

Connor, F. P. 1976. The past is prologue: Teacher preparation in special education. *Exceptional Children* 42: 366–78.

Connor, L. E. 1951. CEC's federal legislative activity. *Exceptional Children* 18: 135–39.

Conroy, M., and H. M. Levin. 1985. *Schooling and work in the democratic state.* Stanford, Calif.: Stanford University Press.

Convention of American Instructors of the Deaf and Dumb. 1851. Proceedings of the Second Convention. *American Annals of the Deaf and Dumb* 4: 1–41.

Convention of Instructors of the Deaf and Dumb. 1850. First Convention of American Instructors of the Deaf and Dumb. *American Annals of the Deaf and Dumb* 3: 32.

Convention of Principals of American Institutions for the Deaf and Dumb. 1884. Fifth Convention of Principals of American Institutions for the Deaf and Dumb. *American Annals of the Deaf and Dumb* 29: 287–88.

Convention of Superintendents and Principals of American Schools for the Deaf. 1913. Proceedings of the Tenth Convention of Superintendents and Principals of American Schools for the Deaf. *American Annals of the Deaf* 58: 443–44.

Copleston, F. 1985. *A history of philosophy.* Vol. 6. New York: Image Books.

Corballis, M. C. 1989. Laterality and human evolution. *American Psychologist* 96: 492–505.

Coveney, K. C. 1942. The growth of special classes in the city of Boston. *The Training School Bulletin* 39: 57–59.

Cox, C. M. 1926. *The early mental traits of three hundred genuises,* vol 2: *Genetic studies of genius.* Stanford, Calif.: Stanford University Press.

Cravens, H. 1987. Applied science and public policy: The Ohio Bureau of Juvenile Research and the problem of juvenile delinquency, 1913–1930. In M. M. Sokal, ed., *Psychological testing and American society, 1890–1939.* New Brunswick, N.J.: Rutgers University Press.

Cremin, L. A. 1961. *The transformation of the school.* New York: Alfred A. Knopf.

Crofts, L. W. 1916. Bibliography of feeble-mindedness in relation to juvenile delinquency. *Journal of Delinquency* 1: 195–208.

Crookshank, F. G. 1924. *The mongol in our midst.* London: Kegan Paul.

Crouter, A. E. 1907. The organization and methods of the Pennsylvania Institution for the Deaf and Dumb. In *Proceedings of the International Conference on the Education of the Deaf held in the Training College buildings, Edinburgh, on 29th, 30th and 31st July and 1st and 2nd August, 1907,* pp. 125–155. Edinburgh: Darien Press.

Cruickshank, W. M. 1967. The development of education for exceptional children. In W. M. Cruickshank and G. O. Johnson, eds., *Education of exceptional children and youth.* Englewood Cliffs, N.J.: Prentice-Hall.

Cruickshank, W. M., ed. 1976. *Cerebral palsy: A developmental disability.* New York: Syracuse University Press.

Csapo, M. 1984. Segregation, integration, and beyond: A sociological perspective of special education. *BC Journal of Special Education* 8: 211–29.

Cubberly, E. P. 1909. *Changing conceptions of education.* Boston: Houghton Mifflin.

Cures for deafness. 1926. *Volta Review* 28: 392–93.

Currier, E. H. 1894. *The history of articulation teaching in the New York Institution for the Instruction of the Deaf and Dumb.* New York: Printed by the New York Institution for the Deaf and Dumb.

Curti, M. W. 1938. *Child psychology.* New York: Longmans Green.

Cypher, R., D. Hinves, D. Baine, and D. Sobsey. 1984. Contemporary considerations in educating students with severe and multiple handicaps. *BC Journal of Special Education* 8: 137–48.

Dalgarno, G. [1680] 1971. *Didascolocophus. (The deaf and dumb man's tutor.* Ox-
    ford: Timo. Halton. Rpt., English Linguistics Series, 1500–1800, no. 286. Men-
    ston, England: Scholar Press. Also *American Annals of the Deaf and Dumb* 9
    (1859): 14–64.

————. [1834] 1971. *The works of George Dalgarno.* Edinburgh. Rpt., New York:
    AMS Press, 1971.

Danielson, F., and C. B. Davenport. 1912. *The Hill Folk: Report of a rural com-
    munity of hereditary defectives.* Eugenics record office, Memoir no. 1. Cold
    Springs Harbor, N.Y.: author.

Daraul, A. 1961. *Secret societies.* London: Muller.

Darwin, C. 1859. *On the origin of the species.* London: John Murray.

————. 1874. *The descent of man and selection in relation to sex.* 2d ed. London:
    John Murray.

Davenport, C. 1910. Report of the Committee of Eugenics. *American Breeders
    Magazine* 1: 126–29.

Davenport, C. B. 1915a. *The feebly inhibited: Inheritance of temperament.* Wash-
    ington, D.C.: Carnegie Institution.

————. 1915b. *The feebly inhibited: Nomadism, or the wandering impulse, with
    special reference to heredity.* Washington, D.C.: Carnegie Foundation.

Davies S. P. 1959. *The mentally retarded in society.* New York: Columbia Univer-
    sity Press.

Davis, W. 1989. The Regular Education Initiative debate: Its promises and prob-
    lems. *Exceptional Children* 55: 440–46.

Day, H., I. S. Fusfeld, and R. Pintner. 1928. *A survey of American schools for the
    deaf.* Washington, D.C.: National Research Council.

Day schools. 1899. *American Annals of the Deaf* 44: 395.

The deaf mutes of Martha's Vineyard. 1886. *American Annals of the Deaf and
    Dumb* 31: 282–284.

Deafness and syphilis. 1894. *Dominion Medical Monthly* 2: 20.

Deafness cure-fakes. 1916. *American Annals of the Deaf* 61: 195.

De Apodaca, R. F., J. D. Watson, J. Mueller, and J. Isaacson-Koiles. 1985. A socio-
    metric comparison of mainstreamed orthopedically handicapped high
    school students and nonhandicapped classmates. *Psychology in the Schools*
    22: 95–101

Defective children, their care, occupations and support. 1915. *Canadian Journal
    of Medicine and Surgery* 38: 4.

Defoe, D. [1720] 1903. The history of the life and surprising adventures of Mr.
    Duncan Campbell. In *The works of Daniel Defoe,* vol. 4. New York: George D.
    Sproul.

De Guimps, R. 1906. *Pestalozzi, his life and works.* New York: Appleton, Century,
    Crofts.

De Hearne, D. 1877. Consanguineous marriages as a cause of deaf mutism.
    American Annals of the Deaf and Dumb 22: 146–57.

De Land, F. 1905a. Gift of speech to world's deaf mutes. *Pittsburgh Leader,* Jan-
    uary 29.

————. 1905b. The real romance of the telephone. *Association Review* 7: 306–26,
    389–99.

———. 1906. The real romance of the telephone, or why deaf children in America need no longer be dumb. *Association Review* 8: 1–27, 120–35, 205–22, 329–444, 406–27.

———. 1912. Marriages of the deaf. *Volta Review* 4: 186–89.

———. 1919a. The Melville Bell symbols for recording speech sounds. *Volta Review* 21: 617–21.

———. 1919b. Some notes about the American Association to Promote the Teaching of Speech to the Deaf, 3. *Volta Review* 21: 663–69.

———. 1923. An ever lasting memorial. *Volta Review* 25: 91–98.

———. 1925. Hereditary impairment of hearing. *Journal of Heredity* 16: 141–44.

———. 1931. *The story of lip reading.* Washington, D.C.: Alexander Graham Bell Association for the Deaf.

D'Elia, D. J. 1969. Dr. Benjamin Rush and the Negro. *Journal of the History of Ideas* 30: 413–22.

Delp, H. A., and M. Lorenz. 1953. Follow-up of 84 public school special class pupils with IQs below 50. *American Journal on Mental Deficiency* 58: 175–82.

de Mause, L. 1974. *The history of childhood.* New York: Psychohistory Press.

———. 1981. The fetal origins of history. *Journal of Psychohistory* 9: 1–89.

Demos, J. 1970. *A little commonwealth: Family life in Plymouth Colony.* New York: Oxford University Press.

Denys, P. 1889. Pioneer work in Canada. *American Annals of the Deaf* 34: 239–41.

de Sanctus, S. 1908. Dementia praecocissima catatonica. *Folio Neurobiol* 2: 9.

Despert, J. L. 1970. *The emotionally disturbed child: An inquiry into family patterns.* New York: Anchor Books.

Deutsch, A. 1949. *The mentally ill in America.* 2d ed. New York: Columbia University Press.

Diderot, D. [1749] 1965. *Lettre sur les aveugles à l'usage de ceux qui voient.* Reprinted in Meyer, P. H. *Diderot Studies.* Geneva: Libraine Druz SA.

———. [1751] 1965. *Lettre sur sourds et muets.* Reprinted in Meyer, P. H. *Diderot Studies.* Geneva: Libraine Druz SA.

Digby, A. 1985. *Madness, morality and medicine: A study of the York Retreat, 1796–1914.* London: Cambridge University Press.

Digby, K. 1665. *The nature of bodies.* London: John Williams.

———. 1827. *The private memoirs of Sir Kenelm Digby, etc, written by himself.* London: Saunders and Otley.

Discussion at Chicago concerning day classes in public schools. 1884. *American Annals of the Deaf and Dumb* 29: 312–25.

Dix, D. 1843. *Memorial to the Legislature of Massachusetts.* Boston: Munroe and Frances.

Dobyns, J. R. 1889. In memory of Miss Mossie McGann. *American Annals of the Deaf* 34: 34–37.

Doermer, K. [1969] 1981. *Madmen and the bourgeousie.* London: Basil Blackwell.

Doll, E. A. 1913. Inexpert Binet examiners and their limitations. *Journal of Educational Psychology* 4: 607–9.

———. 1941. The essentials of an inclusive concept of mental deficiency. *American Journal of Mental Deficiency* 46: 214–19.

———. 1965. *Vineland Social Maturity Scale.* Circle Pines, American Guidance Services.

———. 1983. Deborah Kallikak, 1889–1978: A memorial. *Mental Retardation:* 21, 30–32.

Domich, H. J. 1945. John Carlin: A biographical sketch. *American Annals of the Deaf* 90: 345–54.

Doren, G. A. 1878. The status of the work—Ohio. In *Proceedings of the Association of Medical Officers of American Institutions for Idiotic and Feeble Minded Persons, June, 8–12, 1878, Syracuse, New York,* pp. 103–4. Philadelphia: J. B. Lippincott.

Down, J. L. 1866. Observations on ethnic classification of idiots. *London Hospital Report* 3: 229–62. Also *Journal of Mental Science,* 1867, pp. 121–23.

Doyle, R. P. 1989. The resistance of conventional wisdom to research evidence: The case of retention in grade. *Phi Delta Kappan* 71: 215–20.

Draper, A. G. 1888. Dr. Bell's memoir and criticisms upon it. *American Annals of the Deaf* 33: 37–43.

———. 1889. Deaf and hearing teachers. *American Annals of the Deaf* 34: 158–59.

———. 1895. The attitudes of the adult deaf toward pure oralism. *American Annals of the Deaf* 40: 44–54.

———. 1901. The deaf section at the Paris Congress. *American Annals of the Deaf* 46: 219–22.

———. 1902. Thomas Gallaudet. *American Annals of the Deaf* 47: 392–403.

———. 1904. The education of the deaf in America. *American Annals of the Deaf* 49: 352–63.

Dr. Bell's man-lifting kite. 1908. *National Geographic* 19: 35.

Dr. Bell's tetrahedral tower. 1907. *National Geographic* 18: 671.

Dr. Gordon's report. 1899. *Association Review* 1: 202–14.

Dr. T. H. Gallaudet's philanthropic labors. 1886. *American Annals of the Deaf and Dumb* 31: 73–75.

Dubois, P. H. 1966. A test-dominated society: China 1115 BC–1905 AD. In A. Anastasi, ed., *Testing problems in perspective.* Washington, D.C.: American Council on Education.

Dudley, L. 1880. Shall Massachusetts longer discriminate against the parents of the deaf and the blind? Northampton, Mass.: m.p. (pamphlet). Boston Public Library, Boston, Mass.

Dugdale, R. L. 1877. *The Jukes: A study in crime, pauperism, disease and heredity.* New York: Putman.

Duglison, R. 1854. *A letter to the president of the Board of Managers of the Pennsylvania Institution for the Instruction of the Blind.* Philadelphia: John C. Clark and Son.

Dunlop, F. 1947. The president's message. *Exceptional Children* 13: 225–27.

Dunn, L. M. 1968. Special education for the mildly retarded—Is much of it justifiable? *Exceptional Children* 35: 5–22.

———. 1973. *Exceptional children in the schools: Special education in transition.* New York: Holt, Rinehart and Winston.

Dunscombe, C. 1836. *Report upon the subject of education made to the Parliament of Upper Canada 25 February 1836, through the Commissioners, Doctors Morrison and Bruce, appointed by a resolution of the House of Assembly in 1835 to obtain information upon the subject of education, etc.* Upper Canada: M. C. Reynolds.

Durant, W. 1944. *Caesar and Christ.* New York: Simon and Schuster.

———. 1950. *The age of faith.* New York: Simon and Schuster.

Dwyer, E. 1987. *Homes for the mad: Life inside two nineteenth century asylums.* New Brunswick, N.J.: Rutgers University Press.

E. A. B. 1958. John Broadus Watson. *Canadian Psychologist* 7: 4–8.

Ebbinghaus, H., H. Ruger, tr., and C. Bussenius, tr. 1913. *Uber das Gedachtnis* [Memory: A contribution to experimental psychology]. p. 281. New York: Teachers College, Columbia University.

Eckler, J., and O. Weininger. 1988. Play and cognitive development: Development in preschoolers: A critical review. *Alberta Journal of Educational Research* 34: 179–93.

Edelstein, L. 1937. Greek medicine in its relation to religion and magic. *Bulletin of the History of Medicine* 5: 201.

Edinburgh Encyclopedia. 1813. 8: 13, 14. Edinburgh: printed by A. Balfour and sold by J. Anderson.

Editor. 1915. Nature or nurture. *Journal of Heredity* 6: 227–40.

Editorial comments. 1934. *Council Review* 1: 1–2.

Edminson, J. A. 1949. Gang delinquency. *Canadian Forum* 29: 6–8.

Eliot, C., ed. 1938. *American historical documents.* New York: Collier.

Ellis, J. W. 1990. Presidential address, 1990: Mental retardation at the close of the twentieth century: A new realism. *Mental Retardation* 28: 263–67.

Elwyn Institution for the Feeble Minded. *Annual Reports* 1880–1900 cf. Elwyn, Penn.: author.

Épée, M. C. de l'. 1776. *L'instruction des sourds et muets, par la voie des signes méthodiques; ouvrage qui content le Projet d'une Langue Universalle, par l'entre mise des signes naturels, assujettis a une Méthode.* Paris: Nyon.

———. 1784. *La véritable manière d'instruire les sourds et meuts confirmée par une longue experience.* Paris: Noyen.

———. [1784] 1860. The true method of educating the deaf and dumb, confirmed by long experience. *American Annals of the Deaf and Dumb* 12: 1–131.

Erikson, K. T. 1966. *Wayward Puritans.* New York: Wiley.

Esquirol, J. E. D. [1838] 1845. *Des maladies mentales* [Mental maladies: A treatise on insanity]. Paris: Bailliere. Trans. E. K. Hunt, Philadelphia: Lea and Blanchard. 1845.

Estabrook, A. H. 1916. *The Jukes in 1916.* Washington, D.C.: Carnegie Institution.

Estabrook, A. H., and C. B. Davenport. 1912. *The Nan family: A study in cacogenics.* Eugenics Record Office, Memoir no 2. Cold Springs Harbor, N.Y.: author.

Estes, L. L. 1984. Incarnations of evil: Changing perspectives on the European witch craze. *Clio* 13: 133–47.

Etienne, R. 1976. Ancient medical conscience and the life of children. *Journal of Psychohistory* 4: 131–61.

A eugenics catechism. 1927. New Haven, Conn.: American Eugenics Society.

Excerpts from convention addresses. 1934. *Council Review,* pp. 3–4.

An Extremist, Nowhere. 1873. The perversity of deaf-mutes. *American Annals of the Deaf and Dumb* 18: 262–63.

Fagan, T. K. 1985. Sources for the delivery of school psychological services during 1890–1930. *School Psychology Review* 14: 378–82.

———. 1990. Contributions of Letta Hollingworth to school psychology. *Roeper Review* 12: 157–61.

Fagan, T. K., and F. J. Delugach. 1984. Literary origins of the term "school psychologist." *School Psychology Review* 13: 216–20.

Fairchild, D. 1922. Alexander Graham Bell: Some aspects of his greatness. *Journal of Heredity* 13: 194–200.

Fairchild, H. 1917. The literacy test. *Quarterly Journal of Economics* 31: 447–60.

———. 1924. The immigration law of 1924. *Quarterly Journal of Economics* 31: 447–60.

Fair deaf-mute salaries. 1862. *The Gallaudet Guide and Deaf Mutes Companion* 3 (March): 11–15.

Familyculture, the science of human life. 1927. *Journal of Heredity* 18: 165–73.

Fancher, E. 1985. *The intelligence men: Makers of the IQ controversy.* New York: W. W. Norton.

Fancher, R. E. 1983. Biographical sources of Francis Galton's psychology. *Isis* 74: 227–33.

Farrell, G. 1956a. *Children of the silent night: The story of the education of deaf blind children here and abroad.* Watertown, Mass.: Perkins Institution for the Blind.

———. 1956b. *The story of blindness.* Cambridge: Harvard University Press.

Fay, E. A. 1874. Notices of publications: Review of J. C. Amman's A dissertation on speech. *American Annals of the Deaf and Dumb* 19: 31–34.

———. 1875. Notices of publications: Van Helmont's Alphabeti veve Naturalis Hebraci Brevissima Delineatio, 1667. *American Annals of the Deaf and Dumb* 20: 171–77.

———. 1877. Review of Deaf and Dumb by B. St. John Ackers. *American Annals of the Deaf and Dumb* 22: 115.

———. 1879. Contract between Gallaudet and Clerc, 1816. *American Annals of the Deaf and Dumb* 24: 115–17.

———. 1883. Review of History of deaf-mute education, with special reference to the development of deaf-mute instruction in Germany, 1882. *American Annals of the Deaf and Dumb* 28: 238.

———. 1884. Discussion by the National Academy of Sciences concerning the formation of a deaf variety of the human race. *American Annals of the Deaf and Dumb* 29: 70–77.

———. 1891. The instruction of the deaf. *Science* 17: 122.

———. 1896. An enquiry concerning results of marriages of the deaf, 2. *American Annals of the Deaf* 41: 22.

———. 1898a. The eleventh census. *American Annals of the Deaf* 43: 345–59.

———. 1898. *Marriages of the deaf in America.* Washington, D.C.: Gibson Brothers.

———. 1900. The Paris Congress of 1900. *American Annals of the Deaf.* 45: 406–16.

Fay, G. O. 1886. The education and care of the deaf. In Proceedings of the Thirteenth Annual Session of the National Conference of Charities and Corrections, 215–33, July 15–22, St. Paul, Minn. Boston: Press of Geo. H. Ellis.

———. 1899. Hartford and the education of the deaf. *American Annals of the Deaf* 44: 419–35.

Fay, P. B. 1923. A miracle of the 13th century. *American Annals of the Deaf* 68: 121–22.

Feldman, H. 1970. *A history of audiology.* New York: Columbia University.

Fernald, G. 1918. The problem of the extra-institutional feeble-minded. *Journal of Psycho-Asthenics* 23: 82–91.

Fernald, W. E. 1903. Farm colony in Massachusetts. *Journal of Psycho-Asthenics* 7: 74–80.

———. 1904. Care of the feeble-minded. In *Proceedings of the National Conference on Charities and Corrections* 31, no. 3.

———. 1912a. The burden of feeble-mindedness. *Medical Communications of the Massachusetts Medical Society* 23 and *Journal of Psycho-asthenics* 17: 87–111.

———. 1912b. *History of the treatment of the feebleminded.* Boston: Geo. H. Ellis.

———. 1919a. After-care study of the patients discharged from Waverly for a period of twenty-five years. *Ungraded* 2: 1–7.

———. 1919b. A state program for the care of the mentally defective. *Mental Hygiene* 3: 566–77.

———. 1919c. State programs for the care of the mentally defective. *Journal of Psycho-asthenics* 24: 114–22.

———. 1924. Feeblemindedness. *Mental Hygiene* 8: 964–71.

Ferrari, G. 1906. The deaf in antiquity. *American Annals of the Deaf* 51: 469–70.

———. 1908. *The American institutions for education of the deaf.* Philadelphia: Pennsylvania School for the Deaf.

Ferrier, C. 1897. Letter to Windsor Public Magistrate. In Victoria Industrial School files, Public Archives of Ontario, Toronto.

———. 1923, In *Our boys, Victoria Industrial School magazine,* July-August. Public Archives of Ontario, Toronto.

Fiedler, L. 1982. Pity and fear: Myths and images of the disabled in literature, old and new. In *Proceedings of the literary symposium sponsored by the International Centre for the Disabled in colloboration with the United Nations.* New York: International Center for the Disabled.

Field, J. A. 1911–12. The progress of eugenics. *Quarterly Journal of Economics* 26: 1–67.

Finkelstein, B. 1985. Schooling and the discovery of latency in nineteenth-century America. *Journal of Psychohistory* 13: 3–12.

———. 1988. Teachers as symbolic mediators in nineteenth-century United States. Paper presented at the Standing Committee for the History of Early Childhood Education, Joensuu, Finland, August.

Fitts, A. M. 1916. How to fill the gap between special classes for mentally defective children and institutions. *Ungraded* 11: 1–8.

Flynn, G., and B. Kowalczyk-McPhee. 1989. A school system in transition. In S. Stainback, W. Stainback, and M. Forest, eds., *Educating all students in the mainstream of regular education,* pp. 29–41. Baltimore: Paul H. Brookes.

Fogarty, D. W. 1960. A history of the Halifax School for the Blind. M.A. thesis, Nova Scotia, St. Mary's University.

Formigari, L. 1974. Language and society in the late eighteenth century. *Journal of the History of Ideas* 35: 275–92.

Forness, S. R. 1981. Concepts of learning and behavior disorders: Implications for research and practice. *Exceptional Children* 48: 56–62.

Foucault, M. 1965. *Madness and civilizations: A history of insanity in the age of reason.* New York: Pantheon Books.

Fox, S. J. 1972. Juvenile justice reform: An historical perspective. *Stanford Law Review* 22: 1187–1239.

Franklin, B. M. 1989. Progressivism and curriculum differentiation: Special classes in the Atlanta public schools, 1898–1923. *History of Education Quarterly* 29: 571–93.

Freeman, F. N. 1926. *Mental tests: Their history, principles and applications.* Boston: Houghton Mifflin.

French, R. S. 1932. *From Homer to Helen Keller: A social and educational study of the blind.* New York: American Foundation for the Blind.

French, St. George, M. 1981. Detecting treatable conductive hearing losses which are overlying sensorineural losses. *ACEHI Journal* 7: 97–107.

Friedlander, J. R. 1833. *An address to the public at the first exhibition of the pupils of the Pennsylvania Institution for the Instruction of the Blind at the Music Hall.* Philadelphia: Pennsylvania Institution for the Blind.

Froelich, C., G. McNealy, R. Nelson, and D. Norris. 1944. Gifted children. *Exceptional Children* 10: 207–9.

Fromkin, V., S. Krasten, S. Curtiss, D. Ringler, and M. Ringler. 1974. The development of language in Genie: A case of language acquisition beyond the critical period. *Brain and Language* 1: 81–107.

Fuller, S. 1907. Alexander Melville Bell. *Association Review* 9: 269–72.

Gallagher, J. J. 1972. *The search for an educational system that doesn't exist.* Reston, Va.: Council for Exceptional Children.

Gallaudet, E. M. 1870. Hon. Amos Kendall. *American Annals of the Deaf and Dumb* 15: 41–47.

———. 1876. Dr. Howe and Laura Bridgman. *American Annals of the Deaf and Dumb* 21: 74–79.

———. 1881. The Milan Convention. *American Annals of the Deaf and Dumb* 26: 1–16.

———. 1884. The value of articulation in business. In Fifth Convention of Principles of American Institutions for the Deaf and Dumb. *American Annals of the Deaf and Dumb* 29: 287–88.

———. 1886. History of the education of the deaf in the United States. American Annals of the Deaf and Dumb 31: 136–40.

———. 1888. *Life of Thomas Hopkins Gallaudet, founder of deaf-mute instruction in America.* New York: Henry Holt.

———. 1890. The intermarriage of the deaf, and their education. *Science* 16: 294–99.

———. 1892. Our profession. *American Annals of the Deaf* 38: 1–9.

———. 1894. The proposed union of the Convention and the Association. *American Annals of the Deaf* 39: 47–51.

———. 1895. What is the combined system? *American Annals of the Deaf* 40: 31–35.

———. 1896. Admission of young women to the College. In *Twenty ninth report of the Columbia Institution for the Deaf and Dumb.* Washington, D.C.: author.

———. 1900. The Paris Congress. *Association Review* 2: 478–79.

————. 1907. The present state. In *Proceedings of the international conference on the education of the deaf held in the Training College buildings, Edinburgh, on 29th, 30th and 31st July and 1st and 2nd August, 1907,* pp. 18–22. Edinburgh: Darien Press.

Gallaudet, T. 1856. St. Ann's Church for Deaf-Mutes, New York. *American Annals of the Deaf and Dumb* 8: 172–85.

————. 1858. St. Ann's Church for Deaf-Mutes, New York. *American Annals of the Deaf and Dumb* 10: 29–40.

Gallaudet, T. H. 1815a. Letter to Mason Cogswell. Gallaudet Archives, Gallaudet University, Washington, D.C.

————. 1815b. Letter to Mason Cogswell, February 12. Gallaudet Archives, Gallaudet University, Washington, D.C.

————. 1815c. Letter to Mason Cogswell, July 11. Gallaudet Archives, Gallaudet University, Washington, D.C.

————. 1816a. Letter to Mason Cogswell, April 11. Gallaudet Archives, Gallaudet University, Washington, D.C.

————. 1816b. Letter to Abbé Roch Sicard, May 21. Gallaudet Archives, Gallaudet University, Washington, D.C.

————. 1817. *A sermon upon the opening of the Hartford Institution for the Deaf and Dumb* (pamphlet). Volta Bureau, Washington, D.C.

————. 1819. *An address delivered at a meeting for prayer with reference to the Sandwich mission, in the brick church in Hartford, Oct. 11, 1819.* Hartford, Conn.: Lincoln and Stone.

————. 1821. *Discourse delivered at the dedication of the American Asylum for the Education of the Deaf and Dumb, May 22nd, 1821.* Hartford, Conn.: Hudson.

————. 1825. *Plan for a seminary for the education of the instructors of youth.* Boston: Cummings, Hilliard.

————. 1828. An address on female education. *American Journal of Education* 3: 178–83.

————. 1831. Remarks on seminaries for teachers. *American Annals of Education* 1: 25–26.

————. 1837. Letter to Flora Post, August 1. Gallaudet Archives, Gallaudet University, Washington, D.C.

————. 1844. Letter to Horace Mann, May 13. Gallaudet Archives, Gallaudet University, Washington, D.C.

Galt, J. [1842] 1846. *The treatment of insanity.* New York: Harper and Brothers.

Galton, F. 1865. Hereditary talent and character. *Macmillans Magazine* 7: 157–60.

————. [1869] 1870. *Hereditary genius: An enquiry into its laws and consequences.* London: Appleton.

————. 1873. Hereditary improvement. *Fraser's Magazine,* n.s. 7: 116–23.

————. 1883. *Enquiries into human faculty and its development.* London: J. M. Dent.

————. 1889. *Natural inheritance.* London: Macmillan.

Gardiner, M. 1910. The story of "Visible speech." *Volta Review* 12: 99–102.

Gardiner, R. A. 1958. Alfred A. Strauss, 1897–1957. *Exceptional Children* 24: 373–75.

Garis, R. 1927. *Immigration restriction*. New York: Macmillan.

Garnett, C. B., Jr. 1968. *The exchange of letters between Samuel Heinicke and Abbé Charles Michel de l'Épée*. New York: Vantage Press.

Garrett, E. 1882. Visible Speech; A plan for supplying the demand for articulation teachers; and remarks on methods of giving speech to the deaf. *American Annals of the Deaf and Dumb* 27: 106–9.

———. 1883. A plea that the deaf "mutes" of America may be taught to use their voices. *American Annals of the Deaf and Dumb* 28: 15–20.

Gaw, A. 1906. The development of the legal status of the deaf. *American Annals of the Deaf* 51: 269–75, 401–23.

———. 1907. The development of the legal status of the deaf. *American Annals of the Deaf* 52: 1–12, 167–83, 229–45, 468–89.

Geer, W. C. 1977. The CEC and its roots. *Exceptional Children* 44: 82–89.

Gelb, S. A. 1989. "Not simply bad and incorrigible": Science, morality, and intellectual deficiency. *History of Education Quarterly* 29: 359–80.

Gelzheiser, L. M. 1987. Reducing the number of students identified as learning disabled: A question of practice, philosophy, or policy? *Exceptional Children* 54: 145–50.

Gibbon, E. [1776] 1952. *The decline and fall of the Roman Empire*. Abridged ed. Edited by D. A. Saunders. London: Penguin English Library.

Gilbert, J. B. 1977. Anthrometrics in the U.S. Bureau of Education: The case of Arthur MacDonald's laboratory. *History of Education Quarterly* 17: 169–95.

Gile, B. C. 1916. The menace of suppurating ears. *Volta Review* 18: 403.

Gill, C. 1985. Ancient psychotherapy. *Journal of the History of Ideas* 46: 307–25.

Gillespie, J. A. 1884. The aural instruction of the semi-deaf. *American Annals of the Deaf and Dumb* 29: 244–48

Gillett, P. H. 1870. The organization of an institution for the deaf and dumb. *American Annals of the Deaf and Dumb* 15: 193–209.

Gilman, A. 1984. From widowhood to wickedness: The politics of class and gender in New York city private charity, 1799–1860. *History of Education Quarterly* 24: 59–74.

Givner, D. A. 1962. Scientific preconceptions in Locke's philosophy of language. *Journal of the History of Ideas* 23: 168–74.

Gleason, C. L. 1938. Rollins College honors Dr. Howe. *Outlook for the Blind* 32: 11–12.

Goddard, H. H. 1910. Four hundred feeble-minded children classified by the Binet method. *Journal of Psycho-Asthenics* 15: 17–30.

———. 1911. Two thousand normal children measured by the Binet measuring scale of intelligence. *Pegagogical Seminary* 18: 232–59.

———. 1912. *The Kallikak family: A study in the heredity of feeble mindedness*. New York: Macmillan.

———. 1913. The Binet tests in relation to immigration. *Journal of Psycho-Asthenics* 18: 105–10.

———. [1914a] 1973. *Feeble-mindedness: Its causes and consequences*. New York: Arno Press.

———. [1914b] 1976. What it means. . . . In M. Rosen, G. R. Clarke, and M. S. Kivitz, eds., *The history of mental retardation: Collected papers*. Vol. 2) Baltimore, Md.: University Park Press.

———. [1915a] 1986. *The criminal imbecile: An analysis of three remarkable murder cases.* Littleton, Colo.: F. B. Rothman.

———. 1915b. *School training for defective children.* New York: World.

———. 1916a. *Feeblemindedness.* New York: Macmillan.

———. 1916b. The menace of mental defectives from the standpoint of heredity. *Boston Medical and Surgical Journal* 175 (August): 269–71.

———. 1917. Mental tests and the immigrant. *Journal of Delinquency* 2: 243–77.

———. 1919. *The psychology of the normal and subnormal.* New York: Dodd.

———. 1920. *Human efficiency and levels of intelligence.* Princeton, N.J.: Princeton University Press.

———. 1921. *Juvenile delinquency.* New York: Dodd, Mead.

———. 1927a. *School training of gifted children.* New York: World Book Co.

———. 1927b. *Two souls in one body? A case of dual personality: A study of a remarkable case, its significance for education and for the mental hygiene of childhood.* New York: Dodd, Mead.

———. 1948. *How to raise children in the atomic age.* Mellot, Ind.: Hopkins Syndicate.

Goldstein, M. 1919. The meetings of the Convention and the Association. *Volta Review* 64: 339.

———. 1920. An acoustic method. *American Annals of the Deaf* 65: 472–81.

Golladay, L. 1991. Slide tour: Earlier schools for the deaf and their founders. Paper presented at the First International Conference on the History of Deafness, Washington, D.C., June.

Goodenough, F. 1949. *Mental testing: Its history, principles and applications.* New York: Rinehart.

Goodman, N. G. 1934. *Benjamin Rush: Physician and citizen.* Philadelphia: University of Pennsylvania Press.

Gordon, D. 1921. The menace of delinquency. *Social Welfare* 3: 184–85.

Gordon, J. C. 1885. Deaf mutes and the public schools from 1815 to the present day. *American Annals of the Deaf and Dumb* 30: 121–43.

———. 1892. The new departure at Kendall Green. *American Annals of the Deaf* 37: 121–27.

———. 1894. Recent progress in aural surgery. *American Annals of the Deaf* 39.

Gordon, J. C., ed. 1892a. *Education of deaf children: Evidence of Edward Miner Gallaudet and Alexander Graham Bell presented to the Royal Commission of the United Kingdom, on the condition of the blind, and the deaf and dumb, etc., with accompanying papers, postscripts and an index.* Washington, D.C.: Volta Bureau.

———. ed. 1892b. *Notes and observations upon the education of the deaf, with a revised index to Education of deaf children.* Washington, D.C.: Volta Bureau.

Goshen, C. E. 1967. *Documentary history of psychiatry: A source book of historical principles.* New York: Philosophical Library.

Gould, G. M., and W. L. Pyle. 1896. *Anomalies and curiosities of medicine.* New York: Bell.

Gould, J. 1981. Psychometric tests: Their uses and limitations. In B. Cooper, ed., *Assessing the handicaps and needs of mentally retarded children.* New York: Academic Press.

Gould, S. 1981. *The mismeasure of man.* New York: W. W. Norton.

Graham, R. M., and A. S. Beer. 1980. *Teaching music to the exceptional child.* Englewood Cliffs, N.J.: Prentice-Hall.

Grant, M. 1921. *Passing of a great race.* New York: Scribner and Sons.

Grave, C. E. 1939. Twenty-five years of progress in education at Woods School. *Exceptional Children* 16: 83–89.

Green, F. 1783. *"Vox Oculis Subjecta": A dissertation on the most curious art of imparting speech, and the knowledge of language, to the naturally deaf, and (consequently) dumb, with a particular account of the Academy of Mrrs. Braidwood of Edinburgh in 1783. By a parent.* London: Benjamin White.

Greenberger, D. 1874. Visible speech as a means of communicating articulation to deaf mutes. *American Annals of the Deaf and Dumb* 19: 65–74.

———. 1876. Hill's method. *American Annals of the Deaf and Dumb* 21: 103–16.

———. 1889. Doubtful cases. *American Annals of the Deaf* 34: 93–99.

Greenwood, E. 1957. Attributes of a profession. *Social Work* 2: 45–55.

Greer, J. V. 1990. Shattering the monolith. *Exceptional Children* 56: 286–89.

Gregg, W. R. 1868. On the failure of "natural selection" in the case of man. *Fraser's Magazine* 78: 356–68.

Griesinger, W. [1867] 1882. *Mental pathology and theraupetics.* 2d ed., trans. by C. L. Robertson and J. Rutherford. Rpt., London: New Syndenham Society.

Grob, G. N. 1973. *Mental institutions in America: Social policy to 1875.* New York: Free Press.

Guillie, D. 1817. *Essai sur l'instruction des aveugles ou expose analytique des procédés pour les instruire.* Paris: Imprime por les aveugles.

Gulik, S. 1916. An immigration policy. *Journal of Heredity* 7: 546–52.

Hackett, G. T. 1969. A history of public education for mentally retarded children in the Province of Ontario, 1867–1964. Ed. D. thesis, Ontario College of Education, University of Toronto.

Hagan, J., and J. Leon. 1977. Rediscovering delinquency: Social history, political ideology and the sociology of law. *American Sociological Review* 42: 587–98.

Haines, T. H. 1925. State laws relating to special classes and schools for mentally handicapped children in the public schools. *Mental Hygiene* 9: 545–51.

Halifax Institution for the Blind. 1874, 1875. *Annual report.* Halifax, N.S.: author.

Halifax Institution for the Deaf. 1892. *Twenty-seventh annual report.* Halifax, N.S.: author.

Halifax *Morning Chronicle.* July 13, 1868; April 6, 1870.

Halifax Protestant Industrial School. 1861–62, 1884, 1890. *Annual Report.* Halifax, N.S.: author. Public Archives of Nova Scotia, Halifax.

Hall, G. S. 1904. *Adolescence: Its psychology and relationship to physiology, anthropology, sociology, sex, crime, religion and education.* Englewood Cliffs, N.J.: Prentice-Hall.

Hall, G. S. [1906] 1969. *Adolescence.* 2nd ed. New York: Arno Press.

Hall, M., and L. Dennis. 1968. *Living and learning: The report of the provincial committee on aims and objectives of education in the schools of Ontario.* Toronto: Newton Publishing.

Hall, P. n.d. *The Columbia Institution for the Deaf.* Washington, D.C.: Gallaudet College.

Hallahan, D. P., and J. M. Kauffman. 1982. *Exceptional children: Introduction to special education.* 2d ed. Englewood Cliffs, N.J.: Prentice-Hall.

————. 1986. *Exceptional children: Introduction to special education.* 3d ed. Englewood Cliffs, N.J.: Prentice-Hall.

Haney, W. 1981. Validity, vaudeville, and values: A short history of social concerns over standardized testing. *American Psychologist* 36: 1021–33.

Hansen, A. 1916. The education of the deaf in the Scandinavian countries. *Volta Review* 18: 407.

Hardy, M. I., J. McLeod, H. Minto, S. A. Perkins, and W. R. Quance. 1971. *Standards for education of exceptional children in Canada: The SEECC report.* Toronto: Leonard Crainford.

Hare, E. H. 1962. Masturbatory insanity: The history of an idea. *Journal of Mental Science* 108: 1–25.

Hareven, T. 1969. An ambigious alliance: Some aspects of American influence on Canadian social welfare. *Historie sociale/Social History* 2: 82–98.

Harms, E. 1976. The historical aspect of child psychiatry. In R. Jenlins and E. Harms, eds., *Understanding disturbed children.* Seattle: Special Child Publications.

Harvey, J. 1978. Legislative intent and progress. *Exceptional Children* 44: 234–37.

Haüy, V. 1786. *Essai sur l'éducation des aveugles.* Paris: Imprime par les aveugles.

Hawker, R. 1805. *Witness for God, being the Substance of a Sermon preached in the Parish Church of St. Giles, Cripplegate, on Sunday Afternoon, May 19, 1805, at the Anniversary of the Charity for the Deaf and Dumb.* N.p.: n.p. Tracts 81, Metro Toronto Public Library.

————. [1805] 1905. *The history of the asylum for the deaf and dumb.* London: Williams and Smith.

Haworth, L. 1961. *A history of the Mackay School for the Deaf.* M.A. thesis, McGill University.

Hayman, M. 1939. The interrelations between mental defect and mental disorder. *Journal of Mental Science* 85: 1183–93.

Healy, W. 1915a. *The individual delinquent.* Boston: Little, Brown.

————. 1915b. *Mental conflicts and misconduct.* Boston: Little Brown.

Healy, W., and A. F. Bronner. [1926] 1969. *Delinquents and criminals: Their making and unmaking.* New York: Macmillan. Rpt., Montclair, N.J.: Patterson-Smith.

Heassman, K. 1962. *Evangelicals in action.* London: Geoffrey Bles.

Hebb, D. O. 1942. The effect of early and late brain injury upon test scores and the nature of normal adult intelligence. *Proceedings of the American Philosophical Society* 85: 275–302.

Heber, R. A. 1961. *A manual on terminology and classification in mental retardation.* Rev. ed. American Journal of Mental Deficiency, monograph supplement.

Heck, A. O. 1940. *The education of exceptional children.* New York: McGraw-Hill.

Henderson, R. 1919. Child labour, delinquency, and the standard of living. *Social Welfare* 2: 16–17.

Henry, T. S. 1920. Classroom problems in the education of gifted children. *19th Yearbook, Part 2, National Society for the Study of Education.* Chicago: University of Chicago Press.

Herbert, S. 1971. Darwin, Malthus and selection. *Journal of the History of Biology* 4: 209–17.

Herbst, J. 1988. From citizen teacher to professional. In *Papers of the International Standing Committee on the History of Education,* pp. 143–52. Jounsuu, Finland: International Standing Committee on the History of Education.

Heredity. 1876. *Sanitary Journal* 2 (Sept.): 315–16.

Herodotus. 1954. *The histories.* New York: Penguin Classics.

Hewes, D. W. 1989. Entrance age to public education in the United States, 1642 to 1842. Paper presented at the International Standing Committee on the History of Education, Oslo, August.

Hewett, F. 1974. *Education of exceptional learners.* Boston: Allyn and Bacon.

Hibbert, C. 1975. *The house of Medici.* New York: William Morrow.

Hiedsiek, J. 1898. Hearing deaf mutes, 3. *American Annals of the Deaf* 43; 283.

Hilgard, E. R. 1957. Lewis Madison Terman (1877–1956). *American Journal of Psychology* 70: 472–79.

———. 1987. *Psychology in America: A historical survey.* New York: Harcourt Brace Jovanovich.

Hill, A. S. 1951a. Legislation affecting special education since 1949. *Exceptional Children* 18: 65–68.

———. 1951b. The growth and development of professional organizations. *Exceptional Children* 17: 238–40.

———. 1956. A critical glance at special education. *Exceptional Children* 22: 315–17, 344.

Hill, H. F. (1945). Vineland summer school for teachers of backward and mentally deficient children. *Training School Bulletin* 42: 41–49.

Hincks, C. M. 1918. Feeblemindedness in Canada: A serious national concern. *Social Welfare* 1: 29–30.

———. 1919a. Feeblemindedness in Canada. *Social Welfare* 1: 103–4.

———. 1919b. Mental hygiene. *Social Welfare* 1: 130.

Hinshelwood, J. 1900a. Congenital word blindness. *Lancet,* p. 1506.

———. 1900b. *Letter, word, and mind blindness.* London: H. K. Lewis and Co.

———. 1917. *Congenital word blindness.* London: H. K. Lewis.

History of the first school for deaf mutes in America: How they are educated and how the alphabets are invented and introduced into use. 1885. Weymouth, Mass.: Ira H. Derby.

Hitz, J. 1905. Alexander Melville Bell. *Association Review* 7: 425–28.

Hodgins, F. E. 1919. *Report of the Royal Commission: The care and control of the mentally defective and feeble-minded in Ontario.* Toronto: Wilgrass, printed by order of the Legislative Assembly of Ontario.

Hodgins, G. J. 1889. *Ryerson memorial volume; Prepared on the occasion of the unveiling of the Ryerson statue in the grounds of the Education Department on the Queen's birthday, 1889.* Toronto: Warwick and Sons.

Hodgson, K. [1952] 1973. *The deaf and their problems: A study in special education.* London: Watts. Facsimile ed., Ann Arbor: University Microfilms.

Hoffman, E. 1975. The American public school and the deviant child: The origins of their involvement. *Journal of Special Education* 9: 415–23.

Hogan, D. J. 1985. *Class and reform: School and society in Chicago. 1888–1930.* Philadelphia: University of Pennsylvania Press.

Holburn, C. S. 1990. Symposium: Rules in today's residential environments. *Mental Retardation* 28: 65–66.

Holder, W. [1699] 1967. *Elements of speech.* London. Rpt., edited by R. C. Alston. English Linguistic Series, 1500–1800, no. 49. Menston, England: Scholar Press.

Hollingworth, L. S. 1913. The frequency of amentia as related to sex. *Medical Record* 84: 753–56.

———. 1914. *Functional periodicity: An experimental study of the mental and motor abilities of women during menstruation.* New York: Teachers College, Columbia University.

———. 1926. *Gifted children: Their nature and nurture.* New York: Macmillan.

———. 1942. *Children above 180 IQ, Stanford-Binet: Origin and development.* New York: World Books.

Holman, H. 1914. *Seguin and his physiogical method of education.* London: Pitman.

Holmes, S. J. 1933. *The eugenics predicament.* New York: Harcourt, Brace.

Hoolihan, C. 1985. Too little too soon: The literature of deaf education in 17th century Britain (part 2). *Volta Review* 86: 28–44.

Horace Mann and the common school revival in the United States. 1900. New York: Charles Scribner's Sons.

Horn, M. 1984. The moral message of child guidance, 1925–1945. *Journal of Social History* 18: 25–36.

Houston, S. 1982. The "waifs and strays" of a late Victorian city: Juvenile delinquents in Toronto. In J. Parr, ed., *Childhood and family in Canadian history.* Toronto: McClelland and Stewart.

Howard, F. E. 1935. *Mental health: Its principles and practices with emphasis on the treatment of mental deviations.* New York: Harper and Brothers.

Howard, J. C. 1902. Men and women teachers. *American Annals of the Deaf* 47: 278–81.

How best to teach mutes. 1891. In Ontario Institution for the Education and Instruction of the Deaf and Dumb, *Twenty-first annual report,* pp. 12–17. Toronto: Government Printer.

How do subnormal persons live? 1940. *Exceptional Children* 6: 31–33.

Howe, M., and F. H. Hall. 1903. *Laura Bridgeman.* Boston: Little, Brown.

Howe, S. G. [1848a] 1972. *On the causes of idiocy; being the supplement to the report by Dr. S. G. Howe and the other commissioners appointed by the governor of Massachusetts to enquire into the condition of idiots of the Commonwealth, dated February 26, 1848, with an appendix.* Rpt., New York: Arno Press and the New York Times.

———. 1848b. *Report to the Legislature of Massachusetts upon idiocy.* Boston: Collidge and Wiley.

———. 1852. Third and final report of the Experimental School for Training and Teaching Idiotic Children; also, the first report of the trustees of the Massachusetts School for Idiotic and Feeble-Minded youth. *American Journal of Insanity* 9: 20–36, 97–118.

———. 1854. *A letter to J. H. Wilkins, H. B. Rogers and F. B. Fay, commissioners of Massachusetts for the State Reform School for Girls.* Boston: Ticknor and Fields.

———. 1866a. *Address.* Boston: Walker, Fuller.

———. 1866b. Massachusetts State Board of Charities, *Second Annual Report.* Boston: author.

———. 1866c. *Remarks upon the education of deaf mutes in defence of the doctrines of the Second Annual Report of the Massachusetts Board of State Charities and in reply to charges of Rev. Collins Stone.* Boston: Walker, Fuller.

———. 1874. The co-education of the deaf and blind. *American Annals of the Deaf and Dumb* 19:162.

———. 1875. The comparable happiness of the deaf and the blind. *American Annals of the Deaf and Dumb* 20.

How the deaf mutes were cared for by de l'Épée and Sicard. 1928. *American Annals of the Deaf* 72: 366–77, 458–68.

Hubbard, G. G. 1876. The origin of the Clarke Institution. *American Annals of the Deaf and Dumb* 21: 178–83.

Huey, E. 1910. The Binet scale for measuring intelligence and retardation. *Journal of Educational Psychology* 1: 435–44.

Hughes, J. G. 1980. *American Academy of Pediatrics: The first fifty years.* Evanston, Ill.: American Academy of Pediatrics.

Hutt, R. B. 1923. The school psychologist. *Psychological Clinic* 15: 48–51.

Hutton, J. S. 1869a. Deaf mute education in the British Maritime provinces. *American Annals of the Deaf and Dumb* 14: 65–82.

———. 1869b. Statistics of the deaf and dumb in the lower provinces of British North America. *American Annals of the Deaf and Dumb* 14: 1–20.

Hutton, W. L. 1936. *A brief for sterilization of the feeble-minded. Prepared at the request of the Association of Ontario Mayors at their annual conference, Orillia, June, 1936.* Ontario: Ontario Mayors.

The hygienic value of speech. 1892. *American Annals of the Deaf* 37: 80–81.

Illick, J. E. 1974. Child-rearing in seventeenth century England and America. In L. de Mause, ed., *The history of childhood.* New York: Psychohistory Press.

Inherited deafness. 1879. *American Annals of the Deaf and Dumb* 24: 126.

Institutional reports. 1872. *American Annals of the Deaf and Dumb* 17:

Institution at Hartford for Instructing the Deaf and Dumb. 1818. *North American Review,* 7: 129–32.

Iowa Institution for the Feeble-Minded. 1883. *Ninth Annual Report.* Iowa: author.

Ireland, W. 1877. *On idiocy and imbecility.* London: J. and A. Churchill.

Irvine, P. I. 1971. Henry Herbert Goddard, 1866–1957: A biographical sketch. *Journal of Special Education* 5: 210.

———. 1976a. Dorothea Lynde Dix, a biographical sketch. *Journal of Special Education* 10: 2–3.

———. 1976b. Frank Haven Hall, a biographical sketch. *Journal of Special Education* 10: 120–21.

I. S. F. 1921. Is the male teacher becoming an extinct species? *American Annals of the Deaf* 66: 29–32.

Issel, W. 1979. Americanization, acculturation and social control: School reform in industrial Pennsylvania, 1880–1910. *Journal of Social History* 12: 569–90.

Itard, J. M. G. 1801. *De l'éducation d'un homme sauvage.* Paris: Goiyon.

———. 1804. *Rapports et mémoires sur le sauvage d'Aveyrons. L'idiote et la surdi-mutité, avec une appreciation de ces rapports par Delasiawe.* Paris: F. Alcan.

———. 1807. *Rapport fait à son Excellence le Ministre de l'Interior sur les nou-veaux développements et l'état actuel du sauvage d'Aveyron.* Paris: J. J. Marcel.

———. 1932. *The wild boy of Aveyron,* trans. G. and M. Humphrey. New York: Century.

Jacobs, J. 1869. Dummies. *American Annals of the Deaf and Dumb* 14: 20–23.

Jarvis, E. 1852. On the supposed increase of insanity. *American Journal of Insanity* 8: 333–64.

Jenkins, J. R., and A. Heinen. 1989. Students' preferences for service delivery: Pull-out, in-class, or integrated models. *Exceptional Children* 55: 516–26.

Jenkins, W. G. 1890. The scientific testimony of "Facts and opinions." *Science* 16: 85–88.

Johanningmeier, E. V. 1989. Piety and patriotism in 17th and 18th century American education: The foundation for Horace Mann's common school crusade. Paper presented at the International Standing Committee on the History of Education, Oslo, August.

Johnson, A. B., and C. A. Cartwright. 1979. The roles of information and experience in improving teachers' knowledge and attitudes about mainstreaming. *Journal of Special Education* 13: 453–62.

Johnson, G. O. 1962. Special education for the mentally handicapped—A paradox. *Exceptional Children* 8: 62–69.

Johnson, R. H. 1918. The marriage of the deaf. *Jewish Deaf,* March, p. 77.

Johnson, S. [1775] 1924. *A journey to the Western Isles of Scotland.* London: W. Strahan and T. Caldwell. London: University of Oxford Press.

Jones, A. 1978. Closing Penatanguishene penitentiary: An attempt to deinstitutionalize treatment of juvenile offenders in early twentieth century Ontario. *Ontario History* 70: 227–44.

Jones, J. W. 1918. One hundred years of history. *American Annals of the Deaf* 63: 1–47.

Jordan, D. S. 1913. *The heredity of Richard Roe: A discussion of the principles of eugenics.* Boston: American Unitarian Association.

Juul, K. D. 1978. European approaches and innovations in serving the handicapped. *Exceptional Children* 44: 322–40.

Kaestle, C. F., and M. A. Vinovskis. 1980. *Education and social change in nineteenth-century Massachusetts.* New York: Cambridge University Press.

Kamin, S. 1974. *The history and politics of IQ.* Potomac, Md.: Erlbaum.

Kanner, L. 1943. Autistic disturbances of affective contact. *Nervous Child* 2: 217–50.

———. 1962. Emotionally disturbed children: A historical review. *Child Development* 33: 97–102.

———. 1964. *A history of the care and study of the mentally retarded.* Springfield, Ill.: Thomas.

———. 1973. Historical perspectives on developmental deviations. *Journal of Autism and Childhood Schizophrenia* 3: 187–98.

Karagianis, L. D., and W. C. Nesbit. 1981. The Warnock Report: Britain's preliminary answer to PL94-142. *Exceptional Children* 47: 332–36.

Karier, C. J. 1972. Testing for order and control in the corporate liberal state. *Educational Theory* 22: 154–80.

Karth, J. 1927. In commemoration of the two hundredth anniversary of the birth of Samuel Heinicke. *American Annals of the Deaf* 72: 270–80.

Kassmaul, A. 1859. *Untersuchungen uber das Sedenleben des neugeborenen Menchen*. Leipzig: C. E. Winter.

———. 1877. Disturbance of speech. *Cyclopedia of Practical Medicine* 14: 581–87.

Katz, M. 1968. *The irony of early school reform: Educational innovation in mid-nineteenth-century Massachusetts*. Boston: Beacon Press.

———. 1971. *Class, bureaucracy, and schools: The Illusion of educational change in America*. New York: Praeger.

———. 1973. From voluntarism to bureaucracy in American education. In M. Katz, ed., *Education in American history: Readings on the social issues*, pp. 38–50. New York: Praeger.

Katz, M. B. 1983. *Poverty and policy in American history*. New York: Academic Press.

———. 1986. *In the shadow of the poorhouse: A social history of welfare in America*. New York: Basic Books.

Kauffman, J. M. 1976. Nineteenth century views of children's behavior disorders: Historic contributions and continuing issues. *Journal of Special Education* 10: 335–49.

———. 1981. *Characteristics of childrens' behavior disorders*. 2d ed. Columbus, Ohio: Merrill.

———. 1985. *Characteristics of children's behavior disorders*. 3d ed. Columbus, Ohio: Merrill.

———. 1989. *Characteristics of children's behavior disorders*. 4th ed. Columbus, Ohio: Merrill.

Kaufman, M. J., J. Gottlieb, T. A. Agard, and A. Kukic. 1975. Mainstreaming: Toward an explication of the construct. *Focus on Exceptional Children* 7: 1–13.

Keep, J. R. 1867. Signs in deaf mute education: An explanation in defence of the American system of deaf mute education. *New Englander,* July, pp. 6–16.

Keller, H. 1903. *The story of my life*. Toronto: William Briggs.

———. 1929. *Mainstream, my later life*. New York: Doubleday, Doran.

Kelley, P. A. V. 1976. *Women in Nebraska Hall of Fame*. Omaha: International Women's Year Coalition.

Kelso, J. J. 1893–94. Neglected and friendless children. *Canadian Magazine,* pp. 213–16.

———. 1910. *Children: Their care, training and happiness as future citizens*. Toronto: L. K. Cameron, King's Printer.

Kent, D. 1986. Disabled women, portraits in fiction and drama. In A. Gardner and T. Joe, eds., *Images of the disabled/disabling images*. New York: Praeger.

Kent, J. H. 1922. Rev. Thomas Gallaudet. *American Annals of the Deaf* 67: 327–32.

Kerlin, I. N. 1877. The organization of establishments for the idiotic and imbecile class. In *Proceedings of the Association of Medical Officers of American Institutions for Idiotic and Feeble-Minded Persons*. Philadelphia.

———. 1889. Moral imbecility. In *Proceedings of the Association of Medical Officers of American Institutions for Idiotic and Feeble-Minded Persons, 1887*. Philadelphia: n.p.

———. 1890. The moral imbecile. In *Proceedings of the National Conference of Charities and Corrections,* 1870. Boston: n.p.

———. 1891. *Manual of Elwyn, 1863–1891.* Philadelphia: Lippincott.

Kile, B. C. 1916. The menace of suppurating ears. *Volta Review* 18: 403.

Kim, Y. H. 1970. *The community of the blind: Applying the theory of community formation.* New York: American Foundation for the Blind.

King, L. S. 1958. *The medical world of the eighteenth century.* Chicago: University of Chicago Press.

Kinsey, A. A., official recorder. 1881. *Speech for the deaf: Essays written for the Milan International Congress. Proceedings and resolutions. Report of the proceedings of the International Congress on the Education of the Deaf, Milan, Sept. 6–11, 1880.* Volta Bureau, Washington, D.C.

Kirby, M. D. 1980. Law reform and disabled people. *National Rehabilitation Digest* 3: 19–25.

Kirk, S. A. 1963. Behavioral diagnosis and remediation of learning disabilities. In *Proceedings of the conference on exploration into the problems of the perceptually handicapped child: First annual meeting,* vol. 1. Chicago: Association for Children with Learning Disabilities.

Kirk, S. A., and F. E. Lord, eds. 1974. *Exceptional children: Educational resources and perspectives.* Boston: Houghton Mifflin.

Kitto, J. 1852. *The lost senses: Deafness and blindness.* New York: Robert Carter and Brothers.

Klobas, L. 1985. TV's concept of people with disabilities: Here's lookin' at you. *Disability Rag,* January-February, pp. 2–6.

Knight, E. W., and C. L. Hall, eds. 1951. *Readings in American educational history.* New York: Appleton Century Crofts.

Knight, H. M. 1872. Hallucinations of childhood. In *Proceedings of the Connecticut Medical Society,* May 23.

Knight, I. 1968. *The geometric spirit: The Abbé Condillac and the French Enlightenment.* New Haven: Yale University Press.

Knowlson, J. 1965. The idea of gesture as a universal language in the XVIIth and XVIIIth centuries. *Journal of the History of Ideas* 26: 495–508.

Knox, H. A. 1914. A scale based on the work at Ellis Island, for estimating mental defect. *Journal of the American Medical Association* 62: 741–46.

Koestler, F. 1976. *The unseen minority: A social history of blindness in the United States.* New York: David McKay.

Kozens, J. 1990. A closer look at continuous learning. *ATA Magazine,* March/April, 9–11.

Kraepelin, E. 1896. *Psychiatrie: ein Lehrbuch fur studirende und Aerzte.* Leipzig: J. A. Barth.

Kriegel, I. 1986. The cripple in literature. In A. Gartner and T. Joe, eds., *Images of the disabled/disabling images.* New York: Praeger.

Krug, E. A. 1972. *The shaping of the American high school, 1880–1920.* Madison, Wis.: University of Wisconsin Press.

Krugman, M. 1939. Some impressions of the revised Stanford-Binet scale. *Journal of Educational Psychology* 30: 594–603.

Kugel, R. B., and W. Wolfensberger, eds. 1969. *Changing patterns in residential services for the mentally retarded.* Washington, D.C.: President's Committee on Mental Retardation.

Kussmaul, A. 1859. *Untersuchunger uber des Sedenleben des neugelsoreren Menchen,* Leipzig: C. E. Winter.

———. 1877. Disturbance of speech. *Cyclopedia of Practical Medicine* 14: 581–87.

Kyle, J. 1980–81. Signs of speech: Cooperating in deaf education. *Special Education: Forward Trends* 7-7: 21–29.

Lagemann, E. C. 1989. The plural worlds of educational research. *History of Education Quarterly* 29: 185–214.

Lakin, K. C. n.d. *Demographic studies of residential facilities for the mentally retarded.* Minneapolis: University of Minnesota, Department of Psycho-educational Studies.

La Mettrie, J. O. [1745] 1912. L'historie naturelle de l'âme. Paris. Extract in *Man a machine.* La Salle, Ill.: Open Court.

———. [1748] 1912. L'homme machine. Paris. In *Man a machine.* La Salle, Ill.: Open Court.

Lamson, M. S. 1878. *Life and education of Laura Dewey Bridgman, the deaf, dumb, and blind girl.* Boston: New England Publishing.

Lane, H. 1976. *The wild boy of Aveyron.* Cambridge: Harvard University Press.

———. 1991. Keynote address. Presented at the First International Conference on the History of Deafness, Washington, D.C., June.

Lane, H., and R. Pillard. 1978. *The wild boy of Burindii.* New York: Random House.

Larson, C. A. 1972. Watson's Canadian summer retreat. *Canadian Psychologist* 13: 135–42.

Larson, M. L. 1977. *The rise of professionalism: A sociological survey.* Berkeley: University of California Press.

Laughlin, H. H. 1922. *Eugenical sterilization in the United States.* Chicago: Psychopathic Laboratory of the Municipal Court of Chicago.

———. [1924] 1930. *Eugenical sterilization.* New Haven, Conn.: American Eugenics Society.

———. 1930. Survey of eugenical work in America. In *International Federation of Eugenical Organizations, Report of the Third International Congress of Eugenics.* Cold Spring Harbor, N.Y. Baltimore: American Eugenics Society.

League for Preventative Work. 1916. *Feeble-minded adrift.* Boston: author.

———. 1916–17. *The mental defective and the public schools of Massachusetts.* Boston: author.

Leakey, T. 1991. Rehabilitation. Paper presented at the First International Conference on the History of Deafness, Gallaudet University, Washington, D.C., June.

Lee, J. L. 1944. Editorial. *Exceptional Children* 1: 1–2.

Lee, S., and E. Stevens. 1981. *The rise of literacy and the common school in the United States: Socioeconomic analysis to 1870.* Chicago: University of Chicago Press.

Lenz, F. 1924. Eugenics in Germany. *Journal of Heredity* 15: 223–29.

Lerner, J. 1981. *Learning disabilities: Theories, diagnosis and teaching strategies.* 3d ed. Boston: Houghton Mifflin.

Lesperance, J. 1872. The dumb speak. *Canadian Monthly and National Review* 7: 506–12.

Levin, S. M. 1966. Malthus and the idea of progress. *Journal of the History of Ideas* 27: 92–108.

Lewis, A. 1960. A study of defect. *American Journal of Psychiatry* 117: 289–304.

Lietz, K. 1934. The place of the school for the deaf in the New Reich. *American Annals of the Deaf* 79, 203–4.

Lincoln, W. A. 1918. Venereal disease among the civil population. *Social Welfare* 1: 31–32.

Linden, K. W., and J. D. Linden. 1968. *Modern mental measurement: A historical perspective.* Boston: Houghton Mifflin.

Lippmann, W. 1920. The abuse of tests. *New Republic,* November 15.

———. 1922a. A future for the tests. *New Republic,* November 29.

———. 1922b. The mental age of Americans. *New Republic,* October 25.

———. 1922c. The mystery of the A man. *New Republic,* November 1.

———. 1922d. The reliability of intelligence tests. *New Republic,* November 8.

———. 1922e. Tests of hereditary intelligence. *New Republic,* November 22.

———. 1923. The great confusion. *New Republic,* January 3, p. 146.

Locke, J. [1690] 1894. *An essay concerning human understanding,* vol. 1. Edited by A. C. Fraser. Oxford: Oxford University Press.

———. [1690] 1956. An essay concerning human understanding. In I. Berlin, ed., *The age of enlightenment.* New York: Mentor Books.

———. [1693] 1964. *Thoughts concerning education.* Woodbury, N.Y.: Barron's Educational Series. Also from J. W. Yolton. 1971. *John Locke and education.* New York: Random House.

Lombroso, C. 1891. *The man of genius.* New York: Walter Scott.

Longmore, P. K. 1985. Screening stereotypes: Images of disabled people. *Social Policy* 16: 31–37.

Lord, F. E. 1976. Great moments in the history of the Council for Exceptional Children. *Exceptional Children* 43: 6–8.

Lord, F. E., and S. A. Kirk, 1950. The education of teachers of special classes. In *The education of exceptional children: Forty-ninth yearbook of the National Society for the Study of Education, part 2,* pp. 103–16. Bloomington, Ill.: Public School Publishing.

Love, J. K. 1906. Report on visits to European and American institutions: A plea for the study of the deaf child and for the teaching of speech to the semi-deaf and the semi-mute. *Association Review* 8: 471–84.

Lowenfeld, B. 1956. History and development of specialized education for the blind. *Exceptional Children* 23: 53–57, 90.

Lowenthal, B. 1990. The United States Regular Education Initiative: Flames of controversy. *B.C. Journal of Special Education* 14: 273–77.

Luftig, R. L. 1989. *Assessment of learners with special needs.* Boston: Allyn and Bacon.

Lukoff, I. F., and M. Whiteman. 1961. Attitudes toward blindness—Some preliminary findings. *New Outlook for the Blind* 55: 39–42.

McClure, G. M. 1923. The first state school for the deaf. *American Annals of the Deaf* 68: 97–120.

McConnichie, K. 1983. The Canadian mental hygiene movements in the inner-war years. Paper presented at the Canadian Historical Society meeting, Vancouver.

MacDonald, A. 1902. *Hearing on a bill (HR 14798) to establish a laboratory for the study of the criminal, pauper and defective classes with a bibliography.* Washington, D.C.: Government Printing Office.

MacDonald, C., J. Olson, C. Gunter, and M. A. Winzer. 1984. Education of the deaf in early twentieth century Saskatchewan. *ACEHI Journal* 10: 40–49.

McDonald, R. H. 1967. The frightful consequences of onanism: Notes on the history of a delusion. *Journal of the History of Ideas* 28: 423–31.

MacDonnell, G. M. 1897. The prevention of crime by the state. *Queen's Quarterly* 4: 257.

MacFarlane, A. 1970. *Witchcraft in Tudor and Stuart England: A regional and comparative study.* New York: Harper and Row.

McGann, J. B. 1863. *Home education for the deaf and dumb: First book of lessons.* Toronto: author.

———. 1869. Descriptive remarks on the building in course of erection for a Provincial Institution for the Deaf and Dumb. *American Annals of the Deaf and Dumb* 14: 247–51.

———. 1888. *The deaf mute schools of Canada: A history of their development with an account of the deaf mute institutions of the Dominion, and a description of all known finger and sign alphabets.* Toronto: C. J. Howe.

McGovern, C. M. 1986. *Masters of madness: Social origins of the American psychiatric profession.* Hanover, N.H.: University of New England.

McGill, H. G. 1919. The relation of the juvenile court to the community. *Canadian Journal of Mental Hygiene,* pp. 1–3.

McGrath, W. T. 1962. A new look at juvenile delinquency. *Canadian Forum* 42: 55–57.

———. 1965. *Crime and its treatment in Canada.* Toronto: Macmillan.

Machar, A. M. 1881. Compulsory education. *Canada Educational Monthly and School Chronicle* 3: 327–29.

McHenry, D. C. 1881. School legislation. *Canada Educational Monthly and School Chronicle* 3: 266.

McIlvaine, J. A., Jr. 1909. A plea for the feeble-minded deaf. *American Annals of the Deaf* 54: 444–50.

Mack, J. 1909. The Juvenile Court. *Harvard Law Review* 104.

Mackay School for the Deaf, Montreal [1880]. Application. Located in the archives of the R. J. Williams School for the Deaf, Saskatoon, Saskatchewan.

McLaren, A. 1986. The creation of a haven for "human thoroughbreds": The sterilization of the feeble-minded and mentally ill in British Columbia. *Canadian Historical Review* 67: 127–50.

McLaughlin, C. L. 1920. The Rochester method. *American Annals of the Deaf* 65: 403–13.

McLelland, M. C. 1934. Light from within. *Social Welfare* 15: 31–32, 35–36.

MacMillan, M. B. 1960. Extra-scientific influences in the history of childhood psychopathology. *American Journal of Psychiatry* 116: 1091–96.

MacMurchy, H. 1919. Defective children. *Social Welfare* 1: 135.

McMurrich, W. B. 1872. Industrial schools. *Canadian Monthly* 2: 424–28.

Magdol, M. 1976. An historical perspective to physiological education. In L. Faas, ed., *Learning disabilities.* Boston: Houghton Mifflin.

Mahendra, B. 1985. Subnormality revisited in early 19th century France. *Journal of Mental Deficiency Research* 29: 391–401.

Mallory, G. 1882. The gesture speech of man. *American Annals of the Deaf and Dumb* 27: 69–89.

Malthus, T. [1798] 1963. *Essay on the principle of population.* Homewood, Ill.: R. D. Irwin.

Manitoba School for the Deaf. 1924. *Social Welfare,* November.

Mann, E. J. 1836. *The deaf and dumb: Or, a collection of articles relating to the condition of deaf mutes; their education, and the principal asylums devoted to their instruction.* Boston: D. K. Hitchock.

Mann, L. 1970. Perceptual training: Misdirections and redirections. *American Journal of Orthopsychiatry* 40: 30–38.

————. 1971. Psychometric phrenology and the new faculty psychology: The case against ability assessment and training. *Journal of Special Education* 5: 3–65.

————. 1979. *On the trail of process: A historical perspective on cognitive processes and their training.* New York: Grune and Stratton.

Marriage. 1895. *American Annals of the Deaf* 40: 310.

Marriages of deaf mutes in olden times. 1858. *American Annals of the Deaf and Dumb* 10: 250.

Martens, E. H. 1946. State legislation for the education of exceptional children—Some basic principles. *Exceptional Children* 12: 225–30.

Martin, E. W. 1968. Breakthrough for the handicapped: Legislative history. *Exceptional Children* 34: 493–503.

Massachusetts Institution for the Idiotic and Feeble-Minded. 1885. *Annual Report.* Waverly, Mass.: author.

Massachusetts State Board of Education. *Seventh Annual Report.* Boston: author.

Massachusetts State Board of Charities. 1886. *Annual Report.* Boston: author.

Mathison, R. 1906. Historical sketch of the origin and progress of deaf-mute education. In *Ontario, Department of Education Annual Report,* pp. 413–35. Toronto: L. K. Cameron.

Maudsley, H. 1867. Illustrations of a variety of insanity. *Journal of Mental Science* 14: 153.

————. 1868. *The physiology and pathology of mind.* 2d ed. London: Macmillan.

Mavor, J. 1893. The relation of economic study to private and public charity. *Annals of the American Academy of Political and Social Sciences* 4: 35–60.

Mayne, R. E. 1929. The Bell family and English speech. *Volta Review* 31: 453–456.

Meadow, K. P. 1980. *Deafness and child development.* Berkeley: University of California Press.

Melcher, J. W. 1976. Law, litigation, and handicapped children. *Exceptional Children* 43: 126–30.

Mental survey of Saskatchewan. 1921. *Social Welfare,* May 1, pp. 221–23.

Mercer, C. D. 1979. *Children and adolescents with learning disabilities.* Columbus, Ohio: Merrill.

Mercer, J. R., and J. G. Richardson. 1975. Mental retardation as a social problem. In N. Hobbs, ed., *Issues in the classification of children (vol. 2).* San Francisco: Jossey-Bass.

Meredith, E. A. [1862] 1975. Separate report: Annual report of the Board of In-
    spectors of Asylums, Prisons etc., Province of Canada. In A. Prentice and
    S. Houston, eds., *Family, school and society im nineteenth-century Canada,*
    pp. 271–72. Toronto: Oxford University Press.
Meyer, P. H. 1965. *Diderot studies, VII.* Geneva: Libraire Druz SA.
Meyers, C. E., D. L. MacMillan, and R. K. Yoshida. 1980. Regular class placement
    of EMR students, from efficacy to mainstreaming: A review of issues and re-
    search. In J. Gottlieb, ed., *Educating mentally retarded persons in the main-
    stream.* Baltimore, Md.: University Park Press.
Michal-Smith, H. 1987. Presidential address 1987: Hollywood's portrayal of dis-
    ability. *Mental Retardation* 25: 259–66.
Midelfort, H. C. E. 1968. Recent witch hunting research, or where do we go from
    here? *Papers of the Biographical Society of America* 62: 373–420.
———. 1982. *Witch hunting in southwestern Germany 1562–1684: The social and
    intellectual foundations.* Palo Alto, Calif.: Stanford University Press.
Miles, C. 1944. The epileptic. *Exceptional Children* 10: 205–7.
Miller, R. 1989. Leta Stetler Hollingworth: Pioneer woman of psychology. *Roeper
    Review* 12: 142–44.
Miller, W. B. 1943. Education and the war. *Exceptional Children* 9: 236–39.
Milligan, G. E. 1961. History of the American Association of Mental Deficiency.
    American Journal of Mental Deficiency 66: 357–69.
The miracle of Saint Elizabeth of Hungary. 1880. *American Annals of the Deaf and
    Dumb* 25: 166–68.
Mitchell, S. H. 1971. An examination of selected factors related to the economic
    status of the deaf population. Ph.D. dissertation, American University.
———. 1973. The haunting influence of Alexander Graham Bell. *American An-
    nals of the Deaf* 118: 349–56.
Mohl, R. A. 1970. History from the bottom up: A study of the poor in preindustrial
    New York City, 1794–1830. *Journal of Social History* 70: 87–104.
———. 1971. *Poverty in New York.* New York: Oxford University Press.
Monoghan, E. J. 1989. Noted and unnoted school dames: Women as reading
    teachers in Colonial New England. Paper presented at the Standing Commit-
    tee on the History of Education, Oslo, August.
Monroe, P., ed. 1926. *A cyclopedia of education* 2: 257–65. New York: Macmillan.
Monter, E. W. 1972. The historiography of European witchcraft: Progress and
    prospects. *Journal of Interdisciplinary History* 3: 435–51.
———. 1977. Pedestal and stake: Courtly love and witchcraft. In R. Bridenthal
    and C. Koonz, eds., *Becoming visible: Women in European history,* pp. 119–
    36. Boston: Houghton Mifflin.
Montessori, M. 1912. *The Montessori method,* trans. A. George. New York: Stokes.
———. 1917. *The advanced Montessori method: Scientific pedagogy as applied to
    the education of children from seven to eleven years.* London: Heinmann.
Montreal Catholic Institution for the Deaf. [1885]. Application. Located in the ar-
    chives of R. D. Williams School for the Deaf, Saskatoon, Saskatchewan.
Montreal Institution for Protestant Deaf Mutes. 1886. *Annual Report.* Located in
    the Provincial Archives, Halifax, Nova Scotia.
Moores, D. 1987. *Educating the deaf: Philosophy, principles and practices* 3d ed.
    Boston: Houghton Mifflin.

Morrison, T. R. 1974. Reform as social tracking: The case of industrial education in Ontario. *Journal of Educational Thought* 8: 87–110.

Mott, A. J. 1899. A comparison of deaf and hearing children in their ninth year, 1. *American Annals of the Deaf* 44: 401–12.

———. 1900. A comparison of deaf and hearing children in their ninth year, 2. *American Annals of the Deaf* 45: 33–39.

Mr. Stainer's London day schools. 1884. *American Annals of the Deaf and Dumb* 29: 252–54.

Mundie, G. S. 1919. Specialized care for the defective child. *Social Welfare* 2: 5–6.

M.V.D. 1925. Routing an ancient enemy. *Volta Review* 27: 81–85.

Myers, J. 1976. The efficacy of the special day school for EMR pupils. *Mental Retardation* 14: 3–11.

National Education Association. 1898. *Proceedings, thirty-seventh annual meeting.* Washington, D.C., July.

The National Education Association Meeting: Proceedings of Department XV1. 1899. *Association Review* 1: 107–10.

Neuman, R. P. 1975. Masturbation, madness and the modern concepts of childhood and adolescence. *Journal of Social History* 8: 1–27.

Newcomer, P. L. 1980. *Understanding and teaching emotionally disturbed children.* Boston: Allyn and Bacon.

New York Asylum for the Feeble-Minded. 1862. *Annual Report.* Albany, N.Y.: author.

New York Children's Aid Society. 1855. *Annual Report.* New York: author.

New York Institution for the Deaf and Dumb. 1854. *Annual Report.* New York: author.

New York State Asylum for Feeble-Minded Women. 1893. *Annual Report.* See S. J. Taylor and S. J. Searl, Jr. 1987. The disabled in America: History, policy, and trends. In P. Knoblock, *Understanding exceptional children and youth,* pp. 5–64. Boston: Little, Brown.

Nielson, W. A. 1934. A tribute to Miss Yale. *Council Review,* May, pp. 17, 26.

Nirje, B. 1979. Changing patterns in residential services for the mentally retarded. In E. L. Meyen, ed., *Basic readings in the study of exceptional children and youth.* Denver, Colo.: Love Publishing.

Nix, G. 1981. Mainstreaming: Illusion or solution? *ACEHI Journal* 8, 7–14.

Nordin, F. 1901. Report on the Paris congress. *Association Review* 3: 37–40, 106–18.

Notices of institutions for the deaf and dumb. 1857. *American Annals of the Deaf and Dumb* 9: 123–25.

Numbers, M. 1974. *My words fell on deaf ears.* Washington, D.C.: Alexander Graham Bell Association for the Deaf.

O'Brien, C. H. 1985. The Jansenist campaign for toleration of Protestants in late eighteenth-century France: Sacred or secular? *Journal of the History of Ideas* 46: 523–38.

Olneck, R., and M. Lazeron. 1974. The school achievement of immigrant children, 1900–1930. *History of Education Quarterly* 14: 453–82.

Onania or the Heinous sin of Self-Pollution And All its Frightful consequences, in both Sexes consider'd, etc. 1737. London: author.

On attempted cures of deafness. 1851. *American Annals of the Deaf and Dumb* 3: 244–50.

Ontario Deaf Mute Association. 1906. In Ontario, Department of Education, *Annual Report.* Toronto: Government Printer.

Ontario, Department of Education. 1904, 1905, 1906, 1907, 1911. *Annual Report.* Toronto: Government Printer.

Ontario, Inspector of Prisons, Asylums and Public Charities. 1870, 1876, 1878, 1880, 1881, 1883, 1883. *Annual reports of the Inspector of Asylums, Prisons and Public Charities for the Province of Ontario.* Toronto: Government Printer.

Ontario Institution for the Education and Instruction of the Deaf and Dumb [name varies]. 1871, 1872, 1873, 1874, 1875, 1876, 1879, 1880, 1882, 1884, 1895, 1888, 1889, 1891, 1892, 1893, 1895, 1897, 1900, 1901, 1905. *Annual Reports* [title varies]. Toronto: Government Printer.

Ontario. 1869, 1874, 1875. *Sessional Papers.* Toronto: Government Printer.

Ontario. 1874. *Statutes.* Toronto: Government Printer.

Ordahl, G. 1917. Mental defectives and the juvenile court. *Journal of Delinquency* 2: 1–13.

Orlando, F. A., and J. P. Black. 1975. The juvenile court. In N. Hobbs, ed., *Issues in the classification of children: A sourcebook on categories, labels, and their consequences,* 2: 349–376. San Francisco: Jossey-Bass.

Orton, S. T. 1925. Word-blindness in school children. *Archives of Neurology and Psychiatry* 14: 581–616.

————. 1937. *Reading, writing and speech problems in children.* New York: Norton.

Orwell, G. 1934. *The road to Wighman Pier.* London: Penguin.

Osborn, F. 1974. History of the American Eugenics Society. *Social Biology* 21: 115–26.

Osborn, W. J., and B. J Rohan. 1931. *Enriching the curriculum for gifted children: A book of guidance for educational administrators and classroom teachers.* New York: Macmillan.

OSD. *See* Ontario Institution for the Education and Instruction of the Deaf and Dumb.

Otis, A. S. 1916. Heredity and mental defect: A discussion of the logical aspect of certain controversies. *Journal of Delinquency* 1: 87–100.

Oxley, S. 1930. Some new sidelights on Henry Baker. *American Annals of the Deaf* 75: 6–8.

Palen, I. 1923. Ears that hear not. *Social Welfare 5.*

Park, D. 1969. Locke and Berkeley on the Molyneux problem. *Journal of the History of Ideas* 80: 253–60.

Park, G. E., and J. D. Linden. 1968. The etiology of reading disabilities: An historical perspective. *Journal of Learning Disabilities* 1: 318–31.

Parkinson, J. [1807] 1963. Observations on the extensive indulgence of children. London. In. R. Hunter and I. McAlpine, eds., *Three hundred years of psychiatry, 1535–1860: A history in selected English texts.* London: Oxford University Press.

Passinen, T. M. 1974. Popular science and society: The phrenology movement in early Victorian Britain. *Journal of Social History* 8: 1–20.

Passow, A. H. 1990. Letta Stetler Hollingworth: A real original. *Roeper Review* 12: 134–36.

Pastore, N. 1978. The Army intelligence tests and Walter Lippmann. *Journal of the History of the Behavioral Sciences* 14: 316–27.

Patterson, R. 1926. Romance of the education of the deaf. *American Annals of the Deaf* 71: 177–86.

Paul, J. L., and N. J. Warnock. 1980. Special education: A changing field. *Exceptional Child* 27: 3–28.

Pearl, R. 1927. The biology of superiority. *American Mercury* 12: 200–266.

Peet, D. 1856. The remote and proximate causes of deafness. *American Annals of the Deaf and Dumb* 8: 129–58.

Peet, Edward. 1852. Biographical sketch of Dr. Itard. *American Annals of the Deaf and Dumb* 5: 110–24.

Peet, Elizabeth. 1922. Dactylology. *American Annals of the Deaf* 67: 1–12.

Peet, H. P. [1844] 1882. *A vocabulary and elementary exercise for the deaf and dumb.* New York Institution for the Deaf and Dumb. New York: Baker, Pratt.

———. [1846] 1847. *Address delivered at the New York Institution of the Deaf and Dumb, Dec. 2nd, 1846 by Harvey P. Peet, A.M., President of the Institution, with an appendix containing the proceedings at the dedication of the chapel.* New York: Hovey and King.

———. 1850. Analysis of Bonet's treatise on the art of teaching the deaf to speak. *American Annals of the Deaf and Dumb* 3: 200–211.

———. 1851. Memoir on the origin and early history of the art of instructing the deaf and dumb. *American Annals of the Deaf and Dumb* 3: 129–60.

———. 1852a. Statistics of the deaf and dumb. *American Annals of the Deaf and Dumb* 5: 1–21.

———. 1852b. Tribute to the memory of the late Thomas Hopkins Gallaudet. *American Annals of the Deaf and Dumb* 4: 69–75.

———. 1855. Notions of the deaf and dumb before instruction, especially in regard to religious subjects. *American Annals of the Deaf and Dumb* 8: 1–44.

———. 1857. History of the New York Institution for the Deaf and Dumb. *American Annals of the Deaf and Dumb* 9: 168–83.

———. 1870. Progress in deaf mute instruction. *American Annals of the Deaf and Dumb* 15: 209–16.

Peet, I. L. 1872. The psychical status and criminal responsibility of the totally uneducated deaf and dumb. *American Annals of the Deaf and Dumb* 17: 66–94.

———. 1883. Report of the Standing Committee on the Education of the Deaf and Dumb. In U.S. Conference of Charities and Corrections, *Proceedings of the Tenth Annual Conference held in Louisville, Kentucky, Sept. 24–30, 1883,* pp. 401–21. Madison, Wis.: Midland Publishing.

———. 1884. General view of the education of the deaf and dumb in the United States. *American Annals of the Deaf and Dumb* 29: 1–17.

———. 1890. The life and works of the Abbé de l'Épée. *American Annals of the Deaf* 35: 133–50.

Pendell, E. 1924. Birth control. *Journal of Heredity* 15: 419–20.

Pennachio, L. G. 1986. Toronto's public schools and the assimilation of foreign students, 1900–1920. *Journal of Educational Thought* 20: 37–48.

Pennsylvania Institution for the Feeble-Minded. 1868. *Annual Report.* Located at Boston Public Library, Boston.

Penrose, L. S. [1949] 1966. *The biology of mental defects.* London: Sidgwick and Jackson.

Percival, W. P. 1947. Special education in Quebec and Maritime provinces. *Exceptional Children* 13: 237–41.

Perkins Institution for the Blind. 1832, 1834, 1835, 1836, 1837, 1838, 1839, 1846. *Annual Report of the Trustees of the New England Institution for the Education of the Blind to the Corporation.* Boston: author.

Perkins Institution for the Blind. 1848, 1850, 1851, 1852, 1853, 1854, 1856, 1857, 1858, 1859, 1860, 1861, 1864, 1873, 1874, 1881, 1893, 1894, 1895, 1904. *Annual Report of the Trustees of the Perkins Institution and the Massachusetts Asylum for the Blind to the Corporation.* Cambridge: author.

Perron on the existence of erectile tissue in the mucous membrane of the middle ear. 1888. *Medical Analectic* 5: 402.

Perry, M. E. 1943. *Two hundred and fifty thousand strong.* Victoria, B. C.: author.

Pettengill, B. D. 1872. The instruction of the deaf and dumb. *American Annals of the Deaf* 17: 21–33.

———. 1873. The sign language. *American Annals of the Deaf and Dumb* 18: 1–12.

Phelps, E. 1924. *Restriction of immigration.* New York: H. W. Wilson.

Pinel, P. 1798. *Nosographic philosophique ou la méthode de l'analyse appliqué à la médicine* [The philosophical method of analysis applied to medicine]. Paris: Maradan.

———. [1806] 1962. *Treatise on mental alienation.* Paris. Translated by D. D. Davis. New York: Hafner.

Pintner, R. 1920. Tests of mentality. *American Annals of the Deaf* 65: 278–300.

———. [1923] 1931. *Intelligence testing: Methods and results.* New York: Holt.

Plann, S. 1991. Fray Pedro Ponce de Leon: Myth and reality. Paper presented at the First International Conference on the History of Deafness, Washington, D.C., June.

Pollack, D. 1970. *Educational audiology for the limited hearing infant.* Springfield, Ill.: Thomas.

Pollock, H. 1922. The problem of the unfit. In *International Neo-Malthusian and Birth Control Conference: Report of the fifth conference, Jan. 11–14, 1922.* London: William Heinemann Medical Books.

Poponoe, P. P. 1922. Eugenics in Germany. *Journal of Heredity* 13: 382–84.

———. 1923. Eugenical sterilization: A review. *Journal of Heredity* 14: 308–10.

———. 1928. Eugenic sterilization in California: The number of persons needing sterilization. *Journal of Heredity* 19: 405–11.

———. 1929. *The child's heredity.* Baltimore, Md.: Williams and Wilkins.

———. 1934. The German sterilization law. *Journal of Heredity* 25: 257–60.

Porter, Samuel. 1847. Review of The historie of the Church of England, compiled by Venerable Bede, Englishman, book 5, part 2. London, 1622, Thomas Stapleton (trans). In *American Annals of the Deaf and Dumb* 1: 33–34.

———. 1848a. Bibliographical: An Historical Sketch of the Purposes, Progress, and Present State of the Asylum for the support and education of Indigent Deaf and dumb Children, situate in the Kent Road, Surrey; with the rules of the Society, and a list of its Officers and Governors. London. *American Annals of the Deaf and Dumb* 2: 40.

———. 1848b. Bibliographical: Report of the Institution for the Education of Deaf and Dumb Children, established at Edinburgh, June 25th, 1810, etc. *American Annals of the Deaf and Dumb* 2: 42–43.

———. 1848c. Review of Memoirs of Rev. John Townsend, Founder of the Association for the Deaf and Dumb, and the Congregational school (Boston, 1831). *American Annals of the Deaf and Dumb* 1: 231.

———. 1858. The plans for a community of deaf mutes. *American Annals of the Deaf and Dumb* 10: 136–40.

Porter, Sarah. 1883. Society and the orally restored deaf-mute. *American Annals of the Deaf and Dumb* 28: 186–92.

Potter, H. W. 1933. Schizophrenia in children. *American Journal of Psychiatry* 89: 1253–70.

Powell, F. 1882. Status of the work—Iowa. In *Proceedings of the Association of Medical Officers of American Institutions for Idiotic and Feeble-Minded Persons,* pp. 267–78.

Pratt, E. J. 1920. The social significance of mental defect. *Social Welfare* 2: 263–64.

Prentice, A. 1977. *The school promoters: Education and social class in mid-nineteenth century Upper Canada.* Toronto: McClelland and Stewart.

Pritchard, D. G. 1963. *Education and the handicapped.* London: Routledge and Kegan Paul.

Proceedings of the International Conference on the Education of the Deaf held in the Training College buildings, Edinburgh, on 29th, 30th and 31st July and 1st and 2nd August, 1907. 1907. Edinburgh: Darien Press.

Proceedings of the sixth summer meeting of the AAPTSD, held at Clarke School for the Deaf, Northampton, Mass., June 22–28. 1899. *Association Review* 1: 53–55.

Professor A. Graham Bell's studies on the deaf. 1890. *Science* 16: 117–19.

The project of a school for deaf-mutes in Massachusetts. 1860. *American Annals of the Deaf and Dumb* 12: 195–96.

The psychological examination of recruits. 1917. *Science* 46: 355–56.

Pugach, M., and M. S. Lilly. 1984. Reconceptualizing support services for classroom teachers: Implications for teacher education. *Journal of Teacher Education* 35: 48–55.

Putman, J. H. 1912. *Egerton Ryerson and education in Upper Canada.* Toronto: William Briggs.

Pybas, A. 1909. Compulsory education for the deaf. *American Annals of the Deaf* 54: 356–59.

Quaife, A. 1987. *Godly zeal and furious rage: The witch in early modern Europe.* New York: St. Martins Press.

Rae, L. 1847a. The great peril of Sicard. *American Annals of the Deaf and Dumb* 1: 16–19.

———. 1847b. Introductory. *American Annals of the Deaf and Dumb* 1: 1–6.

———. 1848a. The Abbé de l'Épée. *American Annals of the Deaf and Dumb* 1: 69–76.

———. 1848b. Education of the deaf and dumb in Canada. *American Annals of the Deaf and Dumb* 2: 32–37.

———. 1848c. Historical sketch of the instruction of the deaf and dumb, before the time of de l'Épée. *American Annals of the Deaf and Dumb* 1: 197–208.

Raftery, J. R. 1988. Missing the mark: Intelligence testing in Los Angeles public schools, 1922–32. *History of Education Quarterly* 28: 73–93.

Ramsland, J. 1989. The foundling hospital in eighteenth century London: Social, cultural and educational perspectives. Paper presented at the Australian and New Zealand History of Education Conference, Newcastle, July.

Reinert, H. R. 1980. *Children in conflict.* 2d ed. St. Louis: Mosley.

Report of Bell's fallacies concerning the deaf presented to the Washington Philosophical Society. 1884. *Science* 3: 85.

Report of the Boston Mental Health Survey. 1930. Boston: Boston Council of Social Agencies.

Report of the Committee on Psychological Research. 1901. *Journal of Psycho-Asthenics* 81: 21–26.

Reports of institutions. 1860. *American Annals of the Deaf and Dumb* 12: 175.

Report of the Social Survey Commission of Toronto. 1915. Toronto.

Resnick, L. B. 1981. Instructional psychology. *American Review of Psychology* 32: 659–704.

Resolutions relating to speech teaching, 1868–1900. 1900. *Association Review* 2: 520–26.

Review of Bell's Graphical studies. 1917. *Journal of Heredity* 8: 214.

Review of A report on a system of public elementary education for Upper Canada by E. A. Ryerson. 1848. *Journal of Education for Upper Canada* 1: 175.

Reynolds, M. C. 1975. Trends in special education: Implications for measurement. In W. Hively and M. C. Reynolds, eds. *Domain-referenced testing in special education.* Reston, Va.: Council for Exceptional Children.

Reynolds, M. C., and J. W. Birch. 1977. *Teaching exceptional children in all America's schools.* Reston, Va.: Council for Exceptional Children.

Rhodes, W. C., and M. Sagor. 1975. Community perspectives. In N. Hobbs, ed. *Issues in the classification of children.* Vol. 1. San Francisco: Jossey Bass.

Richards, L. E. 1935. *Samuel Gridley Howe.* New York: Appleton-Century.

Rivera, G. 1972. *Willowbrook: A report on how it is and why it doesn't have to be that way.* New York: Vintage Press.

Roback, A. A. 1937. *Behaviorism at twenty-five.* Cambridge, Mass.: Sci-Art Publishers.

———. 1964. *History of American psychology.* Rev. ed. New York: Collier Books.

Roberts, C. A., and M. D. Lazure. 1970. *One million children: A national study of Canadian children with emotional and learning disorders.* Toronto: Crainford.

Robinson, H. B., and N. M. Robinson. 1965. *The mentally retarded child: A psychological approach.* New York: McGraw-Hill.

Rogers, J. A. 1972. Darwinism and Social Darwinism. *Journal of the History of Ideas* 33: 265–80.

Rosen, G. 1968. *Madness in society: Chapters in the historical sociology of mental illness.* Chicago: University of Chicago Press.

Rosen, M., G. Clark, and M. Kivitz. 1976. *The history of mental retardation.* Baltimore: University Park Press.

Rosenblith, J. F., and J. E. Sims-Knight. 1985. *In the beginning: Development in the first two years.* Monterey, Calif.: Brooks\Cole.

Ross, D. 1972. *G. Stanley Hall: The psychologist as prophet.* Chicago: University of Chicago Press.

Ross, I. 1951. *Journey into light: The story of the education of the blind.* New York: Appleton-Century-Crofts.

Ross, S., H. De Young, and J. Cohen. 1971. Confrontation: Special education placement and law. *Exceptional Children* 38: 5–12.

Rothman, D. 1971. *The discovery of the asylum: Social order and disorder in the new republic.* Boston: Little Brown.

Rousseau, J. J. [1762a] 1963. *Emile.* London: Everyman's Library.

———. [1762b] 1968. *The social contract.* Edited by E. V. Rieu. New York: Penguin Book Classics.

Roweton, W. E. 1990 Leta Stetler Hollingworth: A personal profile of Nebraska's pioneering psychologist. *Roeper Review* 12: 136–41.

The Royal Commission enquiry into the prison and reformatory system of the province of Ontario. 1891. Toronto: Printed by Order of the Legislature, Queen's Printer.

Rudowski, V. A. 1974. The theory of signs in the eighteenth century. *Journal of the History of Ideas* 35: 683–90.

Rury, J., and G. Harper. 1986. The trouble with coeducation: Men and women at Antioch, 1853–1860. *History of Education Quarterly* 26: 481–502.

Rusch, F. R., and L. A. Phelps. 1987. Secondary special education and transition from school to work: A national priority. *Exceptional Children* 53: 487–92.

Rush, B. 1774. An enquiry into the natural history of medicine among the Indians of North America, and a comparative view of their diseases and remedies with those of civilized nations. *American Philosophical Society.*

Russell, C. 1920. The feebleminded in Canada. *Social Welfare,* April 1, p. 2.

Russell, W. 1829. Intelligence. *American Journal of Education* 4: 462.

Ryerson, E. A. 1865. *A special report on the systems and state of popular education on the continent of Europe, and in the United States of America, with practical suggestions for the improvement of public instruction in the province of Ontario.* Toronto: Leader Steam Press.

———. 1868. *Report on institutions for the deaf and dumb and the blind in Europe and in the United States of America with appendices and suggestions for their establishment in the Province of Ontario.* Toronto: Daily Telegraph Printing House.

Saenger, G. 1957. *The adjustment of severely retarded adults in the community.* New York: New York Interdepartmental Health Resources Board.

Sagan, C. 1979. *Broca's brain.* New York: Ballantine Books.

Saleeby, C. W. 1911. *Woman and womanhood: A search for principles.* New York: Mitchell Kennedy.

Salkind, N. 1990. *Child development.* 6th ed. Fort Worth, Tex.: Holt, Rinehart and Winston.

Sanborn, F. 1891. *Dr. S. G. Howe, the philanthropist.* New York: Funk and Wagnalls.

Sanders, W. B. 1970. *Juvenile offenders for a thousand years.* Chapel Hill: University of North Carolina Press.

Sarason, S. B., and J. Doris. 1979. *Educational handicap, public policy, and social history: A broadened perspective on mental retardation.* New York: Free Press.

Sattler, J. M. 1974. *Assessment of children's intelligence.* Philadelphia: Saunders.

————. 1982. *Assessment of children's intelligence and special abilities.* 2d ed. Boston: Allyn and Bacon.

Sawyer, R. C. 1989. "Strangely handled in all her lyms": Witchcraft and healing in Jacobean England. *Journal of Social History* 22: 461–86.

Scheerenberger, R. C. 1982. Treatment from ancient times to the present. In P. Cegelka and H. Prehm, eds. *Mental retardation: From categories to people,* pp. 44–75. Columbus, Ohio: Merrill.

————. 1983. *A history of mental retardation.* Baltimore: Brookes.

Scheier, S. 1931. *Problems in the training of certain special-class teachers.* New York: Columbia University.

Schlepp, M. G. 1923. Causes of defective children: Prenatal development affected by glandular disturbances in the mother—induced by unfavorable environment. *Journal of Heredity* 14: 386–97.

Schmidt, R. R. 1936. *The dawn of the human mind,* trans. R. A. MacAlister. London: Sidgwick and Jackson.

Schwartz, H. 1952. Samuel Gridley Howe as phrenologist. *American Historical Review* 57: 644–51.

————. 1956. *Samuel Gridley Howe: Social reformer, 1801–1876.* Cambridge: Harvard University Press.

Science. 1885.

Scots Magazine. 1767. 31: 12.

Scott, A. G. 1857. History of the Tennessee School for the Deaf and Dumb. *American Annals of the Deaf and Dumb* 9: 117–22.

Scott, W., Sir. 1965. *Heart of Midlothian.* London: Everyman's Library.

Scull, A. 1975. From madness to mental illness: Medical men as moral entrepreneurs. *Archives européenes de sociologie* 16: 218–22.

————. 1976. Mad-doctors and magistrates: English psychiatry's struggle for professional autonomy in the nineteenth century. *Archives européenes de sociologie* 17: 279–305.

Seagoe, M. V. 1975. *Terman and the gifted.* Los Altos, Calif.: William Kaufman.

Sedlak, M. W. 1983. Young women and the city: Adolescent deviance and the transformation of educational policy, 1870–1960. *History of Education Quarterly* 23 (Spring): 1–25.

Seguin, E. 1843. *Hygiene et éducation des idiots.* Paris: Bailliere.

————. 1846. *Traitement moral hygiene et éducation des idiots et des autres enfants erroires.* Paris: Bailliere.

————. 1856. Origin of the treatment and training of idiots. *American Journal of Education* 2: 145–52.

————. [1864] 1976. Origin of treatment and training of idiots. In M. Rosen, G. R. Clark, and M. S. Kivitz, eds., *The history of mental retardation,* vol. 1. Baltimore: University Park Press.

———. [1866] 1907. *Idiocy; And its treatment by the physiological method.* New York: Albany-Brandon Printing.

———. 1876. Education of the deaf and mute. In *Commissioners of the United States, Reports to the International Exhibition held in Vienna, 1873, volume 2.* Washington, D.C.: Government Printing Office.

Seigel, J. P. 1969. The Enlightenment and the evolution of the language of signs in France and England. *Journal of the History of Ideas* 30: 96–115.

Seminary for female teachers. 1831. *American Annals of Education* 1: 341–45.

Senex. 1831. Female education in the last century. *American Annals of Education* 1: 524.

Shapiro, S., E. R. Schlesinger, and R. E. Nesbit. 1968. *Infant, perinatal, maternal and childhood mortality in the United States.* Cambridge: Harvard University Press.

Sheldon, W. H. 1924. The intelligence of Mexican children. *School and Society* 19: 129–42.

Sheridan, L. C. 1875. The higher education of deaf-mute women. *American Annals of the Deaf and Dumb* 20: 248–52.

Shields, S. A. 1990. Ms. Pilgrim's progress and commentary. *Roeper Review* 12: 151–54.

Sibscota, G. [1670] 1967. *Deaf and dumb man's discourse.* London: Printed by H. Bruges. Rpt. edited by R. C. Alston. English Linguistic Series, 1500–1800, no. 8. Menston, England: Scholar Press.

———. 1859. Extract from the treatise of Sibscota on the deaf and dumb. *American Annals of the Deaf and Dumb* 11: 98–111.

Sicard, R., Abbé. 1818. *Théorie des signes.* Paris: De l'imprimerie d'a clo, Truettel et Wurtz.

Siegel, M. 1939. *Population, race and eugenics.* Hamilton, Ont.: author.

Sigmon, S. B. 1982–83. The history and future of educational segregation. *Journal for Special Educators* 19: 1–11.

Silver, M. 1971. Mrs. Alexander Graham Bell. *Atlantic Advocate* 62: 32–39.

Silverman, L. K. 1990. The legacy of Leta Hollingworth. *Gifted Child Quarterly* 33: 123–24.

Sissons, C. B. 1937. *Egerton Ryerson: His life and letters.* Toronto: Clarke, Irwin.

Skinner, B. F. 1989. The origin of cognitive thought. *American Psychologist* 44: 13–18.

Sklar, K. 1973. *Catharine Beecher: A study in American domesticity.* New Haven, Conn.: Yale University Press.

Skodak, M. 1939. Children in foster homes: A study of mental development. *University of Iowa Studies in Child Welfare* 16 (1).

Slack, P. 1985. *The impact of the plague in Tudor and Stuart England.* London: Routledge and Kegan Paul.

Sloan, W., and J. Birch. 1955. A rationale for degrees of retardation. *American Journal of Mental Deficiency* 60: 258–64.

Slusarczyk, K. 1986. The assessment of intelligence in the school age hearing impaired child. M.Ed. thesis, University of British Columbia.

Smith, B. O. 1985. Research bases for teacher education. *Phi Delta Kappan* 66: 184–85.

Smith, J. A., and W. D. Ross, eds. 1910. *The works of Aristotle.* Oxford: Clarendon Press.

Smith, J. A. C. 1980. The right to an appropriate education: A comparative study. *Ottawa Law Review* 12: 367–91.

Smith, J. D. 1985. *Minds made feeble: The myth and legacy of the Kallikaks.* Rockville, Md.: Aspen Systems.

Smith, J. K., and L. G. Smith. 1989. The concept of human nature and education in selected works of B. Rush. In *Education and Enlightenment: The concept of human nature and education (series 111). Selected proceedings of the Third International Conference on Education and Enlightenment,* pp. 81–86. Edmonton: University of Alberta.

Smith, J. L. 1869. *A treatise on diseases of infancy and childhood.* Philadelphia: Lea.

Smith, S. 1876. The silent community. *American Annals of the Deaf and Dumb* 21: 137–45.

Smith-Rosenberg, C. 1971. Beauty, the beast and the militant woman: A case study in sex roles and social status in Jacksonian America. *American Quarterly* 23: 562–84.

The socially inadequate. 1922. *American Annals of the Deaf* 67: 348–49.

Social vice and how to deal with it. 1919. *Social Welfare* 1: 78–80.

Sokal, M. M. 1984. Approaches to the history of psychological testing. *History of Education Quarterly* 24: 419–30.

Sparr, M. P., and W. Smith. 1990. Regulating professional services in ICFs/MR: Remembering the past and looking to the future. *Mental Retardation* 28: 95–99.

Spearman, C. E. 1904. General intelligence objectively determined and measured. *American Journal of Psychology* 15: 201–93.

Spencer, H. 1851. *Social statistics.* London: John Chapman.

———. 1852. A theory of population, deduced from the general law of human fertility. *Westminister Review* 57: 468–501.

Spitzka, E. C. 1883. *Insanity: Its classification, diagnosis and treatment.* New York: E. B. Treat.

———. 1887–88. Cases of masturbation (masturbatic insanity). *Journal of Mental Science* 33: 57, 238; 34: 58, 216.

Spilman, B. W. 1925. Religious freedom for the feeble-minded. *Journal of Psycho-Asthenics* 49: 251.

Splane, R. B. 1965. *Social welfare in Ontario, 1791–1893: A study in public welfare administration.* Toronto: University of Toronto Press.

Sprague, W. B. 1857. *Annals of the American pulpit.* New York: Robert Carter and Brothers.

Sprinthall, N. A., and R. C. Sprinthall. 1987. *Educational psychology: A developmental approach.* 4th ed. New York: Random House.

Statistic of the deaf and dumb. 1859. *American Annals of the Deaf and Dumb* 11: 117.

Stedman, L. 1924. *Education of gifted children.* Yonkers-on-Hudson, N.Y.: World Bank.

Steinberg, M. 1982. The Twelve Tables and their origins: An eighteenth-century debate. *Journal of the History of Ideas* 43: 379–96.

Steiner, B. C. 1919. *Life of Henry Barnard, the first United States Commissioner of Education, 1867–1870.* Washington, D.C.: Government Printing Office.

Stern, W. 1914. *The psychological methods of testing intelligence.* Baltimore: Warwick and York.

Stevens, G. D. 1954. Developments in the field of mental deficiency. *Exceptional Children* 21: 58–62, 70.

Stevenson, G., and G. Smith. 1934. *Child guidance clinics: A quarter century of child development.* New York: The Commonwealth Fund.

Stewart, R. W. 1892. Report of the Standing Committee of the Board on the Deaf, State Board of Charities. *American Annals of the Deaf* 38: 151.

Stockwell, E. G. 1968. *Population and people.* Chicago: Quadrangle.

Stoddard, G. D., Chr. 1940. *Intelligence: Its nature and nurture. 39th Yearbook of the National Society for the Study of Education, pts. 1 and 2.* Bloomington, Ill.: Public School Publishing.

Stoddard, G. D., and B. L. Wellman. 1940. Environment and the IQ. In G. D. Stoddard, Chr., *Intelligence: Its nature and nurture: 39th yearbook of the National Society for the Study of Education, pts. 1 and 2.* Bloomington, Ill.: Public School Publishing.

Stone, C. 1848. On the religious state, and instruction of the deaf and dumb. *American Annals of the Deaf and Dumb* 1: 133–49.

———. 1853. Ohio Institution for Deaf and Dumb. *American Annals of the Deaf and Dumb* 5: 221–39.

———. 1859. Report on the subject of trades for the deaf and dumb. In *American Instructors of the Deaf and Dumb: Proceedings of the Fifth Convention.* Ill.: Courier Steam and Job Printing House.

———. 1869. Address upon the history and methods of deaf mute instruction. *American Annals of the Deaf and Dumb* 14: 95–121.

Strauss, A. A. 1939. Typology in mental deficiency. *Proceedings of the American Association of Mental Deficiency* 39: 44–85.

———. 1941a. The incidence of central nervous system involvement in higher grade moron children. *American Journal of Mental Deficiency* 45: 548.

———. 1941b. Neurology and mental deficiency. *American Journal of Mental Deficiency* 46: 192.

———. 1943. Diagnosis and education of the cripple-brained, deficient child. *Exceptional Children* 9: 163–68.

Strauss, A. A., and L. Lehtinan. 1947. *Psychopathology of the brain-injured child.* New York: Grune and Stratton.

Stribling, F. T. 1842. Physician and superintendent's report. In *Annual reports to the Court of Directors of the Western Lunatic Asylum to the Legislature of Virginia.* Richmond, Va.: Shephard and Conlin.

Strothers, C. C. 1959. The first special education university course in Canada. *Special Education in Canada* 35: 33–34, 75–76.

Struthers, J. 1981. A profession in crisis: Charlotte Whitton and Canadian social work in the 1930s. *Canadian Historical Review* 62: 169–96.

Style, H. W. 1873. A summary of the recorded research and opinion of Harvey Prindle Peet, Ph.D., LL.D, 1. *American Annals of the Deaf and Dumb* 18: 133–62, 213–37.

Suetonius [A.D. 120] 1957. *The twelve Caesars.* Translated by R. Graves. London: Penguin.

Sutton, J. R. 1988. *Controlling delinquency in the United States, 1640–1981.* Berkeley: University of California Press.

Sylvester, R. H. 1913. The form board test. *Psychological Monographs* 14 (whole no. 65).

Szasz, T. S. 1970. *The manufacture of madness.* New York: Dell.

Talbot, M. E. 1964. *Edouard Seguin: A study of an educational approach to the treatment of mentally defective children.* New York: Teachers College, Bureau of Publications.

Taylor H. 1900. The ichtyosaurus, the cave bear and the male teacher. *Association Review* 2: 361–66.

Taylor, R. 1897. A spelling test, 1. *American Annals of the Deaf* 42: 364–69.

———. 1898. A spelling test, 2. *American Annals of the Deaf* 43: 41–45.

Taylor, S. J., and S. J. Searl, Jr. 1987. The disabled in America: History, policy, and trends. In P. Knoblock, *Understanding exceptional children and youth,* pp. 5–64. Boston: Little, Brown.

Taylor Allen, M. B. 1988. "Let us live with our children": Kindergarten movements in Germany and the United States, 1840–1914. *History of Education Quarterly* 28: 23–48.

Teall, J. L. 1962. Witchcraft and Calvinism in Elizabethan England: Divine power and human agency. *Journal of the History of Ideas* 23: 21–36.

A teacher in a small school. 1902. Is the small school a boon to the deaf? *American Annals of the Deaf* 47: 455–63.

Telford, C. W., and J. M. Sawrey. 1981. *The exceptional individual.* 4th ed. Englewood Cliffs, N.J.: Prentice-Hall.

Temkin, O. 1947. Gall and the phrenological movement. *Bulletin of the History of Medicine* 21: 275–321.

Tenny, J. M. 1954. Preparing teachers of mentally handicapped children. *American Journal of Mental Deficiency* 58: 566–72.

Terman, L. M. [1906] 1975. *Genius and stupidity.* Rpt., New York: Arno Press.

———. 1912. Survey of mentally defective children in the schools of San Luis Obispo. *Psychological Clinic* 6: 136–37.

———. 1916. *The measurement of intelligence.* Cambridge, Mass.: Riverside Press.

———. 1917. The intelligence quotient of Francis Galton in childhood. *American Journal of Psychology* 28: 209–15.

———. 1919. *The intelligence of school children.* Boston: Houghton Mifflin.

———. 1920. The use of intelligence tests in the grading of school children. *Journal of Educational Research* 1: 20–21.

———. 1922. The great conspiracy or the impulse impetus of intelligence tests, psychoanalysed and exposed by Mr. Lippmann. *New Republic* 33: 116–20.

———. 1924. The conservation of talent. *School and Society* 19: 363.

———. [1925] 1926. *Mental and physical traits of a thousand gifted children, volume 1: Genetic studies of genius.* Stanford, Calif.: Stanford University Press.

———. 1926. *Genetic studies on genius: Mental and physical traits of a thousand gifted children.* 2d ed. Stanford, Calif.: Stanford University Press.

Terman, L. M., and H. G. Childs. 1912. A tentative revision and extension of the Binet-Simon Measuring Scale of Intelligence. *Journal of Educational Psychology* 3: 61–74, 133–43, 198–208, 277–89.

Terman, L., and M. H. Oden. 1947. *The gifted child grows up: Genetic studies of genius.* Vol. 4. Stanford, Calif.: Stanford University Press.

———. 1951. The Stanford studies of the gifted. In P. Witty, ed., *The gifted child.* Lexington, Mass.: D. C. Heath.

———. 1959. *Genetic studies of genius: The gifted group at mid-life.* Vol. 5. Stanford, Calif.: Stanford University Press.

Terrill, E. 1884. The moral and religious training of deaf mutes. In Ontario Institution for the Education and Instruction of the Deaf and Dumb, *Thirteenth annual report,* pp. 50–51. Toronto: Queen's Printer.

Thomas, K. 1971. *Religion and the decline of magic.* New York: Scribner.

Thomas Braidwood and the deaf mutes. 1888. *Science* 11: 12.

Thorndike, R., E. Hagan, and J. Sattler. 1986. *The Stanford-Binet Intelligence Scale.* 4th ed. Chicago: Riverside.

Thornton, W. 1793. Cadmus: On the mode of teaching the surd, or deaf, and consequently dumb to speak. *Transactions of the American Philosophical society* 3. Also *Association Review* 5 (1903): 462–73.

Three generations of imbecility enough for Supreme Court: Case of Buck vs Bell. 1927. *Journal of Heredity* 18: 493–95.

Thurston, R. H. 1876. *Reports of the Commissioners of the United States to the International Exhibition held in Vienna, 1873.* Washington, D.C.: Government Printing Office.

Thurstone, L. L. 1938. *Primary mental abilities.* Psychometric Monographs no. 1. Chicago: University of Chicago Press.

Tiffany, F. 1890. *Life of Dorothea Lynde Dix.* Boston: Houghton.

Tillinghast, J. A. 1910. Reflections of an ex-educator of the deaf. *American Annals of the Deaf* 55: 245–54, 462–73.

Tinkle, W. J. 1933. Deafness as an eugenical problem. *Journal of Heredity* 24: 13–18.

Tisdall, W. J. 1958. A follow-up study of trainable mentally retarded children in Illinois. *American Journal on Mental Deficiency* 65: 11–16.

Tissot, S. A. [1766] 1985. *Onanism, or a treatise upon the disorder produced by masturbation; or the dangerous effects of secret and excessibe venery,* trans. A. Hume. New York: Garland Publishing.

Toronto. *The World* May 7, 1912.

Townshend, J. 1831. *Memoirs of Rev. John Townshend.* Boston: Crocker and Brewster.

Tredgold, A. F. [1908] 1922. *Mental deficiency.* London: Balliere, Tindall and Cox.

———. 1929. *Mental deficiency (amentia).* 5th ed. New York: William Wood.

Trevor-Roper, H. R. 1969. *The European witch-craze of the sixteenth and seventeenth centuries and other essays.* New York: Harper and Row.

Tropea, J. L. 1987a. Bureaucratic order and special children: Urban schools, 1890s–1940s. *History of Education Quarterly* 27: 29–53.

———. 1987b. Bureaucratic order and special children: Urban schools, 1950s–1960s. *History of Education Quarterly* 27: 341–61.

Tuke, D. H. [1882] 1968. *Chapters in the history of the insane in the British Isles.* Amsterdam: E. J. Bonset.

Tuke, S. 1813. *Description of the Retreat in the Institution in York, for insane persons of the Society of Friends, containing an account of its origin and progress and means of treatment and statement of cases.* Philadelphia: Isaac Peirce.

Tull Boatner, M. 1959. *Voice of the deaf: A biography of Edward Miner Gallaudet.* Washington, D.C.: Public Affairs Press.

Turner, T. A. 1944. Crippled children. *Exceptional Children* 11: 215–16.

Turner, W. W. 1847. Causes of deafness. *American Annals of the Deaf and Dumb* 1: 25–32.

———. 1851. High school for the deaf and dumb. *American Annals of the Deaf and Dumb* 4: 41–48.

———. 1852a. High school for the deaf and dumb. *American Annals of the Deaf and Dumb* 4: 259–61.

———. 1852b. On the proper age of admission of pupils into institutions for the deaf and dumb. *American Annals of the Deaf and Dumb* 5: 146–49.

———. 1858. A contrast. *American Annals of the Deaf and Dumb* 7: 12–15.

———. 1868. Hereditary deafness. In *Proceedings of the National Conference of Principals of Institutions for the Deaf and Dumb,* pp. 91–96. Washington, D.C.: author.

———. 1870. Laurent Clerc. *American Annals of the Deaf and Dumb* 15: 16–28.

The twelfth census of the deaf. 1907. *American Annals of the Deaf* 52: 245–51.

Two out of five feeble-minded. 1917. *The Survey,* September 15, pp. 328–29.

Tyack, D. B., and M. Berkowitz. 1977. The man nobody liked: Toward a social history of the truant officer, 1840–1940. *American Quarterly* 29: 31–54.

Tyler, E. B. 1879. The gesture language. *American Annals of the Deaf and Dumb* 24: 39–45.

Tyor, P. L. 1977. "Denied the power to choose the good": Sexuality and mental defect in American medical practice, 1850–1920. *Journal of Social History* 10: 472–89.

Underhill, O. W. 1923. The deaf man and the printing trades. *American Annals of the Deaf* 68: 318–20.

United States, Bureau of Education. 1917–18. Pamphlet located at Boston Public Library.

United States, Department of Education. 1984. *Annual Report to Congress on the Implementation of the Education of the Handicapped Act,* Washington, D.C.: Office of Special Education Programs.

United States, Department of Labor, Children's Bureau. 1915. *Mental defectives in the District of Columbia: A brief description of local conditions and the need for custodial care and training.* Washington, D.C.: Government Printing Office.

United States, National Conference of Charities and Corrections. 1883. *Proceedings of the fourteenth annual conference held at Louisville, Kentucky, Sept. 24–30, 1883.* Madison, Wis.: Midland Publishing.

Vail, D. J. 1966. *Dehumanization and the institutional career.* Springfield, Ill.: Thomas.

Vaisse, L. 1879. A document brought to life. *American Annals of the Deaf and Dumb* 24: 80–89.

————. 1883. Jacob Rodrigues Péreire. *American Annals of the Deaf and Dumb* 28: 221–26.

Valentine, P. 1991. Thomas Hopkins Gallaudet. Paper presented at the First International Conference on the History of Deafness, Washington, D.C., Gallaudet University, June.

Van Cleve, J., and B. Crouch. 1989. *A place of their own.* Washington, D.C.: Gallaudet University Press.

Veith, I. 1965. *Hysteria, the history of a disease.* Chicago: University of Chicago Press.

Vernon, M. L. 1942. Notes on the early days of the Training School. *Training School Bulletin* 39: 22–25.

Victoria Industrial School. 1887, 1912. Applications. Public Archives of Ontario, Toronto.

————. 1896, 1899. *Annual Report.*

————. 1920. Committal. Public Archives of Ontario, Toronto.

Vineland, The Training School at Vineland. 1892, 1893, 1894, 1895, 1896, 1903, 1904, 1906, 1908, 1911, 1912, 1914, 1918. *Annual Report.* Vineland, N.J.: author.

Vitello, S. J. 1980. The legislative and judicial history of sterilization of mentally retarded persons in the US. In *Sterilization and mental handicap.* Ontario: National Institute for Mental Health.

Volta Review. 1923.

Voltaire, F. A. M. [1738] 1967. *The elements of Sir Isaac Newton's philosophy.* London: Cass.

————. [1738] 1964. Lettres philosophiques; ou Lettres anglaises avec le texte complet des remarques sur les Pensées de Pascal. Paris: Garnier frères.

Vorzimmer, P. 1969. Darwin, Malthus and the theory of natural selection. *Journal of the History of Ideas* 30: 527–42.

Wait, W. B. 1892a. *Education of the blind: Its progress and results.* New York: Bradstreet Press.

————. 1892b. *Origin of the New York Institution for the Blind.* New York: Bradstreet Press.

Walk, A. 1964. The pre-history of child psychiatry. *British Journal of Psychiatry* 110: 6754–767.

Wallin, J. E. W. 1911. A practical guide for the administration of the Binet-Simon Scale for Measuring Intelligence. *Psychological Clinic* 2: 121–32.

————. 1914. *The mental health of the school child: The psycho-educational clinic in relation to child welfare.* New Haven, Conn.: Yale University Press.

————. 1917. *Problems of subnormality.* New York: World Books.

————. 1922a. An investigation of the sex, relationship, marriage, delinquency and truancy of children assigned to special public school classes. *Journal of Abnormal Social Psychology* 17: 19–34.

————. 1922b. A study of the industrial record of children assigned to public school classes for mental defectives and legislation in the interest of defectives. *Journal of Abnormal Social Psychology* 17: 120–30.

————. 1924. *The education of handicapped children.* Boston: Houghton Mifflin.

Wallis, J. 1653. *Tractatus de loquela: Grammatica linguae anglicanae. Cui praefigur, De loquela sive sonorum formastione, tractacus grammaticophysicus.* Oxford: Oxoniae.

————. [1670] n.d. A letter of Dr. John Wallis to Robert Boyle Esq., concerning the said Doctors Essay of Teaching a person Deaf and Dumb to speak and to understand a Language; together with the Success thereof, made apparent to His Majesty, the Royal Society, and the University of Oxford, July 18, 1670. *Philosophical Transactions of the Royal Society,* 1668–1670. Rpt., London: John Martyn.

Walton, J. K. 1979. Lunacy in the Industrial Revolution: A study of asylum admissions in Lancashire, 1848–50. *Journal of Social History* 13: 1–22.

Wang, M. C., M. C. Reynolds, and H. J. Walberg. 1987. Repairing the second system for students with special needs. Paper presented at the Conference on the Education of Children with Special Needs.

Ward, R. D. 1927. The second year of the new immigration laws. *Journal of Heredity* 18: 17.

Warner, M. L. 1942. Early history of the International Council for Exceptional Children. *Exceptional Children* 8: 244–47.

————. 1944. Founders of the International Council for Exceptional Children. *Exceptional Children* 10: 217–21.

Warren, F. 1884. The brain of the school child: A point of education not usually considered. *Sanitary Journal* 7: 6–7.

Warren, J. M. 1851. An account of two remarkable Indian dwarfs exhibited in Boston under the name of Atzec children. *American Journal of Medical Sciences,* April.

Waserman, M. J. 1972. Benjamin Rush on government and the harmony and derangement of the mind. *Journal of the History of Ideas* 33: 639–42.

Watson, J. [1806] 1809. *Instruction of the deaf and dumb; or a Theoretical and Practical View of the Means by which they are Taught to Speak and understand a Language; containing hints for the Correction of Impediments in speech together with a Vocabulary.* London: Darton and Harvey.

Watson, J. B. 1927. The behaviorist looks at instincts. *Harper's Magazine,* July, p. 233.

Watson, R. I. 1963. *The great psychologists.* New York: Lippincott.

Weissman, I. 1959. *Social welfare policy and services in social work education.* New York: Council on Social Work Education.

Weld, L. 1847. The American Asylum. *American Annals of the Deaf and Dumb* 1: 7–14, 93–112.

West, A. M. 1984. *The National Education Association: The power base for education.* New York: Free Press.

West, C. [1848] 1963. Lecture on the diseases of infancy and childhood. London, 1848. In R. Hunter and I. McAlpine, eds., *Three hundred years of psychiatry, 1535–1860: A history in selected English texts.* London: Oxford University Press.

West, M. I. 1981. A spectrum of spectators: Circus audiences in nineteenth-century America. *Journal of Social History* 15: 265–70.

Weyent, R. G. 1968. Who's afraid of John B. Watson? Comments on Behavior: An introduction to comparative psychology. *Journal of Canadian Psychology* 9: 360–68.

Wheeler, F. 1920. Growth of American schools for the deaf. *American Annals of the Deaf* 65: 367–78.

Whildon, P. J. 1926. Letter to Mrs. W. M. Voires, May 24. Rare pamphlets, Volta Bureau, Washington, D.C.

White, C. C., K. C. Lakin, B. K. Hill, E. A. Wright, and R. H. Bruininks, 1987. Persons with mental retardation in state-separated residential facilities: Year ending June 30, 1986 with Longitudinal trends from 1950 to 1986. Project Report Number 24, Minneapolis, Minn.: University of Minnesota Affiliated Program on Development Disabilities.

White House Conference on Child Health and Protection. 1931. Section 3, *Education and training.* New York: Century.

White House Conference on Children in a Democracy. 1940. Washington, D.C.: Government Printing Office.

White House Conference Report. 1930. Section 3, *Education of the handicapped and the gifted.* New York: Century.

Whitton, C. 1919. Child labour. *Social Welfare* 1: 142–44.

Widd, T. 1877. History of Protestant Institution for Deaf-mutes, Montreal Canada. *American Annals of the Deaf and Dumb* 22: 193–204.

———. 1880a. *The Deaf and Dumb and Blind Deaf-Mutes; with interesting Facts and Anecdotes; A short History of the Mackay Institution; An easy Method of teaching Deaf-Mutes at Home; the Audiophone, etc.* Montreal: F. E. Grafton.

———. 1880b. John Barrett McGann. *American Annals of the Deaf and Dumb* 25: 148–50.

Wiederholt, J. L. 1978. Adolescents with learning disabilities: The problem in perspective. In L. Mann, L. Goodman, and J. L. Wiederholt, eds., *Teaching the learning-disabled adolescent.* Boston: Houghton Mifflin.

Wilbur, C. T. 1888. Institutions for the feeble-minded. In *Proceedings of the Fifteenth National Conference of Charities and Corrections, 1888,* pp. 106-13. Boston: Geo. Ellis.

Wilkinson, W. 1905. Day-schools, their advantages and disadvantages. *American Annals of the Deaf* 50: 70–95.

Will, M. C. 1986. Educating children with learning problems: A shared responsibility. *Exceptional Children* 52: 411–15.

Williams, F. E. 1917. Dr. Samuel G. Howe and the beginnings of work for the feebleminded in Massachusetts. *Boston Medical and Surgical Journal* 177: 481–84.

Williams, J. 1891. A correction. *American Annals of the Deaf* 36: 118–20.

Williams, L. A. 1989. Concepts of childhood and adolescence in Enlightenment Scotland. In *Education and Enlightenment: The conception of human nature and education. Selected proceedings of the Third International Conference on Education and Enlightenment,* pp. 87–92. Edmonton: University of Edmonton.

Willis, A. S. 1879. *Education of the blind: Speech in the House of Representatives in the United States, January 17, 1879.* Washington, D.C.: American Printing House for the Blind.

Wilson, A. 1972. *Diderot.* New York: Oxford University Press.

Wines, F. 1888. *Report on the defective, dependent and delinquent classes of the population of the United States: as returned in the tenth census (June 1, 1880).* Washington, D.C.: Government Printing Office.

Wing, G. 1886. The associative feature in the education of the deaf. *American Annals of the Deaf and Dumb* 31: 22–35.

Winkler, H. 1917. Testing immigrants. *The Survey,* November 10.

Winzer, M. A. 1979–1980. Historical perspectives on the education of the deaf in Canada, parts 1–5. *ACEHI Journal* 6: 15–20, 34–38, 50–53, 78–79.

———. 1981a. An examination of some selected factors that affected the education and socialization of the deaf in Ontario, 1870–1900. Ed.D. dissertation, University of Toronto/Ontario Institute for Studies in Education.

———. 1981b. Talking deaf mutes: The special role of women in the methodological conflict regarding the deaf, 1867–1900. *Atlantis* 6: 123–33.

———. 1983. Educational reform in mid-nineteenth century Upper Canada: John Barrett McCann and the deaf mutes. *ACEHI Journal* 9: 155–71.

———. 1986a. Deaf-Mutia: Responses to alienation by the deaf in mid-nineteenth century society. *American Annals of the Deaf* 131: 29–31.

———. 1986b. Early developments in special education: Some aspects of Enlightenment thought. *Remedial and Special Education* 7: 42–49.

———. 1986c. Education, urbanization, and the deaf community: A case study of Toronto, 1870–1900. In *Papers of the Second Research Conference on the Social Aspects of Deafness.* Washington, D.C.: Gallaudet University.

———. 1988. From philosophy to psychology: The development of psychology in eighteenth century France. Presented at the International Council of Psychologists, Singapore, August.

———. 1989a *Closing the gap: Special learners in regular classrooms.* Toronto: Copp Clark Pitman.

———. 1989b. Seeking the roots of childhood emotional disturbance. Paper presented at the meeting of the History of Disability Association, Toronto.

———. 1989c. Working for our supper: Institutional education in nineteenth century North America. Paper presented at the meeting of the Australia and New Zealand History of Education Conference, Newcastle, July.

———. 1991. The oral revolution. Paper presented at the First International Conference on the History of Deafness, Washington, D.C., Gallaudet University, June.

———. 1993. *Children with exceptionalities: A Canadian perspective.* 3d ed. Toronto: Prentice-Hall.

Winzer, M. A., and N. C. Grigg. 1992. *Educational psychology in Canadian classrooms.* Toronto: Prentice-Hall.

Winzer, M. A., and A. O'Connor. 1982. Eugenics: The threat of the feeble-minded. *B.C. Journal of Special Education* 6: 217–29.

Witmer, L. 1907. Clinical psychology. *Psychological Clinics* 1: 1–9.

Witty, P. A. 1965. A decade of progress in the study of the gifted and creative pupil. In W. B. Barbe, ed., *Psychology and education for the gifted.* New York: Appleton-Century-Crofts.

Wolf, J. S., and T. M. Stephens. 1982. Gifted and talented. In N. Haring, ed., *Exceptional children and youth: An introduction to special education.* Columbus, Ohio: Merrill.

Wolfensberger, W. 1964a. Some observations on European programs for the mentally retarded. *Mental Retardation* 2: 280–85.

———. 1964b. Teaching and training of the retarded in European countries. *Mental Retardation* 2: 331–37.

———. 1965. General observations on European programs. *Mental Retardation* 3: 8–11.

———. 1972. *The principle of normalization in human services.* Toronto: National Institute on Mental Retardation.

———. 1975. *The origin and nature of institutional models.* Syracuse, N.Y.: Human Policy Press.

Woodring, P. 1975. The development of teacher education. In K. Ryan, ed., *Teacher education: The 74th yearbook of the National Society for the Study of Education.* Chicago: University of Chicago Press.

Woodruff, L. H. 1848. Primary instruction of the deaf. *American Annals of the Deaf and Dumb* 1: 46–55.

Worcester. A. 1885. How shall our children be taught to pronounce at sight the words of our written language. *American Annals of the Deaf and Dumb* 30: 6–21.

Wright, A. 1915. The manual and oral combination. *American Annals of the Deaf* 60: 219.

Wright, D. 1969. *Deafness: A personal account.* London: Penguin.

Wright, E. 1865. *Juvenile criminals and a plan for saving them.* Boston: Wright and Potter.

Wundt, W. 1894. *Lectures on human and animal psychology.* London: Swan Sonnenschein.

Wyatt, J. M. 1919. Causes of juvenile delinquency. *Social Welfare* 2: 10–11.

Yale, C. 1889. Alice Elizabeth Worcester. *American Annals of the Deaf* 34: 121–26.

———. 1920. Harriet Burbank Rogers, 1834–1919. *Volta Review* 22: 501–6.

———. 1931. *Years of building: Memoirs of a pioneer in a special field of education.* New York: Dial Press.

Yale graduates. 1879. *American Annals of the Deaf and Dumb* 24: 193.

Yerkes, R. M. 1917. How may we discover the children who need special care? *Mental Hygiene* 1: 252–59.

———. 1923. Eugenic bearing on instruments of intelligence in the United States army. *Eugenics Review* 14: 225–45.

Yerkes, R. M., ed. 1921. Psychological examining in the US army. *Memoirs of the National Academy of Sciences,* no. 15.

Yolton, J. W. 1985. French materialist disciples of Locke. *Journal of the History of Philosophy* 25: 83–104.

Young, A. F., and E. T. Ashton. 1956. *British social work in the nineteenth century.* London: Routledge and Kegan Paul.

Young, K. 1923. The history of mental testing. *Pedagogical Seminary* 31: 1–48.

Zainaldin, J. S., and P. L. Tyor. 1979. Asylum and society: An approach to industrial change. *Journal of Social History* 13: 23–48.

Zelder, E. Y. 1953. Public opinion and public education for the exceptional child—court decisions, 1873–1950. *Exceptional Children* 19: 187–98.

Zenderland, L. 1987. The debate over diagnosis: Henry Herbert Goddard and the medical acceptance of intelligence testing. In M. M. Sokal, ed., *Psychological testing and American society, 1890–1939.* New Brunswick, N.J.: Rutgers University Press.

Zetlin, A., and M. Murtaugh. 1990. Whatever happened to those with borderline IQS? *American Journal of Mental Retardation* 94: 463–69.

Zigler, E., R. M. Hoddap, and M. R. Edison. 1990. From theory to practice in the care and education of mentally retarded individuals. *American Journal of Mental Retardation* 95: 1–12.

Zilboorg, G., and G. W. Henry 1941. *History of medical psychology.* New York: Norton.

Zinsser, H. 1935. *Rats, lice and history.* New York: Bantam.

Subject Index

An *f* following a page number indicates a figure; a *t* following a page number indicates tabular material.

Author Index

Abraham, W. 111, 318, 331, 335
Abt, I. A., 146, 386
Achenbach, T. M., 330, 344, 346
Ackerknecht, E. H., 64
Ackers, St. J., 163
Addams, J., 347
Adler, E., 152
Afflech, J. D., 385
Akerley, S., 101, 188
Alexander, F. G., 25
Allport, F. H., 256
Amman, J. C., 36, 37
Anagnos, M., 220
Anastasi, A., 262, 307
Anderson-Inman, L., 385
Andrews, M., 229
Anglo, S., 24
Apter, S. J., 12
Aries, P., 49
Aristotle, 13, 18
Arms, H. P., 298
Armstrong, D. F., 124, 125
Arrowsmith, J. P., 143
Ashton, E. T., 72, 387
Atkinson, H. S., 303
Atkinson, R. C., 255
Atkinson, R. L., 255
Ayres, J. A., 143, 204
Ayres, L. P., 328

Bailyn, B., 77
Bain, D. A., 355
Baine, D., 382
Ball, T. S., 67, 69, 181
Ballard, J., 382
Baller, W. R., 311
Balthazar, E. E., 340
Barnard, H. C., 18, 95, 97, 99, 106, 116, 126,
    174, 235, 239

Barr, M. W., 14, 15, 21, 22, 23, 25, 48, 65, 66,
    67, 68, 114, 132, 158, 159, 177, 180, 212,
    280, 285, 300
Barss, J. N., 292
Bartlett, D., 143
Bates, P., 372
Baynton, D. C., 191
Beck, T. R., 17, 60, 64, 110, 157, 158, 159
Bede, the Venerable, 21, 53, 101, 126, 129,
    147, 152, 154, 155, 161
Beer, A. S., 207, 213
Beggs, R., 108
Belanger, A., 323
Bell, A., 192
Bell, A. G., 34, 86, 87, 88, 98, 99, 101, 126, 129,
    147, 152, 154, 155, 161, 182, 188, 191, 192,
    194, 195, 196, 206, 211, 222, 247, 259,
    279, 288, 295, 296, 298, 299, 300, 301,
    304, 317, 318, 319
Bell, A. M., 192, 194
Bell, L. V., 110
Bell, M. H., 217
Bell, R. Q., 14
Bem, D. J., 255
Bench, P. J., 168, 345
Bender, R. E., 37, 55, 72
Benjamin, L. T., Jr., 355
Bergmann, G., 309
Berkeley, K. C., 236
Berkley, G., 43
Berkowitz, M., 138
Berlin, I., 39, 42, 43
Bernard, R. M., 235
Best, E. M, 285
Best, H., 104, 108, 138, 141, 142, 149, 220,
    221, 323
Biklen, D., 10
Billings, B., 251
Binet, A., 216, 256, 267, 268, 271

455